Multicultural Social Work in Canada

Working with Diverse Ethno-racial Communities

Edited by

Alean Al-Krenawi and John R. Graham

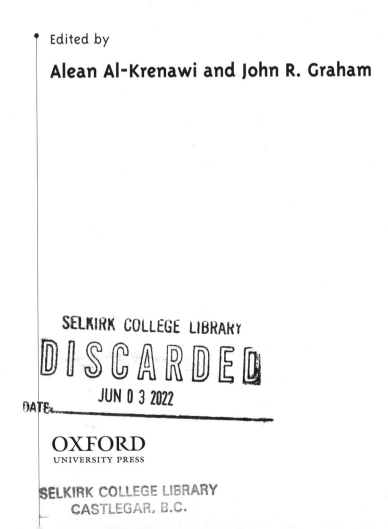

OXFORD
UNIVERSITY PRESS

OXFORD

UNIVERSITY PRESS

70 Wynford Drive, Don Mills, Ontario M3C 1J9
www.oup.com/ca

Oxford University Press is a department of the University of Oxford.
It furthers the University's objective of excellence in research, scholarship,
and education by publishing worldwide in

Oxford New York

Auckland Bangkok Buenos Aires Cape Town Chennai
Dar es Salaam Delhi Hong Kong Istanbul Karachi Kolkata
Kuala Lumpur Madrid Melbourne Mexico City Mumbai Nairobi
São Paulo Shanghai Singapore Taipei Tokyo Toronto

with an associated company in Berlin

Oxford is a trade mark of Oxford University Press
in the UK and in certain other countries

Published in Canada
by Oxford University Press

The National Library of Canada Cataloguing in Publication Data.

Main entry under title:

Multicultural social work in Canada: working with diverse ethno-racial communities.

Includes bibliographical references and index.

ISBN 0-19-541530-2

1. Social work with minorities—Canada.   I. Al-Krenawi, Alean
II. Graham, John R. (John Russell), 1964–

HV3176.M84 2002   362.84'00971   C2002-901289-9

Cover design: Brett J. Miller

1 2 3 4 - 06 05 04 03

This book is printed on permanent (acid-free) paper ∞.
Printed in Canada

Contents

Acknowledgements

Special thanks go to the contributors of this book, for their excellent work in meeting timelines and in coming up with provocative, cutting-edge chapters. The editors are also grateful to several scholars who were involved in the project in other ways. Sincere thanks are extended to Gisele Legault, Université de Montréal, Tat Tsang and Usha George, University of Toronto, Andre Jacob, Université du Québec à Montréal, Keith Brownlee, Lakehead University, and Jacqueline Ismael, University of Calgary. Thanks are extended to Oxford University Press personnel for their continued diligence as the work proceeded towards publication.

Alean Al-Krenawi wishes to thank his wife, Dr Monaor Al-Krenawi, for her support, encouragement, and patience throughout this project. Special thanks go to his parents, brothers, and sisters for their understanding and encouragement. He extends particular thanks to Talal Al-Krenawi, the mayor of Rahat, his hometown, for his emotional support and encouragement. John Graham extends continued thanks to his family. For research assistance, the editors are most grateful to Sigal Shelhav at Beer Sheva, Israel, and Louise Querido at Calgary, Canada.

Contributors

Ramona Alaggia is an assistant professor, Faculty of Social Work, University of Toronto. Dr Alaggia's teaching and research focus is in cross-cultural social work practice, violence in families, and sexual abuse of children. She has worked in the children's mental health field as a clinical social worker, and her publications include proposed approaches for sexually abused children and their families, the role of culture in the sexual abuse of children, and the impact of immigration on families.

Alean Al-Krenawi is the director of the Center for Bedouin Studies and Development and senior lecturer in the Spitzer Department of Social Work, Ben-Gurion University of the Negev, Israel. He and John Graham have published extensively on cross-cultural and international social work and mental health practice in the Middle East.

Ashley Barlow is a student at the University of Calgary with strong interest in Ukrainian-Canadian cultural issues.

Constance Barlow is an associate professor of social work at the University of Calgary and is field education program coordinator at that institution. She has published on field education and clinical services, and maintains an active clinical practice.

Wanda Thomas Bernard is an associate professor and director of the Maritime School of Social Work in Halifax. Her teaching and research interests include Afrocentric social work practice, participatory action research, and child welfare practice. Dr Bernard has published extensively in the area of Afrocentricity and will be editing a volume of papers examining fatherhood in the African Diaspora.

Carole Pigler Christensen is a professor and a former director of the University of British Columbia School of Social Work. She chaired the Canadian Association of Schools of Social Work Task Force on Multicultural and Multiracial Issues in Social Work Education, which helped to initiate new standards of accreditation for Canadian schools of social work. Her research, publications, and theoretical models involve cross-cultural and anti-racist practice.

Peg Delanghe has been involved in community development and organization, including teaching English and assisting newcomers in their adjustments to Canada, for over twenty years. Her area of speciality is community-based health projects involving persons with special needs. She is currently pursuing graduate studies and research with the Canadian Plains Studies Research Center at the University of Regina.

Gary C. Dumbrill is an assistant professor in the School of Social Work, University of Victoria, and a doctoral social work student at the University of Toronto. Gary's teaching and research focus on child welfare, the ways clients experience intervention, and anti-oppressive social work practice. He has worked in the child welfare field in Britain and Canada and as a continuing education trainer focusing on child welfare and anti-racist/anti-oppressive practice.

Douglas Durst, of the Faculty of Social Work, University of Regina, has worked with community groups on issues pertaining to First Nations self-government in various regions of Canada. For over ten years, he has served on the Canadian Council on Multicultural Health and has published widely on social work practice with diverse communities.

David Este is an associate professor in the Faculty of Social Work and is associate director (research) of the Cultural Diversity Institute at the University of Calgary. His teaching and research interests include social work practice with immigrants and refugees, qualitative research methods, diversity in organizations, and the management of human service organizations. He is the co-editor of two recent books: *Professional Social Services in the Multicultural World* and *Macro Social Work Case Studies*.

John R. Graham is professor of social work at the University of Calgary, and formerly the Faculty's doctoral program coordinator. He and Alean Al-Krenawi have published extensively on cross-cultural and international social work in the Middle East.

Ross A. Klein is an associate professor of social work at Memorial University of Newfoundland. Prior to pursuing his PhD, he was involved in Jewish communal work with adolescents. His current teaching centres on research methods for social work, and he is actively engaged in projects involving applied research.

Marie Lacroix is an associate researcher at the School of Community and Public Affairs, Concordia University. She received a doctorate from McGill University in a joint social work program with the Université de Montréal. Her research interests include immigration and refugee policy, refugee claimants and social work practice, multicultural social work, international social work and international development, and community capacity-building.

Brad McKenzie is a professor in the Faculty of Social Work, University of Manitoba. He teaches courses in social policy, program evaluation, and child welfare, and has conducted extensive research in the area of First Nations child and family services.

Sarah Maiter is an assistant professor in the Faculty of Social Work at Wilfrid Laurier University. Her major areas of research, teaching, and practice interest relate to child and family services and to social service provision to diverse populations.

Elsa Marziali is a professor emeritus in the Faculty of Social Work, University of Toronto. Dr Marziali's research focus is on clinical practice outcome studies in fields of mental health and child welfare.

Julia Mirsky teaches in the Spitzer Department of Social Work, Ben-Gurion University of the Negev, Israel. She is a clinical psychologist who, for many years, has been active in the field of immigrant adjustment, including clinical practice, community interventions, consultation, research, and teaching.

Catherine Montgomery is a researcher at the Centre de recherche et de formation, CLSC Côte-des-Neiges, and adjunct professor in sociology at McGill University. Specializing in questions relating to immigration and health services, she is currently beginning a four-year research program on social integration of young immigrants and refugees. She has published on the themes of language and pluralism, social inequalities and immigration, and health practices with immigrant populations.

Vern Morrissette is the director of Métis Child and Family Services for Manitoba. He has worked extensively with Aboriginal organizations and has consulted widely in the field of Aboriginal child and family services.

Narda Razack is an associate professor of social work at York University and field education coordinator with that institution. Her principal areas of research are critical race theory and practice, international social work, postcolonialism, and field education.

Ghislaine Roy has worked in the intercultural field as a social worker, trainer, and professor since 1985. She has published numerous articles and has presented several papers on the subject. She presently works as a social worker in the Service d'aide aux réfugiés et immigrants du Montréal Métropolitain (SARIMM) and as a field researcher in the Centre de recherche et de formation, both part of the CLSC Côte-des-Neiges, a health and social services centre in Montreal.

David Welch is an associate professor at the École de service social, Université d'Ottawa. He has published extensively on social services for people of Franco-Ontarian background, community development, and policy concerns.

June Ying Yee is an assistant professor in the School of Social Work at Ryerson Polytechnic University, Faculty of Community Service. Her scholarly research focuses on race and racism and on access and equity issues for ethno-racial clientele in the areas of health, education, and social services. She has worked in many research capacities in both the local community and teaching environments in the United Kingdom, Calgary, Toronto, and Montreal. Currently, she teaches anti-oppressive practice, focusing on race, gender, class, and sexual orientation issues and conducts training workshops for local agencies.

Preface

This book has been several years in the making. It originated from a conversation with John Graham and Alean Al-Krenawi. Both of us had taught courses in multicultural social work, and we had jointly published over two dozen journal articles on multicultural and international practice, principally among Arab peoples indigenous to the Middle East. One of us (Al-Krenawi) had lived in Canada for several years; the other (John Graham) had lived here all his life, and was teaching in Calgary. Given our research interests, we both had been immersed in diversity and multicultural literatures within and outside Canada. But within Canada, we were increasingly convinced of the need for a single volume that offered insights from many of the country's leading scholars and practitioners of multicultural practice.

This book has been written for introductory and intermediate students and for scholars and practitioners. The first chapter provides foundational knowledge and skills applicable to diverse ethno-racial backgrounds in Canada. It considers how scholars and practitioners currently think about multicultural practice, elaborates the rationale for the book, and discusses several major terms for understanding ethno-racial differences. The remainder of the book is divided into two sections. The next three chapters (chapters 2–4) examine knowledge and skills that are salient for social work practice: Marie Lacroix considers practice with individuals and families; Douglas Durst and Peg Delanghe treat community issues; and Carole Pigler Christensen analyses social policy. In Chapter 5 June Ying Yee and Gary Dumbrill provide striking insight into the influence of the 'white race' upon virtually every aspect of social work practice and contemporary life. In the final chapter in this section, Ghislaine Roy and Catherine Montgomery analyse how to work with people who have immigrated to a new country.

In Section 2, the contributors consider their experiences of multicultural practice in the context of a specific ethno-racial background. In many instances, this background is their own. In all instances, the chapters offer a 'personal narrative'— that is, the writers' stories and research/practice experiences are at the forefront. Close at hand are the nuances, contradictions, and provisional, subjective, and tentative aspects of some practice scenarios. Authors outline how they developed their self-awareness of what it means to be a social worker and how they try both to understand and respond to the lived experience of their clients.

All chapters are strongly wedded to the most current practices and scholarship. Yet in no way are they beacons of truth; they are, instead, a means of conveying a writer's social work experience of identity and difference. From that basis, the reader may undertake comparable self-reflection in relation to *their* ethno-racial background, gender, religion, range of ability, sexual orientation, socio-economic class, and others areas of diversity—all of which help to shape a world view. Before one can understand someone else's world view, it is necessary to understand one's own. From this, differences and similarities with others may come to the fore. Without it, a social worker's assumptions and biases may be imposed, leading to unclear communication, misunderstanding, poor service, early termination, or outright oppression.

It would have been impossible to write about every ethno-racial community in Canada. In the end, the criteria for inclusion comprised a number of factors, among them, ready availability of the country's leading authors who could write about a given ethno-racial community, and the presence of research on practice within a particular community. The editors sought as broad a list of contributors as possible, based on regional affiliation, ethno-racial background, gender, and other areas of diversity. The Canadian context of the book also warranted consideration of practice within and outside Quebec, and in linguistic contexts that include, but are not limited to, English and French.

At the same time that it concentrates on a particular ethno-racial community, each chapter in Section 2 has a unique analytical approach. These varying insights are determined in part by author interest, the particularities of the community itself, and the presence of various research issues in the literature specific to the given ethno-racial group. In Chapter 7, on work with Canadians of Italian background, Ramona Alaggia and Elsa Marziali provide excellent insight into the application of bicultural and intergenerational issues. In Chapter 8, Alean Al-Krenawi and John Graham examine work with Canadians of Arab background, while concentrating more than many other contributors on religion (Islam and Christianity, in particular) and on mental health. Ross Klein and Julia Mirsky, the authors of Chapter 9, offer keen insight into a broad array of issues affecting Canadians of Jewish backgroung, including the impact of systemic barriers such as anti-Semitism. In Chapter 10, which treats Canadians of Ukrainian background, Connie Barlow and Ashley Barlow provide useful historical and contemporary context for working with a particular population, integrating insightful personal narratives to these ends. Work with Canadians of Aboriginal background is the subject of Chapter 11. Brad McKenzie and Vern Morrissette carefully consider the cultural values, world views, and particular sensitivities required in working with people from Aboriginal communities across the country. In Chapter 12, which is on Franco-Ontarians, David Welch concentrates on the political and social policy contexts of working with members of the French-speaking minority in Ontario. The historical and contemporary contexts, and current parameters, of working with African Nova Scotians is the subject of Chapter 13, by David Este and Wanda Thomas-Bernard. Narda Razack grew up in the Caribbean and now lives in Canada. Chapter 14 reflects her multiple identities, providing narrative reflections from a critical/ post-colonial perspective. Finally, Chapter 15, by Sarah Maiter, examines work with Canadians of South Asian background, offering an especially nuanced analysis of such issues as acculturation and direct practice intervention.

Social workers may experience a cultural conflict between aspects of their professional practice and their own world view. Effective coping strategies depend on the given situation. Yet, in all instances, creativity, flexible thinking and behaviour, and the ability to look at the world through multiple lenses, are critical. As the contributors to this volume point out, effective multicultural social work intervention requires, above all else, sophisticated knowledge, skills, and self-reflection.

Chapter 1

Introduction

Alean Al-Krenawi and John R. Graham

Canada is becoming increasingly diverse. Yet, as the following pages elaborate, social work is only beginning to adapt knowledge and practice to the realities of our multicultural country. This introduction begins by outlining the emergence of diverse thinking on social work practice with ethno-racial communities in Canada. It then examines several assumptions that will underlie authors' work in this volume as well as the diverse representations that all the contributors, as a whole, ultimately convey. After providing a brief overview of the content of subsequent chapters, this chapter focuses on some major terms that will be of importance in subsequent chapters, and concludes with some final thoughts on multicultural social work in Canada.

Social Work Then and Now

The classic text by the late University of Chicago scholar Charlotte Towle, *Common Human Needs* (1945), captured the assumptions of social work literature prior to the late 1960s. Assigned to social work courses across the continent, Towle's work, like that of others of her day (Casas, 1985; see Tsang & George, 1998), tended to presume commonality in needs and therefore did not pay great attention to ethno-racial and cultural differences. In Canada, the post–Second World War welfare state adopted similar assumptions, in the form of universal social programs. As with social work practice, particularist assumptions triumphed: for example, dominant patriarchal, heterosexist, middle-class perspectives that ignored ethno-racial minorities and the differently abled were considered the norm (Ursel, 1992; Christensen, 2002). In today's world, in contrast, most scholars would agree that the prevailing perspective should surely be diverse, rather than common, human needs. The translation of this contemporary ideal into practice is fraught with nuance, complexity, and multiple assumptions, as subsequent chapters in this book make clear.

A second historical footnote bears emphasis. In many areas of Canada, a diverse array of charitable and voluntary services dotted the mid- to late-nineteenth-century landscape, prior to the development of a domestic social work profession in the First World War era (Speisman, 1973). These services, like their informal counterparts of familial and community helping, were the main avenues for social care, and many represented, to some extent, particularistic traditions. Specific categories included religion (Protestant, Roman Catholic, Jewish, other), how recently the person has arrived in the country (immigrant-aid associations), race (for example, although most churches that provided charitable services had white congregations, a minority were African Canadian), and gender (many charities were gender-specific, although some served both women and men). Socio-economic class was also a category: members of emerging trade unions and friendly societies, for instance, would have had different class backgrounds than many of those who ran charities sponsored by the social, political, and economic elite (Graham, 1992, 1996; Emery & Emery, 1999; Speisman, 1973; Winks, 1997). Some of these institutional categories continue to define a proportion of social service organizations to this day. But, prior to the development of professional social work in the early twentieth century, such categories may have been even more important in differentiating charitable service organizations and, to some extent, marking the way practice was conceptualized. Further implications are not yet well considered, and it is always difficult to predict conclusions in future scholarship. It is possible, though, that research may one day claim that these past practices in some modest way foreshadowed the profession's current interest in multicultural practice. Perhaps, too, subsequent findings may more fully consider how the emergence of a twentieth-century welfare state and social work profession may have had the paradoxical effect of accelerating homogeneous, rather than heterogeneous, approaches to social services in subsequent decades.

From the 1960s to 1980s, various theories of cultural difference that influenced Canadian social work emerged outside of this discipline. They included models that emphasized inferiority/pathology (Padilla, 1981), deviance (Rubington & Weinberg, 1971), disorganization (Moynihan, 1965), and cultural (Padilla, 1981) and genetic (Herrnstein, 1971) deficiencies (Casas, 1985, cited in Tsang & George, 1998, p. 74). All of these models assumed inferiority of ethnic and racial minority communities. The assimilationist White Paper on Aboriginal peoples, put forward by the federal government in 1969, is a Canadian social policy example that sadly reflected dominant trends (Shewell & Spagnut, 1995). In the same decade, the tragic forced relocation of the African-Canadian members of the community of Africville, in the North End of Halifax, Nova Scotia, is a comparable example of direct social work practice that reflected profound ethno-racial insensitivity (Clairmont & Magill, 1974).

Subsequent Canadian social work continued to be influenced by American literature. The 1970s ushered in a so-called colour-blind approach to social work that is now appropriately seen as glossing over a client's self-identity or social reality (Tsang & George, 1998, p. 75). It was followed in the 1980s and 1990s by models that highlighted cultural difference (Katz, 1985; Sue, 1981), multiculturalism (Johnson, 1990), and cultural pluralism and diversity (Ponterotto & Casas, 1991).

All of these more recent models value cultural difference, and to varying extents understand individual problems within such broader issues as racism, oppression, discrimination, and deprivation (Tsang & George, 1998, pp. 75–76).

More recently, an anti-racist model of social work, well developed in the United Kingdom, has paid still greater attention to integrating individual, organizational, and structural levels of change (Dominelli, 1997). This approach takes 'on board the structured inequality existing between different racialised groups' and works 'on ways in which equality between them can be achieved' (Dominelli, 1997, p. 55). Yet the anti-racist movement, too, has been criticized for lacking sufficient theoretical grounding (Macey & Moxon, 1996; Williams, 1999). Some analysts—including the contributors to the present volume—propose a still different framework: anti-oppression. With anti-oppression, all forms of identity—age, age-cohort status, gender, ethnicity, nationality, race, range of ability, religion, sexual identity, socio-economic class, among others—are the bases upon which one moves towards the awareness of self, of societal inequalities, and of differences among all peoples (Bishop, 1994; Macey & Moxon, 1996). Thus, in Section 2 of this book, authors use the prism of their own lived experience and diverse backgrounds to write about practice with an ethno-racial community. (It should be noted that space limitations preclude this book from engaging equally with *all* areas of diversity; hence, the particular focus on ethno-racial plurality, an area of great complexity and research, incorporating other diversity-related conceptions.)

Recent Canadian literature, like its American counterparts (Lum, 1992; Devore & Schlesinger, 1996), has emphasized a model of cultural competence that enables behaviours, knowledge, attitudes, and policies to respond appropriately to cultural and racial diversity (Este, 1999; Herberg, 1993). As shown in Table 1.1 competence goes well beyond sensitivity. Whereas cultural sensitivity is a skilled awareness of cultural issues, cultural competence is more highly skilled and more knowledgeable, and entails a more change-committed focus to cultural issues (Este, 1999, p. 32). (Elements to consider in culturally competent practice are further elaborated in Section 2 of this book.)

But how does one become culturally competent? One way of understanding is to think about where one might fall along a continuum. One's position might vary over time and in different contexts; the two polarities are, at best, intellectual constructs assisting us to better understand cultural competence. On the one end of the

Table 1.1   The Cultural Sophistication Framework

Dimension	Culturally incompetent	Culturally sensitive	Culturally competent
Cognitive dimension	Oblivious	Aware	Knowledgeable
Affective dimension	Apathetic	Sympathetic	Committed to change
Skills dimension	Unskilled	Lacking some skills	Highly skilled
Overall effect	Destructive	Neutral	Constructive

From Este, 1999, p. 32

continuum is cultural literacy; on the other, experiential phenomenology (see Table 1.2). Some practitioners tend towards the cultural literacy end of the spectrum. Canadian scholars Tat Tsang and Usha George (1998) are critical of this position, which, they argue, presupposes that a social worker's knowledge is superior to a client's. It also assumes that social workers are conversant with a client's culture and with any other cultural system they encounter; that they know what problems exist and how to respond to them; and that social workers are willing to use stereotypical 'culture-specific' intervention techniques (ibid., p. 82). Moreover, cultural literacy tends to place clients in a category, rather than trying to understand the unique intersection of each person's diversities and the nuances of individuality.

In contrast, the more experiential, phenomenological end of the continuum assumes a stance of openness, humility, curiosity, and wanting to know more about a client. A worker's assumptions are more suspended in this model, and worker–client interaction stresses the former's lack of presumption in engaging with the client. Recent scholarship discusses this stance in relation to 1) understanding one's own culture and self, and using this as a basis for understanding others; and 2) using social constructivist principles to guide intervention (Lee & Greene, 1999). The following chapters adhere to this approach, but with some additional consideration. Cultural literacy is not entirely abandoned. For example, several contributors appear to think, and we agree, that some culturally specific techniques *are* tenable, provided they are carried out in experiential-phenomenological ways, and as long as there is space for the client to exercise cultural knowledge/expertise. Likewise, clients may be members of a particular cultural group; but in a thoughtful, experiential-phenomenological model, this should not mean—as a strongly cultural literacy position may assert—a totalizing and limiting set of perceptions that a worker would then hold.

Most of the major books in multicultural social work are British (cf. Dominelli, 1997) or American (cf. Devore & Schlesinger, 1996), with assumptions that are particular to those countries. The present volume is written for a Canadian readership and thus contributes to a nascent Canadian literature (Herberg, 1993; Lie & Este, 1999) and to the distinct issues that confront our country's multicultural reality. Among them are practice with French-speaking people inside and outside of

Table 1.2   Two Models of Culturally Competent Multicultural Practice

Cultural literacy model	Experiential-phenomenological model
Practitioner as expert	Practitioner as learner
Assumes superior knowledge	Naiveté and curiosity
Culture as homogeneous system	Plurality and multiplicity of internalized culture
Client as member of cultural group	Member as unique individual
Culture-specific techniques	Process-oriented techniques
Nearly impossible	Demands critical self-examination

Adapted from Tsang & George, 1998, p. 83.

Quebec, direct practice with various ethno-racial communities in a multicultural Canada, and principles of community and social policy development in a multi-cultural Canada.

Above all, then, we encouraged contributors to write about:

- fluid boundaries of ethnocultural identity that vary from one encounter to the next and are subject to time, geography, and other factors
- social-constructionist narratives that indicate how the writer's experience and world view intersect with the client's
- multiple identities—that is, no single or totalizing portrayal of a particular ethno-racial community; but rather a discussion of the author's particular encounter
- ethno-racial considerations intersecting with all other types of identity: sexual orientation, acculturation, geography, age cohort status, age, socio-economic class, gender, range of ability, religion, national identity; these intersections nec-essarily vary from one person to the next
- the tentative, provisional, and subjective nature of insight, which varies over time and place, and from one person to the next: an opportunity to engage in dialogue.

This book provides some leading Canadian authors with an opportunity to write about social work with diverse ethno-racial communities, emphasizing the more experiential, phenomenological approach to practice, and the intersection of mul-tiple positionalities in the locus of practice. Authors represent, among other diverse social locations, both sexes, different provinces, and various ethno-racial groups, and they come from both inside and outside Canada. They address a wide range of experiences that social workers might expect to encounter during their professional lives: different levels and fields of practice, practice scenarios with various ethno-racial communities, and a variety of social problems.

For this first edition, we wanted a mix of ethno-racially specific analysis and broader general principles. Consequently, the book retains the advantage of both breadth (the chapters in Section 1 being applicable to diverse ethno-racial groups) and depth (the chapters in Section 2 documenting distinct practice strategies as applied to a writer's experience of research and/or practice within a particular ethno-racial context). The way in which we as editors approached a book on multicultural social work in 2002 is different from what would have been the case even five years earlier—or, indeed, might be the case five years hence. Future editions will likely be configured differently. A chapter on work with Canadians of Anglo background struck us as a useful frame of reference for many students, and yet it had to be aban-doned for space considerations. Several authors who had wanted to be involved could not be. They are acknowledged in the beginning of this book. We hope that they might be involved in a future edition. And, of course, a future edition will be differ-ent in ways that cannot be predicted as our knowledge continues to evolve.

We are aware of the nascent state of multicultural social work writing in Canada, and the broad parameters that now define it. Within the framework of multicultural social work that is non-oppressive and is grounded in the experiential-phenome-nological model, we consciously provided latitude for contributors to convey diverse perspectives on social work with a variety of communities. Again, a future edition might adopt a different organization or approach. For the time being, 'diversity' was an apt metaphor on several levels: it reflects the current state of multicultural prac-tice and research in this country, and the variety of approaches not only among schools of social work, but also among both scholars and practitioners. But social work is not the only discipline to be in a state of flux; and multicultural concerns are not the only sub-specialty. As a Canadian historian argues, 'disciplines have been "decentred", metanarratives dismissed' (Friesen, 2000, p. 223): such is the state of much of the most interesting contemporary scholarship across the disciplines. For many reasons, then, readers ought to be exposed to this breadth of perspective within contemporary Canadian scholarship on multicultural social work.

The contributors to this volume can be distinguished from each other by a vari-ety of theoretical assumptions that inform practice and that situate discussion in different practice contexts and personal practice frameworks. Christensen's and Razack's chapters, for example, are highly structuralist in orientation. Durst and Delanghe's chapter, in contrast, proposes different models of community practice, depending, in part, on the situation and the wishes of the community. Some chap-ters are clinical, such as Alaggia and Marziali's contribution on work with Canadians of Italian background. Others, such as Welch's on work with Franco-Ontarians, are referenced to community practice. This is not to suggest the absence of clinical concerns in work with Franco-Ontarians, nor of community issues with Canadians of Italian background. We should likewise note that no book could pos-sibly discuss every ethno-racial community in the country; rather, communities in Section 2 are addressed, in part, in relation to available authors to write on major ethno-racial communities in Canada, and the commensurate availability of litera-ture to research these topics. Similarly, to avoid unnecessary repetition, key areas of knowledge are limited to specific chapters. Thus, for example, genograms are dis-cussed in Chapter 6, some of the major tenets of multicultural theory in Chapter 7, and communication styles in Chapter 8.

At the beginning of the twentieth century, the social work profession emerged in western Europe and North America (the North); during the interwar period, it was transplanted to countries such as Egypt and India (the South). In the post–Second World War era, the profession was globalized; schools of social work proliferated across the South—invariably with cultural assumptions originating in the North (Healey, 1999; Midgley, 1981). As a result, social work in much of the developing world is deeply incompatible with most of the world's divergent cultural, economic, political, and social realities (Healey, 1999; Midgley, 1981, 1999; Ragab, 1990). As a corrective, some observers have called for an indigenization of social work theory and practice—that is, that social work theory and methods be more consciously adapted to the culture in which they are applied (Drower, 2000; Ragab, 1990). Numerous scholars insist upon a profession that is, variously, specific to Africa, (Osei, 1996), India (Nagpaul, 1996a, 1996b), or other countries or regions. These indigenization initiatives often highlight localized approaches to practice, as well as transregional, transnational, and transmigratory ways of conceptualizing practice contexts. They have much in common with similar calls in Canada for models of social work that are ethno-racially appropriate to a wide array of communities, including Aboriginal peoples (Morrissette, McKenzie & Morrissette, 1993), or rural, northern, and remote communities (cf. Delaney, Brownlee, & Graham, 1997). Several contributors in this volume—McKenzie and Morrissette on Aboriginal peoples in Canada, Al-Krenawi and Graham on Arab-Canadian peoples, Este and Thomas-Bernard on African-Canadian peoples—are highly sympathetic towards this movement, and consciously situate their work within it. Indigenization is not of the old, and largely discredited, tradition of cultural literalism. It has everything to do with epistemology. And it is an effort to further—on geographic, ethno-racial, and national terms, among others—the diverse knowledge bases, and world views, that provide the foundation for social work knowledge and practice worldwide.

In other respects, different aspects are emphasized one chapter to the next, depending in part on author interest, and in part on the particularities of the community under discussion. Given its importance to the experiences in Canada of people of Ukrainian background, history is a prominent feature of the chapter by Barlow and Barlow. Klein and Mirsky focus on anti-Semitism, a form of discrimination that has commonalities with other forms of racism but also its own particularities. Some chapters span similar terrain, but each has different nuances, as evidenced by the discussion of migration and acculturation in the chapters by Alaggia and Marziali and by Maiter, or on collectivism and individualism in Al-Krenawi and Graham and by Maiter. In a similar vein, issues of adaptation frequently appear in Section 2. It should be noted that not all chapters in that section need to be read in all instances. Indeed, the entire book can be consulted selectively, to reflect student or instructor interest, to keep readings manageable, or to integrate with readings from outside this book.

The term *multicultural*, which is especially prominent in Canadian public policy and scholarly documents, is used in many chapters in this book. In countries other than Canada, words such as cross-cultural, intercultural, ethnocultural, multiple cultures, and transcultural are commonly used to convey concepts similar to multicultural. However, as one Canadian scholar points out, 'multicultural' alone is accurate when describing Canada's diverse population, 'not only because of different streams of new immigration but also because these other terms [cross-cultural, intercultural, etc.] do not encapsulate the increasing heterogeneity in ethnoculture, race, and religion of Canada's people' (Herberg, 1993, p. xvi). *Multicultural social work*, then, assumes a pluralistic context of many ethno-racial communities involved in social work intervention. Yet not all contributors use the term 'multicultural'. Roy and Montgomery, writing on practice in Quebec, prefer the term 'intercultural practice' for reasons that are particular to practice scenarios they write about in that province. Alaggia and Marziali use the term 'cross-cultural' because of the distinct practice scenarios in their chapter. Such is the current state of social work writing in Canada, and we wanted the book to reflect this fully.

The resulting narrative structures throughout this book are reflexive and subjective windows into the views of the contributors. In no way are they meant as the final word on their subjects. Rather, they are intended to stimulate thought and to provide an opportunity for classroom discussion and reader thinking to unfold in a manner that allows learners to engage with their *own* background, using that as a principle for engaging with the literature and with students and clients of different backgrounds (Holland & Kilpatrick, 1993). The book's fundamental contribution, we think, will be its promotion of diverse views from Canadian authors writing on complex issues, and its implicit encouragement for students to think skeptically and to develop their own distinct views, just as the contributors have done. There is no one right way to look at such complex issues as social work with diverse ethno-racial communities. Nor, as the chapters also illuminate, are there any shortcuts through the thoughtful engagement of self-awareness, attempting to understand the contexts in which one works and continuously engaging with clients and broader social service systems to check and recheck assumptions. The multiple perspectives and diversity represented by the book, we emphasize, are a jumping-off point for encouraging plurality within the classroom, where different views can be conveyed in an open, respectful, and inquiring milieu. The book is also a reflection, in turn, of the diverse practice contexts in which workers may find themselves, with different approaches varying by colleagues, agencies, and communities, and with evolving assumptions over time. The book is especially valuable for readers who are non-linear thinkers and who might be less anxious than others about ambivalence, paradox, and relative states of knowing—all common phenomena, as recent Canadian scholarship so aptly conveys, in social work practice (Miehls & Moffatt, 2000; Rossiter, 2000).

It follows that several principles could be encouraged when using this book in any classroom setting. Diller articulates these very effectively; the following list is taken entirely from his work (1999, p. 22):

- There will be no name-calling, labeling, or blaming each other. There are no heroes or villains in this drama; no good people or bad. Each of us harbors our own negative reactions toward those who are different. It is impossible to grow up in a society and not take on its prejudices. So, it is not a matter of whether one is a racist or not. We all are. Rather, it is a question of what negative racial attitudes one has learned so far, and from this moment on, what one is willing to do about them.
- Everything that is said and divulged in this classroom is confidential, and it is not to be talked about with anyone outside of here. Students often censure, measure their words, and are less than honest in what they say out of fear of either looking bad or of having their personal disclosures treated insensitively or as gossip.
- As much as possible, everyone will personalize their discussion and talk about their own experiences. There is much denial around racism that serves as a mechanism for avoiding responsibility. Only by personalizing the subject and speaking in the first, rather than the third, person can this be avoided.
- You can say whatever you believe. This may, in turn, lead to conflict with others. That is okay. But you must be willing to look at it, take responsibility for your words, and learn from what ensues. Anything that happens during class is a learning opportunity. It can and may be analyzed as part of the process. The class is a

microcosm of the outer racial world with all of its problems, and as such, honest interaction in class can shed valuable light on the dynamics of inter-group conflict.
- Our intention is to create a safety zone where students can talk about race in ways that cannot be talked about in most parts of the real world. Most students have serious questions about race and ethnicity that need to be answered or experiences in relation to them that must be processed and better understood. Significant learning about race and ethnicity cannot proceed without this happening. Opportunities to do so are rare, but only through such occasions can growth and healing begin.

As has been suggested above, approaches to social work practice are in a constant state of flux, reflecting a continuous revisiting of self-awareness and professional re-evaluation over a practitioner's lifetime.

Chapters 2 and 3 elaborate on how clinical and community-level practitioners practise competently, while Chapter 5 focuses on policy issues. Space limitations precluded authors from talking at length about agency administration. It istherefore useful to turn briefly to those strategies that might be incorporated by a social service administrator who is committed to cultural competence. Such an administrator:

- Conducts an introspective examination of cultural values, biases and stereotypes within the agency
- Identifies a personal and professional philosophy that encompasses a respect for cultural differences
- Clarifies the reasons why cultural competence is so important to the organization
- Develops a vision around the 'place' where the organization would be if it functioned as one that strives to be culturally competent
- Understands and thinks through the personal and organizational risks that must be taken in launching cultural competence initiatives
- Assumes responsibility for creating and maintaining a culturally supportive environment for staff and clients
- Provides training and staff development that encourage non-threatening opportunities for open discussion of problems and issues
- Assumes a leadership role in encouraging boards and other advisory bodies to reflect in their membership the cultural mix of the client population served by the agency
- Assumes a leadership role in communicating the significance of cultural competence to the governance of the organization
- Recruits and retains staff who are culturally diverse
- Includes all staff in plans for creating a culturally supportive environment
- Commits to achieving a personal and an organizational lifetime goal of cultural competence. (Este, 1999, pp. 42–3, reprinted by permission of Canadian Scholars' Press Inc. © 1999.)

Major Terms for Understanding Ethno-racial Differences

It is worthwhile reviewing the meaning of key terms used throughout this book. *Culture* is 'the totality of ideas, beliefs, values, knowledge, and way of life of a group of people who share a certain historical, religious, racial, linguistic, ethnic, or social background' (Henry, Tator, Mattis, & Rees, 1995, p. 326). A related concept is *race*, a category 'used to classify humankind according to common ancestry and reliant on differentiation by such physical characteristics as colour of skin, hair texture, stature, and facial characteristics' (ibid., p. 328). It is important to distinguish between race and ethnicity. An *ethnic group* is 'a community maintained by a shared heritage, culture, language, or religion; a group bound together by ties of cultural homogeneity, with a prevailing loyalty and adherence to certain beliefs, attitudes, and customs' (ibid., p. 327). Race, ethnicity, culture, and other aspects of an individual contribute to a sense of *identity*, which is 'a subjective sense of coherence, consistency, and continuity of self, rooted in both personal and group history' (ibid., p. 327). Many communities are not in the majority; that is, they are part of a *minority group*, one that 'is either relatively small in number or has little or no access to social, political, or economic power' (ibid., p. 328). Identity may also be expressed as *nationalism*, which may be defined as a social and psychological force that provides people with a sense of perceived unity and community, based on a shared cultural, linguistic, racial, historical, or geographic experience.

All people have *biases*, or 'opinions, preferences, prejudices, or inclinations formed without reasonable justification that then influence an individual's or group's ability to evaluate a particular situation objectively or accurately' (ibid., p. 326). The key to effective social work and, indeed, human functioning is to ensure that biases are not the final determining factor of the human encounter—that an individual is able to suspend biases and revise them subsequent to lived experience and exposure to new peoples and ideas. Anyone with power—and here we include members of majority groups—is capable of asserting hegemony. By *hegemony*, we mean the 'social, cultural, religious, or moral traditions and ideas that reinforce the power of the dominant group at the expense of other groups' (ibid., p. 327). The assertion of hegemony may lead to *oppression*, which may be defined as 'the domination of certain individuals or groups by others through the use of physical, psychological, social, cultural, or economic force' (ibid., p. 328). An important related notion is *ideology*, 'a complex set of ideas that attempts to explain, justify, legitimate, and perpetuate the circumstances in which a collectivity finds itself' (ibid., p. 327). White hegemony over Aboriginal peoples in Canada, for example, has been perpetuated by a racist ideology of white superiority.

Such concepts lead to the term *disadvantage*—that is, the 'unfavourable and unequal access to resources such as employment, education, and social services' (ibid., p. 326). *Racism* is 'a social system in which one group of people exercises power over another group on the basis of skin colour'. It is 'an implicit set of beliefs, erroneous assumptions, and actions based on an ideology of inherent superiority of one racial group over another, and evident in organizational or institutional structures and programs as well as in individual thought or behaviour patterns' (ibid., p. 329). Racism may be rooted within institutions (*institutional racism*) and societies (*structural racism*). In both instances, *racial discrimination* may arise—that is, 'any discrimination, exclusion, restriction, or preference based on race that has the purpose of nullifying or impairing the recognition, enjoyment, or exercise, on an equal footing, of human rights and fundamental freedoms in the political, economic, social, cultural, or other field of public life' (ibid., p. 328).

In other instances, hegemony influences people of minority communities in different ways. One such manifestation is *acculturation*, 'a process of adaptation and change whereby a person or an ethnic, social, religious, language, or national group integrates with or adapts to the cultural values and patterns of the majority group' (ibid., p. 325). A related term, taking acculturation several steps further, is *assimilation*, 'a process by which an individual or group complete adopts—or is absorbed by—the culture, values, and patterns of another social, religious, linguistic, or national group' (ibid., p. 326). Both acculturation and assimilation are related to the notion of integration. By *integration*, we mean a process 'that allows groups and individuals to become full participants in the social, economic, cultural, and political life of a society while at the same time enabling them to retain their own cultural identity' (ibid., p. 328).

Like so many terms in multicultural theory, acculturation and assimilation are relativist, and are best seen along a continuum. It is helpful, in a limited sense, to know that a client belongs to a particular cultural or ethno-racial community. It is far better, however, to know where the client falls along a continuum that extends from traditional identification to complete acculturation. In this way, the worker avoids the pitfall of assuming that a client personifies all of the presumed cultural values of a particular community (Diller, 1999, p. 97). Finally, one should appreciate the considerable emotional strains associated with acculturation, sometimes referred to as *acculturation stress*. Consider, for example, a family newly arrived in Canada, with limited linguistic facility in a dominant language (English or French), who may need to seek a family translator, schooling for children, employment, housing, and other forms of social support. All of these tasks require considerable commitments of emotion and energy. Such considerations are elaborated in Chapter 2.

Collaborative Relationships and Cultural Competence

Recent literature, much of it in the area of mental health, discusses several ways in which other personnel can be used to enhance a practitioner's culturally competent practice. The first of these is an interpreter.

Interpreter
Interpreters are bilingual people who orally translate communication between clients and practitioners (Cheng, 1987). Often, they are chosen for this role because of convenience or availability (for example, they are among the direct care staff). But sharing a common language does not guarantee understanding: if the interpreter has limited knowledge of or background in the ethnic culture of the help-seeking individual, translations that may be literally correct may not convey the

essence of the individual's response (Singh, McKay, & Singh, 1999). Moreover, interpreters focus on translating only the spoken word and may fail to include very important non-verbal cues. In many cultures, normal social interactions rely very heavily on non-verbal communication (Singh, McKay, & Singh, 1998). Sometimes family members and relatives are asked to provide interpreting services. This practice is problematic for many reasons. It is possible that family members may minimize what they might perceive to be potentially embarrassing details about the individual seeking a social service, thereby depriving the practitioner of relevant information (Glasser, 1983).

In summary, having interpreters does not necessarily enhance, or remove cultural barriers to, communication between the individual and the practitioner. Even when interpreters have had exposure to concepts within the helping professions, they may still lack insight into a client's cultural concepts, rituals, beliefs, and help-seeking practices (Singh, McKay, & Singh, 1999).

Cultural Broker

Cultural brokers may provide an effective alternative, and/or supplement, to interpreters in the delivery of social work services. Cultural brokers are people who are acculturated in a particular minority culture or cultures as well as in the mainstream culture (Herzog, 1972; Paine, 1971). They are able to straddle multiple cultures and function as language and cultural bridges. Cultural brokers are in the unique position of being able to communicate the nuances and values of a minority culture to the mainstream culture, and to communicate the nuances and values of the mainstream culture to the minority culture (Singh, McKay, & Singh, 1999). They are different from cultural interpreters in that they not only make communication possible between speakers of different languages but also enhance the interaction and understanding between people of different cultures.

In mental health, the term cultural broker was introduced by Weidman (1975) to describe an intermediary who works with therapists from the mainstream culture and clients from other cultures. The cultural broker facilitates the understanding of the clinician regarding the nature of the problem as perceived by the individual who is seeking a mental health service. Also, the cultural broker helps the individual to understand how the clinician views and treats the problem (Singh, McKay, & Singh, 1999). Often, there are differences in world views of the individual seeking services and the clinician providing them. Further, both may lack insight regarding each other's expectations, especially those related to the treatment process.

Given the different cultural backgrounds of the clinician and the individual seeking services, it is likely that the expectations of each may only partially overlap. One of the cultural broker's roles, therefore, is to increase this overlap by changing the expectations of both the practitioner and client through informal education. The combination of linguistic, cultural skills, and insight into social/mental health service, constitutes the cultural broker's unique expertise in identifying relevant information related to cultural aspects of a client's problems

(Singh, McKay, & Singh, 1999). A cultural broker has a comparative understanding of how a social/mental health service system within an ethno-racial community may differ from that in the clinician's world, and is able to explain these differences to both the client and the practitioner. Because their usefulness extends beyond mere translation, cultural brokers may also be useful with clients who speak the mainstream language.

Cultural Consultant

Budman, Lipson, and Meleis (1992) used the term cultural consultant to describe the involvement of an Arabic-speaking consultant, a nurse-sociologist, in the case of an Iraqi-American adolescent who was admitted to a psychiatric in-patient unit. The principles that arise may be considered potentially applicable to other social work settings. In the case presented by Budman et al., the cultural consultant could be defined as a type of cultural broker who is, in addition to being acculturated in the minority and the mainstream culture, some kind of a mental health professional. As such, the cultural consultant can not only translate or interpret the interaction between the clinician and the help-seeking individual, but also take an active part in the process of diagnosing and treating the individual. In the case study described by Budman et al., the cultural consultant helped in three areas: cultural interpretation, suggestions to improve psychiatric care, and primary care before and after the client's hospitalization.

In general, the cultural consultant's role is to bridge the gap between the clinician and the individual who is seeking help (and, sometimes, his or her family). This is done by helping to clarify the explanatory model of each side to the other: the client (and sometimes his/her family) and the social service system in the person of the practitioner. To accomplish this, the cultural consultant needs in-depth knowledge of the world views of the health care and social service system, the client, and—where relevant—the client's family. With the goal of helping each to understand the other's framework without favouring or alienating either, the cultural consultant should be familiar with the client's culture and with the social service / mental health system. Ideally, cultural consultants should have experience or training in the psychiatric/helping professional field and should be bicultural and bilingual. Awareness of their own identity, behaviour, and biases is also important. Cultural consultants in social services/mental health can serve as brokers and where relevant, diagnosticians, helping the mental health/social service service system to determine the client's problem, within a cultural context.

Cultural Mediator

The purpose of a cultural mediator (CM) is to mediate between two cultures or world views that present potentially different perceptions and traditions of promoting social welfare in a community: those of the social service practitioner and the ethno-racial community in which the practitioner functions. The CM practice is based on co-operation, and contrasts with other types of mediation that typically involve mediating between two sides that represent different interests (Shemer &

Bar-Gay, 2001). CMs do not necessarily have formal credentials in the helping professions. Their role is to translate the different ways that different cultures (the ethno-racial community and the professional culture of the practitioner) define and solve a problem, and to assist the ways they behave in relation to each other (Al-Krenawi & Graham, 2001; Fry & Fry, 1997). In one case example, CMs who were senior members of several Bedouin-Arab tribes in the Middle East assisted social work practitioners to function more sensitively in this cultural context. They provided concrete advice to social workers, and where required, collaborated with social work roles to help render the latter more culturally sensitive. More than just a cross-cultural translator, the CM also functions as a buffer between cultures, helping to maintain the unique identity of each side (Al-Krenawi & Graham, 2001). CMs encourage the culturally sensitive practice of social work and, ideally, the empowerment of different community groups that are deprived of access to power. Thus, CMs are not perceived as a neutral third side but rather are expected to operate in collaboration with social service delivery, for the sake of both social justice in the community and cultural sensitivity in service delivery (Schellenberg, 1996; for more information see Al-Krenawi and Graham [2001]).

Bridging the Gap between Worker and Client

Several other concepts can assist a social worker to appreciate difference and to engage with a client. Every social group has a world view or 'set of more or less systematized beliefs and values in terms of which the group evaluates and attaches meaning to the reality that surrounds it' (cited in Gudykunst & Kim, 1984, p. 40). World views vary by culture and have considerable variance within cultures. They also have the following functions:

- explaining the world
- evaluating the means and ends of behaviour
- psychologically reinforcing beliefs
- integrating people within a collectivity
- helping people to adapt to change and problems (Gudykunst & Kim, 1984, pp. 40–1).

High and Low Contexts
Anthropologist Edward Hall distinguishes between high and low context cultures. By *context*, Hall means the collection of social and cultural conditions that surround and influence the life of an individual, organization, or community. High context cultures tend to emphasize the collective over the individual, have a slower pace of social change, and tend to value social stability. Some Aboriginal, Arab, and Asian communities may be so described. Low context cultures tend to emphasize the individual over the collective, have a faster pace of social change, and tend to value social flux rather than stability (Hall, 1976). Some western European communities may be so described. In all instances, high and low context are ideal types—that is, they are intellectual constructs that assist observers to appreciate

broad distinctions. To allow for individual and community exceptions, and for variances and nuances among cultures, it is best to conceptualize each community along a continuum of high and low context, rather than as high or low context in an absolute sense.

A client from a high context community may be more collectivist and holistic and less individualist than someone from a low context community. Common to some high context communities is the manifestation of mind-body somatic complaints rather than strictly psychological distress (Dwairy, 1998). In such cases, a bio-psychosocial model of intervention that takes into account mind, body, and socio-cultural context, is especially useful. Thus, in working with some high context communities, it may not be useful to apply an intrapsychic focus, which divides the mind, body, and social context, and which is more commonly applied to members of low context, and often Western, communities (Al-Issa, 1990; Dwairy, 1998).

Someone from a high context community may develop a collective ego identity, where the self is more explicitly embedded within the group; individual aspirations may be secondary to those of the collective. Major life decisions such as who to marry, where to live, or what career to pursue may be more group oriented than in a low context community. In addition, individual independence may be less than what is experienced in low contexts. In a high context community, informal community resources (the nuclear and extended family, community members of status, religious leaders, and others) may be the first recourse for identifying and responding to a problem. In many instances, intervention with individuals of a high context community necessitates a social worker interacting with more than the individual client. Effective collaboration is key to promoting a useful intervention.

Low context cultures tend to be more egalitarian in structure; high context cultures more hierarchical. Such considerations are elaborated in Chapter 8, on work with clients of Arab background. The majority ethno-racial group in Canada tends to be low context, valuing democratic political traditions. But the political system of some clients may be less democratic. For example, the world view of a client who has recently immigrated to Canada may be fundamentally different than majority-group views with respect to perceived authority figures such as social workers. Implications necessarily arise in the worker's ability to develop a sense of trust and to create and sustain a helping alliance. Likewise, a client's experience of human rights—the legislative protection of individuals and groups from arbitrary interference with, or curtailment of, life and freedom—may be different from a worker's. Many countries have human rights traditions that are manifestly different from that of Canada. Similarly, a client may have a different experience of civil society—the collection of social institutions that are not ordinarily focused on the family or state (e.g., voluntary organizations, the media, trade unions, professional associations).

Emic, Etic, Relativism, Absolutism, Universalism
Like models of high and low context societies, 'emic' and 'etic' are ideal types that are frequently used in social work. An *emic* perspective is one from the viewpoint

of members of a particular cultural or ethno-racial group. An *etic* perspective, in contrast, is one that is interpreted from an outside point of view (Pike, 1967). Social workers often bring an etic perspective to intervention, and should attempt to better appreciate a client's emic frame of reference. An especially important emic–etic aspect of intervention is the difference between the client's and the social worker's explanatory model for a particular presenting problem. An explanatory model is a symbolic representation of distress applied to a particular instance of psychosocial distress. It is a culturally based, cognitive attempt to comprehend the origins, progress, and possible outcome of a problem. All such explanatory models are products of social construction—that is, the community, cultural, and other backgrounds of each individual help to determine a world view and perception upon which the individual's model is based (Dean, 1993).

The social worker and the client may have divergent explanatory models, and the way in which each is conveyed to the other person represents a complex process of coding and decoding verbal and non-verbal messages (Kleinman, 1980). Social workers' explanatory models are derived from their professional training and cultural assumptions. Clients' models, in contrast, often arise from their emically based culture and experiences. Moreover, the communication patterns with which clients frame their perception and explanation of a problem are based on words and gestures from a emically based symbolic map that includes a particular cosmological context. Take the example of what is understood in the West to be schizophrenia. A social worker's etic perspective may be based on a bio-psychosocial model, while a client within a high context community may have an entirely different terminology, and may perceive causes with reference to external supernatural powers (Al-Krenawi, 1999a, 1999b; Al-Krenawi & Graham, 1997, 1999).

These notions of emic and etic lead, finally, to the terms relativism, absolutism, and universalism. Relativism avoids imposing values and judgments, and attempts to allow each cultural context to be understood in its own emic terms. Absolutism is an etic perspective taken to its extreme: it applies the same evaluative criteria across cultures in a fixed, unchanging perspective, minimizing the significance of cultural context. Universalism attempts to bridge relativism and absolutism. It assumes, as an example, that such psychological processes as pleasure and pain may be universal, but that they are manifested in culturally specific ways (Pedersen, 1995). Let us, for the sake of illustration, apply these concepts to mental health: in a universalistic framework, all cultures experience mental health problems, but there may be differences in how symptoms are perceived, expressed, and experienced. A relativist position allows a problem to be understood within its own cultural context; among the Bedouin-Arab, for example, there are traditional healers who experience a *baraka*, a type of mental breakdown, which is understood by the culture to be a healing presence from a supernatural power that allows the person to begin a journey of becoming a *dervish*, a well-respected traditional healer (Al-Krenawi, Graham, & Maoz, 1996). Finally, an absolutist perspective assumes that there are no differences across cultures in the ways that mental health problems are experienced or manifested.

The preceding concepts provide a framework for social workers to establish and maintain a working relationship with clients. In essence, they provide greater clarity of distinction between emic and etic aspects of practice. Differentiating between the concepts of emic and etic assists social workers to identify differences and to think more explicitly about integrating a client's world view with social work practice. In many ways, a greater appreciation of the client's—and the worker's—ethno-racially based emic world allows a social worker to overcome assumptions of professional training that otherwise create a strongly etic (that is, professional) biased perception. Especially in Section 2 of this book, contributors, often from the same racial or ethnic groups about which they write, distinguish between the emic and etic, and provide readers with an opportunity to extrapolate principles to their own practice lives. Implicit to the entire book is a hopeful way of looking at the evolution of social work knowledge. To some extent, engaging with a client of a different ethno-racial background enables social workers to grasp beyond their ordinary reach. The accumulated wisdom of these encounters will have a commensurate impact upon the entire profession. We hope that the good that comes from these interventions will render practice less oppressive and harmful.

References

Al-Issa, I. (1990). Culture and mental illness in Algeria. *International Journal of Social Psychiatry*, *36*(3), 230–240.

Al-Krenawi, A. (1999a). Explanations of mental health symptoms by the Bedouin-Arabs of the Negev. *International Journal of Social Psychiatry*, *45*(1), 56–64.

———. (1999b). Integrating cultural rituals into family therapy: A case study with a Bedouin-Arab patient in Israel. *Journal of Family Psychotherapy*, *10*(1), 61–73.

Al-Krenawi, A., & Graham, J.R. (1997). Spirit possession and exorcism: The integration of modern and traditional mental health care systems in the treatment of a Bedouin patient. *Clinical Social Work Journal*, *25*, 211–22.

———. (1999). Gender and biomedical/traditional mental health utilization among the Bedouin-Arabs of the Negev. *Culture, Medicine, and Psychiatry*, *23*(2), 219–43.

———. (2001). The cultural mediator: Bridging the gap between a non-Western community and professional social work practice. *British Journal of Social Work*, *31*, 665–85.

Al-Krenawi, A., Graham, J.R., & Maoz, B. (1996). The healing significance of the Negev's Bedouin-Arab *Dervish*. *Social Science and Medicine*, *43*(1), 13–21.

Bishop, A. (1994). *Becoming an Ally*. Halifax: Fernwood.

Budman, C.L., Lipson, J.G., & Meleis, A.I. (1992). The cultural consultant in mental health care: The case of an Arab adolescent. *American Journal of Orthopsychiatry*, *62*(3), 359–70.

Casas, M.J. (1985). A reflection on the status of racial/ethnic minority research. *Counseling Psychologist*, *13*(4), 581–98.

Cheng, L. (1987). *Assessing Asian Language Performance: Guidelines for Evaluating Limited-English-Proficient Students.* Rockville, MD: Aspen Publications.

Clairmont, D.H.J., & Magill, D.W. (1974). *Africville: The Life and Death of a Canadian Black Community.* Toronto: McClelland and Stewart.

Cross, T.L, Bazron, B.J., Dennis, K.W., & Isaacs, M.R. (1989). *Towards a Culturally Competent System of Care.* Washington, DC: Georgetown University Child Development Center.

Dean, R.G. (1993). Teaching a constructivist approach to clinical practice. *Journal of Teaching and Social Work, 8,* 55–75.

Delaney, R., Brownlee, K., & Graham, J.R. (Eds) (1997). *Strategies in Northern Social Work Practice.* Thunder Bay: Centre for Northern Studies.

Devore, W., & Schlesinger, E.G. (1996). *Ethnic Sensitive Social Work Practice.* New York: Macmillan.

Diller, J.V. (1999). *Cultural Diversity: A Primer for the Human Services.* New York: Wadsworth Press.

Dominelli, L. (1997). *Anti-Racist Social Work.* London: Macmillan.

Drower, S.J. (2000). Globalisation: an opportunity for dialogue between South African and Asian social work educators. *Indian Journal of Social Work. 61*(1), 12–31.

Dwairy, M.A. (1998). *Cross-Cultural Counseling: The Arab-Palestinian Case.* New York: Haworth Press.

Emery, G., & Emery, J.C.H. (1999). *A Young Man's Benefit: The Independent Order of Oddfellows and Sickness Insurance in the United States and Canada, 1860–1929.* Montreal: McGill-Queen's University Press.

Este, D. (1999). Social work and cultural competency. In G. Lie & D. Este (Eds), *Professional Social Service Delivery in a Multicultural World.* (pp. 27–45). Toronto: Canadian Scholars' Press.

Friesen, G. (2000). *Citizens and Nation: An Essay on History, Communication, and Canada.* Toronto: University of Toronto Press.

Fry, D.P., & Fry, C.B. (1997). Culture and conflict-resolution models: Exploring alternatives to violence. In D.P. Fry & K. Björkqvist (Eds), *Cultural Variation in Conflict Resolution* (pp. 9–23). Mahwah, NJ: Lawrence Erlbaum Associates.

Glasser, I. (1983). Guidelines for using an interpreter in social work. *Child Welfare, 57,* 468–70.

Graham, J.R. (1992). The Haven, 1878–1930: A Toronto charity's transition from a religious to a professional ethos. *Histoire sociale/Social History, 25*(50), 283–306.

———. (1996). An analysis of Canadian social welfare historical writing. *Social Service Review, 70*(1), 140–58.

Gudykunst, W.B., & Kim, Y.Y. (1984). *Communicating with Strangers: An Approach to Intercultural Communication.* New York: Random House.

Hall, E. (1976). *Beyond Culture.* New York: Doubleday.

Healey, L. (1999). International social work curriculum in historical perspective. In R.J. Link & C.S. Ramanathan (Eds), *All Our Futures: Principles and Resources for Social Work Practice in a Global Era* (pp. 14–29). New York: Brooks/Cole.

Henry, F., Tator, C., Mattis, W., & Rees, T. (1995). *The Colour of Democracy: Racism in Canadian Society*. Toronto: Harcourt Brace.

Herberg, D.C. (1993). *Frameworks for Cultural and Racial Diversity: Teaching and Learning for Practitioners*. Toronto: Canadian Scholars' Press.

Herrnstein, R. (1971). I.Q. *Atlantic Monthly, 228*(3), 43–64.

Herzog, J.D. (1972). The anthropologist as broker in community education: A case study and some general propositions. *Council on Anthropology and Education Newsletter, 3*, 9–14.

Holland, T.P., & Kilpatrick, A.C. (1993). Using narrative techniques to enhance multicultural practice. *Journal of Social Work Education, 29*(3), 302–8.

Johnson, S.D. (1990). Toward clarifying culture, race and ethnicity in the context of multicultural counseling. *Journal of Multicultural Counseling and Development, 18*, 4–50.

Katz, J. (1985). The sociopolitical nature of counseling. *Counseling Psychologist, 13*, 615–24.

Kleinman, A. (1980). *Patients and Healers in the Context of Culture*. Berkeley: University of California Press.

Lee, M.Y., & Greene, G.J. (1999). A social constructivist framework for integrating cross-cultural issues in teaching clinical social work. *Journal of Social Work Education, 35*(1), 21–7.

Lie, G.W., & Este, D. (Eds) (1999). *Professional Social Service Delivery in a Multicultural World*. Toronto: Canadian Scholars' Press.

Lum, D. (1992). *Social Work Practice and People of Color. A Process-Stage Approach*. Pacific Grove, CA: Brooks/Cole.

Macey, M., & Moxon, E. (1996). An examination of anti-racist and anti-oppressive theory and practice in social work education. *British Journal of Social Work; 26*(3), 297–314.

Midgley, J. (1981). *Professional Imperialism: Social Work in the Third World*. London: Heinemann.

Miehls, D., & Moffatt, K. (2000). Constructing social work identity based on the reflexive self. *British Journal of Social Work, 30*(3), 339–48

Morrissette, V., McKenzie, B., & Morrissette, L. (1993). Towards an Aboriginal model of social work practice: Cultural knowledge and traditional practices. *Canadian Social Work Review, 10*(1), 91–108.

Moynihan, D.P. (1965). *The Negro Family: The Case for National Action*. Washington, DC: US Department of Labor, Office of Policy, Planning and Research.

Nagpaul, H. (1996a). *Modernization and Urbanization in India: Problems and Issues*. New Delhi: Rawat.

———. (1996b). *Social Work in Urban India*. New Delhi: Rawat.

Osei, H.K. (1996). The indigenisation of social work practice and education in Africa: The dilemma of theory and method. *Maatskaplike-Werk / Social-Work, 32*(3), 215–25.

Padilla, A.M. (1981). Competent communities: A critical analysis of theories and public policy. In O.A. Barbain, P.R. Good, O.M. Pharr, & J.A. Siskind (Eds),

Institutional Racism and Community Competence (pp. 20–9). Rockville, MD: US Department of Health and Human Services.

Paine, R. (1971). *Patrons and Brokers in the East Arctic*. Toronto: University of Toronto Press.

Pedersen, P.B. (1995). Culture-centered ethical guidelines for counselors. In J.G. Ponterotto, J.M. Casas, L.A. Suzuki, & C.M. Alexander (Eds), *Handbook of Multicultural Counseling* (pp. 34–52). Thousand Oaks, CA: Sage.

Pike, K. (1967). *Language in Relation to a Unified Theory of the Structure of Human Behaviour*. 2nd ed. Paris: Mouton.

Ponterotto, J.G., & Casas, M. (1991). *Handbook of Racial/Ethnic Minority Counseling Research*. Springfield, IL: Charles C. Thomas.

Ragab, I.A. (1990). How social work can take root in developing countries. *Social-Development-Issues, 12*(3), 38–51.

Rossiter, A. (2000). The professional is political: an interpretation of the problem of the past in solution-focused therapy. *American Journal of Orthopsychiatry, 70*(2), 150–61.

Rubington, E., & Weinberg, M.S. (1971). *The Study of Social Problems*. New York: Oxford University Press.

Schellenberg, J.A. (1996). *Conflict Resolution: Theory, Research, and Practice*. New York: State University of New York Press.

Shemer, A., & Bar-Gay, E. (2001). Cultural mediating among the community. *Mifgash: Journal for Social-Educational Work, 14*, 161–75. (in Hebrew).

Shewell, H., & Spagnut, A. (1995). The First Nations of Canada: Social welfare and the quest for self-government. In J. Dixon & R.P. Scheurell (Eds), *Social Welfare with Indigenous Peoples* (pp. 1–53). London: Routledge.

Singh, N.N., McKay, J.D., & Singh, A.N. (1998). Culture and mental health: Nonverbal communication. *Journal of Child and Family Studies, 7*, 403–9.

———. (1999). The need for cultural brokers in mental health services. *Journal of Child and Family Studies, 8*(1), 1–10.

Speisman, S. (1973). Munificent Parsons and Municipal Parsimony. *Ontario History, 65*(1), 33–49.

Sue, D.W. (1981). *Counseling the Culturally Different: Theory and Practice*. New York: Wiley.

Towle, C. (1945). *Common human needs*. Chicago: University of Chicago Press.

Tsang, A.K.T., & George, U. (1998). Towards an integrated framework for cross-cultural social work practice. *Canadian Social Work Review, 15*(1), 73–93.

Ursel, J. (1992). *Private Lives, Public Policy: One Hundred Years of State Intervention in the Family*. Toronto: Women's Press.

Weidman, H. (1975). Concepts as strategies for change. *Psychiatric Annals, 5*, 312–14.

Williams, C. (1999). Connecting anti-racist and anti-oppressive theory and practice: Retrenchment or reappraisal? *British Journal of Social Work, 29*(2), 211–30.

Winks, R.W. (1997). *The Blacks in Canada: A History*. Montreal: McGill-Queen's University Press.

Knowledge and Skills

Chapters in Section 1 outline some of the knowledge and skills that are necessary for social work in a multicultural Canada. Chapter 2 discusses knowledge and skills required for effective direct multicultural practice with individuals, families, and small groups. It introduces the reader to a process of self-discovery fundamental to multicultural work. Cultural skill areas are outlined as a general framework for developing new skills. New issues relating to migration are introduced as part of a new knowledge base linked to globalization and cultural pluralism. A brief overview of some of the most important direct practice issues is then presented. Concluding remarks offer some fundamental principles for competent direct multicultural practice.

Chapter 3 examines the knowledge, skills, and values necessary for effective social work practice in the domain of community development and organization in diverse community groups. The chapter focuses on four major areas: community development and organizing, unique knowledge, community development skills, and appropriate values for community work.

Chapter 4 addresses the effects of Canadian social policy on those commonly referred to as ethno-racial groups. Emphasis is placed on how Canada's social policies have shaped the experience of those categorized as 'visible minorities'. Consideration is given to aspects of Canadian social policy, and the resulting network of services, institutions, and programs, in historical perspective. Important issues in the formulation and implementation of social policy, as these relate to political ideology, are identified. The chapter closes with a brief consideration of dimensions that would be necessary to consider in order to build an egalitarian, truly inclusive, society.

Chapter 5 explores the issues of race and ethnicity in the delivery of social work by considering the way in which Whiteness attempts to define and delimit them both. Based on an examination of this power, an alternative framework for social work practice develops that frees both Whites and other ethno-racial people from producing and reproducing power dynamics that sustain institutional and societal-wide oppression.

Chapter 6 considers social work practice with those who have immigrated to Quebec. The first part sets out the historical and political framework for understanding immigration in Quebec and examines institutional responses to pluralism. The second section looks more specifically at the positioning of the social worker in this context and at various intervention tools that facilitate practice with immigrants.

Chapter 2

Culturally Appropriate Knowledge and Skills Required for Effective Multicultural Practice with Individuals, Families, and Small Groups

Marie Lacroix

Although the multicultural nature of Canadian society and the pluralism of the Canadian social work context have gained some recognition within mainstream social work practice, myths and prejudices still abound about the 'other'. Very often, fear of the unknown is at the root of our misconceptions. Major cities such as Vancouver, Toronto, and Montreal have historically been areas where immigrants and refugees have settled. However, across Canada, smaller cities and towns still exist where the population remains relatively homogeneous. Many social work students have therefore been insulated from demographic changes and may have never met people originating from different ethnic or even class backgrounds; such students remain 'culturally encapsulated' (Ben-David & Amit, 2000). At the same time, immigrants, refugees, and members of other oppressed and minority groups are joining the ranks of the profession, raising new issues and bringing forth their world views. The multicultural nature of practice, at least in large cities, may also prove to be a new challenge for those social workers who come from more homogeneous and traditional societies.

The concept of diversity emerged in the 1990s to describe the context of practice in increasingly pluralistic western societies. New issues, brought about by the increased mobility of people, massive migrations, and the emergence of a 'global village', are challenging old conceptual frameworks and the foundations of a Eurocentric world view. Within this context what remains unchanged is the mandate of social work, its values and ethics: social work is still committed to humanism, egalitarian ideals, and treating people with respect (Mullaly, 1993). The knowledge base of social work is expanding to include a broader spectrum of populations, and attention is now focused on developing culturally competent practice that considers not only the multicultural and socio-cultural reality of people (Chau, 1991) but also the impact of migration, oppression, and marginalization.

Whereas practice within a context of ethnic and cultural diversity has often been taught as an adjunct to other courses, such as mental health or work with the elderly (Green, 1999), certain authors now advocate infusing multicultural content into all courses (Le-Doux & Montalvo, 1999). Generic skills taught as part of the social work curriculum have increasingly focused on incorporating new skills and knowledge in an attempt to sensitize students to the growing multicultural nature of practice. Yet if practitioners are to intervene competently with different cultural or ethnic groups, immigrants, and refugees, generic skills need translation so that they work in a context where both client and worker may have very different views and points of reference, not only of the world but also of helping relationships and the role of the social worker. Part of our challenge as social work teachers, then, is to offer tools that will enable students to work with diverse populations.

This chapter introduces students and workers to a process of self-discovery fundamental to multicultural practice. The ethnic lens approach (Cox & Ephross, 1998)—knowing one's values and beliefs and how these intervene in the social work process—is the first step to competency in multicultural practice. Cultural skill areas are then outlined as a general framework for developing new skills. New issues relating to migration are introduced as part of a new knowledge base linked to globalization and cultural pluralism. Mass migrations are now challenging notions of rights, citizenship, belonging, and otherness. To practise in a multicultural setting, social workers need to understand some of the issues peculiar to immigrants and refugees. Therefore, a brief overview of some of the most important issues is then presented. The most salient issues in practice with individuals, families, and groups are outlined. Concluding remarks offer some fundamental principles for competent multicultural practice.

Experiential Knowledge

Moving towards Ethnorelativism

The focus for teaching and learning culturally competent social work practice needs to be on developing skills in the cognitive and affective domains to allow students to move from ethnocentricity to ethnorelativism (Krajewski-Jaime et al., 1996; Garcia & Van Soest, 1999). *Ethnocentricity* refers to being centred in one's world view, taking for granted that what members of one's own culture say, think, and do is the only way to approach things, and assuming that all people approach things the same way—or ought to. *Ethnorelativism*, on the other hand, is defined as 'the ability not only to accept and respect cultural differences, but also the empathic ability to shift to another cultural world view' (Krajewski-Jaime et al., 1996, p. 16). To achieve this, experiential components such as critical incidents[1] and intellectual and affective learning (Garcia & Van Soest, 1999; Krajewski-Jaime et al., 1996) are increasingly part of training. *Experiential components* aim at putting students in a situation where they confront their prejudices and biases on an emotional rather than strictly cognitive level. In *critical incidents*, for example, a context for intervention is presented through a story. Workers read the story and are asked about its specific salient values. They are then asked to explain their intervention according to the values expressed in the story. Experiential learning enables students to incorporate knowledge and skills relevant to practice in a multicultural context and move from a cognitive level towards affective knowledge to develop a better understanding of immigrant and minority problems—individual, family, and community—that may lead to use of social services (Christensen, 1992).

Among the new ways of learning, some authors are advocating international field placements as 'offering the possibility of developing new paradigms of intervention and enhancing understanding of cultural difference and structural oppression' (Lyons, 1999, p. 29). One such model is operationalized through a seven-week practicum in a geriatric hospital in Mexico. The placement provides a structured experiential intercultural learning experience in which students confront their ethnocentric perspective: 'Students move through ethnocentric stages, beginning with a denial of essential cultural differences between peoples and ending with the minimization of the importance of these differences and, only then, beginning to move through stages of ethnorelativism to the final internalization of multicultural frames of reference' (Krajewski-Jaime et al., 1996, p. 18). The steps outlined in the model—denial of cultural differences, defence against these differences, minimization of differences, acceptance of differences, adaptation and integration of differences—reflect stages often experienced by students while in the field or engaged in multicultural practice; they provide a framework within which we can develop an understanding of cultural differences.

It is useful to consider that multicultural learning is not a linear, orderly process; rather, it is a process that occurs in complex ways through increasing levels of cultural self-knowledge as an integral part of understanding how responses to culturally different persons are manifested (Nakanishi & Rittner, 1992, p. 29). Social work is about process, not a series of individuated acts (Payne, 1991). It is through this process that we become conscious of our own ethnocentricity and apply skills specific to multicultural practice. The notion of process is therefore central to practice in this environment. As practitioners engage with clients, they will move through several stages, first denying differences, wanting to feel they are all the same, and eventually integrating differences to accommodate the context.

Cultural Skill Areas

Different models and approaches have been developed to work with ethnic and cultural minorities (Green & Watkins, 1998; Cohen-Émérique, 1980, 1993, 2000; Bertot & Jacob, 1991; Dominelli, 1996, 1998; Lum, 1996; Green, 1999; Cox & Ephross, 1998). Whatever the practice model, many writers in this field agree that certain specific knowledge areas are important to multicultural practice. Diller (1999), for example, outlines some major skill areas for practitioners to consider:

- awareness and acceptance of differences in cultures: our ability to recognize how differences may affect the helping process
- self-awareness: our ability to recognize that our culture may have an impact on the helping process
- awareness of the dynamics of cultural difference: our capacity to understand that miscommunication can occur because of the meaning different cultures bear towards such behaviour as eye contact, shaking hands, for example
- knowledge of the clients' culture: understanding the clients' cultural context, their beliefs, how their society is configured
- adaptation of skills: adapting generic social work practice to accommodate cultural differences (e.g., in setting the time or place of meetings); treatment goals can be altered to fit cultural values

New Knowledge Base Related to Migration

Given a rapidly evolving international context, multicultural social work skills have to be developed within a new knowledge base. Globalization means, among other things, large movements of migrants moving about the globe. This is one area social work has only begun to address. Refugees constitute one category of migrants within multicultural practice. Social workers need to be aware of the new social problems and issues brought about by the influx of refugees into Canada. Culturally specific knowledge and skills constitute one level of intervention with refugees. However, in addition to being aware of issues related to culture and ethnicity, practitioners must understand the meaning of migration (Soydan, 1998; Soydan & Williams, 1998), as well as the marginalization often associated with immigration status. Several authors have raised the issue of developing special programs and approaches when working specifically with refugees (Beattie & Randell, 1997; Cohen-Émérique, 1993, 2000; Green, 1999; Jacob, 1993a, 1993b; Lacroix, 2001; Legault, 1996, 2000; Lum, 1996; Pedersen et al., 1989).

Whether voluntary (immigrants) or forced (refugees), migration is a painful experience and always involves a rupture with the past. Among the issues social workers often confront in practice are loss of status and of past identities, under-employment, and non-recognition of educational and professional qualifications (Soydan, 1998, p. 20).

Loss is defined as the separation of an individual or group of individuals from a loved or prized object. The object may be a person or a group of persons, a job, a social position or status, an ideal or fantasy, or a body part (Williams, Zinner, & Ellis, 1999, p. 5). Multicultural reactions to trauma and how people deal with grief, pain, and loss are important elements to consider, and the skills we develop reflect the ability of the worker to learn from a situation: 'Effective helpers allow those they help to instruct them about what or who was lost and the meaning of the loss' (ibid., p. 6).

Post-Traumatic Stress Disorder

Post-traumatic stress disorder (PTSD), which can affect individuals, families, or communities (Williams, Zinner, & Ellis, 2000), is an emerging area in social work.

We need only think of the survivors of the Rwandan genocide, or the women raped in Bosnia, to understand the scope of the problem. According to Lum, the chief symptoms of post-traumatic stress include:

> (1) recurring or intrusive recollections of past traumas; (2) recurrent dreams and nightmares; (3) sad feelings, as if the traumatic events are recurring; (4) social numbness and withdrawal; (5) restricted affect; (6) hyperalertness, hyperactive startled reaction; (7) sleep disorders; (8) guilt; (9) memory impairment; (10) avoidance of activities that might trigger recollection of events; and (11) reactivation of symptoms caused by exposure to events similar to the original trauma (1996, pp. 258–9).

Gender Issues

Social work is only beginning to address issues related to gender and migration. These include women's specific refugee experience (Moussa, 1993), female genital mutilation (FGM) (Shermarke, 1995), rape, and torture. In their study on female genital mutilation among Bedouin-Arab women of the Negev, Al-Krenawi and Graham (1999) stress the importance of appreciating the culturally specific contexts in which the practice is carried out. They argue that 'social work practice needs to be collaboratively applied, rather than arbitrarily imposed' (p. 34). This means that in order to develop 'culturally-specific ways of (re) conceptualizing the custom' (p. 29), the social worker must understand the cultural context and the motivating factors that come into play when women decide to participate in the ritual. In this very sensitive area of FGM, workers and educators are encouraged to read, attend seminars, and talk to people about issues that are traumatic for people seeking help but also, at times, for Western workers, who may never have been confronted with these issues and who may feel profoundly disturbed.

Intervention with Individuals and Families

When presented with an approach specific to multicultural practice, a student once asked what differentiated this approach from any other in social work practice. This is a good question and one that is often overlooked. Indeed, all encounters in practice could be said to constitute a multicultural encounter or episode (Vacc, DeVaney, & Wittmer, 1995). The question was considered in the mid-1980s by Christensen, following the earlier work of Pedersen: 'If we consider the value perspectives of age, sex role, life-style, socioeconomic status and other special affiliations as cultural, then we may conclude that all counselling is to some extent cross-cultural' (Christensen, 1985, p. 63). Such a view serves to demystify multicultural practice, making it less threatening, more approachable. It is important to understand that within a cultural encounter both parties influence each other (Perez-Foster, 1998; Cox & Ephross, 1998; Green, 1999; Cohen-Émérique, 2000). The ultimate goal of practice then, should be 'a real collaborative interaction between two human psyches who together are struggling to understand how they impact on each other' (Perez-Foster, 1998, p. 266).

The Social Work Process

People who seek help do so at times of need and sometimes at great cost to their feeling of self-worth and dignity. The first step in the intervention process is for the worker to recognize that social work emerged within a Eurocentric world view, a Western paradigm (Diller, 1999) with values, beliefs, and approaches specific to Western culture. The following quote offers powerful imagery of what happens when people seek help:

> When the sufferer, trailing a concentrated mix of belief, imagery, and anxiety, appears before an authorized, professional healer [the] disvalued experience is transformed into the clinical 'presenting problem'. The erupting emotions in one's personal life become 'symptoms' to be 'managed'. Clipboards, file folders, closed doors and modulated voices subdue, at least for the moment, disallowed interpretations of crisis. In the clinics and offices of institutional medicine and counselling, physically and functionally set apart from the client's daily life, the interplay of history, biography, and cultural context is usually subordinate to symptom identification, classification, and assessment. (Green, 1999, p. 54)

Here, 'symptom identification', 'classification', and 'assessment' are concepts based on a Western view of the nature of social problems. Although this is how we in the West address social problems, such views may be foreign to communal societies where family and community are involved in problem-solving processes as part of the culture. At the same time, the key notion of process may have been lost in our attempt to quantify, to apply a 'scientific' method to a practice that is, in the end, social (Green, 1999).

Within the social work process, workers need to be attentive to new areas dictated by the cultural traditions of the client. Culture is not static; it evolves and transforms itself through time. Culture defines who we are, our beliefs and values, where we come from, and how we see the world. 'Cultures shape the understanding of one's self-place in the world, as well as define the threshold and boundaries of connection and communication with others' (Perez-Foster, 1998, p. 258). It should be clear that, as social workers, we never meet 'ethnic groups' or 'cultures'. We meet individuals who may or may not define themselves in the ways we perceive them in a particular context (Asamoah et al., 1991). Other issues, such as gender or class, may override issues of culture and ethnicity in any given situation. Therefore, moving towards ethnorelativism means being attentive to those elements. Crucial at the beginning phase of the helping process are a worker's skills in the areas of interviewing, information gathering, developing the helping relationship, rapport and formulation, treatment planning, and intervention. Workers need to evaluate basic facilitative skills such as attending, responding, reflecting, and questioning to see whether or not they work in a multicultural setting (Chau, 1990, pp. 130–1). Plionis and Lewis (1995), for example, warn that 'rephrasing comments actually distorts the original meaning and jeopardizes their integrity because it runs them through the "filter" of others' life experiences' (p. 185). Workers need to develop ethno-sensitive listening skills, tuning in to the client's cultural framework (Cox & Ephross, 1998). Goal development should be based on the client's perceptions of needs (Thornton & Garrett, 1995, p. 70). The social worker's assumption of what the problem is may not be accurate. We should strive for the 'good fit' (Chau, 1991), understanding clients' perceptions of need. The following categories are representative of some of the major areas workers should consider when intervening in a multicultural setting.

Types of Services Asked of Social Workers

At the beginning of the intervention process mutual expectations must be clear for both the client and the worker (Cox & Ephross, 1998). As an illustration, consider the comments of a community worker in Montreal: 'We really had a rough time when the Russians started coming. As soon as we have an office they take us for bureaucrats, they were always criticizing and wouldn't trust anybody with their problems' (personal communication). People often come to Canada with a conception of the reality of daily life in this country that may differ from the mainstream, and the actuality often falls short of their expectations. Social work is a Western profession; in many non-Western societies, problems Western social workers consider worthy of social work intervention are dealt with by the family, the community, traditional healers, or religious leaders. Sensitive clarity of communication is vital to the social work process. Workers should clarify their role and the limits of what is possible in the practice context, whether institutional or community based.

Perceptions

The second step in a helping process involves a process of *decentration* (Cohen-Émérique, 1980, 2000)—that is, of self-discovery of those elements that constitute the foundation upon which our world view is built. This process involves risks: 'recognition of bias can stir feelings of disappointment in oneself, embarrassment, guilt and helplessness' (Plionis & Lewis, 1995, p. 181). Students need to recognize that miscommunication is very often at the root of a failed intervention. Moving towards ethnorelativism starts with understanding that both the worker and the client come to the helping relationship with perceptions, biases, and prejudices about the other. As Cox and Ephross (1998) point out, all ethnic groups distinguish between 'us' and 'them'. To avoid cultural misunderstandings, workers should be interested not only in facts about the other's culture but also in the client's perceptions (Vacc, DeVaney & Wittmer, 1995). Fulher (1995) argues that social workers should clearly realize their own cultural/ethnic background or history. Such self-awareness enables workers to move away from the tendency to impose their own values on others; to not limit intervention/treatment plans; to know when to refer clients elsewhere; and to minimize risks of offending clients by their behaviour. It is only through dialogue that our perceptions can become clear. Perhaps 'the most significant contribution that social work can make to the cultural dialogue is the recognition that it goes on inside all of us' (Martinez-Brawley & Brawley, 1999, p. 29).

Culture Shock

Linked to issues of perception are questions surrounding culture shock. Practice in a multicultural environment can be a very confronting experience both for the worker and the client. It can result in culture shock, which stems from 'value systems, refers to ways of looking and thinking about things, unconscious images, to a vision of the world that determines behaviors and actions' (Legault, 1996, p. 52). Legault, who studied the issue among social workers in Montreal, concludes that culture shock 'leads to misunderstandings of various kinds and extents and can result in intervention problems if not processed and analyzed' (ibid.).

People who come from non-Western societies may have prejudices about the roles of women and men in the West, or about values that may be perceived as having been lost to industrialization and capitalism. For some people, the fact that churches are empty in Quebec may mean that values and morals have been decimated, resulting in high divorce rates and single-parent families. AIDS may be perceived as the result of promiscuous sexual behaviour that does not exist in their societies. The plight of many elderly people in Canada may be incomprehensible to someone from a society in which extended families take care of their elderly, not allowing them to live alone in squalor and poverty.

Upon arrival in Canada, immigrants from traditional or hierarchical societies are confronted with values, ways of thinking, ways of life (including family life and childrearing practices) that are completely foreign and that may precipitate feelings of anxiety, fear, and alienation. Integration services for newcomers are limited (Bertot & Mekki-Berrada, 1999), and few services exist for new immigrants to learn about Canadian society or about its history, elements that would help explain the development of dominant ideas and behaviour (Cox & Ephross, 1998). Social workers have an important role to play in explaining behaviours, values, daily routines, and expectations; this takes time and patience. Similarly, issues confronting newcomers, which are often mirrored back to us, can lead us to question our own values and belief systems.

Ethnorelativism is achieved, therefore, by stepping back from what we know to be true and by listening to what we are saying, doing, and feeling in the context. It means tuning in to the other's reality and how the person may be perceiving the situation. The following categories illustrate some of the major areas where cultural misunderstandings often occur,[2] in working both with individuals and families.

Competence Areas or Areas of Possible Cultural Misunderstanding

Notions of Time and Space

In much of Canada time is structured but it may be more fluid in other societies (Al-Krenawi & Graham, 2000). Although perception of time in Canada may differ from that of other societies, social workers often expect people from other cultures to understand time in the same way they do. Diller (1999) points out that 'European Americans view time as compartmentalized and incremental, and as such, being on time and being efficient with one's time are positive values' (p. 53). Furthermore, 'lateness is often misinterpreted as indifference, provocative, or symptomatic of a lack of basic work skills' (p. 54). Lateness can be particularly irritating for social workers, who often work on very tight schedules. When clients show up late for an appointment or come the next day without an appointment, workers should be aware that the client's notion of time may be very different than the norm. Humour always helps to defuse a situation, and flexibility is a skill all social workers need to develop. As Al-Krenawi & Graham (2000) point out, 'Social workers would do well to clearly establish early on what the rules are regarding appointment times, lateness, and missed sessions' (p. 15).

Canadians live in a vast land and are generally used to maintaining a certain distance when speaking to each other—some call this a 'bubble', or private space. When someone crosses the line, Canadians are inclined to feel uncomfortable. People's proximity can generate feelings of uneasiness and lead to misunderstandings. Situations involving large numbers of people living in small quarters often challenge mainstream values about appropriate space and can lead to misunderstandings, especially when child protection services are involved (Legault & Roy, 2000, p. 201). For example, promiscuity may be suspected when adults and children share the same sleeping quarters. It is important for workers to understand that notions of time and space may have an impact on the relationship with the client and that it is important to reframe these notions within a cultural context.

Notion of the Person

Whereas in Western societies the 'I' is central to the definition of the person, and the autonomy of the individual is valued, non-Western societies tend to use 'we' to encapsulate the notion of person. The individual does not exist without his or her family and community. Thus, it is important to understand that when a meeting is set with an individual, this client may arrive with members of his or her family. Workers need to be prepared to meet with family members and forgo traditional understandings of privacy and confidentiality. For example, in their study on social work practice with Arab clients, Al-Krenawi and Graham (2000) explain that, 'contrary to a Western therapeutic emphasis on the individual, all interventions with Arab clients need to be couched in the context of family, extended family, community, or tribal background' (p. 13). Furthermore, they state that 'among Arab peoples, . . . the group or family identity remains the focus and the individual remains embedded in the collective identity' (ibid.).

Notion of the Family

Definitions of the family in Western societies have become restricted to immediate family members: parents/partners and children. For many societies, definitions of family include the extended family—aunts, uncles, grandparents, cousins, and members of the village or the community. The family may be organized according to a patriarchal structure, which includes a traditional division of labour and control over expression of women's sexuality (Cox & Ephross, 1998, p. 64). Al-Krenawi and Graham refer to the patriarchal organization of Iranian families that 'is to be acknowledged by addressing fathers first and as the head of the family. The social worker should not attempt to change cultural power hierarchies or role patterns since this will alienate the family' (2000, p. 12). They suggest some techniques in working with Iranian families: minimal eye contact and appropriate physical distances. Moreover, when devising an intervention plan based on our notions of autonomy, it is important to consider how this may go against other cultural traditions.

Status and Role of Women within the Family

In many societies, the role of women is still confined to their position as wife and mother. Unmarried women often cannot leave the house without being accompanied by a male family member. Social workers need to understand how this configuration often changes through the migratory process. After arriving in Canada, women often start working outside the home, upsetting traditional roles within the family. In addition, through family reunification, women may have joined their husbands after many years of separation. Estrangement, expectations, and dreams are all issues which, at some point, will need to be addressed in the social work process.

Child rearing Practices and Punishment

The area of youth protection often raises important questions for social workers. There is the possibility of a strong clash between the Western values of the workers—which focus on individualism, autonomy of the person, and democratic authority—and values of collective and traditional societies (Chiasson-Lavoie & Roc, 2000). Issues such as who takes care of the children and the complete authority of the parents over the children are sensitive areas that take on importance in child-protection services. One of the most controversial aspects of practice with families in a multicultural context is how abuse and neglect are defined in Canadian law and how this may contrast with corporal punishment valued in non-Western societies (Morneau, 1999). Perceptions of the social worker's role is often a major stumbling block to gaining trust and co-operation from families where abuse is suspected. In these cases, mistrust, anguish, worry, and anger are often at the root of families' resistance to work with the practitioner. When intervening, it is important for workers to be very clear about their role and to understand the migratory process and consequences of the process on families.

Interpersonal Codes of Behaviour

How people greet each other is an important aspect of the social worker's relationship with clients. It is not uncommon to extend one's hand to someone and not have it met. This should not be taken as a sign of rudeness. Social and religious customs often dictate behaviour; this is especially true in relationships between women workers and men clients. It is impossible to know details about all cultures and what to do in every situation. A good rule is to wait and respond if the client extends his or her hand.

Rituals and Beliefs Surrounding Illness, Mental Illness, and Death

Such rituals and beliefs include folk beliefs, traditional medicine, and what is considered to be a normal part of life and, thus, not to require health care (Cox & Ephross, 1998; Cohen-Émérique, 2000). For the Western world, the medical model is the dominant framework used by mental health workers. One implication of using this model is a tendency to overpathologize (Ridley, 1995, p. 46). As a result, workers may 'overlook the possibility that puzzling behavior is a reflection of social pathologies such as racism, discrimination, poverty, inadequate health care . . .' (p. 46). In the case of Arab mental health clients, Al-Krenawi and Graham (2000) argue that mental health practitioners can learn much from traditional healers, particularly when working with families: 'In traditional healing systems, the healer is active, and the client is passive. The healer directs, advises, guides, gives instructions, and suggests practical courses of treatment, such as rituals, incense burning, or visiting saints' tombs' (p. 18).

Rituals around death also need to be understood. Non-Western cultures may well have strong beliefs about the proper place for the dying person (e.g., at home as opposed to a hospital). Having a client or a member of a client's family die at home may be challenging for a social worker who has not been trained for such an experience. When death does occur at home, such a situation offers the practitioner an excellent opportunity to learn more about the customs of the client and establish a closer relationship with those involved. Non-Western cultures may also have their own ceremonies for the washing of the body and its burial (Cox & Ephross, 1998, p. 77). Many hospitals in large cities serving diverse populations now have protocols to respect these traditions. Workers should therefore be attentive to clients' needs surrounding their traditions.

Religion and Religious Values

The area of religion is still understudied in multicultural practice, and little reference is made to this area in the literature. Yet, practice shows that religion often plays a central role in people's lives. Its importance may be difficult to understand for those who come from secular societies or from a generation, such as in Quebec today, where people have turned away from churches. 'God will provide' may be a sign to some that people have no will of their own or that they have given up the fight. Religious beliefs and spirituality are often a powerful source of grounding and strength for people, and social workers should strive to accompany people through difficult times by understanding their religious beliefs and offering support. Furthermore, as Al-Krenawi and Graham (2000) point out, workers should understand not only how people rely on religion but also how it shapes their world view and actions. As they state: 'Social workers also should appreciate how a religious outlook could cultivate a conservative approach to family problems, marital problems, family matters, and the education of children. Thus, religious concepts may often be explicitly incorporated in the helping process' (p. 17).

Communication Barriers

Social Customs

Westerners tend to have a very direct way of approaching, greeting, and question-ing people. During an initial assessment such tactics may be too direct: questions may be too personal and may be seen as not respecting the codes of the culture regarding privacy and taboo subjects. Eye contact, personal distance, and touching are examples of what Fulher (1995) calls hindrances. These may seem like small matters, yet, as Fulher observes, 'alone one example may not represent "death of the counselling relationship" but hindrances can accumulate and counselling can be less effective' (p. 21).

Interpreters

Social workers may find themselves in situations where they need to work with an interpreter. This raises issues related to privacy and confidentiality for the client, especially if the interpreter is from the same ethnic group, from a different ethnic group within the same country, or from the same community. Clients may feel uncomfortable speaking freely with an interpreter present, fearing that the person knows someone from their family or that word will get around about problems the clients may be having. This raises the important issue of stigma. In non-Western societies where the family takes care of its own problems, someone visiting a worker may be stigmatized for discussing private matters outside the family or the com-munity. The client may be shamed and ostracized by the family, and this may lead to social and emotional isolation. Mental health services are especially stigmatiz-ing for women and could damage their marital prospects or increase the likelihood of separation or divorce (Al-Krenawi & Graham, 2000, p. 14). Clients may also feel uncomfortable using a family member as an interpreter, which may inhibit com-munication (Chiasson-Lavoie & Roc, 2000). In these cases, it is useful to remem-ber to talk with the client; maintain eye contact with the client, rather than with the interpreter; and address the client directly, not the interpreter. Short sentences may help to ensure that translation is not lost. The issue of language spoken also needs to be considered. Languages such as Spanish, which are spoken in different countries, vary according to the speaker's level of education, social class, regional origin, and rural or urban background. For example, Spanish spoken by an edu-cated Colombian is different from the Spanish spoken by an uneducated peasant from Honduras. In addition, the same word may have different meaning in differ-ent countries. In order to avoid serious miscommunication, such issues need to be considered when choosing an interpreter.

Culturally Specific References

Social workers should be self-conscious of their own language (Green, 1999). Many Canadians take for granted common colloquialisms and jargon as well as references to cultural events, institutions, or holidays, but it is important to recognize these may well be incomprehensible to clients from another culture. A sentence such as

'I'll hit the road now' is likely to confuse a client. It is also worth noting that practices such as distributing candy on Hallowe'en, heart-shaped cards for Valentine's Day, and mistletoe at Christmas are not universal!

Client Communication

Communication styles vary across cultures. In a study on culturally sensitive social work practice with Arab clients, Al-Krenawi and Graham (2000) explain that 'Arab communication styles are formal, impersonal, and restrained, rather than candid, personal and expressive' (p. 14). Divulging personal information to someone outside the family or the community may be seen as weak, disloyal, or both. They further state that 'self-disclosure, client affect, and self-exploration are often difficult, particularly if they are perceived as risking damage to family honor. These difficulties should not be constructed as client resistance' (ibid.). In another study, Al-Krenawi and Graham (1997) relate an experience with a client: 'He often revealed his fears and anxiety by quoting Arab proverbs, rather than speaking of his despair outright' (p. 523). It has also been this author's experience that the language used—what is being said to the worker in words—may not be what is actually meant. There is often a respect or reverence for people in authority, such as a social worker, and people may say what they think the authority figure wants to hear. 'Yes, yes, I'll come' may mean 'I don't think so'. In a context of diverse practice, we need to be attentive to the signals, body language, and other non-verbal signs (Cox & Ephross, 1998).

Language of the Client

Green (1999) explains that, like language among social workers, 'client language defines boundaries, conceals "inside" information from those who would attempt to penetrate group boundaries, and helps preserve a sense of specialness and dignity among those familiar with the jargon' (p. 119–20). At times practitioners work with groups or families, and the clients speak among themselves in their own language. At other times, clients may come from different countries but speak a common language. At one point, while this author was working with a group of men from different African countries, the common language was Swahili, not a language spoken by many social workers. It is not easy to step back and allow the group's process to continue without knowing everything being said. Yet, the reality is that social workers cannot control all aspects of an intervention at all times. They need to learn to trust their instincts and offer support and guidance when needed, but also be able to stand back and give back some control to those they are seeking to empower.

Intervention with Families

The process of acculturation is central to intervention with families. Al-Krenawi and Graham (2000) explain that 'acculturation is a central component in conceiving social work services in the West. In providing social work services to an ethnic

Arab family in the West, it is essential to consider the level of acculturation and its different effect on families' (p. 12). How long people have been in the country, their level of social and family support, and the degree of religious affiliation are important factors to consider (ibid.). Katz and Lowenstein (1999) stress the fact that the process of integration into a new country is stressful, both for the individual and for the family (p. 43). Immigrants have left familiar social, cultural, and familial settings and must now enter into a process of adapting to a new context and must reorganize their lives. 'During the process, immigrants may feel helpless, bereaved, stressed, and even in crisis as a result of the loss of familiar coping skills' (Katz and Lowenstein, 1999, p. 48).

Some key points should be mentioned on work specifically with families:

- Workers should be attentive to the migration history of the family and how the family system may have been disrupted by migration (Barudy, 1992), especially in the case of forced migration. As Lum (1996) points out, the immigration process 'is an upheaval and disequilibrium of catastrophic proportions which can be considered a crisis. . . . It involves disintegration of the person's intrafamilial relationships, loss of social identity, and major shifts in the value system and behavioral patterns' (pp. 258–9).
- Workers need to assess how each family member's role has been altered by the migration process, considering how often the family system is shattered by the migration experience, where families may be separated for long periods of time due to immigration bureaucracy. Issues related to family separation and family reunification also need to be taken into account (see Moreau, Rousseau, & Mekki-Berrada, 1999).
- Workers should not rush into a situation to change things without understanding the context: family relationships, roles within the family, separation, intergenerational issues, violence that may be due to stress (Lum, 1996), or breakdown of the family system due to migration.
- Workers should understand the importance of the family and how marriage is regarded. 'The constructions and perceptions of marital quality vary across cultures' (Lev-Wiesel & Al-Krenawi, 1999, p. 51). Moving towards ethnorelativism means understanding the Western view of marriage and family. One study on attitudes towards marriage among Israeli Arabs reaches the conclusion that children, rather than love or social status, are the primary influence in commitment to marriage. This would explain, in part, 'the preference of many Muslim women to suffer a poor marital relationship rather than seek professional intervention' (Lev-Wiesel & Al-Krenawi, 1999, p. 52).
- Workers should educate themselves regarding family values that are prominent in different cultures. For example, 'the family unit is sacred among Arab peoples, who are raised to depend on it as a continual source of support. Extended family members are valued as well. They are expected to be involved and are consulted in times of crisis' (Al-Krenawi & Graham, 2000, p. 14). Workers should therefore expect the family to be involved in the helping process.

- Group work is recommended as the modality of choice in working with families. Cox and Ephross (1998, p. 78) warn that 'social workers should be aware that
what is expected of "good" clients flies in the face of ethnic group norms and
traditions. Finding a way of involving others—family members, other group
members, or others whose life experiences and points of view are compatible—
is a way to normalize the social work client status for many ethnic group members' (p. 78).

Case Examples

Spousal abuse is a serious issue in Canada. Shelters are available to provide temporary housing for battered women and their children. It is not unusual for social
workers to encourage abused women to leave their husbands and avail themselves
of the services at such shelters. But consider the case of violence within a family
recently arrived from Algeria. In one scenario, the abused wife and her four children turn to a shelter for help. After several counselling sessions, the worker, taking a Western feminist approach, counsels the woman to leave her husband. The
woman eventually leaves her husband and the worker is pleased with the outcome.
Yet, consider the repercussions of the intervention. The woman is alienated from
her family, friends, and the community at large. The father has repudiated his children. The woman finds herself without support in a community she does not trust.
The children are having difficulties in school, which are compounded by the fact
that they are learning a new language. Values, beliefs, and the sense of family and
community have been shattered by the intervention.

Now consider what would happen if the worker had taken a different approach,
one more in keeping with the culture of the family. In the second scenario the social
worker, who was from the same community as the client, met with the family as a
group, exploring the issues arising out of the trauma of the migration process.
Issues that were dealt with related to role reversal; loss of status of the father who
had been a professional in his country and was now on welfare; the meaning of family; the husband's expectations when he came to Canada; and changes in the
woman's role. Extended family members and members from the community were
brought in to support the family in its adaptation to the new country. Support networks were established for the husband and wife, and extra help was given to the
children in school. In this case, use of what Green (1999) calls a 'root worker'—a
person of the same ethnic origin—was beneficial to the family. In many such cases,
the worker takes on the role of mediator between the family and the new society,
providing guidance and exploring issues relating to the migration process that have
not been dealt with.

Group Work

Group work, which has a long history in social work, is increasingly used as a particularly effective approach in multicultural practice. It may be especially appropriate for those individuals whose social support networks may be absent or weak

(Al-Krenawi, 1996, p. 304), especially in the case of immigrant or refugee women in Canada who are separated from their families and communities.

Empowerment

Although some authors consider the group as a natural and universal experience, it is not universal to artificially create the different types of groups used in Canadian society to offer help to members through an empowerment perspective. Garvin (1997) argues that groups 'can facilitate empowerment in ways not available to other social work modalities' (p. 277). Empowerment means getting people to do things for themselves, and this is the focus in group work with marginalized and oppressed people. However, social workers often establish a group in response to their own concerns—such as research interests or a heavy caseload—instead of in response to the needs expressed by clients. Another issue to be considered is that primary networks (family and friends) often fulfill the need of newly arrived immigrants and refugees for emotional and psychological support (Legault & Roy, 2000, p. 189). For this clientele, what is often expressed to social workers is material need: finding adequate housing, furniture, help with registering children in school. This type of need may determine different expectations of the group process on the part of group members. Clients may join a group expecting that this is the only way to get their material needs met, not understanding the nature of a self-help group and what may be expected of them in terms of self-disclosure, sharing their experiences about their adaptation process or the impact of the migratory process on their lives. Setting up a group with newly arrived immigrants and refugees requires the worker to be sensitive to the fact that group work may be a foreign concept and that emotional or social needs may be fulfilled by the clients' own community (see Azmi, 1999). For some communities, however, cultural norms and practices may facilitate a group process. In a study on a therapy group with Bedouin widows of the Negev, Al-Krenawi (1996) concludes that groups for widows have played an important role in helping these women deal with their grief. This is due, in part, to cultural customs: 'in Bedouin-Arab society, there is a great emphasis on advice giving. As one saying has it, during a time of crisis or disease, "Ask one who had personal experience of having had the same problems; do not ask an expert". Consequently, the group members were naturally inclined to consider each other the best source of mutual support and advice regarding widowhood. It is a small wonder, then, that group therapy was culturally acceptable' (pp. 314–15).

Groups may be an appropriate approach in rebuilding social networks and social support that may have been lost in migration, in providing material support and information about individuals' rights and validation that their problems are common to those in a similar situation, and in rendering assistance with particular problems (Al-Krenawi, 1996, p. 315).

The Role of the Worker

Group work is premised on an understanding that members can, at the same time, help both themselves and each other. From the outset, the notion of members helping each other raises the issue of the worker's role within the group. The role of the social worker is not central in group work, and this may be difficult for practitioners to accept, especially when they have been trained as 'professionals'. It may be difficult for individuals from hierarchical societies to accept what is considered the non-directive role of the worker, and whose expectations may be high for the worker to take on a more active role in the group (Cox & Ephross, 1998). Flexibility on the part of the worker is therefore needed.

Barriers to Group Process

Group process may be influenced by different factors: age, social class, ethnic origin, immigration status, and political or religious affiliations of the members. It is erroneous to believe that members of one ethnic group constitute a homogeneous mass. For example, refugees coming to Montreal from Bangladesh may be Muslims fleeing political persecution, or Hindus or Christians fleeing religious persecution by the Muslim political majority. Such differences are important considerations in terms of group process and communication. As members of a task-oriented group advocating for the rights of refugees, individuals from these different backgrounds may sit together at the same table, since the commonality between them is their immigration status and needs surrounding their particular legal situation, regardless of their ethnic, religious, or political affiliations. However, should the group be focused on trauma or development of self-esteem, resistance to sitting together in the same room or at the same table would be high. Group process and communication between members of the group may be seriously hindered by factors related to ethnic and religious belonging. If members came from societies where the caste system is in place, this might preclude members from different castes from even sitting together in the same room.

Another barrier to group process is straying from the purpose of the group. In task-oriented groups such as committee meetings or organizing a political event, workers need to stay focused on the purpose of the group, even though other important issues may arise. Working in a task-centred group, such as the group working on advocating for the rights of refugees, often means working with the male leaders of the community. Issues such as the social and economic isolation of their wives, domestic violence, trauma suffered in the pre-migratory process, and lack of social and health services may not be not addressed. It is up to the worker to devise strategies, often in collaboration with women workers from those communities, to address these issues. It may be difficult for a worker to identify needs or issues that are outside of the mandate of the group and not act on them, particularly for women workers who have been trained to work towards empowerment, gender equality, and social justice. However, workers need to stay focused on the task at hand and the objective of the group.

Heterogeneity versus Homogeneity of the Group

There is no consensus on whether it is better to form a group that is heterogeneous or homogeneous in terms of ethnic background, class, age, and gender. Composition of the group is always linked to the objective of the group and the model chosen. Different models are used in group work: socialization, educational, therapy, mutual aid, self-help, social action, and the choice of model will always be the best guide on the composition of the group. Garvin (1997) proposes that when the purpose of the group is not identity or socialization, a heterogeneous group is best suited.

Case Example

A support group for women survivors of torture was set up at the Montreal Women's Centre. Age, ethnicity, immigration status, and social class were not the major elements considered in the formative stage, as the focus was on common experience, and all members had experienced some form of torture. It was this common experience of torture that allowed mutual aid to develop. On the other hand, if the group's goal were to increase women's self-esteem, then age, ethnic background, and immigration status would be important issues to consider. When considering a heterogeneous group, the basic rule should be to ensure that members of the group can relate to other members, either through issues related to ageism, ableism, sexual orientation, social status, oppression, or marginalization. When establishing a group, the worker needs to ensure that members of the group experience the 'mirror' effect—that of finding commonality with other members of the group. There are no easy answers to the question of whether it is better if members are from the same ethnic group or represent different ethnic backgrounds. Research on this topic still in its infancy.

Needs for Effective Group Work

Borrowing from Garvin (1997, pp. 280–1) the following categories reflect information workers should have for effective group work with oppressed populations.

COMMUNICATION

Communication refers to language used by the group members. The common language may be other than French or English. In such a case, Garvin suggests that the worker understand the language or, to compensate for not knowing the language, use an indigenous person as co-facilitator. Language may be a sensitive issue for the workers, and they may resent the fact that members of the group cannot speak the majority language. Flexibility and openness on the part of the worker are required in such cases. Immigrants and refugees will often speak one of Canada's official languages but, if members are from the same ethnic group, discussion among themselves may revert to a common language. Feelings of being an 'outsider' may overwhelm the worker who may feel loss of control over the group or be concerned that his or her authority is diminished by the experience. The worker should understand that this is often part of the process in the group and should be open to the fact that no worker can be privy to everything.

HABITAT

Location is an important consideration in planning a group. When setting up a group for Bedouin widows for example, Al-Krenawi (1996) stresses the importance of having the group meet in a medical clinic. 'The clinic is a modern institution that Bedouin women can visit without interference from their families and with no breach of cultural norms. The absence of stigma in visiting the health care clinic to attend group sessions was one of the main conditions for developing and maintaining the group' (p. 305).

How we utilize physical space is another consideration. How a meeting space is arranged, for example, sets the tone and creates the atmosphere for the group. In Canada, chairs are often arranged in a circle to ensure that all members of the group see each other, thus facilitating communication patterns. Yet, people coming from hierarchical societies are not always comfortable with this custom. For example, a group of Gambian refugees invited to a meeting rearranged the chairs, which had been placed in a circle, into a more formal setting, with rows of chairs and a head table for the leaders. In such a case the worker needs to be flexible and respect the wishes of the group members.

SOCIAL STRUCTURE

Social structure refers to the social stratification of the larger oppressed community with which the members identify (Garvin 1997, p. 281). People originating from highly stratified societies will often reproduce the same configurations in Canada. In these cultures, one's place in society defines who speaks to whom, and in what context. It may be difficult to engage people in open discussion and develop a process of mutual aid if they are from different castes, for example. Workers may use this opportunity, however, to sensitize group members to the egalitarian and democratic ideals that are valued in Canadian society.

GROUP PROGRAM

Any program within the group should be thought out carefully. Attention must be paid to issues of stigma; cultural norms (e.g., being knowledgeable about what girls are allowed to do), customs, and rules; the acceptability of mixed groups; and the nature of taboo subjects (e.g., financial difficulties or problems within the family, which may not be discussed with strangers). Activities involving touching, singing, or disclosure may not be culturally appropriate (Cox & Ephross, 1998).

In a multi-ethnic setting, the viability of group work with strangers needs to be thoroughly evaluated. Careful planning of the group is necessary to ensure that members understand the purpose of the group and what is expected of them in terms of participation.

Conclusion

Within multicultural practice social workers encounter a complexity of cultural, situational, political, social, ethnic, and religious factors. Newly arrived immigrants and refugees are often marginalized because of their status, at times precarious, and may be oppressed for being members of an ethnic minority. In the end, the social worker may act as a catalyst in a process leading to empowerment, helping some people to regain their dignity.

Multicultural practice should not be seen as a set of barriers to effective social work intervention. Nor does it mean that characteristics of different cultural or ethnic groups be studied for competent intervention. Culturally competent practice is a learning process that starts with self-knowledge and moves into a capacity to understand the other's reality. As Roy (1992) states, many 'truths' can coexist. Whether working with individuals, families, or groups, social workers enter into a relationship based on humanistic, egalitarian, and social justice beliefs and values. Empowerment comes from social workers respecting the people they encounter, through knowledge practitioners acquire from practice and from different experiences. Openness to discovering, within oneself, what one believe one's truth to be is the first step towards understanding what other truths may be.

Today, this process of self-discovery is occurring within a theoretical context that is expanding because of what some authors describe as a paradigm shift resulting from postmodern critiques (Leonard, 1994; Green, 1999). How we, in the West, see the world; the underpinnings of our knowledge base, which come from a Eurocentric view; how we have approached learning and knowledge—all of this is being challenged and may have profound repercussions on social work practice generally and multicultural practice specifically.

One of the fundamental implications of the postmodernist approach is to reconsider some of the basic assumptions people make about 'others' based on their ethnic, cultural, or social backgrounds. Standard assessment tools, standard intake interviews, assessment protocols, all based on empiricist assumptions (Green, 1999, p. 40), are now being debated, as is the nature of services offered clients from a diversity of backgrounds. Social workers can take advantage of this exciting time to re-evaluate past notions and misconceptions about those who are culturally and ethnically different from themselves.

To conclude this chapter, an outline of general principles for competent multicultural practice is provided:

- Put yourself in a learning mode, understanding that you can learn from the situation.
- Be aware that multicultural learning is not a linear or orderly process; it takes time, openness, and flexibility.
- Strive for the 'good fit'.
- Understand that you need not be in agreement with the client's beliefs or values and that taking an ethno-relative stance does not mean you are compromising your own values, but, rather, are respecting the other (Cox & Ephross, 1998).
- Be aware that multicultural practice can be a humbling experience. Accept that you will never know everything, that many things may never be shared, for reasons beyond your control.
- When working with men and women and relationships, be prepared to go through the elder, the religious leader, the husband, or other family members.
- Understand that religion may have an important place in people's lives and how they deal with their problems.

- Have tea and/or other culturally appropriate beverages and/or food on hand.
- Use common sense and take the gifts clients may offer as a gesture of appreciation (e.g., earrings, small art pieces representative of their culture, homemade
  foods).
- Meet and sit with the whole family.

Notes

1. For a discussion of experiential components, see Le-Doux & Montalvo, 1999;
   Nakanishi & Rittner, 1992; Weaver, 1998. On critical incidents see Canadian
   Association of Schools of Social Work's web page: http://www.mun.ca/cassw/ar/
   and Montalvo, 1999.
2. Based on the work of Cohen-Émérique (1980) and prepared by G. Aumont for
   the Montreal's Women's Center, date unknown.

References

Al-Krenawi, A. (1996). Group work with Bedouin widows of the Negev in a medical clinic. *Affilia, 1*(3), 303–18.

Al-Krenawi, A., & Graham, J.R. (1997). Social work and blood vengeance. *British
Journal of Social Work, 27*, 515–28.

———. (1999). Social work practice and female genital mutilation: The Bedouin-
Arab case. *Social Development Issues, 21*(1), 29–36.

———. (2000). Culturally sensitive social work practice with Arab clients in mental health settings. *Health and Social Work, 25*(1), 9–22.

Asamoah, Y., Garcia, A., Ortiz Hendricks, C., & Walker, J. (1991). What we call ourselves: Implications for resources, policy, and practice. *Journal of Multicultural
Social Work, 1*(1), 7–22.

Azmi, S.H. (1999). A qualitative sociological approach to address issues of diversity for social work. *Journal of Multicultural Social Work, 7*(3/4), 147–64.

Barudy, J. (1992). Migration politique, migration économique: une lecture sys-
témique du processus d'intégration des familles migrantes. *Santé Mentale au
Québec, 17*(2), 47–70.

Beattie, M., & Randell, J. (1997). Using refugee stories in social work education.
Journal of Multicultural Social Work, 6(1/2), 3–15.

Ben-David, A., & Amit, D. (2000). Do we teach them to be culturally sensitive? The
Israeli experience. *International Social Work, 42*(3), 347–58.

Bertot, J., & Jacob, A. (1991). *Intervenir avec les immigrants et les réfugiés.* Montreal:
Méridien.

Bertot, J., & Mekki-Berrada, A. (1999). *Des services aux demandeurs d'asile:
Pourquoi? Ce qu'en disent les intervenants d'organismes communautaires du grand
Montréal.* Rapport de recherche, Table de concertation des organismes de
Montréal au service des réfugiés. Montreal.

Canadian Association of Schools of Social Work Web page: http://www.mun.ca/cassw/ar/

Chau, K. (1990). A model for teaching cross-cultural practice in social work. *Journal of Social Work Education, 26*(2), 124–33.

———. (1991). Social work with ethnic minorities: Practice issues and potentials. *Journal of Multicultural Social Work, 1*(1), 23–39.

Chiasson-Lavoie, M., & Roc, M.L. (2000). La pratique interculturelle auprès des jeunes en difficulté. In G. Legault (Ed.), *L'intervention interculturelle* (pp. 221–48). Montreal: Gaëtan Morin.

Christensen, C. P. (1985). A perceptual approach to cross-cultural counselling. *Canadian Counsellor/Conseiller Canadien, 19*(2), 63–81.

———. (1992). Training for cross-cultural social work with immigrants, refugees, and minorities: A course model. *Journal of Multicultural Social Work, 2*(1), 79–97.

Cohen-Émérique, M. (1980). Éléments de base pour une formation à l'approche des migrants et plus généralement à l'approche interculturelle. *Annales de Vaucresson, 17,* 117–38.

———. (1993). L'approche interculturelle dans le processus d'aide. *Santé Mentale au Québec, 18*(1), 71–92.

———. (2000). L'approche interculturelle auprès des migrants. In G. Legault (Ed.), *L'intervention interculturelle* (pp. 161–84). Montreal: Gaëtan Morin.

Cox, C.B., & Ephross, P.H. (1998). *Ethnicity and Social Work Practice.* New York: Oxford University Press.

Diller, J.V. (1999). *Cultural Diversity: A Primer for the Human Services.* Wadsworth, CA.: Brooks/Cole.

Dominelli, L. (1996). Deprofessionalizing social work: Anti-oppressive practice, competencies and postmodernism. *British Journal of Social Work, 26,* 153–175.

———. (1998). Multiculturalism, anti-racism and social work in Europe. In C. Williams, H. Soydan & M.R.D. Johnson (Eds), *Social Work and Minorities* (pp. 36–57). New York: Routledge.

Garcia, B., & Van Soest, D. (1999). Teaching about diversity and oppression: Learning from the analysis of critical classroom events. *Journal of Teaching in Social Work, 18*(1/2), 149–67.

Garvin, C.D. (1997). *Contemporary Group Work.* Needham Heights, MA: Allyn and Bacon.

Green, J.W. (1999). *Cultural Awareness in the Human Services.* Boston: Allyn and Bacon.

Green, R.R., & Watkins, M. (1998). *Serving Diverse Constituencies.* New York: Aldine De Gruyter.

Fulher, J. (1995). Getting in touch with your heritage. In N. Vacc, S. DeVaney, & J. Wittmer (Eds), *Experiencing and Counselling Multicultural and Diverse Populations* (pp. 9–27). Muncie, IN: Accelerated Development.

Jacob, A. (1993a). Le processus d'intégration des réfugiés, facteur explicatif majeur dans l'intervention. *Santé Mentale au Québec, 18*(1), 193–210.

————. (1993b). Intégration des immigrants et des réfugiés et intervention. *Intervention, 96*, 7–19.

Katz, R., & Lowenstein, A. (1999). Adjustment of older Soviet immigrant parents and their children residing in shared households: an intergenerational comparison. *Family Relations, 48*, 43–50.

Krajewski-Jaime, E.R., Brown, K.S., Ziefert, M., & Kaufman, E. (1996). Utilizing international clinical practice to build inter-cultural sensitivity in social work students. *Journal of Multicultural Social Work, 4*(2), 15–29.

Lacroix, M. (2001). The refugee claimant experience in Canada: Toward a new understanding. Paper presented at the Troisième Colloque pour étudiant-e-s et jeunes diplômé-e-s, Centre d'études ethniques des universités de Montréal (CEETUM), Montreal.

Le-Doux, C., & Montalvo, F.F. (1999). Multicultural content in social work graduate programs: A national survey. *Journal of Teaching in Social Work, 7*(1/2), 37–55.

Legault, G. (1996). Social work practice in situations of intercultural misunderstandings. *Journal of Multicultural Social Work, 6*(4), 49–66.

————. (2000). Parcours des réfugiés et des revendicateurs du statut de réfugié. In G. Legault (Ed.), *L'intervention interculturelle* (pp. 109–27). Montreal: Gaëtan Morin.

Legault, G., & Roy, G. (2000). Les difficultés des intervenants sociaux aurprès des clientèles d'immigration récente. In G. Legault (Ed.), *L'intervention interculturelle* (pp.185–202). Montreal: Gaëtan Morin.

Leonard, P. (1994). Knowledge/power and postmodernism: Implications for the practice of a critical social work education. *Canadian Social Work Review/Revue Canadienne de service social, 11*(1), 11–26.

Lev-Wiesel, R., & Al-Krenawi, A. (1999). Attitudes towards marriage and marital quality: Comparison among Israeli Arabs differentiated by religion. *Family Relations, 48*, 41–56.

Lum, D. (1996). *Social Work Practice and People of Color.* 3rd ed. Pacific Grove, CA: Brooks/Cole.

Lyons, K. (1999). *International Social Work: Themes and Perspectives.* Brookfield, VT: Arena; Aldershot, Hants: Ashgate.

Martinez-Brawley, E.E., & Brawley, E.A. (1999). Diversity in a changing world: Cultural enrichment or social fragmentation? *Journal of Multicultural Social Work, 7*(1/2), 19–36.

Montalvo, F. (1999). The critical incident interview and ethnoracial identity. *Journal of Multicultural Social Work, 7*(3/4), 19–43.

Moreau, S., Rousseau, C., & Mekki-Berrada, A. (1999). Politiques d'immigration et santé mentale des réfugiés: profil et impact des séparations familiales. *Nouvelles pratiques sociales, 11*(2)/*12*(1), 177–196.

Morneau, S. (1999). Réflexions sur l'intervention en maltraitance auprès des groupes culturels minoritaires. *Canadian Social Work Review/Revue Canadienne de service social, 16*(2), 219–231.

Moussa, H. (1993). *Storm and Sanctuary: The Journey of Ethiopian and Eritrean Women Refugees*. Dundas, ON: Artemis Enterprises.

Mullaly, R. (1993). *Structural Social Work: Ideology, Theory, and Practice*. Toronto: McClelland and Stewart.

Nakanishi, M., & Rittner, B. (1992). The inclusionary cultural mode. *Journal of Social Work Education*, 28(1), 27–35.

Payne, M. (1991). *Modern Social Work Theory: A Critical Introduction*. Chicago: Lyceum.

Pedersen, P.B., Graguns, J.G., Lonner, W.J., & Trimble, J.E. (Eds). (1989). *Counseling across Cultures*. 3rd ed. Honolulu: University of Honolulu Press.

Perez-Foster, R. (1998). The clinician's cultural countertransference: The psychodynamics of culturally competent practice. *Clinical Social Work Journal*, 26(3), 253–70.

Plionis, E.M., & Lewis, H.J. (1995). Teaching cultural diversity and oppression: Preparation for risk, the Coverdale model. *Journal of Teaching in Social Work*, 12(1/2), 175–92.

Ridley, C.R. (1995). *Overcoming Unintentional Racism in Counseling and Therapy*. Thousand Oaks, CA: Sage.

Roy, G. (1992). Devons-nous avoir peur de l'interculturel institutionnalisé? *Nouvelles pratiques sociales*, 5(2), 53–4.

Shermarke, M.A.A. (1995). *Report on the Montreal Consultation of Female Genital Mutilation*. Report for the Federal Interministerial Committee on FGM: Montreal.

Soydan, H. (1998). Understanding migration. In C. Williams, H. Soydan, & M.R.D. Johnson (Eds), *Social Work and Minorities* (pp. 20–35). New York: Routledge.

Soydan, H., & Williams, C. (1998). Exploring concepts. In C. Williams, H. Soydan, & M.R.D. Johnson (Eds), *Social Work and Minorities* (pp. 3–19). New York: Routledge.

Takeda, J. (2000). Psychological and economic adaptation of Iraqi adult male refugees: Implications for social work practice. *Journal of Social Service Research*, 26(3), 1–21.

Thornton, S., & Garrett, K.J. (1995). Ethnography as a bridge to multicultural Practice. *Journal of Social Work Education*, 31(1), 67–74.

Vacc, N.A., DeVaney, S.B., & Wittmer, J. (Eds). (1995). *Experiencing and Counselling Multicultural and Diverse Populations*. 3rd ed. Muncie, IN: Accelerated Development.

Weaver, H.N. (1998). Teaching cultural competence: Application of experiential learning techniques. *Journal of Teaching in Social Work*, 17(1/2), 65–79.

Williams, M., Zinner, E.S., & Ellis, R. (1999). The connection between grief and trauma: An overview. In E.S. Zinner & M. Williams (Eds), *When a Community Weeps: Case Studies in Group Survivorship* (pp. 3–17). Philadelphia: Brunner/Mazdel.

Culturally Appropriate Social Work for Successful Community Development in Diverse Communities

Douglas Durst and Peg Delanghe

On the outskirts of Anytown, Canada, the traveller normally encounters a large signpost boldly announcing the name of the village, town, or city, usually in large white letters on a green background. Also included is the community's population. Another signpost stands some metres further along the road, listing the various religious organizations. Yet another sign lists the numerous community organizations and service clubs—the ubiquitous Lions Club, Elks, and Kiwanis are invariably proudly displayed. This sign is distinctively North America: the idea of service clubs and organizations is a particularly Western phenomenon. Herein lies the caveat for the community organizer in the cross-cultural or multicultural setting.

Canada is a land of immigrants who, because of their personal histories and cultural backgrounds, rarely arrive with the concepts of community service agencies, volunteer organizations, or non-profit community-based structures to assist in meeting community needs. For many immigrants, social programs and services do not exist in their native countries in the same manner as in Canadian society. In Canada, social programs are offered through non-profit organizations, public institutions, and for-profit businesses. In many poor countries, services for financially or socially disadvantaged persons are non-existent, leaving these citizens to beg, borrow, or steal a marginalized existence, often in the midst of opulence and wealth. What limited services may be available are provided through some 'charitable' religious organizations or government-run institution. For these new Canadians, the idea that members of the community would collectively apply their financial and personal skills to a need that is not directly their own is indeed 'foreign'.

Most behaviours are culturally determined. Each culture has its own values, norms, and expectations that reinforce appropriate behaviour and discourage inappropriate behaviour. An important goal of social work is to enable people to make positive changes in their lives, to facilitate and encourage behaviours that empower individuals, and to allow them to make positive changes as individuals and as members of their community.

In recent decades, the profession of social work has recognized the need to develop models of practice that acknowledge and accommodate diversity in race, gender, sexual orientation, and ethnicity (Davis & Proctor, 1989; Iglehart & Becerra, 1995). Social work literature on ethnic-sensitive practice and competence has developed, primarily in the clinical field or in direct practice with individuals, families, and groups (Carlton-LaNey & Andrews, 1998; Devore & Schlesinger, 1996; Gallegos, 1984; Gutierrez, 1996; Gutierrez & Alvarez, 2000, p. 40; Harper & Lantz, 1996; Lum, 1992). Dominelli (1988) focuses on racism and promotes anti-racist social work practice. Generally, the area of community development and community organizations has been neglected; however, there are some works found in the American literature (Bradshaw, Soifer, & Gutierrez, 1993; Burghardt, 1982; Gutierrez & Alvarez, 2000, p. 40; Gutierrez & Lewis, 1994; Rivera & Erlich, 1995). Considering the diversity in Canadian society, an emphasis on community-development practice with diverse populations, including ethnicity and cross-cultural contexts, is long overdue.

This chapter discusses the knowledge, skills, and values necessary for effective social work practice in the domain of community development and organization in diverse community groups. The chapter is organized into four sections: community development and organizing; definitions, models, and strategies; unique knowledge; community-development skills; and appropriate values for community work. The first section introduces essential terms and concepts. The second section explores two key types of knowledge necessary for effective community development: self-knowledge and academic/professional knowledge. The third section examines the broad range of skills required by community workers to effectively carry out their many roles as guide, facilitator, educator, and motivator. The final section reviews the values—of the community worker and the client community—that guide behaviour.

In each section, the concepts will be discussed first in terms of general community development. Where appropriate, specific considerations for working in multicultural and cross-cultural settings will be explored. All knowledge, skills, and values discussed promote or contribute to the goal of community development: enabling communities to make positive change for themselves.

For community workers working in their own culture, cultural knowledge is learned in childhood and may be deeply imbedded in their being. The culture is part of the person and is expressed in subconscious ways in everyday life. When working in a cross-cultural environment, community workers must learn about that culture in order to interact effectively. In a multicultural community or cross-cultural setting, community workers must respect the group's culture: its values, norms, and expectations. This attitude encompasses more than 'respect'. To be effective, workers must possess an understanding of the history of oppressed or disadvantaged groups and how they have striven to improve their communities (Carlton-LaNey & Burwell, 1996). For example, in the United States, the history of civil rights and the efforts of African Americans and others to end discrimination and oppression are essential to understanding and working with African Americans (Munoz, 1989; West, 1990). In Canada, the colonial oppression of First Nations people[1] and the discriminatory and racist immigration policies that affected new Canadians need to be understood and integrated into the subconscious of the social worker: these must be understood as 'given'. Multicultural community work is accepting and embracing cultural and ethnic pluralism, valuing the contributions of all Canadians, and finding ways to enhance their contribution so that Canadian society benefits as a whole. It involves eliminating oppression, racism, and discrimination; removing barriers to social justice; and seeking equality and equity in all sectors of our society. Finally, the reader must remember that the community worker may not be of the dominant cultural group.

Community Development and Organizing: Definitions, Models, and Strategies

Culture refers to the shared collective norms, values, beliefs, and traditions of a group. Race or ethnicity does not necessarily determine culture. 'Ethnicity refers to sharing a common national origin, race, culture and/or language' (McDonald, Pittaway, & Nahmiash, 1995, p. 9). 'Ethnicity is also an abstraction. It refers to the specific aspect of culture of an individual or group that derives from another national cultural heritage' (Herberg, 1993, p. 4). As Fleras and Elliott (1999) state, 'Broadly speaking, ethnicity consists of a shared awareness of ancestral differences as a basis for engagement or entitlement. It entails a consciousness about belonging and loyalty to a particular people, homeland or cultural tradition . . . [It] is a statement of affiliation or attachment involving like-minded people in pursuit of a social activity or goal . . . or "people hood"' (p.108).

Yet, ethnocultural groups are not homogeneous. Among First Nations groups, for example, are many nations with different languages and complex dialects. There are numerous Chinese-Canadian groups, again with different languages and dialects. In addition, the personal experiences of these Canadians vary. Some recent Chinese immigrants come from wealthy and privileged Hong Kong families; others have survived unimaginable horrors in refugee camps. Immigrants may have common cultures and language, and may even have the same extended family, but they may still come out of vastly different environments. The variety of cultural backgrounds and experiences results in differing values, beliefs, and attitudes, which can be quite confusing for the outside community worker. Immigrants who arrived as children will incorporate and develop a new value base from their parents, and the next generation, born and raised in Canada, will create still another cultural mix. 'Ethnoculture is a blend of the old culture and new host culture adapted to a specific environment' (Herberg, 1993, p. 4). Like culture, the ethnicity of an individual is not static but alive and changing.

Definitions of 'community' are wide and varied (Lyon, 1987, p. 3); an early review by Hillery (1955) found ninety-four separate uses of the word. Yet, most definitions include four components: people, location in a geographic space, social interaction, and common ties (Lyon, 1987, pp. 5–6; Wharf & Clague, 1997, p. 5). Hence, the term 'community' may be used to identify a First Nation of Plains Cree living in Saskatchewan, a group of Vietnamese refugees who settled in Halifax twenty years ago, or a group of Bosnian refugees dispersed across southern Ontario. There can also be communities within communities—for example, a sub-group of entrepreneurial Canadian-born Hong Kong Chinese among the Chinese immigrants originally from the mainland.

Community development refers to 'efforts to mobilize people who are directly affected by a community condition . . . into groups and organizations to enable them to take action on the social problems and issues that concern them' (Rivera & Erlich, 1995, p. 3). Community development is characterized by dual emphasis on growth of the individual and of the community (Taylor & Roberts, 1985, p. 3). Rubin and Rubin (1986) state that 'community development involves local empowerment through organized groups of people acting collectively to control decisions, projects, programs and policies that affect them as a community' (p. 20). The goal of community development for marginalized groups in general, and diverse communities in particular, is to close the gap between needs and resources in order to improve the condition or social functioning of individual residents who constitute the community.

Many models, approaches, and perspectives frame and direct community development. Rothman's 1974 article 'Three models of community organization practice' has become a classic in community and social work literature (Wharf & Clague, 1997, p. 8) and is most frequently used in social work curriculum (McNutt, 1995). Rothman identified twelve characteristics of community work, and developed three primary models—locality development, social planning, and social action—based on assumptions about the nature of society, particularly the distribution of power. The three central models are briefly defined below; for a more complete description it is worth reviewing Rothman's updated chapter in Cox et al. (1995).

The *locality development model*, commonly referred to as community development, occurs as a result of a community identifying and resolving its problems cooperatively with outside structures. It is based upon co-operation, participation, and coordination of a broad range of participants (Rothman, 1995, pp. 28–30, 39). It assumes that those in positions of power will support proposals for change from community members and will co-operate in creating change.

The *social planning/policy model* assumes that gathering, presenting, and analyzing facts can resolve problems. It is a logical, rational process that attempts to take a neutral position with regards to politics and power. In this model, community development relies on research and a rational approach to problem solving, and on co-operation among community residents but not necessarily their participation. Power is held by the sponsoring or employing agency and decision making is controlled by 'elites' (ibid., pp. 30–2, 39).

The *social action model* assumes that some individuals, groups, and communities are disadvantaged or oppressed by existing groups or structures. The disadvantaged group needs to organize and demand change from the broader society in terms of equality in treatment and increased resources. In this model, change (community development) occurs only with a redistribution of power from external sources to the community (ibid., 1995, pp. 32–3, 39).

Although useful and practical in most applications, Rothman's three models do not adequately reflect the complexity of community development. In his 1995 chapter, he recognized their limitations and explored the 'interweaving of intervention approaches', creating three bimodal mixtures of the three ideal types (ibid., pp. 46–52). These bimodal models expand the application of his theories and better describe and analyze groups and organizations that apply different community development strategies.

Taylor and Roberts (1985, p. 6) described five models of community work: community development; community liaison; planning; pluralism and participation; and program development and coordination. Expanding on Rothman's original work, Weil and Gamble (1995) listed eight models of community work: neighbourhood and community organizing; organizing functional communities; community social and economic development; social planning; program development and community liaison; political and social action; coalitions; and social movements. The two primary characteristics that differentiate the above models are, first, the roles and strategies used by the community worker and, second, the levels of power and decision making at the community level (Hardina, 2000, p. 6).

The specific activities of the community developer should be determined by the community's strategy or long-range goal meant to address the agreed-upon social change. The American community sociologist Roland Warren identified three strategies that are employed to address the desired change: collaboration, campaign, and contest. *Collaborative strategies* seek social change based on negotiation and agreed action. For example, most of the developing Indian Child and Family Service agencies in Canada are based on tripartite agreements between First Nations Band Councils and the provincial and federal governments (Durst, 1999, p. 196). *Campaign strategies* are persuasive in nature, seeking to change people's or organizations' perspective through education and promotion. In addition to educating, campaign strategies can involve 'shocking' or 'embarrassing' the more powerful party into some action. Television news coverage of the solvent-sniffing children of Davis Inlet, Labrador, shocked the nation and prompted the federal government to take immediate action. Concerns for the health of the individual children was then expanded to concern over the third-world conditions of the entire community. Warren (1971) describes *contest* as confrontation with the intent to pressure the power-based decision-making organizations to implement responses to address the issues of the community. The 1990 Oka standoff was a landmark case (no pun intended) in confrontation by First Nations in Canada. For seventy-eight days, the Mohawk men, women, and children of Kanehsatake and the village of Oka, Quebec, held an armed stand-off against the Quebec police and the Canadian army. This historic event was a culmination of 270 years of resistance and led to the implementation of the monumental Royal Commission on Aboriginal Peoples in 1991 (Costellano, 1999, pp. 92–3). Generally, community development draws upon consensus and co-operative strategies, and social action applies strategies involving contest and confrontation. Depending upon the approach, campaign strategies can be either co-operative/collaborative or confrontational in nature (Warren, 1971).

The orientation that the worker and the community members take will reflect their understanding of issues of power. It will reflect a basic theoretical framework that can be understood and analyzed through sociological theory. Those workers who assume that power is shared and that rational decision-making will lead to social improvements may be applying a *social systems* or a *functionalist* framework. This assumes that all groups in society have common goals and shared values that can best be achieved through co-operation and collaboration. Those workers who assume that power is not shared and that those in positions of power wish to maintain their power, even at the expense of others, subscribe to a *conflict/feminist/ Marxist* conceptual framework. Many feminists see the oppression and exploitation of patriarchy as central to imbalances of power. African Americans have made significant gains by rejecting past power structures and demanding social change. For these groups, the battle is not over.

For the most part, ethnic communities in Canada have been marginalized, but in recent years some groups have become increasingly vocal and active in asserting their wishes. Most Aboriginal communities were traditionally based on egalitarian and co-operative values. Under self-government, many of these communities have seized the autonomy to determine their own needs and the power to develop and carry out plans to meet these needs. The paternalistic practices and policies of the governments of the dominant culture are being relinquished with the recognition of First Nations people's inherent right to self-determination and self-government.

In Canada, schools of social work vary in terms of their general orientation, but a number of schools publicly espouse a conflict/feminist/Marxist framework. These programs reflect the belief that real social change can occur only if there is fundamental change in the way power and resources are distributed. However, most schools in North America have a functionalist or systems framework with a liberal humanitarian understanding. Faculty tend to teach that permanent social change occurs through a re-adjustment of resources achieved through collaboration and co-operation. Implicit in this chapter is the belief that each model has a role in community development and that the worker's approach depends upon the situation and the wishes of the community.

Many immigrants and new Canadians have struggled, often with great personal sacrifice, to 'fit in' and find a comfortable level of social, economic, and, sometimes, political integration. They have sought to minimize conflict, find harmony and balance, and accept some level of discomfort from discrimination and racism. Adjustment and social integration are found through the collaboration and successful co-operation with all members of society. Some groups, such as Canada's

Aboriginal peoples and Black Canadians, have suffered under centuries of oppression, colonialism, discrimination, and blatant racism. Even with efforts of collaboration and co-operation, the experiences of these Canadians have been marked by the continuation and extension of oppression and racism. For many, the most effective response is found in more radical and aggressive tactics for social change. The challenge for the community worker is finding the tactic and style of community development/social action that is appropriate for the community and is comfortable for both the community worker and the community members. A community worker who is trained and ready for aggressive strategies in a community that seeks a collaborative style is bound to experience frustration and failure.

Unique Knowledge

> The integration of social workers' perspectives with clients' unique details supplies the concrete and specific knowledge base for each phase of social work.
>
> Krogsrud Miley, O'Melia, and DeBois, 1995, p. 124

Knowledge is information that is internalized and understood. Problems are identified and resolved through application of sufficient and appropriate knowledge. Community workers acquire knowledge through personal life experience and through professional education and training. Knowledge of self is critical in order for community workers to understand what motivates and shapes their actions. This intimate knowledge of self allows community workers to recognize how their behaviour influences interactions with others and professional decisions. Professional and academic education and training help workers understand human behaviour and also equip them with the requisite knowledge for specific types of community-development initiatives, such as health, economic development, or education.

Self-Knowledge and Personal Life Experience

Community workers are people first and professionals second. Their personal biases, prejudices, strengths, and challenges constitute the foundation upon which the professional is built. To comprehend and influence the behaviour of others, community workers must have a clear and accurate understanding of what directs their own behaviour. All people are biased: one may strive for total objectivity, but as intelligent, sentient creatures, people are inherently both intellectual and emotional. Biases—likes and dislikes—develop over a lifetime; they are often unconscious, the product of an individual's cumulative life experiences and influences. Effective community workers know their biases, strengths, and challenges. A successful community worker recognizes that he or she is but one of many resources available to the client; the worker draws on personal strengths and compensates for deficiencies in order to ensure that clients receive the services and resources they need.

Professional/Academic Knowledge

Knowledge about human behaviour—the worker's and that of the client community—is essential to the community developer. In addition, the community worker requires general knowledge about human interaction and community intervention, knowledge specific to the particular type of community-development initiative planned, and knowledge about the community in which the individual will work.

Social Work Knowledge

Social workers in the community engage in many types of community intervention and development. Depending on the needs identified by the community, social work embraces a wide range of activities: health care, education, economic development, and child care are but a few examples of the many different needs communities may encounter. Specific knowledge about the topic is required for an effective response to a need. For each area of activity, a body of knowledge has developed based upon the cumulative, collective experiences of thousands of individuals over time. These experiences have been organized into pockets of knowledge that can readily be transmitted by an instructor to students in a classroom setting, and by established community workers to novice colleagues in a practical work environment.

The academic training for a specific discipline provides the theories and foundations, which in turn provide the rationale and structure for interaction and activity. This academic knowledge allows the worker to benefit from the vast experiences, both the successes and the failures, of those who have been working in the field.

In order to influence behaviour, the community worker must know and understand what motivates and constrains human behaviour. Social workers use theoretical knowledge to better understand and predict human behaviour in order to help foster positive change (Krogsrud Miley, O'Melia, and DeBois, 1995). The disciplines of both social work and psychology focus on human behaviour.

Ethical/Legal Knowledge

Until recent years, guidelines directing interaction between a researcher or community worker and participants/subjects (human or other animal) were not rigidly regulated. With greater understanding and insight, those working in the fields of human and animal research and interaction have come to recognize the moral obligations of ensuring that study or practice subjects—people and animals—are treated with respect and in such a manner so as to avoid distress or harm. The recognition of this moral obligation is manifested in ethical guidelines or standards. Community workers involved in academic, research, or clinical activities involving interaction with people are expected to adhere to the ethical guidelines applicable to their discipline or institution.

Professional ethics is related to ethical/legal knowledge. Although the community worker may be volunteering, the worker is a 'professional', even though he or she may not be a member of the professional association of social workers. Regardless of the worker's status within the profession, the social work profession has established clear and detailed guidelines for ethical practice and ethical decision-making. These guidelines provide the foundation for ethical practice and must be adhered to. The national professional associations in Canada and the United States make these standards available on the Internet and in published form. Further discussion on values and ethics is presented in the section entitled 'Appropriate Values for Social Work'.

Knowledge of the Community

Before entering a community, community workers need to learn about that community—the who, what, where, when, why, and how that shape and direct community behaviour. Erasmus and Ensign (1991) point out that knowing a community's demographics, history, and culture, and understanding both the formal and informal power systems, helps the community worker identify practical parameters, including barriers or challenges, for community-development initiatives.

Knowing whether a community comprises a hundred or a thousand residents has direct implications for the type and scope of possible community development. Geographic location may have implications in terms of access to resources, or issues related to transportation throughout the seasons. Distance and climate are important considerations in planning interventions or development activities, particularly in areas where distances are vast and the climate can be extreme and unpredictable.

Awareness of the community's history and culture helps the community worker understand the forces that shaped the initial development of the community and the beliefs, values, and traditions that shape the community today. Communities with rigid boundaries—that is, communities where there is little interaction between the residents and those outside, particularly with the larger, dominant society—tend to adhere more strongly to traditional values and norms. The social roles and behaviours within the community are shaped according to its specific culture (Cox & Ephross, 1998, p. 82).

The ability to demonstrate awareness of social and political protocols indicates the community worker is aware of and sensitive to the values and practices that guide social interaction in the community. Acknowledging the importance of these fundamental protocols is the community worker's first step towards building open, trusting relationships with community residents.

The community worker does not work in isolation within the community: her or his role is to mobilize the community so that residents collectively and co-operatively make positive changes for themselves. This mobilization is facilitated through support of the local political decision-making and service-delivery systems. In any group or community, there are two systems of power: formal power (authority) and informal power (influence). Community residents have given those in positions of authority, such as elected or appointed representatives, power to act and make decisions on their behalf. For example, in First Nations communities, the council and head (chief on a reserve, chairperson in a Métis settlement) have authority to make decisions on behalf of the members within their community. Any initiative designed to have an impact on the community must first be discussed by the council (Erasmus & Ensign, 1991, p. 25). Additionally, there may be individuals or groups who, while not elected representatives, have influence by virtue of possessing a particular skill, or are otherwise admired or respected for their demonstrated competence or commitment to community well-being. In First Nations communities, sources of influence may include elders, other community leaders, or friendship centres.

While the community as a whole may wish to work towards its collective betterment, there may not necessarily be consensus on how best to proceed. For example, in attempting to address the problem of violence against women, male band leaders may define the problem and view solutions differently than the worker or the community. One of the roles of the community worker is to align the community, including those individuals with authority or influence, so that all members of the community are working co-operatively towards a common goal.

Krogsrud Miley, O'Melia, and DeBois (1995) stress that 'only clients know what their history has been, what is currently happening to them, and what they would like their future to hold. They know the challenges they face . . . and have abundant information about their resources' (p. 124). Clearly, the best source of expertise about a community is the community residents; they have intimate knowledge about the problem they wish to address. Their perspective provides essential subjective information not available through objective, static reports or other documentation. The community worker needs to discover what the people know about the challenges they wish to address, how they have addressed them in the past, and what similar or other challenges they have successfully resolved in the past. Building on past successes, and avoiding repetition of past mistakes, contributes to positive momentum in achieving goals.

The term 'problem' implies a negative situation—it suggests a lack or barrier of some kind. The worker's fresh view of the situation may provide insights into the fundamental nature of the problem that the community wishes to address. The community worker's outside perspective may also help identify the extent of perceived problems. It is important to be aware of the perceived challenges the community faces, which influence how residents respond to the problem.

While negative elements certainly do exist, it is important to focus also on the positive aspects of a situation, particularly the inherent strengths of the community. Drawing from and building on community strengths—current and potential resources (e.g., people, funds, facilities, programs), as well as local and satellite resources—provides at-hand resources and reduces the need to acquire outside resources. Since the goal of community development is to enable communities to make positive changes for themselves, it is imperative that community resources and structures be self-sustaining so that they function effectively and independently in the long term.

Communities experience challenges as the collective needs of their residents change over time. While all residents may agree that a problem exists, it may be difficult to arrive at a consensus about the true nature and scope of the problem. Before any remedial action can be taken, the problem must first be clearly articulated (Durst, McDonald, and Parsons, 1999). The community worker must first know what the community has determined to be the problem. The problem identification and determination of specific goals provide a starting point for research and action. Understanding how community residents perceive the problem, and their perceptions of needs, is the basis for community work (Cox & Ephross, 1998, p. 93; Durst, McDonald, and Parsons, 1999). The community worker must then make his or her thorough assessment of the situation. Once this process is completed, the community worker must check for congruence between this personal assessment and the community's perception of the problem. When both the community worker and the community have parallel views about the nature and scope of the problem, they can then begin working together to address it.

When the problem has been clearly defined, the community worker must clarify both his or her role and the community's role in addressing the problem. The worker's role may be defined by the mandate of the institution, department, or discipline that the individual represents; however, the worker's overall role is to help the community help itself. Both the community worker and the community must be clear about their respective roles and responsibilities. Assumptions about role expectations may lead to misunderstandings that compromise or confound goal achievement.

The history in many First Nations communities is one of 'outsiders' deciding what is best for the community, a practice that has promoted dependency and passivity (Erasmus & Ensign, 1991, p. 6). Under these paternalistic practices, community workers coming into a community were expected to 'solve a problem', often through an infusion of funds or the implementation of a program developed with no consultation with community residents. As First Nations communities achieve increasing control in determining and addressing their needs, the expectation that the worker will 'fix' the problem is giving way to the proactive view of the community worker as a facilitator.

Community-Development Skills

Skill is a demonstrated competence or mastery—a practised ability. A community worker must be competent in a range of skills associated with many and varied roles as guide, facilitator, educator, and motivator. In this chapter, four broad categories of skills are examined: organizational skills, strategic or political skills, communication skills, and analytical skills. Within each of these categories, several specific types of skills are identified and discussed.

Organizational Skills

The goal of community development is to enable communities to solve problems and take action on their own. In order to accomplish this, communities must establish structures and processes that allow them to communicate about their needs and to act to address them. Many communities have a variety of committees and hold regular meetings to discuss community business. The worker has expertise in identifying additional structures and processes suitable for the community's particular needs. This skill is particularly important if community members do not have a history of organizing to meet shared needs; such community members may lack the knowledge and skills required to build and maintain an organization to meet their needs.

The community worker assists the community to identify, coordinate, and activate resources through established or new structures and processes. The community worker aims to build on community strengths so that the community becomes self-sufficient in its problem-solving efforts.

Strategic/Political Skills

A variety of skills are needed to accurately identify a problem, develop a plan of action, and ensure that the plan is implemented. The successful community worker is adept at recognizing the various and often conflicting concerns of community residents, and in working to accommodate these concerns without compromising the community's collective goals.

Residents in a community may have differing views of the problem and how to address it. The role of the social worker is to help residents work towards a consensus so that each member contributes in a co-operative fashion to resolving the problem. An effective worker assists a community to develop a variety of strategies and activities to address the problem; maximum benefit is derived when all groups work concurrently and co-operatively towards a common goal.

Where discrepancies or conflicts exist between groups of residents, the community worker ensures all parties have the opportunity to express their concerns. When all the concerns have been aired, the worker must be flexible and creative in negotiating a compromise that allows all parties to feel they have been heard and treated fairly.

As discussed in the section on knowledge, an important aspect of 'getting things done' is engaging the support and co-operation of those with authority or influence. Gaining the co-operation and support of the political decision-making and service-delivery systems is an integral component of ensuring that things get done. The community worker must identify both the internal and external sources of authority and influence, and work to secure their co-operation.

In First Nations communities, the internal sources of authority include the chief or chairperson and council members. Internal sources of influence might include elders, other community leaders, and community groups, such as friendship centres. External sources of authority include various levels and departments of government. External sources of influence may be individuals, groups, or agencies with expertise or an interest in some facet of the problem. While these people have no direct control over decisions made in the community, they may provide critical information or direction.

Communication Skills

Communication involves information transmission, reception, and exchange. Clear and accurate information is only one component of effective communications. Information must be transmitted in a manner suitable to both the sender and the receiver. Leigh (1998) offers detailed guidelines for culturally competent communication. In this section, several modes of communication—written, electronic, verbal, and non-verbal—are briefly discussed from the community development perspective.

WRITTEN COMMUNICATION

Western culture relies heavily on the written mode of information transmission. Printed and electronic reports and correspondence are used in a wide variety of disciplines and environments. In order for these transmissions to be effective, they must use language that is unambiguous, free of jargon, and at a level appropriate for the intended readers.

Writing is not a traditional mode of communication among some Aboriginal populations. Like other ethnic cultures with strong oral traditions, important information is passed on verbally through story and narrative. These stories are creative and animated, tactics designed to ensure the information is remembered and retold (Graveline, 1998, p. 65). These elements of story are not part of the so-called factual, objective, linear information transmission of Western culture. For a community worker who is from a Western culture and is working in an Aboriginal community, awareness of the different ways people transmit important information will assist in understanding not only the words but the meanings to be gleaned from spoken dialogue.

ELECTRONIC COMMUNICATION

Simple binary communication started with the telegraph—'a dot and a dash'—and developed into digital electronic technology, revolutionizing the way the world communicates. Technological developments have changed the nature of organizations, including how corporations, governments, and community-based organizations function. Lines of communication and styles of communication are much different than even a decade ago; they require new strategies and the adaptation and application of communicating in 'cyberspace' (McNutt, 2000, p. 97). The community organizer can use electronic technology to communicate to agencies and government departments with instantaneous results. Letters, petitions, and proposals can be distributed around the world with the press of a button. Today, many members of provincial and federal legislatures can be reached with individual e-mail letters.

This technology can also be used to build the organization (McNutt, 2000, p. 100). Members of a community group can be contacted and provided with up-to-date information efficiently and effectively. Sharing information and coordinating events and activities are critical duties for the community worker, and electronic mail can greatly facilitate these functions (Downing et al., 1991). It is easy to develop mailing lists, which can distribute messages, reports, and information quickly and efficiently to group members. In order to recruit members and promote the goals of the organization, a Web page can be developed that outlines the organization, its goals and its activities (Grobman & Grant, 1998; Krause, Stein, Clark, 1998; McNutt, 2000, p. 99; Zeff, 1996). A Web page can also stimulate discussion and debate about central ideas and concerns of the group.

With the prices of computer hardware falling each year and the level of sophistication increasing, it is no longer only the privileged who own computers and use them to communicate. For most community applications, 'last year's' model is more than adequate and frequently comes loaded with useful and practical computer programs. Cutting-edge computer technology is seldom necessary. Community organization using electronic media to communicate generate considerable financial savings on items such as postage and photocopying. For developing and established organizations, computer skills in budgeting, administrative management, spreadsheets, word processing, desktop publishing, and graphic arts replace old mimeographing, silk-screen printing, and IBM Selectric typewriters!

The computer also offers unlimited access to vast amounts of information. Some federal government departments have useful Web pages with important data and information. Statistics Canada's Web site (http://www.statcan.ca) offers, in addition to the 1996 Census, over two hundred tables of continuously updated statistics on a variety of social and economic issues. The site provides daily news offering new data and analysis on economic indicators and new services. The material is available twenty-four hours a day, seven days a week. For those working on Aboriginal issues, Indian and Northern Affairs Canada offers a Web page with the latest data, past and current publications (see http://www.ainc-inac.gc.ca). The entire Royal Commission on Aboriginal Peoples is available on a Web site (see http://www.libraxus.com). Canadian Web pages are also available for many anti-poverty and welfare rights groups and can be an invaluable resource for advocating and struggling against poverty and oppression (see http://www.web.net for links to these sites).

While knowledge and competency with personal computers is an essential skill, it is also a vast and complicated field of expertise. No community worker can provide all the knowledge and skills useful in computer application, but a basic knowledge is helpful, as is a willingness to find a person who can offer advice or training on computer-related issues. Not unexpectedly, young women and men who have grown up with computers frequently have the comfort and expertise to help a community organization with its computer needs. A community developer would be wise to find the right young person and 'plug them in' to the organization.

VERBAL COMMUNICATION

Talking, the verbal transmission of ideas, is perhaps the most common mode of information sharing. Yet, miscommunication can occur, even between individuals speaking the same language. Effective speaking involves more than using the right words; it involves using both words and tone that are appropriate to the situation. The intimate greeting between family members in public is not appropriate between strangers; similarly, the casual language of an informal setting such as a party is not necessarily appropriate for formal or diplomatic business. Using both the appropriate language as well as the appropriate degree of formality demonstrates respect between those engaged in verbal information transmission.

In all cultures, verbal transmission should be appropriate to the occasion. In particular, the community worker should know and follow the verbal and social protocols associated with ceremonies or spiritual activities. These protocols vary among communities, and the community worker must remember that what is deemed appropriate in one community may not necessarily be appropriate in another. In Western culture, verbal discourse is often factual, chronological, linear, and direct, which may conflict with the style of other cultures. Such directness may seem rude or controlling by other groups. Aboriginal communities have strong oral traditions that create flexible, narrative, and non-directive modes of expression.

Non-verbal Communication

When people engage in conversation, they transmit meaning not only by their words, but also by their tone of voice, expressions, gestures, and body position. Effective communication results when there is congruence between the verbal and the non-verbal messages being sent. The individual who says 'I am interested in what is being said, and I respect what I am hearing', but who is gazing off into space, drumming fingers on the tabletop, and emitting heavy sighs, demonstrates impatience. Such displays indicate that the person believes that his or her time and/or opinions are more valuable than those of the person who is speaking. This behaviour does not communicate interest and respect.

Like verbal language, the non-verbal elements of communication are, to a large degree, culturally learned. In Western culture, people commonly use direct eye contact and the animated use of one's hands and arms to reinforce the verbal message. This degree of animation and eye contact is not appropriate in all cultures. Aboriginal communities often display a blend of traditional and Western behaviours. Where direct eye contact might be appropriate for the 'Westernized' resident, others may view it as a challenge or a sign of disrespect. A non-Aboriginal worker is more effective when aware of appropriate communications behaviours in the community.

In Western culture, listening is a dynamic and often animated practice. Active listening, where the listener nods, makes short, verbal affirmations, and maintains direct eye contact with the speaker, is normally considered an indication that the listener is paying attention and understands what is being said. In Aboriginal cultures, members listen intently and non-demonstratively without excessive head nodding or verbal comments or gestures (Graveline, 1998). Aboriginal people have strong connections to the spiritual aspects of their world; they connect with this spiritual dimension through silence and reflection. For this reason, silence is sacred

(Graveline, 1998), and is an integral component of communication. The success-ful community worker is sensitive to these very different listening behaviours, inter-preting and responding to them appropriately.

Analytical Skills

The role of the community worker is to synthesize information to offer new per-spectives on situations and generate options for change (Krogsrud Miley, O'Melia, & DuBois, 1995, p.100). This is achieved by using a variety of analytical skills, including observation and interpretation, assessment, development of an action plan, and evaluation of outcomes.

Well-honed observation skills are essential to community workers, who must assess a situation in order to facilitate the identification of the problem and assist in the development of an action plan. Workers must learn to interpret what they observe as a function of cultural and environmental influences. The person from a tropical country who experiences snow for the first time would likely have difficulty making an accurate conclusion about what they were seeing; if the concept of 'snow' is completely unfamiliar, they have no past experience upon which to draw conclusions about the phenomenon.

People use their past experiences to draw conclusions about what they observe. Over time, as similar experiences are repeated, the step from observation to con-clusion becomes automatic. In familiar environments, community workers are likely to make accurate interpretations and conclusions about the phenomena that are observed; however, they must be wary of drawing similar conclusions in a new environment. Workers in a cross-cultural community must be particularly diligent about drawing conclusions from observed behaviours or situations. Behaviour is culturally determined and, therefore, cannot be evaluated by the standards or norms of another culture.

In order to arrive at an accurate conclusion about a situation or behaviour, the community worker must first understand the norms of the culture. Second, the community worker should observe the community from many perspectives. Finally, the worker must verify his or her conclusions by comparing or discussing them with members of the community who are most familiar with their culture.

Using culturally sensitized observation skills, the community worker is ready to assess with the community the nature of the problem or situation. Some years ago, one of the authors was involved in an assessment of community needs with a Mi'kmaq community in Atlantic Canada (Durst, McDonald, & Parsons, 1999). The problem was violence against women, and many community members believed the solution was some variation of a women's shelter. They had learned about such shelters from television and other media and had envisioned a small facility to be located in the centre of this community of less than seven hundred people. With the community, the author assisted in completing a needs assessment, which uncovered a variety of issues such as confidentiality, cost considerations, and orga-nizational problems. The assessment concluded that a community-based women's health/education centre was a better plan. In the end, the band council approved the centre, which provided a crisis plan to protect women and children in immediate danger but also provided counselling and parenting supports as well as health and social education.

One component of an assessment includes examining the community's past efforts to address the problem. The worker may wish to consider what strategies were successful in the past, what activities were less successful, and what factors apply to the problem that is presently being addressed. Building on past successes reinforces community strengths, and avoiding past mistakes saves time.

With the conclusion of an assessment, the community worker is ready to help the community develop a plan of action to address the problem. The plan should draw from and build on community strengths, while accommodating the constraints and challenges of the situation. Drawing on the community's strengths taps into present and future skills and resources that reinforce the community's ability to make and maintain positive changes.

Another important and sometimes forgotten skill is the ability to evaluate outcomes. Although research and evaluation skills are usually low on a worker's priority list, these skills should be included in the community action. They will be valuable in the early assessment of needs and in the determination of goals and objectives of the organization. They are also necessary in determining whether or not these goals and objectives have been achieved. Clearly, the community worker cannot be superhuman, but these skills must not be forgotten. If the worker does not possess them, they should be accessed through another person.

Appropriate Values for Community Work

Values are the general standards and ideals by which we judge our own and others' behaviour (Horne, 1987, p. 1). Every culture has its own set of values that guides the behaviour of its members. Many values, such as honesty, respect, trustworthiness, co-operation, and compassion, are evident in many different cultures but are expressed in different ways. Community workers must be aware of both their own personal and professional values as well as the values of the community. Sometimes these values conflict and compete, creating ethical dilemmas (Reisch & Lowe, 2000, p. 25). These situations can be difficult to resolve, creating considerable stress for the worker and the community. Reisch and Lowe (2000, pp. 24–6) offer some helpful guidelines for resolving these dilemmas, including the identification of the issues, ethical rules and criteria, and issues of conflict of interest. They also suggest ranking and prioritizing the rules, and listing the consequences of various choices.

Community Workers' Personal and Professional Values

Community workers' personal and professional values reflect their commitment to enabling others to make positive changes for themselves. Indispensable to such work are the values of dignity; respect for oneself, for one's clients, and for individual differences; and confidentiality. First, dignity and respect—including self-respect— are fundamental for community workers, helping them to interact in a positive and successful manner with clients and colleagues. Second, while community workers must recognize the collective values of a community's culture, they must also acknowledge and prize the strengths in individual difference. Each person has a unique contribution to make, regardless of education, training, and experience. Finally, personal and professional confidentiality engenders trust and confidence between the community worker and community residents. This trust builds strong, productive relationships that contribute to goal achievement.

Accountability

Accountability—that is, being responsible for the consequences of one's actions— is important in any relationship. It is particularly important in the relationship between the worker and the community members where the community worker's actions have such significant and long-term ramifications. Earlier in the chapter, it was discussed how the orientation of the community worker must fit the goals and values of the community. The strategies and tactics employed must reflect the value base of both the worker and the community. Community workers must understand that they are accountable for their actions. This raises some questions about civil disobedience and extreme or militant actions.

In order to achieve shared community objectives, workers may be asked to participate in simple distortions and/or exaggerations of the truth or in personal attacks. This situation may not be a problem for one community worker but could be a serious ethical decision for another. In a more extreme situation, this same worker may be asked, encouraged, or even pressured into engaging in questionable tactics such as lying, stealing, or vandalizing property (Reisch & Lowe, 2000). The international organization Greenpeace is well-known for its extreme measures, including illegal activity, which are justified, in the minds of the activists, as ways to generate publicity and exert political pressure on powerful institutions, both government and corporate. In other cases, one protester in Alberta resorted to bombing oil wells and oil installations to publicize his political message, while others in Quebec have assaulted political and corporate executives with cream pies. The judicial courts have taken these actions seriously, handing down sentences that reflect the belief that such actions cannot be tolerated. Finally, some groups and workers may consider violent activities and even terrorism directed at civilians as justified. Although terrorist acts are rare in Canada, the international community, including the United States, has witnessed unspeakable horror in the form of violent terrorism. Ultimately, community workers are accountable for their actions and may need to seriously consider the implications of community action that involves civil disobedience or more extreme acts. Well-respected Canadian scholar Bill Lee expands this discussion and offers some guidelines for making hard choices (Lee, 1999).

Diversity in Values and the Aboriginal World View

Many ethnic communities have been exposed to Western values and practices. For practical purposes, some diverse people and communities have adopted Western practices to facilitate interaction with the dominant Western culture. Community workers in cross-cultural communities must keep in mind that the adoption of Western practices does not necessarily mean adoption of Western values.

Lum highlights some of the differences in values between Western culture and that of ethnic minorities, including Aboriginal cultures: 'The mainstream society tends to emphasize human control of the environment, future orientation, individual autonomy, competitiveness and upward mobility, and the nuclear family. Ethnic minorities focus on harmony with the environment, reminiscence about the past and pleasure in the present, collectivity, self-discipline and endurance of suffering, and the extended family' (Lum, 1992, p. 86). While Lum's generalizations are rather broad, they do identify some of the key areas in which Western and non-Western values differ: the environment, the community, and the family.

Just as each culture has its own norms and values, so, too, does each community, including each multicultural community. Aboriginal communities do, however, share some fundamental values that arise out of their common world view. According to Graveline (1998, p. 52), the Aboriginal world view was the common-sense foundation of early tribal existence. People were dependent on the Earth to provide what they needed for survival; they cherished and nurtured the Earth so it would sustain them physically and spiritually. They cherished and respected all things in the world, including all that is animate and inanimate, visible and invisible, past, present, and future.

Aboriginal values, beliefs, and practices including immanence and spirituality, interconnectedness, harmony, and holism arise out of their world view. This world view recognizes that each person is intimately and dependently connected with all other forms and forces of life, and that a person is whole and healthy physically, mentally, and spiritually, only when that individual is in harmony and balance with the life elements.

Feehan and Hannis (1993) point out that, while Western culture is increasingly scientific and the rejection of spiritual values is common, many Aboriginal people are rediscovering and revaluing their unique spirituality. Graveline (1998, p. 53) posits that Aboriginal spirituality is universal, and that it coexists in all aspects of life—it resides in the essence of the person, in the community, and among the people. The community worker in an Aboriginal community must recognize the value of this process of spiritual rediscovery and incorporate it into a holistic approach to both Aboriginal personal development and the social work interventions practiced in their communities (Feehan & Hannis, 1993, p. 23).

'Aboriginal Traditionalists have long recognized the link between individual responsibility and community well-being' (Graveline, 1998, p.57). For Aboriginal people, this link is the foundation of a network with many complex interrelationships and multiple roles that constitute their community. The community is the dominant system; individuals, families, friends, and extended families are interdependent (Feehan & Hannis, 1993). These complex and interdependent relationships must be foremost in any community-development initiative. The community worker must ensure that initiatives accommodate and strengthen these relationships, which are the foundation of the community itself.

The Aboriginal world view perceives life and the world as cyclical and connected. Past, present, and future are infinite and interconnected, not separate, quantifiable, and controllable by people. For Aboriginal people, time is based on a ceremonial and circular-understanding of order and harmony (Graveline, 1998). For an Aboriginal person, being on time means being in harmony with self and ritual. This is in direct contrast to the Western attitude towards time as an external, artificial, and often arbitrary construct to be measured, parcelled out, and used to control behaviour.

Conclusion

The signposts outside of Anytown, Canada, are changing. New organizations and community groups are showing their presence in towns and villages that were once 'homogeneous' across the nation. These Canadians are expressing themselves and participating in society in new ways through development and organization at the community level, making this nation truly multicultural and multi-ethnic in ways previously unseen. These changes include new ways of social work practice, including community work.

In this chapter we have argued that successful community development is based on the community worker's ability to understand and influence behaviour in order to enable community residents to make positive changes for themselves. Community workers must have a thorough understanding of self—what motivates and constrains their own behaviour—before they can effectively influence the behaviour of others. In addition to knowing and understanding human behaviour, community workers must have knowledge of the community, as well as academic and professional knowledge specific to the type of community development they will pursue.

Social workers in community development must develop competency in a broad range of organizational, strategic/political, communication and analytical skills to address their many roles as guide, facilitator, educator, and motivator. Such workers, by virtue of the vocation of working with people, embrace values that respect all people. Successful community workers know and respect the values of the client community, even where those values differ from their own.

In contemporary ethnic communities, much of the members' knowledge of themselves, and many of their values, are re-emerging from their traditional past, before the disruptive and destructive influences of immigration, forced integration, racism, and, for Aboriginal people, colonialism. For the social worker in a multicultural community, understanding and respecting the self and possessing knowledge, skills, and values of anti-racist and multicultural practice is the foundation for successful community development. Travelling in these new times, it is well worth observing the additions of new groups and organizations that have proudly taken their place on the signposts of each village and town.

Note

1. For the purpose of this report, the term First Nations people is used to described persons who are status Indians as defined by the Indian Act. The phrase Aboriginal people is a broader term used to define all those people who identify as being of Aboriginal ancestry and may be of mixed background. The term is used to include status and non-status Indians and Métis persons.

References

Bradshaw, C., Soifer, S., & Gutierrez, L. (1993). Toward a hybrid model for effective organizing in communities of colour. *Journal of Community Practice, 1*(1), 25–42.

Burghardt, S. (1982). *The Other Side of Organizing.* Cambridge, MA: Schenkman.

Carlton-LaNey, I., & Andrews, J. (1998). Direct practice: Addressing gender in practice from a multicultural feminist perspective. In J. Figueira-McDonough, F.E. Netting, & A. Nichols-Casebolt (Eds), *The Role of Gender in Practice Knowledge: Claiming Half the Human Experience* (pp. 93–125). New York: Taylor and Francis.

Carlton-LaNey, I., & Burwell, N.Y. (Eds). (1996). *African American Community Practice Models: Historical and Contemporary Responses.* New York: Haworth Press.

Costellano, M.B. (1999). Renewing the relationship: A perspective on the impact of the Royal Commission on Aboriginal Peoples. In J. Hylton (Ed.), *Aboriginal Self-Government in Canada.* 2nd ed. (pp. 92–111). Saskatoon: Purich Publishing.

Chow, P., & Saldov, M. (1992). *The Ethnic Elderly in Metro Toronto Hospitals, Nursing Homes, and Homes for the Aged: Communication and Health Care.* St John's: School of Social Work, Memorial University of Newfoundland.

Cox, F., Erlich, J., Rothman, J., & Tropman, J. (Eds) (1995). *Strategies of Community Organization.* 4th ed. Itasca, IL: F.E. Peacock.

Davis, L., & Proctor, E. (1989). *Race, Gender and Class: Guidelines for Practice with Individuals, Families and Groups.* Englewood Cliffs, NJ: Prentice-Hall.

Devore, W., & Schlesinger, E.G. (1996). *Ethnic-Sensitive Social Work Practice.* 4th ed. Columbus, OH: Merrill Publishing.

Dominelli, L. (1988). *Anti-Racist Social Work: A Challenge for White Practitioners and Educators.* London: Macmillan.

Downing, J., Fasano, R., Friedland, P., McCollough, M., Mizrahi, T., & Shapiro, J. (Eds). (1991). *Computers for Social Change and Community Organization.* New York: Haworth Press.

Durst, D. (1994). Understanding the client/social worker relationship in a multicultural setting: Implications for practice. *Journal of Multicultural Social Work, 3*(4), 29–42.

Durst, D., McDonald, J., & Parsons, D. (1999). Finding our way: A community needs assessment on violence in native families. *Journal of Community Practice,* 6(1), 45–69.

Erasmus, P., & Ensign, G. (1991). *A Practical Framework for Community Liaison Work in Native Communities.* Brandon, MB: Justin Publishing.

Feehan, K., & Hannis, D. (1993). *From Strength to Strength: Social Work Education and Aboriginal People.* Edmonton: Grant MacEwan Community College.

Fleras, A., & Elliott, J. L. (1999). *Unequal Relations: An Introduction to Race, Ethnic, and Aboriginal Dynamics in Canada.* 3rd ed. Scarborough, ON: Prentice Hall/ Allyn Bacon.

Freire, P. (1993). *Pedagogy of the Oppressed.* New York: Continuum Books.

Gallegos, J. (1984). The ethnic competence model for social work education. In B. White (Ed.), *Color in a White Society.* Silver Spring, MD: National Association of Social Workers.

Graveline, F.J. (1998). *Circle Works.* Halifax: Fernwood.

Grobman, G.M., & Grant, G.B. (1998). *The Non-Profit Internet Handbook.* Harrisburg, PA: White Hat Communications.

Gutierrez, L. (1996). Understanding the empowerment process: Does consciousness make a difference? *Social Work Research, 19*(4), 229–37.

Gutierrez, L., & Alvarez, A.R. (2000). Educating students for multicultural community practice. In D. Hardina (Ed.), *Innovative Approaches for Teaching Community Organization Skills in the Classroom* (pp. 39–56). New York: Haworth Press.

Gutierrez, L., & Lewis, E. (1994). Community organizing with women of color: A feminist approach. *Journal of Community Practice, 1,* 23–44.

Hardina, D. (Ed.). (2000). *Innovative Approaches for Teaching Community Organization Skills in the Classroom.* New York: Haworth Press.

Harper, K.V., & Lantz, J. (1996). *Cross-Cultural Practice: Social Work with Diverse Populations.* Chicago: Lyceum Books.

Herberg, D.C. (1993). *Frameworks for Cultural and Racial Diversity: Teaching and Learning for Practitioners.* Toronto: Canadian Scholars' Press.

Hillery, G.A., Jr. (1955). Definitions of community: Areas of agreement. *Rural Sociology, 20,* 779–91.

Horne, M. (1987). *Values in Social Work.* Aldershot, UK: Wildwood House.

Iglehart, A.P., & Becerra, R.M. (1995). *Social Services and the Ethnic Community.* Boston: Allyn and Bacon.

Krause, A, Stein, M., & Clark, J. (1998). *The Virtual Activist: A Training Course.* Netaction. Retrieved from http://www.netaction.org/

Krogsrud Miley, K., O'Melia, M., & DuBois, B.L. (1995). *Generalist Social Work Practice: An Empowering Approach.* Boston: Allyn and Bacon.

Lee, B. (1999). *Pragmatics of Community Organization.* 3rd ed. Toronto: Commonact Press.

Leigh, J.W. (1998). *Communicating for Cultural Competence.* Needham Heights, MA: Allyn and Bacon.

Lyon, L. (1987). *The Community in Urban Society.* Chicago: Dorsey Press.

Lum, D. (1992). *Social Work with People of Color: A Process-Stage Approach.* Pacific Grove, CA: Brooks/Cole.

McDonald, L., Pittaway, E., & Nahmiash, D. (1995). Issues in practice with respect to mistreatment of older people. In M.J. Maclean (Ed.), *Abuse and Neglect of Older Canadians: Strategies for Change* (pp. 5–16). Ottawa: Canadian Association on Gerontology.

McNutt, J. (1995). The macro practice curriculum in graduate social work education: The results of a national study. *Administration in Social Work, 19,* 59–74.

———. (2000). Organizing cyberspace: Strategies for teaching about community practice and technology. In D. Hardina (Ed.), *Innovative Approaches for Teaching Community Organization Skills in the Classroom* (pp. 95–109). New York: Haworth Press.

Munoz, C. (1989). *Youth Identity and Power: The Chicano Movement.* London: Verso.

Reisch, M., & Lowe, J.I. (2000). 'Of means and ends' revisited: Teaching ethical community organizing in an unethical society. In D. Hardina (Ed.), *Innovative Approaches for Teaching Community Organization Skills in the Classroom* (pp. 19–38). New York: Haworth Press.

Rivera, F. G., & Erlich, J.L. (1995). *Community Organizing in a Diverse Society.* 2nd ed. Needham Heights, MA: Allyn and Bacon.

Rothman, J. (1995). Approaches to community intervention. In F. Cox, J. Erlich, J. Rothman, & J. Tropman (Eds), *Strategies of Community Organization.* 4th ed. (pp. 26–63). Itasca, IL: F.E. Peacock.

Rubin, H.J., & Rubin, I. (1986). *Community Organizing and Development.* Columbus, OH: Merrill Publishing.

Schwartz, E. (1996). *NetActivism: How Citizens Use the Internet.* Sebastopol: O'Reilly Publishing.

Taylor, S.H., & Roberts, R.W. (Eds). (1985). *Theory and Practice of Community Social Work.* New York: Columbia University Press.

Warren, R. (1971). Types of purposive social change at the community level. In R. Warren (Ed.), *Truth, Love, and Social Change* (pp. 134–49). Chicago: Rand McNally.

Weil, M., & Gamble D. (1995). Community practice models. In R.L. Edwards (Ed.), *Encyclopedia of Social Work.* 19th ed. (pp. 577–94). Washington, DC: National Association of Social Workers.

West, G. (1990). Cooperation and conflict among women in the welfare rights movement. In L. Albrecht & R. Brewer (Eds), *Bridges of Power: Women's Multicultural Alliances* (pp. 149–71). Philadelphia, PA: New Society Publishers.

Wharf, B., & Clague, M. (Eds). (1997). *Community Organizing: Canadian Experiences.* Toronto, Ontario: Oxford University Press.

Zeff, R. (1996). *The Nonprofit Guide to the Internet.* New York: Wiley.

Chapter 4

Canadian Society: Social Policy and Ethno-Racial Diversity

Carole Pigler Christensen

Broadly defined, social policy refers to decisions and resulting guidelines about the allocation of resources and rights in a society, or one of its systems, that constitute a general framework to direct future decisions and actions in a given area of policy concern (Pierce, 1984). Social policy decisions underlie all aspects of social welfare and social services that affect the daily lives of all people living in Canada. Moreover, because social services are a reflection of social policy, access barriers and inequities experienced by ethno-racial groups are directly related to the manner in which policies are carried out by decision makers in agencies where professional social workers are employed. The current interest in cross-cultural and anti-racist social work practice is directly related to demographic changes following the liberalization of Canada's immigration policy during the 1960s. The major purpose of this chapter is to address the effects of Canadian social policy on those commonly referred to as ethno-racial groups. Emphasis is placed, therefore, on how Canada's social policies have shaped the experience of those referred to as being 'other' than the 'two founding nations'—that is, those categorized as 'visible minorities'. Aspects of Canadian social policy, and the resulting network of services, institutions, and programs, are examined in historical perspective. Important issues in the formulation and implementation of social policy, as these relate to political ideology, are identified. Following a brief consideration of the current and evolving social policy issues of concern to ethno-racial minorities, the chapter ends with a vision of how a paradigm shift might lead to the adoption of policies promoting an egalitarian, truly inclusive society.

The following underlying assumptions are central to this chapter. First, historically, social policy was formulated solely to serve the concerns and needs of the 'two founding nations', the French and the British. Second, despite differences in stated ideologies as social policies have evolved over time, the unique concerns of ethno-racial groups have been ignored, or inadequately addressed. Third, even today, social policies are seldom enacted with a multiracial population in mind. Fourth, because social policies profoundly affect social work practice, the implications for working with ethno-racial minority clients, while respecting professional values and ethical standards, must be considered.

The Language of Social Policy: Meanings and Effects

A meaningful discussion of the effects of social policy on *ethno-racial* groups requires an understanding of this term, and other terms used in this paper. Language and labels are closely related to the status various populations are accorded in a stratified society. Although racism remains a taboo subject in Canada, anyone living here for an appreciable length of time becomes aware that identifiable groups are hierarchically arranged and labelled accordingly. Social scientists have long been aware of ethnic stratification, or Canada's 'vertical mosaic', and its implications for individuals and for interethnic and multiracial relations has been discussed by several analysts (Bolaria & Li, 1988; Kalbach & Kalbach, 2000; Porter, 1965; Tennant, 1985). However, social workers, like the general public, are likely to be unaware of the actual history of Aboriginal peoples and ethno-racial minorities. It is seldom taught in Canadian schools or addressed in the popular media.

Throughout this chapter, *dominant group* refers to those whose culture and values are legitimized and transmitted through formal institutions, including governments, educational institutions, the media, and legislated social policies. The dominant group wields most of the social, economic, and political power and determines social policy sanctioned by official sources. In a multicultural society, positions of authority and decision making tend to be occupied by this group. The dominant group in Canada comprises people of British and French (in Quebec) origin, officially referred to as the 'two founding nations', or charter groups, giving them special status. Canadians of European ancestry have generally been assimilated into this group, becoming part of the so-called mainstream—those viewed as 'typical' Canadians having a rightful place here. Policies formulated by the dominant group determine which groups will be allowed to enter the country as immigrants or refugees, and the societal positions they will be allowed to occupy. Those who are not part of the dominant group are perceived as belonging to a *minority group*, and are themselves aware that they lack power and experience varying degrees of oppression and marginalization. Minority status means being part of a group that lacks power, privilege, and prestige in relation to Canadians of the dominant group. Whatever their numbers, members of minority groups seldom hold decision-making positions in the wider society. The intricacies of the process by which social policies underlie and perpetuate dominant–minority relations in Canada are seldom discussed and, therefore, remain somewhat mystifying (Christensen, 2001).

Ethno-racial groups are minority groups in terms of both status and power. The term has two aspects worth noting. First, the term *ethnic* has been associated increasingly with people whose ancestry is other than European. This is, of course, a misnomer, since all people, including the British and the French, are part of an ethnic group, meaning a group bound together by a shared history, culture, traditions, and beliefs. Second, it is informative that, in labelling people of colour as visible minorities, official sources chose a term that differentiates them from Euro-Canadians according to the racialized feature of skin colour. Might this be considered state-imposed racism? Indeed all groups, including 'Whites', can be classified according to the socially constructed racial categories established by eighteenth- and nineteenth-century European scientists, most notably Charles Darwin. Although it has no biological basis, racist ideology has resulted in the belief that the human species is hierarchically arranged into races, having immutable qualities in terms of morals, intelligence, and cultural attributes, with Whites being superior to all others. *Racism* exists when people are treated as if these arbitrarily defined categories truly exist. This was this ideology that guided European colonizers.

Most social scientists now agree that race is a social construct but, too often, they fail to acknowledge its persistent political, economic, and social consequences (Christensen, 1999, p. 296). Racism operates on individual, cultural, and institutional levels, the two latter categories being most difficult to discern. It manifests itself when people take action, including the formulation of social policy, while harbouring a belief system supporting racist ideology. Because of racism in Canada, people of colour are *racialized*—that is, meanings are attributed to their identifiable features so as to give them special, negative, or exotic significance. As an ideology, the concept of race shapes the world view of those indoctrinated by it, even if unconsciously; as a political tool, it maintains systems of inequality.

The term '*communities*' has often been attached to groups that are, in fact, *ethno-racial categories*: people diverse in ethnicity, cultural background, social class, religion, and genealogy, arbitrarily classified as being alike on the basis of identifiable racial features, such as skin colour. For example, people labelled 'Black', whatever their actual genetic and cultural heritage, are viewed as being alike, are expected to conform to popularized dominant-group stereotypes, and are perceived as a community of like-minded individuals. Such ignorance generates difficulties, not only in perceptions, but also in academic research (e.g., American studies often compare Blacks and Whites). Aware of their ethnic diversity, those identified as part of a given ethno-racial community have in common the historical experience of having suffered indignities and injustices (e.g., colonialism); in the present, they share living in the social context of racism.

Marginalized populations experience societal disadvantage, and do not have the power to define themselves in a manner that is readily accepted as legitimate by the dominant culture. This is illustrated by the many names used to categorize various ethno-racial minorities over time by social policy analysts, governments, and official bodies such as Statistics Canada. Equally important is the language in popular use at a given time (e.g., Indian, Eskimo, First Nations; Chink, Oriental, Asian; Negro, coloured, Black, African-Canadian; Hindu, Paki, South Asian). The manner in which groups are classified often dictates the degree to which they are perceived as distinct from, or similar to, the dominant culture. As noted by Li (1988, p. 23), what forms the basis of ethnic or racial groups is not so much inherent traits, whether physical or cultural, but rather the salience given to these characteristics by the dominant group with the power to define socially what constitutes a subordinate group. Once social meaning is attached to ethno-racial characteristics, they become the basis of social stratification. An understanding of this process is essential for a meaningful analysis of the effects of social policy on racialized minorities in Canada.

It is extremely difficult to have an honest discourse about the effects of social policy on ethno-racial minorities in Canada. This is because, given the constant espousal of democratic liberalism, Canadians remain in denial about racism as a commanding force in Canadian society. Canadians prefer to assume that equality of opportunity exists, and that achieved, rather than ascribed, characteristics determine one's life chances. To acknowledge that ethno-racial categorization affects the lives of minorities is to concede that Euro-Canadian hegemony continues to operate and define the structures within which mainstream programs and services are delivered (Dei, 1996). Consequently, any labels that include the term 'race' almost inevitably cause discomfort. At the same time, the term 'mainstream' has become part of the common parlance, clearly implying that some people are inside and others are outside of whatever groups, institutions, or organizations are perceived to be the norm, or the standard, in every imaginable area that can be categorized. With the above in mind, it is possible to examine how social policy decisions have affected the lives of ethno-racial minorities in Canada.

The Need for an Analysis of the Effects of Social Policy On Ethno-Racial Minorities

Traditionally, the very presence of ethno-racial groups (not meant to include Aboriginal people) has been omitted from official accounts of Canadian history, making them virtually invisible. Not surprisingly, the social welfare experiences of these groups, and the barriers to social services that they have faced, have been largely ignored. Similarly, the extensive literature on Canadian social policy has paid scant attention to the effects on neglected populations of policies associated with public education, health, child welfare, income security, housing, and social services. Interestingly, immigration policies have generally not been considered when social policy analyses have been made, despite their impact on ethno-racial immigrant groups. Consequently, social workers have lacked information about how social policy decisions have affected the well-being of ethno-racial minorities over time.

Today, perhaps more than ever, there is reason to give serious attention to the effects of Canadian social policies on ethno-racial minorities. The proportion of people in Canada who are not of European ancestry has grown considerably over the past three decades, but ethno-racial peoples remain numerical minorities in Canada as a whole (approximately 11 per cent of the total population). The number of 'visible minorities' is highest in Ontario (1,682,045 people, or 15.8 per cent of the population); in British Columbia (660,545 people, or 17.9 per cent of the population); and in Quebec (433,985 people, or 6.2 per cent of the population) (Statistics Canada, 1996). These percentages increase considerably when multiple ancestry is reported, as it has been in recent census data. Because the greatest concentration of racial minorities is in major cities where employment opportunities for professionals also exist, social workers who work in these settings will inevitably have clients from diverse ethno-racial backgrounds. Census data indicate that Canada now comprises people from over seventy countries, not including about 800,000 Aboriginal people. Studies conducted in urban areas suggest that certain sectors employing social workers (e.g., the criminal justice system, youth protection, child welfare) have a disproportionate number of clients that are from ethno-racial backgrounds, including minorities of long-standing, immigrants, and First Nations peoples (Henry, Tator, Mattis, & Rees, 2000).

Without proper analysis, the realities of the effects of social policies on ethno-racial groups, although profoundly affecting their daily lives, appear to be unimportant or so complex as to be incomprehensible. Yet, this is far from true. Rather, there has heretofore been little interest in analyzing, researching, and publicly reporting how various ethno-racial groups fare under varying social policy conditions. For example, when unemployment statistics are reported in the media, figures do not indicate whether all people in Canada are experiencing the same rates of unemployment. Furthermore, when policies change the conditions for eligibility for employment insurance, little is known about how this affects minorities already suffering higher levels of unemployment than majority-group Canadians. Recently, Canadian studies have begun to explore this area (Kazemipur & Halli, 2000; Ornstein, 2000).

In the analytical framework that I am proposing, the inclusion of the following variables is considered fundamental to any attempt to understand racialized groups' social policy concerns:

- ethno-racial groups' experiences interacting with the dominant culture (i.e., the degree of economic, social, and political marginalization and oppression) over time;
- variations in the time period over which a particular ethno-racial group entered Canada, whether during a specified period, or over several generations;
- the number of people and demographic characteristics of a particular group;
- the entrance status initially accorded the majority of those from a particular group (e.g., slaves, landed immigrants, or refugees);
- the level of cohesiveness and institutional completeness of an ethno-racial group;
- the circumstances in which Canada found itself at the time of entry (e.g., economic conditions, political climate, attitudes towards immigration);
- the degree to which the ethno-racial minority is a true ethnic group (sharing more than superficial characteristics such as skin colour), interacting voluntarily to maintain valued traditions;

• the status of the immigrant group in the international arena and its effect on power relations globally and in Canada.

Once in Canada, racialized groups find themselves somewhat coerced into assuming a collective identity as an ethno-racial community. Yet, often, members of this 'community' have come from vastly different geographic locations; some may even have been former enemies 'back home'. Some ethno-racial groups come to Canada under a wave of public sympathy, with special settlement social policies enacted by governments for their benefit (e.g., the Vietnamese boat people), while others may be clearly less welcome (e.g., Somali refugees). Currently, Asians from wealthy industrialized countries are sought after as business people, while other Asians come as refugees and face discrimination in the job market. Timing is also a factor. The same ethno-racial group may have been viewed quite negatively during a particular period, and more positively at a later time (e.g., the Japanese during the Second World War, compared to today). Canadian governments have always been sensitive to the political ramifications on the international arena of their treatment of various immigrant groups, and this has a profound effect on how people from various regions are received here. To illustrate, Africa has little or no political significance for Canada, but China is treated with wary respect, as a potentially important trading partner. For the time being, at least, overt racism towards the Chinese in Canada has declined.

Recent research gives clear evidence that ethno-racial minorities often have a very different experience of Canada than do White Canadians (Kazemipur & Halli, 2000). Should their call for attention to their legitimate and serious concerns continue to go unheeded, Canada will allow a great divide between the White population and people of colour to grow, potentially leading to problems for the society as a whole. Events in the United States provide an unenviable example of the disruption to daily life that may result when the harm caused by racial disparity is ignored.

Social Policies and Ethno-racial Minorities in Historical Perspective

There was never a time when Canada was not multiracial, as is obvious from the existence of diverse Aboriginal people prior to the arrival of Europeans. Popular myth suggests that there had never been a significant historical presence in Canada of peoples from outside of Europe. This myth was maintained by the lack of attention to the social policy concerns of non-European groups during Canada's formative years: Aboriginal peoples; slaves brought directly from Africa to Canada (1600s–1833); African fugitive slaves from the colonies before the American Civil War (1700s–1860s); and immigrant groups arriving from Asia (1850s).

Historically, the most important influences on the early formulation of social policy in Canada were the British Poor Laws and, especially in Quebec, the Catholic Church. Three aspects of early thinking about social policy are of particular import. First the provision of social welfare was considered something that the wealthier classes did for, or to, the socially disadvantaged as an act of charity; it was not regarded as a right to which the disadvantaged were entitled. Second, a distinction was made between the deserving and the undeserving poor; able-bodied individuals who were considered to be without the motivation or capacity to improve their condition were labelled as 'undeserving' and received little—if any—assistance. Third, a system of private or voluntary services, dependent on good will and philanthropy, became a cornerstone of the social service structure. Evidently, the social policy provisions described above were envisioned to apply exclusively to those of European ancestry.

At the same time that attitudes were evolving about helping those deemed in need of assistance, a parallel line of thinking towards Aboriginal people and racialized minorities was also evolving. The effects of racialization were most evident in the use of the Indian Act to exclude Aboriginal peoples from policies meant for the general public, in the 'separate and unequal' policies that were applied to immigrant minorities of colour, and in Canada's discriminatory, 'White only' immigration policies (Jakubowski, 1997). The current conditions of ethno-racial minorities cannot be understood without knowledge of the history of social policies that have, to a great extent, determined their place in Canadian society (Christensen & Weinfeld, 1993).

Policies of Exclusion: Separate and Unequal Status and Access

The politics of exclusion must be examined in the context of power relations. Special status was conferred on the dominant cultural groups, the British and French settlers, the 'two founding peoples'. The British settlers brought two attributes of lasting significance with them to the New World. First, they embraced the prevailing racist ideology of Manifest Destiny based on Social Darwinism. They were convinced that they were superior to 'uncivilized' Aboriginal populations and had an absolute sense of entitlement to the lands and resources of the 'New World'. Second, they embraced the philosophy underlying the British Poor Laws, which viewed poverty as a personal weakness and permitted only meagre charitable assistance that was difficult to access (Christensen, 1999). The doctrine claiming that the White race had the 'burden' to 'civilize' other races served as a rationalization for colonial exploitation by the French and the British, and shaped attitudes and social policies that affected racialized groups. The pioneer ethic promised to reward European rugged individualists, and fostered the view that people were in need due to personal, rather than societal, failure. Given these viewpoints, those in need were relegated to second-class status early in Canadian history (Turner, 2001, p. 81). Racialized minorities were excluded altogether from official social policies aimed at alleviating the hardships experienced by European settlers. The most blatant examples of formal policies of exclusion are to be found in the treatment of Aboriginal peoples and racial minorities.

For over four hundred years, separate policy guidelines have been devised and applied exclusively to Aboriginal peoples. Following an initial period of mutual respect and tolerance, relations between the European newcomers and Aboriginal nations worsened, as the colonizers tightened their grasp on the territory that was to become Canada. After Confederation, policies in the Indian Act of 1876 officially codified the systematic subjugation and exclusion of, and deceit and discrimination directed at, Aboriginal people. Among other things, various acts outlined social welfare benefits and services administered under the Department of Indian Affairs, and took control of the land and resources, relegating the original peoples to reserve Crown lands, which they could not sell. Suffice it to say that the results left Aboriginal people, for the most part, in conditions of abject poverty. Their psychological, social, and economic needs have remained largely invisible and poorly understood by most Canadians. For valid and important reasons, Aboriginal Canadians do not wish to be lumped together with ethno-racial minorities. Nonetheless, they have much in common with ethno-racial groups in terms of oppression and marginalization in relations with the dominant culture.

Most Canadians do not know that Blacks were among the earliest people to arrive in Canada, introduced as African slaves in 1608 by the French. The existence of slavery has been all but obliterated from Canadian history, perhaps due to the abject cruelty of the conditions of enslavement and the social policies that supported it. Social policies, adopted under both French and British rule, legalized the import of and active trade in slaves as chattel, from 1628 through 1834, when slavery was abolished in the British territories (Winks, 1971). In 1689, Louis XIV of France gave legal assent for Black slaves to be provided for the fisheries, mines, and agriculture in the French North American colonies. The lives of slaves were regulated by the Code Noir, a social policy that also protected Whites from slave revolt. Marguerite Bourgeoys of the Sisters of the Congregation of Notre Dame in New France was an influential eighteenth-century religious leader who traded in slaves. Despite protests from Canadian Blacks she has, nonetheless, recently been approved for sainthood by the Catholic Church. Of the sixteen legislators in Canada's first Parliament of Upper Canada, at least six were slave owners (Henry et al., 2000, p. 70).

Throughout Canada's earliest history, slaves were to be found in what are now Nova Scotia, New Brunswick, Quebec, and Ontario (Walker, 1976). It is estimated that by 1860 there were 60,000 Blacks in Canada. Yet, due to the harsh conditions endured in Canada, many left for Africa (Sierra Leone, in 1792 and in 1800) or returned to the United States after the Civil War. At a time when the country was sparsely populated, Blacks were, no doubt, a noticeable presence, especially in Nova Scotia, where they lived in sizeable numbers. Many had come from the American colonies as Black Loyalists, 'freed' from slavery in 1783, in exchange for supporting the British. Although loyal to the British during the American Revolution, military policies forced them to fight in segregated armies. In the Canadian colonies, government-supported social policies ensured that Blacks remained unequal, living in segregated communities, and occupying a caste-like status outside of the opportunity structure. They were subject to race riots and the destruction of their homes and were denied land ownership, food rations (during Nova Scotia's famine in 1789), fair wages, and employment opportunities. Many succumbed to malnutrition and disease. Still, former slaves and new settlers formed self-help organizations, often associated with segregated Black churches.

Confederation and the decades that followed did not change discriminatory laws and practices that had thrived in the British North American colonies. Indeed, in the 1950s, Blacks were still regularly denied access to community services, recreational facilities, and restaurants. Legally segregated schools ended in Ontario and in Nova Scotia only in the 1960s. The significance of the early Black settlers' experience goes beyond historical fact, something that their descendants should simply 'get over' and forget about. Blacks are the only 'imported' people to have experienced the caste-like status of slavery in the Americas, a legacy that has continued to shape the daily lives of Black Canadians (Christensen & Weinfeld, 1993).

In the nineteenth and first half of the twentieth century, Chinese and Japanese immigrants were labelled 'Orientals'. Most of these early Asian immigrants settled on the West Coast. Lured by the Fraser River gold rush, they were permitted to enter Canada during the mid-1800s as cheap, casual labour to perform specific menial tasks, such as working on the railroad or in the mines. Referred to as the 'yellow peril', they were generally expected to return to their countries of origin once the need for their labour expired—and indeed, many dreamed of doing so. Chinese and Japanese settlers experienced extreme forms of harassment and oppression, not only from the general public, but also as a result of provincial and federal government policies. Chinese men who had wives in their country of origin were nonetheless considered 'bachelors' for the purposes of immigration and were prevented from bringing their wives to Canada, but there were severe social sanctions for relationships with White women. Chinese men filled menial jobs such as gardening, domestic service, forest clearing, and laundry work. Fearing competition from the low wages paid to the Chinese in Victoria, White workers formed the Workingman's Protective Association, intended to protect them from the threat of cheap Chinese labour, and race riots initiated by Euro-Canadians (such as that in Vancouver in 1907) sometimes occurred. In his 1908 *Report of the Commissioner Appointed to Enquire into the Methods by Which Oriental Labourers Have Been Induced to Come to Canada*, Mackenzie King defended policies restricting immigration on the basis of race, considering it 'natural' that Canada should desire to remain a White man's country for economic and social reasons, and also as a matter of political and national necessity (Christensen, 2001, p. 185; Henry et al., 2000, p. 78). In British Columbia, the Chinese were barred from voting and from entering certain professions, including dentistry and law. The Immigration Act of 1923 barred Chinese immigration; it was not repealed until 1947. Excluded from the welfare benefits available to the dominant group, Asians formed their own benevolent associations. Although Asians were unwelcome for military service in the two world wars, they were allowed to serve in segregated armies when soldiers were desperately needed.

Between 1941 and 1948, during and immediately after the Second World War, the federal government adopted policies forcing assumed 'enemy aliens' that is, Japanese Canadians—to leave their homes for internment camps scattered across Canada. They were forced to do roadwork and to be farmhands in Alberta, Ontario, and the British Columbia interior. In 1988, after a long struggle for recognition of their loss of human rights and property in the 1940s, the Canadian government finally acknowledged wartime atrocities and offered token compensation to Japanese Canadians. Most of the money was used for homes for the aged, who might not be comfortable in homes supposedly available to the general population.

Indo-Canadians, having first come to Canadian shores in the late 1800s, also experienced blatant and long-standing racism and discrimination. They too faced immigration restrictions, were exploited as cheap farm labourers, and were considered too 'exotic' for assimilation. British Columbia barred them from voting in 1907, and in 1908 the federal government passed the Continuous Passage Act, to stem the tide of immigration from India. The act required all immigrants to arrive by an uninterrupted journey from their country of origin. This effectively precluded immigration from India, which had no regular direct shipping lines to Canada. In the infamous *Komagata Maru* incident of 1914, four hundred would-be immigrants from India, who had chartered a boat to bring them to Canada, were held at Vancouver harbour for months before being turned back.

In summary, the social policies adopted throughout Canadian history consistently restricted ethno-racial groups from fulfilling their needs for access to goods and services, land and resources, employment, education, and participation in the civic and political process. Moreover, ethno-racial minorities were stripped of human dignity by these policies, which were designed to humiliate them and to limit their life-chances. Such abhorrent and unjust social policies formed the basis for the concerns of people of colour, and set the stage for their later experience.

For centuries, the European response to racialized groups was to ignore them, or to suggest that if they worked hard, like European immigrants, they could 'get ahead'. Such responses denied the severe impact of social policies supporting and perpetuating systemic racism endured by racialized minorities over time (Christensen, 2001, p. 192). The British North America Act of 1867 assigned responsibility for welfare provisions to the provincial governments, leaving patchwork welfare programs, guided by the Poor Laws, mainly to municipalities (Turner, 2001). However inadequate these programs may have been for majority-group Canadians, they were inaccessible to early Black and Asian settlers. Ethno-racial groups without the resources to help themselves faced disaster during times of economic recession and depression. By the early twentieth century, it was becoming clear to dominant-group social policy makers that the complexities of a capitalist industrialized state demanded more centralized planning, and the federal government became increasingly involved in assuming responsibility for matters relating to health and welfare. Only when universal programs associated with the welfare state were in place, and *overt* racism had diminished somewhat, could ethno-racial minorities hope to benefit from social welfare programs.

Despite significant changes in Canadian social policies in the twentieth century, negative attitudes towards the needy have remained. When unemployment levels are high, immigrants still become scapegoats for society's ills. Minorities are blamed for taking jobs from 'real' Canadians and for taking unfair advantage of the social welfare system. It is certainly no exaggeration to say that many of the major issues that ethno-racial groups have continued to face have been directly caused by systemic racism, institutional discrimination, and the inferior status that they have been accorded for many generations (Ruggles & Rovinescu, 1996; Ujimoto & Gordon, 1980).

Racialization and Immigration Policy

The current attention given to multicultural and ethno-racial groups is the result of their increased numbers in the population, due to changes in immigration policy in the 1960s. Until 1962, immigration policies were clearly designed to promote the immigration of people from northern and western Europe, and to make it almost impossible for migrants from elsewhere to enter the country as permanent residents. For centuries, immigration policies were fertile ground for the manifestation of overt racism towards those labelled 'uncivilized' and/or 'heathen' (non-Christian), and therefore deserving to be dominated and exploited, not assimilated. Interestingly, people who, until quite recently, were openly viewed in this way now live among the Europeans who had colonized them on the basis of such perceptions (Fleras & Elliott, 1999).

The Canadian Immigration Act of 1869 excluded 'undesirables', such as criminals, the diseased, Asians, and Blacks. In 1884, the Royal Commission on Chinese Immigration reported that the people of British Columbia wanted legislation restricting the province to 'people of the European race' (Christensen, 2001). By 1885, head taxes of $100 to $500 were imposed on Chinese people wishing to immigrate to Canada. Restrictive policies were applied to all racial minorities by the time of the Immigration Act of 1910 (Jakubowski, 1997, p.13).

Immigration restrictions of the early 1900s reflected racial stereotypes popularized in the media. Blacks were also unwelcome in the Prairies, where in 1903 J.S. Woodsworth, later a founder of the Co-operative Commonwealth Federation (CCF), described them as impulsive, having strong sexual passions, and lacking willpower (Henry et al., 2000, p. 71). Southern and eastern Europeans and religious minorities (e.g., Jews, Doukhobors, and Hutterites) also faced discrimination at various times. Some practised voluntary segregation, at least initially. Without being identifiable on the basis of colour, and since policies restricting access to land, resources, services, and employment were not generally denied them, by the second generation White immigrants became indistinguishable from 'mainstream' Canadians, unless choosing to remain apart.

Immigration policies became less overtly racist in 1967, with the introduction of an 'objective' point system that considers factors such as age, education, work experience, and prearranged employment in a needed job category. However, observers note that room for bias and racism remain (Christensen, 2001): the point system allows immigration officers to make subjective judgments concerning the potential immigrant's 'suitability'; there are few immigration offices in Third World countries; a landing fee of $975, quotas, tests for French or English proficiency, and medical examinations ensure that only the 'best and the brightest' from 'developing' countries are admitted. Moreover, newly revised policies require applicants to have at least a Masters degree. Recent policies have made it increasingly difficult to sponsor relatives; it is easiest for business entrepreneurs or highly educated young (under age twenty-four) people with guaranteed jobs in Canada to enter the country as independent immigrants. It is worth noting, however, that even legal immigrants, with high levels of education from their countries of origin, often find that their credentials are not accepted, and they are forced to take menial jobs. Despite immigrants' concerns about immigration policies, Canada's population has become increasingly diverse. In 1961, 90 per cent of Canada's immigrants came from Europe, but this number had dropped to 19 per cent by 1996.

Special Status Policies

Legal status remains the basis of exclusion for particular categories of migrants, for whom special social policies were created early in Canada, and remain operational. In contradiction to Canada's reputation abroad as a champion of human rights, this country maintains an exploitative system of migrant-worker, domestic, and caregiver schemes with Third World countries such as Mexico, India, Jamaica, and the Philippines (Bolaria & Li, 1988). Refugees, temporary migrant workers, domestic workers, and illegal immigrants (often working in the garment and restaurant industries) have restricted social welfare benefits and are often exploited due to their vulnerable status. Poor women of colour (often leaving their own children behind) care for the children and homes of affluent Whites; even feminists seeking personal career fulfillment apparently fail to be disturbed by the policies that support such exploitation. People in these various categories represent a source of cheap labour on which the Canadian economy depends. Many fear that they will jeopardize their status with authorities or that they risk reprisals from their employers should they complain or seek forms of help available to the general public. Most often, illegal immigrants have fled their country due to war or persecution, have had no possibility of obtaining legal documents from authorities at home, and hope to gain refugee status in Canada.

Refugees, illegal immigrants, and temporary and migrant workers are generally viewed unsympathetically by Canadians, who are unaware of the vital role that they play in the economy and who tend to perceive them as 'undeserving' aliens. Canadians also tend to be uninformed about how government policies in the international arena (e.g., in co-operation with the World Bank, the General Agreement on Tariffs and Trade, the Multilateral Agreement on Investments and with military operations in the Third World) help to maintain poverty and create refugees in various parts of the world.

Settlement and Integration Policies

When one considers government-funded orientation and settlement services available to immigrants and refugees, matters are complicated by the existence of policies and programs operating at both the federal and provincial levels, in addition to programs operated by the voluntary sector. Most programs offered by non-governmental organizations and volunteers do not involve the services of professional social workers (Christensen, 2001). Generally underfunded (whether by government or other sources) and limited in the range of services offered, agencies providing services specific to ethno-racial groups continue to remain apart from 'mainstream' social services. In most cases, there are no official policies assuring collaboration between mainstream agencies and those serving immigrants and minority populations.

The costs involved in administering programs associated with settling immigrants must not be overlooked. Unaware of historical and present inequities, Euro-Canadians are likely to react negatively to any suggestion of 'special treatment' for ethno-racial groups or for Aboriginal peoples. At the same time, marginalized ethno-racial groups would prefer to be part of the opportunity structure, with equal access to employment and resources, making special policies such as employment equity legislation, for example, unnecessary.

Professional Social Work: Ethno-Racial Issues

Both the conventional and progressive roots of professional social work are to be found in two social movements that developed in late-nineteenth- and early twentieth-century Canada. First, charitable organizations, which were funded by middle-class White businessmen (a precursor of Canada's United Way) and engaged White women as 'friendly visitors' to help the poor and destitute, led to the social casework model. Second, there was the settlement house movement, which viewed poverty as having structural, rather than personal, causes. Those involved in the latter assumed that people were not treated equally in a capitalistic society, and that many people experienced discrimination. They went to the sweatshops and the slums where marginalized European workers were found, and focused on reforming society rather than the individual. This movement was the precursor of community organization, community development, and social action. Yet, despite the rhetoric of the progressive settlement house movement, help was offered almost exclusively to Euro-Canadians. The exclusion of racialized minorities from social services was so ingrained that it was dictated by 'common sense'. Social policy makers and analysts made no mention of how early Black and Asian immigrants were being affected by social welfare policies. In Quebec, social policy has always been related to language, religion, and French-Canadian cultural identity issues. Even French-speaking ethno-racial minorities have found themselves suspended between their allegiance to the collective good and the regular reminder that they are not viewed as part of the Québécois community.

Geared to meeting the concerns of the dominant group, social policies still fail to attend to the unique needs of ethno-racial minorities experiencing systemic racism and structural exclusion. For these groups, societal oppression is experienced not only in lack of access to social services, but in lack of access to full participation in all areas vital to well-being (Christensen, 2001, p. 192). The meaning of 'cross-cultural competence' must move beyond skills and tools that enhance social workers' understanding of ethno-racial groups' cultures to include the ability to incorporate changing structures and institutional practices that are detrimental to clients.

The Ideological Bases and Consequences of Current Social Policies

Ideology is a pervasive set of values and ideas that legitimate particular social and economic conditions and that provide meaning to everyday discourse. If policy makers truly wish to plan strategies for overcoming the consequences of generations of exclusion, it is essential that they examine the current ideologies that inform the construction of social policies, in order to understand why fundamental problems resulting from racialization have persisted over time.

Although recent surveys indicate that racist beliefs are widespread, Canadians are unlikely to express them publicly, speaking instead of adhering to democratic principles. The ideology of *democratic racism* allows commitment to the principles of democratic liberalism, such as fairness, equality, and justice, to coexist with negative attitudes, differential treatment, and discriminatory behaviour towards ethno-racial minorities and Aboriginal people (Henry et al., 2000). Democratic racism obscures both the operation and consequences of racism, as evidenced in mainstream social service institutions (e.g., hospitals, schools, child welfare agencies, family service agencies, and the criminal justice system), in the policy content in the curricula of schools of social work (Canadian Association of Schools of Social Work, 1991; Christensen, 1999), and in the content of the historical and current social policy literature. Serious, in-depth attention is seldom given to the effects on racialized minorities of policy decisions designed for the general public (Ornstein, 2000), much less the daily effects of policies embedded in, for example, the Indian Act and immigration and refugee policies. Canadian feminist literature is no exception. If considered at all, this subject is presented as clearly peripheral (see, for example, most issues of the *Canadian Review of Social Policy* and classic textbooks dealing with social policy). Only in recent decades has the existence of inequality tied to ethno-racial background become more openly acknowledged in Canada (Abella, 1984; Bolaria & Li, 1988; Christensen, 1986a; Kazemipur & Halli, 2000).

The psychological, social, and economic well-being of ethno-racial minorities is greatly influenced by the dominant ideology of the day. The ideology of the political party in power at a given time determines whether the programs that are adopted continue the long history of inequity and discrimination or truly address the needs of ethno-racial minorities. In a political system where majority rule is said to be fair, numerical minorities with limited political power rely mainly on policies and programs that benefit dominant-group Canadians and that *may* also happen to benefit ethno-racial groups (e.g., employment insurance, workers' compensation, medicare, child benefits, public schools). By providing a consistent set of social, economic, and political beliefs, ideology, as doctrine, forms the basis for operating programs (Mullaly, 1997, p. 31). The major ideologies underlying social policies adopted by governments, purportedly to protect citizens and respond to their needs, may be categorized as conservatism, liberalism, and social democracy. Initially, the conservative ideology of rugged individualism shaped Canadian social policy, but following the Great Depression, welfare capitalism, based on liberalism, began to be espoused to protect the general public from the more severe dislocations of the capitalist system. Social democratic ideology was, along with liberalism, a guiding force in formulating policies of the welfare state that took form following the Second World War. However, the economic recession of the 1970s, fuelled by the oil crisis, brought a resurgence of conservatism, which has since influenced the social policies of all political parties. Social policy analysts agree that since the mid-1980s, there has been a policy of devolution, in which social programs have been dismantled.

The next section provides a discussion of how current ideologies, and the social policies based on them, may affect ethno-racial minorities who are in need of social services and who depend on the state to alleviate structural inequalities and the distress that they cause.

Conservatism

Conservatism is suspicious of anything that might upset traditional processes and institutions (Mullaly, 1997). State interference in the affairs of the individual is viewed negatively, and laissez-faire capitalism is favoured. Societal inequalities in terms of status, education, class, and wealth are accepted. Neo-conservative rhetoric is now in vogue among politicians, bureaucrats, and policy makers in many Western countries with governments professing liberal or social democratic ideals. Although it uses somewhat more sophisticated rhetoric, neo-conservative doctrine continues to insist that the 'undeserving poor' are taking advantage of 'the system', and that social services should be privatized and market-driven (Melchers, 1999). The welfare state's social expenditures, including those assisting identifiable 'interest groups', such as ethno-racial minorities, are considered to be responsible for the social and economic problems experienced in recent years. Neo-conservatism fosters a 'residual' approach to social welfare, in which the state intervenes only in cases of emergency when personal wealth is not sufficient (e.g., for the elderly, the disabled, or the chronically ill). In Canada, this philosophy is advanced by the Progressive Conservative Party, the Reform Party, and the Canadian Alliance, to varying degrees.

IMPLICATIONS OF NEO-CONSERVATISM FOR ETHNO-RACIAL MINORITIES

Implicit in the neo-conservative ideology is the longing for the 'good old days', when Canada was (incorrectly) viewed as a homogeneous, 'White' society. Immigration, blamed for social ills (e.g., gangs, drugs, crime, and increasing welfare rolls), would be restricted with regard to numbers and countries of origin. Ideally, European immigrants would again receive preferable treatment. Ethno-racial groups already in Canada would be tolerated, at best, if they could fend for themselves. Those experiencing difficulties due to structural causes (e.g., economic recession, unrecognized foreign credentials) would be viewed as undeserving, lazy, or incapable, and should fall by the wayside. Such attitudes were clearly observable in the Conservative government of Mike Harris in Ontario, which abolished the employment equity office and its related activities as one of its first acts of government (Little, 1999). Neo-conservative immigration policies would emphasize attracting entrepreneurs and would reduce the sponsorship of relatives and the acceptance of refugees. Racialized minorities would be expected to 'maintain their place' in the hierarchical order, and people of colour would be expected to remain separate from the dominant group in private life. Conservative social policies place social workers in the position of controlling the behaviour of minorities, who are perceived as threatening 'traditional' lifestyles and law and order. Intimidation— by, for example, the threat of removing children from 'unfit' parents—is considered necessary to maintain social order. The general public is led (via the media) to associate welfare 'hand-outs' with racialized minorities, and funding cuts are made. For some, Christian 'morality' justifies inequality, and ethno-racial minorities holding other religious beliefs may be viewed unfavourably. Neo-conservatives advocate tolerating high levels of unemployment, while reducing social assistance funds; means tests and workfare; charter schools (which encourage segregation); and building more prisons, which, like medical services, should be privatized. This ideology is antithetical to incorporating the concerns of ethno-racial groups and First Nations, and violates the egalitarian values of the social work profession.

Liberalism

Liberalism is based on a the belief that the freedom of the individual is paramount and should be fostered, while allowing for essential societal constraints. Differences in quality of life are believed to stem from a combination of differences in individual effort or ability, or from imperfections in the system. Individuals can be assisted in alleviating the consequences of personal defects, and appropriate reform measures can correct systemic ills. State intervention is potentially positive, when promoting freedom for the oppressed. Since reform liberals acknowledge that the free market may create inequality, economic freedom must be restrained in some ways. Liberals do not seek to abolish inequality, only to reduce it. Social programs centre on the individual and should not interfere with the impact of market forces on individuals and families. This type of government response is referred to as a 'liberal residual approach' (Kitchen, 2001, p. 235). The power of the state may be used to establish social policies in the areas of, for example, public education, health care, and unemployment insurance, but too much assistance is believed to destroy individual initiative. If there is equality of opportunity, everything positive that furthers the individual's advancement and well-being, such as equal access to education, jobs, social services, and health care, should follow. Systemic inequalities are overlooked.

Despite embracing humanism, today's liberals hold many values in common with neo-conservatives, including individualism and competition in the capitalist free market, as exemplified by the policies adopted by the government led by Gordon Campbell in British Columbia. Neither conservatives nor liberals believe in collectivity, nor do they emphasize community values, the very values that many ethno-racial communities wish to maintain.

IMPLICATIONS OF LIBERALISM FOR ETHNO-RACIAL MINORITIES

Social work practice is based mainly on the residual liberal ideology, with ecological and systems theories being widely used. These models suggest that the current system is perfectly suited to the needs of ethno-racial minorities, if only individuals can be assisted in coping with it, understanding it, and gaining access to it. Consequently, students of social work generally learn most about interventions meant to support or transform individuals and families, using models rooted in liberal ideology. Most curricula do not include required courses allowing students to learn advocacy methods or community mobilization skills useful for working with marginalized ethno-racial minorities facing systemic barriers (Christensen, 1992). Even radical social policy theorists, feminists among them, offer little that can be translated into direct action in response to the concerns of ethno-racial groups (Baker, 1997). Increasingly dependent on free trade agreements and the push towards globalization, those professing liberalism are incorporating 'new world order' social policy platforms, and corporatist-statist policies (i.e., in which corporate interests often merge with those of the state). Such policies, which place the responsibility for helping the needy on their families, rely minimally on the state (Epsing-Anderson, 1989). The liberal-residual welfare system that was formerly in place in Canada, and was helpful to economically deprived racialized groups, is under attack. The corporate sector has convinced many Canadians that the economic downturn of the 1970s and 1980s resulted from social programs that were too expensive to maintain, and that immigration must be curtailed to protect jobs and to avoid abuse of the system. Social policies based on corporate-statist ideology may be supported by immigrants who enter Canada as wealthy entrepreneurs.

Social Democracy

Since the foundation of the Co-operative Commonwealth Federation in the 1930s, and its evolution in the New Democratic Party (NDP) in the 1960s, the ideology of social democracy has been competing with liberalism and neo-conservatism. North Americans often confuse social democracy and Marxist ideology, but the differences are fundamental. Marxism stipulates the need for existing capitalist structures to be demolished and replaced by new institutions; in contrast, social democrats seek to transform capitalist society, through peaceful means and participatory decision making, into a welfare state that responds to people's needs, not to their positions of power. The NDP, which espouses social democratic ideals in Canada, generally places low in national elections (receiving only 8.5 per cent of the vote in the federal election of 1998). Principal among social democratic ideals are equality and social integration, natural rights, self-realization, economic efficiency, and social planning for the common good (Mullaly, 1997). Gross inequalities are unacceptable and are to be alleviated by state programs involving pay equity, progressive taxation, human rights, affirmative action, and some degree of redistribution of resources. The dominant class is perceived as using the power of the state to maintain its institutions, which are used to sustain inequality. Those adhering to this ideology adopt a social conflict perspective, viewing oppression as rooted in competition among groups for valued resources (e.g., wealth, power, privilege, and political control). Citizens are entitled to have their basic needs fully met, by public, rather than private, control of resources, so that education, health, and social services are available to all. Ideally, under a social democratic government, social workers would emphasize prevention and client self-help, rather than adjustment to adverse conditions (Moreau, 1990). Experts would share decision-making power with ordinary people, who would play a role in social policy decisions that affect their lives. In reality, however, the impact of racism on social democratic ideals is blatantly omitted from the ongoing discourse among politicians when stating their priorities.

IMPLICATIONS OF THE SOCIAL DEMOCRATIC IDEOLOGY FOR ETHNO-RACIAL MINORITIES

Social democracy is related to the progressive, critical view of social work practice, often associated with radical social work. Proponents of progressive social work recognize that there is a social policy crisis at all levels of government. This crisis is manifested by a growing gap between rich and poor and by the worsening of conditions for disadvantaged groups, including immigrants and ethno-racial minorities of long standing (Carniol, 2000).

Structural social work theory claims to be the most radical socialist theoretical formulation, promoting social work practice congruent with social work values. Its conceptual framework is believed to include all forms of interlocking oppressions (class, gender, race, sexual orientation, disability, and so on) (Mullaly, 1997, p. 99). Structural social work claims to differ from other socialist theories in the emphasis placed on the need for social workers to *act* in order to change current inequalities that are contradictory to social work ideals. The ideology of social democracy recognizes that concepts such as equality and self-determination are meaningless for people who are powerless to access resources (e.g., adequate incomes, decent housing) and who do not have sufficient control over their lives. The presence and demands of ethno-racial groups, including immigrants, are not considered to be inherently problematic; rather, their concerns stem from Canadian society's being deliberately structured to ensure that entire categories of people will remain in marginalized positions, from generation to generation. Recently, some progressive policy analysts have acknowledged that social policies, and the resulting institutions and services, have not responded to the needs of racialized minorities, and that they are often treated as pathological for not adhering to certain dominant cultural values. Social workers using a social democratic approach would work with those considered deviant, not with the goal of changing them, but acknowledging that society's norms and expectations may create the appearance of deviance among ethnocultural minorities. Community development approaches would be recognized as more effective than individual intervention when dealing with systemic problems. However, like neo-conservatives and liberals, social democrats believe that social work can help to bring about change by working within the existing capitalist system. Such work can become a method of achieving a socialist society.

A Critique of Current Ideologies and Policy Analyses

The problems of ethno-racial minorities have persisted historically, and worsened recently, whether under neo-conservative, liberal, or socialist regimes. Yet, even 'radical' social policy theorists expect radical change to come about, somehow, within the very socio-economic system that has nurtured (historically) and tolerated (presently) inequality based on the concept of 'race', and that still benefits from it. Equality cannot come about in an unequal system. Current ideologies and theories fail to offer methods for challenging ingrained racist belief systems detrimental to ethnocultural minorities and, therefore, to society as a whole. The question for social work practitioners is whether values such as acceptance, self-determination, and 'starting where the client is' can genuinely be applied in a helping context, when society tolerates inequality, unemployment, homelessness, exploitation, and systemic racism. Liberalism has allowed inequalities to increase, as have Canadian governments of all political stripes.

While recognizing the need for an alternative vision of society, several Canadian social policy analysts have recently followed the American example of calling for eradicating *all* forms of oppression, lumping all forms of 'diversity' together. The term *diversity* (once used to refer to culture and race) is now applied to all kinds, and degrees, of marginalization. Depending on the author consulted, this might include children, women, the elderly, the disabled, gays and lesbians, poor people, ethno-racial minorities, and several other categories of the human condition (Armitage, 1996; Carniol, 2000; Mullaly, 1997). Attending to diversity and oppression as generalized concepts, rather than as personal experiences, has had two significant results. First, competition among groups claiming oppression based on diversity is now more evident than ever (Stainton & Swift, 1996, p. 81). One cannot claim to be anti-racist without, at the same time, claiming to be against all other forms of oppression as well. Second, important differences among oppressions are masked. Consequently, unique and all-pervasive forms of oppression resulting from racism are, once again, denied or trivialized. The uniqueness of racism is experienced by ethno-racial minorities who cross other marginalized categories (e.g., disabled, lesbian, elderly) and find racism there too (Ratti, 1993). Effects of racism and discrimination are cumulative and are especially detrimental to older ethno-racial minority women (Daenzer, 1997; Philippine Women Centre of BC, 2000). Problems relating to faulty and limited policy analysis have been clearly delineated by feminist women of colour (Ruggles & Rovinescu, 1996; Caraway, 1991). It could be argued that the current situation represents *symbolic racism*, which manifests itself in behaviours that are rationalized on a non-racial basis while, in fact, maintaining the status quo by continuing discriminatory treatment (Sears & McConahay, 1973).

Throughout the world, the gulf between the rich and the poor is growing, which affects marginalized ethno-racial minorities most severely. There is a dearth of material analyzing the effects of Canadian social policies on racialized minorities from a global perspective, including the effects of market forces on their lives in this country, and in the lives of others of the same ancestry internationally. Canada is now so dependent upon the capitalist system and its global corporate functions that, short of a worldwide revolution, efforts to 'transform the system' in one country are unlikely to improve the collective lives of racialized peoples (Kitchen, 2001; Miles & Torres, 2000; Richmond, 2000).

Current Social Policy Issues Affecting Ethno-Racial Minorities

Access Issues Remain

Paradoxically, it is because racial origin generally fails to be mentioned by policy analysts as a factor having a profound and pervasive affect on the well-being of racialized groups that its significance becomes apparent. It would appear that the expectation that racialized minorities would not be allowed the same life-chances as Euro-Canadians was so ingrained that it was considered a 'natural' phenomenon. Historically, formal and informal barriers to equal access to goods and resources, services, opportunity, and power were deliberately erected by Euro-Canadian decision makers and were not to be questioned, either by the dominant group or by ethno-racial minorities. As discussed below, current conditions call into question how much has really changed.

Unfortunately, access issues remain pervasive at the beginning of the twenty-first century, affecting all ethno-racial minorities, to varying degrees, in all areas of daily life (Christensen, 2001; British Columbia Human Rights Commission, 2000; Vancouver/Richmond Health Board Region, 2000). When one analyzes the effects of social policy on ethno-racial groups, it must be taken into account that racialized minorities do not start their lives in Canada on as equal footing in terms of entrance status. In keeping with a dynamic and constantly evolving ethno-racial hierarchy, they are not all treated the same in terms of acceptance and opportunity. Equal access remains a fundamental social policy issue, wide-ranging and complex in its manifestation, but having effects on services and programs purportedly available to all (Fay, 1997), government policies notwithstanding.

Inadequate and Ineffective Government Policies

Governments have responded to the access concerns of ethno-racial minorities with policy initiatives spurred by various reports that followed the proclamation of Canada's 1971 multiculturalism policy celebrating cultural diversity (e.g., Abella, 1984). By the late 1980s, numerous reports had documented racial discrimination in education (Dei, 1996); hiring and promotion (Henry & Ginsberg, 1984; Husbands, 1999); employment (Working Group on Poverty, 1998); housing (Canada Mortgage and Housing Corporation, 1997; Kazemipur & Halli, 2000); health care (Doyle & Visano, 1987; Intercultural Committee, Greater Vancouver Mental Health Service, 1999); social services (Christensen, 1986b; Christensen, 1999; Sirros, 1987); the media (Fleras & Kuhz, 2001); and the justice system (Henry et al., 2000) right across this country. Blacks and First Nations people also face differential treatment in financial institutions (e.g., obtaining loans, financing business ventures), although this area has received little documented attention. Both of these groups have experienced generations of unequal educational opportunities and the streaming of their children into non-academic courses in schools. Perhaps most importantly, recent studies have indicated that certain ethno-racial immigrant groups have experienced downward mobility in the second generation, with children accomplishing less than their parents did in terms of education and employment (Kazemipur & Halli, 2000). Without adequate government policies to alleviate the current situation, a cycle of unequal access may perpetuate itself.

By the late 1980s, emphasis shifted from cultural to *racial* diversity, as ethno-racial minorities called for policies to alleviate the effects of racism. The federal Employment Equity Act, passed in 1986, sought 'equality in the workplace and to correct conditions of disadvantage in employment' experienced by women, Aboriginal people, visible minorities, and persons with disabilities. However, compliance was made voluntary, no accountability was built into the policy, and no sanctions were imposed for non-compliance, even in government workplaces. In 1988, the Charter of Rights and Freedoms made human rights a legal matter, and a federal Human Rights Commission was established. Provinces enacted similar policies to promote employment equity and encourage inclusiveness, establishing human rights commissions and instituting programs to 'manage' racial and cultural diversity among employees (e.g., racial harassment policies in institutions). It is a matter of concern to ethno-racial groups that the Charter of Rights and Freedoms has a notwithstanding clause, allowing provinces to opt out of certain sections at will; that the federal Multiculturalism Act, passed in 1988, was abolished in 1993; and that the federal Race Relations Directorate was done away with, and the Department of Multiculturalism and Citizenship downgraded federal multiculturalism.

From the 1980s through the mid- to late 1990s both the private sector and many social service and health care institutions called for the elimination of access barriers and focused on cross-cultural and sensitivity-training programs for employees. Some organizations enacted employment equity hiring and anti-harassment policies. Organizational change models, requiring commitment from top-level decision makers were used less frequently. The results of such activities have been mixed, since there is no guarantee that policies promoting equity and inclusiveness will translate into practice (Fleras and Elliott, 2000). Numerous reports from federal, provincial, and municipal sources have shown that, at the beginning of the twenty-first century, little progress had been made towards eradicating the social policy issues facing 'visible minorities'.

Backlash and Social Policy
Currently, backlash from White Canadians who feel that 'things are changing too fast' has become quite apparent. Employment equity policies have been downgraded or even eliminated in some provinces. Although they are generally ineffective, efforts to move towards a more just and egalitarian society are often labelled 'reverse discrimination.' Hate crimes appear to be on the increase, with the Internet serving as the newest method for spreading hateful and stereotyped images of racialized groups (Khanna, 1999). Numerous incidents of racially motivated beatings and murders, and continuous innuendo in the media linking ethno-racial

minorities and immigrants to violence and crime, cause many ethno-racial groups to conclude that 'things are getting worse'. Policies allow the police to carry out internal investigations when blatant acts of violence against ethno-racial minorities and Aboriginal people are committed, and the perpetrators usually receive either no sanction or a shamefully light sentence. Attitudes towards racialized groups, especially those believed to be Muslim, have worsened considerably since the World Trade Center in New York was destroyed by 'dark-skinned people' on 11 September 2001. The recent adoption by the federal Parliament of Bill C-36, the anti-terrorist legislation, legitimizes state policies supporting racial profiling as a reason for arrest and detention. It has strengthened the suspicion among ethno-racial minorities that racism remains deeply ingrained in Canadian society and that the dominant group is not fundamentally committed to inclusiveness, fairness, justice, and freedom for them. When ethno-racial minorities protest, become politically active, or attempt to influence social policy, they are considered a threat and labelled overly aggressive rather than positively assertive. Having been largely excluded from the political process, few ethno-racial minorities are involved when major policy decisions affecting their lives are made. This fact becomes quite evident when one examines the face of Canada's government bodies and decision makers at all levels.

Lack of access to power, privilege, and prestige remains, despite decades of discussion, reports, research, and conferences dealing with the subject of racial discrimination (e.g., Canadian Council on Multicultural Health, Fourth Annual Conference, 1998; the Removing Barriers Symposia, 1998 and 2000; 'End Racism in the 21st Century' Conference, 2000). In preparation for the World Conference against Racism, Racial Discrimination, Xenophobia and Related Intolerance, held in Durban, South Africa, in September, 2001, researchers found that during the past twenty years alone, 3,500 recommendations suggesting how to effectively eradicate discrimination based on race have been made in key reports produced by federal, provincial, municipal, and territorial governments (Jedwab, 2000). These recommendations cover the vital areas of employment, media, immigration, criminal justice, health, education, the military, and housing. The existence of these recommendations provides a strong indication that policy-makers know what should be done, but lack the political will to do it. In short, despite rhetoric about democracy, multiculturalism, equality, and human rights, ethno-racial minorities remain socially and politically marginalized, often by the very policies supposedly designed to eliminate inequality (e.g. the use of referendums, which are intended to disadvantage minority groups; the moderation or elimination of equity policies at the whim of government officials, etc.).

Conclusion

When considering ethno-racial issues, social policy theorists generally make two errors. First, more attention is paid to analyzing the results of disadvantage and oppression than to how to bring about change in the factors that serve to maintain these patterns over time. Linear thinking is not helpful, since these factors operate on multidimensional levels (i.e., past and present; personal and political; conscious and unconscious; local, national, global), aided and abetted by social policies. Second, the prevailing discourse and research studies focus on those deliberately victimized by racism rather than on the perpetrators. A paradigm shift in research emphasis would foster the study of how decision makers operate to keep ethno-racial minorities, individually and collectively, 'in their place' in the established hierarchical order. In other words, more emphasis must be placed on White society (McIntosh, 1990). Policy analysts and social scientists must examine the following questions. What methods are used, who designs them, and by what mechanisms are protests ignored or invalidated? What thinking processes are involved in the practice of democratic racism, and how do they manifest themselves? What can be done to ensure that future generations do not face the same devastating psychological, social, and economic effects of racialization that have been harmful to their forebears? The main difficulty is, of course, that most policy analysts and academics are themselves immersed in patterns that have normalized Eurocentric thought and dominant-group hegemony. The Metro Coalition for a Non-Racist Society, located in Halifax, Nova Scotia, is breaking new ground in Canada, as a predominantly White group that acknowledges responsibility for racism and that is attempting to do something about it (Boyd & the Metro Coalition for a Non-Racist Society, 1998).

By having people from many origins living together, Canada is facing one of the major challenges of the twenty-first century. Often, people of colour who are perceived to be immigrants are Canadians who have been here for two or many more generations. They know no other home. They are not going away. There is a choice to be made about the kind of society Canadians want. The electorate could follow the destructive United States model of racism, creating a permanent underclass perceived to be in need of authoritarian control. This will result in the elite societal group having to maintain power and control by instituting increasingly draconian measures. On the other hand, Canadians could choose to question seriously the direction of current ideologies and their attendant social policies in order to create something better. It might even be possible to elect multiracial governments that dare to state policy positions promoting an egalitarian society and that, once in office, act to institute truly effective policies towards this goal. The elected officials would be held accountable to all Canadians, and not mainly to the economic, political, and corporate elite. The word 'race' would gradually disappear, not because it is taboo, but because it would become irrelevant.

The creation of a fair and just society is possible, but there are minimal prerequisites. First, it would be necessary to challenge the direction of political leaders, whatever party they represent, who form governments that are corrupted by self-interest (remaining in office), greed, and fear of the powerful. Policies that increase national and global inequalities, and that permit corporate ruination of the planetary environment for short-term personal gain, would be unequivocally rejected. As noted by Gil (1976) only governments have the power to create and maintain conditions of social equality. Second, the fear of people who are defined as 'other than my group' would have to be overcome within, and between, ethno-racial categories, as well as by the dominant group in relation to others. This can be approached by creating opportunities to know each other more intimately, as respected and valued individuals, rather than as representatives of a racial category. It is only when we go beyond superficial relationships that similarities, rather than real and imagined differences, are revealed. Third, there must be opportunities, in public forums, to consider seriously the end results of the Western value system emphasizing competition rather than co-operation, the individual rather than the community, and economic gain above spiritual growth, however the latter may be defined by different people. Last, and perhaps most importantly, there is a personal dimension to be considered before one is able to reach out freely to others in a genuine, caring manner. Reaching out to those considered 'different' from oneself requires a 'whole' individual who is self-aware and internally secure and whose capacity for empathy, compassion, and rapport is not limited to 'certain types' of people (Christensen, 1989).

Social workers have a potential role to play in planned change, but it would require the development of new methods and frameworks (Rogers & Summers, 1999) suitable for the realities of a postmodern era, rather than nostalgia for yesteryear. Social policies and practice models must be developed by, and with, ethnoracial minorities, incorporating ways of thinking and doing other than those of the dominant racial and cultural group. In a global age, Canada and the social work profession would only be enriched by becoming truly inclusive.

References

Abella, R.J. (1984). *Report of the Royal Commission on Equality in Employment.* Ottawa: Ministry of Supply and Services Canada.

Armitage, A. (1996). *Social Welfare in Canada Revisited: Facing Up to the Future.* 3rd ed. Toronto: Oxford University Press.

Baker, M. (1997). Women, family policies and the moral right. *Canadian Review of Social Policy, 40,* 47–64.

Bodnar, A., & Reimer, M. (1979). *The Organization of Social Services and Its Implications for the Mental Health of Immigrant Women.* Toronto: Working Women Community Centre.

Bolaria S., & Li, P.S. (1988). *Racial Oppression in Canada.* 2nd ed. Toronto: Garamond Press.

Boyd, J., & the Metro Coalition for a Non-Racist Society. (1998). *Racism: Whose Problem? Strategies for Understanding and Dealing with Racism in Our Communities.* Halifax: Metro Coalition for a Non-Racist Society.

British Columbia Human Rights Commission (2000). *Not Good Enough! Representation of Aboriginal People, People with Disabilities, and Visible Minorities in the British Columbia Public Service.* Findings of public forums held by the BC Human Rights Commission.

Canada Mortgage and Housing Corporation (1997). *Lone Parents, Young Couples and Immigrant Families and their Housing Conditions—A 1991 Census Profile.* Ottawa: CMHC and Statistics Canada.

Canadian Association of Schools of Social Work. (1991). *Social Work Education at the Crosswords: The Challenge of Diversity.* Report of the Task Force on Multicultural and Multiracial Issues in Social Work Education. Ottawa: Canadian Association of Schools of Social Work.

Caraway, N. (1991). *Segregated Sisterhood: Racism and the Politics of American Feminism.* Knoxville: University of Tennessee Press.

Carniol, B. (2000). *Case Critical: Challenging Social Services in Canada.* 4th ed. Toronto: Between the Lines.

Christensen, C.P. (1986a). Cross-cultural social work: fallacies, fears, and failings. *Intervention, 74,* 6–15.

———. (1986b). Chinese residents' perceptions of mainstream social services: Keys to service underuse? *Intervention, 74,* 41–9.

———. (1989). Stages in the development of cross-cultural awareness: A conceptual model. *Counselor Education and Supervision, 28,* 4, 270–87.

———. (1992). Training for cross-cultural social work with immigrants, minorities, and refugees. *Journal of Multicultural Social Work, 2,* 1, 79–97.

———. (1998). Social welfare and social work in Canada. In V. D'Oley & C. James (Eds), *Revisioning Canadian Perspectives on the Education of Africans in the Late 20th Century* (pp. 36–57). Toronto: Cactus Press.

———. (1999). Multiculturalism, racism and social work: An exploration of issues in the Canadian context. In G.-Y. Lie & D. Este (Eds). *Professional Social Service Delivery in a Multicultural World* (pp. 293–310). Toronto: Canadian Scholars' Press.

———. (2001). Immigrant minorities in Canada. In J.C. Turner & F.J. Turner (Eds), *Canadian Social Welfare.* 4th ed. (pp. 180–209). Toronto: Pearson Education.

Christensen, C.P., & Weinfeld, M. (1993). The Black family in Canada: A preliminary exploration of family patterns and inequality. *Canadian Ethnic Studies, 25,* 3, 26–44.

Daenzer, P.M. (1997). Challenging diversity: Black women and social welfare. In P.M. Evans & G.R. Wekerle (Eds), *Women and the Canadian Welfare State: Challenges and Change* (pp. 269–90). Toronto: University of Toronto Press.

Dei, G. (1996). *Anti-Racism Education: Theory and Practice.* Halifax: Fernwood.

Doyle, R., & Visano, L. (1987). *Access to Health and Social Services for Members of Diverse Cultural and Racial Groups in Metropolitan Toronto.* Toronto: Social Planning Council of Metropolitan Toronto.

Epsing-Anderson, G. (1990). *Three Worlds of Welfare Capitalism.* Princeton, NJ: Princeton University Press.

Fay, J. (1997). It's time to get political: The myth of social policy consultation. *Canadian Review of Social Policy, 40,* 87–8.

Fleras, A., & Elliott, J.L. (1999). *Unequal Relations: An Introduction to Race, Ethnic, and Aboriginal Dynamics in Canada.* Scarborough, ON: Prentice Hall/Allyn Bacon.

Fleras, A., & Kuhz, J.L. (2001). *Media and Minorities: Representing Diversity in a Multicultural Canada*. Toronto: Thompson Educational Publishing.

Gil, D. (1976). *The Challenge of Social Equality*. Cambridge, MA: Schenkman Publishing.

Henry, F., & Ginsberg, E. (1984). *Who Gets the Work? A Test of Racial Discrimination in Employment*. Toronto: Urban Alliance on Race Relations and the Social Planning Council of Toronto.

Henry, F., Tator, C., Mattis, M., & Rees, T. (2000). *The Colour of Democracy: Racism in Canadian Society*. Toronto: Harcourt Brace.

Husbands, W. (1999). 'Born in Canada . . . or not: Immigration status and food bank assistance in the Greater Toronto Area.' *Canadian Review of Social Policy / Revue Canadienne de politique sociale, 44*, 57–70.

Intercultural Committee, Greater Vancouver Mental Health Services. (1999). *Multiculturalism and Mental Health: Developing Culturally Competent Systems of Care*. Vancouver: Greater Vancouver Mental Health Services.

Jakubowski, L.M. (1997). *Immigration and the Legalization of Racism*. Halifax: Fernwood.

Jedwab, J. (2000). *A Stock Taking of Recommendations in the Fight Against Racism, Racial Discrimination, Xenophobia and Related Intolerance in Canada*, Volume I (Draft). Commissioned by the Canadian Secretariat–World Conference Against Racism. Ottawa: Canadian Heriatge.

Kalbach, M.A., & Kalbach, W.E. (Eds). (2000). *Perspectives on Ethnicity in Canada*. Toronto: Harcourt.

Kazemipur, A., & Halli, S.S. (2000). *The New Poverty in Canada: Ethnic Groups and Ghetto Neighbourhoods*. Toronto: Thompson Educational Publishing.

Khanna, M. (1999). *Hate/Bias Motivated Acts Perpetrated by and against Youth: A Research Overview*. Prepared for Citizens' Participation and Multiculturalism. Ottawa: Department of Canadian Heritage.

Kitchen, B. (2001). Poverty and declining living standards in a changing economy. In J.C. Turner & F.J. Turner (Eds), *Canadian Social Welfare*. 4th ed. (pp. 232–49). Toronto: Pearson Education.

Li, P.S. (1988). *Ethnic Inequality in a Class Society*. Toronto: Thompson Educational Publishing.

Little, M.H. (1999). The limits of Canadian democracy: The citizenship rights of poor women. *Canadian Review of Social Policy, 43*, 59–76.

McIntosh, P. (1990). White privilege: Unpacking the invisible knapsack. *Independent School, 49*, 2, 31–6.

Melchers, R. (1999). Local governance of social welfare: Local reform in Ontario in the nineties. *Canadian Review of Social Policy, 43*, 29–57.

Miles, R., & Torres, R. (2000). Does race matter? Transatlantic perspectives on racism after 'race relations.' In M.A. Kalbach & W.E. Kalbach, (Eds), *Perspectives on Ethnicity in Canada* (pp. 15–34). Toronto: Harcourt.

Moreau, M. (1990). Empowerment through advocacy and consciousness-raising: Implications of a structural approach to social work. *Journal of Sociology and Social Welfare, 17*, 2: 53–67.

Mullaly, R.P. (1997). *Structural Social Work: Ideology, Theory, and Practice.* Toronto: Oxford University Press.

Ornstein, M. (2000). *Ethno-Racial Inequality in Toronto: An Analysis of the 1996 Census.* Toronto: Institute for Social Research, York University.

Philippine Women Centre of BC (2000). *Canada: The New Frontier for Filipino Mail Order Brides.* Vancouver: Philippine Women Centre of BC.

Pierce, D. (1984). Defining policy for practice. In *Policy for the Social Work Practitioner* (pp. 17–27). New York: Longman.

Porter, J. (1965). *The Vertical Mosaic.* Toronto: University of Toronto Press.

Ratti, R. (Ed.). (1993). *A Lotus of Another Color: An Unfolding of the South Asian Gay and Lesbian Experience.* Boston: Alyson Publications.

Richmond, A. (2000). Global apartheid: Migration, racism, and the world system. In M.A. Kalbach & W.E. Kalbach (Eds), *Perspectives on Ethnicity in Canada* (pp. 329–43). Toronto: Harcourt.

Rogers, G., & Summers, H. (1999). Structuring a learning environment: Guidelines for becoming competent in cross-cultural practice. In G.Y. Lie & D. Este (Eds), *Professional Social Service Delivery in a Multicultural World* (pp. 331–60). Toronto: Canadian Scholars' Press.

Ruggles, C., & Rovinescu, O. (1996). *Outsider Blues: A Voice from the Shadows.* Halifax: Fernwood Publishing.

Sears, D., & McConahay, J., Jr. (1973). *The Politics of Violence: The New Urban Blacks and the Watts Riot.* Boston: Houghton Mifflin.

Sirros C. (1987). *Rapport du comité sur l'accessibilité des services de santé et des services sociaux du réseau aux communautés culturelles.* Quebec: Publications officielles.

Stainton, T., & Swift, K. (1996). 'Difference' in social work curriculum. *Canadian Social Work Review, 13,* 1, 75–87.

Statistics Canada. (1996) *1996 Census of Canada.* Ottawa: Ministry of Supply and Services Canada.

Tennant, P. (1985). Aboriginal rights and the Penner Report on Indian self-government. In M. Boldt & J.A. Long (Eds), *The Quest for Justice: Aboriginal Peoples and Aboriginal Rights* (pp. 321–32). Toronto: University of Toronto Press.

Turner, J. (2001). The Historical Base. In J.C. Turner & F.J. Turner (Eds), *Canadian Social Welfare.* 4th ed. (pp. 80–95). Toronto: Pearson Education.

Ujimoto, K.V., & Gordon, H. (1980). *Visible Minorities: Asians in Canada.* Scarborough, ON: Butterworth.

Vancouver/Richmond Health Board. (2000). *Framework for Diversity: Diversity in Health Services, Human Rights and Employment Equity Initiatives in the Vancouver/Richmond Health Board Region.* Vancouver: Richmond/Vancouver Health Board Region.

Walker, J.W. St. G. (1976). *The Black Loyalists: The Search for a Promised Land in Nova Scotia and Sierra Leone, 1783–1870.* Halifax: Dalhousie University Press.

Winks, R.W. (1971). *The Blacks in Canada*. Montreal: McGill-Queen's University Press.

Working Group on Poverty (1998). *Unfulfilled Expectations, Missed Opportunities: Poverty among Immigrants and Refugees in British Columbia*. Vancouver: M. Spigelman Research Associates.

Chapter 5

Whiteout: Looking for Race in Canadian Social Work Practice

June Ying Yee and Gary C. Dumbrill

Canada's population is becoming increasingly diverse: approximately 50 per cent of people in Toronto, 40 per cent in Vancouver, and 25 per cent in Montreal, Edmonton, Calgary, and Winnipeg are from racial minority groups (Henry, Tator, Mattis, & Rees, 2000). The recognition that an increasing number of people from diverse ethno-racial backgrounds are appearing on workers' caseloads brings to the fore the urgent need to provide culturally relevant and appropriate services. Many social service agencies struggle to find ways to deliver both equitable and accessible services that meet the cultural and linguistic needs of diverse ethno-racial populations (Thomas, 1987; United Way of Greater Toronto, 1991). This struggle focuses on equipping service providers with knowledge about the culture of various ethno-racial communities, in the belief that ignorance and prejudice about cultures different from one's own can lead to cultural insensitivity and discrimination (Devore & Schlesinger, 1999; McGoldrick, 1982). Many within social work practice hold the view that if one can better understand the behaviour, culture, and perspectives of an ethno-racial group, then cultural respect, validation, and acceptance should follow.

A focus on understanding culture creates problems on many fronts. First, this approach detracts from the lived experiences of the oppressed; their 'voice' easily becomes subsumed within the defining forces of the dominant culture, which presents itself as non-ideological, fair, and neutral. Second, a focus on the 'Other' mitigates the responsibility, shared by everyone, to implement far-reaching actions to dismantle systemic, individual, and cultural discriminatory barriers within Canadian social service systems. Social work practitioners can feel good about having knowledge of another culture, and at the same time be oblivious to the fact that they are reproducing the values and norms of the dominant culture and keeping oppressive and dominant structures intact. Finally, at its worst, this approach reduces 'culture' to a static concept and reduces people to celebrations of dress, customs, and behaviours. This reification of the concept of 'culture' further mystifies people's social relations and allows one to make generalizations about people's behaviour without considering their material, lived experiences of racism, classism, sexism, ableism, and heterosexism.

Research shows that, compared to the more privileged sectors of society, society's disadvantaged groups—such as single mothers and ethno-racial minorities—are disproportionately represented among those receiving social work intervention (Jones, 1994; Mayall, 1991; Swift, 1995). Swift builds on Hutchinson's (1992) work in contending that, in child welfare cases, 'the propensity to classify racial and ethnic Others into the category neglect in disproportionate numbers does not apply only to Native people, but to other non-white groups as well' (Swift, 1995, p. 127). She further notes that categories such as 'neglect' 'maintain and legitimize' the present societal inequalities of Native people and non-White groups without any mention of race, which is an important variable in structuring differential outcomes (ibid., p. 127). Ethno-racial communities receive blame for inappropriate conduct, a label readily applied by a child welfare bureaucracy that fails to recognize the underlying causes sustained by racial and ethnic inequality. In turn, child welfare workers do not provide the types of support required by ethno-racial communities to address the larger socio-economic factors that have a negative impact on parenting capacity. This difficulty in naming social processes that perpetuate the stigmatization and devaluing of cross-cultural communities has much to do with Western, liberal democratic societies, which produce male 'white, eurocentric, heterosexual and able-bodied' perspectives and practices through the preservation of their own unnamed power base (Truman & Humphries, 1994).

If one is to understand the production and reproduction of such discriminatory practices, one needs to locate how and why such mechanisms of oppression operate. Several important questions arise from an effort to understand these mechanisms. Why focus on ethno-racial communities in multicultural social work practice in Canada? Does this mean there exists some referential norm that is implicitly being compared to one's understanding of ethno-racial communities? If so, what is this norm? Who really struggles with ethno-racial communities and why? Until such unsettling questions can be answered, the complex processes that allow for the reification of the concepts race, culture, and ethnicity cannot be unpacked. This chapter explores these questions, but first we need to define some important concepts. It is important to understand that *race* as a biological or social category does not exist, and any real reference to the concept is false, other than when race is viewed as being constructed as an ideological effect of social relationships that have become racialized. *Culture*, a fluid, dynamic, and constantly changing aspect of behaviour, is the totality of practices by which groups can be identified according to their heritage. *Ethnicity* refers to the common heritage that particular groups identify themselves as belonging to—for example, Caribbean-Black, Chinese, or Pakistani. Statistics Canada reports commonly use such categories in describing the ethno-racial composition of the country. Although White people are recognized as having an ethnicity, the term 'racial' usually applies to those who have skin colour other than White.

In looking at the broader picture, one could argue that a focus on ethno-racial communities results from the problem that much research in multicultural social work practice has developed from a body of knowledge about race, which defines ethno-racial people by their cultural characteristics. This definition of race does not undertake any socio-political understanding of the contested nature of race and ethnicity. In modern-day society, the term 'race', which we know plays a central role in people's everyday social relations, reconfigures itself without naming itself as race. Winant (2000) has commented on the 'continuing significance and changing meaning of race' and how 'the category of race' has been replaced by 'supposedly more objective, categories like ethnicity, nationality, or class' (p. 182). This categorization of people according to ethno-racial background may appear to serve practical purposes of understanding the particular needs of specific communities, but does this practice address the more sensitive issues around inequality and racism? Or does attempting to understand cultural practices of ethnic groups fall prey to creating generalizations and stereotypes that may not apply, even with a positive evaluation of the culture? In other words, who benefits from the ethno-racial classification system, and what meanings are created about ethnic groups without the consent of the subjugated? For example, can one assume that writers who come from the ethno-racial group they are writing about offer a more credible and authentic knowledge base about that particular culture than someone from the dominant culture could? These questions raise contentious issues about who can be the knower, who can be known, and who benefits from the knowledge.

Furthermore, a focus on race and ethnicity allows social work practitioners to hide behind cultural misunderstandings to explain why ethno-racial communities do not receive the services they need. This reduction of race and ethnicity to identity and culture not only stereotypes the needs and aspirations of diverse communities and unique individual identities but also covers up how 'Whiteness' determines Canada's social service delivery system. To examine Whiteness is to identify how race shapes the lives of both White people and people of colour (Dyer, 1997; Frankenberg, 1993; Gabriel, 1998). Multicultural social work practice cannot be fully engaged in by social work practitioners unless an examination of Whiteness occurs. The problem of dominance cannot be dismantled in society unless an emphasis and focus on ethno-racial communities shifts to the invisibility of the privileged in shaping the experiences of the oppressed. To name Whiteness in social work practice penetrates the insidious nature of discriminatory practice. To do otherwise means colluding with the oppressors and continuing to struggle in the area of diversity at superficial levels without creating real change. More specifically, one could argue that Whiteness—the basis upon which Canada's social service delivery system developed—is responsible for unintentional and intentional forms of discriminatory practices inherent in the wider Canadian society. Understanding the concept of Whiteness unmasks the way the dominant culture shapes the norms and values of Canadian society and reproduces various forms of oppression such as racism, classism, sexism, and other 'isms' in the delivery of social work services.

The mere suggestion that social work practice, which focuses on understanding the culture of specific ethno-racial communities, is vulnerable to reproducing forms of oppression runs counter to the benevolent perspective of Western society's deeply held belief that Canada is a country based on justice, fairness, and equality. Similarly, much multicultural social work practice responds to various cultures as though we live in a land in which all ethno-racial groups are equal and those who deliver services and produce discourses about social work practice are colourless. This assumption, we argue, is wrong; the production of social work knowledge and the delivery of services remain primarily a White, European enterprise. It makes little sense, therefore, to examine the 'differences' of ethno-racial communities without first examining the group that defines these communities as different and the power that enables this group to consider itself the norm. To define and examine Whiteness in Canada and the mechanisms through which White oppression masks its race and power is to deconstruct what is normally not named and, more significantly, to challenge processes that perpetuate the status quo for failing to provide culturally appropriate services.

This chapter explores Whiteness in a process that needs to be mirrored in mainstream social work discourses and within Canadian society as a whole. June Ying Yee, a woman of Chinese heritage, and Gary C. Dumbrill, a white man of British heritage, explore the issues of race and ethnicity in the delivery of social work services not by presenting characteristics of our respective ethno-racial identities but by considering the way in which Whiteness attempts to define and delimit them. Examining this delineation, we unmask how Whiteness invisibly assumes power, situates itself as the norm, and constructs the ethno-racial Other. The impact Whiteness has on social work practice demonstrates the way it maintains hegemony by literally 'whiting out' and obscuring its racial origins. Based on an examination of this power, an alternative framework for social work practice develops that frees both Whites and ethno-racial people—the 'mainstream' and the 'ethnic'—from producing and reproducing power dynamics that sustain institutional and society-wide oppression.

Identifying Whiteness as a Race in Canada

How race affects Canadian social work practice can be easily discerned, provided the race one examines is not White. The influence of the White race on social work practice is hardly discussed in social work texts, reflecting a silence that exists in society as a whole. The significant role that the White race plays in everyday life, often referred to as 'whiteness' (Dyer, 1997; Frankenberg, 1993; Gabriel, 1998; Martinot, 2000; Roediger, 1994), operates so invisibly that Kincheloe (1999) states, 'no one at this point really knows what whiteness is' (p. 162). Despite the elusive nature of Whiteness, Kincheloe (1999) further states that 'most observers agree that it is intimately involved with issues of power and power differences between white and non-white people' (p. 162). Whiteness, therefore, is a form of hegemony that allows one group to use its power to dominate a group in a position of less power.

The presence and impact of Whiteness can be demonstrated in the lives of the authors of the chapter, one from an established Canadian family and the other an immigrant from a foreign country. Many people ask June Ying Yee, a second-generation Canadian and a woman of Chinese descent, 'where do you come from?' Few people ask Gary Dumbrill, a White male, the same question, even though he is a relatively recent immigrant from Britain. These experiences are not unique: many Canadians of colour report being asked where they come from, as though they do not belong in Canada (Drakes, 2000). June's Chinese ethnicity does not belong in the Canadian fabric. Consider the following observation—intended as a 'compliment'—made to June by a White Anglo-Canadian person: 'June, I don't even see you as Chinese.' When June chose to use her middle name, 'Ying', stating she would not pay the expected price, the same White, Anglo-Canadian person responded: 'Oh, you don't want to use that name. It sounds so ethnic.' Such a statement indicates the price of June's acceptance: she has to adopt White, Anglo-Canadian ways and erase her Chinese-Canadian identity as if she were not Chinese. Gary, on the other hand, is rarely considered 'ethnic'; because of his White race, he automatically has a place in the Canadian fabric. He is rarely questioned about where he comes from, even though he is an immigrant from London, England. Many White Anglo-Canadians who do recognize Gary's origins by his accent often enthusiastically ask him questions about Britain's (and Canada's) queen, erroneously assuming he has an interest in the British monarchy.

The above narratives provide evidence of the assumed power of the White race within Canadian society and illustrate the way White Anglo-Canadians and, to a lesser extent, White French Canadians, represent Canada's 'dominant culture'. Furthermore, the examples reveal that the authors have been assigned to fixed positions in society and that the dynamic that accomplishes this circumscription is one of Whiteness. These examples are important because, as will be shown below, naming Whiteness and the ways it attempts to delineate each of us forms the first step in resisting the mould within which it tries to fit us. June, voicing her personal narrative, and coming from a social location that is not a part of the 'White race', challenges the power of Whiteness to define her by her race and ethnicity. Gary's narrative shows that because of his location as a part of the 'White race', the dominant culture absorbs him into a position of racial privilege. By making visible the 'White race', one can challenge and question the power of Whiteness to also define Gary in ways that make him replicate the oppressive practices of Whiteness. By extension, June's and Gary's personal narratives provide an entry point to understanding the way in which Whiteness shapes social work practice. Indeed, June's and Gary's different experience of acceptance as a part of the Canadian fabric is mirrored in social work practice. The concept of 'diversity' in social work acquires meaning only because a reference point exists from which 'difference' can be measured—a reference point of Whiteness. 'Diversity' refers to ethno-racial communities, while the White reference point remains invisible.

Frankenberg (1993) describes the three dimensions of Whiteness that enable it to establish White societal norms: 'First, whiteness is a location of structural advantage, of race privilege. Second, it is a "standpoint", a place from which white people look at ourselves, at others, and at society. Third, "whiteness" refers to a set of cultural practices that are usually unmarked and unnamed' (Frankenberg, 1993. p. 1). Evidence demonstrating the existence of the latter two dimensions—a White standpoint and a set of unmarked cultural practices—can be found in James's (1996) research of ethnicity in Canada. James asked White people to describe their ethnicity: 'To me, ethnicity was something that belonged to people that differed from the so-called average White Canadian—differing perhaps because of language, accent or skin colour. I believe my ignorance regarding my ethnicity is because I belong to the majority in Canada. Because the majority of Canadians are White, English-speaking, descendants of Britain, I have only thought of myself as a Canadian. In essence, I didn't realize I had ethnicity because I did not differ from the stereotypical image of an average Canadian' (James, 1996, pp. 39–40). White people making similar statements view themselves, others, and society from their own White standpoint without recognizing the cultural practices of their own 'ethnicity'.

Other researchers (Bonnett, 2000; Henry et al., 2000; Roger, 2000) have similarly documented the failure of White, English-speaking Canadians to recognize their own ethnicity while seeing and defining Native, Chinese, Somali, and other visibly different people as 'ethnic'. Such ethnocentrism seems innocuous at first but, because Whiteness is also a 'location of structural advantage and race privilege', White ethnocentrism has the power to become the centre of the societal universe. The White standpoint becomes the nation's standpoint, and White cultural practices are constituted as Canada's social norms. Gabriel (1998) explains the power of Whiteness to wield delineating power, in his expansion of Fiske's (1994) definition of Whiteness as 'a set of discursive techniques, including: *exnomination*, that is the power not to be named; *naturalization*, through which whiteness establishes itself as the norm by defining "others" and not itself; and *universalization*, where whiteness alone can make sense of a problem and its understanding becomes *the* understanding' (Gabriel, 1998, p. 13; emphasis in original).

The essence of Whiteness, therefore, lies in its power to establish and maintain a silent discourse that so equates normality with White culture that this culture becomes taken for granted as the norm. The origins of White power date back to the early days of colonialism, European enslavement of others, and capitalism. White European cultural practices were imposed around the world by military and economic might. Today rather than White cultural practices being sustained by military power and subjugation, Whiteness maintains itself by the power to define the subject. The transition from military to ideological domination can be discerned in Canada's history. Mercredi and Turpel (1993) recount how some five hundred years ago the people of Turtle Island met visitors from other lands in 'a momentous event in our collective history' (p. 16). The history that followed involved White Europeans settling, subjugating, invading, and engaging in acts of genocide to dominate Native people. By 1867, the British and French colonizers had formalized the establishment of a political entity called Canada in the northern part of Turtle Island. A part of the colonial subjugation of Aboriginal peoples by the French and British was the building of a national institutional infrastructure, including various levels of government, judicial systems, and educational systems that decimated the cultural practices and infrastructure of First Nations communities (James, 1996). The institutions of colonial rule eventually became the vanguard of White dominance.

The shift from violent methods to predominantly ideological coercion demonstrates the ability of Whiteness to maintain subjugation by adapting to changing historical circumstances. Yet this shift was more apparent than real: ideology has justified and bolstered the rule of Whiteness from its colonial beginnings. Kincheloe (1999) explains how the justification and propagation of White rule are deeply embedded in the ideology of the Enlightenment: 'Whiteness took shape around the European Enlightenment's notion of rationality with its privileged construction of a transcendental white, male, rational subject who operated at the recess of power while giving every indication that he escaped the confines of time and space. In this context whiteness was naturalized as a universal entity that operated as more than a mere ethnic personality' (p. 164). The Enlightenment project utilized 'science' and 'reason' to justify White colonial domination (Kincheloe, 1999). Some writers (Johnson, Rush, & Feagin, 2000) suggest that the 'scientific' categorization of humans by race grew from the need to legitimate the European–American slave trade. In 1775, Johann Blumenbach developed one of the first typologies of race by dividing humans into five biological categories: Mongolians, Ethiopians, Americans, Malays, and Caucasians. He chose the term 'Caucasian' to refer to White Europeans because he believed that Whites had originated in the Russian Caucasus Mountains, where they had been created by God in his own image (Akintunde, 1999; Blakey, 1999). Using a hierarchical scale, Blumenbach ranked the races in order of superiority; since he considered Caucasians as most God-like, other races fell beneath them, their degree of relative inferiority determined by their closeness to the White ideal (Akintunde, 1999; Cameron & Wycoff, 1998). With other races ranked as inferior to Whites, the justification of the enslavement and domination of other races by Whites was possible because it was seen as the natural order of society. The concept of race, therefore, enabled and justified the subjugation of other races by Whites.

Today, with the exception of neo-Nazis and White supremacists, most people recognize Blumenbach's 'science' as flawed. Yet the White race still rules, Whiteness retains normative status, and White understanding continues to be what Gabriel refers to as 'the understanding' (1998, p. 13) (emphasis original). Whiteness maintains dominance, in part, because Blumenbach did not simply construct the concept of race, he constructed an apparatus through which 'White' systemic racial subjugation was justified.

Recognizing 'Whiteness' as a form of domination separates, to some degree, the concept of Whiteness from a description of White people. Separating Whiteness from Whites is important: because biological descriptions of race such as 'White',

'Black', or 'of colour' are now recognized as lacking validity, one cannot claim that Whiteness is a racial characteristic. Although the concept of race has no ontological meaning, race has epistemological meaning: as was shown above in June's and Gary's narratives, 'race' as a social location shapes the way the world is experienced. Race, therefore, gains meaning not as a descriptor of skin colour but as a marker of social location, with 'Whiteness' representing what Frankenberg (1993) describes as a location of structural advantage and race privilege. As such, the term 'Whiteness' transcends race to represent the multiple sites of advantage and privilege of being White, male, middle-class, heterosexual, and able-bodied. Just as these locations transcend race, so does their antithesis of being a person of colour, female, working-class, or lesbian, gay, or bisexual, or of having a disability.

As a construction representing a social location, Whiteness is more than skin colour. Ethnicity can also be included in the construct of Whiteness because, although ethnicity refers to cultural grouping rather than the grouping by racial characteristics, socio-political processes choose which of the vast array of available human characteristics are singled out as signifiers of ethnicity. As shown in June's and Gary's narratives, both Gary's Whiteness and his invisible ethnicity secured his acceptance into the Canadian fabric while June was excluded by her race and ethnicity. Ethnicity, therefore, becomes interconnected with race in the array of social locations forming the power position of Whiteness.

In Britain, understanding race as a political construct resulted in members of a number of subjugated groups recognizing the oppression they experienced as having roots in their social location rather than in their race or ethnicity. Consequently, many South East Asians, South Asians, people of African descent, and even some 'White' Irish rallied together and adopted the label 'Black' (Gabriel, 1998; Kincheloe, 1999). The use of the term 'Black' by these groups was a political rather than a biological statement. It emerged from a solidarity among groups that arose from the development of a shared consciousness about the nature of their common oppression. The inclusion of 'White Irish' as members of the 'Black' group reveals that not all Whites have access to the full privilege and power of Whiteness. Recognizing different access among Whites to the power of Whiteness is important. To act as though everyone is defined only by one aspect of their oppression homogenizes and reduces people to that essence—it essentializes them. Such essentializing must be avoided.

To claim that all White people have equal access to the power of Whiteness is inaccurate and oversimplifies the problem. McIntosh (1998) describes Whites as having an unearned 'invisible knapsack' of privilege that they can draw from. Yet if Whiteness is characterized as an intersection of locations of privilege, all Whites clearly cannot access the same array of privileges. As Gabriel (1998) comments, 'I am not suggesting that Whiteness works for all "Whites" in the same way. Not all White ethnicities are dominant and not all "Whites" are privileged' (p. 4). Clearly, the homeless White male, the White mother on welfare, or the White male CEO of a Fortune 500 company do not form a homogeneous group with equal access to White privilege. Neither are people of colour, women, the working class, lesbian,

gay, or bisexual women and men, or persons with disabilities homogeneous groupings who are equally barred from access to power. Whiteness does not divide the
oppressed from the oppressors in such a neat binary manner. In fact, division into
the binary opposites of Black and White is a form of objectification that denies subjects their ability to act in different ways (Leonard, 1997). In other words, categorization into White oppressors and Black oppressed defines people by race and
denies them the ability to resist that definition—a process Whiteness itself uses to
maintain dominance. The spectre of binary simplicity must not, however, allow
Whiteness to elude interrogation. Without falling into the trap of essentialization,
Whiteness must be named. As Frankenberg (1993) states, 'naming "whiteness" displaces it from the unmarked, unnamed status that is itself an effect of its dominance' (p. 6).

    Because Whiteness profoundly changes the way one engages in social work prac-
tice with 'ethno-racial' others, social workers must understand the nature and place
of Whiteness if they are to fight oppression. Furthermore, understanding Whiteness
raises the question of whether current social work practice combats or supports
Whiteness, especially if Whiteness is a central constituent within such practice.

The Invisible History of Whiteness in Multicultural Social Work Literature

When one recognizes the pervasiveness of Whiteness in Canadian culture, the history of multicultural social work take on new meaning. No longer is the history of
multicultural practice about searching for ways of working with ethno-racial communities; rather, it is a history of how the discourse of Whiteness shapes, defines,
and delineates knowledge about ethno-racial people. Social work, from the anchor
point of the norms and values of the dominant culture, reappropriates the terms
'race' and 'ethnicity' by socially constructing these categories through the lens of
Whiteness. Ethno-racial people are understood from the standpoint of the 'rational'
and 'scientific' nature of White understanding; moreover, Whiteness developed the
terms 'race' and 'ethnicity' and, in so doing, created itself. In this process of racialization, the world is divided into two camps, the definer and the delineated, with
attention given to ethno-racial people, not to Whiteness itself. The object of activity for service providers, who work from a place of Whiteness, focuses on the problems that ethno-racial communities place on the system, rather than laying bare the
invisible domination of the discourse of Whiteness.

    The preservation of race privilege and the predominance of the cultural prac-
tices of Whiteness create the ethno-racial Other. Although White societal norms
manifest themselves in different ways over time, they have determined the knowledge base of earlier and present social work literature. During the 1950s and 1960s,
intergroup conflict between ethno-racial minorities and the dominant culture
group in North America resulted in the creation of the race relations, bias, and
assimilation models. These approaches assumed that racial tensions were caused by
individual prejudice and a lack of cultural contact between members of the main-

stream and ethno-racial people. Mainstream social scientists, including political scientists and sociologists, readily accepted these claims. They coincided neatly with state policy perspectives and the benevolent belief that Canada could not possibly be racist. From this point of view, importance was placed on blaming racial tensions on the ethno-racial groups themselves by focusing on their acculturation and adaptation skills, rather than considering the source of conflict as emanating from the racism of the mainstream group. Inherent in this thinking was an 'us and them' attitude in which Whiteness plays a key role: ways needed to be found for 'them' (ethno-racial Others) to fit better with 'us' (White society). Such ideological forces rest on the assumption that the characteristics of race and ethnicity, or of these Others, need to be identified and scrutinized to mark and objectify ethno-racial people. Once the Other has been objectified, the dominant culture wields power over it, emphasizing the cultural characteristics of minority groups in order to define them, determine their needs, and place them within the hierarchical social order. Although such categorization makes little sense, this process of racialization helps to ameliorate the dominant group's perception that the ethno-racial Other encroaches into the space of Whiteness and potentially threatens to change the Whiteness of the Canadian landscape.

According to authors such as Hall (2000) and Goldberg (2000), a focus on difference and cultures allows people to avoid dealing with the historical presence of racism inherent in society. More significantly, as noted by Back and Solomos (2000), 'the language of culture and nation invokes a hidden racial narrative' (p. 20). Whiteness dominates the narrative of Canadian history and is an integral and defining force of national identity. Yet its very omnipresence renders it virtually invisible: it is simultaneously 'everywhere but nowhere' in the consciousness of both White people and people of colour. For example, one of the striking powers of Whiteness lies in its ability to determine who belongs and who does not belong in the discourse of the nation. Most people are aware that the use of the term 'Canadian' frequently refers to those who are of White British descent, as opposed to people of colour. Take, for instance, the 'hyphenation' of people's identity (e.g., Chinese-Canadian or Japanese-Canadian people) or, the comment that: 'I am a Canadian and I do not need to refer to my ethnicity'. As Back and Solomos (2000) further substantiate, a racial narrative 'is the way [culture and nation] naturalises social formations in terms of a racial/cultural logic of belonging' (p. 21). In everyday social work practice, to emphasize the differences of ethnicity and race not only diverts attention from the way various social locations give differential access to power and privilege, but also removes any awareness about the power of the White professional to socially construct and define 'ethno-racial communities'.

In social service agencies, the dominant culture may constitute itself in the position of power and control, through the privileged social location of Whiteness, and may determine and limit the type of social services, supports, and resources available to ethno-racial communities. A major obstacle mainstream service providers have yet to overcome is their own inability to challenge the way mainstream agencies organize and structure service delivery and to change these systems so that such services fully and equally take into account the rights of the ethno-racial Other. Race evasion on the part of mainstream agencies—that is, failure to acknowledge the role that race plays in structuring service delivery—prevents them from equitably sharing power with and integrating services for ethno-racial communities. Moreover, one questions the contention that agencies are resistant to change because such a viewpoint denies the fact that mainstream agencies, do indeed, make attempts to address the cultural needs of ethno-racial people. For example, many agencies provide workshops on educating mainstream service providers about the culture of ethno-racial communities. A consequence of such action is that the equal rights of the ethno-racial Others are perpetually undermined by the dominant culture. If the ethno-racial Others are not satisfied with the services they receive from mainstream agencies, the reason must be because 'they' are different, and those ethno-racial Others should expect to receive culturally appropriate services only if and when funding becomes available.

Separate from the socio-political interpretations of ethno-racial communities' interaction with the dominant culture, the development of psychological, biological, and social analyses of cultural groups predominated in social work literature, especially from the 1960s to the early 1980s. Tsang and George (1998) expand Casas's (1985) review of cross-cultural understandings of ethno-racial people. They reveal five different models, all of which portray ethno-racial Others in negative terms: the inferiority or pathological model (Padilla, 1981), the deviant model (Rubington & Weinberg, 1971), the disorganizational model (Moynhihan, 1965), the culturally deficient model (Padilla, 1981), and the genetically deficient model (Herrnstein, 1971) (Tsang & George, 1998, pp. 74–5). The discourse of Whiteness, notable in these texts, does not simply portray ethno-racial people as explicitly inferior; it also implicitly portrays the dominant culture as superior, without making any explicit reference to the normality of Whiteness. This notion of White superiority complements the race relations, bias, and assimilation perspectives of the same period by taking for granted that the problem stems from ethno-racial people, not White people. In social work practice, the standard convention for dealing with the problem of race and ethnicity is to teach the ethno-racial Other how to maintain their ethnicity in appropriate 'Canadian' ways, and to assimilate as a 'Canadian' by acting more White, rather than to help build the cultural identities of ethno-racial people in positive ways.

The policy of multiculturalism has not reduced problems of racial inequality, even though the intent of the policy was the acceptance and tolerance of Canada's many diverse cultures. Adopted in 1971 against the backdrop of institutional recognition of British and French cultures and bilingualism, the policy of multiculturalism officially recognized Canada's mosaic of cultures, and did help to propogate the idea that the ethno-racial Other need no longer assimilate and should instead be encouraged to maintain their cultural heritage. In the context of multiculturalism, understanding the ethno-racial Other became very salient and important. Especially in social work practice, the 'cultural literacy' approach of McGoldrick (1982) flourished, as mainstream workers sought expert knowledge of the client's culture to meet the instrumentalist need for a practical hands-on approach of working with those who come from another culture. Cultural fairs and 'ethnic' food lunches became popular, and it was fashionable to develop an appreciation for saris, samosas, and steel bands. Obviously, the cultural literacy approach requires little critical self-reflection on the part of social work practitioners about how their personal values, beliefs, or social locations filter and transform the cultural world of the service user to conform to that of agency's mainstream practices. As long as practitioners remain consciously unaware of their Whiteness, its power remains deeply embedded and invisible in various social work practice approaches, erroneously deflecting attention away from the self to the Other.

Although much of the social work literature on cultural literacy approaches carefully cautions readers to pay attention to the variability of people's experiences and to avoid making generalizations about people's behaviour, many social work practitioners unintentionally fall into the trap of essentializing and circumscribing people's social identities. More importantly, one cannot ignore the reality that the social identities of ethno-racial people intermesh with those of Whiteness. The reason for a focus on the ethnicity of racial minorities may not be so much the fault of the practitioner as the fallacy of the approach itself. As noted by Gilroy (1990), 'at the end of the day, an absolute commitment to cultural insiderism is as bad as an absolute commitment to biological insiderism' (p. 80). In other words, culture cannot be treated as some kind of artifact that the social work practitioner takes for granted as true; rather, social workers should politically critique the appropriation of culture by the person who has the power to speak about it. As further commented by Gilroy, 'in our multi-cultural schools the sound of the steel pan may evoke Caribbean ethnicity, tradition and authenticity yet they originate in the oil drums of the Standard Oil Company rather than the mysterious knowledge of ancient African griots' (p. 80). Without a historical understanding of the role that economic and colonial oppression play in the lives of ethno-racial people, a White 'understanding' of the Other remains, subsequently deepening common-sense notions assumed uncritically in the media, school, and workplace.

Indeed, multiculturalism and cultural literacy approaches perpetuate and maintain Whiteness as the societal referential norm and authoritative voice from which the ethno-racial Other can be defined and measured. As Dyche and Zayas (1995) point out, culture is, 'reified, lifted from its abstract status and the printed page and perceived as a description of real individuals; that is clients are seen as their culture, not as themselves' (p. 391). The safety in examining ethno-racial people's identity through their cultures serves many purposes. First, for social work practitioners, understanding the cultures of ethno-racial people provides a cookie-cutter approach to social work practice and maintains the illusion that we treat everybody the same. Second, this approach colludes with the myth that all cultures in Canada are equal, despite the power of the dominant culture to shape Canadian norms and values. Although the policy of multiculturalism acknowledges the contribution of Canada's ethnic-racial diversity to everyday life, there are limits to which ethno-racial people can transform the Whiteness of the Canadian landscape.

In Eva Mackey's (1996) research on White Canadians' thoughts about multiculturalism, she encountered this comment: 'an interviewee at a festival hesitantly moved towards admitting that Canadian culture should "be first" and that multiculturalism "was dividing the country"' (pp. 26–7).

Such anecdotes point to the larger structures in place and illustrate how Whiteness becomes the underlying dominant mode of understanding embedded within the historical, collective unconscious of Canada. Recognizing such structures, Homi Bhabha states that the unspoken meaning behind multiculturalism, with its emphasis on difference, is nothing but, 'a sham universalism that paradoxically permits diversity [and] masks ethnocentric norms, values and interests' (cited in Jordan & Weedon, 1995, p. 485). Such masking, propagated and further supported by multiculturalism and cultural literacy approaches, takes race completely off the social work agenda. With no mention of race, and much talk about ethnicity, diversity in Canada is reduced to a mosaic of cultural practices and traditions; the ability to conceptualize and critically discuss the historical origins of privilege, power, and racial oppression becomes further obscured. Any person who associates race with inequality is accused of propagating the very phenomena discussed. As argued by Proctor and Davis (1994) and reinforced by Tsang and George (1998), a 'colour-blind practice assumes equality between client and worker and the acknowledgement of racial difference is seen as racism' (Tsang & George, 1998, p. 75). As well, proponents of a colour-blind approach argue that devising solutions from the standpoint of race promotes the polarization of society; however, evading the concept of race denies the extent and degree to which social relationships are, in fact, structured through race. The denial of race oppression promotes the shallow belief that, underneath the appearance of differences, everyone is the same and we are all just human. Yet in every instance of interaction, race configures the perceptions of both the observer and the observed and subsequently plays a role in determining the dynamics of the relationship. To deny this reality is to deny the reality that ethno-racial people experience barriers in access to resources and opportunities in daily life and in their interactions and negotiations with institutions. In general, few would contest that racial-ethnic minorities experience unequal outcomes.

The conflation of the terms race and ethnicity into mere cultural identities removes the possibility for social action that would critically interrogate the underlying dominant mode of understanding, a system that benefits White people and supports a structure of inequality. At the same time, ethno-racial people easily become transformed into a subordinate role, that of the oppressed, in relation to the dominant culture. Notwithstanding the impact of the civil rights movements in the 1960s, the implementation of the policy of multiculturalism in 1971, and the establishment of the Charter of Human Rights and Freedoms in 1985, all of which challenge the power of Whiteness to undermine the rights of ethno-racial communities, there are limits to these multicultural practices. The effectiveness of such social movements and policies must be framed within the context of Whiteness, which still has the ability to reassert its homogenizing power in seemingly neutral and fair ways and to prevent the dismantling of the larger systemic and institutional forms of discrimination still in place. This is why it is important to recognise that the rights of ethno-racial communities must always be understood in the context of Whiteness; otherwise collusion with Whiteness can too easily occur, and with little awareness that this is what is happening.

In the 1980s and through the 1990s, critical discourse on the concepts of race and racism created shifts in the literature on cultural diversity. Critical of the multiculturalism approach, many writers (Dei, 1996; Dominelli, 1997; Gilroy, 1987, 1990; Leah, 1995) argue that the problem of race, class, gender, and other forms of oppression are rooted in the historical, social, political, and economic circumstances of people's material, lived experiences. Known as the *antiracism approach*, some of the key features stand out clearly in opposition to the limitations of the multiculturalism approach. They include an acknowledgement that racism exists in society; that conflict between racial minorities and the dominant group is not due to lack of contact or to cultural misunderstanding between groups, but rather can be traced to power differentials between the dominant group and ethno-racial minorities; and that people's social, political, and economic relationships are racially structured. Dei (1996) provides a comprehensive definition of *antiracism* as 'An action-oriented strategy for institutional systemic change that addresses racism and other interlocking systems of social oppression. It is a critical discourse of race and racism in society that challenges the continuance of racializing social groups for differential and unequal treatment. Antiracism explicitly names the issues of race and social difference as issues of power and equity, rather than as matters of culture and ethnic variety' (p. 252).

Within an antiracism approach, the concept of race transforms from a descriptive variable to an ideological entity in the context of Western, liberal societies. Such societies are characterized by two irreconcilable positions: a strong belief in equality of treatment, irrespective of one's race, gender and class; and the prevalence of discriminatory treatment of people due to race, gender, and class. Much of the antiracism literature acknowledges the existence of the latter reality by proactively engaging in strategies that dismantle concrete barriers and structures that may intentionally or unintentionally exclude ethno-racial people from equal participation in society. More significantly, Whiteness perpetuates racial inequality and subordination. As discussed by Dei, 'the antiracism perspective moves beyond acknowledgement of the material conditions that structure societal inequality; it questions White power and privilege and their rationale for dominance. Antiracism questions the marginalization of certain voices in society and the delegitimation/devaluation of the knowledge and experience of subordinate and minority groups' (Dei, 1996, p. 254).

As was suggested above, even the positive evaluation of ethno-racial communities and their cultures in social service agencies is harmful when such an evaluation rests against the backdrop of the dominant culture. Ultimately, the dominant culture not only sets the parameters by which ethno-racial communities are understood, it also defines whose voices are heard. Although many boards of social service agencies encourage ethno-racial representation, tokenism may ensure the domination of White privilege. To expect, for example, a Caribbean-Black person to be representative of all Caribbean-Black people reduces the individual to a particular aspect of his or her social location and, furthermore, may imply that people have static social identities. More importantly, to state the need for greater representation of ethno-racial perspectives in the national culture of Canada, dominated by Whiteness, can only come across as sounding as though an interest group is speaking. The association of demands for ethno-racial representation with 'interest-group' politics reveals the power of the White, heterosexual, able-bodied, male to be taken as the norm, and not an interest group. An awareness of the marginality of ethno-racial perspectives raises questions about whether the portrayal of the culture of ethno-racial communities can truly be recognized in the context of a White Canada.

Recently, a strong backlash has been aimed at the antiracism perspective; indeed, some critics were once advocates of antiracism. To begin, the implementation of the antiracism perspective in social service agencies has failed miserably in gaining acceptance among key stakeholders who have the power to create change, and this is why possibilities for agencies addressing racism do not occur. Naming racism within an agency causes major internal objections. For example, in an evaluation report of a multicultural organizational change project, a change strategy adopted to help agencies become more culturally accessible to ethno-racial clients, the organization strongly recommended that the word 'racism' be completely taken out; objection to the use of the word was clearly expressed by antiracism change facilitators. Some authors suggest that the omission of the word racism is a form of resistance to change (Henry et al., 2000, p. 283). Yet, a more political analysis of the situation by Humphries (1997) demonstrates how 'much of the radical potential of anti-racism has been re-defined and re-situated, *appropriated and accommodated* within a liberal value base' (p. 295; emphasis in original). Once again, the power of Whiteness, as an ideological force in Canadian society, finds ways to reassert itself and prevent any systemic and structural change, thus perpetuating and maintaining the status quo. Perhaps one could further argue that this is why social service agencies have not moved further ahead in providing culturally appropriate and relevant services to ethno-racial people.

The opposition of many people in Canadian society, especially those in privileged sites of power, to understanding the problem of racial inequality as a consequence of Whiteness prevents the possibilities for any real social change. Even in the United Kingdom, where progressive social work practice tried to raise the level of consciousness of students in training, the power of Whiteness defensively relabelled education about racism as intolerant and damaging to White people. As Humphries (1997) has observed: 'Suffice it to say that the right-wing press and parts of the liberal press, along with one or two prominent academics and politicians criticized both CCETSW [the Central Council for Education and Training in Social Work] and social work courses in universities for being totalitarian, intolerant and vicious in imposing beliefs that racism was endemic in all British institutions, and for forcing white students, on pain of explusion, to confess to their own racism. The words "thought police" and "political correctness" were the key words in this discourse' (p. 290).

Although an antiracism perspective aims to tackle the social relations that underlie discriminatory treatment of ethno-racial people, the power of Whiteness refuses to put its own structures and practices under scrutiny, and race evasiveness helps to maintain Whiteness. For mainstream agencies to adopt an antiracism organizational change model requires decision makers to challenge the underlying cultural practices of Whiteness that are entrenched in the norms and values of the agency. More problematic for many agencies, such acknowledgement of racism puts into question forms of multicultural practice in use today, such as educating mainstream service providers about ethno-racial communities, and shifts the focus onto Whiteness as the barrier to fair and equitable outcomes for ethno-racial communities. Examining Whiteness can be very threatening, to say the least, but it represents a positive move towards a real sharing of power among those who are privileged and those who are perpetually marginalized.

Strategies on How to Combat Whiteness in Canadian Social Work Practice

Strategies to combat Whiteness must begin with social service agencies acknowledging the pervasiveness of Whiteness as a part of Canadian consciousness and national identity. Irrespective of whether the focus is on mainstream, grassroots, or an ethno-specific organization, all agencies operate within the larger environment of the dominant culture. Some agencies may resist the prevalence of Canada's dominant culture, yet if they fail to name Whiteness as the impetus behind dominance, resistance reinforces domination. For agencies to extricate themselves from being a voice in the discourse of Whiteness, the discourse must be recognized. To act as though organizations are not a part of the whole of Canadian society negates the socio-political dimensions of understanding both Whiteness and oppression. As Canadians, we have a core set of values that provide a sense of commonality among all groups of people, irrespective of race and ethnicity, gender, class, ability, and sexual orientation. It is important to recognize that, within these values, Whiteness prevails. These values, in turn, determine those of various subcultures and/or minority cultures (e.g., those who experience social oppression). As stated by Beverly Jones: 'Every society has a dominant culture. But because the dominant culture doesn't have to look outside itself, it remains largely unconscious of its own assumptions and characteristics. The subordinate culture, by contrast, must interact with the dominant culture to survive. By necessity, the sub-culture becomes bicultural, while the dominant culture is observed but not observant' (cited in Poplin, 1992, A23). Thus, recognizing and gaining an awareness of the role that Whiteness plays in socially constructing both the dominant and the oppressed is necessary in bringing about institutional and society-wide change. To avoid such awareness can result only in the continuation and reproduction of present power relations, which exclude various groups of people from equal participation in society.

The critical lesson, especially for those who are committed to social change, is not to underestimate the extent and degree of the power of Whiteness to reconstitute itself continually in order that its own structures and power are never dismantled. Within all organizations, tremendous possibilities for change exist, provided one remembers the cautionary note that 'the master's tools will never dismantle the master's house' (Lorde, 1984, p. 123). Those in positions of power have much at stake in maintaining the status quo, even though they may not be aware of how Whiteness dominates the Other. Discriminatory practices are not always about intent; they are often about how people are socially constructed into positions—one that, for example, enable social work practitioners to unintentionally participate in the creation of systems that do, in fact, exclude the ethno-racial Other. Within this understanding, there is also a recognition of everyone's complicit or explicit involvement in the process of Whiteness, irrespective of one's personal social locations of both privilege and oppression. Thus, just because a person socially locates himself or herself as part of an oppressed group does not necessarily mean that this person is an ally in dismantling the privileged structures of Whiteness. The key issue becomes whether that person's actions proactively demonstrate a dismantling of discriminatory and exclusionary structures, practices, and policies that support a system of privilege and inequality.

The importance of recognizing the Whiteness of Canada helps to draw linkages between the racial narratives of the Canadian national identity and to make visible the taken-for-granted privilege and power of the dominant culture. Furthermore, to acknowledge the Whiteness of Canada requires a deeper understanding of the way the particular knowledge production of people's experiences is legitimated and supported by Canada's social, political, and economic institutions. Unfortunately, many Canadians continue to make comments that attest to the Whiteness of Canada: 'minority groups cannot fit into Canadian society—they change the national identity [and] all we need to do is treat everybody equally' (Henry et al., 1995, pp. 23–7). The first comment assumes that one culture exists in Canada, that of Whiteness, and that the cultures of ethno-racial people threaten the homogeneous power of the dominant culture. In the second comment, as shown in section 15 (2) subsection (1) of the Canadian Human Rights Code, which allows for affirmative action programs, equal treatment leads to inequitable treatment. In other words, if one does not recognize differences in power, one sees no need to level the playing field. The perpetuation of myths that work to the detriment of those who are disadvantaged in society documents the sentiments of many Canadians in the discourse of the wider society and, more significantly, reflects the way mainstream agencies provide services to ethno-racial people. Henceforth, the need to develop alternative discourses that introduce new forms of knowledge production become particularly relevant to challenging differential power relations. As Dei (1996) comments, the importance of 'challeng[ing] definitions of what can be named "valid knowledge" and to privileg[ing] the idea of multiple and collective origins of knowledge rather than competing claims to knowledge' (p. 254) means that the space for authentic dialogue between members of the dominant culture and ethno-racial communities needs to be opened.

Furthermore, all knowledge is historically constituted in the Whiteness of Canadian history and is socially mediated by social service providers in the choices they make when determining which measures to adopt to address the needs of ethno-racial communities. What is known today as standard, conventional social work practice evolved from specific historical processes that constitute the role of Whiteness in Canada as the determining force in terms of which services can meet the needs of ethno-racial people. A central strategy that focuses on dismantling systems of Whiteness should become the priority of social service agencies. This can occur by facilitating an environment that fosters and supports, as an integral part of the agency's functioning, the practice of listening to the different needs of the oppressed. For example, the establishment of service-user committees, which allow ethno-racial groups to partake in the planning, delivery, and evaluation of services, can help democratize the process of ethno-racial participation. Too often, organizations claim to know the needs of the community and develop programs without adequate consultation with community members. As well, social service providers need an understanding and awareness of the way the entrenched norms and values of the dominant culture may limit and constrain the rights of ethno-racial people.

One of the dangers of putting much of the responsibility on Whiteness to eradicating social inequality lies in the obvious problem that to critique Whiteness without acknowledging the many actions taken by people in positions of power to meet the needs of ethno-racial people runs the risk of essentializing Whiteness. Put differently, the process of Whiteness can be oversimplified, and its full and sometimes contradictory characteristics not grasped. Any measures that attack Whiteness are limited because of the extent to which power structures can be challenged, since those who perpetuate Whiteness may not do so intentionally. This limitation can be overcome by recognizing that those in positions of power cannot dismantle discriminatory practices alone; but rather, by not recognizing the power of Whiteness, those in positions of power will only reproduce themselves. In fact, one could argue that much multicultural training has been generated and encouraged by people in positions of power (who benefit from Whiteness). If that is the case, does it not make sense to alert these people to the issues of Whiteness and to expect them to be a key part of developing more critical remedies to discriminatory practice? In other words, before real social change can occur, people must increase their level of awareness and knowledge of how each person, socially located within the dominant culture, can lay bare the social processes that intentionally or unintentionally discriminate.

Many agencies focus on increasing the representation of ethno-racial members among staff, volunteers, and board members, but this approach has failed to eradicate systemically entrenched forms of discrimination. Instead, ethno-racial people may experience further oppression as token representatives of the agency. According to Dei (1996), 'the question of representation, that is, the need to have a multiplicity of voices and perspectives entrenched (and centred) as part of main-stream social knowledge' is crucial (p. 254). But how can that happen if mechanisms and processes are not in place that enable ethno-racial people to share equal space with the privileged? Again, one cannot expect that the efforts of ethno-racial peo-ple to shape Canadian norms and values will come to fruition until the power of Whiteness is confronted directly by those in positions of power. For example, by hiring multicultural outreach workers, who are expected to address the needs of ethno-racial minorities, some agencies have had limited success in providing serv-ices to ethno-racial clientele. These positions, however, are supported largely by transitional funding on a contract basis and do not operate with the same resources as their mainstream counterparts. This is why mainstream agencies continue to rely heavily upon the services of ethno-specific agencies to fill the gaps of their service delivery to ethno-racial clientele (Beyene, Butcher, Joe, & Richmond, 1996).

Hopefully, by rendering the invisible visible, a shared consciousness will develop about the way Whiteness regulates, defines, and delimits everyone in society, irre-spective of race, class, or gender oppression and privilege. The goal of eradicating social inequality, based on multiple oppressions, is a society that successfully sets in place social processes and mechanisms that allow all members of society to relate to one another in truly authentic ways. This requires that the oppressive forces that subordinate the ethno-racial Other are not reproduced. Thus, authentic social work practice is about legitimating the multiplicity of voices, narratives, and histories of those not from the dominant culture. Yet, bringing the voices from the margin to the centre is not enough. Rather, there needs to be a complete reworking of main-stream practices; a process must occur that acknowledges the impact that various practices have on people who occupy different social locations. This may seem like a utopian idea, but the reason such an approach has not worked in the past was the failure to recognize Whiteness. To fail to engage ethno-racial people in a process with those who hold the power to determine services only marginalizes ethno-racial people, maintains their segregation as separate from the dominant culture, and, more importantly, does not provide the changes that would be of real benefit to the oppressed.

Conclusion

This chapter ends by referring back to the authors' narratives of the impact Whiteness has had on them personally and, by example, can bring to the fore impli-cations for social work practice. Currently, social work responses based on a mul-ticulturalism and antiracism ideology would focus on understanding June and eradicating the racial oppression she and Others like her experience. Attempts to combat attitudes that exclude June and Others would rest on educating service providers in the hope that knowledge about the culture of Others would eliminate the problem of cultural insensitivity. Such responses, however, make June, and Others like her, the focus of attention and objectify the racial identity of the Other in the eyes of the observer. The focus on June and Others distracts from the issue of why social service providers do not look at how Gary and those like him are seen as a part of the Canadian fabric. The process that excludes June does not need attention, but the process that includes Gary does. Indeed, if one begins from the premise that race, as a social construct, provides an entry point for oppression to occur, then June's emancipation cannot happen by simply focusing on the methods used to oppress. Rather, the importance of challenging the power that enables race to become a social and political construct should be critically interrogated. Focusing on this power is similar to existing antiracism social work practices, yet it contains a subtle but critical difference: it identifies Whiteness as the source of that power.

Stainton and Swift (1996) articulate anti-oppressive practice and speak of the need to develop a general theory of oppression that unmasks the hegemonic power of Canada's dominant culture. Although they refer to a 'dominant culture', they do not identify the power of Whiteness that lies behind this dominance; consequently, their anti-oppressive remedies focus on social work combating the 'technologies of oppression' and developing 'techniques of emancipation' (Stainton & Swift, 1996, p. 82). Without identifying Whiteness, such anti-oppressive approaches are lacking. As Frankenberg (1993) notes, 'naming Whiteness displaces it from the unmarked, unnamed status that is an effect of dominance' (p. 6). Social work practice that does not make visible the pervasiveness and power of Whiteness can never address the cultural and linguistic needs of ethno-racial communities or lead to emancipation. As Wildman and Davis note, 'Domination, subordination, and privilege are like three heads of hydra. Attacking the most visible heads, domination and subordination, trying bravely to chop them up into little pieces, will not kill the third head, privilege. Like a mythic multi-headed hydra, which will inevitably grow another head if all heads are not slain, discrimination cannot be ended by focusing only on subordination and domination' (Wildman & Davis, 1997, p. 317). Striking at all three heads of the hydra—subordination, domination, and privilege—is key to providing culturally appropriate and relevant services to ethno-racial communities.

The challenge of striking all three heads can be illustrated by again examining the social locations of the authors. The value in Gary acknowledging his site of privilege and Whiteness, or how he occupies sites of privilege, enables him to proactively engage in eradicating systems that perpetuate forms of racism, sexism, and other isms. Gary and those like him, however, may try to avoid association with Whiteness, because most liberal Whites oppose racism, and other oppressive isms, and the very thought that they could be a part of oppressive processes creates considerable discomfort. By drawing attention to his working-class background, how he had dropped out of high school as a teen, or the fact that he gained entry to a British university through a program designed for those disadvantaged in education by the British class system, Gary could easily slip into the trap of avoiding scrutiny. He may protest that 'Whiteness does not work for me!' This response would be of no surprise: as Wildman and Davis suggest, 'whites spend a lot of time trying to convince ourselves and each other that we are not racist' (Wildman & Davis, 1997, p. 13). Avoiding talking about privilege, however, is counterproductive;

the pervasive nature of Whiteness means that nobody escapes having their attitudes shaped by it, especially Whites. While we need to be careful not to essentialize the White identity, we also needs to heed Wildman and Davis's contention that, 'a big step would be for whites to admit we are racist and then consider what to do about it' (Wildman & Davis, 1997, p. 318). Indeed, until Whites recognize that racism, and all other isms associated with Whiteness, is not merely the bigotry of White supremacists and neo-Nazi groups, but a part of everyday society, discriminatory systems, actions, and policies can never be eradicated.

Just as denial often constitutes a White response to being confronted with Whiteness, its opposite—guilt—can also be a common response. Kincheloe (1999) notes that an identity struggle can occur where Whites 'engage in a form of white self-denigration that expresses itself in conceptualization of non-white cultures as superior to white culture—more authentic, natural and sacred' (p. 172). Those adopting a positive evaluation of the cultures of ethno-racial communities fail to understand Whiteness and, more significantly, fail to escape Whiteness. Their portrayal of non-White cultures as 'authentic, natural and sacred' essentializes the Others associated with these cultures. Such White self-pity and guilt do not change the dynamics of power and privileged relationships; they merely make these privileges a little more uncomfortable to own.

Denial and guilt are both counterproductive in the deconstruction of Whiteness. Putting aside these defences, social workers on an individual and institutional level must examine how they and their practice are shaped by Whiteness. Identifying Whiteness can be the catalyst needed to transform current social work practice with ethno-racial communities, which is 'Other-producing', into forms of liberating practice that effectively deal with oppression. Current social work practice of understanding culture must be modified to reveal rather than rest on the invisible hegemony of Whiteness. Indeed, the social work focus on anti-oppressive practice can be effective only when we recognize Whiteness as the root of shared oppressions. Likewise, multicultural practice can be effective only when everyone recognizes that cultures exist in an environment of Whiteness that shapes and forms not only the way race and culture are lived, but also the rules that govern who can know and what can be known.

References

Akintunde, O. (1999). White racism, white supremacy, white privilege, and the social construction of race: Moving from modernist to postmodernist multiculturalism. *Multicultural Education, 7*(2), 2.

Back, L., & Solomos, J. (Eds). (2000). *Theories of Race and Racism: A Reader.* London: Routlege.

Beyene, D., Butcher, C., Joe, B., & Richmond, T. (1996). Immigrant service agencies: A fundamental component of anti-racist social services. In C.E. James (Ed.), *Perspectives on Racism and the Human Services Sector: A Case for Change* (pp. 171–82). Toronto: University of Toronto Press.

Blakey, M.L. (1999). Scientific racism and the biological concept of race. *Literature and Psychology*, *1*(2), 29–43.

Bonnett, A. (2000). *Anti-Racism*. London: Routledge.

Cameron, S., & Wycoff, S. (1998). The destructive nature of the term race: Growing beyond a false paradigm. *Journal of Counseling and Development*, *76*(3), 277–85.

Casas, M.J. (1985). A Reflection on the status of racial/ethnic minority research. *The Counseling Psychologist*, *13*(4), 581–98.

Dei, G. (1996). Critical perspectives in antiracism. *Canadian Review of Sociology and Anthropology*, *33*(3), 247–67.

Devore, W., & Schlesinger, E.G. (1999). *Ethnic-Sensitive Social Work Practice*. Toronto: Allyn and Bacon.

Dominelli, L. (1997). *Anti-Racist Social Work*. London: Macmillan.

Drakes, S. (2000). Many Canadians are made to feel like strangers in their homeland. *Toronto Star*, 29 January.

Dyche, L., & Zayas, H.L. (1995). The value of curiosity and naiveté for the cross-cultural psychotherapist. *Family Process*, *34*(4), 389–99.

Dyer, R. (1997). *White*. London: Routledge.

Fiske, J. (1994). *Media Matters: Everyday Culture and Political Change*. Minneapolis: University of Minnesota Press.

Frankenberg, R. (1993). *White Women, Race Matters: The Social Construction of Whiteness*. London: Routledge.

Gabriel, J. (1998). *Whitewash: Racialized Politics and the Media*. London: Routledge.

Gilroy, P. (1987). *There Ain't No Black in the Union Jack*. London: Hutchinson.

———. (1990). The end of anti-racism. *New Community*, *17*(1), 71–83.

Goldberg, D.T. (2000). Racial knowledge. In L. Back & J. Solomos (Eds), *Theories of Race and Racism: A Reader* (pp. 154–180). London: Routledge.

Hall, S. (2000). Old and new identities, old and new ethnicities. In L. Back & J. Solomos (Eds), *Theories of Race and Racism: A Reader* (pp. 144–53). London: Routledge.

Henry, F., Tator, C., Mattis, W., & Rees, T. (2000). *The Colour of Democracy: Racism in Canadian Society*. 2nd ed. Toronto: Harcourt Brace.

Herrnstein, R. (1971). I.Q. *Atlantic Monthly*, *228*(3), 43–64.

Humphries, B. (1997). The dismantling of anti-discrimination in British social work: A view from social work education. *International Social Work*, *40*(3), 289–301.

Hutchinson, Y. (1992). *Profile of Clients in the Anglophone Youth Network: Examining the Situation of the Black Child*. Montreal: Ville Marie Social Service Centre and McGill University School of Social Work.

James, C.E. (Ed.). (1996). *Perspectives on Racism and the Human Services Sector: A Case for Change*. Toronto: University of Toronto Press.

Johnson, J., Rush, S., & Feagin, J. (2000). Reducing inequalities, doing anti-racism: Toward an egalitarian American society. *Contemporary Sociology*, *29*(1), 95–110.

Jones, J. (1994). Child protection and anti-oppressive practice: The dynamics of partnership with parents explored. *Early Child Development and Care, 102,* 101–14.

Jordan, G., & Weedon, C. (1995). *Cultural Politics: Class, Gender, Race and the Postmodern World.* Oxford: Blackwell Publishers.

Kincheloe, J.L. (1999). The struggle to define and reinvent whiteness: A pedagogical analysis. *College Literature, 26*(3), 162–94.

Leah, R. (1995). Anti-racism studies: An integrative perspective. *Race, Gender and Class, 2*(3), 105–22.

Leonard, P. (1997). *Postmodern Welfare: Reconstructing an Emancipatory Project.* London: Sage.

Lorde, A. (1984). Age, race, class and sex: Women redefining difference. In *Sister Outsider: Essays and Speeches by Audre Lorde.* Trumansburg, NY: The Crossing Press.

McGoldrick, M. (1982). *Ethnicity and Family Therapy.* New York: Guilford Press.

McIntosh, P. (1998). White privilege: Unpacking the invisible knapsack. In P. Rothenberg (Ed.), *Race, Class, and Gender in the United States: An Integrated Study.* 4th ed. (pp. 165–9). New York: St Martin's Press.

Mackey, E. (1996). *Managing and imagining diversity: Multiculturalism and the construction of national identity in Canada.* Unpublished doctoral dissertation, Sussex University, Sussex.

Martinot, S. (2000). The racialized construction of class in the United States. *Social Justice, 27*(1), 43–60.

Mayall, B. (1991). Researching childcare in a multi-ethnic society. *New Community, 17*(4), 553–68.

Mercredi, O., & Turpel, M.E. (1993). *In the Rapids: Navigating the Future of the First Nations.* Toronto: Viking.

Moynhihan, D.P. (1965). *The Negro Family: The Case for National Action.* Washington, DC: US Department of Labor, Office of Policy, Planning and Research.

Padilla, A.M. (1981). Competent communities: A critical analysis of theories and public policy. In O.A. Barbarin, P.R. Good, O.M. Pharr, & J.A. Siskind (Eds), *Institutional Racism and Community Competence* (pp. 20–9). Rockville, MD: U.S. Department of Health and Human Services.

Poplin, M. (1992). Educating in diversity. In P. Drucker (Ed.), *Educating for Results* (pp. A18–24). Baltimore: National School Boards Association.

Proctor, E., & Davis, L.E. (1994). The challenge of racial difference: Skills for clinical practice. *Social Work, 39*(3), 314–23.

Roediger, D. (1994). *Towards the Abolition of Whiteness: Essays on Race, Politics, and Working Class History.* London: Verso.

Roger, K. (2000). 'Making' white women through the privatization of education on health and well-being in the context of psychotherapy. In A. Calliste & G.J.S. Dei (Eds), *Anti-Racist Feminism: Critical Race and Gender Studies* (pp. 123–41). Halifax: Fernwood Publishing.

Rubington, E., & Weinberg, M.S. (1971). *The Study of Social Problems*. New York: Oxford University Press.

Stainton, T., & Swift, K. (1996). 'Difference' and social work curriculum. *Canadian Social Work Review, 13*, 75–87.

Swift, K J. (1995). *Manufacturing 'Bad Mothers': A Critical Perspective on Child Neglect*. Toronto: University of Toronto Press.

Thomas, B. (1987). *Multiculturalism at Work: A Guide to Organizational Change*. Toronto: YWCA of Metropolitan Toronto.

Truman, C., & Humphries, B. (1994). Re-thinking social research: Research in an unequal world. In B. Humphries & C. Truman (Eds), *Re-thinking Social Research: Anti-Discriminatory Approaches in Research Methodology*. Aldershot, UK: Avebury Publishing.

Tsang, A.K.T., & George, U. (1998). An integrated framework for cross-cultural social work. *Canadian Social Work Review, 15*, 73–93.

United Way of Greater Toronto. (1991). *Action, Access, Diversity: A Guide to Multicultural/Anti-Racist Organizational Change for Social Service Agencies*. Toronto: United Way of Greater Toronto.

Wildman, S.M., & Davis, A D. (1997). Making systems of privilege visible. In R. Delgado & J. Stefancic (Eds), *Critical White Studies* (pp. 314–19). Philadelphia: Temple University Press.

Winant, H. (2000). The theoretical status of the concept of race. In L. Back & J. Solomos (Eds), *Theories of Race and Racism: A Reader* (pp. 181–190). London: Routledge.

Chapter 6

Practice with Immigrants in Quebec

Ghislaine Roy and Catherine Montgomery

> Nous, c'est aussi les autres.
> Berthelot, 1990

Any attempt to introduce a pluralist vision into social work in Quebec is an occasion to rethink social work practice in a heterogeneous world in constant flux. This practice is torn between a respect for the history and consensus of the majority on the one hand, and, on the other, the adjustments to be made in light of specific values and migratory experiences of immigrant communities. We are thus confronted with the age-old debate between the universal and the particular: to what extent is it necessary to adapt social work practice? This debate is echoed in current models on the integration of immigrants, which are structured around a civic discourse proposing a form of moral contract between citizens, regardless of their origins. The emphasis on cultural differences, at the forefront of social work models in the 1980s, has shifted towards more universal considerations such as participation and equality. It is in this context that social workers in Quebec practise their profession. This context is explored in greater detail in this chapter. The first part sets out the historical and political framework for understanding immigration in Quebec and examines institutional responses to pluralism. The second section looks more specifically at the positioning of the social worker in this context and some of the intervention tools that facilitate practice with immigrants.

Quebec as a Multi-ethnic Society: A Brief Overview

Quebec, like many other regions of Canada, is increasingly characterized by the multi-ethnic makeup of its population. According to the 1996 census, the number of Quebec residents born outside of Canada represents close to 10 per cent of the total population (Institut de la statistique du Québec, 1999). Pluralism is especially evident in the city of Montreal, which is home to 88 per cent of Quebec's immigrant population (MRCI, 1999). The cosmopolitan character of Montreal is also reflected in the 1996 census, in which 43 per cent of the city's residents declared an origin other than French, British, Canadian, Québécois, or Native (Ville de Montréal, 1998). It would be a mistake, however, to say that pluralism is new to Quebec. On the contrary, the territory of present-day Quebec has been home to a diversity of communities throughout its history. Numerous Native communities, among them the Inuit, the Algonquin, and the Iroquois, inhabited this territory long before the arrival of the Europeans (Dorais, 1992). Even under the French regime, from 1534 to 1760, settlers originating from France came from such linguistically distinct regions that only one-third spoke French as a mother tongue (Trudel, 1973). The others spoke dialects typical of Perche, Poitou, Normandy, and other regions. The arrival of the English, following the British Conquest of 1760, added to this already existing pluralism. Just prior to the American Revolution, in 1776, the population of Canada was approximately 110,000, of which 65,000 were of French origin (Rogel, 1989). Thus, the image of Canada as being a nation of two founding peoples has a long history. Yet, this history masks the fact that numerous other communities occupied the territory of present-day Quebec long before the twentieth century.

The Black community, for instance, has been present in Quebec since the French regime. Most of them slaves, they numbered over one thousand in 1760. Black immigration increased steadily following the American Revolution and throughout the nineteenth and twentieth centuries (Williams, 1998). Irish and Scottish artisans and entrepreneurs, many of whom spoke and traded in French, also formed part of the population of New France. However, the most important wave of Irish and Scottish immigrants arrived between 1815 and 1860, many fleeing poverty and famine in homelands. Political and economic instability in central and eastern Europe during the second half of the nineteenth century also provoked mass migrations from countries such as Russia, Poland, Ukraine, Romania, and Germany. The majority of these European immigrants were Jewish, and there are now very strong Jewish community networks in Quebec. Finally, towards the end of the nineteenth century, Chinese immigrants were recruited as a source of cheap labour for the construction of the railway, victims in many cases of exploitation and discriminatory practices (MAIICC, 1995).

Improved means of transatlantic transportation and communication, increased international trade, and the political upheavals provoked by the two world wars created the conditions for the mass world migrations that marked twentieth-century Quebec. In the early part of the century, Italian and Greek immigrants seeking to improve their life chances settled in Montreal, where many found work in the construction, hospitality, and manufacturing sectors. A second wave of Greek immigrants arrived three decades later, followed in the 1960s by significant migrations from Portugal. Numerically speaking, the Italian, Greek, and Portuguese communities were among the most important to immigrate to Quebec prior to the 1970s, although other groups such as postwar refugees from eastern Europe and immigrants from Haiti and the Caribbean countries of Barbados, Guyana, and Jamaica also arrived during this period (MAIICC, 1995). Like most regions of Canada, immigration patterns have changed dramatically in the past thirty years. While Europe had been a principal source of immigration prior to the 1970s, in recent decades far greater numbers have come from the so-called developing world. According to the 1996 census, 43 per cent of Quebec residents born outside of Canada are of European origin, 25 per cent are from Asia, 22 per cent from the Americas, and 9 per cent from Africa (Institut de la Statistique du Québec, 1999).

Despite the great diversity of communities throughout Quebec's history, their presence has been largely occulted by French–English relations, which have dominated the public scene, both politically and symbolically. Traditionally, new immigrants tended to be closer to the English-speaking community: they lived in predominantly English-speaking neighbourhoods, were employed in work sectors largely controlled by the English-speaking community, and tended to send their children to English-language schools (Levine, 1990; Montgomery and Renaud, 1994; CLF, 1996). Until the 1960s, this situation was just part of the way things worked in Quebec and remained largely unquestioned. But the rise of the nationalist movement in this period challenged the status quo. Symbolized by the slogan 'maîtres chez nous' (masters in our own house), the nationalist movement centred on several fundamental issues: a strengthened Quebec state, an economy controlled by French Canadians (now known as Québécois), and the acknowledgement and promotion of French as the official language of Quebec. At the same time, declining birth rates, increased demand for professional and skilled labour in a growing economy, and the need to ensure the survival of the French language became the impetus for a renewed political project in which new immigrants were to play a central role (Levine, 1990; Rogel, 1989). Since this period, many policies and programs have been adopted in order to foster harmonious relations between francophone and immigrant communities, including language laws, control over the selection of new immigrants, and policy directives on immigration and integration. The term 'integration', used widely in Quebec, has been defined by Perotti as 'a gradual process by which new immigrants become active participants in the economic, social, civic and cultural life of the host country, all the while preserving their own culture' (cited in Gravel & Battaglini, 2000, p. 44).

Of all these policies, perhaps the language laws have received the most attention in past years. The French Language Charter, adopted as Bill 101 in 1977, is certainly the best known of these laws, although it was preceded by Bill 63 in 1969 and Bill 22 in 1974. In addition to affirming the official status of the French language for Quebec society, Bill 101 set up a framework for promoting French-language use in all sectors of public life, including the administrative, public, employment, commercial, and educational sectors (Montgomery, 1998). The language laws were a response to growing concern for the future of the French language in a context where English had become the predominant language in several key sectors of activity, particularly in the economic sphere. In the late 1960s, heated debates on the language of education also drew attention to the anglicization of new immigrants, which further threatened the demographic weight of the French-speaking population. The principal objectives of the laws were global ones: they announced a societal project that acknowledged the historical importance of the 'French fact in America' (Wade, 1968) and that established French as the linking element among the diverse communities that make up Quebec.

Some observers have perceived Bill 101 as a coercive piece of legislation, but it is perhaps better understood as a means of protecting a precious cultural heritage. It should also be emphasized that the recognition and encouragement of cultural diversity is clearly stated in the bill: 'The National Assembly intends to pursue this objective [of francization] in a spirit of justice and openness, in the respect of the institutions of the Quebec community of English expression and those of ethnic minorities' (Preamble, French Language Charter, 1977). Consequently, provisions are made for the protection of English-language institutions and services in Quebec. In the health and social service sector, for instance, there were eighty-four designated English institutions in the public health network in 1995 (CLF, 1996). Although the bill does not give specific protection to ethnic associations or service organizations for new immigrants, a strong existing network serves this clientele, particularly in the community sector. Moreover, since its adoption, the French Language Charter has had a significant impact in terms of the linguistic integration of new immigrants. According to a study undertaken in 1991, for the first time in Quebec's history, French had become a predominant language of use identified by persons whose mother tongue was neither French nor English. More precisely, 45 per cent of these people declared knowing both French and English, 25.4 per cent French only, 22.5 per cent English only, and 6.8 per cent neither of these two languages (CLF, 1996).

Closer relations between francophone and immigrant communities have also been encouraged through changes in the immigrant-selection process. Traditionally, this role belongs to the federal government. Since the 1960s, however, Quebec has acquired significant control over immigration within its territory. Unlike the other Canadian provinces, Quebec has had its own Ministry of Immigration since 1968 and, through a series of Quebec–federal agreements between 1971 and 1991, has acquired increased responsibility for the selection and acceptance of immigrants within its territory (Legault, 2000a). The objective of these agreements was to encourage the selection of immigrants who would be more easily integrated into a society characterized at once by its francophone and multi-ethnic character. At the present time, Quebec retains the exclusive responsibility for selecting independent immigrants and refugees who wish to come to the province and whose applications are processed outside Quebec and for receiving demands for family sponsorship. The responsibility for refugee claimants seeking asylum after having arrived in Quebec remains under federal jurisdiction.

Quebec also retains the responsibility for programs designed to facilitate social, economic, and linguistic integration of new immigrants. Since 1968, a large part of this mandate has been fulfilled by the network of service centres known originally as the Centres d'orientation et de formation des immigrants (COFI), and more recently as Carrefours pour l'intégration, which offer French-language training and practical information sessions on existing resources, day-to-day life in Quebec, and social rights. The government's position on the integration of new immigrants and the adaptation of public institutions to pluralism has also been outlined in two important policy papers: *Autant de façons d'être Québécois* (1981) and *Au Québec pour bâtir ensemble* (1990). All of these measures have a common objective: to foster a relationship between host and immigrant communities that supports and strengthens a societal project in which French is the predominant language of use. This project has also been described as a pluralist one, in which individuals may have multiple sources of identity and yet are united through a single common language (Juteau & McAndrew, 1992). The scope of these global policy orientations extends to all institutions and organizations in the public sector and yet has specific implications for practice with immigrants in the health and social services.

Adaptation of Health and Social Services to Pluralism

Health and social services are key institutions in Canadian society. They are targeted, along with other public institutions, as key domains for social investment. Not only are they present in all stages of our lives, from birth to death, but they are also symbols of our national pride. Public health care systems in Quebec, and in Canada more generally, are cited as being among the best in the world, although the drastic cutbacks of the 1990s are certainly cause for alarm in the future. Like other public sectors of activity, health and social services are not neutral institutions. Instead, it is through these institutions that societal policies and goals are translated from theory into practice. They are both the agents and the barometers of social change and, in this sense, front-line actors in the adaptation of society to pluralism. From this point of view, the very evolution of health and social services in Quebec reflects transformations taking place in society itself with regards to immigration and integration.

Generally speaking, the history of health and social services in Quebec reveals both closure and openness to pluralism. In the nineteenth century, the organization of health and social services reflected a conception of Quebec as a society comprised of two solitudes: the French and the English. Thus were developed the two distinct networks of institutions, divided along ethnolinguistic lines, which are still characteristic of the health sector today. Despite the fact that several other immigrant communities were already established in Quebec during this period, there were few specific services or programs for them within these networks. There were, however, some initiatives set up in the private and community sectors for helping new immigrants. Companies such as the Canadian Pacific Railway, for instance, had their own resources for recruiting immigrant labour, arranging for their immigration papers and even for medical attention when needed. On the community side, some charitable and philanthropic organizations within the Catholic, Protestant, and Jewish communities also offered services to new immigrants. Aside from these isolated initiatives, it would appear that there was otherwise little specific concern for health and social work practice with immigrants during this period (Jacob, 1992).

With increasing public and political awareness for the plight of refugees in the period after the Second World War, some concerted efforts were put into place for facilitating the establishment of new immigrants. The organization of these services also reflected a dualistic conception of Quebec society. On the French side, the Catholic Church created organizations whose specific mandate was to provide support to new immigrants. Thus were established the Centre social d'aide aux immigrants and the Service d'accueil aux voyageurs (SAV) in the 1940s and 1950s. Both organizations provided practical services intended to inform new immigrants of existing resources and introduce to them to Quebec society in general. On the English side, the Traveller's Aid Societies played a similar role (Jacob, 1992; Fiorino, 1996). Despite these initiatives, the idea of adapted services for new immigrants remained relatively marginal in the overall schema of things and had not yet reached the mainstream public institutions.

The Service d'accueil aux voyageurs still exists today, although it has undergone several name changes since its creation in 1955, becoming the Service d'accueil aux voyageurs et aux immigrants (SAVI) in 1961, the Service aux migrants et aux immigrants (SMI) in 1973 and the Service d'aide aux réfugiés et aux immigrants du Montréal métropolitain (SARIMM) in 1993 (Fiorino, 1996). SARIMM is now an integrated regional service in the public health network, where it is a part of the CLSC Côte-des-Neiges. As a public service with expertise in the establishment of new refugees and immigrants, SARIMM remains unique in Quebec.

As was suggested earlier, concern for questions relating to immigration and integration began to emerge only in the late 1960s. This period was also marked by the consolidation and the secularization of the Quebec state and its major institutions, including those in the health and social services sector. An important impetus for change came in 1971, with the implementation of the Castonguay reform on the reorganization of health and social services. Among other things, the reform set up the framework for the creation of a new type of establishment: the Centres locaux de services communautaires (over one hundred in Quebec, including just over thirty in the region of Montreal), more commonly known by their acronym, CLSC. In providing front-line services inspired by a more community-based approach to health and social care, these establishments were intended to improve accessibility to services for the general population. Although the reform made no explicit mention of pluralism (Jacob, 1992), the CLSCs have nonetheless played a key role in terms of services to new immigrants, particularly those situated in multi-ethnic neighbourhoods (Sévigny & Tremblay, 1999). Some of these institutions have acquired an important expertise in terms of practice with new immigrants.

During the 1970s, there were no specific policy guidelines on questions relating to practice with immigrants. This expertise was developed largely through direct experience in the field. A study by Roy (1991), for instance, demonstrated the way in which practitioners in a Montreal social service centre incorporated their experiential knowledge of interaction with immigrant clients in their intervention models. Drawing on their field experience, they developed techniques enabling them to adapt to new situations, such as practice with immigrants. In this process of adaptation, the practitioners become in some ways what we may call 'knowledge builders', in the sense of exercising an implicit knowledge in their patterns of action (Schön, 1983, p. 49).

In addition to this experiential knowledge, societal guidelines and plans of action on immigration and integration have become one of the trademarks of Quebec social policy since the 1970s. The two policy papers mentioned earlier— *Autant de façons d'être Québécois* (1981) and *Au Québec pour bâtir ensemble* (1990)—had implications for all sectors of public activity, although the health and social services were targeted as a particularly important sector for action. In the 1981 policy paper, the guidelines were organized around two axes: the accessibility of services to a multi-ethnic clientele, and their adaptation to the specific needs of this population (MCCI, 1981). Several other initiatives and measures dealing with these themes were also put into place during this period (Legault, 2000a). In 1981, the Comité pour l'implantation du plan d'accès à l'égard des communautés culturelles (CIPACC) examined questions relating to the accessibility of services. Shortly thereafter, a pressure group consisting of fifty member organizations was created in order to defend the rights of access to health and social services for new immigrants. This committee still exists today under the name ACCESSS (Alliance des communautés culturelles pour l'égalité dans la santé et les services sociaux). In 1987, the themes of accessibility and adaptation of the health and social services were also examined at length in two government commissioned reports (Sirros, 1987; Bibeau, 1987).

The second policy paper on immigration and integration, *Au Québec pour bâtir ensemble*, in 1990, was structured around three principal themes: the right to participate in society, the struggle against inequalities, and the use of French as the common public language. While this policy also addressed the themes of accessibility and adaptation, it went significantly further in drawing attention to the inequalities faced by new immigrants and to systemic barriers to integration (Jacob, 1992). The difference in emphasis between the two policies is not only incidental; it reflects a fundamental transformation in the way of thinking about pluralism, integration, and social intervention. This transformation can be described as a movement from a culturalist model to a social contract model and, more recently, to a citizenship model.

Three Visions of Integration and Their Implications for Social Work with Immigrants

With the adoption of the first policy on immigration and integration in 1981, *Autant de façons d'être Québécois*, the notion of culture became the dominant organizing theme for social work practice with immigrants (Jacob, 1992). Hence, the use during this period of the term 'cultural communities' to designate the diverse populations living in Quebec. A few years earlier, it was this term that had announced the changing orientation of the then Ministry of Immigration of Quebec, which became the Ministry of Cultural Communities and Immigration (MCCI) in 1978.

According to the culturalist model, an adequate response to the health and psychosocial needs of the 'cultural communities' required a sound understanding of the cultural universe in which they were situated. *Culture* here referred to the value and belief systems belonging to the different immigrant communities.

With the objective of introducing health and social practitioners to the distinct needs of this clientele, a series of training programs were set up to examine the specific traits and characteristics of the 'cultural communities' (Vietnamese, Haitian, Greek, and so on). During this same period, a number of ethnic associations and organizations were also created to respond to the particular needs of their respective communities. Social work practice with immigrants in this model was structured around the idea of cultural differences. Thus, practice was to be adapted to the values and traits considered distinct from one 'cultural community' to another.

Since the end of the 1980s, the culturalist model has been increasingly called into question (Juteau, 1999). In part, this is attributable to the notion of culture itself and the static way in which it had been defined throughout much of this period as a fixed set of beliefs and values. Cultural communities had been conceived as being homogeneous groupings of individuals, yet it was increasingly evident that this was not so. Theoretical work in the field of ethnic relations drew attention to the dynamic character of ethnicity and identity construction (Juteau, 1999; McAll, 1994; Meintel, 1993). In this work, cultural beliefs and values were conceived of as being products of social processes that evolved across time and according to different contexts. Consequently, the defining characteristics of any given cultural community were not considered as being fixed, but rather as having fluid boundaries. Also, increasing emphasis was placed on the acknowledgement that individuals have multiple forms of identity. In terms of social work practice, this means understanding an individual not only in terms of a strictly ethnic or cultural identity, but also in terms of other forms of belonging, such as socio-economic status, age, sex, professional or educational background, and so on.

From this point of view, there is no one single Vietnamese (or Indian, or Québécois, or Haitian) culture, but rather a continuum of variants depending on a multitude of factors and contexts. The underlying objective of this critique was to avoid 'ethnicizing' health and social issues. The critique also served as a reminder that there are no clear-cut recipes in social work practice with immigrant communities—or any other population for that matter. Overall, the idea was not so much to dispense with the notion of culture altogether, but rather to work towards a more dynamic and complex understanding of health and social issues as being the product of multiple determinants.

The renewed debate on pluralism, which corresponds in part with the adoption of the second policy on immigration and integration in 1990, *Au Québec pour bâtir ensemble*, placed less emphasis on cultural differences than on the acknowledgement of common difficulties faced by many new immigrants as a group. Predominance was given to systemic barriers rather than to cultural ones. While barriers against access remained part of the ongoing debate on social work practice, the reflection also went much further, addressing other types of barriers faced by many new immigrants—inadequate housing and work conditions, exclusion and discrimination—that can hinder long-term life chances. In an attempt to draw attention to the social issues underlying the migration experience, several studies during this period examined the obstacles encountered by new immigrants and refugees (Bertot & Jacob, 1991; Renaud, Carpentier, Ouimet, & Montgomery, 1992; McAll, 1996; Renaud & Gingras, 1998). Furthermore, the obstacles encountered were not seen just as markers of the immigrant condition, but rather as the product of unequal relations between the host society and its minority communities. Whereas training programs in the 1980s were intended to introduce practitioners to different 'cultures', new training models in the universities place greater emphasis on the immigrant experience in a much broader perspective: the context and causes of international migrations; the history of immigration in Canada and Quebec and the socio-political conditions of immigrant selection; the description and critique of immigration policies; the description and critique of dominant ideologies with respect to social integration; the specific situation of refugees and refugee claimants; the mechanisms of inclusion and exclusion of new immigrants; the accessibility and adaptation of health and social services; and other global social issues relating to immigration and integration (Legault, 2000b).

The idea of a social contract, used to describe this second model, is based on the tacit recognition of the rights and responsibilities of all and the ideal of a free and equal society, as set out in the Charter of Rights and Freedoms. There is, thus, a social contract between the host community and new immigrants, and between practitioners and clients. From this point of view, social work practice intervenes not only in a cultural dimension, but also in other dimensions, such as social inequalities. It is not so much cultural differences that become the organizing axis of social work practice with immigrants, but rather the complex weave of relationships, equal and unequal, in which the individual is situated as well as the multiple identities that she or he carries. Generally speaking, the social contract model is more reform-oriented than the culturalist model that characterized the 1980s.

Since the late 1990s, a new model has emerged, in which the 'citizen' is a key actor. The name change from the Ministry of Cultural Communities and Immigration (MCCI) to the Ministry of Relations with Citizens and Immigration (MRCI) in 1996 is itself indicative of a movement towards a citizenship model. While there is little documentation available on this model in the health and social service sector, there has been some reflection on the theme in the educational sector. In many ways, this model would seem to be an extension of the social contract model in that it places particular emphasis on rights and responsibilities. Additionally, it is based on the adherence of members of the society to shared core values such as the promotion of equal opportunity, the use of French as the common public language, and the respect of basic human rights (MEC, 1998).

Whereas the culturalist and social contract models targeted new immigrants as a specific population with specific needs, the citizenship model tends more towards a conception of the 'universal citizen', referring to all members of a society independent of origin or immigration status. In so doing, this model avoids a certain polarization of society into 'ethnics' and 'the rest'. One of the advantages of such an approach is that it avoids some of the more negative aspects related to targeting vulnerable populations. From this point of view, for instance, new immigrants are not singled out as a 'problem' population. Sometimes such labelling, while meant well, may in fact reinforce societal stereotypes. Nonetheless, there is a risk that the obstacles faced by some segments of the population (immigrant or other) may be masked or hidden behind the ideal of the universal citizen as free and equal, creating the illusion that there are no special needs. It is too early yet to see what direction this model might take. At the same time, it is not too late to propose that a more critical understanding of this model must acknowledge that certain categories of the population, such as new immigrants, are sometimes excluded from the basic rights of participation normally afforded by citizenship (McAll, 1995). Like the social contract model, the implications for social work practice from this perspective would mean working towards the inclusion of members of society who face barriers to integration.

These models of integration propose global frameworks for the organization of services in a multi-ethnic context. In this sense, they are ideals of practice. In day-to-day activity, however, practitioners need tools that enable them to negotiate between the ideals of what should be and the complex reality of what is. This process of negotiation is further explored in the next section, both in relation to the positioning of the practitioner in intercultural practice and the tools used in day-to-day practice.

Reflexivity in Action: Intercultural Practice and the Positioning of the Practitioner

Social work involves many actors—the practitioner, the client, the institution, and the society—each of which adds to the complexity of practice. The greatest challenge lies in the ability to integrate and make sense of such disparate elements. Thus, social work practitioners often find themselves at the forefront of complex, multidimensional realities. How do they go about helping their clients solve their problems? This question is even more relevant given that the situations they encounter, particularly in practice with immigrants, are often new and difficult to assess in terms of their own life experiences. What is needed is a certain 'reflexivity in action'—that is, the ability to distance oneself from practice, to reflect on interaction situations in order to build a knowledge arising from the action itself. Essentially, social workers try to link practice, theory, and research into one system (Schön, 1983, p. 303).

In Quebec, this introspection has taken place largely in relation to the development and evolution of what has been called an intercultural approach to practice. The term 'intercultural' itself emerged in the 1970s in opposition to the multiculturalism of English Canada. In the multiculturalism model, minority communities are encouraged to develop and express the specificity of their cultures and institutions. From this model stems the idea of a mosaic of multiple communities, distinct from one another, yet cohabiting the same territorial space. Although Quebec inter-culturalism maintains the idea of promoting minority communities, these communities are seen as being linked on another level through a common language and shared civic values. Despite the stated differences between the two models, several authors have suggested that they often tend, in practice, to designate the same thing (McAndrew, 1995; Legault, 2000a). Nonetheless, the intercultural approach as developed in Quebec does have specific implications with respect to practice.

Generally speaking, the intercultural approach to practice emphasizes a reciprocal relationship between practitioner and client. This reciprocity, as Maalouf (1998) suggests, is a prerequisite to openness: 'In order to advance resolutely toward the other, you need to have your arms open and hold your head high, and you can only open your arms if you hold your head high' (p. 60). The fundamental elements behind reciprocity are trust and respect, without which no successful encounter or intercultural interaction can take place. Whatever the linguistic barriers, trust and respect are built up through countless little gestures, empathy, healthy curiosity, home visits. Thus, 'the more a practitioner gets to know a person in their natural surroundings, . . . the greater the tendency for the practitioner to call upon a wide range of factors to explain his or her situation: isolation, poverty, violence, working conditions, family relationships, housing conditions, state of health' (McAll, Tremblay, & LeGoff, 1997, p. 95). As a result, the intervention model is based on an all-embracing, multidimensional understanding of the social situations experienced by immigrants and refugees throughout their integration process (Bertot & Jacob, 1991; McAll, Tremblay, & LeGoff, 1997). From this point of view, the predominantly culturalist explanations of the 1980s, as described earlier, become just one contributing factor among others in accounting for any intervention situation. Intervention, then, must take into account the complexity of identity construction, which draws on multiple types of affiliations, such as language, age, beliefs, lifestyle, family relationships, artistic taste, influences of origin, profession, social milieu, sexual affinities, personal developments, on so on.

The complexity of identity construction applies not only to the client, but also to the practitioner. Whether from Quebec or elsewhere, the social practitioner is not outside of social relationships, but rather has national, religious, and regional affiliations and belongs to a certain social class, a professional category, and an institution. The internalization of all these forms of belonging defines and orients the professional relationship with clients. As members of the majority group in Quebec, for instance, French-speaking social work practitioners may be tempted to exert 'assimilation pressure' (Sterlin, 1988, p. 22), given the paradoxical context of finding themselves in a situation of being both a majority (in Quebec) and a minority (in Canada). In some cases, this paradoxical relationship may become the backdrop for a practitioner–client relationship in which the 'other's' culture, country, and religion are the object of assessment, while the culture and history of the practitioner remain unquestioned. Social workers need to be aware of this situation and to be capable of maintaining sufficient distance from their own group memberships that these do not interfere in the intervention process. It also means seeing migration in a new light and acknowledging that we are all migrants of sorts, social worker and client alike, whether born in Quebec or elsewhere. The challenge that we as a society and as practitioners must take up is to assume our identity, complete with our complex history, while at the same time allowing different identities in our society to flourish alongside.

The theme of identity also leads us to question a fairly widespread tendency in practice with immigrants, which consists of pairing social workers and clients of the same ethnic origin or, alternatively, in relying on a cultural broker to assist in a practitioner's interventions. This process has been described by Weinfeld (1999) as 'ethnic matching'. It is sometimes taken for granted that a practitioner of the same ethnic background ('homo-ethnic') as the client is in a better position to practise in 'their community' and to provide explanations for its specific characteristics. It is also assumed that the cultural broker will furnish information and insights that will help to unravel complicated situations. This may be true in some cases. Naturally, the homo-ethnic practitioner has a linguistic advantage, in the same way that the cultural interpreter is familiar with the culture of origin. This knowledge, however, should not be taken as an automatic guarantee for success in dealing with certain complex situations. The homo-ethnic practitioner may run the risk of getting trapped in relationships of similarities and allegiance. There is also a question of the positioning of both the practitioner and the client with respect to other forms of belonging, such as personal history, age, generation, migration, and education. Sometimes the proximity between the broker and the client is too great, given that they are members of common social groups, particularly in small cities or small communities. Such situations may in turn inhibit client communication or cultural mediation, thus limiting effective social work practice. In other words, ethnic culture does not determine all choices that an individual makes. One has only to think of all the Algerians, Tamils, Pakistanis, Indians, Congolese, Afghans, Serbs, Chinese, Kurds, and others, newly arrived, 'interpreted' by someone who is of the same origin but who has lived in Quebec for many years or was born there, who belongs to another social class or another generation, who has not experienced political conflicts or family separation. Additionally, many homo-ethnic practitioners and cultural interpreters have studied at Western institutions, so they may very likely use the very same schemas of reference as their Quebec colleagues to understand the specific realities of their ex-compatriots. Thus, although ethnic matching may be beneficial in many cases, it is not a panacea. Practice with immigrants demands a certain capacity to transcend not only one's own ethnocultural affiliation (Québécois or other) but also stereotyped frameworks of reference for interpreting ways of saying and being.

Complementary Models and Intervention Tools: Intercultural Practice in Quebec

Do the above considerations mean that there is an underlying sameness to all social issues, that there are no differences in the way in which social workers handle their interventions with people coming from other cultural universes? Should they aim for social homogeneity by reducing differences? Absolutely not. What we have insisted on so far is the need to include variables other than ethnicity when defining the problems of immigrant populations, and not to try and explain everything by ethnocultural differences.

Those who have left their countries, whether of their own free will or not, have special characteristics that must be taken into account in the evaluation process and in intervention plans. Immigration is a very personal project, sustained by a strong motivation and a deep-seated desire for change. The decision to immigrate must be placed in the political, familial, and historical context that determines the project and for which the immigrant makes enormous sacrifices. 'The migratory project is also the idea of developing the person's potential, to assume his or her own identity in order to rise beyond such limits as poverty, environment, family and social class' (Cohen-Émérique, 1989, p. 84). For some, such as political refugees, there is no migration project as such: they make a total break, abandon all hope of ever returning, and, consequently, experience a grief that has to be worked through. Another characteristic of the special needs of the immigrant that social workers must bear in mind is the status of immigrants in the host country: despite the prevailing discourses of equal rights for all, it is clear that unequal relations exist in many spheres of daily life.

All of these dimensions may play a significant role in ascertaining the needs of new immigrants. Several specific models and tools, complementary to the intercultural approach, have been developed in recent years and have found wide use in Quebec. The interweaving of some of the elements of these various models has created an original composite approach to practice with immigrants.

The French psychologist Cohen-Émérique (1993), for instance, has developed many training sessions for professionals in Quebec's social services. For Cohen-Émérique, the intercultural approach is first and foremost a question of the care relation and of attitude; it is based on respect for the person and for individual world visions and value systems. Care relations, whether intercultural or not, are all built on the same foundations. However, the multiple facets of cultural identity—ethnicity, nationality, region, religion, social class—give a special colour to this approach. Another important aspect of the intercultural approach is that of interaction between two people, each with their own identities and values. Thus, the focus is not solely on 'the other', the client, the immigrant, but also on the subjectivity of the practitioner. The interaction between the two actors becomes the determining element. For Cohen-Émérique, three interrelated stages mark this interaction: the 'decentring' or defining of one's own identity; the penetration of the other's system of reference; and the process of negotiation and mediation between systems of reference.

Bertot and Jacob (1991) emphasize the life situations of refugees and immigrants. From this perspective, living and working conditions, reactions to the host society, communication codes, and group memberships should all be included in any analysis undertaken by a social service agency or social practitioner. These authors believe that by using a strictly psychosocial model of intervention with an immigrant and refugee clientele, a practitioner tends to neglect the influence of social and economic factors affecting their lives. Thus, this intervention model comprises several dimensions: helping clients come to terms with their migration trajectories; aiding in the discovery of personal models for change and fostering awareness of personal capacities for integration; adapting to individual learning styles; working with family support networks; and helping individuals to alter their expectations with regard to new family situations. Generally speaking, this approach consists of juggling the dynamics of social relationships of immigrants, linking their pasts and their futures.

Other researchers (Green, 1982; Devore & Schlesinger, 1981; Lum, 1986) have elaborated models and concepts contributing to a larger acceptance of the cross-cultural sensitivity in social work practice. All these models can be seen as keys to opening multiple universes of perceptions, ways of speaking and of being. The different models employed in Quebec at present share many common features, such as the emphasis placed on the positioning of the practitioner and the client as carriers of cultures and histories, and on the importance of taking into account structural data and characteristics of the host society. After years of reflection, debate, and experimentation, we can say that intervention has reached a certain maturity with regard to diversity. What must be kept in mind is the importance of minimizing differences, consolidating social links, and striving for intercultural convergence in intervention. The models used for interpreting problems are constantly revised, efforts must be made to refine concepts better adapted to today's socio-political realities, and thought must be given to the intervention process. Furthermore, these models and concepts are combined with elements of practice in order to create intervention tools for navigating the twists and turns of practice.

The term *intervention tool* is used here in the sense of an instrument designed to apply the major parameters of an intercultural approach to situations of practice. These parameters can be summarized in terms of knowledge and understanding of the other; acceptance of differences, beginning with a reflection about one's own identity and collective history; openness towards diverse values; integration of factors related to the migratory context; and acknowledgement of the interdependence of a person's needs (Roy, 1993). An intervention tool is never complete; rather, it provides a means of understanding at least some parts of highly complex realities. Moreover, this complexity justifies the need for the complementary development and use of a diversity of intervention tools, which enable social practitioners to deal with a wide range of situations. Four such intervention tools are the set of intercultural assessment guidelines, the genogram, the autobiographical narrative, and the case discussion protocol.

Intercultural Assessment Guidelines

The intercultural assessment guidelines (Figure 6.1), based largely on the work of Cohen-Émérique (1984, 1989, 1991, 1993), set out the principles for assessing situations and problems encountered by individuals whose cultural codes and life

Figure 6.1   Intercultural Assessment Guidelines

Objectives:
- Integrate the psychosocial dimensions of migration and exile into the assessment of intervention situations
- Provide a comprehensive framework of analysis for a culturally sensitive intervention

1. Migration context
- *Pre-migratory context*

Context in the country of origin. Feelings about leaving the country. Dreams about the new country before leaving. Way in which new country was imagined. Perception of social success in the context of migration. Emigration project the result of a family decision or decided by just one family member. Changes aspired to. Traumas affecting departure. Brutal exodus in tragic conditions. Residence in other countries along the way. Time spent in a refugee camp. Help offered during process of departure.

- *Post-migratory context*

Context in the host country. Existing support networks or acquaintances in period of arrival. Conditions of arrival. Time of the year. Significant emotional break made. Individual's financial situation.

- *Plans to return to home country*

Reality or myth. Possible or impossible. Perception of being here 'just for a while'.

- *Lifestyle in home country*

Significance of family: type of family, hierarchical relations, tribal or caste membership. Employment in country of origin. Social class. Political, social, or other involvement: the individual, other members of family, tribe, or clan. Ethnic group membership. Minority status in home country. Religious affiliation and practice.

2. Immigration status
Applicant for refugee status. Refugee. Permanent resident. Sponsored. Other.

3. Investigation into beliefs, world views, values
Type of authority in the family. Each person's role. Types of beliefs and values. Perception of humanity, problems, destiny, happiness, human relations, society. What is the importance of the group in relation to the individual? How do people prefer to come into contact with each other?

4. Group memberships and use of this network
Friends or acquaintances belonging to the same tribe, clan, community. Membership in a well-established cultural community. Allegiances of the community. Member or outsider within community of origin. Network of significant relations (including those who have died). Participation in groups of people sharing the same ethnic origin.

5. Definition of the situation
Client's perception of the problem. Practitioner's perception of the problem. Client often accompanied by a fellow group member. Cultural shocks experienced. Situations that make client feel uncomfortable. Perception of the practitioner and the institution or community group from which services are offered. Difference between client's language and culture and those of the host country. Solutions the client has identified as being useful.

6. Identification of areas of vulnerability
People seeking refugee status, sponsored, no longer sponsored. Inversion of traditional roles. Grieving to be done. Refusal by the Immigration Board. Guilt and anxiety about those who remained behind. Giving birth in the host country. Learning a new language. Drastic changes in living conditions. Cramped living quarters and many people crowded together. Climatic changes and impact on daily life.

Roy, 1996 (based on the work of Cohen-Émérique: 1984, 1989, 1991, 1993).

histories are completely foreign to the practitioner. The purpose of this set of guidelines is to explain behaviours, deduce meaning from life events, trace the origin of problems, and direct the client towards appropriate sources of assistance. It was constructed as a means of gaining access to the client's cultural universe and personal history, drawing on the premises of intercultural intervention more generally. Thus, this tool introduces a framework for a 'culturally sensitive' approach to practice, incorporating pyschosocial dimensions of migration and exile into the assessment of the life situations themselves: pre- and post-migratory contexts; knowledge of the individual's expectations of the host country; lifestyle and conditions in the country of origin; interaction between the client and the practitioner; and family structure, social class, and other contextual variables. Generally speaking, these guidelines serve to contextualize the migratory process in order to better grasp factors of cultural difference and to prevent situations of social exclusion and misunderstanding.

The flexible use of guidelines such as these can help the practitioner to adapt social work practice to different immigrant populations by identifying sources of potential misunderstanding, by creating an opportunity for sharing and getting to know one another, and by acknowledging differences without stigmatizing them.

The Genogram

A *genogram* is a much-used tool among anthropologists and has been borrowed readily by social work practitioners for intervention purposes. Its objective is to trace relationships within families: full-blood relatives, relations by marriage, filiation. It is widely recognized that clienteles of different geographic and ethnocultural origins often have values and experiences very remote from our usual points of reference. The family structure can represent an area of potential major misunderstanding. It is essential to put aside the limiting concepts of the nuclear family, the two-parent family, and a strictly biological sense of filiation, and think instead in terms of extended family, clan, tribe, multiple wives, and other social variables.

The genogram, which can be used at the beginning of or during an intervention process, provides a means of encouraging the client to talk. It enables an individual client or an entire family to reconstruct relationships in time and space, through the recounting of events that have happened to relatives. In addition, the genogram gives the social worker an opportunity to work closely with the client in seeking solutions and explanations while at the same time creating a certain complicity between them. Furthermore, this complicity forms the basis for building a relationship of trust, without which a social link cannot be guaranteed. In such a context, the client, as the recipient of the intervention process, becomes the best guide for explaining individual differences and needs (Brault, 2000).

Autobiographical Narrative

Another intervention tool, adopted from ethnology, is the autobiographical narrative (Figure 6.2). In practice, social workers are always listening to stories or fragments of people's lives. Cohen-Émérique (1991) argues that these stories can be

Figure 6.2   Analytical framework used for an autobiographical narrative

1. Observation of the family environment
   • Arrangement of the room, decoration, meaningful objects

2. Observation of the person and search for meanings in relation to cultural roots, the acculturation process, the degree of identification with majority norms, tensions and conflicts encountered:
   • Physical appearance
   • Non-verbal language: postures, tics, gestures, actions, etc.
   • Verbal language: tone of voice, pronunciation, use of certain expressions, words or themes

3. Analysis of the autobiographical narrative at three levels:
   • Event-based or diachronic level
   • Socio-cultural or synchronic level
   • Psychological level: both diachronic and synchronic

4. Exploration of the dynamics of the interview and the way in which conflicts between different social codes and individual needs are integrated

5. Reflection about the changes required in professional practice and the new knowledge learned in the interview in which the grid was applied

(Cohen-Émérique, 1991, based on the work of Abou: 1986)

used in the intervention process, enabling the client to find meaning in the events that have occurred and, consequently, to create some kind of coherence in situations that, at first glance, seem disorganized. Generally speaking, autobiographical narrative is a form of conversation analysis, which is already an integral part of the practitioner's work, manifested in such activities as listening and reinterpreting requests for help. This intervention tool, adapted from the work of Selim Abou (1986), seeks to discover the social environment as perceived subjectively by the client and to accompany the client in the process of identity reconstruction. It is complementary to the genogram in that it, too, represents a constant interweaving of collective and individual elements, creating a fabric in which social phenomena are seen in both their subjective and structural dimensions.

In concrete terms, the client's conversation is analysed by means of three readings. The first reading corresponds to the establishment of an event history that identifies the chronological succession of events at a given time in the person's life. The second is a thematic reading, which is constructed by the client and relates to his or her life cycle. The thematic reading provides insight into cultural values and social norms, which may be in obvious confrontation with those of the mainstream. There is also the possibility that new models of behaviour and thought processes emerge from the contact of the two cultures. The third reading is a symbolic one, which includes both chronological and thematic aspects and which attempts to understand the impact of social and cultural constraints on the individual's life trajectory. In the interview itself, the practitioner asks the client to describe experiences in different life situations. Throughout this process, several themes may be addressed, such as social roles, family and/or professional status, group membership, and family structures. Thus, individual experience is closely linked to social background and context.

The advantage of this particular intervention tool is that it enables the practitioner to identify personal adaptation strategies developed by clients in order to resolve or overcome conflicts, handle paradoxical situations, discover meanings attributed to events, and share these with the persons concerned.

Case Discussion Protocol

At some point in their careers, social practitioners have all had an opportunity to present a case or sit in on a case discussion initiated by a colleague. They are therefore well aware of what such an exercise implies in terms of systematizing data so as to reach a maximum of clarity and offer valid guidelines. How do they avoid emphasizing one element over another? How do they avoid bias or hasty judgments? Have some practitioners ever felt uncomfortable faced with the volume of information generated, their own incapacity to remember it all, and the obligation to impose some order in the tangled collection of data?

It often seems as if the interpretation tools used by professionals offer only a partial understanding of the complex reality of social problems. This is why it is so important to have tools for interpreting and decoding reality that incorporate the notion of complexity. The case discussion protocol was developed with the objective of facilitating the systematization of information generated in a practitioner–client relationship. This protocol incorporates the idea of complexity, as developed by the sociologist Morin (1991), who denounces the mutilation of reality by knowledge simplification. Firmly believing in the dynamic character, and seeming disorder, of real-life situations, he insists on the need to observe the interplay between the different elements and various actors involved. The protocol was also inspired by Cohen-Émérique (1984), who emphasizes the need to observe differentiating cultural signals, social filters and screens, and distortions in the attribution of meanings, and to identify areas of vulnerability. This is where the proposed case discussion protocol, designed to take into account the myriad dimensions of a given situation, is most useful to social workers, who are usually stuck with organizational models offering simplified responses to complex requests for their services. Case discussion is currently used by social workers to illustrate a situation or problem, justify an orientation, or seek their colleagues' opinions. It involves presenting a case without emphasizing more on one aspect than on another, without being partial, without 'forgetting' elements deemed unimportant, and without becoming trapped in categories.

An intercultural approach to problems obliges practitioners to be open to a client's many differences while remaining highly aware of their own. Since each individual embodies a culture, a world view, and a system of values, what happens when two individuals meet? What happens when one of them is experiencing difficulties relating to cultural differences and a host of other things? Is it possible to take account of all this in a case discussion? The practitioner, like the client, is not excluded from social relationships, and has multiple affiliations. Using figure 6.3, the practitioner first presents a situation in all its dimensions, according to his or her personal frame of reference—filters, definition of the situation, and identification of areas capable of triggering crises. The practitioner then describes the client's frame of reference—filters, definitions of the situation, sensitive areas as defined by the client. In Figure 6.3, the sensitive areas, or those containing elements that could produce a crisis, are examples only and need to be adapted to the context of each situation.

The diagram presented in Figure 6.3 was designed with the objective of reaching a complex definition of the problem. This definition results from practitioners distancing themselves from their personal frame of reference while at the same time seeking the frame of reference of the person needing help. A 'co-definition' of the problem emerges from this process. In a world like ours, obsessed with categorization and labelling of all kinds, it is not an exaggeration to base our principles on this notion of complexity. However, it does present a challenge: how to develop

Figure 6.3   Diagram of a case discussion protocol

Practitioner's frame of references	Filters	Areas of vulnerability	Filters	Client's frame of references
practitioner: age, sex, language	perception and ideas conveyed by public services	childbirth in foreign country	perception of public services	client: age, sex, language
religion, family, region of origin, country		death in foreign country or country of origin		religion, family, region of origin, country
past social class, present social class	perception of immigrants and refugees	role inversion in the family	perception of host country	past social class, present social class, socio-politic status, occupation in country of origin
		"adultification" of one child because of his role as interpreter or else		
	values and beliefs	family violence	values and beliefs	
socio-political context, colonized/ex-colonized, Western/non-Western, majority/minority	etc.	sexual abuse	etc.	socio-political context in country of origin, colonized/ex-colonized, Western/non-Western, majority/minority
		unemployement		
		precarious socio-economic conditions		
		etc.		
Problem as defined in terms of the practitioner's frame of reference				**Problem as defined in terms of the client's frame of reference**

Problem as defined by the practitioner and the client following the decentering stage aimed at gaining access to other's frame of reference

(Roy, 2000, based on the work of Morris: 1991, and Cohen-Émérique: 1984)

a wide variety of approaches to be able to cope with the host of presenting situations. The challenge becomes even more daunting when we consider that social, health care, and other services, including education, are structured around details, divided opinions, standardizing normative frameworks, and simplified indicators of efficiency.

In the preceding discussion, we have identified four intervention tools, although a large number of alternative tools have also been developed by practitioners and researchers: the differential adaptation grid (Sterlin, 1988), which draws attention to variations in adaptation routes; photo-novels based on life situations (Falcon, 1994); the systemic reading of migratory processes (Barudy, 1992); identity strategies, which describe different integration manoeuvres used by immigrants (Malewska-Peyre & Gachon, 1988). In all cases, these intervention tools are designed to obtain a better understanding of intercultural problems and to minimize the distance between theory and practice. In the intervention process itself, they can also act as catalysts for intercultural exchanges between the practitioner and the client. They thus represent a way for the practitioner to work in close collaboration with the client in a common attempt to overcome communication difficulties and reach a mutual understanding.

Conclusion: Intercultural Social Work in the Specific Context of Quebec

Policy planners and social work practitioners in Quebec are increasingly aware of the heterogeneity of the general population and of the special needs of recent immigrants (Gravel & Battaglini, 2000). In the 1970s, this clientele was designated by the term 'cultural communities'. The political context was then one of cultural convergence, and there was a strong tendency to act almost exclusively through the prism of culture—the client's culture, of course. In the 1990s, government policy on the establishment of new immigrants and refugees placed more emphasis on individual integration and social inequality than on cultural differences, thus reflecting changes taking place in society itself, particularly in key intervention sectors such as social work. This orientation, which draws on a civic discourse, encourages the active participation of new immigrants in Quebec society, without reducing individuals to their strictly ethnic particularities. Such an orientation represents a significant transformation in terms of practice with immigrants; it answers the critics of the Quebec government who reproached it for failing to take account of economic conditions, political issues, racism, discrimination, and the migratory processes in its integration policies.

This transformation is also manifest in the development of new intervention models that extend the range of factors to be considered in practice with immigrants. In acknowledging the reciprocity of the practitioner–client relationship, these models also encourage a new openness in which both actors benefit mutually from one another's social codes, values, cultures, and histories. This openness facilitates the intervention relationship, which can only be enriched by this new conception of integration. Despite this openness, intercultural intervention in Quebec retains a paradoxical element: a balance must be found between respect for the specific history of the majority group and accommodation in terms of the values and realities of recent immigrants.

If this search for balance is to succeed, the two parties have a shared responsibility for reconciling particularities and constructing links. At the same time, the pluralism that is found in Quebec does not apply exclusively to the ethnocultural or religious diversity resulting from immigration, but should be understood in all its extended meaning in terms of multiple forms of belonging.

References

Abou, S. (1986). *L'identité culturelle*. Paris: Éditions anthropos.

Barudy, J. (1992). Différentes modalités adaptatives des familles immigrées. Unpublished paper.

Berthelot, J. (1990). *Apprendre à vivre ensemble*. Montreal: Centrale d'enseignement du Québec.

Bertot, J., & Jacob, A. (1991). *Intervenir avec les immigrants et les réfugiés*. Montreal: Méridien.

Bibeau, G. (1985). *Des pratiques différenciées de la santé*. Traité d'anthropologie médicale, l'institution de la santé et de la maladie. Montreal: Presses Universitaires du Québec.

———. (1987). *À la fois d'ici et d'ailleurs: les communautés culturelles du Québec dans leurs rapports aux services sociaux et aux services de santé*. Montreal: Commission d'enquête sur les services de santé et les services sociaux.

Bisaillon, H. (1989). *L'accessibilité des services aux communautés culturelles. Les résultats de la consultation du personnel du CSSMM*. Montreal: Centre de services sociaux du Montréal métropolitain.

Bouthillette, J. (1989). *Le Canadien français et son double*. Montreal: l'Hexagone.

Brault, M. (2000). Le génogramme: un outil d'intervention auprès des réfugiés. In G. Legault (Ed.), *Intervention interculturelle* (pp. 203–21). Montreal: Gaëtan Morin.

Chiasson-Lavoie, M. (Ed.) (1992). *L'approche interculturelle auprès de réfugiés et de nouveaux immigrants*. Montreal: Centre de services sociaux du Montréal métropolitain.

CLSC Côte-des-Neiges. (2000). *Projet jeunesse montréalais: État de situation locale*. CLSC Côte-des-Neiges.

Cohen-Émérique, M. (1984). Choc culturel et relations interculturelles dans la pratique des travailleurs sociaux. *Cahiers de sociologie économique et culturelle, 2*, 183–218.

———. (1989). Travailleurs sociaux et migrants: La reconnaissance identitaire dans le processus d'aide. In C. Camilleri & M. Cohen-Émérique (Eds), *Chocs de culture* (pp. 77–117). Paris: l'Harmattan.

————. (1991). Le récit autobiographique: approche universelle et accès à la connaissance d'un milieu. *Intercultures, 13*, 131–6.

————. (1993). L'approche interculturelle dans le processus d'aide. *Santé mentale au Québec, 17*(1), 71–92.

Conseil de la langue française (CLF). (1996). *Le français langue commune.* Enjeu de la société québécoise. Quebec: Direction des communications.

Devore, W., & Schlesinger, E. (1987). *Ethnic-sensitive Social Work Practice.* Colombus, OH: Merrill Publishing Company.

Dorais, L.J. (1992). Les langues autochtones d'hier à aujourd'hui. In J. Maurais (Ed.), *Les langues autochtones du Québec* (pp. 63–91). Quebec: Publications du Québec.

Falcon, G. (1994). Un photo-roman: outil de pratique interculturelle. *Intervention, 97*, 28–32.

Fiorino, G. (1996). SAVI . . . SMI . . . SARIMM . . . Quarante ans d'intervention sociale auprès des non-résidents, des immigrants et des réfugiés. *Intervention,103*, 48–56.

Gouvernement du Québec (1997). Charte de la langue Française. Quebec: Editeur official du Québec.

Gravel, S., & Battaglini, A. (2000). *Culture, santé et ethnicité: vers une santé publique pluraliste.* Montreal: Régie régionale de la santé et des services sociaux de Montréal-Centre.

Green, J.W. (1982). Cultural Awareness in the human services. Englewood Cliffs, NJ: Prentice-Hall.

Institut de la statistique du Québec. (1999). *La statistique démographique au Québec, bilan 1999.* Quebec: Gouvernement du Québec.

Jacob, A. (1992). Services sociaux et groupes ethnoculturels. *Nouvelles pratiques sociales, 5*(2), 37–49.

Juteau, D. (1999). *L'ethnicité et ses frontières.* Montreal: Les Presses de l'Université de Montréal.

Juteau, D., & McAndrew, M. (1992). Projet national, immigration et intégration dans un Québec souverain. *Sociologie et sociétés, 24*(2), 161–80.

Legault, G. (2000a). Québec, société multiethnique. In G. Legault (Ed.), *Intervention interculturelle* (pp. 41–50). Montreal: Gaëtan Morin.

————. (2000b). Conclusions. In G. Legault (Ed.), *Intervention interculturelle* (pp. 324–7). Montreal: Gaëtan Morin.

Legault, G., & Roy, G. (2000). Les difficultés des intervenants sociaux auprès des clientèles d'immigration récente. In G. Legault (Ed.), *Intervention interculturelle* (pp. 185–203). Montreal: Gaëtan Morin.

Levine, M.V. (1990). *The Reconquest of Montreal: Language Policy and Social Change in a Bilingual City.* Philadelphia: Temple University Press.

Lum, D. (1986). *Social Work Practice and People of Color.* Monterey, CA: Brooks/Cole.

Maalouf, A. (1998). *Les identités meurtrières.* Paris: Grasset.

McAll, C. (1994). Racisme et ségrégation ethnique. In S. Langlois (Ed.), *Traité des problèmes sociaux.* Quebec: Institut québécois de la recherche sur la culture.

————. (1995). Les murs de la cité: Territoires d'exclusion et espaces de citoyenneté. *Lien Social et Politiques, 34*, 81–92.

————. (1996). *Les Requérants du Statut de Réfugié au Québec.* Montreal: Ministère des relations avec les citoyens et de l'immigration.

McAll, C., Tremblay, L., & LeGoff, F. (1997). *Proximité et distance.* Montreal: Éditions Saint-Martin.

McAndrew, M. (1995). Multiculturalisme canadien et interculturalisme québécois: Mythes et réalités. In M. McAndrew, R. Toussaint, O. Galatanu, & C. Ciceri (Eds), *Pluralisme et éducation: Politiques et pratiques au Canada, en Europe et dans les Pays du Sud* (pp. 33–51). Montreal: Faculté des sciences de l'éducation.

McGoldrick, M., & Gerson, R. (1990). *Génogrammes et entretien familial.* Paris: ESF Éditeur.

Malewska-Peyre, H., & Gachon, C. (1988). *Le travail social et les enfants de migrants.* Paris: l'Harmattan.

Meintel, D. (1993). New constructionist approaches to ethnicity. *Culture, 13*(2), 5–9.

Ministère des Affaires internationales, de l'Immigration et des Communautés culturelles (MAIICC). (1995). *Profils des communautés culturelles du Québec.* Quebec: Gouvernement du Québec.

Ministère des Communautés culturelles et de l'Immigration (MCCI). (1981). *Autant de façons d'être québécois.* Quebec: Gouvernement du Québec.

————. (1990). *Au Québec pour bâtir ensemble.* Quebec: Gouvernement du Québec.

Ministère de l'Éducation (MEC). (1998). *Une école d'avenir: Politique d'intégration scolaire et d'éducation interculturelle.* Quebec: Gouvernement du Québec.

Ministère des Relations avec les Citoyens et de l'Immigration (MRCI). (1999). Le MRCI en chiffres. *Bulletin statistique trimestriel du ministère des relations avec les citoyens et de l'immigration, 2*(3). Montreal: Ministère des Relations avec les Citoyens et de l'Immigration.

Ministère de la Santé et des Services sociaux. (1994). *Accessibilité des Services aux Communautés Ethnoculturelles.* Quebec: Éditeur officiel du Québec.

Montgomery, C. (1998). *Fragmented Voices: Language, Community and Rights.* Doctoral dissertation. Department of Sociology, Université de Montréal.

Montgomery, C., & Renaud, J. (1994). Residential patterns of new immigrants and linguistic integration. *Canadian Geographer, 38*(4), 331–42.

Morin, E. (1991). *Introduction: à la pensée complexe.* 2nd ed. Paris: ESF Éditeur.

Plourde, M. (1988). *La politique linguistique du Québec.* Quebec: Institut québécois de recherche sur la culture.

Renaud, J., Carpentier, A., Ouimet, G., & Montgomery, C. (1992). *La première année d'établissement d'immigrants admis au Québec en 1989.* Portraits d'un processus. Montreal: Ministère des Communautés culturelles et de l'Immigration.

Renaud, J., & Gingras, L. (1998). *Les trois premières années au Québec des requérants du statut de réfugiés régularisés.* Quebec: Ministère des Relations avec les Citoyens et de l'Immigration.

Rogel, J.P. (1989). *Le défi de l'immigration.* Quebec: Institut québécois de recherche sur la culture.

Roy, G. (1991). *Pratiques interculturelles sous l'angle de la Modernité.* Montreal: Centre des services sociaux du Montréal métropolitain.

———. (1993). Complexité et Interculturel. *Service Social, 42,* 145–53.

———. (1993). Bouillon de pratiques interculturelles. *Intervention, 96,* 77–87.

———. (1996). Grille d'évaluation en approche interculturelle. Internal document. SARIMM-CLSC Côte-des-Neiges, Montreal.

———. (2000). Le protocole de discussion de cas. et 'Les modèles de pratique'. In G. Legault (Ed.), *L'intervention interculturelle* (pp. 131–58). Montreal: Gaëtan Morin Éditeur.

Roy, G., & Shermarke, M. (1996). Errance d'exil et cul-de-sac institutionnel. *Intervention, 103,* 43–7.

St-Arnaud, Y. (1992). *Connaître par l'action.* Montreal: Presses de l'Université de Montréal.

Schön, D.A. (1983). *The Reflexive Practitioner.* New York: Basic Books.

Sévigny R., & Tremblay, L. (1999). L'adaptation des services de santé et des services sociaux au contexte pluriethnique. In C. Bégin, P. Bergeron, P.G. Forest, & V. Lemieux (Eds), *Le Système de santé québécois: Un Modèle en Transformation* (pp. 77–94). Montreal: Presses de l'Université de Montréal.

Sirros, E. (1987). *Rapport du comité sur l'accessibilité des services de santé et des services sociaux aux membres des communautés culturelles.* Quebec: Publications officielles.

Sterlin, C. (1988). L'intervenant homoethnique en contexte interculturel. *Centre interculturel Monchanin, 21*(3), 21–30.

Trudel, M. (1973). *La Population au Canada en 1663.* Montreal: Fides.

Ville de Montréal. (1998). *Profil socio-économique, Ville de Montréal et ses quartiers.* Montreal: Ville de Montréal.

Wade, M. (1968). *The French Canadians, 1760–1967.* Rev. ed. Toronto: Macmillan.

Weinfeld, M. (1999). The challenge of ethnic match: Minority origin professionals in health and social services. In H. Troper & M. Weinfeld (Eds), *Ethnicity, Politics, and Public Policy: Case Studies in Canadian Diversity* (pp. 117–41). Toronto: University of Toronto Press.

Williams, D.W. (1998). *Les Noirs à Montréal. Essai de démographie urbaine.* Montreal: VLB Éditeur.

Personal Narratives on Social Work with Diverse Ethno-Racial Communities

Chapters in Section 2 provide case study insight into social work within various ethno-racial contexts in a multicultural Canada. Chapter 7 considers practice among Canadians of Italian background. The chapter is particularly focused on clinical concerns. It discusses bicultural and intergenerational issues, as well as challenges faced by Italian immigrant families. Case vignettes are used to illustrate intervention strategies, which are applicable to other cultural groups. In addition, a theoretical model of cross-cultural practice is used to illustrate the integration of fundamental social work principles with sensitivity to cultural issues.

Chapter 8, on social work with Canadians of Arab background, is, like the preceding chapter, particularly focused on direct practice. It is also oriented more than some other chapters in this section to people who have come relatively recently to Canada. It considers the Arab world in context; how to integrate social work 'formal theory' and Arab world views or 'informal theory'; issues of acculturation in Canada; religious, familial, age, and gender constructions; and individual development and group references in Arab culture. Subsequent sections focus on help-seeking strategies in Arab communities, difficulties in establishing and maintaining a helping relationship, and guidelines for effective social work practice in Canada with clients of Arab background.

Chapter 9 discusses social work practice with Canadians of Jewish background. This chapter, which is generic to all levels of practice, is divided into four parts. The first looks at patterns of migration and settlement of Jews in Canada and provides a broad overview of the present Jewish experience in Canada. The second section examines psychological issues and dynamics of migration and resettlement. The next section discusses the Canadian Jewish community and salient cultural and social issues that confront Jewish Canadians. The chapter concludes with a discussion of social work practice and recommendations for culturally appropriate practice with people of Jewish-Canadian background.

Chapter 10 focuses on Ukrainian Canadians. This chapter uses narrative and historical descriptions of Ukrainian experiences in twentieth-century Canada, particularly in western Canada, as a backdrop to considering direct and community practice within this cultural context. It weaves the life and familial histories of the authors into the context of several waves of Ukrainian migration to Canada, considering the children and subsequent generations of Ukrainian immigrants to Canada and the commensurate implications for culturally appropriate social work practice.

Chapter 11, on social work with Aboriginal people in Canada, outlines a general model for multicultural social work practice at all levels of intervention with Canadians of Aboriginal background. It briefly outlines contextual information pertaining to Aboriginal people and then goes on to discuss a general framework for social work practice with Aboriginal people. The balance of the chapter discusses the relationship of this framework to empowerment and healing and, finally, highlights implications for practice.

Chapter 12 is on the Franco-Ontarian community. Focusing on community intervention among a linguistic minority in Canada, it begins by introducing historical patterns of settlement as well as the development of some of the community's social practices and institutions, particularly within the past thirty years. The chapter outlines some of the Franco-Ontarian resistance to policies imposed by the Anglophone majority as well as internal community resistance to practices imposed by the elites, including the Roman Catholic Church. It also discusses some of the ways in which the community has adapted and continued to develop. Finally, it examines a few of the new social welfare practices now being developed within the Franco-Ontarian community that can be seen as alternatives to the existing ways of doing things.

Chapter 13 examines African–Nova Scotian communities. This chapter, like the one preceding it, provides the insight of a geographically specific case study. It focuses on micro and mezzo levels of practice among African Canadians in Nova Scotia. The first part of the chapter introduces African-Canadian history, with particular reference to the African–Nova Scotian community. The second presents an Afrocentric paradigm, a blueprint for human services practitioners working with individuals, families, groups, and organizations within the community. The chapter concludes with a discussion of some major social concerns confronting this community, as well as some pragmatic practice principles and strategies for human service personnel to practise appropriately.

Chapter 14 is on social work with Canadians of Caribbean background. This chapter is highly structuralist in orientation and, in this respect, shares some similarities with Chapter 4. It is relevant to all levels of practice, and begins with an exploration of the complexities of Caribbean cultures that have emanated from the profound influences of colonization, imperialism, and legacies from indentureship and slavery. It considers gender construction, family violence, racism, and the author's understanding of self and culture in relation to social work practice in the context of migration and social structures in Canadian society.

Chapter 15 is on work with Canadians of South Asian background. Like Chapters 7 and 8, this chapter focuses on direct practice. It describes how research about and practice within the South Asian Canadian community demonstrate the problematic tendency of social work to rely on cultural perception more than contextual reality. The chapter also presents a new theoretical approach, which moves beyond the perception of culture to consider the context of culture, in order to provide appropriate services for diverse populations.

Chapter 7

Social Work with Canadians of Italian Background: Applying Cultural Concepts to Bicultural and Intergenerational Issues in Clinical Practice

Ramona Alaggia and Elsa Marziali

Because of the continual arrival of immigrants in Canada, social workers are acquiring experience with helping clients of diverse ethnic, racial, and cultural backgrounds in ways that are respectful, knowledgeable, and effective. Developing an understanding of the specific experiences, problems, and needs of new immigrants is fundamental to implementing good social work practice methods. For immigrant groups, the challenges of settling in a new country are many. Among other things, newcomers need to cope with the demands of acculturation; mourn the loss of country of origin, simultaneously with adapting to the new environment; reorient parenting beliefs and behaviours that conflict with those of the host culture; and deal with prejudice and rejection by members of the country of settlement.

The impact of immigration on individuals and their families is profound. Studies of immigrant families have found that immigration can significantly disrupt parent–child relations, exacerbate high-risk adolescent behaviour, and intensify intergenerational conflict, resulting in problems across generations (Baptiste, 1993; Brice, 1982; Brindis, Wolfe, McCarter, Ball, & Starbuck-Morales, 1995; Cornille, 1993; Lau, 1986). Acculturation to a new country, and culture, is an emotionally and physically taxing process that requires reorganization of the family unit, both psychologically and socially (Alaggia, Chau, & Tsang, 2001; Ward, 1996). With immigration, families experience the loss of extended family members who previously provided reliable support. In some instances, parents and children are temporarily separated, often with one parent staying behind in the country of origin while the other forges ahead to carve out a new life in the country of settlement. For those families who are fleeing the oppressive conditions of wartorn or politically volatile countries, problems with adaptation to a new country are intensified by the traumatic stress of being forced to leave their country of origin. Regardless of specific reasons for emigrating, it is expected that newcomers to Canada will face a host of challenges in their settlement and adjustment.

Patterns of migration over the last century show that, once they have settled, most immigrant groups remain in Canada (Elliott & Fleras, 1990). New generations of children are born here, initiating a process of progressive family acculturation over time. Thus, within each ethnic group, the impact of immigration and subsequent issues of acculturation reverberate through generations of families. All families have unique dynamics shaped by historical events and individual characteristics, as well as by the value and belief systems deeply rooted in their culture. As each family member grows and the family unit as a whole evolves, interfamilial relationships are affected by many factors. The experience of immigrating, the stressful process of acculturation, the maintenance of an identification with their ethnic group, and meeting the challenges of adapting to the host culture place enormous pressures on family systems.

The authors of this chapter come from different but overlapping perspectives in regard to their ethnicity and experiences with Italian Canadians. While one is the daughter of Eastern European immigrants, who married a first-generation Italian Canadian and has two daughters of mixed heritage (Italian and Lithuanian), the other hails from an Italian background, is a first-generation Italian Canadian, and married outside of the Italian community. The combined personal and professional experiences of the authors bring an awareness of (a) the impact of immigration on families, (b) the dynamics of bicultural marriage, and (c) the complexities of negotiating intergenerational and bicultural issues in practice with clients. Both authors are clinicians who have worked with Italian-Canadian clients.

The aim of this chapter is to discuss both bicultural and intergenerational issues and the challenges faced by Italian immigrant families. Case vignettes, drawn from the clinical experiences of the authors, are used to illustrate intervention strategies. Although we use casework examples with Italian-Canadian clients, our approach has broad application to other cultural groups. Because no cultural group can be defined in absolute terms, we refrain from describing characteristics and features of Italians as an ethnic group. Rather, we will introduce cultural concepts relevant to social work practice with culturally different clients. A theoretical model of cross-cultural[1] practice will be used to illustrate the integration of fundamental social work principles with sensitivity to cultural issues.

Historical Background

The end of the nineteenth century heralded the first great influx of Italians to North America. While a large number settled in the United States, immigration policies in Canada created avenues of entry for Italian labourers. Their skills were particularly needed in the construction industry, including work on expanding the Canadian Pacific Railway. Between 1900 and 1915 Italian immigrants were characterized as sojourners who came to work in Canada on a seasonal basis. Although most made several trips back to Italy, the majority eventually settled in the new country. For those immigrants who came from southern Italy, emigration was precipitated by poor economic conditions; lack of opportunity, owing to a heritage of little and poor education; and the decline of agrarian culture (Sturino, 1999). In the second half of the nineteenth century socio-political changes in Italy, which resulted in the unification of the northern and southern regions, brought more hardship to the south, while the north, especially the major cities of Milan and Turin, prospered with massive industrialization projects. Thus, immigration to Canada was viewed as a survival strategy for the men and their families, that eventually resulted in their choosing to stay in Canada.

During the interwar years, particularly following the invasion of Ethiopia by Benito Mussolini in 1935, and throughout the Second World War, Italy's political orientation and military alliances led Western host countries to curtail the immigration of Italians. Although Mussolini was ousted in 1943, and Italy signed an armistice with the Allies, political alliances with 'enemy nations' resulted in Italians being viewed as 'undesirables' (Sturino, 1999). Canada responded with more stringent immigration policies that limited entry to agricultural workers. These policies favoured farmers from southern Italy, who were still struggling in an agrarian environment, as opposed to those living in the more industrialized northern regions of the country.

In 1949 Italy joined the North Atlantic Treaty Organization (NATO). Canada, a member nation of NATO, subsequently signed a bilateral agreement in 1950 that removed the enemy-alien status of Italian Canadians and allowed them to sponsor Italian relatives for immigration to Canada. During this period, many Italians were willing to come to Canada; their home country was struggling to revitalize its economy in the aftermath of the war and had the worst unemployment rate in Europe. In contrast, the Canadian economy was flourishing. As in the historical cycles of immigration to Canada, Italian men found jobs as labourers, primarily in the construction industry. Some went on to own their construction companies (Sturino, 1999). This cyclical pattern of the types of occupation available for immigrants has persisted, including the more recent entry of female Italian immigrants into the service trades. Overall, Italian immigrant families prospered, purchasing homes and settling in ethnically homogeneous areas of the country (Lautard & Guppy, 1990; Sturino, 1999).

In 1957 Italy became one of the founding members of the European Economic Community, and, shortly thereafter, experienced some economic recovery and expansion, which included the implementation of progressive social programs. Partly because of this progress, emigration from Italy slowed considerably in the 1960s. This decline was also attributable of Canada's revised immigration policies, which promoted the entry of skilled and professional individuals. Such an approach to screening immigrant applications continued into the early 1990s. As a result, after 1980 Italian arrivals decreased to less than 2,000 per year, a dramatic decline from a high of over 28,000 in 1958 (Iacovetta, 1992, p. 204; Sturino, 1999).

As a result of immigration trends, Ontario has the largest population of Italian Canadians, followed by Quebec and British Columbia. Numbers of Italian Canadians in each of the remaining provinces fall well under 100,000 with the Northwest Territories and Yukon having the lowest numbers. According to the decennial census of 1991, the four urban centres with the largest number of Italian Canadians are Toronto (387,375, based on the number of people who in the census claimed Italian-Canadian background), Montreal (207,315), Vancouver (60,310), and Hamilton (58,785). Toronto and Montreal have the largest Italian neighbourhoods in Canada. Typically, Italian immigrants have been attracted to large urban centres where work suited to their particular skills was available. Their contribution to the union movement in Canada has been significant, and their active participation in community life has resulted in the development of ethno-specific clubs and agencies (Sturino, 1999). Clearly, Italians represent a significant ethnic group in Canada, claiming a distinct history over several generations.

Another historical trend of interest, and one directly related to the focus of this chapter, is changing attitudes towards intermarriage. Attitudes towards endogamy (marriage within a group, as dictated by law or custom) and rates of intermarriage indicate that Italian Canadians have been relatively open to marriage outside of their ethnic group. In 1941 Italian Canadians had an intermarriage rate of 45 per cent, higher than most major ethnic groups in Canada. In Toronto by 1980, endogamy had decreased from 91 per cent for the first generation to 64 per cent for the second generation, and 29 per cent for the third generation (Sturino, 1999). It is important to view these numbers within the context of important cultural factors. Most significant among these is that 70 per cent of all 'mixed marriages' are with other Roman Catholics, and it is widely recognized that religion is a powerful vehicle for ethnic identity and cultural transmission. Given these trends, it can be expected that Italian Canadians face intergenerational and bicultural issues on a day-to-day basis and throughout the course of the family life-cycle. When these issues escalate to levels that cannot be resolved within the family, they may seek intervention from helping professionals.

Overview of Developments in Cross-cultural Social Work Practice

Changes in ethnic demographics across North America have dramatically increased the need for culturally sensitive approaches to social work practice. In response to these needs, a number of conceptual models for cross-cultural practice have evolved over the last three decades. Earlier models of cross-cultural practice, which focused primarily on personality and behavioural deficits, have been largely replaced by ethnic-sensitive models that include sensitivity to racism and oppression. For the purposes of this chapter, an overview of the evolution of several important models of cross-cultural practice will be presented as the background for understanding and engaging in ethnic-sensitive work.[2]

Deficit models of social work practice dominated cross-cultural work during the 1960s (Casas, 1985). From this perspective, minority group clients were perceived as having 'deficits' by virtue of their ethnic heritage, which differed from the dominant culture of the host country. Interventions stemmed from an assessment approach that viewed the immigrant client as being inferior and deficient. Non-White clients, whether immigrant or native born, were particularly discriminated against by these approaches to practice.

Later, so-called colour-blind models of practice were developed to address the inadequacies of the deficit-model approach (Cooper, 1973; Thomas & Sillen, 1976). The aim of colour-blind models was to view minority clients as no different than any other client. While this attempt at 'normalizing' clients, regardless of ethno-racial status, was well intended, the client's uniqueness could be ignored. In this model, fundamental aspects of diversity were minimized, and clients' ethnic and racially specific life experiences were dismissed as non-relevant to the clinical relationship and the change process (Griffith, 1997).

Following these earlier approaches, the concept of cultural competence emerged, with the aim of developing programs to train social workers and organizations for competency in practice with diverse clients. It is believed by the profession that the ultimate achievement of cultural competency engages the practitioner in a never-ending process of knowledge and skill acquisition, including self-observation in the context of cross-cultural interactions. Respect for the cultural integrity of the client interacts continuously with the process of cultural self-awareness (Devore & Schlesinger, 1999; Green, 1999). Today, advanced abilities in intercultural communication were identified by a number of authors as an important aspect of culturally competent practice (Gudykunst & Kim, 1984; Leigh, 1998; Ruben, 1989). As a result, competence in communication and relationship-building skills continue to be emphasized in most contemporary cross-cultural models.

Elements of culturally competent practice vary across models, but all require professionals to adhere to some fundamental beliefs. These include self-awareness of one's own culture and its limitations; the ability to be open to and value difference; acknowledgement of the importance of the client's cultural identity; sensitivity to multiple diversities; and the appreciation of culturally based individual and community resources (Cross, 1988; Falicov, 1995; Green, 1999; Pinderhughes, 1989). From an ecological perspective, culturally competent models of practice address issues of culture from micro, mezzo, and macro perspectives of intervention. However, implementation of culturally competent models of practice have occurred mostly at the micro, clinical level of practice and in organizations that support this work.

Professional Training and the Development of Cultural Competency Standards of Practice

Throughout the 1980s, schools of social work revised their educational programs to expand theoretical and practice models beyond a Eurocentric perspective and to advance the teaching of cross-cultural practice approaches that were sensitive to a broad definition of diversity (racial, ethnic, religious, economic, physical ability, etc). As a result of these curricular changes across social work programs, cultural competency standards for professional practice were proposed. The adoption of standards has been slow, owing to the proliferation of multiple definitions of efficient and effective culturally competent practice. The issue of identifying a coherent set of standards is further complicated by the fact that the acquisition and implementation of culturally competent strategies must be tested within both clinical and socio-political approaches to change. For example, it could be argued that, without standards that apply to observing change at the macro-structural level of intervention, competency standards that apply at the clinical practice level cannot be effectively evaluated. Whereas the problems of individuals can best be understood and managed in the context of societal factors such as racism, discrimination, and deprivation, approaches to the extinction of all forms of oppression must evolve from a structural perspective (Dominelli, 1993; Henry, Tator, Mattis, & Rees, 1995; Mullaly, 1994). Clearly, societal reinforcement of oppressive beliefs and practices will not be eliminated through models of clinical practice; but the experienced effects of oppression on both the client and the social worker can be understood and managed in the change process. Ultimately, understanding the interaction among societal oppressive forces, the client's experiences of oppression, and the worker's self-observations of prejudicial attitudes will determine which clinical practice strategies maximize positive outcomes for the client (Bishop, 1994).

An attempt at articulating the minimum standards for culturally sensitive practice have been included in the Canadian Association of Social Workers (CASW) Code of Ethics, which was revised in 1994. These include the following:

1.2   A social worker in the practice of social work shall not discriminate against any person on the basis of race, ethnic background, language, religion, marital status, sex, sexual orientation, age, abilities, socio-economic status, political affiliation or national ancestry.

. . .

1.7   Where possible, a social worker shall provide or secure social work services in the language chosen by the client.

. . .

4.1   The social worker shall respect the client and act so that the dignity, individuality and rights of the person are protected.

. . .

10.1   A social worker shall identify, document and advocate for the elimination of discrimination.

10.2   A social worker shall advocate for the equal distribution of resources to all persons.

10.3   A social worker shall advocate for the equal access of all persons to resources, services and opportunities.

. . .

10.6   A social worker shall promote social justice.

Although it is useful to formulate a code for ethical, professional cross-cultural practice, there have been few attempts to generate theoretical and practice models that would reflect the efficacy of applying these standards to actual clinical practice. Although as yet untested, three theoretical models for competent cross-cultural practice have been developed over the last decade. A review and critique of each models follows.

Three Theoretical Models of Cross-cultural Practice

Three contemporary models of cross-cultural clinical practice are gaining saliency: the cultural literacy model (LaFramboise & Foster, 1992), the experiential-phenomenological model (Dyche & Zayas, 1995), and the integrated framework for cross-cultural practice (Tsang & George, 1998). While each represents a different perspective, the models are best viewed as located on a continuum of cross-cultural approaches, with differing emphases on acquiring knowledge about specific cultures and understanding diversities. Differences in clinical strategies used in cross-cultural work are less clearly articulated.

Among the assumptions of the *cultural literacy model* are that the practitioner is responsible for obtaining knowledge about various cultural groups, that each culture is predominantly homogeneous, and that culturally based interventions are applied. These assumptions are reflected in the work of a broad spectrum of clinical professions—psychiatry, psychology, nursing, and clinical social work—some of which have developed ethnic-specific approaches to assessment and treatment (Lam, 1998; McGoldrick, Giordano, & Pearce 1996; Sue & Sue, 1987; Watts, 1992). Although this model represents an important contribution to clinical work with diverse clients, it has significant limitations. First, complete knowledge of all cultures and diversities is impossible. Second, when cultural groups are assumed to be internally homogeneous, an individual client is cast into a role that may not reflect her of his unique experiences. Third, it is unrealistic to specify intervention strategies that are uniquely responsive to each cultural group, since there is no evidence to support the efficacy of such an approach.

The *experiential-phenomenological model* evolved from a belief that it is impossible for practitioners to be knowledgeable about all cultures. Instead, this model promotes a practitioner stance of openness and curiosity with all culturally diverse clients. The aim is for the practitioner to acquire understanding of each client's unique experiences of her or his culture, race, gender, and class. Specific intervention strategies are not recommended; rather, the practitioner responds to the interaction with each client as it evolves (Dyche & Zayas, 1995). The experiential-phenomenological approach uses the therapeutic narrative as the vehicle for discovering elements of the client's culture, for exploring subjective experiences with acculturation, and for understanding the client's unique stresses in the acculturation process (Reichelt & Sveaass, 1994). The clients are the experts, and the worker acknowledges and values clients' unique experiences with oppression both within and outside their cultural group. This stance contributes to the building of mutual trust within the therapeutic relationship. Chosen change strategies are specific to the clients' narratives about their subjective experiences of prejudice and oppression.

Although the experiential-phenomenological model focuses on understanding the clients' subjective experiences of their culture, this model has been criticized for imposing on clients the task of 'educating' the practitioner. Some argue that the client is burdened with informing the practitioner about relevant cultural factors rather than being the recipient of the practitioner's understanding of culturally sensitive issues (Brown, 1991). These criticisms neglect the importance of understanding the client's subjective experiences with oppression. It is the evolving interaction between the client's cultural context and that of the worker that ultimately determines the quality and outcome of their work together. Through this interaction they inform each other of their respective cultural similarities and differences. Essential to the process is the practitioner's ability to become aware of her or his own prejudicial beliefs and attitudes.

The *integrated framework for cross-cultural practice* proposed by Tsang and George (1998) is based on an ecological perspective. The model integrates three practice-related constructs: personal attitudes, professional knowledge, and professional skills. The development of culturally sensitive attitudes is viewed as imperative for effective professional practice. These 'attitudes' include a commitment to justice and equity, open acceptance and valuing of difference, readiness to learn from the client, and critical self-reflection. Professional knowledge targets the systemic context of culture, including the process of acculturation, internalized meanings of culture, and understanding the dynamics of cross-cultural communication. The aim is to address issues of diversity at the individual, social, and political levels of intervention. For example, external factors, both social and political, affect the process of acculturation for each individual. Simultaneously, the individual's internalized system of cultural meanings—that is, how the client views self within the context of her or his cultural group—needs to be understood. Finally, the nuances of communication across cultural boundaries convey meanings that can only be understood by the interacting participants. *Professional skills*, the third focus of the model, refers to the social worker's ability to interact with a client in a cross-cultural context that is effective and meaningful. The working relationship evolves from mutual acknowledgement of and respect for difference. When this is achieved, the client feels safe to reveal experiences with external and internal expressions of culturally based conflicts. The challenge for the social worker is to shift and change intervention strategies constantly, commensurate with the client's unique cultural views and beliefs. The worker must accommodate the client's world view, regardless of how much it matches or differs from that of the worker. Ultimately, the shaping of a positive and productive treatment relationship will depend on the worker's ability to communicate understanding and acceptance of the client's unique cultural identity.

In summary, Tsang and George (1998) propose a comprehensive theoretical and practice model for cross-cultural clinical work. Of the three models reviewed, it is the only one that is being tested empirically in a treatment-outcome study with cross-cultural client–worker dyads.

Our approach to cross-cultural practice is consistent with that of Tsang and George. It provides a clinical perspective that integrates basic social work practice principles with an approach that stresses the importance of acquiring cultural sensitivity through monitoring of the clinician's own prejudicial beliefs as well as those reflected by the host culture. Although this model of practice deals adequately with important issues concerning sensitive cross-cultural practice, understanding the process of acculturation and its effects on family adaptation to a new culture is not well articulated in the model. Yet it is the stress of finding one's way in the new host country that frequently leads a client to request help from a social service agency.

Regardless of the model used, two issues are critical for competent cross-cultural work: 1) respect for cultural differences between client and worker, and 2) on-going self-examination for prejudicial beliefs and behaviours on the part of all practitioners. Clinical cross-cultural work must include, as well, knowledge of systemic discrimination and social inequities; embedded in these global forms of oppression are the sources of prejudices within the individual social worker and within the profession as a whole. All social work practitioners share the task of increasing awareness of and eradicating systemic discrimination. However, clinical social workers need to incorporate in their methods of intervention specific approaches that address pervasive societal discriminatory practices.

Acculturation: Implications for Intergenerational and Bicultural Family Conflict

The process of acculturation is defined as both a state and a process: 'As a state, the amount or extent of acculturation is typically defined and measured in relation to culture-specific cognitive, behavioural, and affective markers . . . with related indices, such as level of education, socioeconomic status, media usage, and patterns of friendship. In contrast, acculturation as a process is viewed in a broader context and explores dimensions of change over time. This perspective encompasses a range of conceptual frameworks' (Ward, 1996, p. 124). From a clinical practice perspective, it is more relevant to focus on acculturation as a process.

Following immigration to a new country, family members experience disorientation and disorganization (Berry, 1988; Berry, Kim, Minde, & Mok, 1987; Ward, 1996). The subsequent acculturation process is emotionally, psychologically, socially, and physically demanding. Acculturation is a major life event characterized by stress, and one that requires adaptive responses. On the micro level, there has been a great deal of interest in the study of the effects of acculturation on physical and psychological well-being (Berry et al., 1987). Ward's (1996) theoretical model of acculturation combines individual and societal factors for understanding the multiple stressors of acculturation. Individual characteristics that influence the acculturation process include personality dimensions, language fluency, type of training and work experience, and adequacy of coping strategies. Macro factors that affect the success of acculturation include the socio-political, economic, and cultural characteristics of the host country, as well as discriminatory beliefs and attitudes held about newcomers by the host society (see Ward, 1996, pp. 128–9 for full description of the model).

The outcome of the immigrant settlement process determines the degree of acculturation achieved and results in a redefinition of ethnic identity. Each family member across generations is affected by the primary acculturation process experienced by the newcomer family. Berry and his colleagues (1987) describe four outcomes of the acculturation process that are useful for culturally sensitive social work practice with individuals and families: separation/isolation, integration, cultural assimilation, and marginalization.

The first outcome of acculturation, separation/isolation, can occur when immigrant families avoid contact with the host culture and instead strive to retain most of their original ethnic identity and ties. This is observed in communities, such as Little Italys, where immigrants maintain their original language and function with little or no knowledge of the official language of the dominant culture. They can work, attend the local church, and participate in social activities exclusively in their own Italian community while relying on others (usually their children) for communication with the host culture.

A second outcome of acculturation, integration, occurs when families retain some of their ethnicity while simultaneously incorporating some cultural aspects of the host country. For example, family members may speak the language of their country of origin at home, but converse in the language of the host country outside of the home. Also, they may observe their own distinct cultural traditions and holidays as well as partake in those of the host country.

A third outcome, cultural assimilation, occurs when families renounce most, or all, connections with their ethnic origins and adopt the traditions, language, and other significant cultural aspects of the host country. These families sometimes anglicize their names to 'blend in', to deflect discrimination, or to protect themselves from persecution, as exemplified by postwar Jewish immigrants (Pinderhughes, 1989). Another result of assimilation is the loss of the language of the country of origin, especially by second and third generations of immigrant children. Assimilation, as an outcome of acculturation, has been the dominant paradigm in Canada.

The fourth outcome of acculturation, marginalization, is the most devastating: ethnic groups entirely lose their heritage ties and cultural identity while at the same time being excluded from making connections with the dominant culture. This is frequently the outcome for those groups who are victims of civil war in their country of origin or who are members of indigenous communities, such as First Nations people in Canada. In this country, we witness the impact of colonialism in the disproportionate rate of poverty and incarceration among Native communities. Historically, oppressive policies and practices—the enforced placement of Aboriginal children in residential schools, for example—coupled with inadequate support services most often provided by members of the dominant culture, have reinforced the destruction of First Nation cultures.

Most groups who immigrate to a new country locate themselves between outcomes one and three of the acculturation process. Understanding the degree of acculturation achieved by immigrant groups requires an analysis of the respective experiences of individual family members. Often, family acculturation precipitates intergenerational conflicts that are not easily resolved. For example, first-generation children may be assigned the task of achieving a form of cultural adaptation that is acceptable to the family as a whole. Conflicts arising from confused intergenerational expectations result in family stress. It is at this juncture that outside help from social service workers may be sought.

Case in Point: Joseph was expected to take over the family business in land development and construction. His father, an Italian immigrant, worked hard to build a successful operation and fully expected to retire with the knowledge that his capable son was taking the reins of the company. Yet Joseph had developed an interest in theatre and he pursued studies in dramatic arts, much to the dismay of his parents, who viewed this as a frivolous hobby. After graduating, Joseph, who felt he had no aptitude or interest in his father's work, nonetheless took over the family business. Initially, Joseph worked with his father, but the latter died. Now in his forties, Joseph found that running the company by himself required long hours and offered few personal rewards. Ultimately, about a year after his father's death, Joseph's wife brought him in for counselling for his unhappiness and depression.

Joseph's father wanted his son to appreciate not only the value of the business that he had built but also the struggles he had faced in setting up a successful business in a new country. Confronting language barriers, financial stress, and unfamiliar bureaucratic processes (e.g., zoning by-laws, licensing procedures) allowed him to establish himself as a credible business person. At the same time, he expected his son to inherit his own culturally based gender attitudes. As an only son, Joseph was expected to carry on the family business; his two sisters were absolved from this responsibility. As the dutiful son, Joseph fulfilled his father's wishes while denying his own aspirations. It is not surprising that, after his father's death, he was faced with a mid-life crisis.

Therapy focused on understanding unresolved family-of-origin issues. Initially, the meaning of immigration for the family as a whole was explored. The impact on Joseph of the Italian views of gender roles was explored and its effect on his parenting of his one son were clarified. For example, Joseph and his wife were in crisis with their adolescent son, whose rebelliousness included serious truant behaviour. Joseph grappled with the irony of his role as the dutiful son and his son's seeming aimlessness. He eventually came to the conclusion that he had countered his father's overbearing expectations by taking a laissez-faire approach to parenting his own children. This insight prompted Joseph and his wife to alter their parenting style.

Parent–child conflicts are to be expected in every family, especially during specific developmental stages. Tension occurs when the degree of attachment to the ethnic culture varies among family members and across generations. Children are especially vulnerable because they participate in an educational system that requires the acquisition of a new language as well as new beliefs and behaviours that contrast with the family's culture of origin. In parallel, the parents may be committed to retaining the language, religious practices, cultural values, belief systems, customs, and rituals of their country of origin. This clash in expectations within the family invariably precipitates problems between generations, especially between immigrant parents and their adolescent children who confuse psychological separation from parents with separation from their ethnic culture in favour of the host culture.

Case in Point: Lena's mother discovered birth control pills in her fifteen-year-old daughter's dresser drawer. Mr and Mrs G., immigrant Italians and practising Roman Catholics, strongly disapproved of their daughter's sexual relationship with her boyfriend, of whom they otherwise approved. Mr and Mrs G. had been brought together in an arranged marriage in Italy, and while they did not wish to impose this type of arrangement on their daughter, they pressured her either to terminate the relationship or to have her boyfriend make a formal commitment. Lena felt caught between her parents and boyfriend. She did not want to terminate the relationship, but she was not ready for a long-term commitment. The relationship between Lena and her parents was full of conflict, and her father was verbally abusive, making, among other things, derogatory sexual remarks. Fights between Lena and her parents sometimes resulted in her leaving home for two or three nights. The school social worker intervened, concerned that Lena's twenty-year-old boyfriend was sexually exploiting her. She began exploring child welfare involvement and recommended family counselling.

The initiation of sexual activity by adolescent children is of concern to most parents, but for families whose culture places a strong taboo on premarital sexual relations, the intergenerational conflicts are intense and highly stressful for the whole family. For Mr and Mrs G., the notion of premarital sexual relations was unacceptable for moral and religious reasons. Despite their Catholic faith, the G.'s accepted the use of birth control, but they could not condone their daughter's use of contraceptives because they opposed her having sexual relations outside of marriage. Thus, neither of her parents was able to show approval of the fact that Lena was behaving in a mature and responsible manner to protect herself against pregnancy. Instead, Lena looked to her older married sisters for support and advice about using birth control. The possibility of child welfare involvement created enormous anxiety for the family. In Italy, intervention by a government-mandated service would be experienced as an embarrassment to the family. They perceived the child welfare system as taking children away from parents and were completely unprepared for this 'Canadian way' of dealing with private family matters. Despite the efforts of the school social worker, who spent considerable time explaining child welfare legislation and how it applied to Lena, who was a minor, the parents were unable to co-operate. The father never did understand that his behaviour towards Lena was emotionally abusive and could be constituted abusive according to child welfare law. Because Lena was close to her sixteenth birthday and stated that she was in a mutually consensual sexual relationship, the child welfare approach was abandoned. The family was referred to an agency that served the Italian community, and their conflicts were addressed from a culturally sensitive family systems perspective.

Intergenerational conflicts related to acculturation are further heightened by bicultural issues that erupt when adult children form unions with partners outside their own ethnic group. It is widely accepted that culture is passed down from generation to generation, and disruptions in the transmission of culturally based values and beliefs, such as marrying outside one's ethnic group, can threaten the integrity of the family unit. Bicultural unions frequently precipitate anxiety, anger, and guilt within each partner's family and potentially affect every level of the family system: the individual, the couple, their children, the grandparents, and the ethnic communities involved. Due to different experiences with the initial process of acculturation, extended family members may differ as to the reasons for rejecting intimacy with persons outside of their ethnic or racial group. Among the reasons for objecting to bicultural unions are ethnic loyalty; religious convictions; and maintenance of language and ethno-specific values, beliefs, and customs. When the couples' families share some of these belief systems, family tension is reduced. When they differ, especially in terms of the value placed on religious beliefs, socioeconomic and educational aspirations, and the retention of language, there is the greater likelihood of resistance, fear, and conflict between the couple and between their respective extended families (McGoldrick & Preta, 1984). Ethnic-based values, which are strongly reinforced within an ethno-racial group, determine the extent to which marriage outside of the group can be sanctioned. These cultural values and beliefs regarding ethnic intermarriage shape the attitudes of all family members. When intermarriage first occurs within an ethnic group, the need for an attitudinal shift is painfully obvious. When intermarriage has taken place in previous generations and/or is common within the ethnic group, it is more readily accepted.

In summary, the type of acculturation experienced by each partner in a bicultural relationship and by each member of their respective families determines the extent of accommodation of the bicultural union.[3] Differences need to be negotiated and resolved between the partners, and between them and their families. When partners of bicultural unions have children, bicultural conflicts resurface, often in the form of differences in child-rearing practices. The case of Maurizio and Susan illustrates the family conflicts that arise in cross-cultural marriages. This is followed by the case of Mrs R., which illustrates intergenerational conflicts within the Italian immigrant culture.

Case 1: Bicultural Issues

Maurizio (age twenty-five) and Susan (twenty-four) had been married for one year when they contacted a family services agency seeking marital counselling. Maurizio and Susan had had a brief courtship, which resulted in Susan becoming pregnant. They married quickly and quietly, and, for financial reasons, moved in with Maurizio's parents. Susan had just completed teacher's college, and Maurizio worked as a service technician for a large telecommunications company. Susan secured a teaching position after the birth of their son, and her mother-in-law was providing child care for the baby, then aged nine months.

Maurizio is the youngest of four sons in an Italian family. Because of the circumstances and their hopes for their youngest son to marry an Italian woman, his parents disapproved of the marriage. Susan is the only daughter of Dutch immigrants. Although her parents like Maurizio, they were apprehensive because of the precipitous nature of the marriage. They had hoped Susan would launch her career before having a family. Susan grew up in a small farming community north of Toronto, where her parents owned a gardening and supplies store. Maurizio's parents immigrated to Canada after the birth of his oldest brother. Living in a predominantly Italian neighbourhood, Maurizio's parents retained their Italian customs, language, and friends. Their mastery of the English language was poor. Maurizio's father was a labourer, having dug tunnels for the Toronto subway system and worked various contracts that he secured through his Italian community contacts. The work was hard, with no benefits or security; however, the family was frugal and saved money diligently.

Susan had concerns about living with her in-laws. The first conflict occurred upon the birth of the baby. Maurizio's family had a naming tradition, which meant that the grandson should be named after his paternal grandfather, Piero. Susan objected to this, and Maurizio supported her because he felt the name was too 'ethnic'. The couple compromised, choosing the name Peter. They also had their son baptized in the Roman Catholic Church the in-laws belonged to, even though Susan is not Catholic. Despite the compromises, the couple felt that the situation went downhill following these events. Maurizio's mother insisted on doing all the cooking, doting on her son and grandson, and both parents spoke only Italian. Although Susan was picking up the language, she could not easily engage in conversation, and Maurizio acted as interpreter.

Maurizio acted quiet, even somewhat shy, and was caught in the middle between his parents and his wife. There were concerns that he was depressed. His style was to try to mediate the conflicts and make peace. Susan was engaging and sociable and made her opinions known. Lately, Maurizio and Susan were arguing a lot about his parents, their living arrangements, and their career goals. Susan wanted her husband to go back to school to pursue a more gratifying career. His parents felt that Maurizio's job was a good one: he made decent wages and had excellent benefits. Maurizio was unsure about what he wanted to do but felt certain that going back to school would be a financial setback. By the time they sought counselling, Susan believed that Maurizio was always siding with his parents. Their conflict escalated when Susan threatened to move herself and the baby to her parents' farm for the summer break.

The therapist perceived boundary issues and developmental problems in the relationship but also felt there were cultural issues that were not being addressed. The therapist was from an Anglo background and did not feel competent in dealing with these specific cultural groups. She requested a consultation with someone who had experience in working with Italian families, who reinforced her working assessment and interventions but suggested exploring cultural entry points and expanding the assessment to ask about the couple's respective cultural backgrounds. The therapist felt she was being culturally sensitive and knew how to probe the meaning of each partner's culture in their lives today.

The therapist started with a family systems approach that focused primarily on boundary issues, especially between Maurizio and his parents. However, this did not produce much progress in the therapy. The focus then shifted to the couple and their conflicts. They were asked to list their goals for the next five years. This task-focused approach provided safer ground for dialogue. Although they both agreed that they would like to move out and set up their own household, Maurizio's timelines were open-ended. He expressed the bonds of loyalty that he felt towards his family of origin, and these were represented primarily as loyalty to his Italian cultural and ethnic identity. He acknowledged his parents' need to maintain Italian traditions with their grandson, as well as their fears that Susan would undermine their wishes. By having the families live in the same household, his parents felt assured about their influence on their grandson. The parents' concerns about Susan and Maurizio loosening their bonds with the Italian culture were well founded—most of their other grandchildren were losing their ability to converse in Italian. In another disclosure, Maurizio admitted that, unlike his wife, he had never enjoyed school and had struggled to get his college diploma. He differed from Susan regarding the value of post-secondary education. By contrast, Susan's parents were acculturated to a greater degree into Canadian society. They wished to have some of their cultural traditions observed but usually only around holidays and special times of the year. They put a high value on formal education and career aspirations because they had had to struggle to carve out a living without the benefit of a Canadian education.

Despite the differences in type of acculturation achieved by their respective families of origin, Maurizio and Susan shared many of the experiences common to children of immigrant parents. Both had managed the challenges of growing up as children of newcomer Canadians. They shared the experiences of being singled out as being 'different' in school, functioning as translators and family ambassadors for their parents, having to be more mature in order to represent their families in the host culture, and having to respond to the stereotypical views of their ethnic backgrounds. Eventually Susan acknowledged some envy of the strong ethnic identity of Maurizio's family in contrast to her own diminished sense of ethnicity (e.g., loss of her parent's native language). This made her feel that her son would be more connected with his Italian heritage than his Dutch roots. This therapeutic focus on cultural dynamics within and between the families of origin proved to be useful in identifying the problematic issues of a bicultural union and the impact on raising children. As well, sharing a common bond as first-generation Canadians helped the couple to join in their efforts to resolve their differences.

After a number of months in therapy, Maurizio and Susan worked on reconciling their conflicts and developed a plan. Susan asked her parents for a deferred loan to finance a down payment for a house. The couple was looking for a house close enough to the home of Maurizio's parents for regular contact but far enough away that it was not in the Italian district. Initially, Maurizio's parents felt slighted but, as a supportive gesture, his mother offered to continue to provide free child care. The couple accepted this offer and viewed it as beneficial to maintaining Peter's sense of Italian identity. Maurizio decided not to pursue further schooling for the moment and instead sought to concentrate his efforts on achieving financial stability. Susan respected his decision and agreed it was more practical since they were planning a second child. On follow-up, Maurizio and Susan reported that their relationship was in good shape. Maurizio's parents were adjusting to the new situation, although the relationship with their daughter-in-law remained strained. They would never accept an invitation for dinner at Maurizio and Susan's home: they preferred to see the family on their own turf. In general, familial tension had decreased, and issues of ethnicity were discussed and responded to as these came up.

Case 2: Intergenerational Issues

Mrs R., a seventy-five-year-old Italian immigrant, was referred by her family doctor and brought to the session by a son and daughter. The therapist met with all three for half an hour, with Mrs R. for half and hour, and then reconvened with the son and daughter present (the session was conducted in Italian). When the family doctor made the referral, his main concern was with the high doses of various psychotropic medications that Mrs R. had been taking for many years. He had only recently become her GP, but had learned from Mrs R.'s children that their mother had been depressed since immigrating to Canada over forty years earlier. She was reclusive and relied on her husband to interact with the outside world regarding managing the children and family home. The children, two daughters and two sons, had a business in which they were partners but that did not involve their parents. Their father, now retired, had been a labourer in the construction business. He passively accepted his wife's affliction. Mrs R. obtained her medication from a psychiatrist whom she had been seeing for over fifteen years. No psychotherapy was provided. According to her children's report, Mrs R. told the psychiatrist which medications worked best for her, at which dose level, and the psychiatrist would write the prescriptions.

During the initial joint session with her children, Mrs R. denied all of their concerns regarding the number and amounts of drugs she was taking. They countered that they would often find her disoriented, with slurred speech. Their fear was that she was 'destroying brain cells' and would eventually need to be institutionalized. None of these voiced concerns had an impact on Mrs R. When I asked the children to leave the session, Mrs R. resisted saying that there was nothing she had to say to me that she hadn't said in front of her children. I shared with Mrs R. her GP's desire to wean her off of the medications and to prescribe a more limited level of medications. Mrs R. refused to discuss this possibility; she was happy with her psychiatrist and had no intention of leaving him. When I asked her how she planned to deal with her children's concerns, she said that she did not want them to be involved; she would manage her medications on her own. She was very critical of her husband for bringing her to this country; had she remained in Italy she would not need the drugs. She dated her depression and ill health from the time she stepped foot in Canada.

By the end of our meeting, it was agreed that we would invite her children back into the session so that she could tell them that she did not want them to interfere in her drug taking and did not want to hear about their concerns. Mrs R.'s children were not pleased with this outcome, but I reinforced her wishes, stating that they had done all they could to help her and that now they needed to leave their mother to manage her own health issues. We clarified what this would mean in practice; for example, Mrs R.'s youngest son would no longer fill her daily dose pill box. Mrs R. was not happy about this and insisted that her son should continue to carry out this task. I challenged her, reminding her that she wanted to take full responsibility for her drug intake; to continue to rely on her son would re-involve her family, which she had stated clearly she did not want. It was clear to the son and daughter how Mrs R. manipulated them with her complaints about her health and her persistence in taking high doses of medication. I reassured the son and daughter that they would continue to visit with their parents but that they would no longer voice concerns regarding their mother's health, nor would they attempt to intervene. If she deteriorated, she would know that she could not blame them: she was fully in charge of her treatment, with her psychiatrist. Mrs R. reiterated that she trusted her psychiatrist and would remain in treatment with him. Her son and daughter had expected a different outcome from the session (that their mother would agree to psychotherapy with me and would terminate her contact with the psychiatrist). I spoke with the GP; he agreed that nothing more could be done and that all his previous efforts to influence Mrs R. had failed. He would reinforce with the children their withdrawal from her treatment.

This case illustrates an acculturation outcome in which, following immigration, Mrs R. refused to engage with the host culture. Her husband was left to mediate between his wife's adherence to her Italian culture and the new Canadian culture, so that their children could achieve a form of acculturation that straddled both. Mrs R.'s depression following immigration may have been precipitated by her inability to mourn the loss of her country, culture, and the support of an extended family. No doubt, her husband's and children's guilt about her unhappiness caused them to accommodate Mrs R. in ways that were ultimately harmful. During the early stages of her depressive illness, Mrs R. 'shopped' around for an Italian-speaking psychiatrist until she found someone who would prescribe medications according to her specifications. She angrily rejected her family's concerns regarding her health.

The approach taken in the management of the case was one that respected Mrs R.'s world view about her life in Canada. She had had little control over the decision to immigrate, but she could not change the past. Under these circumstances, her only way to deal with the resentment and depression at having lost her country of origin was to numb the pain with medication. Her children needed to respect their mother's right to be in charge of her life, even if she were harming herself. She was not interested in talking about her depression or its sources. In fact, she barely tolerated the session, which she had agreed to attend only to appease her children's concerns.

Application of Cross-cultural Practice Concepts to Bicultural and Intergenerational Issues

Although interventions from several theoretical frameworks (e.g., systems, ecological, developmental) were employed in both of these cases, we will concentrate on how cultural dynamics were probed to address specific problems. Central to our case analyses is an understanding of the process of acculturation and its impact on family adaptation to a new culture. As well, interventions are generated from the integrated framework for cross-cultural practice proposed by Tsang and George (1998). Finally, adherence to social work principles, as detailed in the Canadian social workers professional code of ethics, is highlighted.

In the case of Maurizio and Susan, the need to respond to the unique representations of two distinct ethnic groups overwhelmed the therapist. As a social worker, she had to integrate her knowledge of the various cultural literacy models of practice with being culturally self-aware, as well as being aware of the dominant culture's perceptions of the Italian and Dutch immigrant groups. The challenge was to articulate her cultural sensitivity to each partner. In other words, how does one implement the strategies used typically in couples therapy when the focus of the problems and their resolution has to do with bicultural issues, especially when the worker is not a member of either culture and has her own unique experiences of yet a third culture.

The first part of the work required the therapist to accept her discomfort in inquiring about cultures with which she was largely unfamiliar. According to Tsang and George (1998), the integration of culturally sensitive attitudes requires the therapist to demonstrate a firm commitment to social justice and equity, accept and value difference, and be critically self-reflective. As a member of the dominant culture, the therapist had little personal knowledge of or experience with the impact of immigration and the process of acculturation. Yet, she was well aware of the negative impact of structural and institutional policies, especially on immigrant and refugee groups currently immigrating to Canada. How had these policies affected Maurizio and Susan's parents when they first immigrated to Canada? What were the current negative affects?

Next, the therapist had to show her acceptance of cultural/ethnic difference as well as reflect on her own social/cultural prejudices. The therapist proceeded by readily revealing her limited knowledge of the couple's respective cultures and by inquiring about their respective cultural experiences. This approach requires a stance of readiness and openness to hear the clients' personal narratives about their experiences within their cultural groups and with the host culture. The therapist's acceptance of the couple's portrayal of their ethnicity and cultural identity, and her empathic acceptance of cultural differences between the couple, and between herself and the couple, enhanced the on-going assessment and strengthened the therapeutic alliance.

Arriving at an assessment of the influence of cultural differences on bicultural marriages requires exploration of cultural meanings within the original family context of each partner. This exploration results in the construction of a family genogram, a means of graphically mapping the family relationships and dynamics that includes ethnocultural dimensions as key factors in explaining family system tension and conflict. Sample question directed to each partner are:

- Could you describe your experience of being a first-generation Italian/Dutch Canadian?
- How similar, or different, are you from your parents (and siblings) today?
- Tell me about your grandparents and/or other extended family.
- What is it like being married to someone from an Italian/Dutch background?
- How are your cultures similar? Different?
- How do your parents (extended family and cultural group) view marriage outside of your culture?
- How do they regard child rearing?
- What was it like growing up as a child of newcomers?
- What kind of a neighbourhood did you live in? Was it culturally diverse?
- Did you experience discrimination? If you did, how did you deal with it?
- What do you hope for your children in terms of ethnic ties?

The acquisition of professional knowledge, according to the integrated model of sensitive cultural practice, requires the therapist to understand the process of acculturation as experienced by newcomer families, the impact of this experience on the internalized meanings of the culture retained by subsequent generations, and the dynamic significance of cross-cultural communication. The therapist came to understand that Maurizio's parents, in contrast to Susan's, had achieved a degree of acculturation that left them separate from the host culture; they felt more comfortable retaining close ties to their Italian heritage. They lived in an Italian neighbourhood, participated in Italian social clubs, spoke primarily Italian, and retained Italian religious and cultural values and customs. Probably because the Dutch culture had more in common with the host culture, Susan's parents achieved an integrated degree of acculturation. The task for the therapist was to understand the impact of parental acculturation on Maurizio and Susan's internalized meanings of their respective cultures. She also had to try to understand the nature of communication across their respective cultures, between them, and between their families. Maurizio's internalized view of his cultural heritage was reflected in his desire to fulfill his and his parents' hopes for maintaining Italian traditions within his own family. This contrasted with Susan's looser ties with her Dutch culture, despite the fact that she mourned the loss of parts of her ethnic identity. Initially, communication across cultural boundaries and belief systems was conflicted and confused by strong emotional reactions—anxiety, frustration, disillusionment, and disappointment. However, as the couple gained greater comfort in revealing their respective cultural identities and differences, they were able to understand and empathize with each other's cultural bonds. This resulted in improved cross-cultural communication between them.

The professional skills component of the integrated framework was grounded in the therapist's openness about her lack of knowledge about the couple's respective cultural experiences, the therapist's empathic understanding of the couple's portrayal of their parents' experiences with acculturation, and the therapist's ability to convey the importance of acknowledging, valuing, and accepting cultural difference. Within this therapeutic context, Maurizio and Susan were able to be open about their cultural differences while respecting each other's viewpoint with regard to ongoing relationships with their families of origin.

In the case of Mrs R., two operative social work principles supported a culturally competent approach. First, providing social work services in the language of the client (CASW, 1994, Section 1.7, p. 10) was an important accommodation. Despite Mrs R.'s reluctance to attend the interview arranged by her children, knowing that the session would be conducted in Italian probably contributed to her agreement to participate. Her past attempts at finding Italian-speaking psychiatrists indicated how important it was for her to communicate in her own language rather than having her children function as translators, which they did regularly for both parents. Second, the therapist acted in a manner that respected the client's dignity and individuality (CASW, 1994, Section 4.1, p. 13), even when there was considerable pressure from the client's children and the referring doctor to advise Mrs R. to terminate her relationship with her psychiatrist. The therapist's interventions supported Mrs R.'s taking control of her mental health needs. This approach seemed to reassure Mrs R. and contrasted with the absence of control that she probably experienced when she came to Canada against her wishes.

While the above-noted social work principles provide useful guidelines for cross-cultural practice, their application, especially when addressing the ethical complexities of work with Mrs R. and her family, illustrates the importance of being able to communicate in the client's language. In most clinical situations this type of language fit between client and therapist is rare. Language barriers may be addressed by the use of interpreters from the client's own cultural group, but their availability is limited and their services expensive. Also, the process of translation is awkward and sometimes inaccurate, often interfering with the development of a good working bond with the client. On a final note, it is not advisable to ask family members, especially children, to function as interpreters. Children who interpret their parents' communication with the outside world are susceptible to being scapegoated, and viewed by the family as responsible for resolving conflicts with the host culture.

Despite these reservations about addressing cross-cultural language barriers, it is highly impractical to expect a match between social worker and client on the basis of cultural background and language. Rather, each therapist needs to be flexible and creative in selecting strategies for dealing with language barriers. Most newcomers have some ability and desire to speak the language of the host country. Thus, what is required of the therapist is a patient, receptive stance and the use of simplified versions of the language. In situations where the language barrier prevents optimal therapeutic work, referral to an ethno-specific agency or therapist will be necessary. If such services are unavailable, professional social work therapists have the responsibility of advocating for the development of ethnically relevant services for their clients.

Conclusions

In this chapter we have attempted to highlight some fundamental principles that apply to cross-cultural social work practice. Theoretical models for approaching culturally sensitive practice with clients of all cultures and diversities have been critiqued. We believe that Tsang and George's (1998) integrated model for understanding and working in a cross-cultural context is particularly relevant. Conceptually, the integrated model accommodates domains of knowledge that apply to all levels of social work practice—micro, mezzo, and macro. For our discussion of the Italian culture, we emphasized understanding the process of acculturation as well as addressing the specific issues of intergenerational cultural conflicts and the problems that arise in bicultural unions. Finally, we illustrated, through the discussion of clinical cases selected from the practices of the authors, the ways in which cross-cultural theoretical models of practice are reflected in therapeutic work with Italian clients. Future development and refinement of theoretical models of sensitive cross-cultural clinical practice will need to be tested empirically. The results of these studies will lead to important knowledge development, which we hope will advance optimal approaches for helping clients from diverse groups.

Notes

1. The term 'cross-cultural', rather than 'multicultural', is used in this chapter because of its preferred use in the practice literature reviewed. As well, the term 'bicultural' is used in examining unions of people from two distinctly different cultures.
2. An extensive review of culturally based practice models exceeds the scope of this chapter; for a comprehensive critical review of conceptual models of cross-cultural social work practice see Tsang and George (1998).
3. 'Intermarriage' is a term frequently used in the sparse practice literature available in this area. The authors, however, use the term 'bicultural unions' to acknowledge the diversity of relationships formed in modern-day families.

References

Alaggia, R., Chau, S., & Tsang, A.K. (2001). Astronaut Asian families: Impact of migration from the perspective of the youth. *Social Work Research and Evaluation: An International Journal, 2*(2), 295–306.

Baptiste, D.A. (1993). Immigrant families, adolescents and acculturation: Insights for therapists. *Marriage and Family Review, 19*(3/4), 341–63.

Berry, J.W. (1988). *Understanding the Process of Acculturation for Primary Prevention.* Minneapolis: Minnesota University, Refugee Assistance Program, Mental Health Technical Assistance Center.

Berry, J.W., Kim, U., Minde, T., & Mok, D. (1987). Comparative studies of acculturative stress. *International Migration Review, 21*, 491–511.

Berry, J.W., Poortinga, Y.H., Segall, M.H., & Dasen, P.R. (1992). *Cross-cultural Psychology: Research and Applications.* Cambridge: Cambridge University Press.

Bishop, A. (1994). *Becoming an Ally: Breaking the Cycle of Oppression.* Halifax: Fernwood.

Brice, J. (1982). West Indian families. In M. McGoldrick, J.K. Pearce, & J. Giordano (Eds), *Ethnicity and Family Therapy* (pp. 123–33). New York: Guilford.

Brindis, C., Wolfe, A.L., McCarter, V., Ball, S., & Starbuck-Morales, S. (1995). The associations between immigrant status and risk-behaviour patterns in Latino adolescents. *Journal of Adolescent Health, 17*(2), 99–105.

Brown, L. (1991). Antiracism as an ethical imperative: An example from feminist therapy. *Ethics and Behaviour, 1*(2), 113–27.

Canadian Association of Social Workers. (1994). *Social Work Code of Ethics.* Ottawa: Canadian Association of Social Workers.

Casas, M.J. (1985). A reflection on the status of racial/ethnic minority research. *Counseling Psychologist, 13*(4), 581–98.

Cooper, S. (1973). A look at the effect of racism on clinical work. *Social Casework, 54*, 76–84.

Cornille, T.A. (1993). Support systems and the relocation process for children and families. *Marriage and Family Review, 19*(3/4), 281–98.

Cross, T.L. (1988). Service to minority populations: Cultural competence continuum. *Focal Point, 3*(1), 1–4.

Devore, W., & Schlesinger, E.G. (1999). *Ethnic-Sensitive Social Work Practice.* 5th ed. Toronto: Allyn and Bacon.

Dominelli, L. (1993). *Anti-Racist Social Work.* London: Macmillan.

Dyche, L. & Zayas, L.H. (1995). The value of curiosity and naivité for the cross-cultural psychotherapist. *Family Process, 34*, 389–99.

Elliott, J.L., & Fleras, A. (1990). Immigration and the Canadian mosaic. In P. Li (Ed.), *Race and Ethnic Relations in Canada* (pp. 51–76). Toronto: Oxford University Press.

Falicov, C. (1995). Training to think culturally: A multidimensional comparative framework. *Family Process, 34*, 373–88.

Green, J.W. (1999). *Cultural Awareness in the Human Services.* 3rd ed. Boston: Allyn and Bacon.

Griffith, M.S. (1977). The influence of race on the psychotherapeutic relationship. *Psychiatry, 40*(1), 27–40.

Gudykunst, W.B., & Kim, Y.Y. (1984). *Communicating with Strangers: An Approach to Intercultural Communication.* New York: Random House.

Henry, F., Tator, C., Mattis, W., & Rees, T. (1995). *The Colour of Democracy: Racism in Canadian Society.* Toronto: Harcourt Brace.

Iacovetta, F. (1992). *Such Hardworking People: Italian Immigrants in Postwar Toronto.* Montreal: McGill-Queen's University Press.

LaFramboise, T.D., & Foster, S.L. (1992). Cross-cultural training: Scientist-practitioner model and methods. *Counseling Psychologist, 20*(3), 472–89.

Lam, C.M. (1998). Adolescent development in the context of Canadian-Chinese immigrant families. *Canadian Social Work Review, 15*(2), 177–92.

Lau, A. (1986). Family therapy across cultures. In J.L. Cox (Ed.), *Transcultural Psychiatry.* London: Croom Helm.

Lautard, H., & Guppy, N. (1990). The vertical mosaic revisited. In P. Li (Ed.), *Race and Ethnic Relations in Canada* (pp. 189–208). Toronto: Oxford University Press.

Lay, C., & Verkuyten, M. (1999). Ethnic identity and its relation to personal self-esteem: A comparison of Canadian-born and foreign-born Chinese adolescents. *Journal of Social Psychology, 139*(3), 288–99.

Leigh, J.W. (1998). *Communicating for Cultural Competence.* Toronto: Allyn and Bacon.

McGoldrick, M., Giordano, J., & Pearce, J. (Eds). (1996). *Ethnicity and Family Therapy.* New York: Guilford Press.

McGoldrick, M., & Preta, G. (1984). Ethnic intermarriage: Implications for therapy. *Family Process, 23.*

Mullaly, R. (1994). *Structural Social Work.* Toronto: McClelland and Stewart.

Nguyen, H.N., Messé, L.A., & Stollack, G.E. (1999). Toward a more complex understanding of acculturation and adjustment: Cultural involvements and psychosocial functioning in Vietnamese youth. *Journal of Cross-cultural Psychology, 30*(1), 5–31.

Phinney, J.S. (1996). Understanding ethnic diversity: The role of ethnic identity. *American Behavioral Scientist, 40*(2), 143–52.

Pinderhughes, E. (1989). *Understanding Race, Ethnicity and Power: The Key to Efficacy in Clinical Practice.* New York: Free Press.

Poortinga, Y. (1992). Towards a conceptualization of culture for psychology. In S. Iwawaki, Y. Kashima, & K. Leung (Eds), *Innovations in Cross-cultural Psychology* (pp. 3–117). Amsterdam: Swets and Zeitlinger.

Reichelt, S., & Sveaass, N. (1994). Therapy with refugee families: What is a 'good' conversation? *Family Process, 33*, 247–62.

Ruben, B.D. (1989). The study of cross-cultural competence: Traditions and contemporary issues. *International Journal of Intercultural Relations, 13*(3), 229–40.

Sturino, F. (1999). Italian-Canadians. In P.R. Magocsi (Ed.), *Encyclopedia of Canada's Peoples*. Toronto: University of Toronto Press.

Sue, D., & Sue, S. (1987). Cultural factors in the clinical assessment of Asian Americans. *Journal of Consulting and Clinical Psychology, 55*(4), 479–87.

Thomas, A., & Sillen, S. (1976). *Racism and Psychiatry*. Secaucus, NJ: Citadel Press.

Tsang, A.K.T., & George, U. (1998). An integrated framework for cross-cultural social work. *Canadian Social Work Review, 15*(1), 73–94.

Ward, C. (1996). Acculturation. In D. Landis & R.S. Bhagat (Eds), *Handbook of Intercultural Training*. 2nd ed. (pp. 124–47). Thousand Oaks, CA: Sage.

Watts, R.J. (1992). Elements of psychology of human diversity. *Journal of Community Psychology, 20*, 116–131.

Chapter 8

Social Work Practice with Canadians of Arab Background: Insight into Direct Practice

Alean Al-Krenawi and John R. Graham

At some point in their lives, people have had the feeling of being misunderstood. This experience is especially resonant for some social work students who encounter a body of knowledge that may not always adapt readily to their home community. Historically, social workers of various ethno-racial groups tended to have been trained in schools of social work under models that have highly Western assumptions. One of the authors (Alean Al-Krenawi) conveys his personal and professional experiences as a Bedouin-Arab who received undergraduate and advanced social work training in schools of social work in Israel and Canada. After his first university degree, he practised for an eleven-year period. Especially early in his career, he noticed apparent dissonances between his home culture, with which he worked and lived on a daily basis, and the assumptions derived from the profession of social work. One of his most decisive career moments was the gradual discovery that it is essential to bend any social work knowledge, practice, theory, or skill in the direction of the community with which one works. 'Walking with the wind, rather than against it' became a metaphor that guided subsequent work with his community and contributed to his growing comfort in mediating between cultural and professional assumptions. If there is any one unifying theme for this chapter, walking with the wind would be the most resonant (Al-Krenawi, 1998a).

Al-Krenawi and this chapter's co-author, John Graham, a non-Arab born and raised in central Canada, have published extensively on direct social work and mental health practice with Arab peoples, especially the Bedouin-Arab. For this reason, significant portions of this chapter are referenced to direct practice. Likewise, because of the authors' experiences in and outside Canada, the breadth of literature on practice in the Arab world, and the recentness of much immigration to Canada from the Arab world, portions of this chapter concentrate on practice implications from the vantage point of people who are relatively new to Canada, in addition to those who have been in Canada for some time. The chapter has relevance, therefore, to domestic and international practice. As with the other chapters in this section, the present analysis draws from the authors' collective experiences, and is subject to the confines of their perceptions. Readers are encouraged to engage with the chapter and to use it as a basis for further developing their appreciation of self-awareness as well as the prospects of working with clients of Arab background.

The chapter considers a wide range of topics: the Arab world in context; how to integrate social work views ('formal theory') and Arab world views ('informal theory'); issues of acculturation in Canada; religious, familial, age, and gender constructions; and individual development and group references in Arab culture. Following a discussion of these topics, we turn our attention to help-seeking strategies in Arab communities, difficulties in establishing and maintaining a helping relationship, and guidelines for effective social work practice with clients of Arab background.

The Arab World in Context

This chapter refers repeatedly to the Arab world, by which we mean a highly diverse collection of twenty-two countries stretching over fourteen million square kilometres, from northern Africa through to the Arabian peninsula, and including Morocco, Egypt, Jordan, Lebanon, Syria, and Saudi Arabia. By describing such as the Arab world, we in no way intend to imply that significant portions of Canada, where people of Arab background live, are not also part of an Arab world. Yet, for clarity's sake, this chapter will distinguish between countries from which people of Arab background originate and those communities in Canada where there are people of Arab background.

Arab demographic growth has been phenomenal. In 1977, people in the Arab world numbered less than 150 million; this has since increased to 275 million, or about 5 per cent of the world population, and is projected to double again by 2024. People of Arab background constitute a significant—and growing—proportion within Western countries such as Australia (210,000), Canada (144,050) France (2,000,000), Britain (210,000), Israel (1 million), and the United States (700,000) (Al-Krenawi & Graham, 1998; Hopkins & Ibrahim, 1997; UNESCO, 1996). The populace is also young. Today, 52 per cent of the people in the Arab world are under the age of twenty; the equivalent percentage worldwide is 32 per cent, and in more advanced industrialized countries 20 per cent. Literacy rates in the Arab world are low: in 1995 no more than 45 per cent of the population over ten years of age was literate. Technical skills and infrastructure are likewise sparse. Economic participation in the Arab world is such that 30 per cent of the populace carries the remaining 70 per cent. In more economically developed countries, in contrast, economic participation rates are as high as 60 per cent. Average life expectancy in the Arab world has increased markedly over the last half-century: in 1960 it was forty-five years; in 1996 it was sixty-three years. The latter figure compares to sixty-four years worldwide and seventy-seven years in advanced industrialized countries (Al-Krenawi & Graham, 1998).

Arab societies are highly diverse. Thus, any generalizations necessarily obscure and neglect differences in an effort to explain and illuminate potential commonalties. All that follows, therefore, is tentative and provisional. As many scholars conclude, people in Arab countries may have a strong identity based on ethnic, linguistic, sectarian, familial, tribal, regional, socio-economic, or even national identities. Consequently, outside observers may perceive a lack of unity, based in part on their perceptions of social and class distinctions, political disunity or fragmentation, or religious differences. At the same time, Arab societies share many attributes. These include, but are not limited to, a common physical and geographic environment and a collective history (Barakat, 1993, p. 33). Countries in the Arab world are profoundly transitional, balancing modern phenomena such as oil exploration with traditional structures such as tribal castes (ibid., pp. 24–6). Economies tend to be largely dependent on other countries and may be underdeveloped. As one sociologist remarks, 'its material and human resources have been harnessed for the benefit of a small segment of the population and on behalf of antagonistic [geopolitical] external forces' (ibid., p. 26).

Several historical factors have been influential. One of the earliest and most significant occurred in the period 622 to 900, during which time Islam spread throughout the Arab world. That era gave way to several struggles with Christendom, throughout what is commonly called the Crusade period, with particular focus on Jerusalem and other sites sacred to both religions. Then, in the fifteenth and sixteenth centuries, the Arab world fell to the Ottoman Empire. Later, in the nineteenth century, European countries vied for control in the region. In 1948, the United Nations' plan to partition Palestine into two states—one for Jewish (Israel) the other for Arab peoples—ignited a political reaction that coincided with the fall of many old regimes in the Arab world, and with the rise of new regimes. At certain points, some of these new regimes were committed to greater independence from colonial powers, closer pan-Arab co-operation, and greater social reform and equality. An especially significant historical event is the defeat of Syria, Egypt, and Jordan during the 1967 Arab–Israeli war. That event led to the Israeli occupation of part of Jerusalem and the West Bank (formerly part of Jordan) and Gaza (formerly part of Egypt). Some historians see 1967 as a marker for the slowing down of pan-Arab unity or co-operation, and for increasing dependence upon the superpowers (United States and the Soviet Union) (Barakat, 1993; Hopkins & Ibrahim, 1997). The resurgence of Islamic loyalties since the 1980s, which coincided with the resurgence of Arab autonomy, has provoked internal energies within the Arab world (Abudabbeh & Aseel, 1999, pp. 284–5).

All such historical experiences have contributed to the world views of many people of Arab background. People from the Arab world who emigrate to Canada may have experienced, either directly or indirectly, the wars and complex geopolitics of the Middle East in the past half-century. Canadians of non-Arab background may have several preconceived biases towards people of Arab background. Their initial context might be with the OPEC oil-producing countries. People of Arab background have been targets of racism in Canada. Popular equations of Islam with terrorism, or of Arab peoples with terrorist organizations, provide fertile ground for discrimination. During the Gulf War in the early 1990s, for example, Canadians of Arab background experienced systematic and overt discrimination (Kashmeri, 1991); likewise such has been the case in the aftermath of the events of 11 September 2001 in the United States. Racism may well be exacerbated by the visibility of people of Arab background—that is, by the way in which people of Arab background may dress or be otherwise distinguished from some others in Canadian society.

Immigration of people from Arab countries has increased substantially over the past thirty-five years. According to Statistics Canada census information, in 1961, 0.5 per cent of the immigrant population hailed from 'West Central Asia and the Middle East' (note that this broad category includes both Arab and non-Arab countries). This figure increased to 1.9 per cent in 1961–70, 3.1 per cent in 1971–80, 7.1 per cent in 1981–90, and 7.9 per cent in 1991–96 (see the Statistics Canada Web site, at http://www.statcan.ca/english/census96/nov4/table1.pdf). The 1996 Canadian census indicated that people of Arab origin number 188,435 across the country, constituting 0.7 per cent of the total population. In certain metropolitan areas, the presence of people of Arab background is higher. In Montreal and Ottawa, for example, the proportions are 2.2 per cent, in Toronto 0.9 per cent, and in Edmonton 0.8 per cent (http://www.statcan.ca/english/Pgdb/People/Population/demo28e.htm).

Formal Theory, Informal Theory, and Mediating Social Context

Any social work intervention involves two or more individuals, each of whom is distinct from the other. Such differences could include, but are not limited to, conceptions of race, culture, gender, age cohort, life stage, sexual orientation, region, nationality, creed, or religion. As scholars have long concluded, each such difference influences a worker's approach to a client and a client's approach to a worker (Ibrahim, 1985). A second and equally important way of thinking about differences between social workers and clients is the concept of 'formal' and 'informal' theories (Al-Krenawi, 1998b, 2000a). Social workers may be seen to bring to any encounter a body of professional knowledge, values, and skills, the totality of which may be considered 'formal theory'. Clients bring to the encounter the sum total of their life experiences—with the knowledge, values, and skills that they imply—all of which may be seen as an informal theory. Often, this informal theory is strongly anchored to a client's culture. Likewise, workers process their understanding of formal theory through their own culture. Formal and informal theories, however, interact in a particular social milieu, and that person-in-environment context is the apex upon which any social work intervention is shaped. Take the example of a social worker of Italian background who works with a Muslim family of Arab background. The family head is from Jordan. The social worker has learned that the client has two wives, one of whom lives in Canada, the other in Jordan. Thinking of family in polygamous terms immediately challenges the worker's formal theory; likewise, the worker's cultural assumptions of what ought to constitute a family are potentially called into question. The worker may be aware that his or her assumptions are manifestly different than those of the husband; the worker may need to determine their congruence, or lack of congruence, with the assumptions of other family members.

Because social work emerged as a profession in Western countries such as the United States, the United Kingdom, and France, precepts of democracy, liberalism, and individual rights tend to dominate its assumptions. The popular slogans of the 1776 American Declaration of Independence (life, liberty, and the pursuit of happiness) and of the French Revolution of 1789 (liberty, equality, fraternity) epitomize these cultural values. Social work's sister disciplines, which have similar individualistic assumptions, have influenced social work and may have helped reinforce Western notions in social work. In psychology, for example, Abraham Maslow's hierarchy of needs emphasizes self-actualization as an ultimate, and profoundly individualistic, ideal. Likewise, Erik Erikson's notion of individual development stresses stages in which individuals separate from their parents and develop an autonomous, and again strongly individualistic, sense of self. Conceptions of individuation (Jung), autonomy (Mahler), and inner growth/becoming human (Rogers) prevail among other psychologists. To their credit, social work's earliest thinkers appreciated the individual in larger contexts, be it family, community, or society. But individualistic notions nonetheless are strongly resonant: individual autonomy, individual achievement, and individual choice making capacity in social work thinking. In other respects, social work has been committed to human rights and self-determination, as expressed in individual and community contexts.

Among some cultures, a client's informal theory may be highly collectivist, in contrast to the worker's formal theory, which, as we note above, is often individualistic. Categories such as 'individualist' and 'collectivist' are ideal types—that is, broad conceptions that help us to understand particular phenomena. While these ideal types may obscure and neglect differences within a category, they are nonetheless helpful in illuminating and explaining differences between two or more categories. It is sometimes useful to conceive individualism and collectivism along an individualist-collectivist (IC) continuum, with worker and client falling somewhere between the two polarities. IC refers to the degree to which the person's world view encourages, fosters, and facilitates the needs, wishes, desires, and values of an autonomous and unique self over those of a group (Mead, 1967; Triandis, 1972). Individualists may be inclined to perceive themselves as separate and autonomous individuals. Collectivists, in contrast, may conceive of the individual in far less isolation from others within the same community—they may see themselves as fundamentally connected with others (Markus & Kitayama, 1991). In individualist world views, personal needs and goals take precedence; in collectivist world views, they may be secondary to the goals of a group. The social context in which a worker–client interaction occurs is necessarily variable. Many who read this textbook will expect to practise in Canada, a diverse society with fairly individualistic historical influences. Others may choose to practise in societal contexts that are more clearly collectivist.

Acculturation, Assimilation, Discrimination

Acculturation is the process of adapting and adjusting to life in a new country. *Assimilation* occurs when one moves away from one's original cultural identity to a different culture. Within the individual, tensions between acculturation and assimilation may occur. Similar dynamics may also co-exist between family members (children born in Canada versus parents who immigrated to Canada, for example). In both instances, notions of acculturation and assimilation may be fluid and changing. Some evidence suggests that people of Arab background, particularly those affiliated with Islam—a minority religion in countries such as Canada—'find acculturation to be more difficult than have other immigrants' (Faragallah, Schumm, & Webb, 1997, p. 182). Some scholars see the United States as having a stronger tradition of assimilation than does Canada (Lipset, 1990), and so transnational comparisons are not entirely reliable. However, research from the United States indicates that Americans of Arab background, more so than other Middle East immigrant groups, have tended to perceive themselves as having feelings of being an outsider and of wanting to return ultimately to their homeland (Georgeski, cited in Faragallah, Schumm, & Webb, 1997, p. 182).

Processes of acculturation are influenced by age, gender, education, the recentness of arrival, and generational status (a newly arrived immigrant to Canada may have a different sense of acculturation than, say, a third-generation Canadian of Arab background). People of diverse backgrounds may choose to live in Canada sometimes, and in a different country at other times, possibly returning to an Arab homeland. Processes of acculturation (coming to Canada) and reacculturation (returning to one's initial homeland) may occur. Social workers may encounter cultural conflict, confusion, disharmony, and disintegration within families as a result of acculturation (Abu-Baker, 1999). Given the differences between some aspects of the Canadian experience and those associated with a client's Arab background, there may be intergenerational tensions. People of Arab background, like those from other cultures, may have the feeling of leading multiple lives: one life (often in the home/family context) in closer accordance with Arab cultural traditions; another life with greater reference to broader Canadian society. In the interaction between these two contexts, the propensity to identify with one's own experience of culture may be reinforced.

Religion

Small portions of northern Israel, Lebanon, and Syria adhere to the Druze religion (a faith tradition premised on transmigration of souls and the reception of religious knowledge in the middle years of one's life); small numbers in these countries follow other religions beyond this (Lev-Wiesel & Al-Krenawi, 1999). Most people of Arab background, however, are either Christian or Muslim. Approximately fourteen million Arab people, less than 10 per cent of all Arabs, follow the Christian faith. Lebanon has the highest portion of Christians; they constitute nearly half the population. Most follow the Eastern Orthodox or Catholic traditions. In all other Arab countries, Christians are in a minority, with the highest percentages in Sudan, followed by Syria, Egypt, Jordan, and Palestine. The largest Christian congregation in the Middle East is the Coptic Orthodox Church, numbering nearly six million, most of whom are in Egypt. Although a minority within the Arab world, Christians nonetheless have been important leaders in the intelligentsia, the professions, and in political activities of the period following the Second World War (Abudabbeh & Aseel, 1999, pp. 285–6).

The majority of Arab peoples are Muslim. After Christianity, Islam is the world's second largest religion, representing 19.4 per cent of the world's population and having high rates of population growth (Al-Krenawi & Graham, 2000b). This religion originated in the seventh century, with Allah's revelation to the Prophet Muhammad, via the angel Gabriel, of a sacred book called the Koran, which Muslims believe to be the word of God (Al-Krenawi & Graham, 2000b). The Koran is further supplemented with the Prophet's own sayings (the *hadith*) and practices (*Sunna*). Specific strictures on marriage, property division, prayer, and other family and individual matters, are therewith elaborated. An important part of the religion is the *Shari'a*, those revealed laws to which Muslims must adhere. They cover marriage, divorce, child custody, and other aspects of life. Another important aspect is the Five Pillars of Islam:

1. The *Shahada*, also known as the profession of faith, is the belief that there is no other god but Allah and that Muhammad is His last prophet. Islam therefore insists on the submission of the faithful to the oneness of God. 'Say: He is God, the one and only' (Koran, 112, v. 1–4) is one of many Koranic verses emphasizing the monotheistic character of Islam.
2. The *Salat* is the imperative to pray five times daily: at dawn, noon, mid-afternoon, sunset, and evening. These prayers can be performed anywhere. Although individual prayer is allowed, group prayer is preferred.
3. The *Zakat* is payment of alms to the needy on behalf of one's family and business. 'It was customarily calculated as an annual payment of two and one half percent of all capital assets, savings, and current income above a specified threshold' (Azmi, 1991, p. 223). Exact rates, however, could be flexible, in part according to the need established by the imam, or local Muslim cleric.
4. The *Siam* is the requirement of fasting from food, drink, and sex during daylight hours during the month of Ramadan, which immediately precedes the celebration of the date upon which Allah revealed the Koran to the Prophet Muhammad. Ramadan ends with a three-day celebration, Id Al-Fitr, the breaking of the fast. The Siam emphasizes self-discipline and reflection rather than abstinence and self-mortification.

5. The *Hajj* is a pilgrimage to Mecca, a holy city where Allah revealed the Koran to the Prophet Muhammad. This pilgrimage should be undertaken at least once in a Muslim's lifetime, if one is financially, mentally, and physically able to do so.

In anthropological terms, Muslim societies tend to be high context. They tend to emphasize the collective over the individual, have a slower pace of societal change, and experience a greater sense of social stability than low context societies, which tend to revere the individual and which are fast-paced societies in continual transition (Hall, 1976). Muslims, therefore, may view social stability as the achievement of social peace. This imperative may be reinforced by an emphasis upon the collective over the individual—on the Umma, or community of all Muslims, extending to the global level. 'Help each other in the acts of goodness and piety and do not extend help to each other in sinful acts or transgression behaviours' (Koran, 5, v. 2). The Prophet Muhammad advised Muslims: 'Help your brother [the Muslim] whether he is the oppressor or the oppressed.' When the Prophet was asked how to help a fellow Muslim if he is the oppressor, he replied: 'Hold his hand from oppression' (Al-Juzuyyah, 1993). The prophetic Hadith points out that 'Every one of you is a shepherd and each one of you is responsible for his flock' (Nagati, 1993).

This sense of collective responsibility is further reinforced by how Muslims tend to view their place within society. Islam, it should be emphasized, is not concerned with the welfare of the individual alone; it seeks to achieve a wider societal well-being. While ensuring the individual's freedom, it places equal stress on mutual responsibility. This principle, in turn, is two-dimensional. The individual achieves balance between thought and action (internal), while caring for the collective welfare of society (external) (Azmi, 1991; Dean & Khan, 1998; El-Azayem & Hedayat-Diba, 1994). But this individual-societal consonance is best realized through total submission to the will of God. As stated in the Koran, 'My worship and my sacrifice and my living and my dying are all for Allah, Lord of worlds' (Koran, 6, v. 163).

Family, Age, and Gender Constructions

Most social roles in Arab societies are influenced by age and sex, and the basic social structures are the nuclear and extended (*hamula*) family. Among some communities in the Arab world, collections of hamula are a tribe. Age is an important determinant of social status and power. Deference and respect from an individual in a subordinate position may require the person in a superior social position to look after that individual. For both sexes, advanced years and experience are associated with wisdom and knowledge; hence the popular Arab expression 'anyone who is a day older than you in age is a year older than you in understanding'. In some communities, post-menopausal women, especially mothers of powerful men, may have considerable power and both formal and informal social influence upon virtually all aspects of family life (Al-Krenawi & Graham, 2000a).

The Arab school system throughout the Middle East and North Africa is strongly representative of Arab culture (Chaleby, 1987b). At many Arab schools, the curriculum is based largely on rote learning and on remembering facts, rather than on developing individual interpretations and analysis. Conformity, rather than independent thought and creativity, often predominates (Chaleby, 1987b). The teacher may be a strong authority figure, reinforcing society's hierarchical, authoritarian nature and its insistence upon respecting one's elders. Adults are likely to be perceived as a source of knowledge, wisdom, and authority (Barakat, 1993; Sharabi, 1975). From early childhood, the individual may learn that knowledge and wisdom are passed on by the old to the young, and not vice versa (El-Islam, 1989).

Arab societies can be patriarchal, where the father is the head of the family and a powerful, charismatic figure. In such a family structure, the father commands subordination and respect as the legitimate authority for all family matters (Al-Krenawi, 1999a; El-Islam, 1983). This same patriarchal structure extends throughout all levels of society. The father of the nuclear family may be subordinate to his own father, who in turn defers to the authority of the head of the clan. All clan heads are subordinate to the head of the tribe or hamula. The tribal or clan leader also serves as the spiritual and practical father of the whole group: he represents the collective to the outside world, oversees the rules for the clan or tribe, and guides their actions. In effect, the patriarchal structure creates a complete and autonomous society within a society, functioning as a single unit (Morsy, 1993; Shalhoub-Kevorkian, 1997). The formal idea of family in Arab societies extends family identity and membership backward through all ancestors in the male family line, ongoing in the present time, and on to future descendants who have yet to appear. One's sense of family is not bound by time or limited only to important living kin. While the father may be considered the head of the nuclear family household and is responsible for the family's economic and physical well-being, he still shows deference and loyalty to his living or dead father and older brothers as well as to his living or dead mother and older sisters. Elders in the father's extended family are also respected.

As one scholar points out, Arab women, particularly in Muslim society, have been viewed as 'powerless, subservient, and submissive' (Al-Haj, 1987, p. 103). In many Arab communities, female social status is closely aligned to matrimony and maternity, especially the raising or boys (Al-Sadawi, 1977, 1995). The mother is included in the extended family of her husband. As a mother, she is the emotional hub of her nuclear family of creation, responsible for offering support to her husband and nurturing their children (Al-Haj, 1987). While wielding tremendous emotional power and often acting as the relational and communication link between father and children, she may appear to have little public power and authority and may appear to defer to her husband, his mother, and the elders in the husband's extended family (Al-Krenawi, Maoz, & Reicher, 1994; Shalhoub-Kevorkian, 1997).

The family is considered sacred to Arab life, and many families are the locus of decision for major life events: who to marry, where to live, and (for men) what career to pursue. Psychosocial problems, likewise, may be collectively articulated and resolved within family structures. Within Arab communities, it is common for social workers to work collaboratively with family and extended family members to deal with large numbers of people in resolving a problem that an outsider might consider to reside with the individual. Family structures, like other social relations in Arab society, may be authoritative and hierarchical, but one should be cautious about too rigid an application of social work terminology in this instance. Take the social work notion of closed and open families. If workers proceed with unchecked biases, they may wrongfully assume that families in the Arab community are 'closed'—that is, that the family has strict regulations limiting transactions with the external environmental, as well as incoming and outgoing objects, information, and ideas (Hepworth & Larsen, 1986). In point of fact, Arab families may be far more 'open'—that is, more accepting of external influences such as the primary, secondary, and higher education of children, as well as accepting of outside personnel such as social workers. True, to the outsider, roles within families, and between family members and their environment, might appear to be rigid and inflexible. Likewise, intrusion from an outsider may initially be viewed with suspicion and concern; hence, as noted in the proceeding guidelines section, a social worker would have to be particularly diligent in order to strike an effective helping alliance.

Age and gender are important in determining external and internal boundaries. A teenage boy, for example, may more easily socialize with peers outside of the home than would his female counterparts. Such behaviour may appear less threatening to family honour, harmony, and stability. Within the family itself there are mediating influences upon social roles; a grandmother, mother, or father, for instance, may dissuade a teenage daughter from wearing certain clothing, or a teenage son from undertaking certain behaviours such as late night parties. Family coalitions may occur in order to mobilize family pressure. A daughter may enlist a mother or grandmother to mediate between her and the father to convince him to agree to an activity the daughter wants to undertake.

In many Arab regions outside Canada, arranged marriages are common; in some instances these may also occur in Canada. Women are especially vulnerable to several problems arising from such a practice. Divorced women in the Arab world suffer emotionally and socially (Brhoom, 1987). A divorced woman's marital prospects may be poor; in many Muslim societies, they are usually restricted to becoming the second wife of a married man, or the wife of a widower or older man (Al-Krenawi & Graham, 1998; Brhoom, 1987). Mothers in Arab communities are known to endure years of marital problems in order to avoid the stigma of divorce or the prospect of losing their children (Al-Krenawi & Graham, 1998). This possibility can be especially severe within Muslim societies, since Islamic conventions hold that fathers have custody over boys after the age of seven and girls after the age of nine (Amar, 1984).

In general, social workers are trained to work with families, many of which comprise a father and a mother. Yet Muslim-Arab countries—like those in other parts of the world such as Asia or Africa—also contain polygamous family structures

(Al-Krenawi, Graham, & Al-Krenawi, 1997). Social workers in Canada may encounter clients who are in polygamous relationships, or who are from polygamous families. As a proceeding section points out, there are significant psychosocial impacts associated with polygamy. These family structures, like their attendant intervention principles, are therefore fundamentally different from monogamy. According to Islam, a man may have upwards of four wives if he treats each wife equally—providing for each sufficiently and sharing his life and resources equally among each wife and their children. In some Arab communities, wealth and polygamy are correlated, and a well-to-do man can afford to have more than one wife. In other instances, a man may take another wife if the first wife has not been perceived to have produced enough male heirs, or if there are other sources of marital conflict (Abu-Baker, 1992; Al-Krenawi, 1998b). In practice, in some Muslim-Arab communities the most recently married wife is sometimes seen to have greater favour with the husband. The man's marriage to a new wife may be seen to the other wife or wives as an affront. Polygamous families may be associated with tension, conflict, and disharmony (Lev-Wiesel & Al-Krenawi, 2000). A man's co-wives may be compete with each other, and children of one wife may rival children of another (Al-Krenawi, 1999b; Al-Krenawi & Graham, 1999a, 1999b; Al-Krenawi, Graham, & Al-Krenawi, 1997; Chaleby, 1985, 1987a; El-Islam, 1975; Lev-Wiesel & Al-Krenawi, 2000). The academic achievement, social adjustment, and family conflict of children of polygamous families may be greater than those of monogamous families (Al-Krenawi, Graham, & Slonim-Nevo, in press; Al-Krenawi & Lightman, 2000).

Individual Development in Arab Societies

An earlier generation of psychological theory asserted that, during the course of human development, individuals undergo an important psychosocial separation from their parents, leading to the formation of a unique, autonomous identity (Erikson, 1963; Mahler, 1968). But as recent diversity research insists, individual development in Africa, Asia, South America, or the Middle East may occur differently (Sue & Sue, 1990). In these societies, the collective identity of the family remains focal (Hofstede, 1986), and the individual is embedded within this collective identity (Al-Krenawi & Graham, 2000a; Dwairy, 1998; Sharabi, 1975).

If one were to examine Arab communities in contrast with those in the West, eight differences would be especially salient:

1. Group affiliations, and interdependence rather than competition, may prevail (Rotheram & Phinny, 1987). A 'collective ego identity' may reference behaviour and social strictures to the group.
2. Orientations may appear to be passive and accepting (Rotheram & Phinney, 1987). For example, a client may not easily divulge personal or family problems and may appear immediately unwilling to co-operate with suggested tasks.
3. Authoritarian hierarchies rather than egalitarianism may characterize social organization.

4. External locus of control: individuals may learn that occurrences in life are determined by external powers such as family, social leaders, life experiences, or God. This perspective may be reinforced by a community or family context that is collective. Responsibility for behaviour is less oriented to the isolated individual and more oriented to the individual in relation to others within the community (Al-Krenawi, 1999b, 2000a; Bazzoui, 1970; West, 1987).

5. Unindividuated self: the psychological autonomy and individuation described by many Western psychosocial theories may bear only limited relevance to the common pattern of psychosocial development in collectivist Arabic cultures (Dwairy & Van Sickle, 1996; Gorkin, Masalha, & Yatziv, 1985; Timimi, 1995). Personal identity may be more strongly derived from the family, self-concept may be enmeshed in the family concept, and an individual's needs, attitudes, and values may stem from those of the family. Thus, if a family member contradicts social norms, the entire family may be seen to have been shamed; conversely, if a family member is successful in professional or remunerative terms, it is to the credit of the entire family (Al-Krenawi, 2000b).

6. Interpersonal rather than intrapsychic sources of distress: Individuals may be conditioned through external threats of sanctions, making external controls more significant than internal (superego) ones. Shame (which is group oriented) rather than guilt (which is individual oriented) may more often regulate behaviour (Gorkin et al., 1985; Sharabi, 1975, 1977), and interpersonal coping strategies become more effective than intrapsychic defence mechanisms (Dwairy & Van Sickle, 1996).

7. Communication styles may be restrained, impersonal, and formal rather than overt, personal, and expressive (Rotheram & Phinney, 1987).

8. Indirect expression of emotions: In Arabic societies, people may avoid directly expressing negative emotions such as anger and jealousy towards family members (West, 1987). Individuals may be expected to exhibit emotions congruent with Arab societal norms and to avoid expressing them in certain contexts, such as in a clinical social work intervention. Other emotions may be articulated through acting-out behaviours—which may be the reason a social worker is seen—or through body language (Dwairy, 1998; Sharabi, 1975).

One of the dilemmas individuals invariably experience is the choice between conformity and self-referenced objectives. This dynamic is especially prominent during adolescence and early adulthood and among those who immigrate to Canada and experience acculturation. When the conformist choice is adopted, the individual accepts support provided by the family and social environment in exchange for realizing a more pronounced expression of individuality. If the self-referenced choice is made, the individual asserts that he or she has the right to self-expression and personal decision, but social support of the family and traditional community may be reduced. Traditional social norms of Arab society may, from early childhood, condition the individual towards choices that are seen to conform with community norms (Dwairy, 1998). Moreover, the forces that encourage conformity remain in place during adulthood. Young couples, for example, may continue to require the economic and social support of extended family members. This support may be seen as a covert agreement that encourages the couple to conform to community and broader familial norms. As one psychologist emphasizes, such behaviour should not be perceived as transference of a child-parent role, but as an adaptive response to authority (Dwairy, 1998).

Dynamic social harmony is the major social rule governing many meaningful interpersonal relationships generally. It requires varying degrees of social co-operation, adaptation, accommodation, and collaboration by all individuals in the social hierarchy. In Arab societies, social hierarchy and social roles are based more on family membership and on social position, gender, age, social class, and social position than on qualification or ability.

Help-Seeking Strategies in Arab Communities

Social services have a limited presence in the Arab world, and in Canada some first-generation social work clients of Arab background may have a limited appreciation of the nature and scope of social work intervention. In Egypt or Jordan, for example, although social work practice occurs, it is often perceived to be restricted to the provision of instrumental support. Likewise, the Arab world, in comparison to Canada, has an extremely limited welfare state (Ismael & Ismael, 1995; Ragab, 1995). Here again, notions of entitlement to a program, or to an income security payment, may be limited. Thus, in all instances, a social worker in Canada would have the potential of letting the client of Arab background know more about the comparatively greater breadth and depth of available services.

As illustrated in Figure 8.1, help-seeking strategies may be collective and collaborative. Individuals may initially perceive a problem, but its further articulation and resolution take place with family members. As part of the help-seeking process, family members influence the individual's perception, as well as the selection of available choices to resolve a problem. Here, informal and formal sources of help are especially important. In some instances, informal sources may suffice; in others, professional (formal) sources are used. Informal sources may be utilized prior to, concurrent with, or subsequent to the utilization of formal sources (Al-Krenawi, 1995; Al-Krenawi & Graham, 1999c, 1999d, 1999e).

The Arab world has a wide variety of informal sources of help, and these are often integrated with life in Canada, upon immigration to this new land. Particularly important are family members, but beyond them are a wide variety of traditional healers and community members of status, who may be consulted by the individual, family members, or both. For example, 60 per cent of a sample of patients at the University Clinic in Cairo, Egypt, had consulted traditional healers before coming to see a psychiatrist (Okasha, 1999). In two different psychiatric clinics, between 49 and 53 per cent of a sample of patients had seen a traditional healer the year before seeking psychiatric assistance (Al-Issa & Al-Subaie, in press). Research in other Arab countries indicates that age, sex, social class, and education

Figure 8.1   Help-seeking Strategies

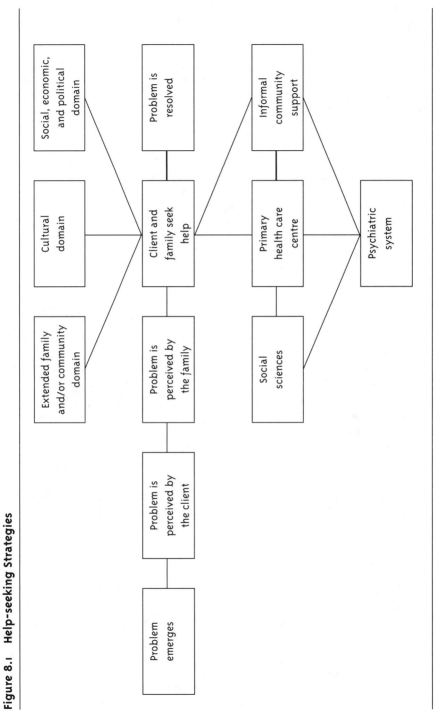

Al-Krenawi 1995, p. 225.

tend not to influence choices between a psychiatric system and traditional healing (Al-Subaie & Al-Hamad, 2000). Among traditional healers are amulet writers, the Dervish, Koranic healers, and others who provide tangible support, advice, and consultation during such life events as mourning, distress, crises, traumas, or various mental or physical illnesses. Recent scholarship argues that these centuries-old traditional healing systems can teach much to professionals. Possible lessons include the ability to strike and maintain effective helping alliances, to work collaboratively with family and community members, and to discern and use culturally appropriate strategies and idioms (Al-Issa, 2000; Al-Krenawi & Graham, 1996a, 1999b, 1999d, 1999f; Al-Krenawi, Graham, & Maoz, 1996; Gorkin & Othman, 1994; Graham & Al-Krenawi, 1996). Important community members of status may also be used to resolve problems, by providing advice, direction, or by mediating between problems that involve more than one family, as marital problems often do. Such cultural mediators are especially important in sensitive areas such as child welfare, or marital disputes, among other areas of conflict resolution elaborated in the guidelines section below (Al-Krenawi & Graham, 2001; Salem, 1997).

As illustrated in Figure 8.1, social context is essential to defining and resolving a problem. A first-generation immigrant to Canada is likely to find the context of the new country different from that of the homeland. Canada has a comprehensive welfare state, a more elaborate and older tradition of professional social services, and a way of delivering services that is significantly different in scope and nature than what may occur in the Arab world. Research on social service utilization among minority Arab peoples in advanced industrialized countries suggests lower rates of utilization, higher rates of early termination, and many barriers to service delivery, including gender dynamics, language barriers, culturally inappropriate services, communication styles, and techniques of intervention (Al-Krenawi & Graham, 2000a; Al-Krenawi, Graham, & Sehwail, 2000).

Difficulties in Establishing and Maintaining a Helping Relationship

In this section we examine a variety of difficulties that may arise for social workers who are trying to establish and maintain successful helping relationships with clients of Arab background. These are obviously not the only problems that may arise; rather, they provide a basis for elaborating some strategies for culturally appropriate practice. Specific problems therefore are described and are followed by intervention strategies that may help to address the difficulty.

1. Clients of Arab origin may have a negative view of social services, owing to a possible lack of exposure to the welfare state, a possible perception that social services are stigmatizing, or other reasons. Consequently, they may tend to mistrust, underutilize, and/or prematurely terminate these services.

   Intervention response: A cultural gap potentially leading to mistrust could occur when a non-Arab social worker comes into contact with an Arab client. Therefore, the social worker's first task is to establish a functional helping alliance. To that end, knowledge about the religious, cultural, and national background of the client is essential. Before an intervention plan is formulated, a client history could be taken. It could include such information as length of time outside the country of origin, reasons for and conditions under which emigration occurred, level of social/family support available, and perceived degree of religious affiliation. Work with recently arrived immigrants has especially germane nuances. There may be a difference, for example, between the Arab client who is here as a student, and who is struggling with issues of sexuality, and a middle-aged man who has left a country in turmoil and is suffering from a post-traumatic stress disorder. An assessment of the client's personal background and level of acculturation could alert the worker to potential cultural conflicts.

2. Clients of Arab background and their families may imbue the practitioner with a great deal of authority and, in so doing, place the onus on the practitioner to provide a solution to their problems with little or no input from themselves. Clients may want to conform—at least on the surface—to what is advised or prescribed because disagreeing may be equated with confronting, which may be considered rude. The social worker may perceive the Arab client to be passive during the assessment interview and this helping process in general.

    Intervention response: The worker must develop a comprehensive understanding of Arab views of social work practice, and must accept that the client may appear to be passive. Additionally, the professional should develop techniques that will encourage trust and openness between client and clinician, as elaborated in this guidelines section.

3. Arab clients may express problems through bodily complaints (somatization). Therefore, especially in a health or mental health setting, they may expect the setting to provide physical or medical treatment. The expression of conflict, whether internal or external, and the expression of negative feelings are not always well accepted in Arab culture (Al-Issa, 1990). The anxiety that may accompany a depressed mood may be negatively viewed as 'thinking too much' and/or as narcissistic self-preoccupation. Physical symptoms, however, may be acknowledged as legitimate, morally acceptable expressions of pain. Even the way the language is used lends itself to a confusion of psyche and soma, as depressive symptoms are depicted in physical imagery, especially involving the chest and abdomen. For example, as pointed out by Bazzoui (1970), 'the average Iraqi patient describes his depression as a sense of oppression in the chest, a feeling of being hemmed in, or in other cases, a hunger for air. On being asked if he feels sad, downcast or depressed, one is struck in many cases by the unawareness of the patient of his mood' (p. 196). Likewise, because of the religious stigma against taking one's life, suicidal feelings may not be divulged easily. While working in Saudi Arabia as a psychiatrist, Dubovsky (1983) discovered that 'if asked directly if they are having thoughts of killing themselves, most depressed patients reply that they are good people and would never entertain such thoughts. If, however, potentially suicidal patients are asked if

they wish that God would let them die, they usually will reply in the affirmative' (p. 1457).

Intervention response: Somatic problems are an important point of entry into many social work interventions. As several scholars point out, such complaints may be especially useful in establishing and maintaining a helping alliance with female clients (Racy, 1980). Intervention strategies that may arise in somatic contexts are elaborated above and below.

4. The family's involvement in an intervention may be considerable. In some cases, the family will intervene on behalf of the 'individual client', although they too may lack in trust while they expect much from the practitioner. To elaborate the lack of trust: the family, for example, might try to control the interview by answering the questions directed at the client while withholding information they may perceive as embarrassing (Meleis & La Fever, 1984).

Intervention response: These cultural constructions can best be utilized by social workers' willingness to accommodate the involvement of Arab families. Social workers could profitably educate themselves regarding Arab family values so that they can share sensitively with family members the necessary requirements for a workable helping relationship. They should not necessarily consider family involvement as overprotection, co-dependency, or enmeshment. Likewise, they should reconsider what would constitute intrusion on helping based on the client's expectations, not on Western standards. Cordial use of key familial leverage points may be important, although this must be done with great sensitivity to gender and age dynamics. An unknowing worker may perceive a client to be passive. Regardless of gender, the client may project authority onto the worker, which in turn may be a useful means of encouraging clients to follow through on various contracted functions—keeping a diary, performing certain tasks, coming to the next appointment, and so on.

5. Cultural expectations regarding gender and age can complicate the helping relationship. Cross-gender social worker–client relations may have complex nuances. Some male clients, for example, may have difficulty accepting a female social worker's directions. When this occurs, it does not necessarily arise from the male client himself but may stem from a male family member in a position of authority such as a father, uncle, older brother, or any older male family member (Irani, 1999).

Intervention response: Cross-gender practitioner–client relations, or those that involve different ages, may be more restrained and formal than same-gender or comparable age relations. A client's eye contact with the practitioner may be minimal, and in some instances, the practitioner's use of such terms as 'sister' and 'brother' to address clients of the opposite gender may be helpful (Mass & Al-Krenawi, 1994). Social workers need to be sensitive to gender considerations in other respects, and as much as possible style interventions to be as sensitive and culturally appropriate as possible. Regarding Iranian families, Jalali (1982) comments, that 'the patriarchal organization of the family is to be acknowledged by addressing fathers first and as the head of the family. The social worker should not attempt to change cultural power hierarchies or role patterns since this will alienate the family' (p. 308).

6. Time concepts of the worker may be different from those of the client. Differences in temporal perception can present challenges in working with people of Arab background. Arab people's notion of time is more fluid than, and not as structured or determined as, in the West, and a practitioner from the West may perceive a client of Arab background as not very time-bound. In the Arabic language there are no clear distinctions between various forms of past and future. Psychologically speaking, this can be viewed as advantageous in that it fosters flexibility in one's adaptation to life circumstances, with an ability for prompt readiness when facing the unforeseen. It is a disadvantage, however, when one lives in cultures that require a different type of time-sensitive attitude. Thus, making and keeping appointments at fixed times or starting and ending sessions promptly might be a source of difficulty. Moreover, in a clinic or hospital setting, the family may have difficulty with limited visiting hours.

Intervention response: Early in the helping relationship, the social worker would do well to establish clearly the rules regarding appointment time, lateness, and missed sessions. Also, workers need to adapt their own practice to the time notions of clients, maintaining as flexible an approach as possible (Dwairy & Van Sickle, 1996).

Guidelines for Social Work Practice with Clients of Arab Background

Social work practice with Arab peoples requires several ethno-specific approaches. In this section, these approaches are described and briefly elaborated upon (several are adapted from Al-Krenawi & Graham, 2000a).

1. *Social services may be stigmatizing and may have perceived influences upon family pride.* Clients of Arab background, like those from other non-Western societies, may find psychiatric or psychological intervention (Fabreka, 1991), and family and marital therapies (Savaya, 1995) stigmatizing. For women, mental health services have several potential stigmas. These include the perception of jeopardizing marital prospects or of increasing the likelihood of separation or divorce. Among Muslims in the Arab world, seeking treatment could be used by a husband or his family as leverage for obtaining a second wife (Al-Krenawi, 1999b; Bazzoui & Al-Issa, 1966; Chaleby, 1987a; Okasha & Lotalif, 1979). Stigma may be avoided or reduced by integrating mental health services into non-stigmatizing frameworks or physical settings, such as general medical clinics (Al-Krenawi, 1996). Social services in general may be stigmatizing to family pride, especially if they are perceived to imply notions of poverty or need. In all instances, it is helpful to deliver services in sensitive and flexible modes. A family may decline to show up for an appointment if it is anticipated that a different family of Arab background may notice them entering a social service or mental health clinic, with the stigma that this entry implies. As elaborated

below, stigma may also be attenuated by more culturally appropriate approaches.

2. *Contrary to a Western therapeutic emphasis on the individual, interventions with clients of Arab background may need to be couched in the context of the family, extended family, or community.* Traditional family values, norms, and roles are reinforced throughout one's lifetime. Among clients of Arab background, the suppression of individual impulses may be considered important, and loyalty to traditional authority a priority; socialization processes may stress conformity over individual independence (Hopkins & Ibrahim, 1997, p. 175). The importance of the group is reinforced in daily interactions. Rather than adopting Euro-American ideals of conjugal isolation and withdrawal from the extended family, Arab social structures are dominated by daily interaction with near and extended kin (Holmes-Eber, 1997). Since individuals' interests unite with those of their group of allegiance, and the general good may supersede the personal, individual problems engage members of the group in common pursuit of solutions (Al-Krenawi & Graham, 2000a). Indeed, change may not be possible without the participation of dominant members of a family. Practitioners, therefore, must make special effort to appreciate the family's authority (Al-Krenawi & Lev-Wiesel, 1999).

3. *Religion is an important context in which problems are constructed and resolved.* Religion is a focal point of the Arab world view, whether it is based on Christianity, Islam, or minority religions such as Druze. All such religious orientations assume a visible and invisible world, the latter being the potential source of spirits, angels, the devil, the Divine, and/or sorcery. Major life experiences such as birth, marriage, childrearing, mutual aid and charity, and death are fundamentally based in religion. Psychosocial problems may be articulated using religious nomenclature and may be experienced and understood within a religious framework. Religious terminology and concepts may be essential to a social work intervention.

4. *The Arab client may perceive psychosocial problems to be based on one, two, or three of the following: the biomedical, the human, or the supernatural realm.* A client of Arab background may believe that his or her problems are caused by external elements. A physical or mental illness, or family or marital problem, may be perceived as resulting from several external causes, including the intervention of supernatural elements such as spirits or the participation of other people in the supernatural via such avenues as the evil eye or sorcery (Al-Krenawi, Graham, & Maoz, 1996; El-Islam, 1982; Morsy, 1993; Sanua, 1979; West, 1987). Likewise, the existence of external factors such as unemployment or discrimination, or any events external to the individual, may be readily appreciated by the Arab client; here, clear separation of the individual and the problem is a potentially helpful tool for leading to partialized solutions (White, 1989). Research indicates no correlation between clients' educational level and the perception that the problem is caused by supernatural forces (Khalifa, 1989; El-Islam & Abu-Dagga, 1992). A worker should appreciate the cause of the

problem or illness from the perspectives of the clients, their family, and the society to which they belong. It is possible to bridge the gap between formal and informal theories by using clients' idioms of distress in the intervention process (Al-Krenawi, 2000a; Bilu & Witztum, 1995).

5. *Communication may be restrained, formal, and impersonal. Idioms of distress might rely upon a complex system of metaphors and proverbs.* Clients of Arab background may bring with them communication styles that are based on proverbs and culturally bound metaphors that have developed via the collective experience of the culture. Part of everyday language, these metaphors and proverbs encapsulate collective wisdom, values, and ways of thinking. Personal and/or family conflict, therefore, may be conveyed using such language, and in a manner that the Western practitioner may interpret as restrained, formal, impersonal, indirect, circular, or non-specific (Al-Krenawi, 2000a). For instance, a woman who is depressed may describe a heart that has fallen down; a man who is feeling hopeless may convey a proverb that is highly fatalistic, such as 'the person who has no fortune does not need to work hard, because the future is already determined' (Al-Krenawi, 2000a).

   Intervention techniques commonly used in the West may have limited applicability to clients of Arab background. Self-disclosure, client affect, and self-exploration may be difficult, especially if they are perceived to risk family or collective honour, and these dynamics should not be construed as client resistance. Decoding a client's expressions is especially important. A worker of Arab background, or one who has knowledge of the metaphors and proverbs, could convey responses using such language. For example, a worker may respond to the fatalistic, hopeless man with a proverb that conveys hope and greater optimism about the future. 'Don't give up if you fail once. You must continue to try, since the more you try the more you increase your chances to pass a difficult situation.'

6. *Interventions are most successful when they are short-term and provide direction.* A worker who maintains too rigid a timeframe could be perceived to be cold or unreasonable. Directive treatment, especially that which uses short-term cognitive or behavioural theoretical assumptions, may be especially useful in working with clients of Arab background. The clients bring various problems that they feel are urgent to an intervention; some scholars point to the necessity of dealing with these problems that a client immediately identifies first and foremost, and in ways that convey practitioner warmth and empathy (Ibrahim, 1999). The worker may represent a symbol of authority, not unlike the client's parents, and may take on the role of a *hakim*, or wise counsellor, in the eyes of the client (Al-Krenawi & Graham, 2000a). Interventions that are directive, with clear and concrete targets, and those that provide guidance, advice, explanations, and instructions, are all often helpful. The client may reject overly philosophical or abstract intervention (Lev-Wiesel & Al-Krenawi, 1999).

7. *Several gender and cultural aspects can assist a worker to sustain a helping alliance.* In situations where the client and social worker are of the same sex, the social

worker should take into consideration the client's need for expressions of intimacy and occasionally relax the formality that is the norm in Western helping. Conversely, when worker and client are not of the same sex, the former should maintain even greater distance than normal, for fear of engaging in what might be perceived of as sexual impropriety (Mass & Al-Krenawi, 1994). Minimal eye contact may commonly occur as a result of a cross-gender helping relationship (Al-Bostani, 1988; Rizvi, 1989), and should not be interpreted as client resistance to treatment. Other cross-gender dynamics are noted in the preceding section.

8. *Clients often utilize social services and informal community supports (such as traditional healers, traditional mediators, religious leaders, or other community members of status) concurrently or in succession.* Implications for this integration are elaborated in item 9, below.

9. *When a problem is experienced, the family is involved at the earliest stages in identifying its nature and possible means of resolution.* Clients and their families may first seek assistance from a wide network of community resources, and indeed these may be involved at the earliest stages as well. Some problems may never come to a professional from outside the community. In other instances, informal resources are used before, concurrent with, or after a professional intervention. Scholarship has encouraged professionals to utilize these resources, to collaborate with them where appropriate, and to learn from them many of the community-specific nuances of helping (Al-Krenawi & Graham, 1996a, 1996b, 1997a, 1997b, 1999d, 2000a). In instances of conflict between two or more extended families—and these often are implicit in marital or child welfare concerns—community mediators from related families may be fruitfully used to resolve disagreements in culturally appropriate ways (Al-Krenawi & Graham, 2001). Community mediation, the *wasit*, is a long-standing practice in the Arab world, involving community members of status who resolve problems quickly, and with minimal loss of pride among participants, using culturally appropriate idiomatic (metaphors/proverbs) and practical (traditional meals) constructions (Al-Krenawi & Graham, 1999d, 2001; Lee & Armstrong, 1995). Traditional healers, including amulet writers, the dervish, and Koranic healers, are widely consulted to identify and treat psychosocial problems related to anxiety, spirit possession, marital disharmony, mourning, and stress. Many such positions, including the dervish, are open to female or male participation (Al-Krenawi, 2000b; Al-Krenawi, Graham, & Maoz, 1996). Ultimately, practitioners can learn much from informal networks of traditional healers, cultural mediators, and others, particularly with respect to working with families.

Informal community resources are especially prevalent in the Arab world. They and the client share a common world view that stresses the importance of their joint origin and helps them to understand the problem, its sources, and optimal ways of relating to it (Al-Krenawi, 2000b; Torrey, 1986). The use of rituals may resonate culturally and religiously with a client. These have specific purposes and differ from one community to the next. Specific rituals related to mourning, sickness, child-birth, anxiety, and other life events may be prescribed, and, we argue, could be inte-grated with a social work intervention. This is not to suggest that social workers should appropriate such practices, but rather that they should appreciate that they are part of the client's world view and therefore could potentially supplement a social work intervention (Al-Krenawi & Graham, 1999c; El-Islam, 1967; Graham & Al-Krenawi, 1996). Community support providers may well render assistance that is culturally appropriate in other ways: it is directive, involves the group, resonates with the client as appropriately authoritative, and takes into account the familial and community ecological maps as well as the spiritual and temporal realms.

Conclusion

Integrating the guidelines discussed above, Table 8.1 compares culturally compe-tent social work practice adapted for an Arab population to help that is suitable for a Western population. This model of intervention, adapted from Al-Krenawi (1999a), compares Western principles of talking therapy with the cognitive-behav-ioural assumptions that could be usefully adapted to Arab communities.

This chapter has emphasized approaches at the level of the individual, family, group, and community, all through a prism of a predominantly collectivist culture. These principles are necessarily situated to time and place. Accordingly, like all knowledge, they are best seen as provisional, tentative, and processed through the unique perspective of the individual. As Max Siporin (1985) once pointed out, to know oneself is to know others. Self-reflection is as important to culturally respon-sive practice as it is to other aspects of the profession (Weaver, 1998). It is the means

Table 8.1   A Comparison of Talking Therapy Suitable for Western and Arab Populations

Western talking therapy	Adapted for Arab communities
Based on self-discovery	Based on explanations and instructions
Some guidance given by the social worker	More guidance provided by the social worker
Use of indirect methods to find a solution to the problem	Use of direct methods such as advice and suggested solutions
Social worker and client are on a more equal footing	A teacher–pupil relationship may exist between social worker and client
The social worker's words are perceived as suggestions or advice	The social worker's words may be perceived as instructions
The social worker may be more passive and the client more active during helping encounter	The social worker may be more active and the client more passive during helping encounter

by which formal and informal theories are both recognized and reconciled. With peoples of Arab background, as with those of other ethno-racial communities, may social workers and their clients walk together, and with, rather than against, the wind.

References

Abu-Baker, A. (1992). *Polygamy in Islam*. Cairo: Maktabat Al-Tourath Al-Islami (in Arabic).

Abu-Baker, K. (1999). Acculturation and reacculturation influence: Multilayer contexts in therapy. *Clinical Psychology Review, 19*(8), 951–67.

Abudabbeh, N., & Aseel, H.A. (1999). Transcultural counseling and Arab Americans. In J. McFadden (Ed.), *Transcultural Counseling* (pp. 283–98). Alexandria, VA: American Counselling Association.

Al-Bostani, M. (1988). *Psychology and Islam*. Beirut: Dar Al-Balaha (in Arabic).

Al-Haj, M. (1987). *Social Change and Family Processes*. London: Westview.

Al-Issa, I. (1990). Culture and mental illness in Algeria. *International Social Psychiatry, 23*, 219–43.

Al-Issa, I. (Ed.) (2000). *Al-Junun: Mental Illness in the Islamic World*. Madison, CT: International Universities Press.

Al-Issa, I., & Al-Subaie, A. (in press). Native healing in Arab-Islamic societies. *Transcultural Psychiatry*.

Al-Juzuyyah, I.Q. (1993). *Natural Healing with the Medicine of the Prophet*. Philadelphia: Pearl.

Al-Krenawi, A. (1995). *A study of dual use of modern and traditional mental health systems by the Bedouin-Arab of the Negev*. Unpublished doctoral dissertation, University of Toronto.

———. (1996). Group work with Bedouin widows of the Negev in a medical clinic. *Affilia, 11*(3), 303–18.

———. (1998a). A constructivist approach and its implementation to direct practice in a multicultural society. *Society and Welfare, 18*(2), 253–67 (in Hebrew).

———. (1998b). Family therapy with a multiparental/multispousal family. *Family Process, 37*(1), 65–82.

———. (1999a). Culturally sensitive mental health therapy with Arab peoples. In C. Rabin (Ed.), *Being Different in Israel: Ethnicity, Gender and Therapy* (pp. 65–82). Tel-Aviv: Ramot, Tel-Aviv University Press (in Hebrew).

———. (1999b). Women of polygamous marriages in primary health care centers. *Contemporary Family Therapy, 21*(3), 417–30.

———. (2000a). Arab clients' use of proverbs in the therapeutic setting. *International Journal for the Advancement of Counselling, 22*(2), 91–102.

———. (2000b). *Ethno-Psychiatry among the Bedouin-Arab of the Negev*. Tel-Aviv: Hakibbutz Hameuchad (in Hebrew).

Al-Krenawi, A., & Graham, J.R. (1996a). Social work practice and traditional healing rituals among the Bedouin of the Negev. *International Social Work, 39*, 177–88.

———. (1996b). Tackling mental illness: Roles for old and new disciplines. *World Health Forum, 17*, 246–8.

————. (1997a). Nebi-Musa: A therapeutic community for drug addicts in a Muslim context. *Transcultural Psychiatry, 34(3)*, 377–91.

————. (1997b). Spirit possession and exorcism: The integration of modern and traditional mental health care systems in the treatment of a Bedouin patient. *Clinical Social Work Journal, 25*, 211–22.

————. (1998). Divorce among Muslim Arab women in Israel. *Journal of Divorce and Remarriage, 29*(3/4), 103–19.

————. (1999a). Globalization, identity, and social work practice: What can we learn from the perspective of working with Arab peoples? In T.I. Shereen (Ed.), *Globlization: Challenges and Responses* (pp. 271–86). Calgary: Detselig.

————. (1999b). The story of Bedouin-Arab women in a polygamous marriage. *Women's Studies International Forum, 22*(5), 497–509.

————. (1999c). Gender and biomedical/traditional mental health utilization among the Bedouin-Arabs of the Negev. *Culture, Medicine, and Psychiatry, 23*(2), 219–43.

————. (1999d). Conflict resolution through a traditional ritual among the Bedouin-Arabs of the Negev. *Ethnology: An International Journal of Cultural and Social Anthropology, 38*(2), 163–74.

————. (1999e). Social work and Koranic mental health healers. *International Social Work, 42*(1), 53–65.

————. (2000a). Culturally sensitive social work practice with Arab clients in mental health settings. *Health and Social Work*, 25(1), 9–22.

————. (2000b). Islamic theology and prayer: Relevance for social work practice. *International Social Work, 43*(3), 289–304.

————. (2001). The cultural mediator: Bridging the gap between a non-Western community and professional social work practice. *British Journal of Social Work, 31*, 665–86.

Al-Krenawi, A., Graham, J.R., & Al-Krenawi, S. (1997). Social work practice with polygamous families. *Child and Adolescent Social Work Journal, 14*(6), 445–58.

Al-Krenawi, A., Graham, J.R., & Maoz, B. (1996). The healing significance of the Negev's Bedouin. *Dervish. Social Science and Medicine, 43*(1), 13–21.

Al-Krenawi, A., Graham, J.R., & Sehwail, M. (2002). Bereavement responses among Palestinian widows, daughters, and sons following the Hebron massacre. *Omega: Journal of Death and Dying, 44*(3), 241–55.

Al-Krenawi, A., Graham, J.R., & Slonim-Nevo, V. (in press). Mental health aspects of Arab adolescents of polygamous/monogamous families. *Journal of Social Psychology.*

Al-Krenawi, A., & Lev-Wiesel, R. (1999). Attitudes toward and perceived psychosocial impact of female circumcision as practised among the Bedouin-Arab of the Negev. *Family Process, 38*(4), 431–44.

Al-Krenawi, A., & Lightman, E.S. (2000). Learning achievement, social adjustment, and family conflict among Bedouin-Arab children from polygamous and monogamous families. *Journal of Social Psychology, 140*(3), 345–55.

Al-Krenawi, A., Maoz, B., & Reicher, B. (1994). Familial and cultural issues in the brief strategic treatment of Israeli Bedouin. *Family Systems Medicine, 12*, 415–25.

Al-Sadawi, N. (1977). *The Psychological Struggle of the Arab Women.* Beirut: Al-moasasa Al-Arabia (in Arabic).

———. (1995). Gender, Islam, and orientalism: Dissidence and creativity. *Women: A Cultural Review, 6*, 1–18.

Al-Subaie, A., & Al-Hamad, A. (2000). Psychiatry in Saudi Arabia. In I. Al-Issa (Ed.), *Al-Junun: Mental Illness in the Islamic World.* Madison, CT: International Universities Press.

Amar, A. (1984). *Islam and Marriage.* Jaddh, Saudi Arabia: Dar-Al-fiker Al-Arabi (in Arabic).

Azmi, S.H. (1991). Traditional Islamic social welfare: Its meaning, history and contemporary relevance. *Islamic Quarterly, 35*(3), 80–165.

Barakat, H. (1993). *The Arab World. Society, Culture, and State.* Los Angeles: University of California Press.

Bazzoui, W. (1970). Affective disorders in Iraq. *British Journal of Psychiatry, 117*, 195–203.

Bazzoui, W., & Al-Issa, I. (1966). Psychiatry in Iraq. *British Journal of Psychiatry, 112*, 827–32.

Bilu, Y., & Witztum, E. (1995). Between sacred and medical realities: Culturally sensitive therapy with Jewish Ultra-Orthodox patients. *Science in Context, 8*(1), 159–73.

Brhoom, M. (1987). The phenomenon of divorce in Jordan. *Deraast, 13*(12), 189–205 (in Arabic).

Chaleby, K. (1985). Women of polygamous marriages in inpatient psychiatric service in Kuwait. *Journal of Nervous and Mental Disease, 173*(1), 56–58.

———. (1987a). Women of polygamous marriages in out-patient psychiatric services in Kuwait. *International Journal of Family Psychiatry, 8*(1), 25–34.

———. (1987b). Social phobias among Saudis. *Social Psychiatry, 22*, 167–70.

Dean, H., & Khan, Z. (1998). Islam: A challenge to welfare professionalism. *Journal of Interprofessional Care, 12*(4), 399–405.

Dubovsky, S. (1983). Psychiatry in Saudi Arabia. *American Journal of Psychiatry, 140*(11), 1455–9.

Dwairy, M.A. (1998). *Cross-cultural counseling: The Arab-Palestinian Case.* New York: Haworth Press.

Dwairy, M., & Van Sickle, T.D. (1996). Western psychotherapy in traditional Arabic societies. *Clinical Psychology Review, 16*(3), 231–49.

El-Azayem, G.A., & Hedayat-Diba, Z. (1994). The psychological aspects of Islam: basic principles of Islam and their psychological corollary. *International Journal for the Psychology of Religion, 4*(1), 41–50.

El-Islam, M.F. (1967). The psychotherapeutic basis of some Arab rituals. *International Journal of Social Psychiatry, 13*, 265–8.

———. (1975). Clinical bound neurosis in Qatari women. *Social Psychiatry, 10*(1), 25–9.

———. (1982). Arabic cultural psychiatry. *Transcultural Psychiatric Research Review, 19*(1), 5–24.

———. (1983). Cultural change and inter-generational relationships in Arabian families. *International Journal of Family Psychiatry,* 4(4), 321–29.

———. (1989). Collaboration with families for rehabilitation of schizophrenic patients and the concept of expressed emotion. *Acta Psychiatrica Scandinavica,* 79(4), 303–7.

El-Islam, M.F., & Abu-Dagga, S. (1992). Lay explanation of symptoms of mental ill health in Kuwait. *International Journal of Social Psychiatry,* 38(2), 150–6.

Erikson, E. (1963). *Childhood and Society.* New York: Norton.

Fabreka, H. (1991). Psychiatric stigma in non-Western societies. *Comprehensive Psychiatry,* 32(6), 534–51.

Faragallah, M.H, Schumm, W.R., & Webb, F.J. (1997). Acculturation of Arab-American immigrants: An exploratory study. *Journal of Comparative Family Studies,* 28(3), 182–203.

Gorkin, M., Masalha, S., & Yatziv, G. (1985). Psychotherapy of Israeli Arab patients: Some cultural considerations. *Journal of Psychoanalytic Anthropology,* 8(4), 215–30.

Gorkin, M., & Othman, R. (1994). Traditional psychotherapeutic healing and healers in the Palestinian community. *Israel Journal of Psychiatry and Related Sciences,* 31(3), 221–31.

Graham, J.R., & Al-Krenawi, A. (1996). A comparison study of traditional helpers in a late nineteenth century Canadian (Christian) society and in a late twentieth century Bedouin (Muslim) society in the Negev, Israel. *Journal of Multicultural Social Work,* 4(2), 31–45.

Hall, E. (1976). *Beyond Culture.* New York: Doubleday.

Hepworth, D.H., & Larsen, J.A. (1986). *Direct Social Work Practice: Theory and Skills.* New York: Dorsey Press.

Hofstede, G. (1986). Cultural differences in teaching and learning. *International Journal of Intercultural Relations,* 10(3), 301–20.

Holmes-Eber, P. (1997). Migration, urbanization, and women's kin. *Journal of Comparative Family Studies,* 28(2), 54–73.

Hopkins, N.S., & Ibrahim, S.E. (Eds). (1997). *Arab Society: Class, Gender, Power and Development.* Cairo: American University in Cairo Press.

Ibrahim, F.A. (1985). Effectiveness in cross-cultural counseling and psychotherapy: A framework. *Counseling Psychologist,* 13(4), 625–38.

———. (1999). Existential worldview theory and cultural identity. In J. McFadden (Ed.), *Transcultural Counseling* (pp. 23–55). Alexandria, VA: University of South Carolina Press.

Irani, G.E. (1999). Islamic mediation techniques for Middle East conflicts. *Middle East Review of International Affairs,* 3(2), 1–18.

Isajiw, W.W. (1999). *Understanding Diversity: Ethnicity and Race in the Canadian Context.* Toronto: Thompson Educational Publishing.

Ismael, J., & Ismael, T.Y. (1995). *Social Policy in the Arab World.* Cairo: American University in Cairo Press.

Jalali, B. (1982). Iranian families. In M. McGoldrick, J. Pearce, & J. Giordano (Eds), *Ethnicity and Family Therapy* (pp. 288–309). New York: Guilford Press.

Kashmeri, Z. (1991). *The Gulf Within: Canadian Arabs, Racism, and the Gulf War.* Toronto: James Lorimer.

Khalifa, A.M. (1989). Beliefs and attitudes of Egyptian students related to mental health disease. *Egyptian Journal of Psychology, 11*(3), 103–17 (in Arabic).

Lee, C.C., & Armstrong, K.L. (1995). Indigenous models of mental health intervention. In J.G. Ponterotto, J.M. Casas, L.A. Suzuki, & C.M. Alexander (Eds), *Handbook of Multicultural Counseling* (pp. 441–56). Thousand Oaks, CA: Sage.

Lev-Wiesel, R., & Al-Krenawi, A. (1999). Attitudes towards marriage and marital quality: A comparison among Israeli Arabs differentiated by religion. *Family Relations, 48*(1), 51–6.

Lev-Wiesel, R., & Al-Krenawi, A. (2000). Perception of family among children of polygamous families as reflected in their family drawings. *American Journal of Art Therapy, 38*(4), 98–106.

Lipset, S.M. (1990). *Continental Divide: The Values and Institutions of the United States and Canada.* New York: Routledge.

Mahler, M. (1968). *On Human Symbiosis and the Vicissitudes of Individuation: Infantile Psychosis.* Volume 1. New York: International University Press.

Markus, H.R., & Kitayama, S. (1991). Culture and the self: Implications for cognition, emotion, and motivation. *Psychological Review, 98*(2), 224–53.

Mass, M., & Al-Krenawi, A. (1994). When a man encounters a woman, Satan is also present: Clinical relationships in Bedouin society. *American Journal of Orthopsychiatry, 64,* 357–67.

Mead, M. (1967). *Male and Female: A Study of the Sexes in a Changing World.* 2nd ed. New York: Morrow.

Meleis, A., & La Fever, C. (1984). The Arab American and psychiatric care. *Perspectives in Psychiatric Care, 12*(2), 72–86.

Morsy, S.A. (1993). *Gender, Sickness, and Healing in Rural Egypt: Ethnography in Historical Context.* San Francisco: Westview Press.

Nagati, M.A. (1993). *The Tradition of the Prophet and Psychology.* Cairo: Daar Al-Shorok Press (in Arabic).

Okasah, A. (1999). Mental health in the Middle East: An Egyptian perspective. *Clinical Psychology Review, 19*(8), 917–33.

Okasha, A. & Lotalif, F. (1979). Attempted suicide: An Egyptian investigation. *Acta Psychiatrica Scandinavica, 60,* 69–75.

Racy, J. (1980). Somatization in Saudi Women: A therapeutic challenge. *British Journal of Psychiatry, 137,* 212–16.

Ragab, A. (1995). Middle East and Egypt. In T.D. Watts, D. Elliott, & N.S. Mayadas (Eds), *International Handbook on Social Work Education.* (pp. 281–304). London: Greenwood Press.

Rizvi, S.A.A. (1989). *Muslim Tradition in Psychotherapy and Modern Trends.* Lahor: Lahor Institute of Islamic Culture.

Rotheram, M.J., & Phinney, J.S. (1987). Ethnic behavior patterns as an aspect of identity. In J.S. Phinney & M.J. Rotheram (Eds), *Children's Ethnic Socialization: Pluralism and Development.* Newbury Park, CA: Sage.

Salem, P.E. (1997). A critique of Western conflict resolution from a non-Western perspective. In P.E. Salem (Ed.), *Conflict Resolution in the Arab World: Selected Essays* (pp. 11–24). Beirut: American University of Beirut Press.

Sanua, V.D. (1979). Psychosocial interventions in the Arab world: A review of folk treatment. *Transcultural Psychiatric Research Review, 16,* 205–8.

Savaya, R. (1995). Attitudes towards family and marital counselling among Israeli Arab women. *Journal of Social Service Research, 21*(1), 35–51.

Shalhoub-Kevorkian, N. (1997). Wife-abuse: A method of social control. *Israeli Social Science Research, 12*(1), 59–72.

Sharabi, H. (1975). *Introduction to the Study of Arab Society.* Jerusalem: Salah Eldin.

———. (1977). Impact of class and culture on social behavior: The feudal bourgeois family in Arab society. In L.C. Brown & N. Itzkowitz (Eds), *Psychological Dimensions of Near Eastern Studies.* Princeton, NJ: Darwin Press.

Siporin, M. (1985). Current social work perspectives on clinical practice. *Clinical Social Work Journal, 13*(3), 198–217.

Sue, D.W., & Sue, D. (1990). *Counselling the Culturally Different: Theory and Practice.* 2nd ed. New York: Wiley.

Timimi, S.B. (1995). Adolescence in immigrant Arab families. *Psychotherapy, 32*(1), 141–149.

Torrey, E.F. (1986). *Witchdoctors and Psychiatrists.* Northvale, NJ: Jason Aronson.

Triandis H.C. (1972). *The Analysis of Subjective Culture.* New York: Wiley.

UNESCO (1996). *1996 Statistical Yearbook.* New York: UNESCO.

Weaver, H.N. (1998). Indigenous people in a multicultural society: Unique issues for human services. *Social Work, 43*(3), 203–11.

West, J. (1987). Psychotherapy in the eastern province of Saudi Arabia. *Psychotherapy, 24*(1), 105–7.

White, M. (Ed.). (1989). *The Externalization of the Problem and the Reauthoring of Lives and Relationships. Selected Papers.* Adelaide: Dulwich Center.

Chapter 9

Social Work with Canadians of Jewish Background: Guidelines for Direct Practice

Ross A. Klein and Julia Mirsky

Given the size of the Jewish population in Canada—just over 1 per cent of Canadians—people of Jewish background comprise a very small minority in this country. It is a minority group that can be invisible to many social workers because Jews are generally white-skinned, from the same European homelands as many other Canadians, and assimilated into Canadian society. In this chapter, we focus on social work practice with people of Jewish-Canadian background.

The chapter is divided into four parts. The first part looks at patterns of migration and settlement of Jews in Canada and provides a broad overview of the present Jewish experience in Canada. As will be seen, many Jews, like other Canadians, are relatively recent immigrants—either first or second generation. For this reason, the second part looks at psychological issues and dynamics of migration and resettlement. In the third part we discuss the Canadian Jewish community and salient cultural and social issues that confront Jewish Canadians, including anti-Semitism, assimilation and loss of a Jewish identity, and demographic concerns. The chapter concludes with a discussion of social work practice and recommendations for ethnic-sensitive practice with people of Jewish-Canadian background. While some readers may be tempted to skip to this part of the chapter, appreciation for the discussion in the last section depends on understanding the three sections that precede it.

A Demographic Primer

Measuring the number of Jews in Canada is difficult, given that being Jewish is both a religious and an ethnic heritage. In the 1991 census, when asked for religious affiliation, 318,070 Canadians (roughly 1.2 per cent of the population) identified their religion as Jewish. When asked about ethnic origin, 369,565 Canadians (roughly

1.4 per cent of the population) claimed their ethnic origin to be Jewish. Based on these figures, *The Encyclopedia of Canada's People* estimates the Canadian Jewish population in 1991 at approximately 356,000, or just over 1.3 per cent of the total population (Weinfeld, 1999).

Periods of Immigration

Jews were among the first people to land in Canada. In 1677, Joseph de la Penha, a Jewish trader from Rotterdam, was driven by a storm onto the coast of Labrador. He promptly claimed the territory for William III, who was the ruler of Holland and soon to reign as King of England. Some twenty years later, de la Penha saved William's life when the vessel on which the king was sailing was caught in a violent storm and began to sink. As a reward, William granted to de la Penha title over Labrador. De la Penha never settled in the area, though 225 years later one of his descendants verified their title to the territory by filing a claim with England's Privy Council.

Had de la Penha taken up residence in Labrador at the time, it is unclear whether he would have been welcome. When Cardinal Richelieu founded the Company of New France in 1627 to develop and explore the French territories in North America, he stipulated that they be open only to French Catholics. Jews were among those explicitly disallowed from settling in the area. The practice was further 'reinforced by the infamous Black Code of 1685, which decreed that officials in every French possession in the world "drive out . . . all Jews . . . as enemies of the Christian name"' (Abella, 1990, p. 3).

It wasn't until the British capture of Quebec and Articles of Capitulation in 1760 that Jews were allowed to enter New France. Prior to 1760, any Jews who arrived in Quebec were required to renounce their religion and convert to Catholicism, or they were deported back to France. During this same period, several Jewish merchant families had resettled in Halifax from the British colonies in what was to become the United States. By 1752, Halifax was home to about thirty Jews. It wasn't until the mid-nineteenth century that relatively large numbers of Jews began to land in what is now Canada.

JEWISH IMMIGRATION TO FRENCH CANADA

The first Jews to settle in Quebec were Sephardic Jews (the word *spharad* means Spain in Hebrew)—Jews who were expelled from Spain and Portugal during the Inquisition. In the early 1760s, a number of Jewish families had settled in parts of Quebec, including Trois Rivières and Montreal. By 1768, enough Jews had arrived at Montreal to warrant the establishment of the Spanish and Portuguese Synagogue, the sixth oldest Jewish congregation in North America.

The Jewish community grew slowly. In 1831, of the 107 Jews in all of Canada, about 50 were in Montreal. The Jewish community had gained considerable recognition in these early years: in 1829, it was officially recognized by the legislature of Lower Canada for the purpose of maintaining a registry of births, deaths, and marriages; in 1832, the legislature guaranteed to Jews full rights and privileges, including the right to own land. This is significant in that it corrected a situation in which the civil rights of Jews had been in doubt. Among other things, it gave Jews the right to hold elected office, something that had been denied until that time. In 1808, and again in 1809, Ezekiel Hart was elected to the Legislative Assembly as a representative of Trois Rivières, but was prohibited from taking his seat because of his religion (Elazar & Waller, 1990, p. 69).

The Jewish population of Montreal continued to grow over the next several decades. By the early 1860s, there were over five hundred Jews in Montreal alone. This number doubled in the twenty years that followed. The new immigrants included Sephardic as well as Ashkenazic Jews (whose name derives from *Ashkenaz*, the Hebrew name for Germany). Ashkenazic Jews immigrating to Canada originated from Germany, Poland, Russia, and east-central Europe, and began settling in large numbers in the mid-1800s.

JEWISH IMMIGRATION IN THE MID-NINETEENTH CENTURY

The emergence of a Jewish community in Toronto coincides with the first substantial wave of Jewish immigrants to North America in the period between 1840 and the 1880s. Comprised mainly of German settlers, and eastern Europeans who had migrated to Germany on their way to the New World, these immigrants headed to the Americas for both economic and political reasons. The majority of these immigrants went to the United States—by 1877 there were 277,000 Jews in that country. To a lesser degree, they moved to Canada, where the Jewish population in 1881 had reached 2,455.

During this time, Jewish communities emerged in a number of Canadian cities. The community in Toronto, which largely comprised Jews of English origin as well as some from the United States and Montreal, was formally established in 1849. By 1860, there were seventy-five Jewish families in that city. Jewish communities also formed in such places as Lancaster, Cornwall, London, and Windsor, all in Ontario. By 1860, Hamilton had a community that was large enough to support a synagogue. In the 1850s and 1860s, viable Jewish communities also developed in Halifax and in Saint John. The Jewish community of Canada almost doubled in size between 1871 and 1881.

TOWARD THE TWENTIETH CENTURY: IMMIGRATION FROM EASTERN EUROPE

The greatest wave of Jewish immigration took place between the 1880s and the 1920s. The Jewish population in Canada grew from 2,455 in 1881 to over 156,000 in 1931. By comparison, the Jewish community in the United States grew from 280,000 in 1877 to 4.5 million in 1925. The majority of these immigrants came from the western borders of the Russian Empire and Romania. Their movement out of these areas was associated in large part with increased anti-Semitism and with pogroms in Russia in 1881. As these immigrants moved to Canada, they went beyond the traditional areas where Jews had settled. Ukrainian Jews settled in Winnipeg; others settled further west, including on the prairies and the West Coast.

Those who arrived in Canada in the late 1800s and early 1900s were different than those who had come earlier. Immigrants in the early 1800s and before were predominately merchants, traders, and professionals. Many of these brought their wealth with them; others (like David David, who was a founding partner of the Bank of Montreal) brought skills that gave them the ability to accumulate their wealth after they arrived. However, those who immigrated between 1870 and 1900 tended to be small merchants, clerical workers, artisans, unskilled labourers, or in unspecified occupations. Over 70 per cent of Jewish immigrants after 1920 were skilled labourers and artisans, a much higher proportion than among the general immigrant population arriving in Canada or the United States.

Jewish immigration to Canada was sustained at substantial levels until 1931, when it was drastically reduced by government policy. 'With the onset of the Depression, economic insecurities fed antisemitic prejudice to help close the doors even to desperate Jewish refugees from Nazi Germany. Arrivals throughout the 1920's had averaged several thousand per year, but in the next decade, despite the rise of antisemitism in Europe, the numbers declined to several hundred' (Weinfeld, 1999, p. 862).

Anti-Semitism also affected Jews who had already settled in Canada. Referring to the time between 1930 and 1945 as 'the Dark Years', Abella (1990) describes the social tone of the day. For example, in 1934, fourteen interns walked off the job at Notre Dame Hospital in Montreal (joined by interns from five surrounding Catholic hospitals, as well as by the clergy of neighbouring parishes), refusing to work with a Jew. Samuel Rabinovich had graduated first in his class at the University of Montreal but ended up having to resign from his position in the face of the protests. One Quebec newspaper wrote that 'Jews . . . had now learned their place, and "it is not in Quebec"' (p. 180). At roughly the same time, the Regina General Hospital refused to hire two Jewish radiologists, citing that a Jewish appointment would be unacceptable both to the staff and the public at large. As well, there were violent confrontations in Toronto, Winnipeg, and Vancouver as Jews and anti-Jewish gangs confronted one another.

The situation is reflected in a study commissioned by the Canadian Jewish Congress in 1938. It reported that quotas and restrictions had become a way of life. According to the study, few of the country's teachers and none of its school principals were Jewish; banks, insurance companies, and large industrial and commercial interests excluded Jews from employment; department stores did not hire Jews as salespeople; Jewish doctors could not get hospital appointments; there were no Jewish judges, and Jewish lawyers were excluded from most firms; universities and professional schools devised quotas against Jewish students and they did not hire Jewish faculty; few civil servants were Jews, and the exceptions were rarely promoted.

If a Jew found it difficult to find a job or receive an education, it was perhaps even more difficult to find a suitable place to live or to vacation. Increasingly, restrictive covenants were put on various properties, preventing them from being

sold to Jews. Signs sprang up at beaches and resorts throughout the nation informing Jews that they were not welcome. A Laurentian hotel warned 'No Jews or Dogs
Allowed.' A Toronto beach posted a 'No Jews Allowed' sign. A tourist camp in Gimli,
Manitoba, put up signs warning Jews to keep away. Throughout Ontario's Muskoka
area, various hotels issued warnings that Jews should keep out (Abella, 1990,
p. 182).

IMMIGRATION AFTER THE SECOND WORLD WAR

Jewish immigration to Canada resumed after the end of the Second World War. The
first wave arrived between 1947 and 1952. During these years, a total of 34,000 Jews
came to Canada, of whom 11,064 had been displaced by the war. Immigration as a
consequence of the war continued through the mid 1950s. In 1956, just over 2,000
Jews arrived in Canada; the following year over 6,000 arrived. Many of these immigrants were survivors of the Holocaust. Though not strictly orthodox in the religious practice, these people were firmly rooted in Jewish rituals and traditional
Jewish culture. Although larger numbers of Holocaust survivors settled in the
United States than in Canada, the proportion, relative to the size of the Canadian
and the American Jewish communities, was greater in Canada. As a result, the background and experience of these people had greater impact on the Canadian Jewish
community than it did south of the border.

Jewish migration to Canada has continued to this day. Most immigrants have
come in waves associated with political events in their homeland. There were, for
example, large numbers of migrants following the failure of the 1956 revolution in
Hungary. In the ten years from 1955 to 1965, approximately 20,000 francophone
Sephardic Jews from North Africa (primarily Morocco) arrived in Montreal. In
1968, a number of Jews arrived from Poland, following their expulsion by the Polish
government. In the period beginning in the mid-1970s until the mid-1990s, more
than 20,000 Jews immigrated to Canada from the Soviet Union. These Jews differed
from most that had come before them. Under Soviet control, with its suppression
of religious freedom, many of these immigrants were unfamiliar with the Jewish
religion and culture. These circumstances have posed a unique problem for the
Jewish community in its integration of these newcomers into Jewish communal life.

Most recently, Jewish migration to Canada has included thousands of Israelis.
Many of these immigrants are Sephardic in origin. They, too, pose a quandary for
the Canadian Jewish community. On the one hand, there is a desire to welcome
these newcomers into the community. However, given the Jewish community's support for Israel and Zionism, to be too welcoming could be seen as undermining
Israel's interests. In addition to Israelis, recent immigrants have come from
Ethiopia, South Africa, and Latin and South America.

Before shifting our attention to Jewish culture and community life, we discuss
psychological issues and dynamics of migration. It is helpful to bear in mind that
Jewish immigrants continue to arrive in Canada, and that many Canadian Jews are
first-generation Canadians. The discussion that follows provides insight into their
experience, as well as the experience of immigrants generally.

Psychological Aspects of Migration

Immigration is a major life event that may have long-lasting and far-reaching psychological consequences. Although some attention has been devoted recently to the positive, development-enhancing aspect of this life transition, psychological distress has been long recognized as an integral part of the experience of migration. The modern approach to the study of migration views this psychological distress as a normative and temporary reaction to stress, and focuses on attempts to identify factors that affect this reaction. During the last two decades, research into these aspects has notably expanded and has resulted in an enormous and heterogeneous body of professional literature. This part of the chapter will review research into the psychological aspects of migration; it then presents theoretical models that may help conceptualize its psychological essence.

Research into the Risk and Resilience Factors in Migration

The contemporary psychological approach to migration rests on two complimentary assumptions (Murphy, 1977). The first is that psychological distress of immigrants is a situational and transitional reaction that may be best conceptualized as an 'adjustment disorder' (*DSM*, 1998). It is a subjective mental distress that may occur in adjustment to a major life change and may temporarily affect the individual's professional, scholarly, and social functioning. It may be expressed in a variety of psychological symptoms, such as anxiety, depression, obsessive-compulsive symptoms, poor self-esteem, hopelessness, and helplessness, as well as psycho-physiological symptoms (Berry, 1992; Westermeyer, 1989; Orley, 1994).

The second basic assumption in migration research is that numerous risk factors operate in migration. These risk factors cause some groups of immigrants to be at greater risk for psychological distress and psychopathology, while certain protective factors may render other immigrants more resilient to the stresses of migration. Consequently, contemporary research has focused on the study of risk and resilience factors for the psychological well-being of immigrants. The most important factors will be identified and discussed below.

Objective conditions no doubt affect the psychological well-being of immigrants, but they will be referred to only briefly since the focus here is on psychological determinants and processes. The most important condition affecting the psychological well-being of immigrants is the circumstances of migration. For example, previous trauma, either in the homeland or en route, as is the case with many refugees and exiles, is associated with high psychological distress and adjustment difficulties in the new country (Vega, Kolody, & Valle, 1987). In general, the more difficult the pre-migration experiences, the more complex the cultural adaptation process (Jacob, 1994). The objective life conditions in the new country—the socio-economic and professional status of the immigrants and their living arrangements—also affect the psychological well-being of immigrants (Brody, 1994; Scott & Scott, 1989; Vega et al., 1987; Orley, 1994).

Time is one of the most intriguing and most controversial of the factors in migration. Since psychological distress and functional impairments are viewed as normative and temporary phenomena in migration, it is assumed that with time an improvement occurs in the psychological state and functioning of the immigrant. Indeed, most of the studies show that, with the passage of time, the psychological well-being of immigrants improves (Scott & Scott, 1989; Henner, Weller, & Shor, 1997). However, a growing number of studies show that psychological distress may persist among some immigrants for years, even decades (Flaherty, Kohn, Levar, & Birz, 1988; Orley, 1994; Zilber, Lerner, & Kertes, 1996; Mirsky, 1997).

Along with their objective conditions, immigrants also bring cultural baggage to their new homeland. Consequently, cultural factors are often the focus of research in this field. Some studies explore what may be termed as *cultural character*—that is, a set of traits that seems to be common to a certain culture. For example, a higher level of narcissism was found among American women of Caucasian origin, compared to those of Hispanic or Asian origin (Smith, 1990). Similarly, a series of studies found that subjects in countries of the former communist block tended to exhibit characteristics that had higher social desirability than did English subjects (Hanin et al., 1991). Only a few studies have examined the association between cultural traits and psychological reactions in migration. One area of study has focused on the effect of cultural distance between the homeland and the new country. Researchers concur that the larger this distance, the greater the adjustment difficulties of immigrants and the higher their psychological distress (Furnham & Bochner, 1986; Westermayer, 1989; Brody, 1994; Berry, 1997).

One of the main social factors that is being studied in the context of migration relates to attitudes that prevail towards the immigrants in the host country (Westermayer, 1989). Rejection, prejudice, and discrimination put at risk the psychological well-being of immigrants, as does the pressure for assimilation into the culture of the host country and the abandonment of the original culture (Berry, 1992; Brody, 1994; Jacob, 1994; Orley, 1994; Alderete, Vega, Kolody, & Aguilar-Gaxiola, 1999). Social support, in contrast, is one of the most potent factors reducing stress in migration (Vega et al. 1987; Scott & Scott, 1989; Berry, 1992; Furnham, 1990; Flaherty et al., 1988; Mirsky & Barasch, 1993; Lerner & Zilber, 1996). Often, this support is provided by the ethnic community of fellow immigrants. Although ethnic enclaves are often perceived as negative phenomena by mainstream society, many researchers agree that, as a rule, they are temporary, supportive, transitional structures that facilitate the adjustment of immigrants into the host society.

The family may be another source of support in migration, but its supportive function is not self-evident. Immigration may affect the structure, hierarchies, and values of the family as a system and reveal differences among individual family members in their reactions to stress (Ekblad, 1993; Jacob, 1994; Levenbach & Lewak, 1995). New adaptational tasks require changes in roles and in relationship patterns in the family, and these changes may cause conflicts and distress (Ben-David, 1994; Chambon, 1989; Hertz, 1993; Slutzki, 1998).

Changes that occur in immigrant families may limit the ability of the family to extend support to the children (Berry, 1992; Ekblad, 1993; Roer-Strier, 1996). Immigrant parents may be threatened by the new environment, and their attitudes may affect the adjustment of their children (Aronowitz, 1984, 1992; Slonim-Nevo, Sheraga, & Mirsky, 1999) Having been uprooted from their habitual cultural environment, they may lose confidence in their parental role and skills. This may be compounded by the tendency that the young are typically faster to gain orientation in the new environment—learn the new language and new skills; parents may grow to rely, even depend, on them. Additional complications arise in the case of immigrant adolescents. Despite their independence struggles, adolescents still need their parents. In normal circumstances, adolescents commonly withdraw from the family into a group of peers. The peer group alleviates the painful process of emancipation from childhood dependencies. It provides the adolescent with a feeling of belonging and acceptance and often becomes a 'surrogate family' (Blos, 1967; Erikson, 1968). However, with migration there is loss of the peer group, which may deprive adolescents of a major source of support and stability and make it more difficult to separate and gain independence from their parents (Rosenthal & Feldman, 1990). The level of cohesiveness and solidarity of the family is a factor that influences its ability to contain these tensions and to continue providing support to its individual members.

Two main questions are addressed by those who study the role of personality factors in migration: 1) Are there personality characteristics that differentiate immigrants from those that do not immigrate and, if so, what are they? 2) How do various personality variables influence the adjustment of immigrants? Contemporary studies suggest that personality does play a role in the decision to immigrate. For example, a study comparing Indian citizens planning to immigrate to Canada with a matched group who did not plan to immigrate found that personality factors alone predicted to a large extent the decision to immigrate. Traits that seemed to typify the potential immigrants were curiosity, the search for excitement, interest in the world around them, and internal locus of control (Winchie & Carment, 1988). Other studies have also found that immigrants are typified by relative personal freedom and independence (Scott & Scott, 1989). In the search for answers to the second question, some studies focus on the motivation for immigration and the expectation of the immigrants. It is agreed that those who freely choose to immigrate experience less difficulties in the process of adjusting to a new society than do those who were coerced (Brody, 1994). People who are certain that they will improve their lives with migration (for instance, those who immigrate to get a better job), and individuals who have realistic information and expectations of the new country, are likely to adjust with relatively few problems (Vega et al., 1987; Furnham, 1990).

Among other personality-related factors that have been studied are mental health and symptomatology. A positive association was found between sound mental health before and after immigration (Scott & Scott, 1989), while psychiatric symptomatology is associated with psychopathology following migration

(McKelvey, Webb, & Mao, 1993). Personal flexibility and openness to change were found to assist adjustment, while a dependent personality style was associated with psychological distress after migration (McKelvey et al., 1993; Scott & Scott, 1989). One's sense of self-efficacy and optimism were among the strong predictors of coping and health in migration (Jerusalem, 1993). As in other situation of stress, personal maturity was found to be helpful in psychological adjustment (Furnham & Bochner, 1986).

Numerous demographic parameters have been studied in relation to immigration. The most important are gender and age. It has been shown that women immigrants suffer higher rates of psychological distress than do men (Scott and Scott, 1989). However, such gender differences are not specific to migration; they reflect a universal pattern of gender differences in reporting psychological distress: women no doubt react differently to stress but are also more likely to acknowledge and report their psychological experiences (Lerner & Zilber, 1996).

Among the different age groups of immigrants, adolescents have received much attention; however, studies investigating the effects of immigration on the psychological well-being of adolescents have produced variable and inconclusive results. Several literature reviews identify adolescent immigrants as a group at risk for psychological distress (Aronowitz, 1984), and so do some recent studies (Beiser, 1990; Ekblad, 1993). Yet, other studies fail to demonstrate higher psychological distress among immigrant adolescents than among their non-immigrant peers (Scott & Scott, 1989; Klimidis, Stuart, Minas, & Ata, 1994). Psychological distress among immigrant adolescents is typically attributed to immigration-related losses, which complicate the process of identity formation that is focal at this developmental phase (Blos, 1967; Erikson, 1968; Mirsky, 1997). The severity of such losses, and the consequent degree of disruption of psychological well-being, may certainly be affected by personal, familial, and cultural variables. The difficulty in establishing a consistent understanding of the effects of migration on adolescents stems from the close psychological resemblance between the two processes and the fact that they may reinforce or inhibit each other.

Theoretical Conceptualizations of Migration

Theoretical conceptualizations of psychological processes that take place in migration have been suggested by many psychological schools. However, these conceptualizations are seldom based on systematic empirical studies, and such studies are seldom based on theoretical models. It is therefore not the predictive validity of the model, but the theoretical orientation of the researcher, that dictates such conceptualizations. In line with this tendency, the following will favour a psychodynamic conceptualization of psychological processes in migration. This theoretical framework is not among the ones most widely applied to migration. The most popular models for understanding the psychological aspect of migration derive from stress theories, including the model of acculturation developed by John Berry. Berry's model focuses on the changes that occur in the behaviour, attitudes, skills, and values of the individual as a result of the encounter with the new culture. Berry delineates a number of acculturation styles that lie on the axis of the immigrants' willingness to accept the new culture and hold on to the old one. This process may be accompanied by 'acculturation stress', which may manifest itself in various psychological symptoms (Berry, 1992, 1997).

Only recently have psychodynamic psychologists applied their tools of analysis to the understanding of migration. Various orientations were suggested as helpful in understanding the psychology of migration. Some models rest on the paradigm of mourning (Pollock, 1989), others on the object-relation and Kleinian theories (Garza-Guerrero, 1974; Stein, 1985a, 1985b; Grinberg & Grinberg, 1989), and still others on the self-psychology model of Kohut (Antokoletz, 1993) and on the Mahlerian model of separation-individuation. As an illustration, the last conceptualization will be presented in more detail.

The conceptualization of migration as a separation-individuation process proposes that migration re-evokes early conflicts between dependency and independence needs and presents an additional opportunity for the resolution of this conflict (Mirsky & Kaushinsky, 1989; Mirsky, 1990; Gottesfeld & Mirsky, 1992). (Adolescence is also considered a separation-individuation process (Blos, 1967); thus, in the case of adolescent immigrants the two processes overlap.) The decision to immigrate represents a transient solution of the conflict: dependency needs are temporarily pushed aside, and the desire for change, development, and independence prevails. This is achieved through the defence mechanism of splitting. The homeland is devaluated and acquires an 'all bad' quality, while the land of destination is idealized. Immigrants who contemplate migration are prone to idealize their future independence and achievements, which they associate with migration. To an extent, this idealization is adaptive. Like in the 'practising' substage of the original separation-individuation, in immigration the euphoric mood helps the immigrant in acquiring mastery in the new environment.

Nevertheless, a painful realization of separateness and of loss eventually takes the place of euphoria. Immigrants realize that they have lost many things dear to them, things that were part of their identity. This is the most painful and stressful stage of migration, when the initial unresolved conflict resurfaces and the immigrant is again torn between dependency and independence, between old attachments to the homeland and newly created emotional bonds with the new country, between old and newly acquired self-representations. In an unconscious attempt to undo the fact of immigration and out of deep feelings of nostalgia, the splitting mechanism is mobilized again. This time, it is the homeland that is idealized, while the new country is assigned the 'all bad' quality. Through a prolonged interpsychic as well as interpersonal negotiation, similar to the 'rapprochement' subphase in the original separation-individuation, a genuine resolution of the conflict occurs and an integrated representation of both countries is accomplished.

The group of peer-immigrants is particularly important at this stage, as it is in adolescence, since it offers a temporary asylum from the external environment and the internal conflict. Immigrants need a group of peers with whom to share and work through their experiences of anger towards the new country and of nostalgia towards the old. At the final stage of adjustment, an open-ended process of developing an integrated self-representation, which will include old as well as new components, may begin. For adolescent immigrants, it is at the same time a process of developing an adult identity and adult identifications; therefore, for them, it is particularly significant.

As can be seen, this conceptualization not only gives insight into the experience of the individual immigrant, but helps identify risk periods and factors and suggest direction for preventive and therapeutic interventions.

The Canadian Jewish Community

The Jewish community in Canada is heavily concentrated in urban areas. More than 75 per cent of the Jewish population is found in Toronto or Montreal; more than 95 per cent are found in metropolitan areas that have a Jewish population of more than 1,000 persons. Given the recentness of much Jewish migration to Canada, the community includes a substantial proportion of immigrants. Many of the community leaders were born abroad, and most of the others are children of immigrants (Elazar & Waller, 1990, p. 428). Immigration continues, with two-thirds of the Jewish community's growth from 1981 to 1991 attributable to immigration. 'The 30,080 Jews who immigrated to Canada in the same decade (i.e., 1981–91) represented 8.75 per cent of the Jewish community' (Berdichewsky, 1997, p. 87).

According to Weinfeld (1999), it is difficult to overemphasize the communitarian basis of contemporary Jewish life in Canada. This orientation is based in part on traditional religious practice, which requires that prayer take place only in the presence of a minyan (a quorum of ten men), and on religious orientations, which prescribe a sense of responsibility for the needs of other Jews and which highly values altruistic charity. It is also an artifact of the Jewish experience: given the hostilities and realities of anti-Semitism, Jews have traditionally needed to band together and depend on one another.

The Formal versus the Informal Community

As with any community, the Jewish community can be understood in terms of both formal and informal properties. An informal community is constituted by the network of social relationships. The Jewish community, as distinct from most other ethnic communities, has a high level of integration among its members. Weinfeld (1999) refers to this as a sort of informal solidarity. He points out that over three-quarters of adult Canadian Jews in 1990 claimed that 'most of their friends' were Jewish, and a study in Toronto found that between 50 and 55 per cent indicated that their three closest friends were Jewish. These patterns are further reflected in housing patterns, where people of Jewish background live in close proximity to one another, often in neighbourhoods that have a high proportion of Jews. This may be further encouraged by the location of synagogues, Jewish community centres, Jewish schools, and kosher butchers, bakeries, and other merchants.

The formal community is represented by several different types of organizations. Most visible are religious organizations: temples and synagogues. Temples and synagogues fall into one of four distinct denominations in Judaism: Orthodox, Conservative, Reform, or Reconstructionist. These denominations are distinguished by the degree to which they adhere to traditional religious observance. The Reform movement, which emerged in nineteenth-century Germany, espouses a liberal, rational, and universalistic philosophy. Religious practice is not as rigid as in other denominations and, unlike Conservative or Orthodox Jewish practice, religious services are not conducted in Hebrew. Conservative Judaism developed in the United States in the late nineteenth and early twentieth century. It seeks to synthesize elements of Reform and Orthodox practice to create a more traditional form of religious expression than Reform Judaism, but not as traditional as Orthodox Judaism. Orthodox Jews (including the Tascher sect of ultra-orthodox Jews who reside in Montreal) strictly follow Jewish law and Jewish tradition, and are traditional in their religious expression. Reconstructionism is the newest and smallest denomination in Judaism. It is an offshoot of Conservativism that blends traditional and progressive elements. Among Canadians who identify themselves as Jewish by religion, about 19 per cent are Orthodox, 37 per cent are Conservative, 11 per cent are Reform, 1 per cent are Reconstructionist, and 32 per cent are 'other', which includes designations such as 'traditional' or 'ultra-orthodox'.

Identity as Jewish by religion is not reflected by formal membership in a synagogue. In 1990, only two-thirds of Jewish adults were members of a synagogue. As well, many Jews (particularly Reform and Conservative Jews) are selective in their religious observances. Canadian Jews tend to observe those religious rituals that are infrequent, can be invested with universalistic or modern themes, have a counterpart in the Christian calendar, and are child centred. This inclination may explain why more Jews light Hanukkah candles than fast on Yom Kippur, the most important religious holiday. Hanukkah comes once a year and lasts eight days. It parallels Christmas in its timing and in the practice of gift giving. It celebrates the struggle for freedom by Jews against imperialist invaders, a universalist message. Finally, it is profoundly child centred, focused on giving gifts, lighting candles, and spinning the dreidel (toy spinning top). (Weinfeld, 1999, p. 875). Among Canadian Jews, Passover seders are the most faithfully observed rituals (by 92 per cent), followed by lighting Hanukkah candles (87 per cent), and fasting on Yom Kippur (77 per cent). Fifty-six per cent of Canadian Jews light Sabbath candles, 15 per cent refuse to handle money on the Sabbath, and 46 per cent maintain a kosher home.

Not surprisingly, levels of religious observance and participation in formal religious services are highest in large urban communities and decrease with the diminishing size of the local Jewish community. Jews living in smaller communities, or in rural areas, are less likely to be involved in day-to-day Jewish life. This is largely a reflection of their environment and the absence of formal organizations. However, many of these Jews still consider themselves Jewish, either by religion, culture, or ethnicity.

Aside from formal religious organizations, there are several other formal elements of the Jewish community in Canada. These include national fraternal and quasi-political organizations (e.g., B'nai B'rith and the League for Human Rights, National Council of Jewish Women, Hadassah-WIZO, Canadian Jewish Congress, and Canadian Zionist Federation) as well as local philanthropic organizations and agencies (e.g., Jewish federations, Jewish hospitals and schools, and Jewish community centres).

On a national level, the Canadian Jewish Congress (CJC) serves as the official voice of Canadian Jewry and represents Jewish issues and concerns to provincial and federal governments. It acts on matters affecting the status, rights, and welfare of Canadian Jews. Most Jewish welfare federations and community councils are associated with the CJC, as are most other Jewish organizations. B'nai B'rith, an international fraternal organization, which sponsors the League for Human Rights, has remained independent of the CJC structure.

At a local level, Jewish communities in most metropolitan areas are organized around a welfare federation. These federations are responsible for collecting funds for the United Jewish Appeal (an organization that provides funding to national and international Jewish charities, including support for resettlement and welfare services in Israel) and for disbursing funds to a variety of local welfare, social, cultural, and recreational agencies. The fundraising efforts of welfare federations are largely separate from the activities of other national and Israel-related organizations and from the fundraising undertaken by other Jewish institutions such as schools and synagogues. According to a 1990 survey, 41 per cent of the Jewish community in Canada made a contribution of $100 or more to their local federation's appeal; the average contribution was $1,700 (Weinfeld, 1999).

All of the organizations that constitute the formal structure of the Jewish community in Canada rely heavily on voluntary participation and lay leadership. In 1990, 47 per cent of Canadian Jews claimed to belong to a Jewish organization, 31 per cent indicated that they performed volunteer work in a Jewish organization, and 25 per cent indicated that they sat on a board or a committee (Weinfeld, 1999). This level of participation is considerably higher than is the norm for other ethnic groups and ethnic communities in Canada.

The Jewish Family

Stereotypes of the Jewish family tend to focus on an overprotective mother who is skilled in the use of guilt. In reality, there is no clear indication that Jewish mothers are more overprotective than any other group of mothers. However, Jewish mothers do tend to exercise considerable power within the family unit, in contrast to their lower status in traditional religious Judaism. The tension between status at home and status in the religious community has led many Jewish women to embrace feminist issues and principles.

While, like other women, Jewish women face strong expectations for filling the role of wife and mother, they are also pressured to acquire advanced education and a career. Their attainment of high levels of education has direct implications for their employment opportunities and status, but also underlies egalitarian spousal relations. The idea that Jewish women should play an economic role dates back to the Old World. Wives assumed a dual burden as mothers and breadwinners while husbands who were so disposed spent their days at religious study and prayer. Traditionally, Jewish fathers were also involved in childrearing and were concerned about the religious dimensions of the home; in North America this function has been largely overtaken by their role as breadwinners (Weinfeld, 1999, p. 871).

It is difficult to make any broad and general statements that characterize the Jewish family in a unidimensional way. There are some commonalities, such as an emphasis on educational attainment and on traditional Jewish values of charity and good will. The actual practice of religion for many Jewish families is reflected in their celebration of selected Jewish holidays and of rituals that are associated with events in the life cycle: circumcision, or a corresponding symbolic ceremony for females, after birth; the bar mitzvah for boys at age thirteen and bat mitzvah for girls at age twelve, which mark puberty and transition to adulthood; a Jewish marriage ceremony; and practices around death (the period of mourning and the annual commemoration).

Although marriage of Jews to non-Jews is increasing—in 1990 14 per cent of all Canadian Jews lived in intermarried families—there continues to be a strong proscription against intermarriage. According to a study done in 1990, two-thirds of third-generation Toronto Jews expressed a belief that it is important to marry within the religion. The problem of intermarriage is greatest for Jews living outside large Jewish communities. In large communities, social connections tend to be more homogeneous and marriage partners are easier to find. In smaller and rural communities, there is greater integration into the non-Jewish world and fewer potential partners are available. Rates of intermarriage in the Atlantic provinces, for example, are as high as 50 per cent.

A discussion of the Jewish family would be incomplete if we didn't address the issue of poverty. Popular stereotypes notwithstanding, poverty is as much a problem among Jews as it is for other segments of the Canadian population. Poverty is greatest among the elderly and among recent immigrants. One-third of Jews age sixty-five or over live in poverty (23.7 per cent of men; 37.6 per cent of women). As well, the 1991 census indicates that 31.1 per cent of Jews immigrating between 1971 and 1981 lived in poverty, as opposed to 29.1 per cent for non-Jewish immigrants; 28.8 per cent of those immigrating before 1941 lived at the time in poverty (Torczyner, 1993). Not unexpectedly, poverty is also related to educational attainment. Rates of poverty among Jews with post-secondary education are identical to those of non-Jews. Rates of poverty among those who have not completed a post-secondary degree are lower for Jews than for non-Jews; however, they still run as high as 34 per cent among those with no high school education (compared to 41 per cent for the general population) and 18.3 per cent among those who have some high school education (compared to 25.5 per cent for the general population) (Torczyner, 1993).

Issues for People of Jewish Canadian Background

A number of issues confront the Canadian Jewish community. The most visible is anti-Semitism. Anti-Semitism can be defined as hostility directed at Jews solely because they are Jews. It is not caused by the actions or beliefs of Jews, but rather is a result of attitudes and behaviour that arise regardless of what Jews do or what they believe. Quite simply, anti-Semites are antagonistic towards Jews for who they are and what they represent (Mock, 1996).

In reporting on a study of Jewish women and their experience with anti-Semitism, Nora Gold (1997) provides some insight and illustration of the experience of anti-Semitism at different times in the life cycle and in different settings. Her respondents reported such things as being asked, 'Have you eaten a non-Jewish baby lately?' One worked in a store that has a 'jew-me-down' sale; others were called 'dirty Jews' or 'Christ-killers' or were chased home from school by boys throwing rocks at them. Women were picked on by anti-Semitic teachers, deprived of jobs for which they were qualified, and told by non-Jewish children in the neighbourhood that they couldn't play because they were Jewish. One woman in charge of the anti-racism initiative in a large agency was called 'a Jewish princess' by a colleague, who received only the mildest of reprimands. Another woman reported that a noose was hung from the tree in her backyard, and several women have had swastikas painted onto their doors. A third woman related the following incident: she had picked up an old brooch for $5 at a garage sale; when she cleaned it off and took it in to have it appraised, it turned out to be worth $500. A few days later, when she was telling this story to people at work, boasting about her 'find', was told, 'Well, what do you expect? You're a cheap Jew' (Gold, 1997, p. 2). These incidents were made even more traumatic by the fact that they were trivialized or dismissed when recounted to non-Jewish friends and colleagues. As Gold points out, the respondents experienced a kind of secondary victimization. For example, one woman was told she was being too sensitive—that 'jewing down' was just an expression and it didn't really mean anything.

There are several forms in which anti-Semitism can be expressed (Gold, 1996). One is invisibility. In this form, Jewish uniqueness, oppression, and diversity are not seen or, if they are seen, are denied. With all of its attention on multicultural diversity and sensitivity, it would be reasonable to expect that there would be some content in social work curricula on people of Jewish background. To the contrary, a review of books on ethnic-sensitive practice and of course content on practice with racial and ethnic minorities reflects the invisibility of Jews, as a distinct group, to social work educators and students. Invisibility is also seen in attempts to deny or trivialize the Holocaust.

A second form of anti-Semitism is the adherence to myths and stereotypes about Jews. Common misperceptions include beliefs that all Jews are rich and that Jews control the banks and the media. There are stereotypes about the appearance of Jews, about Jews being materialistic, and about Jews being pushy. Jewish women are further marginalized through the stereotype of the Jewish mother and the JAP (i.e., the Jewish American Princess). In each of these cases, views about Jews are constructed independent from any one individual and are applied as though they reflect each individual who is Jewish or who has a Jewish name.

The third form that anti-Semitism takes is anti-Zionism. In this case, the crucial point is not that someone is critical of Israel—many North American Jews are critical about certain policies and practices of the government of Israel—but that the person questions the right of Israel to exist. Anti-Zionists question whether there should be a Jewish homeland, and whether Jews even deserve to have a homeland. This position may be viewed as a direct extension of the belief that Jews as individuals do not have a right to exist. By questioning Israel's very existence (as opposed to questioning a policy of the government of Israel), one takes a stance that is generally recognized as a covert form of anti-Semitism, but that is couched in less obviously discriminatory language than other, less subtle forms (Gold, 1996).

There is little question that most people of Jewish-Canadian background have had some experience with anti-Semitism. While the effects of anti-Semitism are difficult to gauge, Shaffir (1989) suggests that it has an impact on the internal organization of the Jewish community (i.e., the external threat increases internal solidarity) and on the individual. At one extreme, an experience with anti-Semitism may strengthen an individual's Jewish identity and their commitment to Jewish practices. On the other, 'such an encounter may hasten an individual's attempts at assimilating into the larger society at the expense of maintaining any identification as a Jew' (Shaffir, 1989, p. 8). Ironically, anti-Semitism is often directed at people who are assumed to be Jewish, and not solely at those who are observant or practising Jews.

A second issue confronting the Jewish community in Canada is assimilation. Assimilation can be organized around a number of dimensions. For example, we can distinguish between *structural assimilation* (interaction among members of different ethnic groups and equal access to power and privilege with society's major institutions), *cultural assimilation* (the degree to which an ethnic group adopts the cultural traits of the dominant society), and *psychological assimilation* (the degree to which individuals identify with the dominant society and accept that society as the home base or as the prime focus of allegiance).

There is little doubt that Jews have assimilated into the larger society. This assimilation has consisted primarily of the cultural variety where Jews have successfully adapted to, and have become intimately familiar with, the prevailing norms and expectations of middle-class Canadian society. It has also consisted of assimilation into the formal levels of Canadian society. 'At the same time, however, Jewish identity continues to remain high. While Jews may have acquired the perspectives, or ways of thinking, of the dominant group, attempts to identify with it are limited. Jews continue to identify themselves as Jews and are so identified by others' (Shaffir, 1989, p. 6).

Despite Shaffir's observations, and the fact that Jewish assimilation has been minimal compared to the experience of comparable ethnic groups from Europe, assimilation remains a continuing threat to the Jewish community. Intermarriage, increasing structural assimilation, and the effects of anti-Semitism threaten the continuing existence of a viable Jewish community in Canada. Simply, as individuals increase their identification with the dominant society, and decrease their identification with the Jewish community, the vitality of the community becomes threatened. Elazar and Waller (1990) present a more optimistic view in suggesting that 'as the role of religion in Canadian society has declined, a sort of Jewish ethnic or secular identity has emerged' (p. 438). This approach to Jewish identity describes a substantial number of Canadian Jews.

A further threat to the Jewish community in Canada relates to demographics. There is a dual problem of below-average, below-replacement fertility levels in Canada and the fact that the current population is aging. While immigration may be one source of renewal for the community, it is difficult to anticipate whether significant numbers will be added to the Jewish population. Weinfeld (1999) suggests that it is likely that the proportion of Jews in the Canadian population will decline in coming years. The effect of the shrinking size of the community is unclear, but it is an issue of considerable concern to community leaders (Elazar & Waller, 1990).

Social Work Practice with Canadians of Jewish Background

In the context of an ethnic-sensitive orientation to practice, several general suggestions can be made with regard to social work with Jewish clients (see Gold, 1993; Beck, 1991). First, a social worker must take the issue of Jewish identity and anti-Semitism seriously. Jewish identity refers to more than religion. It embodies Jewish culture and history and is reflected in identification with the ethnic group, separate from an identification by religion. Many Jews have a dual identity—Canadian and Jewish. This duality is often resolved by labelling oneself as a Jewish Canadian rather than a Canadian Jew. Part of taking Jewish identity seriously is to understand the difference between these two expressions.

One factor that defines Jewish identity is anti-Semitism. Social workers must be aware of the nature of anti-Semitism and of its forms of expression, as they would be with other forms of racism. They need to be aware of the subtleties of anti-Semitism and of how it is experienced differently during different life stages, an awareness that will undoubtedly influence both a practitioner's general work as well as work specifically with Jewish clients. The practitioner must not tolerate anti-Semitism generally, whether among other clients or colleagues. As well, because the profession is concerned with promoting social justice, anti-Semitism should be included in each social worker's anti-racism agenda (Mock, 1996; Kropf & Isaac, 1992).

A second suggestion for preparation to work with Jewish clients is to become familiar with Jewish history and customs and with the history of anti-Semitism and its cumulative effects. As an ethnically diverse population, Jews have a unique history. This history does not comprise just biblical times, but includes expulsion from Spain during the Inquisition, ghettos and pogroms in nineteenth- and twentieth-century eastern Europe, the Holocaust, and insidious forms of anti-Semitism. These have a cumulative effect on the ethnic group and its members. Jewish culture and Jewish ethnicity is a reflection of these historical experiences. Through an understanding of this history, one is better equipped to work with clients who are part of that culture.

Separate from knowledge of the culture of Jews as an ethnic group, a social worker must also have an understanding of Jewish religious customs and practices. When working with a Jewish client, a social worker must be aware of the observance of the Sabbath and of dietary laws, as well as celebration of rites of passage and of holidays. Although individuals vary widely with regard to the degree to which they observe these customs and practices, the social worker needs to avoid the embarrassment of suggesting an appointment on a Jewish holiday; of encouraging a client who observes the Sabbath to take part in a self-improvement program that is held all day on a Saturday; of failing to acknowledge the significance of a bar mitzvah or a bris; or of offering snacks that are non-kosher. Because many Jews are well assimilated in the dominant Canadian culture, these points would not likely be issues for them. However for many others, this knowledge, and the sensitivity it produces, is an important element in the social worker's ability to develop an effective helping relationship.

A third suggestion for those working with clients of Jewish-Canadian background is to understand how lifespan developmental tasks are influenced by minority status. Although we all go through the same developmental stages and tasks, these may take on a different shape when one is not part solely of the dominant culture. There are two sets of identity issues around growing up and being Jewish: those associated generally with life's developmental tasks and those associated with the development of one's Jewish identity (Beck, 1991). While the former tasks are common and are supported by the dominant culture, tasks associated with Jewish identity are often not supported. Jewish identity is a different issue and takes different forms at different times in one's life. For a child, being Jewish may be a distinguishing characteristic. In some settings this may be a positive distinction; in others it may have negative consequences. For teenagers, Jewish identity is just one more identity issue with which they must grapple. As discussed later, it is also common for adolescents to deal with their orientation to Zionism at the same time. For an adult, Jewish identity may be influenced by having children. Because Jewish identity is not something that is generally supported by the dominant culture, it can be a source of stress and difficulty. Remaining part of a Jewish community is one way in which many cope with this stress.

Fourth, the social worker working with people of Jewish-Canadian background should understand the pressures Jewish culture places on marriage and childrearing. This pressure may be felt more strongly by women than by men, yet for both it comes with a strong proscription against marriage outside the group. These pressures are accentuated among those of Jewish background, as compared to other ethnic groups, because of the Holocaust and the many millions of Jews that were exterminated. It is not just a matter of valuing marriage and children—it is compounded by the issue of survival as a group. It is perhaps difficult for those not in a minority status to understand the dynamic associated with this fact, and with the reality that one's group constitutes barely 1 per cent of the Canadian population.

The final suggestion for social workers engaged with clients of Jewish Canadian background is to be familiar with the processes of migration and with the effects— both short- and long-term—of immigration to a new country and a new culture. It is important to keep in mind that many Jews living in Canada are immigrants. Even though many of them arrived in their youth or early adulthood, the processes around acclimation to a new culture and society are relevant in gaining a full understanding of the client(s).

Social Work Practice and the Life Cycle

In an effort to draw together our discussion, we will look at developmental issues about which social workers should be familiar if their work includes clients of Jewish background. A number of issues—anti-Semitism, for example—cut across developmental stages of the life cycle; others, such as Jewish identity, are more salient at some times than at others. Based on categories suggested by Devore and Schlesinger (1991), we briefly discuss common issues in each of the following stages of the life cycle: childhood, adolescence, adulthood (including mate selection, childrearing and later adulthood), and old age. The issues discussed are in addition to those that are part of normal development in the dominant culture and society.

CHILDHOOD

The main issue during the childhood years, particularly if there is greater contact with peer groups that include people who are not of Jewish background, is being introduced to and coping with anti-Semitism. Experiences vary, but they tend to begin in childhood years. They may continue regularly or be relatively sporadic. The initial experience often has disproportionate impact. A colleague recently shared his first experience with anti-Semitism, which occurred when he was growing up in a rural part of Ontario. When he was seven or eight years old, it was somehow mentioned on the school bus that he was Jewish. Another youngster began to stare at him, and continued to stare until they both got off the bus. Finally, he asked what the other was staring at, to which the child replied 'I am looking for your horns'. He had no idea what all of this meant, but when he shared the experience at home his parents provided his first orientation to anti-Semitism and racism in Canadian society. These experiences are a potential source of stress, depending on perceptions of how threatening they are and on the impact of being different than the dominant society.

Feelings of difference may also be associated with celebration of Jewish holidays. Several holidays (Hanukkah, Purim, Passover) include a child focus, and are often celebrated among the family. Some children may find it increasingly difficult to participate in these holidays while at the same time maintaining a place in school and social groupings that include small numbers of Jewish children. For example, because Christmas is a major focus in public schools, but is not celebrated by Jewish families, Jewish children face the challenge of reconciling it with their own religious beliefs and customs. This is not always easy, and it may not be stress free.

In late childhood, many Jewish children begin preparation for their bar or bat mitzvah. These ceremonies are rites of passage for the transition from childhood to adulthood. They are common celebrations in larger Jewish communities, but are less common in rural areas with small or no Jewish congregations. However, even in larger communities, not all children choose to have a bar or bat mitzvah. This decision may reflect religious identity or other individual or family issues.

ADOLESCENCE

A major task during adolescence is identity formation. It is during this period that youth begin to confront life's issues and begin to formulate an identity and self image. Jewish adolescents must work through two additional issues related to identity. One is their Jewish identity: this may be a decision about religiosity or about pride in an ethnic heritage. The other, closely related, is an attitude about Israel and Zionism. Through participation in Jewish youth organizations (e.g., synagogue-based youth groups, B'nai B'rith Youth Organization) and in Jewish culture, adolescents are encouraged to identify with Israel as a Jewish homeland and to understand Israel's place in the diaspora. Each individual works through these issues and resolves his or her own position, but it is a journey through which most Jewish adolescents must travel. The journey often includes, as part of finding one's roots, travel to Israel in order to view sites that are meaningful and significant in Jewish history.

Anti-Semitism may also be an issue during adolescence, although by that time most Jewish children have become accustomed to so-called normal expressions of anti-Semitism. These expressions may be stressful, but by their teenage years most youth understand that racism is simply a part of living in the dominant culture. There may be isolated difficulties for some adolescents when there are increases in expressions of anti-Semitism, and also in school situations where anti-Semitism (including denial of the Holocaust) is tolerated, but generally anti-Semitism is something to which one becomes increasingly accustomed with age and experience.

Adolescence is the time during which dating begins. As already stated, there is a strong proscription against intermarriage within the Jewish community. This proscription is applied more strictly in areas that support a larger Jewish community and where there is greater likelihood that youth can find other Jews as dating partners, but it is also something that is likely to be experienced in many smaller communities. Dating non-Jews may be tolerated during the high school years, but often a university is chosen where there is greater likelihood that Jewish dating partners will be found. The choices made around dating are in some ways a reflection of the identity formation already discussed, although they also contribute to formation of identity: if one's dating partners are largely non-Jews, the nature of one's Jewish identity is likely to be affected.

ADULTHOOD

Issues around dating and mate selection continue into the early adult years. Jewish young adults experience considerable social pressure to seek out Jewish dating partners and ultimately to choose a marital partner who is also Jewish. As indicated above, because of the Holocaust and the need to rebuild the community, these pressures are perhaps greater among Jews than other ethnic/minority groups. These expectations can be a source of stress for the individual. Young people may perceive themselves as potentially letting down parents or family, or they may feel obliged to date and marry someone whom they might not otherwise have chosen. All young adults must confront and work through many issues around dating, mate selection, and marriage. For Jewish young adults these issues are further complicated by the fact of being Jewish and by the pressures to remain within the group.

Despite the proscription against intermarriage, many Jews do marry outside their religion. While intermarriage may produce some elements of difficulty in the marital relationship itself, difficulties are most likely to be experienced with the arrival of children. The couple must decide about how dual religions will be handled, in what religion the child(ren) will primarily be raised, and how observation of religious holidays will be handled. Some couples may work through these issues with ease, while others may experience marital discord. Even where both partners are Jewish, couples still have to negotiate around issues of Jewish identity and participation in Jewish rituals and customs. Each partner brings her or his own Jewish identity to the new unit, and together they must generate a common identity that will reflect the environment in which they will live and in which they will raise their children.

As families grow and children age, adults will likely have to continue to work through issues of anti-Semitism. Some of the issues may emerge through the experience of one's child in school or with peer groups. In these cases, the parent must provide needed support to the child, and, depending on the case, may attempt to intervene in the situation. For most parents, bearing and tolerating racism directed at themselves is completely different from having to tolerate racism directed at their children. These are difficult issues for parents and something with which a social worker may become involved, either as an advocate for the child or family or as an agent working for a school or other community agency or organization.

Anti-Semitism may also be experienced directly. Adults may deal with anti-Semitism in the workplace, in the local community or neighbourhood, and/or in organizations. As a rule, these experiences do not cause problems that require professional intervention. Nevertheless, they are part of the life experience of these adults, and any intervention on other issues may become associated with experiences of anti-Semitism, either currently or in past. Anti-Semitism is not a unique or new issue at this stage of life. It is simply something with which one continues to deal and which escalates and de-escalates in saliency with historical time and events.

OLD AGE

Poverty is a particular problem among the elderly population, and social workers involved with Jewish seniors may find themselves dealing with issues associated with poverty. Several other challenges arise at this stage of the life cycle as well. These include alienation from one's family; a lack of surviving family members—

something that is altogether too common as a consequence of the Holocaust; and difficulty in continuing to participate in religious observance. With reduced mobility, elderly people may have greater difficulty travelling to synagogue, or they may find themselves placed in a residential facility that creates further isolation from the Jewish community. In either case, elderly folks may find it increasingly difficult to continue to engage in Jewish rituals and customs, and this may be a source of considerable stress.

Social work practitioners working with people of Jewish-Canadian background should be familiar with these stresses and how they might be minimized. They must also have an understanding of Jewish views around death, around mourning and bereavement, and around burial. Jewish practices are quite different than those common in the dominant culture—for one thing, Judaism prohibits desecration of the body, which means that an autopsy cannot be performed—and without an understanding of these practices, intervention is bound to be problematic. The notions of heaven and hell that are common in Christianity are not notions common among Jews; as well, there are clearly defined rituals for mourning and bereavement that differ from those commonly found in the dominant Canadian culture. Familiarity with these rituals is necessary if one is to intervene with an individual or family at this time.

Conclusions

Social work with Canadians of Jewish background requires an understanding and awareness of the Jewish community in Canada. It also requires a basic knowledge of Jewish history. This chapter lays the groundwork for understanding the Jewish community and for gaining the sensitivity needed for working with people of Jewish background. Those who plan to work directly in the Jewish community or with clients of Jewish background will want to undertake additional reading.

References

Abella, I. (1990). *A Coat of Many Colours: Two Centuries of Jewish Life in Canada.* Toronto: Lester and Orpen Dennys.

Alderete, E., Vega, W., Kolody, B., & Aguilar-Gaxiola, S. (1999). Depressive symptomatology: Prevalence and risk factors among Mexican migrant farm-workers in California. *Journal of Community Psychology, 27*(4), 457–71.

Antokoletz, J.C. (1993). A psychoanalytic view of cross-cultural passages. *American Journal of Psychoanalysis, 53*(1), 35–54.

Aronowitz, M. (1984). The social and emotional adjustment of immigrant children: A review of literature. *International Migration Review, 28*(2), 237–57.

———. (1992). Adjustment of immigrant children as a function of parental attitudes to change. *International Migration Review, 26*(1), 89–110.

Beck, E.T. (1991). Therapy's double dilemma: Antisemitism and misogyny. In R.J. Siegel & E. Cole (Eds), *Jewish Women in Therapy: Seen but Not Heard* (pp. 19–30). New York: Harrington Park Press.

Beiser, M. (1990). Migration: Opportunity or mental risk? *Triangle, 29*(2/3), 83–90.

Ben-David, A. (1994). Family function and migration. *Journal of Sociology and Social Welfare, 34*, 121–37.

Berdichewsky, B. (1997). *Cultural Pluralism in Canada: What It Means to the Jewish Community*. Vancouver: Canadian Jewish Congress.

Berry, J. (1992). Acculturation and adaptation in a new society. *International Migration Quarterly Review, 30*, 69–85.

———. (1997). Immigration, acculturation and adaptation. *Applied Psychology: An International Review, 46*(1), 5–68.

Blos, P. (1967). The second individuation process in adolescence. *Psychoanalytic Study of the Child, 22*, 162–78.

Brody, E. (1994). The mental health and well being of refugees: Issues and directions. In F. Marsella, T. Bornemann, S. Ekbald, & J. Orley (Eds), *Amidst Peril and Pain: The Mental Health and Wellbeing of the World's Refugees* (pp. 57–68). Washington, DC: American Psychological Association.

Chambon, A. (1989). Refugee families' experience: Three family themes—family disruption, violent trauma and acculturation. *Journal of Strategic and Systemic Therapies, 8*, 3–13.

Devore, W., & Schlesinger, E.G. (1991). *Ethnic-Sensitive Social Work Practice*. 3rd ed. New York: Macmillan.

Diagnostical Statistical Manual (DSM). (1998). 4th ed. Washington, DC: American Psychiatric Association.

Ekblad, S. (1993). Psychosocial adaptation of children while housed in Swedish refugee camp: Aftermath of a collapse of Yugoslavia. *Stress Medicine, 9*, 159–66.

Elazar, D.J., & Waller, H.M. (1990). *Maintain Consensus: The Jewish Polity in the Postwar World*. Latham, MD: University Press of America.

Erikson, E. (1964). *Insight and Responsibility*. New York: Norton.

———. (1968). *Identity: Youth and Crisis*. New York: Norton.

Flaherty, J., Kohn, R., Levav, I., & Birz, S. (1988). Demoralization in Soviet-Jewish immigrants to the United States and Israel. *Comprehensive Psychiatry, 29*(6), 588–97.

Furnham, A. (1990). Expatriate stress: The problem of living abroad. In S. Fisher & C. Cooper (Eds), *On the Move: The Psychology of Change and Transition* (pp. 275–301). London: Wiley.

Furnham, A., & Bochner, S. (1986). *Culture Shock: Psychological Reactions to Unfamiliar Environments*. London: Methuen.

Garza-Guerrero, A. (1974). Culture shock: Its mourning and the vicissitudes of identity. *Journal of American Psychoanalytic Association, 22*(2), 408–29.

Gold, N. (1993). On diversity, Jewish women, and social work. *Canadian Social Work Review, 10*(2), 240–55.

———. (1996). Putting antisemitism on the anti-racism agenda in North American schools of social work. *Journal of Social Work Education, 32*(1), 77–89.

———. (1997). Canadian Jewish women and their experiences of antisemitism and sexism. In R.J. Siegel & E. Cole (Eds), *Celebrating the Lives of Jewish Women:*

Patterns in a Feminist Sampler, Binghamton, NY: Haworth Press. Retrieved from www.utoronto .ca/wjudaism/journal/vol1no1/v1n1gold.htm

Gottesfeld, J., & Mirsky, J. (1992). To stay or to return: rapprochement processes in the migration of adolescents and young adults. *Journal of Contemporary Psychotherapy, 21*(4), 272–84.

Grinberg, L., & Grinberg, R. (1989). *Psychoanalytic Perspective of Migration and Exile*. New Haven, CT: Yale University Press.

Hanin, Y., Eysenk, S., Eysenk, H., & Barrett, P. (1991). A cross-cultural study of personality: Russia and England. *Personality and Individual Differences, 12*(3), 265–71.

Henner, T., Weller, A., & Shor, R. (1997). Stages of acculturation as reflected in depression reduction in immigrant nursing students. *International Journal of Social Psychiatry, 43*(4), 247–56.

Hepperlin, C. (1991). Immigrant adolescents in crisis: A model for care. In B. Ferguson, & E. Browne (Eds), *Health Care and Immigrants* (pp. 122–45). Sydney, Australia: McLeannon and Petty.

Hertz, D.G. (1993). Bio-psycho-social consequences of migration stress: A multidimensional approach. *Israel Journal of Psychiatry and Related Science, 30*(4), 204–12.

Jacob. A. (1994). Social integration of Salvadoran refugees. *Social Work, 39*(3), 307–12

Jerusalem, M. (1993). Personal resources, environmental constrains and adaptive processes: The predictive power of a theoretical stress model. *Personality and Individual Differences, 14*(1), 15–24.

Klimidis, S., Stuart, G., Minas, I.H., & Ata, A.W. (1994). Immigrant status and gender effect on psychopathology and self-concept in adolescence. *Comprehensive Psychiatry, 35*(5), 393–404.

Kropf, N.P., & Isaac, A.R. (1992). Cultural diversity and social work practice: An overview. In D.F. Harrison, J.S. Wodarski, & B.A. Thyer (Eds), *Cultural Diversity and Social Work Practice* (pp. 3–12). Springfield, IL: Charles C. Thomas.

Lerner, Y., & Zilber, N. (1996). Psychological distress among recent immigrants from the former Soviet Union to Israel: II. The effect of the Gulf War. *Psychological Medicine, 26*, 503–10.

Levenbach, D., & Lewak, B. (1995). Going home or going to pieces. *Contemporary Family Therapy: An International Journal, 17*(4), 379–94.

McKelvey, R., Webb, J., & Mao, A. (1993). Premigratory risk factors in Vietnamese Amerasians. *American Journal of Psychiatry, 150*(3), 470–3.

Mirsky, J. (1990). Individuation through immigration to Israel: Psychotherapy with immigrant adolescents. *Journal of Contemporary Psychotherapy, 20*(1), 47–61.

———. (1997). Psychological distress among immigrant adolescents: Culture specific factors in the case of immigrant adolescents from the former Soviet Union. *International Journal of Psychology, 34*(4), 221–30.

Mirsky, J., & Barasch, M. (1993). Adjustment problems among Soviet immigrants at risk. Part II: Emotional distress of elderly Soviet immigrants during the Gulf War. *Israel Journal of Psychiatry and Related Science, 30*(4), 233–43.

Mirsky, J., & Kaushinsky, F. (1989). Migration and growth: Separation individuation processes in immigrant students in Israel. *Adolescence, 24*(95), 725–40.

Mock, K. (1996). Anti-semitism in Canada: Realities, remedies, and implications for anti-racism. In C.E. James (Ed.), *Perspectives on Racism and the Human Services Sector: A Case for Change* (pp. 120–33). Toronto: University of Toronto Press.

Murphy, H. (1977). Migration, culture and mental health. *Psychological Medicine, 7,* 677–84.

Orley, J. (1994). Psychological disorders among refugees: Some clinical and epidemiological considerations. In F. Marsella, T. Bornemann, S. Ekblad, & J. Orley (Eds), *Amidst Peril and Pain: The Mental Health and Wellbeing of the World's Refugees* (pp. 193–206). Washington, DC: American Psychological Association.

Pollock, G. (1989). On migration—voluntary and coerced. *Annual of Psychoanalysis, 17,* 145–58.

Roer-Strier, D., (1996). Coping strategies of immigrant parents: Directions for family therapy. *Family Process, 35,* 363–76.

Rosenberg, L. (1939). *Canada's Jews: A Social and Economic Study of Jews in Canada.* Montreal: Canadian Jewish Congress.

Rosenthal, D., & Feldman, S. (1990). The acculturation of Chinese immigrants: Perceived effects on family functioning of length of residence in two cultural contexts. *Journal of Genetic Psychology, 151*(4), 495–514.

Scott, W., & Scott, R. (1989). *Adaptation of Immigrants: Individual Differences and Determinants.* Sydney, Australia: Pergamon Press.

Shaffir, W. (1989). Canadian Jewry: Some sociological observations. In E.Y. Lipsitz (Ed.), *Canadian Jewry Today: Who's Who in Canadian Jewry* (pp. 3–10). Downsview, ON: J.E.S.L. Educational Products.

Slonim-Nevo, V., Sheraga, Y., & Mirsky. J. (1999). A culturally sensitive approach to therapy with immigrant families: The case of Jewish emigrants from the former Soviet Union. *Family Process, 38*(4), 445–62.

Slutzki, C. (1998). Migration and disruption of social network. In M. McGoldrick (Ed.), *Re-visioning Family Therapy: Race, Culture and Gender in Clinical Practice* (pp. 360–9). New York: Guilford Press.

Smith, B. (1990). The measurement of narcissism in Asian, Caucasian and Hispanic American women. *Psychological Reports, 67*(3), 779–85.

Stein, H. (1985a). Culture change, symbolic object loss and restitutional processes. *Psychoanalysis and Contemporary Thought, 8(3),* 301–32.

———. (1985b). Culture shock and the inability to mourn. In M. Boyer & G. Grolnick (Eds), *The Psychoanalytic Study of Society.* Vol. 11 (pp. 157–72). Hillsdale, NJ: Analytic Press.

Torczyner, J. (1993). The persistence of invisible poverty among Jews in Canada. In R.J. Brym, W. Shaffir, & M. Weinfeld (Eds), *The Jews in Canada* (pp. 379–94). Toronto: Oxford University Press.

Vega, W., Kolody, B., & Valle, R. (1987). Migration and mental health: An empirical test of depression risk factors among immigrant Mexican women. *International Migration Review, 21*(3), 513–29.

Weinfeld, M. (1999). Jews. In P.R. Magocsi (Ed.), *Encyclopedia of Canada's Peoples* (pp. 860–81). Toronto: University of Toronto Press.

Westermeyer, J. (1989). *Psychiatric Care of Migrants: A Clinical Guide.* Washington DC: American Psychiatric Press.

Winchie, D., & Carment, D. (1988). Intention to migrate: Psychological analysis. *Journal of Applied and Social Psychology, 18,* 727–36.

Zilber, N., & Lerner, Y. (1996). Psychological distress among recent immigrants from the former Soviet Union to Israel: I. Correlates of level of distress. *Psychological Medicine, 26,* 493–501.

Zilber, N., Lerner, Y., & Kertes, J. (1996). *Comparative Study of Immigrants from the Former Soviet Union, One and Five Years after Their Immigration to Israel. Psychological status; Risk factors for psychological distress.* Jerusalem: JDC-Israel, Falk Institute for Mental Health and Behavioral Studies.

Chapter 10

Social Work with Canadians of Ukrainian Background: History, Direct Practice, Current Realities

Constance Barlow and Ashley Barlow

In 1908, Hryn and Maria Lashta, citizens of Bukovina, Ukraine, arrived in Canada. They were typical of the immigrants of that time: almost without exception, most of the 200,000 Ukrainians who entered Canada between 1881 and 1914 were peasant farmers from the towns or the Crown land of Bukovina and Galicia (Hryniuk, 1991; Martynowych & Kazymyra, 1982). They might have been enticed to go to Brazil, where, in 1892, hundreds of Ukrainians settled in the jungle. However, Hryn and Maria heard that conditions on Brazilian coffee plantations, where they would be working, were unfavourable, even for hard-working farmers. The climate was deadly for those who could not combat tropical diseases, but more alarming were the reports of massacres of Ukrainian settlers in the Brazilian jungles. Therefore, they listened with interest when agronomist Dr Osyp Leskiv, on his scouting visits to Ukraine for the Canadian government, spoke of free land, stable government, and safer living conditions on the Canadian prairies. Hoping to create a better future for themselves and their children, Hryn and Maria, along with relatives, friends, and other fellow Ukrainians who were mostly strangers, collected at the railway station to begin their journey to the foreign land of Canada, knowing they would never return to their Ukrainian homeland. The first leg of this journey took them to Lviv. From there they continued overland to Hamburg and Antwerp, and then by ship to Quebec City. From there, they rode the train to Winnipeg, where Hryn got his first job, as a construction worker with the Canadian Pacific Railroad; he remained with the CPR until he had saved enough money to purchase a homestead in Malonton, Manitoba. Because the land was stony and of poor quality, he and Maria moved to Meath Park, Saskatchewan, where they acquired a new homestead and purchased an additional 180 acres of land from the Hudson's Bay Company.

On their journey from the Ukraine, the Lashtas carried with them what they thought they would need: axes, sickles, linens, eating utensils, and the clothes on their backs. Their most important cargo was their seeds—the key to survival for Ukrainian farmers. Maria and Hryn also brought along their 'cultural baggage', something that would have considerable impact on their lives and those of their descendants. Hryn and Maria's four children—Bill, Jean, Steve, and Elsie—represent the first generation of Canadian-born Ukrainians. We, the authors, descendants of Elsie, are second- and third-generation Ukrainians.

Ethno-sensitive social work practice with Ukrainian Canadians is enhanced by understanding that Ukrainian Canadians today are a diverse group whose experience in Canada has been shaped by politics in their homeland. They consist of first-wave immigrants, who would be over eighty years of age, and their descendants; interwar and postwar immigrants and their descendants; Soviet Ukrainian Jews; and current immigrants from the former Soviet Union. On the whole, each wave had different pre-immigration experiences and faced varied resettlement issues that led to their distinct integration into Canadian society.

Ukrainian settlement in Canada occurred in three mass migrations (Swyripa, 1999). The first wave, from 1891 to 1914, saw 170,000 Ukrainians enter Canada, mostly from Galicia and Bukovina, with some from Greater Ukraine (which, at the time, was in the tight grip of the tsarist Russia). The second wave, during the interwar years, 1919–39, brought approximately 68,000 settlers from the territory of the western Ukraine. The third wave, from 1947 to 1954, consisted primarily of 34,000 displaced persons (DPs) and war refugees. After the Second World War, the Soviet Union, in firm control of this region, united virtually all Ukrainian ethnic territories into a single state (Swyripa, 1991). With Sovietization came the liquidation of the Greek Catholic Church, the introduction of large-scale industry and collective agriculture, and the prohibition of all emigration, except for a group of approximately 10,000 'undesirable' ethnic Ukrainians and Soviet Jews (Swyripa, 1999). As citizens of the Soviet state, Ukrainians' language and culture were suppressed. Between World War II and perestroika, Ukrainian citizenship was not recognized and Ukrainians were requested to identify themselves as Soviet. After Mikhail Gorbachev's ascension to power in 1985 and subsequent Ukrainian independence in 1991, restrictions on foreign travel eased. Currently, limited numbers of Ukrainians meeting Canadian immigration standards are being admitted into Canada. As of the early 1990s, over 85 per cent of the Ukrainian population in Canada was Canadian-born (Swyripa, 1999).

The First Wave of Immigration, 1890–1914

The first wave of Ukrainians entered Canada later than many other immigrants and settled on the northern rim of the prairies, in a belt from north of Winnipeg to north of Edmonton. There, they rolled back the forests and prepared the rich soil for cultivation (Darlington, 1991). The new immigrants worked hard, and under difficult conditions. A favourite Ukrainian expression often used by parents to get their children hurrying along, 'hko storshi stow shtane obrow' (whoever gets up first gets to wear the pants), encapsulates the experience of these new immigrants. As Kostash (1980) has noted, poverty walked with new immigrants. Their goal was survival; to be fed, clothed, and housed gave them a sense of security.

Although immigration from Ukraine satisfied the long-range economic plans of the Canadian Pacific Railway and Ontario capitalists hungry for cheap labour, it appalled and disgusted many others, particularly Anglo-Saxon conservatives. Their attitude reflected the prejudice that existed in Canadian society against peasant and working-class immigrants. According to such prejudices, Ukrainians were viewed as the scum of Europe—physical and moral degenerates not fit to be classified as White—and English-speaking settlers demanded that the Ukrainian newcomers be segregated. 'It must be thoroughly disheartening to any respectable English speaking settler to find himself surrounded by a colony of Russian serfs [Ukrainians] . . . hemmed in by a horde of people little better than savages—alien in race, language, and religion, whose customs are repellent and whose morals he abhors' declared the *Winnipeg Telegram* at the turn of the century (10 August 1899). Anglo-Saxon pioneers feared that block settlement would dilute the British character of the West 'through the creation of foreign enclaves resistant to assimilation' (Lehr, 1991, p. 39). Yet, even in the face of increasing demands to cease Slavic immigration, the Canadian government held fast, primarily because the minister of the interior, Clifford Sifton, saw that the Ukrainian pioneer was good material for settlement (Hryniuk, 1991).

First-wave Ukrainian immigrants, along with other ethnic settlers, have not forgotten the prejudices they suffered, notwithstanding the generally favourable reception they received from federal officials. Their resentment of people of British origin is part of the legacy they leave their descendants. Connie Barlow's journal entry (December 1998) confirms Myrna Kostash's statement that 'the bitterness of their parents' experience would be the ghost at the next generation's feast' (Kostash, 1980, p. 55).

I'm friendly with one of Stephen Leacock's grand nephews, who like his famous uncle teaches economics. Over an urban, civilized lunch in an elegant Calgary restaurant, I cannot stop myself—I ask him if he knows what Leacock wrote of Ukrainians and all continental European immigrants. That he called them 'herds of proletariat' and worried that they would be incapable of carrying on the work of the Anglo-Saxon heroes that arrived before them. That he feared the federation of Canada would be dragged down to the depths of their ignorance.

As I look beyond the silver and crystal of this table (so unlike anything my grandmother could have imagined), I wonder what he himself might believe about my grandparents. I'm torn because I like and admire him and am intrigued by his foreignness—his school years spent in a private boys' school, his upper middle class, Anglo-Saxon roots.

We move on to 'safer' subjects, to preserve the relationship. But at a certain level, I want an apology and some acknowledgment for the outrage I feel about what was written and spoken about the Ukrainians. An outrage that my grandfather would surely have felt, if he had had access to those newspapers. And if he could have read them in that strange English language. But he had heard the word—we all did—'Bohunk!' And he had heard them laugh at his name and at the unpronounceable names of his neighbours and friends.

To some extent, Ukrainian Canadians developed an internalized stigma as a response to being assigned a lower value than their Anglo-Saxon counterparts, and they carried with them a sense of shame at being poor (Kostash, 1980). As a result, many changed their names to ones that blended into the dominant society—Capochinsky became Capp, Lewinischuk became Lewis, Denesuik became Dennis. This, some would say, was in reaction to a negative self-image (Lopata, 1975). Others might call it a bid for anonymity and acceptance.

Connie Barlow's journal continues (July 1999):

> We're sitting at the dining room table. Ashley, my daughter, is here. Linda, my only sister, sits between her daughter Candace and Ashley. Along with them are the changing faces of their 'Anglick' [a Ukrainian term generally applied to those of British ancestry] boyfriends and our [Linda's and my] enduring Anglick husbands. We talk about the perogies and the other Ukrainian dishes that are laid before us by my mother, who sits next to Brett, my 17-year-old son.
>
> Here we are together, three generations of Ukrainians. We, the second and third generations, sit comfortably with our Anglo-Saxon names, relieved to have been released from the foreign sounding names that claimed and revealed us when we were children.
>
> I ask about whatever happened to Ukrainian jokes. Brett answers with a hint of disdain that there are no such things anymore. I wonder if we have been so completely assimilated that jokes are no longer necessary to separate us. Linda, however, obliges by telling a joke—'There were these Ukrainians from Edmonton who were travelling to Vegreville. As they got closer to the city, they saw a sign that read "Vegreville Left", so they turned around and went back to Edmonton.'
>
> The Anglicks at the table laugh quietly (they know that too boisterous laughter from them would be greeted with icy stares). My mother looks uncomfortable—she dislikes the jokes but always obliges a teller with a forced laugh and strained smile. For that is the Ukrainian way.

Not all Ukrainians retreated into caution or jumped on the Anglo-Canadian bandwagon. Some were outraged by the persecution and expressed themselves through political organizations (Martynowych & Kazymyra, 1982). The differences in Ukrainian responses to Canadian society—along a continuum of submission to outrage—galvanized with Canada's declaration of war in 1914. The Canadian government questioned the loyalty of the Ukrainian newcomers, labelled them enemy aliens, and prohibited them from serving in the Canadian army. By June 1915, over 5,000 Ukrainian nationals referred to as 'aliens' were interned (Isajiw, 1991; Swyripa, 1991). Their internment, widespread threats and harassment from the Anglo community, and the suppression of Ukrainian newspapers and meetings led some Ukrainians to conclude that Canadian society was unrelentingly hostile and repressive. Their varying responses to persecution were one of the first divisive elements in the Ukrainian-Canadian community and marked the beginning of the tension among Ukrainian Canadians that remains evident today (Swyripa, 1991).

The Second Wave of Immigration: The Interwar Years

Although the First World War ended the 'Great Migration' that brought 2.5 million people to Canada, more settlers were required to tame the remaining forests and keep the railways viable. So important were new settlers to the Canadian National and Canadian Pacific railways that their agents became key players in the settlement of a new wave of immigrants.

The experiences of second-wave immigrants differed from those of the previous generation in a variety of ways (Martynowych, 1991; Osborne, 1991). First, the Ukrainian homeland had changed. With the fall of the independent Ukrainian republic to Communist forces in 1917, Ukraine (as it was known) ceased to exist and its provinces were partitioned among Poland, Romania, and Czechoslovakia, while Greater Ukraine fell under Soviet control.

Second, western Canada, where many second-wave Ukrainian immigrants settled, had seen its cultural and physical landscape transformed since the arrival of first-wave immigrants. The development of the West was well under way: railway lines were established, land had been cleared, and cities and towns dotted the prairies. On the outer rim of many a Western town stood the onion-domed church and detached bell-tower that were the most visible symbols of a Ukrainian community.

New immigrants settling in these established Ukrainian enclaves found communities divided by economic, religious, and political differences (Martynowych, 1991). During the First World War and the interwar years, Ukrainian-Canadian farmers, businessmen, and professionals in Canada experienced economic prosperity because of high agricultural prices; labourers, in contrast, faced unemployment or underemployment and, in some cases, internment. Such economic disparities created tension in what had been a homogeneous, tightly knit Ukrainian community.

Divisiveness engendered by religious practice is a complex issue that reflects the immigrants' connection to religion in the old country. In Ukraine, clerics formed an elite who were paid by the state and who possessed power and privilege similar to that of nobility. Peasants were brought up to fear God, revere the benevolent emperor, respect the authority of the bishops and priests, and obey their superiors

(Yuzyk, 1982, p. 146). However, many immigrants looked upon the clergy with distrust and suspicion and were further disenchanted when few chose to follow them to the New World (Kostash, 1980). With the absence of Ukrainian priests in Canada until 1912, religious leadership devolved to members of the lay intelligentsia—young men disenchanted by the unresponsiveness of the traditional churches. These men influenced religious and secular institutions and were instrumental in forming the Ukrainian Greek Orthodox Church and the Independent Greek Church (Martynowych, 1991), a situation that created tension between traditionalists and reformists and further polarized the Ukrainian-Canadian community. Older settlers looked no further than the Ukrainian Catholic or Russian Orthodox Church for spiritual direction; but the younger, nationally and socially conscious immigrants, whether farmers, small businessmen, or labourers, moved towards the Greek Orthodox Church, which was established in Canada in 1918. They did so because 'it encouraged lay participation in church government and promoted Ukrainian solidarity and economic self-reliance' (Martynowych, 1991, p. 486).

A third significant issue that divided the Ukrainian-Canadian community was the political situation in Ukraine. The revolution and armed struggle there during the war years led to the emergence of opposing groups in Canada: socialists who supported the Soviet regime and nationalists who favoured an independent Ukrainian nation. The antagonism between these groups was bitter, and members of the Ukrainian-Canadian left were 'shunned, ostracized, and dismissed as traitors by their nationalist opponents' (Osborne, 1991, p. 453).

The Third Wave of Immigration: The Years Following the Second World War, 1947–1954

Immigration after the Second World War had a profound effect on the social, religious, and political life of Ukrainian-Canadian communities. As was the case with the second wave, pre-migration experiences of third-wave immigrants were vastly different from those of their predecessors (Luciuk, 1991). Immigrants of the first and second waves believed that resettlement in Canada would ultimately lead to a better life for them and their children. By contrast post–Second World War immigrants were homeward-oriented revolutionary activists who had been forcibly ejected from their homeland for opposing the Soviet takeover of Ukraine (Kunz, 1981; Luciuk, 1991).

Expelled from their homeland, millions of Ukrainians became refugees during the war. Thirty-four thousand of them arrived in Canada from camps in Europe, where they had 'spent several years cloistered together, exposed to daily proselytizing of a militant nationalist minority and feeling threatened by the nearby Soviet power' (Luciuk, 1991, p. 119). As a result of this exposure, the majority came to share a revolutionary and nationalistic world view. Their immigration, however, occurred in a climate where allied governments disapproved of any manifestations of pro-Soviet or Ukrainian nationalistic sympathies.

Resettlement was spearheaded in Europe by members of the Ukrainian Canadian Committee (UCC), a government-supported body whose role was to secure asylum for displaced persons and supply them with food, housing, clothing, and protection against persecution. In Canada, the UCC coordinated Ukrainian resettlement operations. Its leaders, who considered Ukraine a distant land and Canada their homeland, were intent on ensuring that incoming migrants conformed to their idea of how Ukrainian life should be organized. They were concerned about how their own community and the community at large would view the arrival of this highly politicized group (Luciuk, 1991). Despite this internal tension, postwar immigrants established a strong presence in Canada, valuing Ukrainian culture and scholarship and reviving the use of the Ukrainian language. Driven by the belief that their work would someday be needed in Ukraine, they focused on activities not permitted in the Soviet Union, such as studying and writing books on Ukrainian history. Their hard work was not in vain; with the implementation of glasnost in Ukraine, scholars there are requesting such materials (Isajiw, 1991).

The Descendants of Ukrainian Immigrants

The experience of the early Ukrainian immigrants left its imprint on subsequent generations, who live with the contradiction of paying respect to their roots and endorsing their own Canadian experience. Isajiw (1991) found that the first Canadian-born generation demonstrated a strong desire to become part of the society at large, but remained indebted to its ethnic group for much of its socialization. The result was a type of double socialization that produced cognitive inconsistencies and dissonance as well as divided feelings, desires, and loyalties. Kostash (1980) observed that this generation made a compromise between the two cultural solitudes and lives somewhere between the Anglo-Saxon manor, double locked from the inside, and the fallen-down Ukrainian cottage in the bush. 'Canadian identity was their birthright, Ukrainian loyalty a learned response', she notes (p. 367). They are likely to have, to a greater or lesser extent, internalized the stigma of being assigned a lower value than other groups in Canadian society and to have struggled along the continuum of being ashamed of and having pride in their Ukrainian roots.

Ashley Barlow wrote in her journal (1999):

> This journal entry is about my grandmother, Elsie, daughter of my great grandparents Hryn and Maria. Partly it's written to pay tribute to her life, and partly to portray the role of women in Ukrainian communities.
>
> Grandma was the youngest of four children. Jean, her sister, was fifteen years older, and although they were not close due to the age gap she learned a lot by watching her. Jean attended school until the eighth grade, which was typical for girls at that time. When she was eighteen, she married a northern Saskatchewan farmer and became a farmer's wife. Grandma didn't want the same life as her sister and knew that educa-

tion was the key to a different future. When it came time for her to quit school after grade eight, she had to cry and scream for her mother to let her continue. Her mother and father said, 'Girls don't need school.' Why would they spend their scarce dollars on educating a girl when she would remain at home, be looked after by her husband, and raise children? What was the purpose of education for a farmer's wife?

The fact that Ukrainian-Canadian women were schooled at all is a minor miracle. Grandma's life to this point did not follow the usual course of a Ukrainian girl born in northern Saskatchewan, where most girls married, became housewives and farmers' wives, and basically worked their fingers to the bone. And it happened differently for Grandma because her mother Maria had a deep love for learning and it was she who instilled the love of reading in her children. So finally, after considerable nagging on Grandma's part, she was allowed to finish high school and attend a teachers' college. Because there was a shortage of teachers in rural Saskatchewan, she immediately got a teaching job close to home. Being a teacher in a small prairie community was a coveted position. All the farm boys would chase after them because they were usually pretty, young, educated, and respectable. Grandma's first husband, Mike, my grandfather, was one of those boys. They married and she continued to teach. The predictable income that teaching offered was the lifeblood that sustained their struggling farm.

When Mike died years later, grandma was fifty. She returned to school and got her Bachelor of Education degree. Life was not easy for her: she faced many obstacles and endured tragedies, but today she is a snow-bird who golfs in Phoenix all winter and gardens in Calgary during the summer. What would her parents think of that!

I think she led an extraordinary life. She succeeded in a patriarchal society where women were not supposed to be more than wives and mothers. While the enormity of her losses over the years would have hampered or even destroyed some women, she overcame losses, poverty, and restrictions of her sex to become a financially independent woman, a successful mother, teacher, and grandmother.

Canadian-born Ukrainians today are keenly aware of the struggles of their immigrant ancestors. They are compelled to honour that struggle in subtle ways that can be seen primarily in lifestyle choices. The honouring of hard work; the maintenance of the 'garden' and attention to food that is hearty, well cooked, and plentiful; the strong pride characterized by an independent nature that will only reluctantly ask for help; and the hesitancy of publicly acknowledging their Ukrainian heritage—these are elements of the legacy of first-wave immigrants that have left a definite imprint on later generations.

Although present-day Canadian attitudes towards Ukrainians remain undefined, Isajiw (1991) noted that they are basically positive ones, and this is reflected in Canada's multicultural policy. Though Ukrainian Canadians are still more strongly involved in agriculture than is the general population, they have made a decided move into the middle class, to the point of equality with most ethnic groups in Canada, and, in some cases, beyond it. In his book *The Vertical Mosaic*, Porter (1965) placed Ukrainians on the middle of a ladder-like hierarchy of immigrant groups in Canada. Recent studies indicate that Porter's depiction of ethnic and racial stratification in Canada is still relevant (Christensen, 1995).

Ukrainian Canadians Defined and the Implications for Social Work Practice

Critical to social work practice with Ukrainian Canadians is understanding of the religious, spatial, and ethnic diversity among theses people. Time of arrival in Canada (for example, before of after the Second World War), place of settlement (prairie west or urban east), and linguistic and geographic categories (Galicians, Bukovinians, Ruthenians, Little Russians) are primary factors that contribute to their distinctions.

The first wave of immigrants were 'peasants of means', largely illiterate farmers whose adage was 'We worked hard, we suffered, and we overcame' (Kostash, 1980, p. 20). Canadian writers (Darlington, 1991; Ferguson, 1991; Kostash, 1980) have noted two aspects of Ukrainian-Canadian society, perpetuated by these immigrants and their descendants, that drew special attention and distinguished them from other groups: their propensity for hard work and their particular devotion to education. The spirit of self-advocacy and self-sufficiency, which originated in their homeland, became a defining characteristic of Ukrainian immigrants in Canada. Social welfare in early Ukrainian-Canadian communities was the outcome of years of oppression in the homeland and was based on the human instinct of helping others survive.

Most Ukrainians of the first and second wave aspired, even in the face of ridicule and exclusion, to become equal participants in Canadian society while maintaining their cultural identity. Homeward-looking and educated refugees who arrived following the Second World War saw Canada not as their chosen land, but as a country offering temporary asylum until they could return to an independent Ukraine. Their politics and lack of interest in assimilation clearly distinguished them from first- and second-wave immigrants, and from their descendants, with whom they shared Canadian soil. By the 1950s, the Ukrainian-Canadian community emerged divided on issues related to expression of religious faith, participation in Canadian society, and attitudes to politics in Ukraine.

A distinction particularly relevant when considering social work practice with Ukrainian Canadians was made by Magocsi (1991), who noted that by 1950 there were two distinct groups within the Ukrainian community in Canada: 'Canadians of Ukrainian background' and 'Ukrainians who live in Canada'. Canadians of Ukrainian background are people of any generation who consider themselves first and foremost Canadian. They are Canadians, like many others, who have ancestors that came from somewhere else—in this case the Ukraine. They are likely to have minimal or no knowledge of the Ukrainian language, rarely attend a traditional Eastern Christian Ukrainian church, and probably do not belong to a Ukrainian organization. They express only passing concern with events in Ukraine. Magocsi ventured that perhaps 75 per cent of the 800,000 or so

Ukrainian Canadians fall into this category, which could be called the silent majority.

By contrast, Ukrainians who live in Canada include people born in Canada as well as those born in the old country. They consider themselves Ukrainian first, prefer to speak Ukrainian, attend Eastern Christian religious services, follow events in their homeland, and dream that they or their grandchildren will one day return to a free and independent Ukraine. According to Magocsi (1991), 'being a Ukrainian living in Canada is most difficult for those people born and educated in Canada. These people often have split personalities and sometimes suffer from great internal psychological discord' (p. xiii). They are people who speak English with no accent, are well educated, and hold respectable jobs. In short, they function as indistinguishable members of Canadian society but struggle to be Ukrainian in a non-Ukrainian culture. Preservation of their Ukrainian identity may take the form of speaking Ukrainian whenever possible, marrying other Ukrainians, and faithfully attending Ukrainian religious events. They are also more likely to challenge government agencies for financial support, which they see as legitimate compensation for their sacrifices to Canadian society.

Bishop (1994) offers insight into the dichotomy of being 'Ukrainian and living in Canada' with her observation that 'the more the oppressor group can separate and distinguish itself from the oppressed group, the greater its capacity to create and carry out policy, reserve resources, and build an ideology of oppression—all part of taking and maintaining control. The oppressed group has to make a choice and most are split over it' (p. 71). The dilemma for Ukrainians living in Canada is that if they decrease differences, they have a better chance of accessing the privileges and resources offered by mainstream society. However, if they maintain separateness, they are more likely to preserve an identity and spirit that allows their oppression to continue, so that they can move, as a group, toward liberation. Magocsi (1991) wondered about the long-term viability of the latter category, the Ukrainians who live in Canada, whose existence is driven by the sense of identity, commitment, and duty to their homeland and a desire to sustain what they believe was being lost there. Now that revolutionary change has toppled Communist rule and Ukraine has become a free, democratic country like its European neighbours, what will be the focus of Ukrainians living in Canada?

The changes that have taken place in Ukraine since 1985 have met with varying responses from the Ukrainian community in Canada (Isajiw, 1991). Differences are revealed in attitudes towards visits to Ukraine and visitors from Ukraine. Until perestroika, Soviet contact with the West was maintained by official designates of the government, and relations with the West were looked upon with suspicion. Since 1985, Soviet citizens have been allowed to travel to the West and re-establish connections with kin.

However, Ukrainian Canadians differ in their attitudes to visiting a liberated Ukraine. Immigrants who arrived in Canada prior to the Second World War, unlike their postwar counterparts, are motivated by a desire to re-establish family ties rather than to pursue ideological goals. The third generation is involved to some extent in the 'roots phenomenon', interested in rediscovering its identity and learning about Ukrainian culture (Isajiw, 1991). These Ukrainian-Canadian descendants have a 'recreational' interest in Ukraine—as a place to travel in the summer—but, as Isajiw (1991) notes, they are not ideologically committed to helping with the restructuring process taking place in Ukraine today.

The Fourth Wave: Soviet Immigration

The Soviet Ukrainian Immigrant

Social workers meeting current Ukrainian immigrants may be confused about their citizenship, so some clarification is necessary. Not all Soviets were Russians; indeed, ethnic Russians made up only somewhat over half of the Soviet population (Castex, 1992). The former Soviet Union comprised fifteen republics, including Russia, Byelorussia, and Ukraine. Prior to achieving independence in 1991, Ukrainians, like Russians and Byelorussians, were considered Soviet citizens. Now, all of these peoples have had their ethnic identities reinstated. It is significant that, despite an oppressive Soviet regime, the Ukrainian ethnic identity remained strong, with the Ukrainian language continuing to be taught at home and used in churches and fraternal organizations.

Commonalties are also evident among current immigrants from the former Soviet Union. They all experienced life under a communist Soviet regime and lived through the political and social changes since glasnost. Classified as 'White ethnics' in their new country, they are less likely to face issues of devaluation based on physical characteristics such as skin colour. Nonetheless, they may feel a lack of acceptance in Canadian society because they are considered 'Soviets' and originate from a country that, during the Cold War, Canadian people 'loved to hate' (Kropf, Nackerud, & Gorokhovski, 1999). In some respects, classifying Soviet immigrants as 'White ethnics' is problematic: it fails to recognize their diversity. 'Many white ethnics have their cultural practices and belief systems subsumed under the dominant culture since they are viewed only as white. Diverse cultural groups such as Jewish, Italian, Irish, and Polish individuals are often not considered to have unique or distinctive cultural practices' (Kropf, et al., 1999, p. 112).

The Immigration of Soviet Jews

The Soviet regime banned immigration for all but a select group of ethnic minorities, primarily Soviet Jews. In the 1970s, some 200,000 Jewish refugees left the USSR seeking asylum from oppression and persecution (Shwamm, Greenstone, & Hoffman, 1982). Soviet society was anti-Semitic, and Jews were not allowed full participation; they experienced educational discrimination, political alienation, and financial restrictions because of their Jewish identity (Salitan, 1989). The better-educated Jewish immigrants from Russia proper were raised in the traditions of Russian culture and identified themselves with the Russian intelligentsia. They were likely, on the whole, to have a limited knowledge of Jewish culture. Those from Ukraine and Byelorussia were more likely to be workers and craftspeople whose

Jewish culture was still very much alive (Feigin, 1996). Moreover, they lacked an eagerness to learn about it, and were characterized by widespread atheism (Schwamm et al., 1982).

In the 1980s, with the Soviet invasion of Afghanistan and consequent deterioration in international relationships, immigration from Soviet Union was curtailed. Later in the decade, with perestroika, the number of Jews permitted to leave the Soviet Union jumped from 900 to 21,000 (Ivry, 1992; Simon, 1985). Since 1991, the émigré population shifted from being primarily Jewish to a much more diverse group who were leaving for reasons such as economics and family reunification rather than political oppression.

What follows is a true account of the experiences of one Soviet Ukrainian Jew:

> I was 38 years old when we immigrated to Canada. I'm now fifty-eight, and I look my age. In the late 60s and 70s, Jews in the Soviet Union were allowed to go to Israel but what the Soviet Union was gaining from this, I don't know. My husband was a Jew, but I am not, and at that time in the country, Jews were oppressed and couldn't really get good jobs and their chances for higher education were restricted. My husband was a lucky one because he was able to go to school and is now an engineer. I have a Master's degree in languages and speak five languages.
>
> In 1979 our son and daughter were in high school and my husband was in his early 40s. He made the decision to immigrate because he said, 'There is no way my son will die in Afghanistan.' So, like a good wife, I agreed. But I cried and cried because I did not want to go and leave my family. I was patriotic. I had a good job as a teacher and took my students on tours of historic sites in the Soviet Union.
>
> I was proud of my country and I wanted my students to be proud. I would go to work with very red eyes but, of course, could not tell anyone what we were planning. It was so hard because I was devoted to my country but also devoted to my family. But I also heard Canada was a good country. In Ukraine, one of our salaries went to pay for food and the other for clothes, utilities, and transportation. We had no car.
>
> We told everyone that we were going to Israel because it was more acceptable to go there. We even got a letter of invitation from a woman in Israel who said she was my cousin. These 'invitations' were required by the Soviet government as proof of reunification. Obtaining a visa was not an easy process so we had to hire a lawyer. We also needed permission from our parents to leave and I begged them not to give us permission but they said, 'You must go with your husband.'
>
> Our son wanted to go because he liked the western music and jeans. He was already assigned to military duty, so it was crucial for us to act quickly. He was a member of the Young Communist League and they said to him, 'Let them go, we will take care of you if you stay.' We advised him to say, 'I go because I love my parents.'
>
> As soon as we asked to leave, both my husband and I lost our jobs. We had to sell everything just to survive—crystal, furniture, and jewellery. The only money we had when we left was from the apartment—we could sell it back to the government and get what we paid. They took away our passports and left us with only our exit visas. We were stateless. I was afraid.

After six months of waiting, we were allowed to leave, with just two suitcases each. We went first to Czechoslovakia and then by train to Vienna. I loved Italy. The children did not want to leave Italy because they could have bananas. In Ukraine they had bananas just once. Even though Italy was beautiful, I felt anxious because we were stateless.

It was only when we arrived in Italy that we told the Immigrant Aid Society HAISUS that we did not want to go to Israel; instead we wanted to go to Canada. So we flew to Toronto and then Calgary. I remember first seeing Calgary from the airplane and I said to my husband, 'You said it was a city, but it is just a village. How can you expect me to live in a village after living in beautiful Kiev.'

In the Soviet Union there was religious persecution. For 2,000,000 people, there were only 11 churches. Grandparents couldn't bring their grandchildren to church. The government had people sitting at the church doors and would turn away the children. But we have God in our souls. And I thank God for what we have.

Today, we live in a beautiful house in the suburbs. Our children both went to university. My husband works for an oil and gas company and I teach and do translations. I also do resettlement work with Soviet immigrants. I'm happy, but have not been back to Kiev. I want to go now, to visit the graves of my parents. I have missed them terribly. (C. Barlow interview with 'Oksanna Kravchek', August 2000)

Social Work Practice with Soviet Ukrainian Immigrants

Effective social work practice with Soviet Ukrainian immigrants begins with sensitivity to their values and cultural norms and an awareness of their experience with the social welfare system. Because they lived under a communist regime, they present unique resettlement issues. Generalizations from the experiences of prior waves of Ukrainian immigrants cannot be extended to this group. The following, a summary of current research on resettlement issues of Soviet Ukrainian immigrants, is a preliminary and by no means exhaustive guide to social work practice with the most recent wave of Ukrainian immigrants. It offers a description of their pre-migration experiences and outlines resettlement issues. Attitudes to health care, social welfare, employment, and family are described and helping strategies outlined.

The Pre-migration Experience

Castex (1992) has observed that 'whether the resettlement in the host society proceeds smoothly may depend as much on what happened before the date of arrival as it does on the actions of the service providers and the situation of the host society' (p. 144). When working with Soviet Ukrainian immigrants, knowing the time of arrival to Canada serves a dual purpose: it provides information about the likely stage of a client's adaptation and offers clues about the emotional and financial stresses experienced by families before they left the Soviet Union.

Most Soviet Jewish immigrants arrived in Canada between 1972 and 1981, with approximately six thousand settling in Toronto. When a family applied to emigrate, its members were placed in jeopardy (Drachman & Haberstadt, 1992) because, at this time, emigration was considered a betrayal of the Soviet government. They entered into limbo, waiting for a departure date that could take months and even years. Adults were required to quit their jobs, while children, whose routines and social relationships vanished, spent a good part of their time 'sitting on a suitcase'. As well, application to emigrate led to expulsion from the Communist Party and subsequent harassment and humiliation. An additional stress was that an applicant required the consent of both parents to emigrate, regardless of the nature of the relationship or the age of the applicant. If parents consented, they too were harassed and viewed as traitors. Soviet regulations favoured families and extended families emigrating as a unit, alleviating the state's burden of caring for the elderly. This policy could create considerable tension if family members disagreed about the desirability of emigration (Castex, 1992). Families understood that if they did not emigrate together, there was little hope of reunification in the future.

Most émigré families spent between and a month and a year in transit, much of this time spent in Italy awaiting a visa. Upon arrival in Canada, they would likely be both unaware of their destination's customs, work situations, and employment opportunities and unable to speak the language (Barankin, Konstantareas & deBosset, 1989). Immigrants arriving after 1990, however, are more likely to speak English and therefore are less burdened by resettlement issues related to language (Castex, 1992).

Resettlement Issues

Soviet Ukrainian Jews experienced a myriad of resettlement issues that discouraged them and challenged resettlement workers (Brodsky, 1982; Drachman & Halberstadt, 1992). Gulens (1995) wrote, 'I am convinced that in Soviet citizens, we witness major distortions in psychological make-up brought about by being born into, growing up in, working in and forming families in a totalitarian environment' (p. 267). After the Cold War, Westerners believed there would be few differences between 'us' and 'them', as prior differences were attributed to the Soviet Union's separate and idiosyncratic ideology. Yet differences became evident and were likely to be labelled, by both Soviet and Western observers, as Soviet pathologies (Gulens, 1995).

A social worker whose aim is to establish an effective helping relationship with Soviet immigrants can be guided by reflection on how the responses of Soviet immigrants, while perhaps frustrating to the Western social worker, were adaptive strategies in the Soviet context. Understanding that these strategies, although maladaptive in Canadian society, were crucial to survival in the Soviet Union can sensitize a social worker to the experiences of the Soviet immigrant. Simultaneously, individual variables to be considered when working with Soviet immigrants include age of immigration, gender, religion, marital status, education level, languages spoken, reasons for immigrating, and family structure.

What follows is a discussion of adaptive strategies that have shaped the behaviour of citizens living in totalitarian Soviet society. Some have observed that people living under totalitarian governments behave in ways similar to long-term prison inmates who, over time, become limited in their abilities to express former sentiments, attitudes, and abilities (e.g. Kohak, 1992). They become 'jail smart', learning how to derive the benefits that the system has to offer. Initially, in an effort to preserve the attitudes and habits of freedom as they hope for release, they refuse to think and act like prisoners. Kohak (1992) believes that if the oppression of Soviet citizens had ended within twenty years, the citizens would have emerged stronger from the experience. Having experienced despotism, they would have come to value and work towards a society based on democratic principles. However, years of oppression over two generations resulted in deeply ingrained habits and skills that, although adaptive during communist rule, are maladaptive when people 'become their own masters'. Those ingrained habits and skills include maintaining anonymity, promising but not promise keeping, erasing the distinction between truth and reality, being skeptical, distrusting authority yet being dependent on the state, masking emotions, and relying on family and intimate friends for emotional support.

Maintaining anonymity: To survive in the Soviet Union, a low profile was necessary. The Soviet regime insisted on a total monopoly on initiative, and any spontaneous act was suspect. Thus, citizens avoided making decisions, taking responsibility, and displaying a forceful personal identity. 'The adaptive strategies were to think nothing until told, then agreeing, though not too vehemently' (Gulens, 1992, p. 201). Even the act of picking up a piece of paper tossing in the wind might draw the unwanted attention of Soviet authorities.

Promising but not promise keeping: Making a promise earns good will, but keeping a promise may be maladaptive in Soviet society, as it requires reacting to a past situation. To survive, one must be vigilant and responsive to new emerging conditions. A promise may be kept if it is seen as advantageous to the new situation.

Erasing the distinction between truth and reality: In the Soviet Union, free expression of observation, opinions, and emotions was suppressed. Decisions about what was true were made by the state, and citizens were expected to support the state without question. Kohak (1992) notes that truth is a fundamental human need and that lying makes everything precarious. When citizens were asked to repeat lies, they were faced with three options. The first, refusing to lie, was hazardous and would likely lead to incarceration; the second option was believing the lie and becoming indoctrinated. The third option—erasing the distinction between the truth and a lie—was an option chosen by many: maybe Chernobyl is safe and maybe not; maybe there are Siberian prison camps and maybe not. Make-believe became the rule, as evidenced by the Soviet expression 'We pretend to work and they pretend to pay us.' As a result of years of unreliable or nonfactual information, Soviet citizens have developed a reduced ability to accurately distinguish between fact and rumour (Kohak, 1992; Gulens, 1995).

Skepticism: Privately Soviet citizens noted the mismatch between reality and rhetoric. For years they were told to accept the shabbiness of their lives in the name of social justice, but daily they witnessed inequities and injustices. Daily, citizens experienced how Communism discredited idealism and turned noble causes into mockery (Kohak, 1992; Gulens, 1995). Citizens came to disbelieve in altruism and suspected any act of charity as being driven by an ulterior motive or hidden agenda.

Distrusting authority but remaining dependent on the state: Fostered by lifelong bondage, a striking characteristic of Soviet citizens is their profound distrust of and anger at authorities and their paradoxical belief that 'someone up there' is looking after them. Decisions related to employment, education, and health care were made by the state. The long-term effect on the citizenry was a reluctance to take the initiative and assume responsibility, to make decisions, and to make realistic and appropriate plans for the future (Gulens, 1995).

Masking emotions: In the context of a repressive Soviet regime, where 'correct thought', 'correct answers', and 'group decisions' were expected, Soviet citizens learned to mask their true feelings and thoughts. Gulens (1995) wonders whether Soviet citizens are even aware of their deeper, more subtle emotions and how to express them. Western social workers may note that a Soviet Ukrainian client demonstrates little reaction through facial expression, posture, and tone of voice, although such a client may frequently sigh and display expressions of hopelessness and helplessness. This behaviour may, in part, be a remnant of encounters with representatives from the Soviet state. When Soviet citizens approached authorities for help, they were often blamed for their troubles and chastised for seeking justice, while being informed how fortunate they were to hold such superior positions in the world. Authorities told them, 'don't bother us with your small troubles. We have more important work to do' (Kohak, 1992; Gulens, 1995; Mamali, 1996). Ultimately, Soviet citizens learned to keep their troubles to themselves and rely on family members and trusted intimate friends for support. One immigrant woman who belonged to the Soviet Workers' Union noted that members might get together to talk about common problems after work, but personal problems were not mentioned. Most people feared being labelled as needing mental or emotional help, as this could lead to dismissal from work. They spoke of personal difficulties only within their families or to intimate friends, but mostly they tried to solve their problems on their own (Hahn, 1992).

The strategies for living that emerged as a result of living under an oppressive government permeated all aspects of life and influenced relationships with authorities, family, and friends. Of particular interest to social workers assisting Soviet Ukrainian immigrants is the immigrants' views of social welfare, mental health, and the family.

The Soviet Ukrainian Immigrants' View of Social Welfare

New immigrants who are accustomed to services such as housing, employment, occupational training, and medical and dental care may become distressed when they learn that such benefits are not readily available to them in Canada. Difficulty obtaining work or resuming occupations for which they are highly trained and in which they are experienced is also very stressful for them. Because many immigrants have come from upper economic and educational levels in Soviet society, they are hesitant to take on what they consider menial jobs, believing that, as in the Soviet Union, advancement would take years (Schwamm et al., 1982).

Their experiences in the Soviet Union also influence how immigrants utilize social services (Drachman & Haberstadt, 1992). In Soviet society, civil organizations were discouraged; therefore, new immigrants may become confused as to how to respond to organizations, such as the Jewish Family Services, that attempt to build connections among them. Lack of responsiveness to overtures of assistance is based on the belief that family matters belong in the family (Belozersky, 1990; Brodsky, 1982). Smith (1987), a keen observer of Soviet life, has offered insight into such behaviour. He noted a kind of 'deliberate schizophrenia' in which Soviet citizens divide their existence so that their public lives differ from their personal relationships. He observed that 'this happens anywhere to some degree, of course, but Russians make this division more sharply than others because of political pressures for conformity. So they adopt two very different codes of behaviour for their two-lives-in-one. They may be taciturn, hypocritical, careful, cagey, and passive in one; in the other they are voluble, honest, direct, open, and passionate. Because their public lives were so supervised, they invested highly in friendships' (p. 105).

Voluntary service organizations are foreign concepts to these new immigrants, and Canadian service providers are seen in the same light as government employees, who, as in the Soviet Union, must be manipulated if the client is to receive service. Belozersky (1990) wrote, 'In a system in which an individual has very few rights and is constantly at the mercy of small and big bureaucrats, they learned to manipulate this system to survive. When faced with survival tasks upon their arrival in the United States, many immigrants almost instinctively begin to employ the only methods they knew. Because they have no frame of reference for which to understand the difference between state and voluntary agencies, they see any resettlement agency as a continuation of the state and any caseworker as a bureaucrat who must be manipulated' (p. 126). Because voluntary agencies and the social work profession did not exist in the Soviet Union, professional caregiving within a voluntary social service agency was unknown and alien (Brodsky, 1982; Belozersky, 1990).

The Soviet View of Mental Health and Mental Health Practitioners

Soviet immigrants are likely to believe that mental health and psychosocial problems are physical and that the predominant mode of treatment is pharmacological rather than psychodynamic. They are more likely to consult physicians for help with mental health concerns and expect either verbal or pharmaceutical prescriptions for their problems (Drachman & Haberstadt, 1992; Mokkovekov & Donets, 1996). Of importance when attempting to understand this view is that the Russian word for physician is *terpevt* or 'therapist'.

In the Soviet Union, psychiatry was used as a form of social control; therefore, psychiatrists are looked upon with suspicion. Traditional talk therapy may be viewed as strange and therapists seen as incompetent because patients do not appear to be getting what is needed. Since relocation can intensify physical and mental health problems, this attitude of distrust towards mental health practitioners may foster resistance to psychiatric treatment or psychosocial intervention among high-risk immigrants. Their personal experiences, as well as their observation of the fates of others, led Soviet citizens to suspect that commitment to a mental institution was the outcome of outspoken criticism of the state (Reich, 1979). Soviet psychiatry and (by association) other paid helpers were agents of a repressive state (Castex, 1992). For this reason, such immigrants are unaccustomed to discussing personal problems outside close family and friendship groups.

The Soviet Immigrants' Families

For reasons rooted in cultural history, the Soviet family, often characterized by strong parental control, may best be described as matriarchal (Imbrogno & Imbrogno, 1986; Gray, 1990; Kropf et al., 1999). Because of wars and communist oppression, millions of men were killed, spent years on the front in Siberia, disappeared during Stalin's reign of terror, or became alcoholic (Smith, 1987). Out of necessity, women assumed control of their families. In the early years of the Soviet regime, Lenin had promised total equality of the sexes; however, tradition did not catch up to ideology—after an 'equal' day at work, women still did most of the housework (Belozersky, 1990). Even today in dual-career families, women perform most household and childrearing tasks.

Althausen (1993) has noted a melancholic strain in the Soviet psyche that may be attributable, in part, to the totalitarian oppression of the Stalin era (1936–53). During that time, most families feared that one of its members (usually the father) would be denounced as an enemy of the people and whisked away by the secret police, never to be seen again. In an effort to save themselves, Soviet citizens may have denounced family members or friends. Thus, the normal fabric of human relations was destroyed (Conquest, 1991). The consequence was alienation from the state, an attitude of 'laying low' (Feigin, 1996), and a collective family trauma that may surface when Soviet immigrants are asked to provide a family history. The telling of the family story may become overwhelming and result in rejection of future contact with social workers or agencies.

Due to the housing crisis in Soviet cities, three generations often lived together. Two generations often cared for a single child, as one-child families were common (Feigin, 1996; Smith, 1987). The *babushka* or *Baba* (grandmother) played a central role in the family and was an indispensable aid to mothers who worked outside the home. Communal living resulted in strengthened family ties, increased tolerance for personal discomfort, little privacy, and a narrow psychic space, which might be interpreted by the Westerners as enmeshment. Yet what might be perceived as over-involvement could, by the standards of Soviet immigrants, be a normal filial bond (Althausen, 1993). Minuchin (1974) noted that, by sharing resources, extended families are an adaptation to situations of stress and scarcity: grandparents provide child care and hunt for scarce goods while parents work.

In light of their homeland experiences, the intergenerational family relationships are of particular significance. The fear of separation was a powerful motivator for elderly parents to migrate with their children, and, on arrival in the new country, they often relied on their adult children to be their cultural guides. In return, grand-parents helped their children with child care and household maintenance. Yet, as family members differentiated and separated in order to adjust to a new culture, elderly parents felt the loss of their customary control (Althausen, 1996). They also experienced loss of status in the family and sensed fewer opportunities to regain their status. Moreover, while their middle-aged children saw the sacrifices of immigration as being rewarded in the future, elderly parents were less likely to see themselves as having a future in Canada. As atheists and members of the Communist Party, they also felt threatened if their children began attending church.

Another consideration for social work practitioners is related to illness among aging parents. Ukrainian adult children, who see the care of aging parents as their responsibility, not the responsibility of the state, may feel guilt and shame at leaving their parents in the care of the system. Immigrants likely perceive social workers as the system's bureaucrats, who need to be manipulated—either flattered, bribed, or, in some cases, threatened—to ensure that their parents get the best possible treatment (Althausen, 1993).

Finally, recent findings have demonstrated that families who lived in the spectre of the Chernobyl disaster are a particularly vulnerable (Van Den Bout, Havenaar, & Meijler-Iljina, 1995). Health-related concerns remain a primary consideration. In addition, it was found that evacuees and mothers of children under eighteen years of age from the vicinity of Chernobyl had more Chernobyl-related worries and a lower sense of control over their lives in comparison with counterparts living outside Chernobyl's sphere (Havenaar et al., 1996).

Intervention Strategies

Based on the resettlement issues presented, this section recommends strategies for working with Soviet Ukrainian immigrants. Castex (1992) suggested that refugees can be better understood by examining ways in which family systems and individuals deal with stress, loss, and grief and by understanding the renegotiations of appropriate family roles and behaviours after immigration. Also, consideration must be given to the pre-immigration experience related to political or ethnic violence and to Chernobyl. Feigin (1996) cautions us not to assume that clients were merely victims of oppression, a mass of suffering citizens repressed by brutal imperialists in the Kremlin. Such a simplistic, one-dimensional view fails to honour the spirit of loyalty and connection that Ukrainian immigrants, like most others, feel towards their homeland.

Drachman and Halberstadt (1992) see education as an effective helping strategy for new immigrants. Because they may enter the country with unrealistic expectations about employment and standards of living, new immigrants should be informed of the following: differences between the two countries in terms of entitlement to service; issues of certification to practise in the professions in which émigrés have been trained; potential for lowered status due to retraining and language barriers; additional economic expenditures for retraining; differences in the cost of housing; and the nature of the free market.

Use of Ukrainian- or Russian-speaking personnel to provide services was seen as a valuable aspect of resettlement work (Althausen, 1996). With Soviet Jews in Dallas, Texas, resettlement work was based on genuine caring of 'Jew-to-Jew' at every stage of the settlement program: meeting new arrivals at the airport, locating appropriate housing, providing interpreters, and offering orientation programs (Schwamm et al., 1982).

Brodsky (1982) presented a model for working with Soviet immigrants based on socialization theory with an emphasis on mutuality and activity. By conceptualizing the social worker as a socializing agent, she advised the social worker to temper the professional stance and behave informally. Effective strategies included adapting helping skills to meet the needs of the client population and bridging the cultural gap by offering high levels of empathy, warmth, and genuineness. The following themes guided Brodsky's practice with new immigrants: the need for greater informality, recognition of the importance of the extended family, and prompt addressing of immigrant needs. She noted that 'reflecting an informal atmosphere, rather than having the more traditional décor consisting of desk and hard chairs, an office might contain a small couch and comfortable chairs casually arranged in a circle. Such a circular seating formation seems especially appropriate for Russian clients who, when seen in a group on the street, are usually talking in a circle, as if to form a natural barricade against dangerous intruders' (Brodsky, 1982, p. 17). The importance of the family in resolving issues cannot be ignored; including the primary caretaker, Baba, in discussions can expedite closure. Social workers must also be cognizant of the fact that families immigrate as extended networks, and, when planning around housing, schools, and neighbours, they should try to honour the support this network provides.

Finally, social workers assisting these immigrants should understand that waiting in line was customary in the Soviet Union. People waited for consumer goods, for an apartment (for sometimes up to twenty years), and for their exit visas. They expect to do the same in Canada. Hence, making active responses to crisis, arranging frequent appointments, and giving immediate feedback can go a long way to establishing trust and rapport.

Summary

This chapter outlined particular features of Ukrainian-Canadian immigrants that can inform social work practice. A notable feature of this ethnic group is that their integration into Canadian society was shaped by social, economic, and political forces in their homeland.

First and second waves of immigrants came to Canada motivated by economic interests. Canada represented escape from poverty and a hope for the next generation. Despite challenging resettlement issues, they had no desire to return to their homeland and were highly motivated to become full participants in Canadian society. The third wave consisted of displaced persons and war refugees who saw Canada as a haven from oppression but dreamed, one day, of returning to the homeland.

The fourth wave of immigrants included mainly Russian and Ukrainian Jews escaping the religious persecution of an oppressive Soviet regime. This group, along with recent Ukrainian immigrants, lived under repressive conditions that presented particular resettlement issues outlined in the latter portion of this chapter.

Epilogue

Hyrn and Maria's final resting place is a tiny cemetery outside a village in northern Saskatchewan, just miles from their original homestead. At first glance, it might appear that the two white crosses are all that is left of these stalwart pioneers. However, a careful examination of their family history reveals that their descendants, although not operators of the huge tracts of farmland that surround the graveyard, are nevertheless equal participants in Canadian society in their jobs as teachers, pharmacists, and technicians.

References

Althausen, L. (1993). Journey of separation: Elderly Russian immigrants and their adult children in the health care setting. *Social Work in Health Care, 19*(1), 61–75.

———. (1996). Russian families. In M. McGoldrick, J. Giordano, & J.K. Pearce (Eds), *Ethnicity and Family Therapy.* 2nd ed. New York: Guilford Press.

Barankin, T., Konstantareas, M., & deBosset, F. (1989). Adaptation of recent Soviet Jewish immigrants and their children to Toronto. *Canadian Journal of Psychiatry, 34*(6), 512–18.

Belozersky, I. (1990). New beginnings, old problems: Psychocultural frame of reference and family dynamics during the adjustment period. *Journal of Jewish Communal Service, 67*(2), 124–30.

Bishop, A. (1994). *Becoming an Ally: Breaking the Cycle of Oppression.* Halifax: Fernwood.

Brodsky, B. (1982). Social work and the Soviet immigrant. *Migration Today, 10,* 15–20.

Castex, G.M. (1992). Soviet refugee children: The dynamic of migration and school practice. *Social Work in Education, 14*(3), 141–52.

Christensen, C.P. (2001). Immigrant minorities in Canada. In J.C. Turner and F.J. Turner (Eds), *Canadian Social Welfare.* 4th ed. (pp. 180–210).Toronto: Allyn & Bacon.

Conquest, R. (1991). *Stalin: Breaker of Nations.* New York: Viking.

Darlington, J.W. (1991). The Ukrainians impress on the Canadian West. In L. Luciuk and S. Hryniuk (Eds), *Canada's Ukrainians: Negotiating an Identity* (pp. 53–80). Toronto: University of Toronto Press.

Drachman, D., & Haberstadt, A. (1992). A stage of migration framework as applied to recent Soviet 'emigres'. *Journal of Multicultural Social Work, 2*(1), 63–78.

Feigin, I. (1996). Soviet Jewish families. In M. McGoldrick, J. Giordano, & J.K Pearce (Eds), *Ethnicity and Family Therapy.* 2nd ed. New York: Guilford Press.

Ferguson, B. (1991). British-Canadian intellectuals, Ukrainian immigrants and Canadian national identity. In L. Luciuk and S. Hryniuk (Eds), *Canada's Ukrainians: Negotiating an Identity* (pp. 307–25). Toronto: University of Toronto Press.

Gray, F. (1990). *Soviet Women: Walking the Tightrope.* New York: Doubleday.

Gulens, V. (1995). Distortions in personality development in individuals emerging from a long-term totalitarian regime. *Journal of Baltic Studies, 26,* 267–84.

Hahn, D. (1992). Soviet Jewish refugee women: Searching for security. *Women and Therapy, 13*(1/2), 79–87.

Havenaar, J., Van Den Brink, W., Van Den Bout, J., Kasyanenko, A., Poelijoe, N., Wohlfarth, T., & Meijler-Iljina, L. (1996). Mental health problems in the Gomel region (Belarus): An analysis of the risk factors in an area affected by the Chernobyl disaster. *Psychological Medicine, 26*(4), 845–55.

Hryniuk, S. (1991). 'Sifton's pets': Who were they? In L. Luciuk and S. Hryniuk (Eds), *Canada's Ukrainians: Negotiating an Identity* (pp. 3–17). Toronto: University of Toronto Press.

Imbrogno, S., & Imbrogno, N.I. (1986). Marriage and family in the USSR: Changes are emerging. *Social Casework, 67*(2), 90–100.

Isajiw, W.J. (1991). The changing community. In L. Luciuk & S. Hryniuk (Eds), *Canada's Ukrainians: Negotiating an Identity* (pp. 254–68). Toronto: University of Toronto Press.

Ivry, J. (1992). Paraprofessionals in refugee resettlement. *Journal of Multicultural Social Work, 2*(1), 99–117.

Kohak, E. (1992). Ashes, ashes . . . Central Europe after forty years. *Daedalus, 121*(2), 197–215.

Kostash, M. (1980). *All of Baba's Children.* Edmonton: Hurtig Publishers Ltd.

Kropf, N.P., Nackerud, L., & Gorokhovski, I. (1999). Social work practice with older Soviet immigrants. *Journal of Multiculturalism in Social Work, 7*(1/2), 111–26.

Kunz, E. (1981). Exile and resettlement: Refugee theory. *International Migration Review, 15,* 42–52.

Lehr, J.C. (1991). Peopling the prairies with Ukrainians. In L. Luciuk & S. Hryniuk (Eds), *Canada's Ukrainians: Negotiating an Identity* (pp. 30–53). Toronto: University of Toronto Press.

Lopata, H.Z. (1975). The Polish-American family. In C.H. Mendel & R.W. Habenstien (Eds), *Ethnic Families in America: Patterns and Variations* (pp. 15–40). New York: Elsevier.

Luciuk, L.Y. (1991). 'This should never be spoken or quoted publicly': Canada's Ukrainians and their encounter with the DPs. In L. Luciuk and S. Hryniuk (Eds), *Canada's Ukrainians: Negotiating an Identity* (pp. 103–23). Toronto: University of Toronto Press.

Magocsi, P.R. (1991). Preface. In L. Luciuk and S. Hryniuk (Eds), *Canada's Ukrainians: Negotiating an Identity* (pp. 11–15). Toronto: University of Toronto Press.

Mamali, C. (1996). Interpersonal communication in totalitarian societies. In W.B. Gudykunst, S. Ting-Toomey, & T. Nishida (Eds), *Communication in Personal Relationships across Cultures*. Thousand Oaks, CA: Sage Publications.

Marganoff, P., & Folwarski, J. (1996). Slavic families: An overview. In M. McGoldrick, J. Giordano, & J.K. Pearce (Eds), *Ethnicity and Family Therapy*. 2nd ed. (pp. 649–57). New York: Guilford Press.

Martynowych, O.T. (1991). *Ukrainians in Canada: The Formative Period, 1891–1924*. Edmonton: Canadian Institute of Ukrainian Studies.

Martynowych, O. T., & Kazymyra, N. (1982). Political activity in Western Canada, 1896–1923. In M.R. Lupul (Ed.), *A Heritage in Transition: Essays in the History of Ukrainians in Canada* (pp. 85–107). Toronto: McClelland and Stewart.

Minuchin, S. (1974). *Families and Family Therapy*. Cambridge: Harvard University Press.

Mokkovekov, A., & Donets, O. (1996). Suicide in Ukraine: Epidemeology, knowledge and attitudes of the population. *Crisis, 17*(3) 124–34.

Osborne, B. (1991). Non-preferred people: Inter-war Ukrainian immigration to Canada. In L. Luciuk and S. Hryniuk (Eds), *Canada's Ukrainians: Negotiating an Identity* (pp. 81–102). Toronto: University of Toronto Press.

Porter, J. (1965). *The Vertical Mosaic*. Toronto: University of Toronto Press.

Reich, W. (1979). Gregorenko gets a second opinion. *New York Times Magazine*, 13 May. Pp. 43–5.

Salitan, L.P. (1989). Domestic pressures and the politics of exit: Trends in Soviet emigration policy. *Political Science Quarterly, 104*, 671–87.

Schwamm, J., Greenstone, K., & Hoffman, H. (1982). Resettling newcomers: The case of Soviet Jewish immigration. *Arte, 7*(2), 25–36.

Simon, R. (1985). Soviet Jews. In D.W. Haines (Ed.), *Refugees in the United States* (pp. 181–193). Westport, CT: Greenwood Press.

Smith, H. (1987). *The Russians*. New York: Ballantine.

Swyripa, F. (1991). Wedded to the cause: Ukrainian-Canadian women. In L. Luciuk & S. Hryniuk (Eds), *Canada's Ukrainians: Negotiating an Identity* (pp. 30–53). Toronto: University of Toronto Press.

———. (1999). Ukrainians. In P.R. Magocsi (Ed.), *Encyclopedia of Canada's Peoples* (pp. 1281–311). Toronto: University of Toronto Press.

Van Den Bout, J., Havenaar, J.M., & Meijler-Iljina, L., (1995). Health problems in areas contaminated by the Chernobyl disaster: Radiation, traumatic stress or chronic stress? In R.J. Kleber, C. Figley, & B. Gersons (Eds), *Beyond Trauma: Cultural and Societal Dynamics* (pp. 213–32). New York: Plenum Press.

Yuzyk, P. (1982). Religious life. In M.R. Lupul, (Ed.). *A Heritage in Transition: Essays in the History of Ukrainians in Canada* (pp. 143–72). Toronto: McClelland and Stewart.

Chapter 11

Social Work Practice with Canadians of Aboriginal Background: Guidelines for Respectful Social Work

Brad McKenzie and Vern Morrissette

In the foreword to his 1992 book, Rupert Ross relates the story of the Seneca orator Red Jacket, who first rejected the overtures of European missionaries with words that meant 'Kitchi Manitou has given us a different understanding' (p. 7). The understanding that Aboriginal reality is different is becoming more generally accepted in North America today, and this understanding is associated with increased interest in the differences in world views between Aboriginal people and dominant society (Hamilton & Sinclair, 1991; Royal Commission on Aboriginal Peoples (RCAP), 1996; Voss, Douville, Little Soldier, & Twiss, 1999; Weaver & White, 1997). Yet acceptance of these differences has emerged only after considerable struggle by Aboriginal people to assert the uniqueness of their values and traditions as well as their inherent right to control their own destiny amid the colonizing influences of Euro-Western society.

The purpose of this chapter is to outline a general model, including a discussion of selected strategies and approaches, for multicultural social work practice with Canadians of Aboriginal background. Given the diversity of Aboriginal people, and the unique traditional practices associated with different nations, this is a daunting task. While it is impossible to represent the diversity of Aboriginal social work approaches in a single chapter, there are common characteristics and experiences across Aboriginal nations that permit the construction of a general framework and related guidelines for practice.

The chapter is organized into four sections. In the first section, contextual information pertaining to Aboriginal people is briefly outlined. Much of this information reflects characteristics of underdevelopment. The relationship of these characteristics to structural causes, of which colonization is the most important, is discussed. The extent of social problems remains a major challenge, but it is equally important to note that Aboriginal people should not be viewed simply as passive victims of colonization. Many have demonstrated resilience in reconstructing their relationship in Canadian society in ways that respect cultural values and traditional practices; as well, many continue to struggle against both past and present injustices. The second section outlines a general framework for social work practice with Aboriginal people. The relationship of this framework to empowerment and healing is discussed in the third section. Implications for practice, including some examples of cultural models of practice, are highlighted in the final section.

The term *Aboriginal* is used to refer to the indigenous inhabitants of Canada; thus it includes what Section 35 of the Constitution Act of 1982 refers to as Indians, Métis, and Inuit. The term *First Nations* refers to those defined as status Indian under the Indian Act, although the term is also used to refer to one of the many nations or groups of First Nations people living in Canada. It is more common to refer to a nation as a major group of Aboriginal people with a shared sense of national identity within a specific area of the country (e.g., Mohawk, Cree). As this implies, a First Nations community or a Métis community, which refers to a relatively small group of Aboriginal people residing in a single locale, would not normally constitute an Aboriginal nation. The term *Inuit* (meaning 'the people') refers to distinct Aboriginal peoples whose geographic origins were primarily the northern territories of Canada. The term *Métis* refers to distinct Aboriginal peoples whose early ancestors were of mixed heritage (First Nations or Inuit and European) and who associate themselves with a culture that is distinctly Métis.

In Canada, the 1996 census identified 799,000 of Canada's 28.5 million people (2.8 per cent) as Aboriginal. However, given the incomplete enumeration of some reserves and other Aboriginal communities, and the reliance on self-reported identification, the number of Aboriginal people is somewhat underreported. Approximately 61 per cent of Aboriginal people in 1996 identified as First Nations, and approximately 47 per cent of this population lived on one of the 2,597 reserves across Canada (Fleras & Elliott, 1999, p. 170). These reserves were created by a total of sixty-one treaties, and the interests of First Nations are represented by 633 chiefs who constitute the Assembly of First Nations (ibid., p. 170). Among provinces, the highest numbers of Aboriginal people live in Ontario and British Columbia. However, Manitoba has the highest ratio of Aboriginal people (11.7 per cent reported as Aboriginal in 1996). Using Manitoba data as an example, the Aboriginal population of that province in 1991 included 54.2 per cent who were of First Nations origin (status Indian and Inuit), 33.3 per cent who were Métis, and 12.4 per cent who were other Aboriginal (primarily non-status Indians). Many of the latter group are those who lost status through enfranchisement or through intermarriage with a non-status male. In 1996, in Manitoba, approximately 32 per cent of the Aboriginal population lived on reserve, 37 per cent lived in Winnipeg, and 31 per cent lived in other communities off-reserve. If only First Nations people are considered, approximately 58 per cent of this population lived on reserve (Manitoba Bureau of Statistics, 1997, p. 4).

Aboriginal Experiences

Economic and Social Conditions

In the past, Canada has been ranked by the United Nations as the best place to live in the world. Yet Fleras and Elliott (1999) note that Aboriginal people on reserves are ranked sixty-third on a human development index. On reserves, unemployment is three times the national average—indeed, on some reserves more than 90 per cent of the population is unemployed—and is a major cause of social problems leading directly to poor housing, poor health, a cycle of poverty, and cultural disintegration (Drost, Crowley, & Schwindt, 1995). Individual incomes on reserves are half those of the average Canadian. Urban migration is an incomplete solution to these problems: approximately 56 per cent of Aboriginal people in cities were living in poverty in 1995, compared to 24 per cent of non-Aboriginal people (Lee, 2000).

The Aboriginal population is growing more rapidly than the general population. Children under fifteen accounted for 35 per cent of all Aboriginal people in 1996, as compared with only 21 per cent of Canada's total population (Statistics Canada, 2000). In the 1996 census, almost one-third of Aboriginal children under the age of fifteen lived in lone-parent families, twice the rate within the general population (Statistics Canada, 1998).

Health and social problems are more common among Aboriginal people than among the general population. Despite major improvements, infant mortality rates are still twice as high in First Nations communities as in Canada as a whole. Suicide rates among the Aboriginal population average two to seven times that of the population of all of Canada, and chronic diseases such as diabetes and heart disease are increasing (Federal, Provincial, and Territorial Committee on Population Health, 1999). The incarceration rates of Aboriginal people are five to six times the national average (RCAP, 1996), and Aboriginal children are overrepresented among those taken into care by the child welfare system. For example, it is estimated that Aboriginal children make up 21 per cent of Manitoba's population under the age of 15 yet approximately 78 per cent of the children in care are Aboriginal (Joint Management Committee, 2001, p. 7). Despite the evolution of First Nations control over child welfare services on reserves, and the growth of Aboriginal foster homes, including extended family caregivers, many of these children are still placed in non-Aboriginal foster and residential care facilities.

Aboriginal women are among the most severely disadvantaged people in Canada. Economically, they are worse off than both non-Aboriginal women and Aboriginal men. A study by the Ontario Native Women's Association (1989) found that eight out of ten Aboriginal women had experienced physical, sexual, psychological, or ritual abuse, and that these factors were related to drug and alcohol abuse in Aboriginal communities (p. 8). Such issues (physical abuse as well as abuse of drugs and alcohol) are associated with problems of child care and help to explain the disproportionate rate of family breakdown in Aboriginal communities. Historical and social factors work against equal recognition of Aboriginal women within both Aboriginal communities and Canadian society. This is aptly illustrated by the number of women who have lost status because of their marriage to non-Aboriginal males. Although the offending section of the Indian Act was repealed by Bill C-31, and those women deprived of status can now apply for reinstatement, such status disappears completely for third-generation children in these circumstances (see Weaver, 1993, for a full discussion of this issue).

General socio-economic conditions, like those just described, are important to recognize when developing a model for social work practice with Aboriginal people, but there are limitations to such data. First, conditions and circumstances vary considerably among individuals, groups, and communities. Second, any description of these problems is incomplete without a discussion of causality. Finally, this information reflects a problem-focused description that gives inadequate attention to the strengths and resiliency of Aboriginal people. These positive characteristics must be recognized in developing a strengths-based model of practice.

Etiology of Social Problems

The imposition of a colonial framework on Canadian–Aboriginal relations has had powerful, negative effects on Aboriginal people over nearly four hundred years of contact. Government policies have deliberately undermined the viability of Aboriginal communities, divesting them of their land, culture, and tribal authority (Frideres, 1998). The treaties, which created reserves to deal with the 'Indian problem', and the Indian Act were instrumental in this process. Legislation was a particularly important tool in controlling Aboriginal people and divesting them of their resources. The 1857 Act for the Gradual Civilization of the Indian Tribes in Canada sought to eliminate 'Indian' status through the voluntary or forced relinquishment of status as an Indian person, and the Indian Act bestowed sweeping state powers on the federal government to regulate all aspects of reserve life. Until 1960, when the right to vote in federal elections was finally extended to them, First Nations peoples could vote only if they had become enfranchised (i.e., had given up their Indian status). In other cases, marginalization resulted from the sometimes well-intended but always misguided efforts to 'civilize' and 'assimilate' Aboriginal people. The early role of the missionaries, and the continuing influence of organized Christian churches in Aboriginal communities, played a major role in the colonization of Aboriginal people.

Of particular importance is the role of residential schools and, after 1960, the effects of intervention by the mainstream child welfare system. Residential schools were initially described by their proponents in glowing terms. However, this description masked a disastrous goal: institutionalized assimilation by stripping Aboriginal people of their language, culture, and connection with family. The results, for many, have included a lifestyle of uncertain identity and the adoption of self-abusive behaviours. Such behaviours, often associated with alcohol and violence, reflect a pattern of coping sometimes referred to in First Nations communities as 'the residential school syndrome'. Although this picture is sometimes painted without regard to the positive effects experienced by some who attended residential schools, these experiences do not in the final analysis detract from the generally held purpose of the schools, or the preponderance of negative effects experienced by students in these institutional settings. Founded and operated by Protestant and the Roman Catholic churches, but funded primarily by the federal government, the schools operated in all territories and seven provinces. The number of schools reached a peak of eighty in 1931, and most were concentrated on the prairies (Fleras & Elliott, 1999, p. 181). Throughout Canada, between 100,000 and 125,000 Aboriginal children (about one in six) entered the system. By the mid-1980s, all but four schools, which continued to operate under Aboriginal jurisdiction, had been closed (Miller, 1996).

In a study undertaken in Manitoba (Manitoba Joint Committee on Residential Schools, 1994), interviews were conducted with forty-three former students who attended residential schools between 1940 and 1970. Respondents related stories of excessive discipline and abuse, ridicule, humiliation, and demeaning punishment. Almost half of respondents disclosed experiences of sexual abuse. Although most of the sexual abuse was perpetrated by caregivers, older children, who may have learned this behaviour in the schools, were also involved. Three other types of trauma were identified as having lasting effects on adult adjustment and parenting. One was lack of love in most relationships with caregivers and teachers. Second was the denial of cultural expression, such as language, in conjunction with the ridicule heaped on Aboriginal practices, including spiritual beliefs. This pattern can be thought of as a form of spiritual abuse. Finally, the loss of a family experience, including the opportunity for positive bonding with parents, was identified as having a continuing impact on intergenerational parenting practices. One respondent offered this evaluation: 'it robbed me of my family life because I don't think I learned how to love—my whole childhood was stolen from me'. As adults, former students of residential school often turned these negative experiences inward, affecting self-esteem. Many reported an inability to walk in either the Aboriginal or non-Aboriginal worlds, of becoming 'a person without an identity', and of resorting to alcohol and substance abuse.

The residential school system was an obvious instrument of colonialism, but McKenzie and Hudson (1985) demonstrate the parallels between this system and actions of the child welfare system in the 1960s and 1970s. Like the residential school system, the child welfare system separated Aboriginal children from their families, communities, and culture. Power and decision-making authority remained within the dominant society, and decisions were often made in an arbitrary fashion, with little attention to longer-term outcomes for individuals or communities. The devaluation of indigenous people is a particularly significant characteristic of the colonial relationship, and in the child welfare system little attention was paid to the ways in which Aboriginal communities had traditionally handled child-care problems. The result was the denial of kinship care patterns and the removal of almost all Aboriginal children to cross-cultural foster and adoptive homes within the dominant society.

A colonial relationship may also encourage the adoption of behaviours associated with domination and victimization. For example, the adoption of authoritarian forms of leadership within Aboriginal communities is regarded by some as an outcome of colonialism. Another outcome is internalized perceptions of inferiority, leading to self-defeating responses such as alcoholism, violence, and abuse. Although a less likely phenomenon today, internalized perceptions of community and cultural inferiority caused some Aboriginal parents to adopt the belief that placement outside their home community and culture was in the best interests of their children.

Although the effects of the residential school system and the 'sixties scoop' in child welfare are essential aspects of understanding Aboriginal reality, not all problems can be fully explained by these developments. Other structural causes such as systematic racism, poverty, and inadequate opportunities are also important. As well, individuals make choices about their own patterns of behaviour, and even if structural causes affect these choices, the individual's responsibility to engage in healing needs to be recognized.

Resilience and Restructuring

Problem analysis in social work has often failed to acknowledge the strengths and resilience of those who are disadvantaged, although recent attention to the strengths perspective has brought more balance to assessment processes. This is particularly important in appreciating the responses of Aboriginal people to centuries of oppression. On an individual basis, many of those who attended residential schools not only survived the experience, but have emerged to play a leadership role among Aboriginal people. At the collective level, cultural traditions and practices, including the role of the extended family, have survived to become key elements in the renewal of Aboriginal communities and their way of life.

Institutional restructuring has also emerged as a major strategy in the remaking of Aboriginal–White relations in Canada. This movement has been coupled with a renewed interest in the resolution of land claims and the development of a form of autonomous self-governance. Although many Aboriginal people are understandably skeptical, in 1998 the Minister of Indian Affairs apologized to Aboriginal people for decades of systematic discrimination, theft of their lands, and the physical and sexual abuse of Aboriginal children. The Statement of Reconciliation was general in focus, but particular attention was given to those who suffered the tragedy of residential schools, and some funding for the victims of residential schools has been provided.

Four eras in Canadian policy-making affecting Aboriginal people are outlined by Fleras and Elliott (1999): the Assimilation Era (1867–1945), the Integration Era (1945–73), the Devolution Era (1973–90), and the Conditional Autonomy Era (1990 and beyond). The more dramatic institutional changes began in the Devolution Era, with First Nations communities gaining local control over educational services. The development of First Nations child and family service agencies followed, beginning in the early 1980s, and health services have been the focus of more recent attention. Service delivery models in child welfare have involved federal funding, adherence to provincial standards and legislation, and First Nations administrative responsibility for service delivery. Although the development of such service models in child welfare have produced many positive results, including an increase in culturally appropriate services (McKenzie, 1997), several limitations have also been recognized. For example, jurisdictional control has been limited by the required adherence to mainstream legislation and standards in child welfare, a requirement that contradicts the views of many Aboriginal people regarding the inherent right to self-government and the fiduciary responsibility of the federal government. As well, Aboriginal control of child welfare services off-reserve has been slow to develop. Jurisdictional control is an important element in developing culturally appropriate services (McKenzie, 1995), but the diversity of cultural identification among Aboriginal people and the fact that both Aboriginal and non-Aboriginal helpers often lack knowledge and understanding of Aboriginal traditions have restricted the development of such services.

The current era in Aboriginal–Canadian relations is characterized by three significant issues. One is the growing acknowledgement of Aboriginal self-government rights. While the federal government regards these as contingent rather than sovereign or absolute rights, there is some evidence of this government's interest in the development of practical, negotiated arrangements for some form of autonomous self-government (Fleras & Elliott, 1999). In this context, one can anticipate continuing claims to self-determination legitimated by a belief in the inherent right of self-government. A second, and related, development is the importance of land claims settlements based on Aboriginal title. Aboriginal title confers Aboriginal rights of use over land and resources where ownership has not been legally extinguished and transferred to the Crown. Finally, there is the increased recognition in Canadian society of a distinct and broadly accepted world view among Aboriginal people. Growing understanding of the uniqueness of an Aboriginal world view and of related cultural practices and traditions is an important strength that can inform social work practice with Canadians of Aboriginal background.

An Aboriginal Perspective for Social Work Practice

The general framework outlined in this chapter incorporates attributes of the structural model of practice (Mullaly, 1997) that focus on some of the dynamics related to oppression and the importance of connecting the personal with the political in assessment and intervention. These principles are not inconsistent with approaches that have emerged in feminist models of practice, the strengths approach, and the empowerment model of practice. However, an Aboriginal perspective for social work practice focuses on the particular nature of oppression experienced by Aboriginal people and the role of cultural values and traditions in re-establishing individual and collective well-being. Thus, attention is directed to the distinctiveness of an Aboriginal world view and to colonialism as the primary form of oppression affecting Aboriginal people. Colonization is the source of historical trauma and unresolved grief for many Aboriginal people: it resulted in personal and collective losses including family connections and a way of life. A sense of both self and collective identity are critical factors in responding to oppression because it is this knowledge of 'who we are' that affects personal well-being and the nature of interrelationships with others. Cultural identity, particularly among those who do not identify with the dominant culture, is at the centre of who a person is, and the loss of self-identity and self-worth is often associated with coping difficulties. In this context, colonization is not simply a historical event; instead, its effects continue to obscure the world view of Aboriginal people and their related values and traditions. Thus, social work practice, which attempts to empower Aboriginal people, must pay particular attention to its effects on self-identity and the need to reconstruct a positive concept of self and community. For many Aboriginal people, this will include a reconnection with cultural values and some of the traditional practices that help to define Aboriginal well-being.

Recognition of the importance of these factors suggests that effective social work practice with Aboriginal people begins with the adoption of a particular framework or perspective that includes five core elements:

- an understanding of the world view of Aboriginal people and how this differs from the dominant Euro-Canadian world view;
- recognition of the effects of the colonization process;
- recognition of the importance of Aboriginal identity or consciousness;
- appreciation for the value of cultural knowledge and traditions in promoting healing and empowerment; and
- an understanding of the diversity of Aboriginal cultural expression.

These elements, proposed as cornerstones of a framework or perspective for social work practice with Aboriginal people, are described in the sections that follow.

Understanding the World View of Aboriginal People

The first element in the framework is recognition of an Aboriginal world view that differs from that of dominant Canadian society. A *world view* can be defined as a set of related ideas or views to which members of a distinct culture subscribe (Overholt & Callicott, 1982). According to Delaney (1995), world views represent religious, political, social, and physical information about people and the societies they create. Once accepted, a world view becomes a 'recognized reality' that serves to socialize its citizens and to create a political culture. A particular world view is transferred to citizens through institutions such as the family, teachings, and religion; in that process, particular values, attitudes, beliefs, and opinions are adopted (Magstadt & Schottem, 1988). Although specific beliefs and practices vary among different groups of Aboriginal people, it has been demonstrated that several common traditional values exist (DuBray, 1985; Hamilton & Sinclair, 1991; RCAP, 1996; Red Horse, 1980). These general values contribute to the distinctiveness of a world view among Aboriginal people and to the importance of recognizing cultural differences between Aboriginal peoples and Euro-Canadian society. *Culture* can be defined as ways of life, shared behaviour, social institutions, systems of norms, beliefs, values, and world views that allow people to locate themselves within the universe and that give meaning to their personal and collective experience. Traditional Aboriginal cultures typically reflected a more communal approach to helping, group and family reciprocity, and a more holistic relationship with nature and other persons. As well, these cultures placed a high value on traditional spirituality, elders, and the extended family or clan system (Hamilton & Sinclair, 1991).

Like others, Aboriginal people sought fundamental truths and an understanding about their place in the cosmos. The genesis of an Aboriginal world view emerged from a close relationship with the environment. Six interrelated metaphysical beliefs have helped to shape this relationship: all things exist according to the principle of survival; the act of survival pulses with the natural energy and cycles of the earth; this energy is part of some grand design; all things have a role to perform to ensure balance and harmony and the overall well-being of life; all things are an extension of the grand design and, as such, contain the same essence as the source from which it flows (Gitchi-Manitou); and this essence is understood as 'spirit', which links all things to each other and to Creation. In response to these beliefs, accepted as truths, Aboriginal people developed a way of life consistent with the lessons and teachings that Creation provided. This evolved into a symbiotic, intimate, spiritual, and sacred relationship with the earth, and these principles were reflected in relationships among people and with the environment. Meaning systems and social constructs evolved to shape a way of life; thus, mother earth, the family, clan, nation, the world, and the universe all became part of the circle of life. As Nabigon and Mawhiney (1986) suggest, Aboriginal people did not see themselves as separate from the natural world; rather, they were an extension of that same world.

An Aboriginal view of life as a sacred and spiritual journey is captured in other writings. For example, Longclaws (1994) speaks of 'centredness' as the goal for balancing the spiritual and the physical and for 'living responsibly in the natural order of life' (p. 28). Ermine (1995), in discussing the differences between Aboriginal and Euro-Canadian world views, describes the Aboriginal 'nature' of attaining knowledge and truth through a spiritual, sacred, and inner-focused journey. This process or journey requires a deep reverence and respect for the earth, along with an intimate understanding of the natural order (Creation) and the interdependence of all things. The purpose of this knowledge is to maintain harmony and balance between all living things and to ensure that the knowledge to achieve and maintain this is transmitted to the next generation. Such beliefs reflect a spiritual tradition, but the practical side of these beliefs is embedded in survival. Historically, this knowledge was used to regulate the nature of one's relationship to the resources in the environment and to guide behaviours to ensure continued survival.

Aboriginal people, like others, embraced the symbolic as a means to understand themselves and their relationship to each other and to their environment. Berger and Luckmann (1967) refer to this as the creation of symbolic meaning systems.

Thus, Aboriginal ancestors constructed stories and legends and adopted specific ceremonies, physical symbols, practices, community customs, and traditions as means to codify and transmit this knowledge to future generations. These were expressed as values and belief systems and were transmitted through traditional teachings, prescribed roles and familial structures, and rites of passage.

In contrast, the Euro-Canadian world view, based on a more linear model of thinking, is immersed in a history of science and scientific reasoning. It rests on a firm belief about human objectivity in the outward pursuit of knowledge and truth. The dominant world view in Western societies does have spiritual and symbolic attributes, but these are generally segmented from secular forms of knowledge. The secularization of knowledge as science, reason, and technology has led to a fragmentary world view that stands in sharp contrast to the spiritual and sacred interconnectedness of the Aboriginal world view. This premise—integration of spiritual and secular knowledge—leads to a whole different way of being in, and of, the world. Social work practitioners unable to comprehend this fundamental difference risk adopting not only an ethnocentric approach to knowledge development but also the application of methods of practice that fail to appreciate how well-being is defined for many Aboriginal people in Canada.

An Aboriginal world view contains three major value constructs that are particularly important to social work practice. The first is the importance of spirituality, and the connection between spirituality and nature, including the metaphysical aspects of this relationship. A second, related concept is that of holism. These two value constructs reflect the importance of interconnections between the physical and spiritual world, between the individual and the environment, and between mind, body, and spirit, as central to well-being. Reciprocity between human beings, the natural world, and the spirit world involves ceremonies, gift giving, and the acknowledgement of these exchanges in achieving a balanced life. At the individual level, the interconnections between emotional, mental, physical, and spiritual development are recognized, both as sources of potential problems in coping and as aspects of human functioning that must be given equal attention in the healing process. These principles are reflected in the medicine wheel, which illustrates the interconnections between the emotional, mental, physical, and spiritual aspects of well-being. The importance of holism is not inconsistent with the ecological model, although the latter is used in social work primarily to understand relationships between individuals and their immediate economic and social environment. In addition, the emphasis on specialization and the related separation between methods of intervention contradict the basic tenets of holism as expressed within an Aboriginal world view.

The third value construct in the Aboriginal word view important to social work practice is the value of the collective. Recognition is given to healing both at the individual and collective level, but it is the emphasis placed on extended family and the clan system that is particularly important to Aboriginal communities. In research pertaining to the development of child welfare standards in First Nations communities, McKenzie, Seidl, and Bone (1995) reported that respondents more frequently defined their family as including extended family members first, and then members of the immediate or nuclear family. As well, a significant number of respondents noted that the community was 'a kind of family' (p. 642). In child welfare, this value construct has led to the development of policies that prioritize placement with extended family members, or with foster care providers within the same community, when children are removed from their parental home.

The Effects of Colonization

The second element of the framework for effective social work practice with Aboriginal people is an understanding of the dynamic effects of the colonization process. The marginalization of Aboriginal people has been well documented (Fleras & Elliott, 1999; Frideres, 1998; Kellough, 1980; RCAP, 1996) and outcomes associated with this process were summarized earlier in this chapter.

Frideres (1998) explains the predominant elements of any colonization process in the following fashion: incursion of the colonizing group into a geographic area, forced or voluntary; the dismantling of the social and cultural structures of indigenous people; the imposition of external political control leading to economic dependence; the provision of low-quality social services; and racism and the establishment of a colour line. In a similar way, Kellough (1980) discusses the structural and cultural attributes of colonization. Structural colonialism involves efforts to extract wealth from the colonized, leading to their economic dependence on the dominant society. Cultural colonialism, according to Kellough, is complementary to structural colonialism in that it aims at overcoming resistance by 'civilizing' or 'assimilating' the colonized. Thus, it becomes an ideological instrument of structural colonialism.

Colonialism has been generally accepted as a key factor in explaining some of the social problems in Aboriginal communities; however, attention to the psychological effects of colonization, and the use of this knowledge to inform approaches to social work practice with Aboriginal peoples, requires further attention. An important attribute of the colonization process is the notion of *mystification,* which describes the ways colonizing strategies are legitimized as necessary for the salvation of Aboriginal people. Two examples of this were the role of organized religion in degrading and marginalizing Aboriginal spirituality, and the role of government in outlawing such practices as the sun dance. The devaluation of Aboriginal history also led to policies, such as the Indian Act, that excluded Aboriginal people from full and equal partnership in Canadian society unless they conformed to the expectations of dominant society. The devaluation of Aboriginal history was accomplished in two ways: by either ignoring Aboriginal history altogether or depicting it as primitive and uncivilized. Mystification of a people's history through devaluation destroys their collective consciousness and paves the way for assimilation. While some churches have recently made efforts to incorporate selected Aboriginal traditions and ceremonies, others remain less sympathetic. The result is that many Aboriginal people are discouraged from trying to incorporate traditional Aboriginal beliefs within contemporary Judeo-Christian practices.

Education is a key instrument in the transmission of a people's history, a fact well understood by those who developed residential schools. By denying the validity of this history, cultural inferiority was reinforced. Although educational curricula that include a celebration of Aboriginal history and traditions have been developed, particularly for Aboriginal communities, but such curricula are not adequately incorporated in most school programs.

Social work practice in a post-colonial era must involve a 'two worlds' approach, where there is evidence of collaboration and equal partnership in the evolution of policy and practice affecting Aboriginal people. This approach requires continuing efforts to identify the colonial process and its ongoing impact on Aboriginal people, on Canadian people in general, and on the social work profession in particular. Within social work, Aboriginal concepts and practices are beginning to be accepted; however, too often these are marginalized or viewed as secondary to the strategies and techniques emerging from the dominant paradigm.

Two implications are particularly important. First, social workers must critically examine the underlying ideology of dominant approaches to both education and practice and must incorporate approaches based on an Aboriginal world view. Second, efforts to promote structural change must be directed at the institutions and practices in dominant society that continue to oppress Aboriginal people and that fail to promote partnerships for social development based on equality and a fundamental respect for diversity.

The Importance of Identity

Mystification had damaging effects on Aboriginal people because it has socialized them to devalue their own culture and sense of collective identity. The process of mystification, which is designed to reinforce the belief that the colonizer is the sole carrier of a valid culture, can be understood as a form of oppression. Mullaly (1997) describes this process as cultural imperialism. It arises when the dominant group, sometimes without realizing it, projects its experience and culture as representative of all humanity. This allows differences to be defined as deviant and inferior. In this process, Aboriginal people experience a double and paradoxical oppression: stereotypes are used to define them, and at the same time their experiences and perspectives are marginalized. The result is an altered sense of Aboriginal consciousness, where Aboriginal culture and traditions are accepted as inferior and those of dominant society are regarded as superior.

For some Aboriginal people, even efforts to conform to the norms of dominant society fail to ensure acceptance. They experience rejection and feel they do not belong in either world. For others, the lack of a strong self-identity leads to their acceptance of prescribed roles as inferior and subordinate. Some may begin to act out these roles, inadvertently reinforcing the stereotypes perpetuated by dominant society. A cycle of oppression is established in which both the oppressed and those generally responsible for the oppression come to believe that individuals are solely responsible for their present predicament. Given a fragmented perspective on Aboriginal history and a limited understanding of colonization, there is an all too common tendency to blame the victims, including whole communities. The result of these processes is a devalued sense of both self and group identity.

Cultural Knowledge and Traditional Practices for Healing

The fourth element of the framework for effective social work practice with Aboriginal people recognizes that empowerment or healing for many Aboriginal people requires cultural reconstruction. By reinforcing Aboriginal culture, and the values and traditions on which it is built, people who have experienced the effects of colonization can return to their own culture as a source of strength in developing their own self-identity. Support for the importance of this element is based both on theoretical arguments and on experiential evidence from those who have already embarked on this healing journey.

The theoretical argument is summarized first. In attaching value to Aboriginal culture, it is important to distinguish between a categorical and transactional view of ethnicity. Green (1995) notes that the *categorical* view emphasizes ethnic identity as a function of traits such as appearance, dress, and speech patterns. This restricted view of cultural practices often leads to the protection of folk practices as cultural expression, while expecting minority group conformity to other social, cultural, and economic imperatives in dominant society. A *transactional* view of ethnicity focuses on the nature of interaction between dominant society and the subordinate group. In this approach, the social boundaries set by each group become a focus for analysis, and these boundaries shift over time. For example, as Aboriginal consciousness regarding inequality and other differences has grown, group solidarity has been reinforced. As well, this consciousness of culture reinforces a positive self-identity that encourages Aboriginal people to redefine their position from one of inferior status to one of equal or superior status. Although these developments can increase intergroup polarization on occasion, an interactional view of group relations suggests that group differences do not mean people are different in all respects. Overlapping experiences, common goals, and shared attributes provide opportunities for partnerships and collaboration, even though important differences may be recognized. The model of overcoming oppression discussed here depends on the reclamation of culture and the celebration of differences within a context that promotes such an approach. Thus, it does not depend on Aboriginal people alone; it must also be supported by non-Aboriginal people, including social workers, who become allies, advocates, and facilitators of such a process.

The importance attributed to cultural differences and their relationship to identity is reinforced by Kawulich and Curlette's (1998) discussion of life tasks. Work, social relations, and intimacy are three life tasks that are generally applied within the dominant culture in assessing social adjustment. However, these authors argue that identity and spirituality are also important to examine in understanding differences between American Indian and mainstream cultures.

From an experiential perspective, there has been a significant growth in the number of Aboriginal people who are incorporating traditional values and practices as aspects of their own healing or self-development; as well, there has been an increase in the adoption of traditional practices as aspects of the helping process (Heilbron & Guttman, 2000; McCormick, 2000). Of particular importance to social work is the growing evidence that traditional values and practices are associated with well-being and a reduction in social problems. One example is a qualitative study of six Aboriginal adults who exhibited characteristics of resilience during their lives after attendance at residential schools (Nichol, 2000). Although all described the residential school experience as traumatic, each person told a story of an adult life experience that had become productive and self-satisfying to them. Among other factors that seemed to support resilience was the commonly experienced reconnection to Aboriginal spirituality and many of the traditional values and practices of Aboriginal culture. In another study, Fox, Manitonabi, and Ward (1984) found that an increase in the suicide rate among a tribal band was associated with modernization and related factors such as family upheaval, substance abuse, and loss of identity. Five years later, following the introduction of a multidimensional prevention and intervention program based on traditionalism, the suicide rate had dramatically decreased.

Increasing attention is being paid to the role of elders in helping and healing in the Aboriginal context. As noted in the Manitoba Aboriginal Justice Inquiry, 'Elders have long been considered the ones who bridge the ancient traditions and beliefs and the modern day influences that come into play in the day-to-day lives of Aboriginal men and women' (Hamilton & Sinclair, 1991, p. 19). Elders, medicine people, and traditional teachers are often used as advisors, role models, and mentors; as well, they may provide leadership in the use of sacred ceremonies and spiritual healing. While the use of elders and other traditional methods are important to social work practice, not all Aboriginal people will be amenable to these approaches, particularly in the early stages of intervention.

Differing Aboriginal practices such as non-interference and sharing, which arise from related values, have been described elsewhere (Clarkson, Morrissette, & Regallet, 1992; Good Tracks, 1973), and these also have particular significance to the helping relationship. However, one needs to be cautious in generalizing instrumental values and practices to all Aboriginal people: these are often overshadowed by the variability that exists within and across groups and communities.

Diversity in Aboriginal Cultural Expression

A distinct Aboriginal world view can be identified, but cultural diversity among Aboriginal people requires further consideration. One issue is the nature and scope of traditional practices and the particular meaning of these practices within different Aboriginal cultures. For example, Cree and Ojibway people may have somewhat different interpretations of the medicine wheel. Knowledge about such differences is gained by learning, through study and experience, about the particular traditions and practices of individual nations. In this regard, elders and respected teachers are important sources of information. As noted earlier, cultural values and traditions play a significant role in shaping Aboriginal identity and self-esteem, and it is important to assess the extent to which particular individuals and communities incorporate traditional cultural practices. The identification of differences in the expression of Aboriginal identity is a key element of the assessment process. Figure 11.1 illustrates a model for understanding these differences.

This model, which reflects revisions to an earlier model developed by the authors, is based on our continuing analysis of trends in Aboriginal–non-Aboriginal relations (see Morrissette, McKenzie, & Morrissette, 1993). Although the model should be regarded as tentative, its general validity is strengthened by the fact that it has some similarity to other models that have been developed to help understand cultural group identity and behaviour. For example, Williams and Ellison (1996) outline a cultural continuum of American Indian expression that includes four styles of living: traditional, marginal, middle-class, and pan-Indian, with each contributing to a somewhat different sense of family. According to these authors, traditionalists live in accordance with culturally prescribed customs, whereas marginal and middle-class American Indians are caught between two worlds, often experiencing socio-cultural stress. Pan-Indians struggle to re-establish lost traditions in ways designed to encompass tribal variations, and it is the reformation of traditions to encompass the mixing of several different traditional forms distinguishes them from traditionalists. Somewhat different approaches to intervention are recommended for each group.

The Waywayseecappo First Nation developed a spousal abuse program model (Waywayseecappo First Nation, 1992) based on a framework that defined five types of cultural expression: the universalist, the traditionalist, the assimilated, those who were transforming their identity, and those who were in a state of anomie. Universalists understand their own culture, but also accept other cultures and incorporate some of these practices in their life. Traditionalists rely primarily on traditional practices and values for day-to-day living, whereas the assimilated primarily adopt the values and related practices of the dominant society. Those who are transforming are beginning to explore their identity, and those experiencing anomie are caught between two worlds or lost to both.

These models reinforce the importance of considering the association between cultural identity and healing; however, the categorical approach to culture, and the tendency to regard types such as the assimilated in negative terms, is problematic. A more complex and interactive approach to understanding the acculturation process is required. Walters (1999) notes that much of the American research on Indian acculturation assumes that acculturation is synonymous with identity. Thus, as one acculturates to the dominant society one's ethnic identity is lost. This reflects a deficit model of acculturation in that it assumes that individuals replace their traditions with the traditions of the dominant culture and become assimilated with continued contact. A strengths perspective recognizes that Aboriginal people may adopt some customs from other cultures and integrate these while acquiring or maintaining some or all of their Aboriginal values, traditions, and practices. These Aboriginal values may also be used to buffer them against negative colonizing processes in the dominant society. Thus, Aboriginal people could simultaneously

Figure 11.1 Contemporary Expressions of Aboriginal Identity

Traditional cultural expression		Aboriginal/mainstream cultural expression			Non-traditional cultural expression	
Contempory traditional	Traditional	Transitional	Ambivalent	Mainstream dominant	Assimilated	Marginalized/ alienated
• Integration and reconciliation of two world views • Adoption of personal/collective healing model • Use of traditional practices • Ability to clarify and work to resolve cultural conflicts	• Adoption of segregated lifestyles • Adoption of personal/collective healing model • Use of traditional practices • Recognition of heightened cultural conflict	• Recognition of personal/collective cultural conflicts • Challenges to mainstream values/customs • Exploration of cultural answers • Persuit of historical/cultural knowledge • Openness to change	• Beginning recognition of personal cultural conflicts • Confusion between Aboriginal/mainstream values/customs • Hesitancy to embrace cultural/traditional knowledge • Ambivalence to change	• Mystified understanding of colonial experience • Acceptance of mainstream/Christian values/customs • Ascription to Aboriginal self-identity • Acceptance of negative stereotypes of Aboriginal identity • Resistance to change	• Enfranchisement, forced or voluntary • Ascription to mainstream values, beliefs, and practices • Possible minimal ascription to Aboriginal identity • Separation from Aboriginal community	• Alienation from Aboriginal/mainstream society • Powerlessness/hopelessness • Multiple social problems common • Self-destructive behaviors common • Possible adoption of pseudo-culture as resistance to marginalization

be both highly acculturated and ethnically identified with Aboriginal culture and traditions.

In her research on identity and acculturation with American Indians, Walters (1999) hypothesized that identity attitudes were formed by cognitive and affective attitudes towards self (self-identity), a person's cognitive and affective attitudes towards other American Indian people (group identity), the social environment, and institutional responses (p. 166). The author also incorporated a four-stage approach to identity formation based on acculturation styles in the model. The first stage is *internalization,* where negative, colonizing self- and group-identity attitudes are internalized and dominant culture is overvalued. The second stage is *marginalization,* where there is an awakening of consciousness about being caught between two worlds. The third stage, *externalization,* involves the shedding of internalized stereotypes and colonizing attitudes. Finally, *actualization* involves the achievement of integrated identity attitudes and the adoption of healthy psychological buffers to combat further internalization of colonizing attitudes. Walters found that, while identity predicted acculturation styles to some degree, there was a distinction between the two. For example, she found that those with higher levels of externalization and actualization styles tended not to replace Indian values and behaviours with those of the dominant society even though they may have adapted to some of the norms and customs of the dominant society. Results also suggested that one could hold internalized negative attitudes about oneself as a Native American person and towards Native American people as a group without identifying with the dominant culture; in addition, one may still retain some of the behavioural customs and norms that reflect identification with Native American culture. Finally, those with high levels of marginalization may not experience any acculturation style and are likely to experience higher levels of negative mental health outcomes such as depression, low self-esteem, and anxiety. These findings provide some empirical support for the model outlined in Figure 11.1. First, they reinforce the distinction between identity attitudes and acculturation. Although these are related concepts, important differences must be recognized. Second, they support the importance of socio-historical factors, including colonization, in shaping Aboriginal identity.

The continuum of identity expression illustrated in Figure 11.1 highlights the importance of culture to a sense of shared identity, a common past, and a sense of belonging. Culture, and its differentiated effects on identity, is particularly important to the assessment stage in social work practice. In addition, it may assist Aboriginal people in understanding their own expression of cultural identity. Coupled with an understanding of the effects of colonization on individual and collective identification with Aboriginality, it also avoids self-blame and permits one to choose an approach to healing consistent with identity aspirations.

Not all Aboriginal people will embrace traditional values and practices; nonetheless, practitioners using this model must develop an adequate understanding of Aboriginal cultures and traditions to apply these concepts to the assessment process. Of particular importance is an understanding of the conflicting values that may be experienced in establishing one's identity, and the fundamental right to choose from a range of conventional and traditional helping strategies within each stage of cultural expression. Greater knowledge of traditional practices will be required if these form part of the intervention strategy, and social workers should refer to elders or those with specialized forms of traditional knowledge when intervention methods, such as the sweat lodge, are indicated.

Three general types of cultural expression are identified in the model. These are traditional, a combination of Aboriginal and mainstream expressions, and the non-traditional. Variations are also found within each general category.

TRADITIONAL FORMS OF CULTURAL EXPRESSION

Among traditionalists there are those who reject close association with most of the lifestyle or occupational choices within mainstream society. Individuals, and occasionally communities, attempt to exercise their lifestyle without interference from mainstream values and practices. Often individuals live or return to live on the land or on reserves because they feel that this enables greater opportunities for incorporating a traditional lifestyle and managing the cultural conflicts that emerge from the dominant society. A second type of expression within the traditional category is the 'contemporary traditional', where individuals integrate traditional practices and approaches to healing within a lifestyle that includes participation in contemporary institutions, including employment in mainstream or Aboriginal organizations. In some cases integration of traditional culture and Christianity occurs. For example, Nichol (2000) identified people who were respected elders within their communities and who still incorporated some aspects of Christianity, including church attendance, into their life. An important attribute of those adopting a contemporary traditional form of Aboriginal expression is the ongoing ability to recognize and address most conflicts between the dominant society and Aboriginal values in ways that enable them to positively assert their own identity as Aboriginal people. In effect, these individuals walk in two worlds, and are generally able to reconcile these perspectives in establishing their sense of identity.

Somewhat different approaches to helping may be required with these two subgroups. For example, it is likely that traditional people will generally prefer traditional forms of practice, while those who reflect a contemporary traditional perspective may select either conventional or traditional forms of intervention, or a combination of approaches.

ABORIGINAL/MAINSTREAM FORMS OF CULTURAL EXPRESSION

This group includes those who are in the process of reconciling values and practices from Aboriginal and Euro-Canadian world views as part of their identity. Two characteristics distinguish this group from those who have integrated traditional practices and values as part of their identity. One is the presence of significant, unresolved conflicts in integrating values and practices emerging from Aboriginal and Euro-Canadian world views. The other is the lower level of awareness of both the knowledge and traditions of Aboriginal people and the effects of colonization on one's individual and collective identity.

People in this group commonly express three different types of cultural identity. One type includes those primarily acculturated to mainstream values, and this may include an identification with Christian beliefs and practices. While individuals may identify as Aboriginal, they may also apply negative stereotypes to other Aboriginal people, indicating a mystified understanding of the colonial experience. Those who fall under this mainstream-dominant form of identity expression are more likely than the other two groups in this category to resist change. A second type includes those who are more ambivalent about their own forms of cultural expression. While these people may recognize cultural conflicts between the dominant society and Aboriginal traditions, they often experience a degree of confusion about these differences. They may either lack an understanding of traditional Aboriginal knowledge and practices or may hesitate to embrace these traditions. The third type includes those who possess a greater understanding of cultural conflicts, and are more actively exploring some of the answers and directions to be found in the old ways. This type or subgroup can be described as 'transitional' because they are more open to changes involving the incorporation of traditional cultural knowledge and practices than are the other two groups in this category.

Many Aboriginal people express some combination of Aboriginal and mainstream identification, and many of those requesting social work services may experience some of the stresses in identity expression summarized above. Those who adopt primarily mainstream values and expressions are likely to prefer conventional models of assessment and intervention and to be more resistant to questions concerning their personal and collective identification as Aboriginal people. However, methods of practice may include the sharing of information on the effects of colonization and its impact in shaping behaviours and stereotypes of Aboriginal people.

Those who display attributes of ambivalent acculturation generally express greater awareness of the conflicts between Aboriginal and mainstream values and customs, and the social worker has more opportunities to explore the effects of the colonial experience with these individuals. However, the helper must be sensitive in exploring these issues; negative stereotypes about other Aboriginal people and some resistance to Aboriginal values and traditions may be apparent. The role of the practitioner as an educator and information provider is particularly important in this context.

Those who are in a transitional stage are more likely to be actively seeking cultural information, and the practitioner's role as an ally and facilitator in acquiring cultural knowledge will be important. In addition, a more direct helping role may involve exploring the impact of this information in dealing with value conflicts, identity, relationships, and adjustment difficulties.

NON-TRADITIONAL FORMS OF CULTURAL EXPRESSION

The third major type of identity expression occurs among Aboriginal people who embrace non-traditional values and practices. Two different groups are those who are assimilated and those who are either marginalized or alienated. Those who have been assimilated, or adopt only mainstream values, beliefs, and practices, may reflect this identity expression because of enfranchisement, the effects of socialization as a result of being removed from their culture and communities, or a choice in lifestyle and cultural patterns. These individuals are unlikely to play an active role in traditional Aboriginal activities, even though they may identify as having Aboriginal heritage and may participate in Aboriginal community activities that are more generic in nature. Those who are alienated or marginalized may have lost their identification with Aboriginal values and traditions for many of the same reasons as those who are assimilated. While they may identify as Aboriginal, this is not reflected by any comprehensive understanding of traditional values, customs, and practices. Alienated or marginalized individuals also do not incorporate Euro-Canadian values and practices very consistently; thus, they remain marginalized or alienated from the dominant society as well. This loss of identity, which may be related to colonization and intergenerational patterns of family dysfunction, often leads to hopelessness and to related problems of violence, substance abuse, and suicide. Individual expressions of alienation are also reinforced by poverty, unemployment, lack of opportunity, and a cycle of abuse such that individual problems become collective in scope.

There is an important distinction between those who are alienated and those who are marginalized. Alienated individuals are largely unattached to any consistent self-identity or sense of belonging, whereas those who are marginalized may establish a pseudo-identity that replaces either the adoption of core Aboriginal or mainstream values. The development of Aboriginal gangs—which provide for acceptance, a sense of identity, and, in some cases, a sense of family—can be understood in this way. Unfortunately, the sense of collective identity that emerges from this type of marginalization is often associated with other adjustment problems, including criminal activity.

For those who have chosen an assimilated lifestyle, social work practice is likely to be based on conventional methods. At the same time, some of those who identify primarily with Euro-Canadian values and customs may experience conflicts, such as racism, that are related to their ethnic identity. In these circumstances, it may be important to explore cultural conflicts and their connection to colonization. Those who have adopted mainstream values because of forced assimilation may experience periodic difficulties in adjustment due to cultural conflicts, and these may be expressed through substance abuse, self-abuse, or depression. Conventional methods of exploring grief and trauma are relevant in these circumstances, but sharing a cognitive understanding of the effects of colonization and the relationship of this to cultural conflicts is also important.

Individual strategies may be relevant for those who are alienated or marginalized; however, group and community-focused approaches are likely to be more important. Thus, a focus on identity and culture must be matched with opportunities for education, recreation, and employment.

Although the continuum of Aboriginal identity expression in Figure 11.1 proposes general categories and types of cultural expression, individuals may exhibit characteristics from more than one category or type. In addition, people may move from one category or type to others over their life span. Indeed, the concept of a healing journey, as it applies to identity formation and consolidation, is based on the fundamental principle that one's cultural identity may change over time. Similarly, groups or communities may adopt values and practices that result in a shift in their collective identity, although this process of transformation typically occurs over an extended period of time. It is also important to stress that identity formation involves personal choices that are influenced by social networks and other forms of affiliation. As well, intergenerational processes, including one's family, play an important role. Finally, although individuals have ultimate responsibility for their identity and behaviour, the influence of historical patterns of socialization and the cultural influences of institutions, including the media, in dominant society should not be underestimated.

Empowerment and Healing in Aboriginal Social Work Practice

Conceptual Foundations

Empowerment in social work is difficult to define because it is applied to different dimensions or levels of practice (Gutiérrez, GlenMaye & DeLois, 1995). For example, Labonté (1990) identifies a continuum of empowerment from personal to political action. At the personal level, empowerment is enhanced by building self-concept and self-esteem; at the interpersonal or group level, knowledge and skills to promote individual and collective power are gained through experiences shared with others. Community empowerment, which involves the use of resources and strategies for structural change, may include advocacy and political action. A fundamental principle in empowerment is the requirement that clients assume control over decisions affecting them, and take actions on their own behalf. Thus, while social workers can assist in the empowerment process with their clients, they cannot perform this function for them.

Empowerment is intended to address both the personal and structural dimensions of problems; yet, too often in social work it is restricted to the personal dimension. Therefore, it is important to emphasize the following aspects of empowerment.

- It attempts to redress problems of inequality and powerlessness and how these are maintained by institutions and structural arrangements.
- It reflects both a goal and a process of interaction, which requires skills in forming partnerships with clients and a focus on strengths and competencies.

- It occurs at different levels, including the personal, interpersonal, and political, but the personal must be linked to the political in order to realize the full potential of empowerment.
- Empowerment for clients can be initiated and sustained only by clients.
- Social workers can assist in this process but, in order to do so, they must feel empowered both personally and through their employing agencies.

The Aboriginal concept of healing is also important to consider, although the extensive use of this term gives rise to problems of definition that are similar to those encountered with empowerment. Healing and wellness in an Aboriginal world view involve a commitment to *holism*—that is, achieving harmony and balance between the spiritual, physical, mental, and emotional components of one's being. Healing begins with an emphasis on the development of inner strengths, and involves a process or healing journey that is inseparable from spirituality and related concerns for the past and for the future. Healing is an active process, and although it is something that individuals do for themselves, it is something families and communities must do as well (Assembly of First Nations, 2000). Healing is important to the concept of Aboriginal empowerment because it contextualizes personal empowerment as a quest for harmony and balance. Cultural content, particularly in relation to identity and spirituality, is embedded in the Aboriginal concept of healing, and there is implicit recognition of the need to deal with any adverse effects from colonization. While the concept of empowerment gives more explicit attention to structural forms of oppression, healing enriches the concept of empowerment for Aboriginal people by recognizing the cultural dimensions of the process and the importance of self-development as an 'inner journey'.

The framework for practice outlined in this chapter avoids prescribing models of practice based on an overly simplistic or stereotypical view of culture or ethnicity. Thus, methods of intervention need to be designed to respond to particular difficulties experienced by service users and based on choice and cultural preferences. At the same time, some conventional models of assessment and intervention are more consistent with the Aboriginal perspective for social work practice advanced here than are others. These include the ecological model (Compton & Galaway, 1994), the structural model (Mullaly, 1997), the strengths-based approach (Saleebey, 1997), and community work approaches (Rubin & Rubin, 2001). These models are relevant to Aboriginal social work practice, but they are insufficient because they do not explicitly address issues related to colonialization and the attributes pertaining to cultural competence. For example, in comparing the ecological and medicine wheel models, Longclaws (1994) notes that the medicine wheel approach places more emphasis on spirituality, the subjective role of the helper in interacting in a more personal and equal manner with clients, and the importance of the inner journey as an aspect of healing. Intervention strategies associated with the structural model (Mullaly, 1997, pp. 170–9)—consciousness-raising, normalization, redefining personal troubles in political terms, and building collective understanding and responses through group methods—are important. However, these strategies must include explicit attention to the effects of colonization and identity expression within an Aboriginal model of practice. Community work approaches that involve the active participation of community members and local control over the change process are also important, but as Absolon and Herbert (1997) argue, these approaches need to be distinguished from efforts to transfer conventional models of 'development' to Aboriginal communities. In addition, specialized attention needs to be given to the nature of oppression experienced by Aboriginal women, who are marginalized and victimized through patriarchy within the dominant society and, often, through the particular power arrangements that exist within their own communities.

Three Levels of Intervention

Empowerment-oriented practices in social work practice with Aboriginal people must include attention to the cultural dynamics at three levels of intervention: intrapersonal, interpersonal, and community. Intervention at each level is important, but empowerment as an outcome is most likely when intervention involves activities at all three levels. At the intrapersonal level, cultural assessment must focus on issues pertaining to the altered sense of identity and how this relates to present coping and behavioural patterns. As the personal relationship between the social worker and the client evolves, a more active role may be assumed by the practitioner in challenging, clarifying, and linking attitudes to behaviours and promoting personal responsibility for change.

At the interpersonal level, connections can be made between personal issues and those affecting the group or community. Knowledge and understanding of the effects of colonization and their impact on the collective identity of Aboriginal people are particularly important at this stage. The role of the practitioner as educator in linking an individual's experience to that of the group or collective is important in normalizing experiences and promoting both individual and collective change. The use of cultural methods and techniques such as ceremonies and the talking circle can help to build group solidarity and begin to create a positive sense of collective identity.

At the community or structural level, it is important for the practitioner to make connections between personal experiences and structural factors. Although the framework for understanding colonization included in this chapter may help in introducing an understanding of the effects of historical and structural factors, promoting empowerment through social action and structural change is particularly difficult. For service users, initiatives may begin with personal healing and be reinforced through sharing and group solidarity. But if the structural effects of colonization are to be addressed, social work practice must incorporate strategies oriented to community building and policy change.

Empowerment efforts oriented to these goals are not the sole responsibility of service users; social workers should be expected to collaborate with service users and other relevant actors in building community capacity and addressing problems of inequality affecting Aboriginal people. Two developments are important to consider in advancing the goal of empowerment at the community level. One is the renewed interest in community approaches that incorporate a model for community building (Ewalt, Freeman, & Poole, 1998; McKenzie, 1999). Community building focuses on the strengths of communities by using community capacity to address emerging needs and problems through collective action. While capacity building is an important goal, it is important to recognize that it is not a substitute for funding or services that must be provided by the state. Thus, consciousness raising, critical thinking, and critical education are methods that can help link community action with decolonization and prevent community-based strategies from becoming simply a means of off-loading service responsibility to communities. For example, the willingness of people to become involved in learning about fetal alcohol syndrome and effects (FAS/E) may be used to advocate for and create a more responsive range of school-based supports for children with FAS/E. A second development, which emerges from the Aboriginal framework for practice proposed in this chapter, is the use of cultural values and traditional practices to establish principles for alternate forms of relationships and services within Aboriginal communities. This model, which is depicted in Figure 11.2, includes efforts to re-establish economic and social relationships based on communal models of caring and a more sustainable approach to economic development.

Community healing practices based on these principles are receiving increased attention. One example is the community healing circle model of responding to sexual abuse, which was developed in Hollow Water First Nation in Manitoba (Aboriginal Corrections Policy Unit, 1997). As well, more collective approaches to economic development, where benefits accrue to the First Nations community rather than an individual or private corporation, are modelled along these principles. Finally, the development of services and organizations controlled by Aboriginal people can help to promote culturally appropriate practices.

Cultural Models of Practice

A wide range of cultural practices needs to be considered in developing social work methods that respect traditional Aboriginal values and teachings. These can be conceptualized along a continuum based on different degrees of specialized knowledge. It needs to be stressed that the use of these practices should adhere to the protocols and traditions that exist within the particular culture. In this section, we briefly summarize some of these practices.

The circle is commonly used as a traditional model or method of practice, and circles can also be used in the educational process (Graveline, 1998). Most circles adhere to the principle of confidentiality: issues raised and discussed within the circle remain there. Sharing and healing circles are based on the principle that healing begins with an understanding of self. Each person is encouraged to participate in sharing personal experiences within the circle; however, all individuals make a choice about the depth and level of sharing with which they feel comfortable. Ceremonial items such as the eagle feather, sweet grass, or other medicines may be

Figure 11.2:   Back to the Future: Using Traditional Knowledge as Guidelines to Collective Empowerment

Note: The three outer-most circles define different eras in Aboriginal history. Of these, the circle closest to the centre identifies the pre-contact era, when society was based on the clan system with complementary roles and responsibilities. The second circle identifies the effects of colonization, and the third circle proposes principles for Aboriginal healing and empowerment based on traditional values and practices relevant to a post-colonial era. The development of this model acknowledges contributions from those who have struggled to keep cultural knowledge and traditional practices alive. These include elders, traditional teachers, and those who have passed to the Spirit World. Contributions from David Blacksmith, Wilfred Buck, Larry Morrissette, Linda Clarkson, Robert Daniels, Marilyn Fontaine, and Judy Williamson helped inform this model.

used in conjunction with circles, and it is common to circulate an eagle feather, stick, or stone around the circle as each person speaks. Some circles are support oriented while others are more therapeutic in focus. For therapeutic circles, a good facilitator is essential.

Antone and Hill (1990) describe four types or levels of circles: talking circles, sharing circles, healing circles, and spiritual circles. The talking circle involves the discussion of issues or topics, and related feelings and body pain may be identified. Talking circles can be used in a wide variety of circumstances to facilitate group communication. The sharing circle involves telling one's life story and sharing more intimate feelings with others. A high degree of trust and self-disclosure enables an individual to release painful emotions with the support of others. The healing circle involves connecting with the body for the release of painful emotions. Full self-disclosure is key to the healing process. The spiritual circle incorporates attributes of other types of circles; in addition, it encourages people to use their intuitive ability to tap into unconscious memories. The intent is to reconnect with the individual's spiritual gifts, which can then be reclaimed or strengthened. At this stage, forgiveness is possible, and cultural teachings and practices are integrated as aspects of one's life.

Ceremonies play a particularly important role in traditional practices. These may include the use of smudge (i.e., burning sweet grass) as a cleansing process, the use of the purification ceremony (commonly called the 'sweat lodge'), the pipe fast (often called the 'vision quest'), naming ceremonies, and the sun dance. The infusion of these ceremonies into the treatment process is often referred to as the 'red road approach' (Nabigon & Mawhiney, 1986). Although social workers need to have some knowledge of such approaches, these methods of practice are carried out by elders and traditional teachers.

The medicine wheel is an important and powerful construct that can be used to assist both the assessment and intervention processes in social work practice. For example, Nabigon and Mawhiney (1986) demonstrate how the Cree medicine wheel can be used to guide assessment and intervention in healing individuals, groups, and communities. Longclaws (1994) uses the Anishinabe medicine wheel to illustrate how traditional practices are organized within a holistic framework to address needs that arise during the life cycle. The medicine wheel approach to healing includes several important principles. First, there is an emphasis on the personal or the 'inner journey' needed to begin the healing process. Understanding and healing begin at the individual level and move to encompass others, including all living things and one's relationship with the environment and the Creator. Second, the concept of balance between the four directions—the east (spiritual), the south (emotional), the west (physical), and the north (mental)—is critical to healing and to living a balanced, healthy life. The four directions can be used to identify and analyze issues that the individual, family, organization, and community need to address in order to restore balance. A third principle is the importance of the spiritual. While this is not necessarily regarded as more important than other dimensions, it is often neglected in more conventional practice models.

The medicine wheel has also been used as an organizing framework for program and community planning. West Region Child and Family Services (1993) used teachings from the medicine wheel to design a model for dealing with family violence in the First Nations communities that they served. The medicine wheel was also used as an organizing framework for the community healing model developed at Hollow Water for dealing with sexual abuse (Aboriginal Corrections Policy Unit, 1997). The healing approaches included in this model focus on the victim, offender, their families, and the community in a series of thirteen steps based on a circle approach to healing. This service model has enabled the community to begin to break the cycle of abuse; in addition, the outcomes, measured in terms of recidivism rates, are as good or better than those associated with purely conventional approaches.

Cultural methods of practice do not exist in isolation. As indicated, they are closely connected to belief systems about a specific problem or context. It follows that culturally appropriate interventions with Aboriginal people may involve the development of a number of different approaches and policies within any particular field of practice. Examples from the field of child welfare can be used to illustrate this general point. First, Aboriginal control over child welfare services has led to a model of alternate care that prioritizes placements with extended family, other families within the local community, and resources that include caregivers with a cultural background similar to that of the child. Second, a child-saving orientation is replaced with a stronger emphasis on family support and community building. Finally, the principle of permanency planning, where priority is given to placement within a permanent home, even if this is outside the cultural and familial context, is modified in favour of an intermittent flowing pattern of care. Such an option places more emphasis on community and family connections, even if this includes several caregivers (Ricks, Wharf, & Armitage, 1990, p. 43).

Conclusion

This chapter has outlined a general framework for social work practice with Canadians of Aboriginal background. It includes five general guidelines, which, we argue, will help to develop cultural competence for social work with Aboriginal people. These guidelines are: to understand the world view of Aboriginal people and how this differs from the dominant Euro-Canadian world view; to recognize the historical and continuing effects of colonization on Aboriginal people; to understand the importance of Aboriginal identity to healing; to recognize the value of cultural knowledge and traditions and to be able to appropriately incorporate these in practices oriented to healing and empowerment; and to be aware of the diversity of Aboriginal cultural expression and the manner in which this diversity affects identity formation and approaches to social work practice.

These guidelines suggest that effective social work practice with Aboriginal people and communities must reflect a commitment to both political and personal change. Political objectives are associated with the concept of social justice and strategies that incorporate an agenda for decolonization and community building. Such strategies will be determined and led by Aboriginal people, which is consistent with principles associated with empowerment. Social work practice is also concerned about personal change and the connections that must be made between the personal and the political. The Aboriginal concept of healing, and the role of culture in helping to shape the nature and scope of this journey, is particularly relevant to this dimension of practice.

The effects of colonization have continuing implications for Aboriginal social work practice because they shape many of the initial meanings attached to the roles of service user and social worker, particularly if that worker is non-Aboriginal. In a sense, all of us carry the baggage of colonization, either as victims or oppressors. This role may also be affected by the institutional role associated with the employing agency. For example, if a social worker is employed by a child welfare agency, the social control role associated with this function represents another potential barrier to relationship building.

Aboriginal social workers have several potential advantages in providing services to other Aboriginal people. First, the initial ability to establish trust based on shared history and world view may be enhanced. Although social workers from the same community as clients will share a sense of community history, they may also have to contend with family or community expectations that may conflict with their professional responsibilities. Second, Aboriginal social workers may possess cultural knowledge, including language, that enhances cultural competence and communication with clients. Knowledge of an Aboriginal language is particularly important in facilitating communication, especially for those service users who are more comfortable communicating in their own language. However, it is important to note that not all Aboriginal social workers possess cultural knowledge and skills pertaining to traditional practices. In addition, non-Aboriginal social workers provide a wide range of services to Aboriginal people. Thus, the development of Aboriginal cultural competence is an important priority for social workers in general.

Aboriginal cultural competence begins with an understanding of the effects of oppression, particularly in relation to colonization, and an ideological commitment to the aspirations of Aboriginal people as self-determining. Such a commitment includes the right to institutional control over their own services and the provision of social work services informed by cultural practices and traditions. A second requirement is cultural learning. After a social worker has acquired knowledge about Aboriginal cultures, he or she can move to the development of cultural competence through the development of skills that will enable effective social work practice within a particular Aboriginal culture, or across cultures. A basic understanding of colonization and a general commitment to Aboriginal aspirations are important, but these elements should not be equated with cultural competence. Indeed, the integration of knowledge and self-reflection with practice skills to achieve cultural competence is a complex process. For example, the assessment stage in practice must include attention to the psychosocial effects of colonization and other forms of oppression. Interventions can then be designed to promote personal healing and change oppressive social conditions. Methods should include the use of indigenous strategies, as appropriate. The utilization of local community and cultural resources reinforces a strengths approach, and resources such as elders and extended family are particularly important. Finally, the use of culturally based standards for evaluating success is important. Essential to the evaluation stage is the willingness of the social worker to engage in the process of mutual learning, where efforts are made to incorporate community and cultural standards that do not contradict more universal principles based on social justice.

The development of skills for social work practice with Aboriginal people is not confined to practice wisdom gained through experience. Indeed, more attention should be devoted to the integration of cultural learning in social work programs. As well, the development of cultural competence requires a commitment to continuous learning based on collaboration and partnerships with Aboriginal people affected by these services.

References

Aboriginal Corrections Policy Unit. (1997). *The Four Circles of Hollow Water*. Ottawa: Supply and Services Canada.

Absolon, K., & Herbert, E. (1997). Community action as a practice of freedom: A First Nations perspective. In B. Wharf & M. Clague (Eds), *Community Organizing: Canadian Experiences* (pp. 205–27). Toronto: Oxford University Press.

Antone, B., & Hill, D. (1990). Traditional healing: Helping our people to heal. Unpublished paper, Tribal Sovereignty Associates, P.O. Box 4066, Station C, London, ON.

Assembly of First Nations (2000). *First Nations and Inuit Regional Health Survey*. Ottawa: Assembly of First Nations.

Berger, P., & Luckmann, T. (1967). *The Social Construction of Reality*. New York: Anchor.

Clarkson, L., Morrissette, V., & Regallet, G. (1992).*Our Responsibility to the Seventh Generation: Indigenous People and Sustainable Development*. Winnipeg: Institute of International Sustainable Development.

Compton, B.R., & Galaway, B. (Eds) (1994). *Social Work Processes*. 5th ed. Pacific Grove, CA: Brooks/Cole.

Delaney, R. (1995). Social policy: A Northern perspective. In R. Delaney & K. Brownlee (Eds), *Northern Social Work Practice* (pp. 230–1). Thunder Bay, ON: Lakehead University Centre for Northern Studies.

Drost, H., Crowley, B.L., & Schwindt, R. (1995). *Marketing Solutions for Native Poverty*. Toronto: C.D. Howe Institute.

DuBray, W. (1985). American Indian values: Critical factors in casework. *Social Casework*, 66, 30–7.

Ermine, W. (1995). Aboriginal epistemology. In M. Battiste & J. Barman (Eds), *First Nations Education in Canada: The Circle Unfolds* (pp. 101–12). Vancouver: UBC Press.

Ewalt, P.L., Freeman, E.M., & Poole, D.L. (1998). *Community Building: Renewal, Well-Being and Shared Responsibility*. Washington, DC: NASW Press.

Federal, Provincial and Territorial Advisory Committee on Population Health. (1999). *Toward a Healthy Future*. Second Report on the Health of Canadians. Ottawa: Government Services Canada.

Fox, J., Manitonabi, D., & Ward, J.A. (1984). An Indian community with a high suicide rate. *Canadian Journal of Psychiatry, 29*, 425–7.

Fleras, A., & Elliott, J.L. (1999). *Unequal Relations: An Introduction to Race, Ethnic and Aboriginal Dynamics in Canada*. 3rd ed. Scarborough, ON: Prentice Hall.

Frideres, J. (1998). *Aboriginal Peoples in Canada: Contemporary Conflicts*. 5th ed. Scarborough, ON: Prentice Hall.

Good Tracks, J.G. (1973). Native American non-interference. *Social Work, 18*(6), 30–5.

Graveline, F.J. (1998). *Circle Works: Transforming Eurocentric Consciousness*. Halifax: Fernwood.

Green, J.W. (1995). *Cultural Awareness in the Human Services*. 2nd ed. Boston: Allyn and Bacon.

Gutiérrez, L., GlenMaye, L., & DeLois, K. (1995). The organizational context of empowerment practice: Implications for social work administration. *Social Work, 40*(2), 249–58.

Hamilton, A.C., & Sinclair, C.M. (1991). *The Justice System and Aboriginal People*. Report of the Aboriginal Justice Inquiry of Manitoba. Vol. 1. Winnipeg: Queen's Printer.

Heilbron, C.L., & Guttman, M. (2000). Traditional healing methods with First Nations women in group counselling. *Canadian Journal of Counselling, 34*(1), 3–13.

Joint Management Committee (2001). *Aboriginal Justice Inquiry: Child Welfare Initiative: Promise of Hope, Commitment to Change*. Winnipeg: Manitoba Family Services and Housing. Retrieved from: www.aji-cwi.mb.ca.

Kawulich, B.B., & Curlette, W.L. (1998). Life tasks and Native American perspectives. *Journal of Individual Psychology, 54*(3), 359–67.

Kellough, G. (1980). From colonialism to economic imperialism: The experience of the Canadian Indian. In J. Harp & J.R. Hofley (Eds), *Structured Inequality in Canada* (pp. 343–77). Scarborough, ON: Prentice Hall.

Labonté, R. (1990). Empowerment: Notes on professional and community dimensions. *Canadian Review of Social Policy, 26*, 64–75.

Lee, K. (2000). *Urban Poverty in Canada: A Statistical Profile*. Ottawa: Canadian Council on Social Development.

Longclaws, L. (1994). Social work and the medicine wheel framework. In B.R. Compton & B. Galaway (Eds), *Social Work Processes*. 5th ed. (pp. 24–33). Pacific Grove, CA: Brooks/Cole.

McCormick, R.M. (2000). Aboriginal traditions in the treatment of substance abuse. *Canadian Journal of Counselling, 34*(1), 25–32.

McKenzie, B. (1995). *Aboriginal Foster Care in Canada: A Policy Review.* Unpublished Report for the Royal Commission on Aboriginal Peoples. Ottawa.

———. (1997). Connecting policy and practice in First Nations child and family services: A Manitoba case study. In J. Pulkingham & G. Ternowetsky (Eds), *Child and Family Policies* (pp. 100–14). Halifax: Fernwood.

———. (1999). Empowerment in First Nations child and family services: A community-building process. In W. Shera & L.M. Wells (Eds), *Empowerment Practice in Social Work* (pp. 196–219). Toronto: Canadian Scholars' Press.

McKenzie, B., & Hudson, P. (1985). Native children, child welfare, and the colonization of Native people. In K. Levitt & B. Wharf (Eds), *The Challenge of Child Welfare* (pp. 125–41).Vancouver: UBC Press.

McKenzie, B., Seidl, E., & Bone, N. (1995). Child and family service standards in First Nations: An action research project. *Child Welfare, 74*(3), 633–53.

Magstadt, T.M., & Schotten, P.M.(1988).*Understanding Politics: Ideas, Institutions and Issues.* New York: St Martin's Press.

Manitoba Bureau of Statistics (1997). *Manitoba's Aboriginal Populations Projected 1991–2016.* Winnipeg: Manitoba Native Affairs Secretariat.

Manitoba Joint Committee on Residential Schools (1994). *Proposal for a Manitoba Healing and Resource Centre for First Nations Affected by Residential Schools.* Winnipeg: Assembly of Manitoba Chiefs.

Miller, J.R. (1996). *Shingwauk's Vision: A History of Native Residential Schools.* Toronto: University of Toronto Press.

Morrissette, V., McKenzie, B., & Morrissette, L. (1993). Towards an Aboriginal model of social work practice: Cultural knowledge and traditional practices. *Canadian Social Work Review, 10*(1), 91–108.

Mullaly, B. (1997). *Structural Social Work: Ideology, Theory and Practice.* 2nd ed. Toronto: Oxford University Press.

Nabigon, H., & Mawhiney, A. (1986). Aboriginal theory: A Cree medicine guide for healing First Nations. In F.J. Turner (Ed.), *Social Work Treatment: Interlocking Theoretical Approaches.* 4th ed. (pp. 18–36). New York: Free Press.

Nichol, R. (2000). *Factors Contributing to Resilience in Aboriginal Persons Who Attended Residential Schools.* Unpublished MA thesis, University of Manitoba, Winnipeg.

Ontario Native Women's Association. (1989). *Breaking Free: A Proposal for Change to Aboriginal Family Violence.* Thunder Bay, ON: Ontario Native Women's Association.

Overholt, T., & Callicott, J.B. (1982). *Clothed-in-Fur and Other Tales: An Introduction to an Ojibwa World View.* Washington, DC: University Press of America.

Red Horse, J. (1980). Family structure and value orientation in American Indians. *Social Casework, 61,* 462–7.

Ricks, F., Wharf, B., & Armitage, A. (1990). Evaluation of Indian child welfare: A different reality. *Canadian Review of Social Policy, 25,* 41–7.

Ross, R. (1992). *Dancing with a Ghost: Exploring Indian Reality*. Markham, ON: Octopus.

Royal Commission on Aboriginal People (1996). *Report Summary*. Report of the Royal Commission on Aboriginal People. Available: inac.gc.ca/rcap/report/index.html.

Rubin, H.J., & Rubin, I.S. (2001). *Community Organization and Development*. 3rd ed. Boston: Allyn and Bacon.

Saleebey, D. (Ed.) (1997). *The Strengths Perspective in Social Work Practice*. 2nd ed. New York: Longman.

Statistics Canada (1998). *1996 Census: Aboriginal Data*. Retrieved from: www.statcan.ca/ english/census96/jan13/can.html.

——— (2000). *Aboriginal Population by Age Groups, 1996 Census*. Retrieved from: www.statcan.ca/english/Pgdb/People/Population/demo38c.htm.

Voss, R.W., Douville, K., Little Soldier, A., & Twiss, G. (1999). Tribal and shamanic-based social work practice: A Lakota perspective. *Social Work, 44*(3), 228–41.

Walters, K.L. (1999). Urban American Indian identity attitudes and acculturation styles. *Journal of Human Behavior in the Social Environment, 2*(1/2), 163–78.

Waywayseecappo First Nation (1992). *Waywayseecappo Spousal Abuse Program*. Waywayseecappo, MB: Waywayseecappo First Nation.

Weaver, H.N., & White, B.J.(1997). The Native American family circle: Roots of resilience. *Journal of Family Social Work, 2*(1), 67–79.

Weaver, S. (1993). First Nation women and government policy, 1970–1992: Discrimination and conflict. In S. Burt, L. Code, & L. Dorney (Eds), *Changing Patterns: Women in Canada* (pp. 92–150). Toronto: McClelland and Stewart.

West Region Child and Family Services. (1993). *The Medicine Wheel Approach to Dealing with Family Violence*. Rolling River, MB: West Region Child and Family Services.

Williams, E.E., & Ellison, F. (1996). Culturally informed social work practice with American Indian clients: Guidelines for Non-Indian social workers. *Social Work, 41*(2), 147–51.

Chapter 12

The Franco-Ontarian Community: From Resistance to New Social Solidarity and Practices

David Welch

The purpose of this chapter is not to present an exhaustive study of the Franco-Ontarian community, but rather to highlight some of the elements that contribute to an understanding of the social construction of the community and the development of some of its social practices. During this process, we discuss some of the main socio-economic transformations of this community that, in turn, have transformed social practices that led to new ways in which the community sees and defines itself.

The historical patterns of settlement are examined first, followed by the development of some of the community's social practices and institutions, most notably those in social and health services and, to a limited extent, in schooling. Emphasis in terms of the examination of social services is placed on developments in the last thirty years. The chapter will discuss Franco-Ontarian resistance to policies imposed by the anglophone majority as well as resistance to practices imposed by internal elites, including the Roman Catholic Church. It will also review some of the ways in which the community has adapted and continues to develop. Finally, it will examine some of the new social practices now being developed within the Franco-Ontarian community, which can be seen as alternatives to existing ways of doing things.

It is important to keep in mind that Franco-Ontarians have not been passive objects in the development of their community and of Ontario; they have been active participants who have made particular social and economic choices. These choices have permitted the Franco-Ontarian family and community to survive and, in turn, have helped to assure its continual development.

The Early Development of Social Institutions and Practices in French-Speaking Ontario

Early French-Canadian Settlement in Ontario

The earliest permanent French-speaking settlement in Ontario was established in 1749, when French Canadians settled near a Huron village along the south shore of the Detroit River, across from Fort Detroit (now the city of Detroit, Michigan), which had been founded in 1701. In order to avoid harming the lucrative fur trade and draining population away from the scattered settlements along the St Lawrence River, agriculture was developed only enough to feed the local garrison and fur traders. Consequently, the number of families was small and the population relatively mobile.[1] This early population gradually increased and took up new lands along the south shore of Lake St Clair. As new settlers arrived from Quebec in the 1840s, the French-Canadian population increased: by 1871 there were about 14,000 French Canadians in this region, in Kent and Essex counties (Brodeur, 1979).

The Ottawa Valley lumber industry brought the first French Canadians into eastern Ontario. As seasonal workers, thousands of young French-Canadian men worked in the woods in the winter and on the timber rafts down the Ottawa and St Lawrence Rivers in the spring, returning to Lower Canada (Quebec) in the summer (Greening, 1972). By the 1840s, French Canadians began taking up land in the counties of Prescott and Russell, the low, flat, swampy lands between the Lower Canadian border and the emerging city of Bytown, later called Ottawa. The region's proximity to Lower Canada, the union of Upper and Lower Canada into the province of Canada in 1841, and the common economic forms within the French-Canadian community all helped to transform the community into a single social and economic entity on both sides of the Ottawa River. Furthermore, in founding the diocese of Ottawa in 1847, the Catholic Church included territory from what would become in 1867 Ontario and Quebec. By the 1880s, the majority of the population in Eastern Ontario was French Canadian (Choquette, 1984; Gaffield, 1987).

From its beginnings, Ottawa, which was founded in 1827 at the time of the construction of the Rideau Canal, was always at least 25 per cent French Canadian, a segment of the population that was concentrated in Lower Town, around the market. This working-class population, whose men laboured in the local lumber mills, very quickly founded its own parishes and social, health, and educational institutions (Brault, 1942; Vallières, 1980).

Further French-Canadian settlement in Ontario occurred in 1828, when the British military base on Drummond Island was moved to Penetanguishene, on the shores of Georgian Bay. Many French-Canadian and Métis voyageurs followed, to be joined in the 1840s by settlers from Lower Canada. Some of the new arrivals took up land, while others worked in the expanding lumber mills along Georgian Bay (Marchildon, 1984).

The building of the Canadian Pacific Railway (CPR) in 1882–3 brought the first French Canadians to northeastern Ontario (Brandt, 1979). Thousands of French Canadians from Quebec and eastern Ontario worked on the construction gangs.

Encouraged by the CPR (which wanted to sell land along the railway) and by the Catholic Church (which was seeking to stop the exodus of French Canadians to the New England cotton mills), families took up land in the region. Later, as mines were opened and new towns, situated around the sawmills, were founded, more French Canadians moved into the region. By 1901, there were 15,000 French Canadians, constituting about 42 per cent of the population (Brandt, 1976). Although the northeastern part of the province was settled at different times, from the 1880s until the 1930s, the various French-Canadian agricultural settlements, being generally homogeneous, followed quite closely the familiar patterns seen earlier in eastern Ontario and Quebec, with life centred around the parish.[2]

The National Policy of 1879 promoted industrial development in Canada and led to the migration of thousands of French Canadians to the emerging industrial centres of Ontario, stanching, to some extent, the flow to the New England states. By 1881, there were 2,230 French Canadians in Toronto (Trudelle & Fortier, 1987); in 1931, there were 4,846 in Cornwall, concentrated in the textile industry (Scheinber & McIntosh, 1995; Sylvestre, 1984). Much the same process occurred in Welland during the First World War (Schneiderman, 1972; Trudel, 1982). As in the more rural areas, the population tended to settle around their own French parishes and schools, and often chose to work in factories where French Canadians were concentrated, thus assuring the daily use of the French language in spite of their minority status.

The Beginnings of French-Language Social Services

One of the earliest examples of social organization within the Franco-Ontarian community was the volunteer work done by women, both in the cities and the rural areas. Women worked as midwives or healers and they organized community services. As well, the community established various charitable institutions—hospitals, orphanages, and shelters for the aged—usually under the direction of women's religious congregations. Situated mainly in Ottawa and Sudbury, these institutions remain even today prominent in the larger community. For instance, the Hôpital général d'Ottawa was founded in 1845 to serve the Catholic community, largely French Canadian. In the same city, St Joseph's orphanage was founded in 1865 and the St Charles home for the aged in 1871 (Brault, 1942). Later, similar institutions were founded in northeastern Ontario. The development of and interaction between these community social practices laid the foundation for today's French-language social services in Ontario.

By the beginning of the twentieth century, women had begun to set up their own autonomous (i.e., independent from male organizations) organizations in order to better deliver social services to the community. One of the most important organizations was the Fédération des femmes canadiennes françaises (FFCF), founded in 1914 by Almanda Walker-Marchand (Desjardins, 1991). Though its initial mission was to assist in the war effort, very quickly the FFCF expanded to the various parishes across French Canada outside of Quebec and began to diversify its work to the larger social service field (Brunet, 1992). For instance, in 1916 and in 1921, the FFCF gave relief to many of the victims of the devastating forest fires that raged across northeastern Ontario. The FFCF was, to a large extent, a national organizaton, and in 1923–4 it affiliated with the Canadian Council on Child Welfare. Later, in the 1930s, the FFCF became very active in the struggle of the Dionne family to regain custody of their quintuplets. It also worked to ensure that the girls received Catholic and French-language schooling (Welch, 1994–5).

In 1937, the Union catholique des fermières de l'Ontario (UCFO) was founded, with the expressed aim of increasing social services, especially in the rural areas. Not unlike the FFCF, the UCFO was one of many Franco-Ontarian women's groups that remained closely linked to the Catholic Church, with the mission of providing social services to the poorest sectors of the community.

There were also volunteer organizations that had both social and economic objectives. The Saint Vincent de Paul Society, founded in Ottawa by French Canadians in 1860, was responsible for giving help to the poorest families in Lower Town, a largely French-Canadian neighbourhood of Ottawa. In 1874, members of the society asked for meat from the local butchers and heating wood from the local saw mills and farmers to ensure that the poorest survived the winter (Brault, 1942). During the economic crisis of 1875–80, along with the Soeurs de la Charité, the Saint Vincent de Paul Society organized a community kitchen for the poor.

To help combat unemployment during the Great Depression of the 1930s, the Franco-Ontarian elite and its main umbrella organization, the Association canadienne-française d'éducation de l'Ontario (ACFEO), founded the Oeuvre des Chômeurs, an early form of unemployment centre for young men. The centre offered direct financial aide, housing for those most in need, and counselling to help the unemployed find work. It hoped that its activities within the Franco-Ontarian working class would counterbalance whatever influence the Communist Party might have with young unemployed men (Gravel, 1980). At the same time, the ACFEO began looking at ways to create a youth centre for young Franco-Ontarians to counterbalance the YM/YWCA, which was seen as a Protestant, anglophone organization. In 1957, the Patro St Vincent was founded as a sport and recreation organization for young boys.

In the mid-nineteenth century, under the leadership of both lay and religious elites, Franco-Ontarians began setting up co-operatives. One of the first was a mutual aid society called the Union St-Joseph (now Union du Canada), which was initially founded by French-Canadian workers in 1863 in Ottawa. In its early years, the society had only about 700 members; however, by 1910 its membership had increased to around 8,000, and it had 145 local councils around the province. The insurance policies covered from 50,000 to 60,000 persons out of a total Franco-Ontarian population of about 203,000 (Comeau, 1982). The Union St-Joseph, in spite of its co-operative spirit and its aim to furnish non-profit services, rejected all social and economic practices that might have been seen as promoting state intervention. Although it was ready to defend the identity interests of Franco-Ontarians, the union rejected any state intervention on social issues as being too socialistic or communistic (Grimard & Vallières, 1986). This narrow social and economic vision would best be summed up in a book published in 1939. The author, Charles Leclerc, wrote that: 'la Saint Joseph s'inscrit en faux contre les doctrines entachées de socialisme, qui demandent à l'État de se constituer en une sorte de providence, qui veulent faire peser sur tous les citoyens indifféremment le poids de la subsistance d'un certain nombre, qui veulent tuer l'initiative individuelle, et entraver la compétition. . . . Plutôt que de verser, même modérément, dans les théories à saveur socialiste, elle rappelle que le Christ a dit qu'il y aurait toujours des pauvres et que c'est eux qu'il a aimés'[3] (Leclerc cited in Grimard & Vallières, 1986, p. 195).

The same vision of Franco-Ontarian self-reliance was present in the founding of the first caisses populaires, a form of parish credit union. The ones in Ontario were established on much the same model as those in Quebec; indeed, Alphonse Desjardins, who had founded the first caisses populaires in Quebec, resided in Ottawa for many years. The caisses, which grew quickly in number after the Second World War (a period when Franco-Ontarians were able to save, seeing prosperity, often for the first time), allowed community members to save and borrow, thereby ensuring that money stayed in the community. Today, the various caisses populaires in French-speaking Ontario have over $4 billion in deposits.

From the eighteenth century onwards, French Canadians established their own autonomous schools. As restrictions were placed on these schools in the 1880s, and later, especially between 1912–27, Franco-Ontarians undertook large-scale campaigns of civil disobedience. This resistance to state oppression allowed the French-speaking Catholic Church to become far more active in the social and economic life of the community, over time becoming, in a sense, the main governing institution (Choquette, 1984). At the same time, there was some resistance to educational models imposed on the community by the church, especially when this led to higher taxes on the largely impoverished population (Welch, 1993). As a result of continual resistance by the community against state educational policies, the provincial government was forced over time to recognize the language rights of Franco-Ontarians and, thereby, certain limits to its own state power.

In contrast to their relative autonomy in educational matters, Franco-Ontarians had little control over health and social services, and most of these services that developed in Ontario, other than those administered by French-speaking religious congregations and charitable organizations, were unilingual English. Often these services were administered by non-profit organizations, such as Children's Aid Societies, functioning almost entirely in English, regardless of their funding sources, even in cities such as Ottawa and Sudbury that had large Franco-Ontarian minorities. French-language services became increasingly marginalized as new state-funded services were organized; the most vulnerable were particularly affected by this marginalization of French-language services (Carrière, 1995; Pettey & Ouimet, 1988).

This indifference to francophone needs can be understood when one remembers that French Canadians remained excluded from positions of economic and political power. In the industrial workforce, francophones never rose above the level of foremen; they forever remained the subsistence farmers, the lumberjacks, the servants, the semi-skilled railway workers, and the surface workers for the mines. The inequalities of capitalism along with hostility against French Canadians excluded them from positions of any influence over the wider socio-political institutions of the province.

During the 1930s and the 1940s, contrary to the situation in Quebec, where the state supported many of the initiatives that emerged out of civil society, the Ontario government, closely linked to the interests of capital, gave far less support to various co-operative projects, even less to those of the Franco-Ontarians. Thus, the social and economic projects of the community, whether of the private or public sector, were born and nurtured on the margins of the activities of the dominant English-speaking society. In spite of their limits, these various initiatives showed Franco-Ontarians that they were capable of organizing themselves and of creating and managing new organizations that were a reflection of their own community.

From this brief outline of Franco-Ontarian settlement patterns and the creation of distinct social institutions, certain conclusions can be drawn. From the beginning of permanent European colonization in Ontario during the eighteenth century, Franco-Ontarians have played an active role in the economic and political development of the province (Jaenen, 1993; Welch, 1988). Founding relatively homogeneous villages, throughout eastern, northeastern, and southwestern Ontario, the French Canadians who moved to Ontario managed to preserve many of their unique cultural forms. Their social and economic strategies allowed them to survive—'continuing to live when others have disappeared or perished'—even though they were 'on the frontier of the dominant economic system' (Berger, 1979, pp. 196–9). In many regions there were enough Franco-Ontarians to establish schools, parishes, social organizations, and, later, co-operatives and caisses populaires. Many of these same patterns were reproduced in the urban centres of Ottawa, Cornwall, Hawkesbury, Sudbury, Toronto, and Welland. These first initiatives, whether in schooling or the social and health services, were marked by the large-scale mobilization of women, farmers and workers. Working together, usually as volunteers, they founded a multitude of self-help and pressure groups that led to new social and economic forms such as co-operatives.

The autonomous institutions that were created laid the basis for a Franco-Ontarian civil society that, over time, gave the community a distinct social life and the means to distribute resources within the community. Although they were a minority within the province, Franco-Ontarians continued to see themselves as being part of a larger French-Canadian society, with links to French Canadians elsewhere, including the Franco-Americans of New England.

Many of the organizations founded by Franco-Ontarians, and under the leadership of the emerging middle class, had a very conservative moral vision. Their aim was to help the less fortunate without questioning the underlying social and economic inequalities that existed. In spite of the limits of their actions, their strategies built on a belief in social solidarity and assured the survival of Franco-Ontarians as a distinct community in a larger society that was undergoing very rapid change.

Accelerated Urbanization and Transformations in Franco-Ontarian Institutions

The period during and after the Second World War, with its rapid industrial expansion, saw the complete transformation of the economic and socio-cultural face of Ontario. The province completed its transformation to industrial capitalism, becoming more and more integrated into the North American economy. These changes had an important impact on the Franco-Ontarian community. In the space of only a few years, the community went through a massive population displacement from the countryside to the regional cities of the north, and from the north to the industrial cities of the south. Parallel to these demographic changes, thousands of Québécois and Acadians settled in the manufacturing cities of southern Ontario and in some of the mining cities in the northern part of the province (Vallières, 1980).

This increased proletarianization led to new identities, embodied, for example, in unions, which led to new social relationships within the community and to frequent conflicts between the expanding working class and the various elites, who had differing class interests. Frequently, the traditional Franco-Ontarian elite did not support miners and lumber workers as they fought to improve their working conditions; in some cases they openly supported the mine owners (Arnopolous, 1982; Pelletier, 1987). To help temper these social and economic changes, Franco-Ontarians established new institutions (schools, caisses populaires, recreation centres) that were better adapted to the urban environment.

It is important to note that many Franco-Ontarians experienced a rapid improvement in their standard of living and general working conditions after they abandoned subsistence agriculture and forestry. In the mines and the pulp mills, in construction, in the factories, and in the ever-expanding service sector, wages increased far more quickly than the cost of living. However, the transition did not improve the economic situation of all Franco-Ontarians. Unionization had led to better wages for many, but there remained a segment of the population without the skills to profit from postwar prosperity, living in either rural or urban poverty and forming a kind of economic underclass. Many Franco-Ontarians, along with the Québécois and Acadians who had left the rural areas of their respective provinces for Ontario cities, continued to feel the effects of over a hundred years of economic subsistence. Often with few of the necessary skills, and with high rates of illiteracy, they found it difficult to profit from the economic opportunities offered by the city, regardless of the region. For these people, being French Canadian continued to mean a life of poverty and misery, perpetuating in the city the historic conditions of the countryside. In a sense, the country had followed them to the city.

With greater industrialization and urbanization, and with the disappearance of subsistence agriculture and forestry, Franco-Ontarian women had a lesser role to play in direct economic production, giving them less recognition and status within the family. Even on the remaining farms, mechanization resulted in less need for the farm work of the wife and children. The gap between the public world of waged work and the private lives of women, organized primarily around childrearing and domestic labour, widened (Proulx, 1982, 5). Women were limited to the home and the constant care of children, leading to their greater social isolation. The state gradually took over many of the tasks centred around the social services formerly provided informally by women, and it now demanded credentials that most women did not have. In northeastern Ontario, the best-paying jobs were in the mining and lumber industry, both of which excluded women, limiting them to low-paying service jobs and making them even more financially dependent on men. Thus, urbanization and better wages, though improving the situation of Franco-Ontarian men, in many cases did little in the short term to change the situation of Franco-Ontarian women. As families migrated to the cities and their children became even more exposed to the dominant Anglo-Canadian culture, the tasks of women, who were seen as the principal defenders of the language and culture, became even more demanding. Many experienced feelings of guilt when, in some cases, their children lost use of the French language.

Urbanization and industrialization increased the dangers of assimilation. As they became more urbanized, Franco-Ontarians tended to use the social and health services of the majority, which operated almost solely in the English language. Schooling faired somewhat better: in the north and the east, Franco-Ontarians frequently dominated the separate (Catholic) school boards. In the south, new schools were created only after strong opposition from the existing English-speaking Catholic boards.

The Franco-Ontarian Community and New Relationships with the State

In the 1960s, the Ontario government became far more interventionist in almost all sectors of socio-economic life, as did the governments of the other provinces. In the name of reform and the improvement of society, the Ontario government spent millions of dollars to transform educational, social, and health services across the province. The 1960s also brought about greater recognition of Franco-Ontarian rights, most notably through new legislation that allowed the establishment of solely French-language elementary and secondary schools. The federal Official Languages Act (1969), following the recommendations of the Royal Commission on Bilingualism and Biculturalism, also helped to increase the bilingual presence in federal government institutions, especially in the Ottawa area. These reforms coincided with the breakdown of what had been referred to as French-Canadian society, a sense of a common identity across French Canada, constructed around the Catholic Church and a common language (Martel, 1997). During the 1960s, people began to see themselves differently, identifying more with their province, seeing themselves as Québécois, Franco-Ontarians, Franco-Albertans, and so on.

These changes over the course of the 1960s led to a historical transformation in the attitudes of the Franco-Ontarian elite towards the state, especially at the provincial level. Traditionally, the religious and secular elites had turned to the family and to religious institutions for the protection of Franco-Ontarian identity as well as for the development of educational, social, and health services. Secularization and greater state intervention increased the distance between the elites and their community, and people looked outside the community for resources (Carrière, 1993; Juteau and Séguin-Kimpton, 1993). In the future, the rights won from the state, and responsibilities delegated by it, would increasingly determine the power and influence of the Franco-Ontarian elite and the degree of autonomy the community would retain.

Even with the right to new schools, struggles between Franco-Ontarian community organizations on one side and many English-speaking Ontarians and the government on the other continued for another fifteen years before a relatively complete network of French-language secondary schools was established across the province. These struggles—in places such as Kapuskasing, Penetanguishene, Iroquois Falls, Sturgeon Falls, Windsor, and Mattawa, to name only a few locales—led, in turn, to many divisions within the Franco-Ontarian community during vicious fights over the control of ever-decreasing resources (Welch, 1991–2). Moreover, it took over twenty-five years to establish three French-language community colleges in the province.

In the arena of social services, it was only in the 1970s in eastern Ontario and in the early 1980s in northeastern Ontario that the provincial government began to allocate funds for French-language services. Because there were no obligations to provide services in French, both government agencies and private state-subsidized organizations did little to increase services to the French-speaking population (Carrière, 1995). The Franco-Ontarian community remained dependent on the limited French-language services offered on a voluntary basis and, decreasingly, by religious institutions. Yet, more and more of the old French-language or bilingual hospitals, usually in areas with a concentrated Franco-Ontarian population, were being replaced by new facilities, that, while providing better services, tended to function far more in English than in French. Thus, in some cases, in the name of modernity, Franco-Ontarians lost control of institutions that they had managed for generations.

Franco-Ontarians also lost control of their neighbourhoods. For example, in the name of urban renewal and in spite of large-scale opposition, large parts of Lower Town in Ottawa, once about 80 per cent French speaking, were demolished. The establishment of low-rent housing brought in non-francophone people; other renovations brought in a wealthier English-speaking population. Lower Town is now only about 40 per cent francophone. In the process, the social fabric of the neighbourhood was destroyed, eliminating many of the collective self-help projects. The same process happened in the Moulin à Fleur neighbourhood in Sudbury and in the Sacré-Coeur parish in the Cabbagetown area of Toronto. In the new suburbs of Ottawa, Sudbury, and Toronto, it became difficult to re-create a similar community life: there was now greater dispersion of the population, and greater distances between schools and community centres. New social practices tended to be centred around middle-class interests, leaving less for the original working-class culture that once flourished in the inner cities.

In some ways, the French Language Services Act (1986) was an important step forward for the Franco-Ontarian community. A victory after years of pressure from the Franco-Ontarian community, it assured that, in certain designated areas of the province, provincial government services would be provided in both English and French. Its application showed a somewhat increased respect for the 550,000 Franco-Ontarians in the province, and had, as a secondary effect, the creation of hundreds of jobs for community members in public and semi-public services. However, all municipal services were excluded from the act, and non-governmental agencies receiving government funding were left to decide for themselves if they wanted to apply for bilingual service designation (Carrière, 1994). Even in cities such as Ottawa, which has declared itself bilingual, services for the francophone population are often not clearly defined and are left to the good will of public servants. Frequently, given the cutbacks of the past ten years, designated positions remain unfilled by bilingual personnel, or they are filled by people speaking very little French.

New Visions, New Social Practices

New social practices have emerged out of the many reforms that directly affected the Franco-Ontarian community since the 1960s. As the state was pushed to grant greater recognition and space to the Franco-Ontarian community, many Franco-Ontarians turned away from the more traditional elite to a more 'modern' one, advocating the importance of working with the government to bring about what were perceived as needed reforms. Others went even further and sought French-language services distinct from, but parallel to, those offered in English (based in part on the New Brunswick model of services), rather than spending huge amounts of energy on attempting to make existing English-language services bilingual.

Out of these various mobilizations, some social practitioners went beyond the historic demands for French-language services. They began advocating for the establishment of totally new services that were not simply translations of English-language services with all their 'professionalism' and lack of citizen participation. These advocates proposed original, more democratic, social practices that reflected the culture and needs of the community, especially its more vulnerable members (C'est le Temps, 1981, p. 112; Tissot, 1981, p. 95). This process re-enforced a break with the traditional leadership, who frequently remained far more preoccupied with increasing the number of educational institutions and who tended to ignore the importance of developing social services (Coderre and Dubois, 2000). It was as if the elite perceived social services to be solely for 'the less fortunate' or 'those with problems', an attitude that demonstrated a difficulty in understanding that new daycare centres, or shelters for women victims of violence, were real community needs that touched all sectors of the community.

Some of the most dynamic alternative projects have come out of various women's organizations, around the need for better daycare, shelters for battered women, and immigrant information services for women. In some cases, new organizations were created—for example, Ontaroises de l'Est, Franco-femmes in the northern part of the province, and the Réseau des femmes du Sud de l'Ontario in the south (Cardinal & Coderre, 1990). In other cases, some of the more traditional women's organizations restructured their activities, integrating new perspectives and objectives.

Other community practitioners become directly involved in economic as well as social issues. They actively supported striking forestry workers during the Elk Lake mill strike of 1980 in northeastern Ontario and the AMOCO textile strike of 1981 in eastern Ontario (Andrew, Archibald, Caloren, & Serge, 1986). They also supported striking Union du Canada office workers, although this went against the tradition of not striking against the co-operative movement. These actions were new attempts to link social issues with the basic economic realities of many of the community members, even when this meant coming into conflict with the more traditional leadership.

In the 1970s and 1980s, social activists recognized the importance of the welfare state in financing the multitude of projects that were cropping up in French-speaking Ontario. Franco-Ontarians were not only trying to 'catch up' to the anglophone majority, but were proposing new ways of looking at and doing things. Although such reassessments led to frequent tensions among Franco-Ontarians as to what should be prioritized, few people questioned the greater reliance of the community on the financial resources of the provincial government. Some raised the issue that large numbers of the most active people in the Franco-Ontarian community were enticed into jobs with state agencies, thereby creating a 'brain drain' away from the various regions and towards government ministries in Toronto. Even those who continued to work independently frequently found themselves dependent on the government for continued funding of their activities, making them vulnerable to cutbacks (Welch, 1995).

Owing in part to the relative openness of the Peterson Liberal and the Rae NDP governments to French-language services, few questioned the tendency of the provincial government to impose conditions on the forms these services might take. This facilitated an increase in government power to define what might be considered proper boundaries for Franco-Ontarians and to determine, to a certain extent, what were and what were not acceptable practices. This greater dependency, which some characterized as co-opting, made it more difficult for Franco-Ontarians to work out their own compromises or to adapt to rapid changes within and outside their community, and in turn to create their own collective solutions (Welch, 1995). Most of the demands of the community did little to question established notions of the social, economic, and political order.

Neo-conservatism and Its Effects on the Franco-Ontarian Community

The election of the Harris Conservative government in June 1995, with its cutbacks in social programs and transfer of government programs to the private sector, has had extremely negative effects on Franco-Ontarian social and educational institutions as well as community-based projects. Since the 1995 election, the policies of the Conservative government have put people on the defensive in an attempt both to retain what has already been won and to achieve further reforms. Neo-conservative notions that one succeeds or fails on one's own ability, hard work, risk taking, and personal initiative (Browne, 2000) and that there is no civil society, only individual enterprise and self-reliance, are attitudes that go against the historical understanding of many Franco-Ontarians, who believe that the 'social' does indeed exist and that society cannot be reduced to simple self-interest. They have learned over the years that the state's attempts to redistribute national wealth and assure a greater respect for minorities have generally benefited the community. People have discovered by trial and error that civil society, in spite of its limitations, has benefited the majority within the community and that the private sector has little interest in the limited benefits to be won from the social or educational needs of the Franco-Ontarian community.

On a number of levels, Franco-Ontarians remain vulnerable in this period of continuing cutbacks. The functional illiteracy rate within the community is about 25 per cent and many in the community are poor (Coderre and Dubois, 2000). Although the vast majority of Franco-Ontarians are urbanized, many are isolated and dispersed in small towns, far from the main networks of services. As is the case for other minorities, overall schooling costs for Franco-Ontarians have tended to be higher than those for the English-speaking majority, though their budgets have often been smaller. Because francophone students are relatively dispersed, transportation eats up a significant part of Franco-Ontarian educational budgets. French-language books are more expensive than their English-language counterparts, and schools tend to be smaller, leading to higher per capita costs. Any cuts in government funding can potentially be very harmful.

In spite of the progress made over the years, Franco-Ontarian institutions, which are generally more recently established and less wealthy than those of the majority, have had fewer reserves to cope with cutbacks. Many, such as the *centres medicosociaux communautaires* (French-language community health clinics), had only recently been created, with limited, and often special, funding. In other cases, such as shelters for battered women, one French-language institution must provide services to a very large area. Once this sole service is cut, the French-speaking population is left with only English-language services. In November 1995, for example, all funding for social services was cut at Toronto's *centre médico-social communautaire*, leaving 1,200 francophones without any services in their language. It was estimated that only about 5 per cent of the former clients had the financial resources to consult with a French-speaking social worker in private practice. Similar cuts occurred in Hamilton and Welland.

When cutbacks occur, the seniority rules and bureaucratic organization of many social services mean that, unless a position is designated as French language, French-speaking employees, who often have less seniority than their English-speaking counterparts, have been laid off or transferred and replaced by employees who speak only English. The ability to speak French and to have an understanding of some cultural aspects of the local community has often been overridden by other considerations.

One of the reasons the Harris cutbacks have hit Franco-Ontarians disproportionately hard is that, whether because they did not know about the programs or were not well placed to gain access to them, Franco-Ontarians were relatively slow in taking advantage of the willingness of preceding governments to fund new initiatives. As a result, Franco-Ontarians were only just establishing several new cooperative housing projects when the Harris government cut almost all funding for such projects in 1995.[4] As another example, French-language non-profit daycare was far less developed than that existing in English and has therefore been more affected by the cutbacks.

The trend of the Conservative government has been to cut overall funding and then leave the decisions on what to cut to the local communities.[5] This in turn has led to divisions within the community. People have been forced to: ask—and answer—very difficult questions. Do we cut salaries or jobs? Which services should be kept and which should be dropped? Since many of the parallel services established in recent years by Franco-Ontarians have been relatively small, such decisions have led to some bitter divisions among social practitioners, particularly in smaller communities.

Financial cutbacks have not been the only means by which to marginalize a community, or at least certain sectors of it. Closely linked to the actual cutbacks has been a vicious neo-conservative discourse that presents all demands that are contrary to a particular narrow view of society as being from a 'special interest group'. The Harris government broke any commitment to discuss policy with large sectors of civil society and accommodate their concerns, scorning the intermediary role that social organizations have historically played in Ontario. In June 1996, the government abolished without warning the twenty-five-year-old Conseil de l'éducation franco-ontarienne, a Franco-Ontarian advisory agency on all matters pertaining to schooling, including post-secondary education. Now, all decisions on schooling are in the hands of politicians and educational bureaucrats, leaving broad sectors of the community out in the cold. The government gives legitimacy to some groups and not to others, especially those seeking greater equality, notably for women, children, low-income people, people with disabilities, and visible minorities. Because so many Franco-Ontarians work directly or indirectly for state-funded institutions with the mandate of providing French-language services, family incomes have been left extremely vulnerable to cutbacks and the consequent layoffs.[6] In this context, not all Franco-Ontarians have been affected by cutbacks in the same way: important class, gender, racial, occupational, and regional differences exist.

Given its other destructive policies, it may at first seem surprising that the Conservative government has not sought to reform the French Language Services Act. Yet, why change something that already has so many exceptions to it? A more effective way has been simply to limit funding and to allow services to whither. An example of this trend was the cut in March 1996 of 35 per cent of the annual budget of l'Office des affaires francophones, the government commission that has as its mandate the protection of gains made under the French Language Services Act. Another danger for the community has been the tendency of the leadership to concentrate its energies on the protection of the French Language Services Act, while the Conservative government has cut welfare, education, social housing, community services, transfers to municipalities, and so on, thereby affecting the most vulnerable in the Franco-Ontarian community.

The cutbacks certainly led to an initial feeling of hopelessness within the Franco-Ontarian community. Franco-Ontarian social interventionists began voicing their opposition to government policies by refusing to participate in the government's dirty work of deciding who and what would be cut.[7] However, many community spokepersons, with the exception of certain women's groups, have tended to be low-key in their criticism, as if their silence will lead to Franco-Ontarians remaining unnoticed and therefore being less affected by the cuts! One notable exception ended up being one the largest mobilizations within the Franco-Ontarian community since restrictions on French-language schooling in the early twentieth century. A rally in Ottawa in March 1997 brought together over 10,000 people opposed to the closing of Montfort hospital, the only French-language university hospital outside of Quebec. This mobilization and the subsequent court decision resulted in the survival of the hospital, although service was cut back.[8]

Other Franco-Ontarians have proposed that, instead of trying to catch up to the majority by re-creating the same services in French, the community should begin looking at new alternative solutions that depend less on government control and funding and more on community creativity and resources. Based on years of involvement in the Franco-Ontarian community they have begun to pose new questions. Are some alternative projects less vulnerable to government cutbacks than others? What role should the state play in the continued development of the Franco-Ontarian community? In a milieu characterized by massive cuts and an unsympathetic government, the sense of social obligation that is a core value of many Franco-Ontarians has led some social service practitioners to seek new alternatives (Powell and Guerin, 1997).

Franco-Ontarian Alternatives in the Social Service Sector

Those who have been seeking new alternatives in social practices base their thinking on two premises. First, many have criticized the tendency of government to be too paternalistic, bureaucratic, and top-down in its dealings with the social sector. The welfare state has been shown to have important weaknesses and limitations. Second, some believe that, though the state has played a role in supplanting or absorbing some of the activities that had previously been the responsibility of the volunteer sector, it should be kept in mind that government policies and financial support have led to the formation of many new social practices (Browne, 2000). By studying the changing role of the state, and how civil society is changing its social and economic role, we can better grasp the role of new approaches to social and community development, and how this role might change over time.

Contrary to what neo-conservatives proclaim, many social interventionists and professionals have not been blind defenders of the status quo in education and social services. On the contrary, they have been critical of the increasing bureaucratization and dehumanization of the state and its actors, be they teachers, community activists, or social workers. In recent years, the notion that social issues are merely 'technical problems to be resolved administratively by experts, instead of political issues to be resolved through a democratic process by service users and providers' (Browne & Landry, 1995, p. 111) has been contested. At least since the 1970s, some Franco-Ontarian social activists have been critical of the welfare state, not limiting their criticisms to issues of weaknesses in the provision of French-language schooling and services. Yet, while criticizing government as being too rigid, hierarchical, and impersonal, these activists have continued to defend the notion that the state has an important role in providing, through the system of taxation and disbursement, the financial means for organizations to provide services as defined democratically by the community.

In recent years, these advocates have been supporting the struggle for lesser government control but, at the same time, have rejected the transfers of service provision to the private sector. Many Franco-Ontarians have realized that the private sector, with its notions of profit, makes many of the vital services needed in the community simply uneconomical, except for the wealthiest. Consequently, they have defended the idea that, although funding and overall regulation should be provided by the state, these funds should be transferred to community-based groups, which can better mobilize volunteer efforts while providing the necessary services. In practice, this can lead to a greater number of options, since the community-based groups would be alternatives to state agencies, thereby providing 'the advantage of the qualitative (flexibility, proximity to clients, capacity for innovation, etc.) and quantitative (expected lower costs)' (Browne & Landry, 1995, p. 370). As pointed out above, Franco-Ontarian community service providers would also provide services that better respect both the language and culture of the community. It is not a question of 'better managing poverty and social exclusion' (Ninacs, 1998, p. 31) but rather an attempt to link present-day practices with those of the past, urban practices with those of the rural areas, and social issues with those that are more economic in nature. This means that the state must respect the autonomy of organizations within civil society, so that they can continue to be strengthened with a diversified presence and with a recognized legitimacy to participate in problem solving. In the end, respect for this autonomy becomes a means of strengthening both citizenship and democracy (Ninacs, 1998).

When we speak of *civil society*, we are referring to the multitude of social spaces, groups, and organizations that have been created by citizens outside the formal arena of the state and the market sector and that might, at times, appear to be a form of 'creative chaos' (Powell and Guerin, 1997, p. 25). As has been shown earlier in this chapter, civil society that goes back to the beginnings of the Franco-

Ontarian community has remained one of the key building blocks of this community. Over time, this presence of an active civil society has resulted generally in increasing trust and co-operation, leading to relatively high levels of social cohesion within the community. In these times of rapid social change and cutbacks in many social sectors, some Franco-Ontarians regard their community organizations as one means by which they can win back the social, economic, and even political power that they have lost. In a sense, people recognize that democracy has permitted the growth of civil society and that, in turn, civil society has permitted the development of a more effective and more inclusive democracy—one that, in spite of its limits, has benefited Franco-Ontarians.

At the same time, it is important to keep in mind that civil society remains a terrain of struggle that is mined with frequently undemocratic power relations and many different forms of exclusion. Franco-Ontarians have, at times, lived the contradiction where different people with opposing interests within the community can all sing the praises of civil society, without recognizing unequal power relationships. Many strong advocates of civil society can also be defenders of the status quo or can have conservative views about any notion of bottom-up democracy.

In different parts of the province, Franco-Ontarians have been looking for new ways to cope with cutbacks and develop new alternatives. In Sudbury, women's groups have combined their services, not only to save money but also to provide support for women directly affected by the government's measures. A women's work co-operative is one initiative to create new jobs for women based on local needs and talents. In Hearst, a city in northeastern Ontario, a women's co-operative tree nursery, the Maison verte, was founded in 1981 under the direction of a local women's group called Parmi-elles. Starting up with some federal funding, the project has provided eight full-time and about thirty-five part-time jobs. The participants are now growing millions of tree seedlings and garden plants and are building new greenhouses to grow tomatoes for the local market (Kihumbi, 1999).

In Noëlville, a small town near Sudbury, a new co-operative was founded that brought together the social and economic needs of the town. The Coopérative de santé et de logement de la Rivière-des-français, which currently has three hundred, members was founded in 1997 to provide a series of health and social services, including a housing co-operative for seniors so that they might remain in the immediate region. Rather than concentrating the housing in one town, it is to be shared among three villages. When completed, the various projects will have created at least fifteen new jobs, and the same number indirectly (Dennie, 1999b).[9]

On a larger scale, Franco-Ontarian women participated in the organization of the International Women's March that was held throughout the world in October 2000. In collaboration with anglophone groups, Franco-Ontarian women's groups sought to unite their struggles with others across the world in the struggle against poverty and violence against women (Gérome, 2000). Previous to the October demonstration, many related activities were organized for Franco-Ontarian women in the province.

These few examples show that the institutions of the Franco-Ontarian community, not unlike those in many other communities living in Ontario and elsewhere in Canada, are up to the challenge of providing new forms of services and even job creation.[10] Starting from grassroots initiatives, although they have recognized the importance of government funding and sought its assistance, they have attempted to avoid the over-professionalization of state agencies. At the same time, they have been confronted by the challenge of avoiding these same tendencies within their own organizations, of becoming too bureaucratic, too professionalized, and, in the end, anti-democratic. New forms of social practice have permitted these organization to reach populations that have often been neglected, notably francophone immigrants (especially women) and those with relatively little schooling.

Alternatives have helped to rekindle self-confidence in communities that, over the years, have suffered losses in population (especially younger people), and local actions have reinforced sentiments of social solidarity. As had often happened in the past, new practices have helped reinforce existing French-language institutions and have helped to create new ones often better adapted to new needs in the communities (Coderre and Dubois, 2000; Bagaoui and Dennie, 1999; Welch 1999). A final challenge has been the need to avoid becoming inward-looking, thereby developing other forms of intolerance and exclusion, and to find new ways of uniting their actions with those in other communities who have common interests. It has become a 'struggle between very different values; the logic of competition versus the logic of community; the logic of machines and machine efficiency versus the logic of people trying to make a life for themselves and participate meaningfully in their society' (Menzies, 1996, p. xv). In the end it becomes a question of whether 'the local [will] be an extension of global uniformity, or the global [will] be an extension of local diversity' (Menzies, 1996, p. 19).

Conclusion

The different social practices in the past and those of today have played a vital role in the survival and development of the Franco-Ontarian community. Although the early leaders of the community did not question the socio-economic status quo to any degree, they developed practices that permitted self-help and the means to help others in need. They aided in overcoming deficiencies in some basic needs such as housing, health, and schooling, to name only a few areas. But these practices also answered community preoccupations with retention of cultural identity, community recognition, and communitarization, or sense of community. In time, this sense of identity led to the creation of networks and the grounding of practices, customs, and traditions.

As government intervened far more within the community in the 1960s, and the welfare state was reaching its peak, many Franco-Ontarians began to recognize the importance that the state had in the development of new social projects. Social practitioners spent much of their energy in creating new French-language social services to answer the needs of their community. Others went further, seeking to develop services that went beyond a question of language and questioning the objectives and practices of more traditional social services. Such goals led to frequent conflicts with more traditional practitioners and with community leaders.

In recent years, with the crisis of the welfare state and the rise of neo-conservatism, new practices have been developed by practitioners who seek greater autonomy from the state while recognizing that the state has an essential role to play in developing overall policy around social issues and in the continued financing of the social services. These new social practices promote the notion that, although services are still financed by the state, they can be administered in a way that is more democratic and inclusive. Historically, Franco-Ontarians have been part of a frequently excluded minority, but they have continued to develop their creativity as a community. It is certainly not coincidental that many of the recent and most original social practices have come from low-income Franco-Ontarians, immigrant women, and those living in relatively isolated regions. It is out of these common, and yet diverse, efforts that new ways of seeing and doing will continue to emerge, allowing new forms of social practice to be developed.

All these new actions lead one to ask how can people unite the new practices within the Franco-Ontarian community with those elsewhere. A start might be the formation of new alliances to develop power alternatives to the wealthy minority who control an ever greater part of the world's wealth and whose greed is leading the world to environmental and human destruction. As they have done in the past, Franco-Ontarians must continue to create alternative centres of power at the grassroots level, and must continue to be preoccupied with greater gender equality, the struggle against poverty, and a concern with the environment that permits the long-term sustainability of local communities and the active participation in decision-making by local communities (Langdon, 1999). For Franco-Ontarians, this focus entails making choices, as they have throughout their history, based on the options available, and, in turn, fulfilling them to bring about changes. In the end, Franco-Ontarians remain with a collective understanding that they have something to share together and with others—a desire to build a certain social consensus between people on what kind of world they want.

Notes

1. By 1786, the population on both sides of the Detroit River was about 2,000. Although the majority of the population was French Canadian, a significant new population was developing owing to the frequent marriages between French-Canadian men and Native women, thereby creating a particular symbiotic relationship between Native women and the French-Canadian fur traders. By the late eighteenth century in the Great Lakes region, a new nation, known as the Métis, was emerging—a people who were neither French Canadian nor Native, but who spoke French as well as Native languages, were Catholic, and worked for the fur companies (Peterson, 1985). Penetanguishene, founded by Métis

and French-Canadian voyageurs, was another example of these permanant French-Canadian and Métis settlements (Marchand, 1989).

2. It was in this environment that the Dionne quintuplets were born. Their grand-parents had come from Quebec in the 1890s to settle in the region around Corbeil. Out of the 104 families in Corbeil, 102 were French Canadian (Welch, 1994–5).

3. 'The Saint Joseph condemns those ideologies that are tainted with socialism, for they demand that the State act as a kind of providence by imposing on all citizens the duty of looking after a certain number. These ideologies seek to destroy all individual initiative and prevent competition . . . rather than fall, even moderately, into the trap of socialistic theories. One must remember that Christ said that there would always be the poor amongst us and it is them that he has loved most of all.' [my translation]

4. The Coalition franco-ontarienne sur le logement estimated that only about 2 per cent of co-op housing projects had been directed towards francophones, even though they form 5 per cent of the population. However, in 1994 in Ottawa, it was estimated that about 50 per cent of the new co-operative housing projects accepted by the NDP provincial government that year were directed towards the French-speaking community, when the community formed only about 25 per cent of the total population (Pilon 1994). Of the 385 co-op housing projects stopped by the Harris government, 13 were for francophones (Racine, 1995).

5. The effects of downloading responsibilities on local municipalities with fewer resources was seen in May 2000 in Walkerton, Ontario. The province had closed its own water-testing labs, forcing municipalities to rely on private labs that charged twice as much. Regular inspections were stopped after the layoff of a large number of Ministry of the Environment employees. Lab reports were no longer sent to either the Ministry of the Environment or the local district health council. In the end, in order to save money, Walkerton, along with many other municipalities, simply cut corners—in this case, with fatal results.

6. It has been estimated that, in the mid-1990s, about 32.5 per cent of Franco-Ontarians, as opposed to 25.4 per cent of anglophones, worked in the public and para-public sectors (Grenier, 1996).

7. For instance, in March 1996, a representative from the Social Services Department of the Regional Municipality of Ottawa-Carleton came to speak to a group of French-speaking community workers about what role they might play within the context of the Harris government's plans regarding workfare for those receiving social assistance. The community representatives present angrily made it very clear that they were unwilling to do the government's work and betray the very population with whom they have been working over the years. They made it clear that, with regard to workfare or any other program perceived to be coercive, the regional government was on its own.

8. The optimism of the community was dashed when, in December 1999, the provincial government decided to appeal a divisional court decision that

ordered that the Montfort hospital be kept opened to prevent the assimilation of Franco-Ontarians. The government appeal stated that it had no obligation to prevent Franco-Ontarian assimilation and that the lower court decision distorted the Canadian Constitution. The Ontario Court of Appeal that gave its decision in December 2000 rejected the appeal of the Ontario government by stating that the government had not given 'serious consideration to the importance of Montfort to the Survival of the Franco-Ontarian minority'. In February 2002 the provincial government announced that it would not appeal to the Supreme Court.

9. Although there are many new social practices being developed in French-speaking Ontario, in the past they have often not been documented. Since 1995, a new journal called *Reflets: Revue ontaroise d'intervention sociale et communautaire* is being produced jointly by the schools of social work at Laurentian University and the University of Ottawa. Because researchers and social activists are thus being encouraged to write articles, more of these new practices are being documented and studied. For instance, an article by Coderre and Dubois (2000) documented a number of very creative projects in low-income Franco-Ontarian neighbourhoods of Ottawa.

10. Presently, there are at least twenty relatively new community economic development projects in French-speaking Ontario that are seeking to link social issues with local economic development (Dennie, 1999a).

References

Andrew, C., Archibald, C., Caloren, F,. & Serge, D. (1986). *Une communauté en colère: La grève contre Amoco Fabrics à Hawkesbury.* Hull, QC: Éditions Asticou.

Arnopoulos, S.M. (1982). *Hors du Québec point de salut?* Montreal: Libre Expression.

Bagaoui, R., & Dennie, D. (1999). Le développement économique communautaire: Nouveau départ pour le mouvement associatif Franco-Ontarien? *Reflets: Revue ontaroise d'intervention sociale et communautaire, 5,* 1, 75–94.

Berger, J. (1979). *Pig Earth.* London: Writers and Readers Publishing Cooperative.

Bouchard, L., & Cardinal, L. (1999). Conditions de possibilités des services en français en Ontario dans les domaines de la santé et de services sociaux: Un enjeu pour les femmes, *Reflets: Revue ontaroise d'intervention sociale et communautaire 5,* 2 , 111–22.

Brandt, G. (1976). *J'y suis, j'y reste: The French Canadians in Sudbury, 1883–1913.* Unpublished PhD dissertation, York University, Toronto.

———. (1979). The development of French Canadian social institutions in Sudbury Ontario, 1883–1920. *Revue de l'Université Laurentienne, 11,* 2, 5–12.

Brault, L. (1942). *Ottawa, capitale du Canada de son origine à nos jours.* Ottawa: Éditions de l'Université d'Ottawa.

Brodeur, R. (1979). *Villages et visages de l'Ontario français.* Toronto: TV Ontario.

Browne, P.L. (2000). The neo-liberal uses of the social economy: Non-profit organizations and warfare in Ontario. In E. Shragge & J-M. Fontan (Eds), *Social Economy: International Debates and Perspectives*. Montreal: Black Rose Books.

Browne, P.L. & Landry, P. (1995). The 'third sector' and employment. Unpublished paper, Canadian Centre for Policy Alternatives, Ottawa.

Brunet, L. (1992). *Amanda Walker-Marchand (1868–1949): Une féministe*. Ottawa: L'interligne.

Cardinal, L. (1990). Reconnaître une histoire: Le mouvement des femmes francophones hors Québec. *Femmes d'action, 19*, 15–16.

———. (1991). Éducation et identité: L'expérience des femmes francophones vivant en milieu minoritaire. *Éducation et francophonie: femmes et éducation, 19*, 3, 23–6.

———. (1992a). Théoriser la double spécificité des Franco-Ontariennes. In M.-L. Garceau (Ed.), *Relevons le défi! Actes du colloque sur l'intervention féministe dans le nord-Est de l'Ontario* (pp. 177–88). Sudbury, ON: Université Laurentienne.

———. (1992b). La recherche sur les femmes francophones vivant en milieu minoritaire: Un questionnement sur le féminisme. *Recherches féministes, 5*, 1, 5–29.

Cardinal, L., & Coderre, C. (1990). Les francophones telles qu'elles sont: Les Ontaroises et l'économie. *La revue du Nouvel-Ontario, 12*, 151–81.

Carrière, F. (1993). La métamorphose de la communauté franco-ontarienne, 1960–1985. In C.J. Jaenen (Ed.), *Les Franco-Ontariens* (pp. 305–40). Ottawa: Les Presses de l'Université d'Ottawa.

Carrière, R. (1994). La loi 8 et les services sociaux destinés aux familles francophones. Paper presented at the *Colloque familles francophones: Multiples réalités*, Sudbury, ON, 3–5 November.

———. (1995). La loi 8 et les services sociaux destinés aux familles francophones. In C. Bernier, S. Larocque, & M. Aumond (Eds), *Familles francophones: Multiples réalités* (pp. 279–91). Sudbury, ON: Institut franco-ontarien.

C'est le temps, groupe (1981). Se prendre en main. *Revue du Nouvel-Ontario, 3*, 110–14.

Choquette, R. (1984). *L'Église catholique dans l'Ontario français du XIX siècle*. Ottawa: Édition de l'Université d'Ottawa.

Coderre, C. (1995). Femmes et santé, en français s'il vous-plaît. *Reflets: Revue ontaroise d'intervention sociale et communautaire, 1*, 2, 3–71.

Coderre, C., & Dubois, M. (2000). Solidarité et citoyenneté : Initiatives pour contrer la pauvreté chez les francophones dans Ottawa-Carleton. *Reflets: Revue ontaroise d'intervention sociale et communautaire, 6*, 2, 61–86.

Comeau, G. (1982). *The role of the Union Saint Joseph du Canada in the Organization of the Association canadienne-française d'Ontario*. Unpublished MA thesis, University of Montreal.

Desjardins, M. (1991). *Les femmes de la diaspora canadienne-française: Brève histoire de la FNFCF de 1914 à 1991*. Ottawa: Fédération nationale des femmes canadiennes-françaises.

Dennie, D. (1999a). Entrevue avec Éthel Côté, directrice générale du Conseil de la coopération de l'Ontario. *Reflets: Revue ontaroise d'intervention sociale et communautaire, 5,* 1, 18–25.

———. (1999b). Je refuse de laisser mourir mon village. *Reflets: Revue ontaroise d'intervention sociale et communautaire, 5,* 1, 152–8.

Gaffield, C. (1987). *Language, Schooling, and Cultural Conflict.* Montreal: McGill-Queen's University Press.

Gérôme, M. (1996). Bénévolat des femmes vieillissantes à l'aube de l'an 2000. *Reflets: Revue ontaroise d'intervention sociale et communautaire, 2,* 2, 58–81.

———. (2000). La marche mondiale des femmes en l'an 2000 en Ontario français. *Reflets: Revue ontaroise d'intervention sociale et communautaire, 6,* 1, 192–6.

Gravel, J. (1980). *Quelques aspects de la vie des franco-ontariens durant les années de la Grande Dépression (1930–1939).* Unpublished MA thesis, York University, Toronto.

Greening, W.E. (1972). The lumber industry in the Ottawa Valley and the American market in the nineteenth century. *Ontario History, 62,* 134–6.

Grenier, G. (1996). Analyse de la performance économique de la population franco-ontarienne. Paper presented at the *Colloque l'Ontario français, valeur ajoutée?* Université d'Ottawa, 26 April.

Grimard, J., & Vallières, G. (1986). *Travailleurs et gens d'affaires canadiens-français en Ontario.* Montreal: Éditions Études Vivantes.

Jaenen, C.J. (Ed.) (1993). *Les Franco-Ontariens.* Ottawa: Presses de l'Université d'Ottawa.

Juteau, D., & Séguin-Kimpton, L. (1993). La collectivité franco-ontarienne: Structuration d'un espace symbolique et politique. In C.J. Jaenen (Ed.), *Les Franco-Ontariens* (pp. 265–304). Ottawa: Presses de l'Université d'Ottawa.

Juteau-Lee, D. (1983). Ontarois et Québécois: Relations hors-frontières? In D.R. Louder & E. Waddel (Eds), *Du continent perdu à l'archipel retrouvé: Le Québec et l'Amerique francaise.* Québec: Presses de l'Université Laval.

Juteau-Lee, D., & Roberts, B. (1981). Ethnicity and Femininity: (d')après nos expériences. *Revue canadienne des études ethniques, 8,* 1, 1–23.

Kihumbi, M. (1999). La Maison verte: Un cas réussi de développement économique communautaire. *Reflets: Revue ontaroise d'intervention sociale et communautaire, 5,* 1, 176–83.

Langdon, S. (1999). *Global Poverty, Democracy and North-South Change.* Toronto: Garamond.

Marchand, M. (1989). *Les voyageurs et la colonisation de Pénétanguishene (1825–1871): La colonisation française en Huronie.* Sudbury, ON: La Société historique du Nouvel-Ontario.

Marchildon, D. (1984). *La Huronie.* Ottawa: Le Centre franco-ontarian de ressources Pedagogiques.

Martel, M. (1997). *Le Deuil d'un pays imaginé: Rêves, luttes et déroute du Canada français. Les rapports entre le Québec et la francophonie canadienne (1867-1975).* Ottawa: Presses de l'Université d'Ottawa.

Menzies, H. (1996). *Whose Brave New World?* Toronto: Between the Lines.

Mianda, G. (1998). Être une immigrante noire africaine francophone à Toronto: Vécu et perception des rapports de genre. *Reflets: Revue ontaroise d'intervention sociale et communautaire, 4*, 1, 34–52.

Michaud, J. (1999). Les femmes francophones et le travail obligatoire: Un enjeu pour l'économie sociale. *Reflets: Revue ontaroise d'intervention sociale et communautaire, 5*, 1, 95–113.

Ninacs, W.A. (1998). *A Practitioner's Perspective on the Social Economy in Quebec.* Victoriaville, Quebec: Human Resources Development Canada.

Pelletier, J. (1987). *Le conflit minier.* Toronto: TV Ontario.

Peterson, J. (1985). Many roads to Red River: Métis genesis in the Great Lakes region, 1680–1815. In J. Peterson, & J.S.H. Brown (Eds), *Being and Becoming Métis in North America.* Winnipeg: University of Manitoba Press.

Pettey, D., & Ouimet, R. (1988), *Quand je suis malade, je ne suis pas bilingue.* Ottawa: Association canadienne pour la santé mentale, Section d'Ottawa-Carleton.

Pilon, F. (1994). 360 logements pour les francophones. *Le Droit*, 26 August.

Powell, F., & Guerin, D. (1997). *Civil Society and Social Policy: Voluntarism in Ireland.* Dublin: A. & A. Farmer.

Proulx, P. (1982). *La part des femmes il faut la dire.* Ottawa: La Fédération des femmes canadiennes-françaises.

Racine, J-L. (1995). Des couts considérables et une injustice flagrante aux francophones. *Le Droit*, 1 August.

Scheinber, E., & McIntosh, R. (1995). *The Mills of Cornwall: Family, Work and Ethnicity in a Late Nineteenth Century Ontario Town.* Paper presented to the Canadian Historical Association, 25–27 August, Montreal.

Schneiderman, E. (1972). *A Community Profile of Welland, Ontario's French-speaking Population.* Unpublished MA thesis, University of Buffalo.

Sylvestre, P. (1984). *Cornwall.* Ottawa: Le Centre franco-ontarien de ressources pédagogique.

Tissot, G. (1981). L'auto-détermination. *Revue du Nouvel-Ontario, 3*, 91–6.

Trudel, C. (1982). *Welland.* Ottawa: Association des enseignants franco-ontariens.

Trudelle, C., & Fortier, P. (1987). *La paroisse du Sacré-Coeur: Toronto se raconte.* Toronto: La société d'histoire de Toronto.

Vallières, G. (1980). *L'Ontario français par les documents.* Montreal: Éditions Études Vivantes.

Welch, D. (1991–2). La lutte pour les écoles secondaires franco-ontariennes. *Revue du Nouvel-Ontario, 13–14*, 109–31.

———. (1994–5). The Dionne quintuplets: More than a showcase—Five Franco-Ontarian children. *Revue d'études canadiennes, 29*, 4, 36–64.

———. (1995). The Franco-Ontarian community and the provincial educational state: A relationship for greater self-autonomy or a new Trojan horse? *Canadian Ethnic Studies, 27*, 2, 145–65.

———. (1999). L'économie social en Ontario français: analyse historique, pratiques actuelles et recherche de sens. *Reflets: Revue ontaroise d'intervention sociale et communautaire, 5*, 1, 54–74.

Chapter 13

Social Work Practice with African Canadians: An Examination of the African–Nova Scotian Community

David Este and Wanda Thomas Bernard

Despite the longstanding presence of African Canadians in Canada, this community is virtually ignored in the literature dealing with social work practice in this country. This should not be surprising as, even today, the majority of texts used in Canadian schools of social work continue to reflect and articulate the Eurocentric perspective, which is still the dominant world view guiding social work practice. The majority of social work practitioners possess very little knowledge about the African-Canadian community, the prevailing issues that confront the community, and the particular strengths possessed by African Canadians as a collective entity. The lack of this knowledge leaves these individuals ill prepared to work effectively with African Canadians as individuals, as families, as groups, or at the community level. Quite frequently, the theoretical perspectives and interventions used by social work practitioners have limited value and, as a consequence, African Canadians continue to be an oppressed group within Canadian society.

Since the early 1990s, writers such as Christensen (2001, 1998, 1993), Thomas-Bernard, White, and Moore (1993), Daezner (1997) and others have attempted to fill this void in the Canadian social work literature. Despite these valuable contributions, the African-Canadian experience from a social work perspective continues to be marginalized. Although African Canadians represent only about 2 per cent of the total Canadian population, their exclusion from Canadian social work literature is not justified. A thorough understanding of the African-Canadian experience would necessitate that this community receive an increased visibility in all aspects of social work practice in this country.

One of the challenges associated with writing about social work practice and the African-Canadian community is that the community is not homogenous in nature.

There is considerable cultural variation in the community, with individuals and families coming from Africa, the Caribbean, and the United States. Much to the surprise of some Canadians, the community also includes African Canadians who are part of a long historical tradition in Canada.

The material in this chapter augments the existing literature on social work practice with all African Canadians. However, the specific focus of this material is on one of the oldest sectors of the community in Canada, African Nova Scotians. There are several reasons for focusing on this particular African-Canadian community. First, the African–Nova Scotian community is unique in the sense that it has been part of the Canadian landscape for well over two centuries. Second, the community also represents not only the largest group of African Canadians in the Atlantic provinces, but also, numerically, the largest group of African Canadians whose birthplace is Canada. Although the majority of the 573,860 Black Canadians reported in the 1996 census live in Ontario and Quebec, particularly in Toronto and Montreal, the same census indicates that 3.1 per cent of the African-Canadian population resides in the province of Nova Scotia. This represents a total of 18,105 African Nova Scotians (Statistics Canada, 1996); however, some believe that this is a conservative figure. Although there is a large concentration of African Nova Scotians in the Halifax-Dartmouth region, it is important to note that there are over forty African–Nova Scotian communities scattered throughout the province (Hamilton, 1994).

Another reason for the focus on the African–Nova Scotian community stems from the belief that the experiences of this community clearly illustrate that its social concerns are long-term in nature and provide a strong indication that traditional social work methods and practices have, for the most part, not changed the overall socio-economic status of most African Nova Scotians. In response to this situation, all human service programs should critically review their curricula to ensure that practitioners possess the knowledge base and skill competencies that are required to deal with the impact on African Canadians of decades of exclusion from virtually all aspects of Nova Scotian society, particularly the domains of education and employment.

This chapter is divided into three major sections. The first provides an introduction to the discipline of African-Canadian history with a historical review of the African–Nova Scotian community. This review establishes the context for understanding some of the prevailing social issues confronting the African–Nova Scotian community and the larger society in which this community is situated. Also provided are examples of how the African–Nova Scotian community, through its own initiatives, has attempted to deal with exclusionary practices of the dominant group. In the second section, a description of the Africentric[1] paradigm, which provides a blueprint for human service practitioners working with individuals, families, groups, and organizations within the community, is presented. This theoretical perspective provides both philosophical and practice principles that, ideally, should ensure that human service programs are responsive to the unique challenges that exist and, at the same time, utilize the strengths of African Nova Scotians and their communities. The chapter concludes with a discussion of some of the major social concerns confronting African Nova Scotians. This last section also presents pragmatic practice principles and strategies designed to ensure that social workers or other human service professionals working with the African–Nova Scotian community will be effective in enhancing the quality of life experienced by members of the community.

An African-Canadian Historical Perspective

The Discipline of African-Canadian History

Until recently, the historical experiences of African Canadians remained virtually neglected, despite the fact that members of this community have been part of Canadian society since the seventeenth century. Scholars such as Fred Landon and William Riddell wrote extensively on various aspects of the African-Canadian experience. However, the majority of Canadian social scientists ignored the contributions of African Canadians to Canadian society. Perhaps even more depressing is that many of the leading scholars were not even aware of the African-Canadian presence, thus reinforcing the image of African Canadians as the 'invisible people'. When African Canadians were discussed in general histories of Canada, they were referred to as 'Sambos' or 'savages from Africa' (Tulloch, 1975) or were referred to only by 'the standard and misleading references to the underground railroad' (Walker, 1980, p. 3).

During its embryonic stage, the discipline of African-Canadian history received a welcomed addition with the publication of Robin Winks's *The Blacks in Canada: A History* in 1971. Scholars working in the discipline subsequently rejected Winks's overall interpretation of African-Canadian history as a depressing story. However, the book made an important contribution: it was the first general survey on the subject matter and is filled with immense detail on a wide range of topics. Since the publication of this volume, several other accounts of the African-Canadian experience, both at a national and regional level, have been published. Some of these provide a balance to the negative portrayal presented by Winks.

A discrepancy exists within the discipline of African-Canadian history. Most of the research on African Canadians has concentrated on the experiences of groups in Nova Scotia and Ontario. Settlement patterns dictated the geographic focus of the research: the majority of Black immigrants, whether they were loyalists, refugees or fugitive slaves, settled in these two provinces. The early development of African-Canadian communities in Nova Scotia during the 1780s and Ontario during the 1820s, along with the presence of a relatively sizeable African-Canadian population in the provinces throughout their history, resulted in the development of a sustained African-Canadian historical tradition. More recently, research documenting the experiences of African Canadians in other parts of the country, most notably British Columbia, Alberta, and Quebec, has increased. As a result, a more complete profile of the African-Canadian experience exists, allowing historians and other social scientists to compare and contrast the experiences of African Canadians in different parts of the country.

Upon arrival in Canada, the majority of people of African descent attempted to integrate into the mainstream society, or at least expressed this desire. However, the presence of the 'colour line', or what is described by scholars such as Walker (1980) and Tulloch (1975) as subtle racism, effectively excluded the majority of African Canadians from becoming members of the broader society. When they attempted to pursue their rights, African Canadians were rebuffed. They were fighting racist attitudes, attitudes that could not be destroyed even when African Canadians protested their secondary status. Rejected by and alienated from the dominant group, African Canadians turned inwards and created their own institutions to help them survive. Reliance on their own institutions resulted in the formation and consolidation of a distinct culture (Walker, 1980, 1995).

African–Nova Scotian Community: A Historical Review

In order to comprehend the challenges confronting the contemporary African–Nova Scotian community, and the strengths possessed by this community in dealing effectively with prevailing social concerns, it is important to be aware of the historical experiences of this population. Because both individual members and the community as a collective entity continue to be affected by what occurred in the past, social work practitioners must have a firm understanding of what transpired in this history.

According to a number of scholars (e.g., Winks, 1997; Walker, 1995), the first person recorded as coming directly from Africa to what was to become Canada, and the first known African slave in Canada, was a young male who was baptized in 1633 as Oliver Le Jeune. This individual worked as a household servant for approximately twenty years. Slavery had reared its ugly head in New France as early as 1628. However, the phenomenon became more extensive in the eighteenth century, when both African and Indian slaves existed in the region. Walker (1995) contends that the majority of African slaves came from the French West Indies or the British colonies in North America.

The province of Nova Scotia was not an exception to the presence of this 'peculiar institution'. Prior to the American War of Independence, approximately one hundred slaves existed in the region. Pachai (1997) in his discussion on slavery writes, 'In September 1751, an advertisement appeared in the Boston Evening Post, offering ten Blacks from Halifax for sale; they were described as caulkers, carpenters, sail-makers and rope-makers. The sale of slaves by public auction was common in Nova Scotia in the eighteenth century' (p. 11). Following the American Revolution, approximately 1,200 Black slaves were brought to the Maritimes in 1783 with the White Loyalists who settled in the region (Walker, 1995).

The first major migration of Blacks to Nova Scotia occurred during and immediately after the American Revolution. Approximately 3,500 free Black Loyalists migrated to Canada, with the majority settling in the Maritimes. They ventured to Nova Scotia believing that they would receive large land grants, justice, education, and equal status with their White Loyalist counterparts. However, as noted by historians such as Walker (1976, 1980, 1995) and Pachai (1990), the British failed to live up to their promises. As Walker (1995) states, 'their [Black Loyalists'] civil rights were curtailed and there were many restrictions imposed on them by a White majority that considered them more suitable for slavery than for equality' (p. 142). The majority of Black Loyalists did not receive any land. Those who managed to obtain land settled in rural and isolated communities on barren lots. This pattern led to the development of separate Black settlements, with the largest community located at Birchtown, which had a population of over 1,500. Other communities were located at Brindley Town, Preston, and Little Tracadie (Walker, 1995).

With farming virtually impossible, given the inferior quality of the land, most of the Black Loyalists were forced to find some other means of supporting their families. Some became tenant farmers, renting land from White farmers under sharecropping agreements, while others became indentured servants. Yet, the majority of these African–Nova Scotian men and women worked as day labourers in the major towns. Walker (1980) notes that their employers exploited the Black Loyalists, paying them approximately one-quarter of the rate for Whites. The Black Loyalists performed a variety of tasks, including clearing land, laying roads, and erecting public buildings (Walker, 1980).

Failure of the British to fulfill promises made to the Black Loyalists served as a catalyst for two related experiences encountered by African Nova Scotians. First, because they were last in line, from an economic and social perspective, the negative experiences encountered by the Black Loyalists served as the beginning of over two centuries of racism, exploitation, and oppression by the politically, socially, and economically dominant group—White Nova Scotians. Second, the experiences fostered the emergence and development of a distinctive Black culture, which helped to sustain the strength and tenacity members of the African–Nova Scotian community required in order to survive and make meaningful contributions in a very hostile and demeaning environment.

The conditions experienced by the Black Loyalists became so deplorable that in 1792 when an opportunity to migrate from Nova Scotia emerged through the Sierra Leone Company, about 1,200 African Nova Scotians left for Sierra Leone in West Africa. In describing the reasons for this migration, Pachai (1997) remarks:

> They [the leaders] and their followers left because of a combination of three expectations that had remained largely unfulfilled: free grants of sufficient land, full independence and security of life and property. Even then, before their departure, they had to prove that they were free in status, free of debt and of character; furthermore their statements had to be certified by those of their countrymen [Whites] who were least willing to see them go because of their proven skills, cheap labour and market produce. (p. 20)

The mass exodus had detrimental effects on African–Nova Scotian communities. Several community leaders, such as the minister David George, departed. Initially, the economic status of those African Nova Scotians who remained did not change. However, Walker (1995) asserts that, within a decade after the exodus, the economic position of the community improved. African Nova Scotians who worked in indentured positions and as apprentices qualified in various trades, and the demand for labourers increased.

The second influx of Blacks to the province occurred during the summer of 1796, with the arrival of the Maroons from Jamaica. A very proud people, the Maroons were defeated during the British takeover of Jamaica. After they settled in the Halifax region, the Maroons worked as labourers in the building of the city's citadel. According to Walker (1980), attempts were made to convert the Maroons to Christianity and an agricultural mode of subsistence. However, these efforts were rejected by the Maroons and, after a four-year stay in Nova Scotia, most of this community also left for Sierra Leone.

In the early part of the nineteenth century, the Black community received another group of African Americans—the Black refugees from the War of 1812. The British adopted the same strategy they had used during the American Revolution, calling on the slave community to join the British in their struggle against the Americans. Once again, the promises of freedom and land were made. Approximately 2,000 Black refugees were located in the Maritimes, the majority within the Halifax region. Once they arrived in the province, the Black refugees were basically left on their own. Although they received clothing, provisions, and farm implements, once again the land they received was inadequate to sustain any type of economic independence. In describing the plight of this group of African Nova Scotians, Walker (1995) commented: 'At the same time, a post-war depression combined with the arrival of thousands of labourers from the British Isles meant there were fewer jobs available for the blacks. To supplement their government rations, they cut trees on their allotments for sale as firewood, and when that was gone, they attempted to find work with neighbouring White farmers or in the city of Halifax' (p.146). Public sentiment towards African Nova Scotians became more negative, and by 1815 the Nova Scotia assembly attempted to ban further Black immigration. White Nova Scotians believed that Black people were lazy and were consequently dependent on the White community; thus, they were seen as a negative influence on the economy (Walker, 1980, 1979).

In the face of their exclusion from the dominant group, and in reaction to discriminatory and racist behaviour by White Nova Scotians, African Nova Scotians established their own communities such as Preston, Hammond Plains, and Halifax. As part of their development process, these communities developed institutions that helped to preserve the unique history and contributions of the African Nova Scotians.

Walker (1979), Grant (1980), and Pachai (1990) all argue that the most important institution in African–Nova Scotian communities proved to be the church. David George, who arrived in Halifax in 1785, carried out most of the early religious work among the Black Loyalists. He contributed to the mass conversion of Black residents to the Baptist denomination. During the first half of the nineteenth century a Black Baptist revival took place, which resulted in the development of churches within the Black communities. The African Baptist churches provided

African Nova Scotians with a sanctuary in which to escape their day-to-day existence and, just as important, a place to worship. Walker (1979), in describing the role the Black churches played in the community, stated:

> The Black church harboured and succoured a distinct view of life that is rich and satisfying to its members. It is of course, a Christian definition of the meaning of life, a Gospel oriented definition that has survived despite the increasing materialization of mainstream society. If Blacks hold values that are distinct from White society's, those distinctions can be traced to the central importance of the Gospel in black community life, as preserved and transmitted by the Black church. (p. 27)

Walker also asserts that African-Canadian preachers provided leadership to Blacks and were instrumental characters who held the African–Nova Scotian communities together no matter how depressing their conditions: 'The Black pastors inevitably became the natural leaders of their local communities for they represented the first all-black institution in most of their congregations' lives' (Walker, 1979, pp. 86–7).

Education was highly valued by African Nova Scotians. Starting in 1785, schools were built for the Black Loyalists in centres such as Halifax, Preston, Brindley Town, Birchtown, and Shelburne. Walker (1980), in commenting on the provision of education, remarked: 'In each case [i.e., Black community] the teachers were local blacks and in most of them the teacher was also a preacher. . . . Each of the major black communities had its own school which, with the chapel, encouraged the development of a distinctive community spirit' (p. 34). As Grant (1980) notes, following the arrival of the Black refugees, other schools were established in Black communities. These schools proved to be important: for many decades, they provided the only formal education for Black children. The quest for education by African Nova Scotians remained a high priority during the nineteenth and twentieth centuries.

By the middle of the nineteenth century, the African-Canadian community in Nova Scotia was firmly entrenched. From 1861 to 1901, the population of the community experienced a slight increase. In 1861, there were approximately 5,900 Blacks residing in the province; in 1881, 7,062 persons of African descent were listed in the census (Grant, 1980).

During the period from 1854 to 1918, the most important institution in the community was the African United Baptist Association. The driving force behind this association was Richard Preston, who arrived in Halifax with the Black refugees in 1815. In 1832, after being ordained as a minister in London, he returned to Halifax, where he organized and assumed the leadership of the African Baptist Church on Cornwallis Street. For over twenty years Preston organized several Black Baptist churches throughout the province. In 1854, he convened a meeting of all Black Baptist churches to form a parent organization known as the African United Baptist Association (AUBA), an organization that is still in operation. It continues to deal with issues of racism and exclusion in all spheres of Nova Scotian society, concerns that were prevalent in the middle of the nineteenth century (Grant, 1980; Pachai, 1997; Walker, 1995). Through the AUBA, the affiliated Black Baptist churches served as vehicle for cementing social cohesion within African–Nova Scotian communities. The churches served as the focal point of community members for social, educational, and spiritual purposes. In the area of advocacy, the AUBA lobbied for equitable educational opportunities for African Nova Scotians. Education was believed to be the mechanism by which community members would enhance their social mobility and economic progress (Este, 1979).

The churches also provided opportunities for African Nova Scotians to enhance and develop their leadership skills. Throughout the community's existence, various church leaders have led the struggle against the racism, discrimination, and exploitation encountered by African Nova Scotians. Despite the work done by the AUBA in the area of education, the resistance put forth by the dominant culture for equitable education opportunities proved to be strong. Throughout the middle of the nineteenth century, school segregation for African–Nova Scotian children was the norm. During this period, Nova Scotia law allowed school commissioners from any municipality, with the approval of the government, the right to establish separate schools if they considered them necessary (Grant, 1980; Henry, 1973). However, only a limited number of these schools were established; the distinct residential separation of most African Nova Scotians itself resulted in the presence of segregated schools, a practice that existed in Nova Scotia until the 1950s (Winks, 1969; Walker, 1980).

Community leaders and parents realized that the presence of segregated schools meant unequal standards and inferior education. Walker (1995), in writing about the schooling system, commented that: 'Black schools in Halifax went only to the level of Grade 7. Teachers and equipment were inferior and common schools could refuse admission to black children even though black householders were paying taxes for those schools' (p. 160). He continues: 'the combination of provincial policies and racial discrimination ensured that many of Nova Scotia's black schools were in the hands of black teachers. It also ensured that black children did not generally receive an education equivalent to the one obtained by Whites. They entered the workforce, which limited their occupation horizons, their incomes and their status in the broader society' (p. 160). Yet, as highlighted in the BLAC Report on Education (1994), members of the African-Canadian community did not passively accept the status quo: 'Many lessons have been learned as one examines the history of education and the Black community in Nova Scotia. . . . The lessons also demonstrate centuries of incredible fortitude as Black Nova Scotians, especially in their role as parents, struggled to gain access to an education system that prepares the dominant population for a wide variety of roles in society while excluding Black children' (p. 1).

A number of important developments within the African–Nova Scotian community during the period from 1900 to 1930 demonstrated the desire possessed by African Nova Scotians to improve their circumstances in a province where racism and discrimination prevailed. The AUBA continued to be a dominant force within the community. Through its annual meetings, the association stressed the importance of strong, effective leadership and unity in the community. Pachai (1990) also notes that the association advocated pragmatic solutions to address the prevalent social and economic challenges facing African Nova Scotians. The array of contributions of the AUBA was quite remarkable, given that it did not have a centralized location from which it could direct its activities.

One of the reasons for the sustainability of the AUBA rests with the critical contributions of African–Nova Scotian women. These women recognized the importance of the churches to the spiritual and social life of the community. In order to ensure that the churches possessed the fiscal resources required to organize community-based activities, African–Nova Scotian women focused on an array of fundraising activities. In particular, the Ladies Auxiliary of the AUBA was a very effective community organization and was instrumental in the planning of the First Congress of Coloured Women in Canada, held in Halifax in 1920 (Hamilton, 1994).

The Black Baptist churches paid particular attention to African–Nova Scotian youth. A leader in this sphere was James R. Johnston, who became the first African Nova Scotian to graduate from Dalhousie University Law School (Pachai, 1990; Winks, 1997). As early as 1900, Johnston recognized the need for an organization that would provide vocational training for African–Nova Scotian youth. From 1908 to 1917, he worked to develop an institute that was patterned after the Hampton Institute in the United States, where African Americans were provided with different types of vocational training. It took Johnston a considerable amount of time convincing church officials and civic leaders in Halifax of the need for such a school before they allowed it to open in 1917. However, three weeks after opening, the facility was destroyed in the Halifax explosion of 1917.

The other major development was the establishment of the Nova Scotia Home for Coloured Children. The impetus for the home came from the need for a facility to care for neglected and orphaned African–Nova Scotian children. James A.R. Kinney, who became clerk for the AUBA in 1915, was instrumental in the establishment of the home. Building on the work of James Johnston and Reverend Moses Puryear, a committee headed by Kinney was organized with the task of approaching the provincial government for financial support to build the home. Kinney persuaded the government to purchase a 211-acre farm and to provide funds for a building (Pachai, 1990; Winks, 1997). The Nova Scotia Home for Coloured Children was officially opened on 6 June 1921 and continues to work with African–Nova Scotian youth.

The Nova Scotia Home for Coloured Children was just one of several community initiatives that emerged with the goal of improving the quality of life for African Nova Scotians. The Halifax Coloured Citizen Improvement League and the Criterion Club were other organizations that advocated for equality for community members. These organizations, like the AUBA, provided opportunities for African Nova Scotians to take on important leadership roles.

The Nova Scotia Association for the Advancement of Coloured Peopled (NSAACP) was founded in 1945 through the inspiration of another major community leader, Reverend William P. Oliver. The NSAACP maintained that education was the most effective means through which to secure equal treatment from the dominant group. In 1949, Oliver established an urban and rural life committee within the AUBA through which churches could conduct adult education courses in their own communities (Walker, 1995).

Despite the existence of community-based groups and organizations, the overall plight of the African–Nova Scotian community continued to be affected by racism and discriminatory practices that were meant to exclude members of this community from mainstream society. In the area of employment, the majority of African–Nova Scotian males were relegated to jobs as tradesmen and unskilled labourers and as porters for the railway companies. African–Nova Scotian women were largely limited to employment as domestics. Very few African Nova Scotians worked as professionals. As Pachai (1990) notes, individuals who were descendants of the Black Loyalists or refugees did not hold the majority of these professional positions; rather, the ranks were dominated by individuals who migrated to Nova Scotia from the Caribbean or Africa.

The prolonged segregation of schools perpetuated the limited employment opportunities for African Nova Scotians, and members of the community continued to be consigned to the lower end of the socio-economic ladder. The plight of African Nova Scotians is captured in the following excerpt from a two-year study (1959–61) involving African Nova Scotians in the Halifax region and Africville, a community located in the city: 'The survey found that Blacks earned less than the mean city income; that Blacks were unemployed for many more weeks than the average for all unemployed; that Blacks were concentrated more in "menial jobs". . . . The explanation offered for this situation found racial prejudice on the part of White employers, while fear of being rebuffed or rejected led to disadvantaged Black employees to accept the lowest positions' (quoted in Pachai, 1990, p. 209). Nonetheless, as part of a consistent pattern of behaviour, African Nova Scotians persisted in their fight against racism in the areas of education, employment, and housing. The NSAACP under Oliver was instrumental in advocating on behalf of the African–Nova Scotian community: 'The association insisted upon "full citizenship" for black Nova Scotians, which meant that the same standards of rights and responsibilities must be applied to blacks and Whites. . . . The NSAACP promoted education for both children and adults' (Walker, 1995, p. 166).

The 1960s ushered in a new era in the struggle against White racism in Nova Scotia. New efforts and new perspectives were spurred on by the civil rights movement in the United States and by African and Caribbean countries' gaining their independence from colonizing powers. Walker (1995) argues that Halifax youth leader Burnley 'Rocky' Jones represented the new Black consciousness in Canada: 'Jones articulated an intellectual message not often heard in Canada before. . . . Jones and his colleagues identified the problems as systemic, as the responsibility not just of a few overt racists but of society as a whole' (Walker, 1995, p. 168). Jones's work in Nova Scotia, along with other events involving African Canadians throughout Canada—such as the 'racial violence' that occurred at Sir George

Williams University in 1969—contributed to what Walker (1995) describes as the new Black consciousness. One of the results was the development of an umbrella organization, the National Black Coalition of Canada (NBCC). The NBCC possessed the mandate to coordinate the efforts of various African Canadians who were organized to address the concerns of the African-Canadian community.

The relocation of residents from Africville in the mid-1960s represented another concrete example of the power possessed by the dominant group and their disregard for the value of African–Nova Scotian culture. Africville, an African–Nova Scotian community located in the North End of Halifax, was the home of Black refugees. As in other African–Nova Scotian communities, the church, Seaview African Baptist, was the major institution for members of the community. Walker (1980) describes Africville's status during the first half of the twentieth century, noting that it 'lacked most of the facilities enjoyed by adjacent White neighbourhoods. It had no paved roads or bus service, no sewers or running water. In the 1930s a city dump was located beside them, leading to rat infestation and pollution of the well water supply. . . . There were no streetlights. . . . Few jobs were available, leading to employment in menial labour or domestic service in Halifax, [and] to chronic unemployment and poverty' (p. 103).

By the 1950s, the community had become the target of White urban planners who believed that Africville represented an 'American-style ghetto'. Studies were completed by planners who repeatedly recommended that the physical community be destroyed and the residents relocated. For several years, residents of the community resisted, arguing that relocating would involve uprooting friendships and family relations, would destroy the centrality of the church, and would force the community into the difficulties of adapting to a new location. In essence, the residents of Africville advocated the maintenance of their community, which possessed a distinctive culture and history. However, between 1964 and 1968 Africville was destroyed, the property was expropriated, and residents were relocated to rental accommodations in downtown Halifax (Walker, 1995; Alexander & Glaze, 1996).

The latter part of the 1960s witnessed the creation of a number of organizations dedicated to addressing the needs of African Nova Scotians and advocating on the community's behalf. The Black United Front (BUF) was formed in 1968 as an umbrella organization with the clear goal of achieving economic, political, and social power for African Nova Scotians. One of the organization's major goals was to unite all African–Nova Scotian communities into a conscious community for action, with the objectives of improving employment and educational opportunities and increasing cultural awareness (Walker, 1980, p. 169).

In 1970, the Black Educators Association (BEA) was formed. The association provided a forum in which African–Nova Scotian students, parents, and teachers could share their concerns about the education system in the province. Other major activities of the BEA included assisting in the placement of more Black teachers within the school system throughout the province, providing professional development for its membership, offering different education opportunities for students, and developing culturally relevant educational materials (Upshaw, 1994).

During the last three decades of the twentieth century, the preservation of the distinct African–Nova Scotian culture became a major priority of the community. In 1983, the Black Cultural Centre (BCC) was opened to preserve the unique culture of African Nova Scotians and provide the opportunity for all to learn about the experiences of this particular group. Many events take place at the Centre, such as concerts, plays, and educational activities including workshops and lectures.

At the same time as the BCC was established, important African–Nova Scotian writers and artists were emerging, including poets such as George Elliot Clarke, Maxine Tynes, and George Borden. Other creative artists, such as playwrights George Boyd and Walter Borden and filmmaker Sylvia Hamilton, have contributed to an enhanced sense of community and culture.

In the area of politics, the most notable achievement was the election of Wayne Adams as the MLA from the riding of Preston. Adams became a cabinet minister in 1993, when the Liberal party formed the government in Nova Scotia.

Despite these accomplishments, African Nova Scotians continue to experience racism and discrimination. For example, a recent demographic analysis of African Nova Scotians in Halifax in comparison to African-Canadian communities in Toronto and Montreal found that African Nova Scotians had the highest percentage of people who did not complete high school and the lowest levels of people attending university (Torczyner, 1997, pp. 33–4). The continued exclusion of African Nova Scotians from equitable employment, education, and other forms of social and economic opportunities has contributed to a series of challenges that are confronting the African–Nova Scotian community. These are discussed in further detail in the third section of this chapter. The following section provides an examination of Afrocentrism, including the reasons for its emergence and the major principles underlying this specific world view.

The Africentric Paradigm

The Africentric World View

Within the social work literature dealing with diversity and culturally competent practice, one of the dominant themes since the early 1990s has been the need for social work practitioners to acquire an understanding of the world view of different client groups (Jeff, 1994; Moore, 1994). For example, Moore comments that 'the culturally skilled [practitioner] actively attempts to understand the worldview of his (her) client without negative judgements' (p. 34). This literature maintains that an understanding of world views will enable human service practitioners to become more effective in their practice with an array of client systems, including individuals, families, and communities. English (1991), in commenting about the value of understanding world views, states: 'Worldviews of African Americans and other ethnic minorities are useful as a source of knowledge for achieving four distinct goals: assessing the client's cultural background and fundamental orientation towards life; diagnosing problems and planning treatment; empowering African

American and ethnic-minority families and individuals; and designing innovative child welfare programs and interventions' (p. 22).

English (1991) defines world views as 'the way in which people perceive their relationship to nature, other people, and objects. They determine how people behave, think, and define events. Worldviews also are significantly influenced by culture. Thus, world views are said to vary by racial/ethnic group' (p. 1). Along similar lines, Schiele (2000) defines the term in the following manner: 'A worldview can be defined succinctly as the overarching mode through which people interpret events and define reality. It is a racial or ethnic group's psychological orientation toward life. It provides a group with a structure for expressing its own cultural truths, a way to organize its experiences and interpretation into a logical and fairly stable conceptual scheme' (p.1).

Since the 1980s, scholarship describing and articulating the Africentric world view has increased. In commenting on the reasons for the attractiveness of Africentrism, Mazama (2001) stated: 'Today, Afrocentricity is widely discussed in the United States of course, but also in Africa, Europe, South and Central America, and the Caribbean. In short, it has become a formidable Pan-African force that must be reckoned with. The reason for its appeal lies both in the disturbing conditions of African people and the remedy that Afrocentricity suggests' (p. 387). In relation to human services, especially in the United States, Great Britain, and Canada, the philosophy underlying the Africentric world view is serving as the blueprint guiding social work practice with individuals, families, groups, and communities of African descent.

According to Schiele (2000), Africentric human service can be defined as 'methods of human service practice that arise from the socio-cultural and philosophical concepts, traditions and experiences of African Americans' (p. 11). There is general consensus that some of the traditional beliefs and practices of African cultures have survived among African Americans (Jeff, 1994; Turner, 1991). Although the majority of writing on the Africentric perspective focuses on African Americans, the basic tenets of Africentrism are applicable to African Canadians. Within the Canadian context, African Nova Scotians represent one of the most exploited and oppressed groups. As discussed in our historical review of the African–Nova Scotian community, for over two centuries this community has consistently experienced severe forms of racism, discrimination, and exclusion at the hands of the dominant group. Africentrism is viewed as a contemporary approach to changing the racial oppression Blacks encounter, particularly in North America (Asante, 1987).

One of the primary reasons for this development of Africentrism in social services is the growing realization that the majority of theoretical approaches and practice models in social work are Eurocentric in nature, thus negating the unique cultural aspects and experiences of African descent. Although Eurocentic theories and models have recently attempted to acknowledge the existence of the unique cultural values of people of colour, as evidenced by the use of terms such as 'ethnically sensitive', 'ethnic minority', or 'cross-cultural', writers such as Schiele (2000) maintain that European values still serve as the basis premise for these models:

'These human service paradigms usually underscore the following: 1) how racial discrimination and minority status have blocked opportunities and caused disproportionate psychosocial pain for people of colour; 2) how the human service practitioner should be aware of the cultural values and nuances of a consumer of a different racial/ethnic group; and 3) how the human service practitioner should be cognizant of his or her biases and preconceptions when working with someone of another racial/ethnic group' (p. 9).

Advocates of the Africentric paradigm also contend that there is a need for a theoretical approach and practices that are liberating in nature and that deal with the racism, oppression, and exploitation experienced by people of colour and, in particular, people of African descent (Jeff, 1994; Mazama, 2001). As Swigonski (1999) remarks, 'Social work practice from an Afrocentric perspective challenges the social work profession to work with clients to develop alternative social structures that are empowering and that confront the hegemony of existing systems and structures of oppression and domination' (p. 16).

A second, related factor prompting the emergence of Africentrism as a guide for practice stems from the limited effectiveness of traditional programs and services in dealing with social and economic issues that confront people of African descent. 'In the absence of a strong commitment to enfranchise urban youths, Black community leaders have turned away from traditional agencies for help in addressing today's problems. They have instead begun to initiate their own models that are culturally relevant to their communities' (Jeff, 1994, p. 100). Writers such as Mincy (1994) contend that, without culturally relevant programs, groups such as young Black males will continue to be in a state of crisis, experiencing limited academic success and with increasing rates of incarceration often resulting from drugs and related crimes. Jeff (1994) is more explicit in commenting on the value of Africentrism: 'It is a practical, positive philosophy that strengthens the individual while respecting other perspectives. Afrocentric-based programs allow social agencies to use a culture-based model that is effective in transforming troubled African American youths into productive citizens' (p. 113).

Another factor strengthening the emergence of Africentrism as a human service perspective stems from the strong expressed desire by members of the African-Canadian community to have a greater voice, and indeed control, in conceptualizing, developing, implementing, and monitoring programs that address the unique needs of African Canadians. Underlying this position is the belief that, without greater control over the types of programs and services that are developed and delivered, African Canadians will continue to be confronted by the same social and economic issues.

An additional factor that has contributed to the emergence of Africentrism as a social science perspective is the assertion of the need to acknowledge and stress African ideas and values at the core of the study of African and African-American culture and life (Jeff, 1994). One of the leading scholars on Africentrism, Asante (1987), contends that he was motivated to develop an alternative way of knowing as a result of the dominance of Eurocentric values and beliefs, which proved to be inconsistent and incongruent with Africentric values. 'Misunderstandings between Europeans and others provoked in me an interest in alternative perspectives . . . [and] a critical re-evaluation of social phenomenon' (p. 6).

Africentric writers argue that slavery and Eurocentric cultural oppression had an extremely negative impact on African Americans and vilified African culture. Yet, they maintain that not all the customs, values, and beliefs of African culture were destroyed. Moreover, a 'uniquely Afrocentric world view provides the key to identifying those elements in African American life and culture which are distinctively African' (Hill quoted in Mincy, 1994, p. 103). Given the dominance of the Eurocentric perspective, proponents of Africentrism assert that, for centuries, the history of Africans and African Americans was distorted and negatively portrayed, when it was acknowledged at all. As a consequence, 'Afrocentricity is concerned with the systematic reconstruction of the human record to accurately reflect the prodigious influences African people have had on world history' (Rowe quoted in Jeff, 1994, p. 102).

Everett, Chipungu, and Leashore (1991) accentuate the positive attributes related to Africentricity: 'The Afrocentric perspective describes the ethos of African and African Americans and the values that guide the way African Americans interact with the world around them. It goes beyond issues of institutional oppression to offer a global view of the peoples of the African diaspora. It counteracts the all-too conventional application of a deficit model, to the behaviors of people of color. It elicits a proactive stance toward behaviors, beliefs and attitudes of African Americans by emphasizing strengths' (p. 5). In essence, proponents such as Everett, Chipungu, and Leashore view Africentrism as a mechanism that attempts to build character and self-esteem within people of African descent. The perspective strongly affirms the importance and value of Black life. Africentrism also recognizes the array of contributions made by persons of African descent.

Major Principles

The Africentric perspective is based on a number of philosophical principles that have implications for social work practice with African Nova Scotians. Of particular importance are the principles of the interconnection of all things, the spiritual nature of human beings, the importance of collective identity, and a recognition of the affective dimension. The following discussion highlights some of these fundamental tenets.

THE INTERCONNECTION OF ALL THINGS

This principle that all things are interconnected represents the cornerstone of the Africentric perspective. Turner (1991) and Graham (1999) contend that in African philosophy people are perceived as being connected to everything in their environment, including all human beings. A critical aspect of this principle is one's relationships with others. The maintenance of relationships provides individuals with a sense of purpose in life and with connections to both families and community.

According to this principle, the goal for all people, not just people of African descent, is to have positive social relationships, which in turn facilitate the development of self-esteem and the social competencies required in the contemporary world. These are important goals for human service practice with African Nova Scotians, especially in light of their living in an environment where racism and exclusion are commonplace.

THE SPIRITUAL NATURE OF HUMAN BEINGS

Another critical tenet of the Africentric perspective is an emphasis on the spiritual dimension. In this context, spirituality refers to the non-material or invisible substance that connects all elements in the universe (Schiele, 2000). In contrast to Eurocentrism, which stresses the materialistic aspect of life, Africentrism maintains that the non-material aspects of human beings are just as important. As a result, proponents of the perspective stress the importance of the oneness of mind, body, and spirit (Schiele, 2000; Graham, 1999). The focus is on a holistic view of individuals, where the mind, body, and spirit are inseparable. Hence, this belief is directly tied to the principle of interconnection.

An important concept and process embedded within the Africentric conceptualization of spirituality is morality. In describing this concept, Schiele (2000) contends that, from an African humanistic viewpoint, there is no separation between spirituality and morality. He further asserts 'that the human's ability to be moral and caring is believed to be linked with God's model of morality and care' (p. 26). From a human service perspective, adherence to this relationship between spirituality and morality should ideally result in a decrease in the suffering that human beings experience. From a practice perspective, Africentrism stresses that it is the responsibility of everyone in society to help alleviate conditions that have a negative impact on the quality of life of individuals, families, and communities (Schiele, 2000).

For African Nova Scotians, who continue to be subjected to attitudes and behaviours that deny them equitable treatment in Canadian society, there is an ongoing need for the community to deal with the injustices faced on a daily basis. However, proponents of Africentrism also argue that members of the dominant groups need to take responsibility for addressing the salient social and economic issues that confront the African–Nova Scotian community.

COLLECTIVE IDENTITY

In contrast to the Eurocentric focus on individualism and materialism, Africentrism stresses the importance of the collective identity. This emphasis on the collective nature of human beings translates into the collective being responsible for individuals (Turner, 1991; Schiele, 2000). This sentiment is captured by the expression, 'whatever happens to the individual happens to the whole group and whatever happens to the whole group happens to the individual' (quoted in Turner, 1991, p. 47). This principle is also directly related to the principle of connectedness.

Turner (1991) provides a series of examples of how the collective identity is operationalized in daily African and African-American life. The reverence towards

African elders by others in the community represents one of the strongest expressions of the collective identity. In African cultures, children are taught at a very young age to respect elders: 'within the family and by extension the clan and community African elders are treated with respect' (Turner, 1991, p. 50). Elders in the community are highly valued for the collective wisdom they possess and the contributions they make to their communities. In the case of African–Nova Scotian communities, the mere fact that the elders survived in a hostile environment where educational and employment opportunities were limited is a testament to the strengths possessed by elderly African Nova Scotians. They endured the challenges associated with living in Canadian society. It is important to stress that not only did elderly members of the community persevere, they contributed to the development of a distinctive African–Nova Scotian culture, which continues to exist. These individuals—through their stories captured in the oral tradition, their photographs, and other forms of documentation—provide insight into the African–Nova Scotian community as well as the broader Canadian society.

An important sub-theme related to the provision of respect for elders is the belief that elders will be looked after and provided for by members of their family. Adherence to this belief reflects recognition by younger generations of the array of contributions made by elders to both family and community life and, hence, the sense of communal responsibility for this particular part of the community.

The existence of the consanguineal family structure, which prevails in African communities, represents another expression of the collective identity. The basic premise of the consanguineal structure is that the family, as an institution, includes all individuals related through the bloodline as well as those related by marriage. The term 'extended family' is also used to describe this particular family structure (Turner, 1991). This conceptualization of family is extremely important for social workers working with African Nova Scotians as either individuals or collective entities. The presence of the extended family continues to be an important form of social support, assisting members of the community, who reside in a society where racism and discrimination are part of the daily reality.

In virtually every society, parents have the responsibility of raising and taking care of their children. However, within African communities, instead of this responsibility being placed entirely on the biological parents, parenting is a collective responsibility: 'everyone assumed responsibility for discipline. If neighbours saw someone's child misbehaving they admonished the child and informed the parents later' (Turner, 1991, p. 48). Graham (1999) uses the African proverb 'It takes a village to raise a child' to capture the essence of this perspective. The collective responsibility for children also brings to the forefront the value of children within African and African-American communities.

THE AFFECTIVE DIMENSION

A fourth distinctive attribute of the Africentric world view is the strong recognition of the affective dimension possessed by individuals. According to this view, a person's emotions are a vital aspect of the process of self-exploration and knowledge generation. Indeed, Schiele (2000) asserts that 'emotions are the most direct experience of self' (p. 28). The emphasis on this dimension does not negate or deny the rational aspect of individuals. Instead, the Africentric world view stresses that the affective and rational dimensions are interrelated. In describing the relationship, Schiele remarks: 'thoughts do not occur independently of feelings, nor do feelings occur independently of thoughts. Thoughts are no more supreme to emotions than emotions are to thoughts' (ibid., p. 28). In focusing on the relationship between feelings and thoughts, it is argued that the Africentric perspective provides social workers with a more holistic understanding of the experiences of client systems.

The values promoted by the Africentric world view are congruent with the basic values that form the cornerstone of social work practice. However, the profession, as evidenced by the African–Nova Scotian experience to date, has not operationalized these values to benefit the African–Nova Scotian community. The challenges for social work practitioners working with African Nova Scotians is to ensure that an array of creative interventions are used not only to deal with the daily social and economic issues that prevail but also to address the range of structural and systemic barriers that have denied members of the community their rightful place in Nova Scotian society. As Swigonski (1996) states, 'Social work practice from an Afrocentric perspective challenges the social work profession to work with clients to develop alternative social structures that are empowering and that confront the hegemony of existing systems and structures of oppression and domination' (p.160).

Mapping the Terrain for African Nova Scotians within the Current Social, Political, and Economic Environment

This section discusses some of the major social issues that currently confront the African–Nova Scotian community. These challenges are the direct consequence of a long legacy of direct exclusion from all aspects of life in the province.

African Nova Scotians continue to face a chilly climate as they travel the terrain of Canada's political, economic, and social system. African Nova Scotians have always faced systemic racism and discrimination in all sectors and structures of Nova Scotian society; however, as we face the new millennium, it appears that the terrain has become even more difficult. In this section, we map that terrain. We begin with a discussion of the social, economic, and political exclusion that African Nova Scotians face, and we discuss the impact of this exclusion. The chapter concludes with a discussion of the role of social work in dealing with these issues and an illustration of how Africentric theory is used in a practice situation.

Social and Economic Exclusion in Nova Scotia

African-Canadian views on social and economic exclusion are rooted in a critical perspective on poverty that eschews an individual analysis for a more structural analysis of the problems. This goes beyond the class-biased model of poverty to the structural realities that exclude marginalized people from mainstream society. People marginalized from the mainstream of society experience oppression in various forms on a daily basis. As Bishop (1994) explains, class is often the glue that helps to keep oppressive structures in place. Living in poverty is not just about economics; it involves systemic exclusion from ordinary things that many take for granted. For example, people who are excluded from the social and economic life of their communities have no sense of entitlement or sense of their right to participate in their communities. African Canadians who live in Nova Scotia are disproportionately represented among the economically and socially disadvantaged.

In Nova Scotia, where an individual needs to earn $13 per hour to move out of poverty, the minimum wage is $4.50 per hour. Recent provincial and federal budgets focus more on tax breaks for upper-income Canadians and do little to address the systemic conditions that contribute to the cycle of poverty. The reality of absolute and relative poverty goes unnoticed. Furthermore, because African Canadians are overrepresented among the poor, economic deprivation is not only part of their legacy, it is part of their present; and, unless things drastically change in the next few years, it will also be part of their future. A vision of change and hope lies in a critical analysis of the concept of social exclusion, which draws attention to the processes whereby people become deprived and to the multidimensionality of the deprivation they face (Das Gupta, 1999).

According to Coleman (2000), women in Atlantic Canada earn only 81 per cent of the hourly wage of their male counterparts; those with identical education and training still earn about 10 per cent less than men. One in five women in Atlantic Canada lives in poverty, and 70 per cent of single mothers live below the poverty line. Furthermore, the majority of the region's poor children live in single-parent families. African-Canadian women in Atlantic Canada are disproportionately listed among poor and single-headed households. It is important that we understand the impact of living on the margins and of social and economic exclusion. Coleman (2000) asserts that low-income-earners have higher rates of hospitalization and health service usage and that low-income families pass on poverty and lower functional health to their children. There is an urgent need to implement policies that will reduce poverty, and to challenge systemic conditions that help to perpetuate poverty and exclusion. African Nova Scotians are concerned that their voice is not heard, and that there is a lack of political will to deal meaningfully with their lived reality. Some observers believe that the absence of political clout has a great impact on the ability of African people in Nova Scotia to change their conditions.

African Nova Scotians and the Political Arena

African Nova Scotians have historically been excluded from the political arena, both locally and nationally. They lack collective political power, and there is a leadership vacuum in the African-Canadian community, nationwide. The members of the community either lack trust in the political system—sometimes for valid reasons, sometimes because of internalized oppression and colonialism—or they fail to acknowledge effective political leadership. Members of the community are so locked outside the political process that there now appears to be widespread apathy about political issues. Members of the community lack awareness about the political power that they do have; thus, they cannot exercise it.

African people in Nova Scotia lack a political voice. Provincial boundaries were redrawn in 1991 to create a Preston-area riding, with an expectation that an African Nova Scotian would run for each of the major parties and, hence, would be elected to the provincial legislature (Saunders, 1994). This was the government's attempt at positive action to redress systemic discrimination in the political arena. Although African Nova Scotians were elected in two elections, in the most recent election the seat was won by a White male candidate. Two things are important to note here: first, the riding is predominately White, although it holds the largest African population in the province; second, the plan to elect an African Nova Scotian could work only if all of the major parties nominated African–Nova Scotian candidates. To be effective, positive action must be legislated; it requires more than good will. Although the member of the provincial legislature for the Preston riding served the whole constituency, when the incumbent was an African Nova Scotian, there was an unspoken and unacknowledged expectation by the community that the individual was actually representing all of the African population in the province. Many people did not realize the impact of this voice in the provincial legislature until it was lost. A similar experience has recently occurred at the federal level, when during the 2000 election, the one African–Nova Scotian member of Parliament lost his seat after a four-year term in office. This has been a devastating loss for the community, and African Nova Scotians feel that they are not represented at either level of government. Norman Cook has helped to create, and chairs, a group called the African Canadian Dialogue, a vehicle to develop the political power of African Canadians. The group has representatives from most of the major cities in Canada and has the potential to become the political voice for African people across the country. Forming this group is an important step, as the historical lack of political representation, lack of political power, and exclusion from many social and economic realms have had a devastating impact on the development of African–Nova Scotian people and communities.

The Impact of Social, Economic, and Political Exclusion

Poverty, high unemployment, underemployment, and lack of education and marketable skills are symptomatic of the reality of the social, economic, and political exclusion experienced by African Canadians. The unemployment rate for Canadians of African origin is one-and-a-half times higher than that for the total population. This community has the lowest rate of self-employment of all racial groups (Douglas, 1998). Bernard's (1996) research with men of African descent in Halifax and in Sheffield, England, reveals that they share the same experience: they have a high rate of unemployment and the lowest rate of self-employment of any ethno-cultural group. Furthermore, men of African descent in Halifax and Sheffield spend more of their incomes outside their communities than any other group in this Western society.

Although often proclaimed the best country in the world in which to live, Canada has invested little in African-Canadian people. Economic policies have focused on a dramatic downsizing of government and in the public sector, and on less government intervention and more power being handed to big business. The economy and economic growth are left to the private sector, where capitalism prevails and the goal is making profits. Government does not seem to understand the need to redress systemic discrimination with effective policies and procedures. The private sector demonstrates even less understanding of the need for such programs and, moreover, shows a lack of commitment to develop such understanding.

In Nova Scotia, economic growth and job creation lag far behind the rest of Canada. As Cook (1998) states, private-sector funding is market-driven, and the descendants of Africa in Canada have never highlighted their market potential. Douglas (1998) argues that African Nova Scotians suffer from collective economic weakness. There is a lack of support for Black businesses, and the low business-participation rate is tied to high unemployment. Although the youth unemployment rate in Canada is high, the rate for African-Canadian youth is even higher, particularly for males, who continue to drop out (or be pushed out) of public school at an alarming rate (Dei, Mazzucca, McIssac & Zine, 1997). No business sector exists in the African–Nova Scotian community to assist youth who are unemployed and unskilled.

Marginalization from the political and economic mainstream has had a devastating impact on African-Canadian societies. Bernard and Bernard (2002) argue that this history of marginalization and oppression, in addition to the systemic barriers to social and economic resources and power, has had a devastating impact on the emotional and psychological well-being of African-Canadian people. Christensen (1998) refers to these phenomena as the cycle of unequal access, and argues that extraordinary interventions are required if the cycle of psychological trauma that results from such limitations is to be broken. We see the results of that trauma in the daily-life realities of African Nova Scotians. For example, African Nova Scotians are at greater risk for major health problems such as diabetes and hypertension; family and social problems, including violence and abuse; identity and self-esteem problems; and mental health challenges. Little attention is paid by researchers to the impact of racism on one's emotional and physical health, or to race as a determinant of health. Yet systemic racism is reflected in the overrepresentation of African Canadians in mandated services such as child welfare, and underrepresentation in voluntary services such as counselling. In some child welfare agencies, African Nova Scotians, who constitute less than 4 per cent of the population of the province, make up approximately 25 per cent of the caseload. The Association of Black Social Workers (1988) and Barkley (1985) have documented that Black people constitute a high percentage of social service caseloads in child welfare and corrections. However, few Black people use voluntary counselling services in family service or mental health agencies. How much of this tendency reflects earlier practices, where Black families and communities had to rely on each other for support (Saunders, 1994)?

African Nova Scotians have a rocky terrain to navigate if they are to survive in the twenty-first century. The African–Nova Scotian community cannot dictate what role the social work profession will play in challenging this rocky terrain for and with African Canadians. However, it is important to be cognizant of and concerned about the growing conservatism among professionals, including social workers, in African-Canadian communities. Este and Bernard agree with Cook's (1998) position that many of the most talented and successful African Canadians see little or no relationship between their life chances and service to their communities. Canadians of African origin have never produced a document such as W.E.B. Dubois' *Talented Tenth*, which fixed the minds of young African-American university graduates to their responsibility to community. Talented young Canadians of African origin see little to gain financially or socially from participation in their communities at this point in Canadian history. Furthermore, in Nova Scotia, the community experiences the impact of a resource drain as many of its highly educated young people leave the area for permanent jobs in other parts of the country, or in the United States, because they cannot get jobs in the province. The terrain is rocky in this country, but if one is not part of the solution, one becomes part of the problem.

Given the history of marginalization, the legacy of oppression and exclusion, and the current rocky terrain that African Nova Scotians must negotiate today, it is a miracle that the community survives. The cycle of unequal access (Christensen, 1998) leads to low self-esteem, a sense of hopelessness, internalization of oppression and racism, anger, anxiety, and the destruction of self and/or others. For some, survival is by any means necessary; for others, strategies of survival and notions of success are rooted in African-centred values and traditions (Bernard, 1996). For many, the struggle to survive is reflected in the overrepresentation of African Canadians in the negative statistics on high school dropout rates, the prison population, and people living with addictions. The development of culturally relevant services, including the use of Africentric theory in social work in Nova Scotia, has been a priority for African–Nova Scotian social workers and the Association of Black Social Workers (ABSW). However, no agency in Nova Scotia is specifically mandated to provide services to African people. There is an expectation that the social service needs of African-descended people will be met by mainstream agencies. Yet we know that African Nova Scotians are overrepresented among clients using mandated services such as child welfare and addictions counselling, and underrepresented among those who seek help voluntarily (Bernard, 1988; Bernard, Lucas-White, & Moore, 1993; Bernard, Benton, & Baptiste, 2001). The challenge for social workers and social work educators is to prepare all social workers for practice with African people, as well as other marginalized groups. In the next section we explore ways in which social work can be a catalyst for change in services to African–Nova Scotian individuals, families, and communities.

Social Work Interventions

Schiele (1996) stresses three main objectives in Africentric practice:

- Afrocentricity seeks to promote an alternative social science paradigm that is reflective of the cultural and political reality of African Americans;
- It seeks to dispel negative distortions about African people; and
- It seeks to promote a world view that will facilitate human and social transformation. (p. 289)

Applying this approach in practice, Schiele (1996) asserts that the first step is assessing the social inequalities and consequences of social policies on individual problems. Interventions should include approaches that enhance the positive potential of all individuals and the ethic of caring. The helping process is characterized by reciprocity and the personalization of the professional relationship. Clients are seen as the experts of their own experiences, and there is a focus on empowerment and social justice for all human beings.

Phillips (1990) identifies the following philosophical principles: harmony, balance, interconnectedness, affective epistemology, authenticity, and cultural awareness. Theoretical underpinnings of Africentric practice (Asante, 1999; Karenga, 1978; Collins, 1990; Schiele, 1996) include the following principles:

- to centre the experience of African people as agents of their own liberation
- to be rooted in the African value system
- to foster and develop a collective consciousness
- to analyze contextual and structural realities.

From the philosophical and theoretical underpinnings of Africentricity, the following practice principles were adopted (Asante, 1999; Karenga, 1978; Collins, 1990; Schiele, 1996):

- to view individual problems holistically and as rooted in family, community, and social structures
- to promote individual and collective consciousness raising
- to recognize a collective consciousness
- to analyze critically the intersecting nature and the lived reality of oppression
- to focus empowerment on both individuals and the collective, building on strengths
- to seek social change and social transformation.

How are these principles put into practice with African–Nova Scotian clients, and do they make a difference? What are the implications for practice with this client group, given their historical marginalization and their lack of access to mainstream services? Bernard and Bernard (2002) engaged in a research project that explored

Africentric theory with African–Nova Scotian social workers and human service practitioners. The study found that African–Nova Scotian social workers and human service workers were aware of the impact of racism on themselves and their clients, and how this informs their practice. There is a cultural connectedness with their clients and communities. They pay attention to affective knowledge, and they practice from a holistic perspective. They indicated that their life experiences and collective consciousness were important in their practice, as was an analysis of historical and current political and structural realities that have an impact on them as workers and on their clients. Participants also indicated that there were a number of gaps in services to African–Nova Scotian clients and that there was a lack of culturally appropriate services available to this client group. These findings all suggest an engagement with Africentric theoretical principles (Bernard, Benton & Baptiste, 2001). To help illustrate the ways that Africentric theory is used in practice, one of the authors of this chapter (Bernard) developed the following composite case example, based on her practice with African–Nova Scotian clients. Pseudonyms are used for the clients to protect their identities.

CASE EXAMPLE

Mary, an African–Nova Scotian single parent of a thirteen-year-old son, Dan, was referred for counselling by the employee assistance program (EAP) at her office. Mary, who is forty-one years old, has been divorced for ten years. She left a six-year marriage because of her partner's alcohol addiction and violence, and has been on her own with her son since he was three years old. The elder of two children, Mary comes from a working-class family in Halifax, and both her parents are still living. Over the years, her parents and her sister have given her a lot of support. Mary has been with Company X for twenty years. Although she has a college diploma in office management, she has worked as a receptionist for this company since she joined them shortly after graduation. Mary is active in her church and community and is a highly regarded community member who belongs to some voluntary organizations. Recently, Mary and Dan moved from inner-city Halifax to a suburb, as she was able to purchase her first home.

Dan is a Grade 7 student at his local junior high school and is active in community groups. Since his parents' divorce, he has had no contact with his father. He has always experienced difficulty in school and has not adjusted well to the transition from an inner-city junior elementary school to a suburban junior high school. Dan has been angry a lot lately, and has begun to ask his mother about his father. He has received a number of detentions and a five-day suspension for fighting.

The EAP referral letter cited poor work performance as the reason for the referral; it noted that counselling was mandatory, as Mary was at risk of being terminated. The letter also noted that Mary had a negative attitude towards others in the office and contributed to a poisoned work environment. Mary was falling asleep at work and, owing to problems with her son, had many absences. Although she did not readily agree to the referral, she ultimately had no choice. She asked to be referred to an African–Nova Scotian counsellor.

Mary's own assessment of the workplace issues differed significantly from that of her employer. While she agreed that she had a negative attitude at work, she believed that the problem was caused by her co-workers. Mary was the only person of colour in her office and had been systematically excluded from the office social scene for the past five years. Moreover, she had applied for twenty-nine transfers to other jobs within the company, some of which were potential promotions, but she had been denied each time. She felt that both the social exclusion and the lack of opportunity for employment mobility she experienced were because of individual and systemic racism. When her anger and frustration about the way she was being treated became uncontrollable, she decided to disengage, and she stopped speaking to her colleagues unless the matter was related to work. In addition, Mary had problems with her son, who was experiencing academic and social difficulties in school. He was subject to racist name-calling, was fighting with his peers, and missed his friends from the old neighbourhood. Dan was frequently expelled for fighting, and the school did not take up his allegations of racism. Finally, Mary was experiencing extreme fatigue, had difficulty sleeping, and was suffering weight loss due to a loss of appetite.

ASSESSMENT AND INTERVENTION

An Africentric assessment of this case focused on both individual and structural issues. Mary was in danger of losing her job, she was showing physical and physiological symptoms of stress, and she was having difficulty with her teenage son. Parenting on her own after a divorce, she was the sole support for her family. She and her son were the possible victims of systemic and individual racism, along with gender and class oppression. Interventions in this case had to be multifaceted to address both the short- and long-term needs of Mary and her family. Mary's own description of her case indicated that she had a good analysis of the issues that were affecting her, but she did not know how to deal with them. Each of the Africentric practice principles that were outlined above are discussed below to illustrate how these are used in practice.

Viewing Individual Problems Holistically and as Rooted in Family, Community, and Social Structures

As part of the assessment process, Mary was initially referred for a full battery of medical tests to determine the cause of her health-related problems. She was given stress leave from work while the tests were being completed. The practitioner engaged Mary in an assessment of her problems and worked with her to design strategies and interventions that would assist her. She was linked with supports in the education system to deal with the issues pertaining to her son. Individual counselling focused on her strengths, such as her ability to deal with the multiple oppressions that framed her life and the strategies that she had used to deal with everyday racism and sexism.

Promoting Individual and Collective Consciousness Raising
During the intervention, the negative behaviours that Mary exhibited in the work-place were reframed as survival strategies that she used to deal with the racism she was experiencing. Interventions also focused on helping Mary develop a critical understanding of this racism and the links between her experiences and her physical and emotional health problems. Mary had been denied twenty-nine opportunities for promotion in a company where she had worked for twenty years. Mary's assessment of the systemic nature of this problem was validated through the assessment process. Eventually, Mary was able to lay a formal complaint with the human rights commission to investigate the allegations of racism in her workplace.

Mary was raising her son on her own with no support from his father. She had never expected child support or depended on Dan's father to assist her in any way with the boy's upbringing. Mary's fear for her own safety, and her concern that violent behaviour would be passed on from father to son, kept her from seeking support from her ex-husband. In the course of the intervention, Mary was linked to a local parents group that was examining issues pertaining to child support and mandatory payment through the family court system.

Eventually, Mary became aware of the way in which stress affected her both physically and emotionally. Medical tests revealed that Mary had narcolepsy and situational depression. The ongoing human rights investigation created more stress in the office. Mary was eventually transferred to another job in the company—on her thirtieth application. She joined a parents' support group in her local community to assist with the challenges of raising her son and dealing with his problems at school. She continued in individual counselling to deal with depression and other issues that she identified as important to her. Although Mary had left an abusive relationship, she had never talked with anyone about the ways in which that abuse affected her sense of self and her ability to trust others. After she had dealt with the more immediate concerns, she began to deal with those issues in counselling.

Recognizing a Collective Consciousness
Linking Mary with support groups outside her family provided her with opportunities to see her individual struggles as part of a much larger system. Individual consciousness created a greater sense of a collective consciousness as an African–Nova Scotian woman and single parent who was experiencing stress and oppression in the workplace and at home. As a result, Mary became involved in wider movements for change.

Analyzing Critically the Intersecting Nature and the Lived Reality of Oppression
By understanding the lived reality of life as a Black single parent in danger of losing her job, the practitioner was able to connect with Mary in a meaningful way. Mary had just purchased her first home, and she believed that she was finally getting back to the lifestyle in which she had grown up. Her parents had always worked, and they owned their own home. It was important for Mary to recognize that her own economic situation was affected by her gender (women are more

negatively affected by divorce than are men) and her race (she was locked out of promotions in the company due to systemic racism). Mary had never consciously thought about the ways in which the intersecting and interlocking oppressions of race, class, and gender had affected her life, her family, and her community. She had never linked her personal struggles to wider political, structural, and societal conditions. Through individual and collective consciousness raising, Mary was able to develop a more critical and reflective analysis of her own experiences and the impact of these intersecting oppressions.

Focusing Empowerment on both Individuals and the Collective, Building on Strengths

Mary received affirmation of her strength and tenacity in dealing with workplace oppression and maintaining her employment. Her strengths as a single mother and as an active community member were also recognized. Linking her with others in similar situations provided Mary with a broader network of supports to assist with the various problems she was experiencing. While she was on extended sick leave, Mary was able to reflect on her experiences and develop the capacity to continue to fight for her rights. The assessment gave her the evidence she needed to deal with the workplace problems. The counselling interventions helped her to gain strength and confidence in her own abilities to cope and to change. She was able to take back control over her life and to connect with various types of support in her community.

Seeking Social Change and Social Transformation

Mary went on to become very active in her union and in the wider community. She won her human rights case of systemic racism and became an advocate for other women in similar employment situations.

Summary

Social work can be a catalyst for change in the social conditions that African Nova Scotians are living with. Having African-Canadian social workers in the system who are also working to fight systemic barriers does help, but there is a need for more involvement of other workers as well. Securing the involvement of other social workers has implications for social work education in this country. The Dalhousie University School of Social Work is the only school in Canada that offers an elective in Africentric social work. One objective of that course is to examine the relevance of Africentric social work for non-Africans. Should other schools consider offering such an elective, or should this be core content in other courses? What is the best way forward to obtain social change and social transformation for Africans in Nova Scotia? What strategies are needed to redress the systemic inequalities of the past?

A review of social work literature used in the majority of Canadian schools would lead one to conclude that African Canadians are indeed an 'invisible population'. Most social work students graduate with little or no orientation to the needs, issues, and strengths of African Canadians at individual, family, and community levels. There is an underlying assumption that the knowledge and skills provided in the Bachelor of Social Work and in the specialized Masters of Social Work programs are sufficient to deal with the array of social problems confronting a population such as African Canadians. However, in reviewing the historical and contemporary experiences of the African–Nova Scotian community, it becomes quite apparent that social work interventions that are Eurocentric in nature have not been effective in altering the circumstances of this particular community. On the contrary, without greater attention to systemic issues such as racism, discrimination, and exclusion, mainstream social work theories and practice methods will continue to contribute to the oppression experienced by African Nova Scotians.

From a practice perspective, the emergence of Africentrism as a philosophy with specific principles that guide practitioners' work with African Nova Scotians and their communities definitely offers the hope of addressing the particular concerns confronting African Nova Scotians. In order for social workers to be effective in working with this population, it is imperative that practitioners have a solid understanding of the historical and current experiences of the community, along with a basic comprehension of the tenets of Africentrism. From a practice perspective, practitioners must thoroughly understand, and participate with members of the community in the development of, practice methods and models that are culturally relevant. Jeff (1994), in describing the promise of Africentrism, remarks: 'Afrocentrism offers African-American youth positive values such as incorporation and enfranchisement that can help reduce the distance between them and their social environment. It fosters knowledge and human development through critical thinking, diligent study and analysis' (p. 105).

It is imperative that social workers working with African Canadians not solely focus on the problems that confront this community but also stress the positive attributes. The mere fact that, for example, African–Nova Scotian communities exist is a testament to the strength of the members of this community, past and present, in a society that continues to deny equitable treatment in virtually all spheres of society, particularly the educational and employment domains. Hence, social workers need to work with African Nova Scotians in the ongoing struggle to address exclusionary practices. Failure to take on these challenges in an active manner would represent the negation of the values that form the foundation of the profession of social work values—values that are congruent with those guiding Africentric practice.

Note

1. The term *Africentric* is used here to mean 'African-centred'. The term originally coined by Asante was *Afrocentric*; however, the authors have chosen to use *Africentric* as better reflecting the word's derivation (from 'Africa') except in quoted material.

References

Alexander, K., & Glaze, A. (1996). *Towards Freedom: The African Canadian Experience.* Toronto: Umbrella Press.

Asante, M.K. (1987). *The Afrocentric Idea.* Philadelphia, PA: Temple University Press.

———. (1988). *Afrocentricity.* Trenton, NS: African World Press.

———. (1999). *Afrocentricity,* Presentation made in Halifax, NS, 20 March.

Association of Black Social Workers. (1988). *Preserving the Black Family.* Conference proceedings. Halifax, NS: Association of Black Social Workers.

Barkley, J. (1985). *An Examination of the Attitudes and Knowledge Base of Non-Black Social Workers, Counsellors and Social Service Workers Regarding the Black Community in an Urban Area of Nova Scotia.* Unpublished MSW thesis, Dalhousie University, Halifax.

Berkerie, A. (1994). The four corners of a circle: Afrocentricity as a model of synthesis. *Journal of Black Studies, 25*(2), 131–49.

Bernard, C., & Bernard, W.T. (2002). The association of Black social workers and child welfare in Nova Scotia. In B. Wharf (Ed.), *Community Work Approaches in Child Welfare.* Toronto: Broadview Press.

Bernard, W.T., (1988), Black Families and Family Therapy in Nova Scotia. D. Moore and J. Morrison (Eds), in *Work, Ethnicity and Oral History.* Halifax, NS: International Education Center.

———. (1996). *Survival and Success: As Defined by Black Men in Sheffield, England, and Halifax, Canada.* Unpublished doctoral dissertation, University of Sheffield.

Bernard, W.T. & Bernard, C. (1999) Creative Intervention: African Centered Community Support for Children and Families. *National Child and Youth Care Journal, 13,* 1, 73–85.

Bernard, W.T., Benton, W., & Baptiste, R. (2001), *Africentric Perspectives in Social Work: Views From Nova Scotia,* Unpublished Project Report, Halifax, NS.

Bernard, W.T., Lucas-White, L., & Moore, D. (1993). Triple jeopardy: Assessing life experiences of Black Nova Scotia women from a social work perspective. *Canadian Social Work Review, 20*(2), 256–76.

Bernard, W., & Thomas, G. (1991). Social services sensitivity training project report. *Canadian Social Work Review, 10*(2), 237–45.

Bishop, A. (1994) *Becoming An Ally* (Chapters 5 and 8). Halifax, NS: Fernwood.

Black Learners Advisory Committee (1994). *BLAC report on education: Redressing inequity—empowering Black learners. Volume 1-Summary.* Halifax, NS: Black Learners Advisory Committee.

Christensen, C.P. (1998). Social welfare and social work in Canada: Aspects of the Black experience. In V. D'Oyle and C. James (Eds), *Re/visioning: Canadian Perspectives on the Education of Africans in the Late 20th Century* (pp. 36–55). York, ON: Captus Press.

———. (2001). Immigrant minorities. In J. Turner & F. Turner (Eds), *Canadian Social Welfare.* 4th ed. Scarborough, ON: Allyn and Bacon.

Christensen, C.P., & Weinfeld, M. (1993). The Black family in Canada: A preliminary exploration of family patterns and inequality. *Canadian Ethnic Studies, 25,* 26–44.

Coleman, R. (2000) Women's Health in Atlantic Canada: A Statistical Portrait. The Maritime Center of Excellence For Women's Health (Ed.), in *A Portrait of Women's Health. Volume One.* Halifax, NS: The Maritime Center of Excellence For Women's Health.

Collins, T. (1990). *Black Feminist Thoughts: Knowledge, Consciousness and the Politics of Empowerment.* New York: Routledge.

Cook, N. (1998). *Resources.* Presented at the Conference 'Dialogue on the Future of Descendants of Africa in Canada' sponsored by the Afro-Can Dialogue, Ottawa.

Coppock, N.W. (1990). *Afrocentric Theory and Applications. Volume 1: Adolescent Rites of Passage.* Washington, DC: Basbab Associates.

Daenzer, P. (1997). Challenging diversity: Black women and social welfare. In P. Evans & G. Wekerle (Eds), *Women and the Canadian Welfare State: Challenges and Change* (pp. 269–90). Toronto: University of Toronto Press.

Das Gupta, M. (1999). *Social Exclusion and Poverty.* Villa Borsig Workshop Series 1999. Available online at http://www.dse.de.

Dei, G. (1996). A Black African Canadian student's perspectives on school racism. In I. Alladin (Ed.), *Racism in Canadian Education* (pp.42–61). Toronto: Harcourt Brace.

Dei, G., Mazzucca, J., McIssac, G., & Zine, J. (1997). *Reconstructing 'Dropout': A Critical Ethnography of the Dynamics of Black Students' Disengagement from School.* Toronto: University of Toronto Press.

Douglas, L. (1998). *Financial challenges facing Canadians of African origin.* Presented at the Conference 'Dialogue on the Future of Descendants of Africa in Canada' sponsored by the Afro-Can Dialogue, Ottawa.

English, R. (1991). Diversity of world views among African American families. In J. Everett, S. Chipungu, & B. Leashore (Eds), *Child Welfare: An Afrocentric Perspective* (pp. 19–35). New Brunswick, NJ: Rutgers University Press.

Este, D. (1979). *The Emergence and Development of the Black Church in Canada with Special Emphasis on Union Church in Montreal, 1907–1940.* Unpublished cognate essay, University of Waterloo, Waterloo, ON.

Everett, J., Chipungu, S., & Leashore, B. (Eds) (1991). *Child Welfare: An Afrocentric Perspective.* New Brunswick, NJ: Rutgers University Press.

Graham, M. (1999). The African-centered world view: Toward a paradigm for social work. *Journal of Black Studies, 30*(1), 103–22.

Grant, J. (1980) *Black Nova Scotian.* Halifax: Nova Scotia Museum.

Hamilton, S. (1994). Naming names, naming ourselves: A survey of early Black women in Nova Scotia. In P. Bristow et al. (Eds), *We're rooted here and they can't pull us up: Essays in African Canadian women's history* (pp. 13–40). Toronto: University of Toronto Press.

Henry, F. (1973). *Forgotten Canadians: The Blacks of Nova Scotia.* Don Mills, ON: Longman.

Jackson, M. (1995). Afrocentric treatment of African American women and their children in a residential chemical dependency program. *Journal of Black Studies, 26*(1), 17–30.

Jeff, M.F.X. (1994). Afrocentricism and African American male youths. In R.B. Mincy (Ed.), *Nurturing Young Black Males* (pp. 99–118). Washington, DC: Urban Institute Press.

Karenga, M. (1998). *Kwanzaa: A celebration of family, community, culture.* Los Angeles, CA: University of Sankore Press.

McNeil, S. (1997). *The Association of Black Social Workers Fees for Service Program: An Evaluation.* Unpublished report, Maritime School of Social Work, Dalhousie University, Halifax.

Mazama, A. (2001). The Afrocentric paradigm: Contours and definitions. *Journal of Black Studies, 31*(4), 387–405.

Mincy, R.B. (1994). Introduction. In R.B. Mincy (Ed.), *Nurturing Young Black Males* (pp. 7–22). Washington, DC: Urban Institute Press.

Moore, Q. (1994). A whole new world of diversity. *Journal of Intergroup Relations, 20*(4), 28–40.

Oliver, P. (1953) *Brief History of the Coloured Baptists of Nova Scotia, 1782–1953.* Halifax, NS: Fernwood.

Oliver, W. (1989). Black males and social problems: Prevention through Afrocentric socialization. *Journal of Black Studies, 20*(1), 15–39.

Pachai, B. (1990). *Beneath the Clouds of the Promised Land: The Survival of Nova Scotia's Blacks.* Volume 2. *1800–1989.* Halifax: Black Educators Association.

———. (1997). *People of the Maritimes: Blacks.* Halifax: Nimbus.

Phillips, F.B. (1990). NTU psychotherapy: An Afrocentric approach. *Journal of Black Psychology, 17*, 1, 55–74.

Saunders, C. (1994). *Share and Care: The Story of the Nova Scotia Home for Coloured Children.* Halifax: Nimbus.

Schiele, J.H. (1996). Afrocentricity: An emerging paradigm in social work. *Social Work, 41*(3), 284–94.

———. (2000). *Human Services and the Afrocentric Paradigm.* New York: Haworth Press.

Statistics Canada (1998). *1996 Census: Ethnic Origins, Visible Minorities.* Ottawa, ON: Author.

Swigonski, M. (1996). Challenging privilege through Afrocentric social work practice. *Social Work, 41*(2), 153–61.

Torczyner, J. (1997). *Diversity, Mobility and Change: The Dynamics of Black Communities in Canada.* Montreal: McGill Consortium for Ethnicity and Strategic Social Planning.

Tulloch, H. (1975). *Black Canadians: A Long Line of Fighters.* Toronto: NC Press.

Turner, R.J. (1991). Affirming consciousness: The Afrocentric perspective. In J.E. Everett, S.S. Chipungu, & B.R. Leashore (Eds), *Child Welfare: An Afrocentric Perspective* (pp. 36–57). New Brunswick, NJ: Rutgers University Press.

Upshaw, R. (1994). Education programs in Nova Scotia. In V.D. Oyley (Ed.), *Innovations in Black Education in Canada* (pp. 41–8). Toronto: Umbrella Press.

Walker, J. St. G. (1976). *The Black Loyalists: The Search for a Promised Land in Nova Scotia and Sierra Leone*. Halifax: Dalhousie University Press.

———. (1979). *Identity: The Black Experience in Canada*. Toronto: Ontario Educational Communications Authority.

———. (1980). *A History of Blacks in Canada: A Study Guide for Teachers and Students*. Hull, QC: Minister of State for Multiculturalism.

———. (1984). *Racial Discrimination in Canada: The Black Experience*. Ottawa: Canadian Historical Association.

———. (1992). *The Black Loyalists: The Search for a Promised Land in Nova Scotia and Sierra Leone*. 2nd ed. Toronto: University of Toronto Press.

———. (1995). African Canadians. In P. Magocsi (Ed.), *Encyclopedia of Canada's Peoples* (pp. 139–76). Toronto: University of Toronto Press.

Winks, R. (1969). Negro school segregation in Ontario and Nova Scotia. *Canadian Historical Review, 1*, 164–91.

———. (1971). *The Blacks in Canada: A History*. Montreal: McGill-Queen's University Press.

———. (1997). *The Blacks in Canada: A History*. 2nd ed. Montreal: McGill-Queen's University Press.

Chapter 14

Social Work with Canadians of Caribbean Background: Post-colonial and Critical Race Insights into Practice

Narda Razack

> The Caribbean as a geographical region appears to present few problems of definition. Socially however, the area is not a unit. It is differentiated internally by different metropolitan associations, by various religious, linguistic, and cultural affiliations, by different racial-population ratios, and by historical differences. . . . Clearly differentiae of this order rule out the possibility of a uniform pattern.
>
> Barrow, 1996, p. 32

Caribbean Canadians are often referred to as 'West Indians', a term that reflects the colonial legacy left in the wake of Columbus, who had initially embarked on a voyage to capture the East Indies and found himself in the 'West' (Henry, 1999). Caribbean Canadians are those who have migrated to the North from the archipelago of islands stretching in a 2,400-kilometre arc from the tip of Florida to the coast of Venezuela. First and subsequent generations of Caribbean Canadians are included in this analysis. Caribbean Canadians are a very diverse, complex group; their physical, cultural, and linguistic characteristics vary from island to island and among the population of individual islands. These differences result from the various invaders and settlers who instilled their culture into the inhabitants, forcing the development of hybrid nations. For example, the word 'callaloo' is often used in Trinidad to describe the unique blend of various ethnic and cultural backgrounds that exists among its peoples.

This chapter begins with an exploration of the complexities of Caribbean cultures that have emanated from the profound influences of colonization, imperialism, indentureship, and slavery. Consideration of the forces of colonization and imperialism are critical to an understanding of Caribbean culture and ethnicity. Immigration patterns are highlighted to underscore the socio-economic and cultural realities that affect adaptation behaviour and settlement patterns in the host countries. Post-coloniality and neo-colonialism are also key concepts to consider in order to understand the lives of Caribbean Canadians in a White-dominant society. Caribbean Canadians also include citizens with Caribbean ancestry. This chapter tries to acknowledge the importance of differences both within groups and among islands while capturing the essence and flavour of Caribbean peoples. However, although the Caribbean contains a microcosm of people from all over the world, the majority of people are African-Black, with a large concentration of Indo-Caribbean people in Trinidad and Guyana. Some Caribbean Canadians are migrants thrice over and come with a unique blend of histories and cultures. These diasporic locations and identities are significant considerations.

Racism is a palpable dynamic in Canadian society and will be underscored throughout the chapter, especially as it emerges in the law, media, social services, education, and health. Racism plays a significant role in the lives of Caribbean Canadians. Despite the significant number of Caribbean peoples in Canada, concentrated especially in major cities, there are few social work publications and limited research devoted to studying to this very vibrant group. It is not surprising, therefore, that many social workers lack the core knowledge about Caribbean people with respect to their culture, history, and social values that would facilitate a meaningful and helpful process. Moreover, the making of Caribbean-Canadian identities is crucial to the understanding of Caribbean Canadians.

The discussion in this chapter includes the construction of violence and the Canadian family. By discussing violence in the context of social work with Canadians of Caribbean background, no implication is intended regarding the degree or incidences within the community or in comparison with other ethno-racial communities in Canadian society. Woman abuse, in particular, will be discussed from a feminist and narrative perspective, together with a brief analysis of an interview with a social worker who co-leads groups for Caribbean men who have assaulted their partners and have been mandated to attend counselling. These discussions are intended to help the reader appreciate alternative perpectives for direct practice with Caribbean women and men in such situations. The narrative is intended to provide insight into work with people of Caribbean background and to act as a potential beginning point for considering practice in family violence with peoples of other diverse ethno-racial backgrounds.

Issues relating to youth and adolescent identity will illustrate core social work concepts for working effectively with Caribbean Canadians. The school system is paramount in shaping the lives of young Canadians of Caribbean ancestry. Within these institutions, identity is shaped; sadly, there many youth suffer the harshness of racism on a daily basis. Critical, reflective, and transformative pedagogical and practical perspectives will also be discussed with an anti-racist focus to determine their applicability to work with Caribbean Canadians. This theoretical and practice framework will include a critical global feminist and transnational perspective together with an analysis of critical race theory for social work. The construction of identity is central to this analysis.

The Politics of Identity

> . . . looks count for everything, and I *know* people see what they want to see. If they're looking for a new member, I'm it. If they are looking for a scapegoat, I'm it. If they're looking for a specimen, I'm it. If they're looking for an excuse, I'm it. I'm it.
>
> Hernandez-Ramdwar, 1994, p. 2

Many Caribbean people are of mixed-race parentage; thus, issues regarding mixed-race identity can acutely affect the Caribbean Canadian. Glick (1985) states that Whites have firmly established themselves at the top of the hierarchy, with Blacks and Aboriginal people at the bottom and mixed-race people occupying the rungs in between. In the days of slavery, mixed-race peoples had little status, for they were subservient to Whites and were viewed with disdain by Blacks. According to Edmondson (1974) the Caribbean 'was at one time the laboratory of modern political and economic imperialism and the incubator of modern internationalized racism' (p. 76). Class also plays a significant role in the organization of family and behaviours, and Caribbean Canadians are from many different ethno-racial backgrounds. Therefore, it is essential for social workers to understand these various markers of identity.

This chapter is consciously reflective; therefore, it is important to locate myself as a Caribbean Canadian to account for certain biases that may invariably creep into this chapter. My racialization process began in Trinidad, where there is a large Indian and African population with a minority of Chinese and Portuguese and, according to Selvon (1979), 'the other elements that are sandwiched between them' (p. 23). As a new immigrant to Canada, I became acutely aware of the subtleties of language and meanings surrounding difference, and I realized that my identity would be constructed primarily through historical and social meanings of race. Skin-colour racism and other structural disadvantages that are inflicted on Caribbean Canadians prevent their full participation and citizenry in Canada. Calliste and Dei (2000) relate the importance of race identity and describe how one becomes racialized, thereby receiving differential status and privilege: 'Recognition of the complex, dynamic and fluid nature of racial identity implies that in different historical contexts individuals and groups are racialized as different and subject to differential and discriminatory/unequal treatment. Race (like gender and class identities) is fundamental for engaging in society. Race identity influences the social and political practices in which we choose to engage' (p. 29).

At my first place of employment in Canada, a hospital, I was exoticized by those around me, who characterized me as Middle-Eastern, Greek, Latin American, South Asian, or Jamaican (when people know you are from the Caribbean, they automatically assume you are Jamaican). I hung on to my 'Trini' identity and still fiercely protect this rootedness, especially when faced with rank hostility and dissonance in various employment settings, most recently within a university, where I teach and do research. While I was employed at a counselling agency, my difference was seen as a benefit, since I was able to attract 'other' clients. As a member of an ethnic minority employed in academia and other professional positions, one can easily be cast into the role of 'native informant', where one can gain privilege from being a part of the institution and, in turn, buy into the dominance that this role accords. According to Sherene Razack (2000), we can become 'stand-ins for the South, . . . go to conferences, . . . and represent "women of colour" completely eliding the differences between us and poor women of colour in the North and in the South' (p. 41). However, in the North, there is also a penalty, as we are not fully accepted as authentic, especially when the focus of our work is on race, discrimination, and oppression. Knowledge production is still the domain of the dominant White group, and one has to conform in order to meet expectations. Learning the culture is ongoing, and these societal distinctions can be very elusive and difficult for a social worker from the dominant group to fully understand.

Conceptualizing this chapter has been particularly challenging because my professional identity has been shaped by my British and Western education and strongly marked by struggles and challenges that have become etched onto my various identities; these same struggles and challenges frame the lives of many Caribbean Canadians. Identities change with each new experience and challenge, and these shifting locations allow me to reflect on how my Caribbean-ness continues to inform my work and world view. It is imperative for social workers, whether Caribbean or other, to understand the culture, ethnicity, commonalities, uniqueness, and histories that characterize Caribbean Canadians.

Because our history is so steeped in colonization and imperial practices, Caribbean Canadians have to negotiate learning differently within mainstream institutions, and must map the terrain for gaining knowledge. University posed challenges for me as a mature student; the differences were overwhelming because I lacked knowledge of the academic environment. I am deeply aware of how schools harbour a culture of racism that affects many Caribbean-Canadian youth (Dei, 1996; S. Razack, 1995). As a university student I attended lectures in classrooms that were exclusively the domain of White people. I learned White theories, as the texts were traditional and sustained the hegemony of Western British narrative. I still observe how non-White students tend to gravitate towards each other (as we did in graduate school), and I am more keenly aware of how their realities can be subjugated in the classroom. As a professor I am continuously challenged to include all voices while being sensitive to the needs of particular groups.[1] When I was in graduate school my research and subject interests focused on race and oppression; these were viewed as 'my interest areas' and not intrinsic to the curriculum. Globalization and internationalism were absent from my courses, and I constantly bridged the divisions of micro/macro teachings. Generally, the students who chose to focus on policy and community were viewed as 'radical', advocates who were politically motivated in their work. My own practicum experiences highlighted differences and power imbalances relating to gender, race, and class. My White male supervisor held on to his power in very distinct ways to compensate for his lack of knowledge of issues pertaining to race and oppression (see N. Razack, 2001). I continually observe the entrenchment of racism and hegemony in practice. These are the challenges Caribbean peoples face within the dominant society.

Producing new meanings in social work has been vital for me in order to stay rooted within the profession, since I have noted contradictions, especially relating to caring, empathy, and measures of control and dominance (Margolin, 1997; Razack, 2000). There continue to be inconsistencies and dissonance in the theoretical base of the profession. The absence of critical race theory for social work is another form of exclusionary practice, especially for practice in a city as ethnically diverse as Toronto. The Caribbean-Canadian identity is largely constructed by race and the racialization process. Race marks the non-White individual within the academy, in the classroom, and in the community. It is therefore critical for us as academics, students, practitioners, and clients to struggle constantly to understand these socially constructed differences. We must strive both to analyze how knowledge is produced and to seek to impart this knowledge in non-imperialist, non-racist, non-sexist, and non-homophobic ways. These are challenges we face as Caribbean peoples living within the dominant society. The challenges also rest with those from the dominant culture to be aware of the factors that affect the lives of Caribbean Canadians and to accept their own implication and complicity within oppressive structures.

Historical Mappings within the Caribbean

If social workers are to understand how the legacies of slavery and indentureship shape the lives of Caribbean people, they must have a historical analysis of the Caribbean. A historical mapping corrects distortions and repairs erasure of this information. History also relates to present reality: the lens used to analyze a current situation can be extended to include one's ancestry and also more recent circumstances that preceded and followed immigration. Although issues relating to immigration and history may not be presenting problems for the Caribbean-Canadian client, undoubtedly it is up to the social worker to be able to view how these legacies are ineluctably wrapped around the body of the Caribbean Canadian. Understanding the nuances of the culture and the effects of slavery and indentureship, colonization, imperialism, and transnationalism is integral to viewing social problems. In addition, it is vital to discuss the cultural variety among Caribbean peoples and how they are raced in today's society, in order to avoid homogenizing groups, stereotyping, and marginalization. It is particularly important to understand how culture and gender can be insidiously substituted for race, and how those in the North become our imperial saviours (S. Razack, 1998).

The Caribbean was originally inhabited by Carib and Arawak peoples who were largely eliminated by the White settlers who took hold of the economy and purchased blocks of land. Soon after, the settlers realized that they needed to expand their labour force, and slaves were brought from Africa. Thus, their capitalist ambitions demanded that waves of people be uprooted from Africa to fill the labour gap.

Not only were these Africans torn from their homeland, but insidious forms of imperialism and colonization prevented them from practising their culture and religion, and from maintaining their family values (Baksh-Soodeen, 1998). They were unwilling victims of a trade in human merchandise (Glick, 1985), and there were rebellions and uprisings to gain freedom. The legacies of slavery and colonization remain etched in Caribbean history and among its peoples.

After slavery was abolished, Blacks in the Caribbean continued to bear the stamp of inferiority and remained on the lowest end of the social and economic ladder. Plantation owners needed more labourers, and a new wave of indentured workers came from Portugal, China, and, to a much larger extent, India. In the second half of the nineteenth century, over 400,000 Indians arrived to work on the plantations. Trinidad and Guyana have the largest number of Indo-Caribbeans, constituting half or more of the population. It should be noted that many of these indentured labourers brought their families and maintained their culture, religion, family values, and traditions. In these two islands, the differences between Indo- and African Caribbeans are keenly apparent through their culture, religion, personality, and fundamental attitudes and values (Mohammed, 1998). Moveover, Indians tended to settle in rural areas where agriculture was the mainstay for subsistence and survival. Indo-Caribbeans did not entirely defer to the ruling elite and managed to retain their culture and identity.

As time progressed, earlier forms of colonization were replaced by imperialism, in which White officials directed the functioning of the islands. European norms, standards, and values permeated the Caribbean. Racism was a political stratagem designed to forever disrupt and denigrate Black-Caribbean people. Whites held power and privilege while Blacks were viewed as inferior and substandard (Glick, 1985). The islands were divided along racial colour lines, which affected each person's position in society. Many mixed-race children were born as a result of plantation owners' control over the female slave's body. These offspring with lighter skin colour were given higher positions than those with darker skin colour. Marriage was disallowed in slavery; thus common-law unions flourished (Henry, 1999).

In the 1960s, those Caribbean islands that were colonies of Britain began to gain their independence. Today, few islands are still under the rule of former imperial powers. Yet, the European standards for education that were instilled during colonial rule continue to influence local realities. Education is viewed as one way to increase mobility. But even with education, job opportunities are limited; thus, migration is seen as one of the few available options. Unemployment is high and economic disadvantage prevails throughout the islands. The legacies of colonialism, slavery, and indentureship are evident in the way in which Caribbean people operate today. The music, food, religion, family values, and traditions are all of hybrid variety. Although, apart from Trinidad and Guyana, the majority of the Caribbean population is African-Black, islanders vary in terms of dialect, customs, and values (Henry, 1999). Some of these differences are more evident upon immigration.[2]

Immigration

In this section, I describe the patterns of immigration to Canada for Caribbean peoples while illustrating the inherent racism in Canadian immigration policies. This depiction allows us to view the hostile terrain unto which the Caribbean person arrives and the concomitant issues that emerge. It is helpful for the social worker to be aware of the institutional structures that the Caribbean immigrant has to negotiate prior to arrival. Racism has been a dynamic within immigration and continues to be so; indeed, the process of immigration in Canada is mired in racism (see Richmond, 1993; Jakubowski, 1997). However, prior to arrival, the Caribbean immigrant may be unaware of this history and may therefore not immediately recognize the climate of hostility that surrounds entry into Canada. The immigration-planning process in the home country does not involve education about issues like racism, privilege, and power in Canadian society. The recognition of systemic inequalities that are so embedded in Canada can affect the psyche of the Caribbean-Canadian immigrant, and each individual's response varies. Many Caribbean people have sustained relationships with the immigration system because they continue to sponsor relatives. Often, these relationships are fraught with difficulties: the current points system favours immigrants with capital, so some visitors tend to remain in the country as illegal immigrants. For the social worker, knowing about these systems allows for an understanding of privilege and power and how post-colonial space is shaped.

Jakubowski (1997) examines the legalization of racism in immigration and explains that, although there have been changes to address the blatant message that non-Whites are not welcome, the present shift from restrictive to a non-discriminatory immigration policy is only 'in principle'. The earlier overt and explicit racist and ethnocentric immigration system was abandoned over thirty years ago. However, adopting a non-racist immigration policy does not mean that racism is not still apparent, for racist criteria are still employed in the way in which immigrants are chosen, especially for Caribbean people (Simmons, 1998). Discrimination still exists within immigration law, but capitalism has replaced the old blatant racist regime in favouring Whites and avoiding non-Whites as refugees and immigrants. The Caribbean body, which historically has been viewed as not being able to stand the rigours of winter, and as soiling the colour of the majority, is still not welcomed (Simmons, 1998). Preferred immigrants were originally drawn from European countries and the United States. However, this pool did not provide the labour needed to sustain industry, and in the 1880s, when Chinese people were allowed in as cheap labour, the term 'race' became more significant in its inclusion rather than its exclusion.[3] This 'inclusion', or entry into Canada, was by no means a significant swing to acceptance. For example, early Chinese immigrants were subjected to severely harsh and abusive conditions, culminating in a 'head tax' of five hundred dollars on each incoming immigrant—an amount equivalent to the price of a house in Vancouver at that time (Fleras and Elliott, 1999, p. 63).

According to Fleras and Elliott (1999), 'push' factors in immigration allow people to flee from political situations and 'pull' factors relate to the anticipation of a better lifestyle (p. 248). In the late 1950s, Caribbean women came to Canada as domestics and were exploited by their employers in extensive ways (see Calliste, 1996; Bakan & Stasiulis, 1996). From the early 1960s to the mid-1970s, there was an influx of Caribbean immigrants to Canada. These immigrants were from all socio-economic strata and included doctors, nurses, teachers, dentists, clerical workers, domestics, and short-term migrant farm workers (Fleras & Elliott, 1999, p. 248). Caribbean immigration to Canada reached its peak in the mid-1970s. The vast majority of Caribbean Canadians settled in Ontario, with the remainder in Quebec and British Columbia (Henry, 1999). Caribbean-Canadian parents commonly left their children 'back home' in the care of grandmothers in order to work and become more established before having them rejoin the family. Re-integration has caused conflict within the Caribbean family unit, and further difficulties arise in the education system because of the challenges young children experience in the acculturation and settlement process. Re-integration is still part of the immigration process and problems still occur among these families. Henry (1999) also refers to the 'double lap' phenomenon, whereby Caribbean people migrated to Great Britain and then to Canada.

Caribbean communities are not homogeneous, and class differentiation marks the community in Canada. Gradation in skin colour also affects one's status in the Caribbean, with lighter skin sometimes bearing 'privilege' (Henry, 1999). In Canada, there is a hierarchy, or rather a scale of significance, for minority groups. Aboriginal and African people have historically occupied the bottom rung of the ladder with White people at the top. However with the recent events of 11 September 2001, 'Brown' people, especially those with Middle Eastern physiological characteristics, have faced significant racism. These trends illustrate the shifting and pervasive nature of race and racism. Of immigrants from the Caribbean, later arrivals tend to be less educated than the earlier wave, and according to Henry (1999), a growing 'underclass' is developing. Opportunities are unequal when racism and discrimination create barriers to employment and education. The media and the law also serve to repress Caribbean people: the notion of the 'Jamaican criminal' continues to haunt young African-Caribbean men. Accessibility is another issue, especially in employment; systemic discrimination is still a reality and works to limit Caribbean Canadians to a lower-class reality (Henry, Tator, Mattis, and Rees, 1995).

The Caribbean Family

The Caribbean family emerged from the stronghold of slavery, which, intermingled with the legacies of indentureship, colonization, and immigration, has created hybridized family relationships. Legal marriages were not allowed during the slave era, and family relationships were constrained and severely disrupted. European colonizers stripped authority from men; meanwhile, women were subject to the whims of the white colonizers, and many mixed-race children were born (Thakur, 1994). Thus, in contemporary Canada, the Caribbean family is a mix of European, African, and South Asian culture and traditions, and this can precipitate new problems. In addition, with every new generation there are many more mixed marriages in Canada, creating new mixed-race identities. As one author points out, 'Mixed race people can experience racism from either one of their parents' backgrounds. Some mixed race people experience racism at its worst: within the family network and by society's imposed reactions to them. Others may experience only isolated incidents in comparison' (Thakur, 1994, p. 349).

Families can be based in legal marital unions, common-law relationships, or more casual alliances; this, in itself, is not unusual in most parts of the world. However, the type of union, especially common-law and casual, can affect the family dynamics. Children who would naturally be raised in an extended community in the Caribbean are thrust into a hostile, racist, and unfriendly environment in Canada, at the same time losing this extended family. Problems are exacerbated for some families when those children who spent many of their formative years in the Caribbean are re-integrated with their families in Canada, and have to face a different cultural environment, one in which their culture is misunderstood and their dialect ridiculed (James & Walker, 1991).

Family life for many Caribbean-Canadian families can be fraught with difficulties. Henry (1999) contends that the most striking cultural pattern that continues to plague the family life of Caribbean immigrants is proportionately high rates of single motherhood (p. 336). A significant number of children are raised without a father and/or the extended family supports more readily available in the Caribbean. This situation can be devastating for the family, particularly the child. During and after immigration to Canada, separation is a key social issue, with frequent travelling and shifts occurring within families. Consequently, marriage breakdowns occur quite frequently during the first three years after migration, and the dynamics of male–female relationships may contribute to these situations (Henry, 1999). Undoubtedly Western influences continue to shape the Caribbean family as technological advancements export and promote Western and European media content, at times perpetuating a new form of colonization (Faist, 2000). The influences of globalization are significant in the Caribbean, and, after immigration, the family is faced with more upheavals and expectations. Work patterns shift as both parents have to work long hours to be financially solvent. Many times the woman is more successful gaining employment, which can negatively affect the marital relationship.

Religion and class considerations also affect the Caribbean-Canadian family. The Caribbean is predominantly Christian, and in Trinidad and Guyana there is a large Hindu population and a substantial Muslim minority. Religiosity is a major influence on values, culture, tradition, and lifestyle. Social status plays a significant role in shaping politics, family, and gender relationships. In Trinidad for example, there are several public religious holidays to recognize the value of various religions. These recognitions promote an acceptance and understanding of religious differences that are not so evident in other countries. Class continues to be influential in adaptation and settlement, with those who are not as privileged economically sometimes having more adjustment issues after migration. Generally, global racism plagues migrant Caribbeans and their offspring in Canada. At times, Blacks have been stereotyped in Canada as being, lazy, sexually over-active, criminally inclined, and genetically programmed to be inferior (James & Walker, 1991).

Making the Connections

Social workers who work with Caribbean-Canadian clients must understand the historical background of the Caribbean immigrant and family. Inseparable from history is the force of colonialism and post-coloniality, which continues to affect identity, status, behaviours, culture, language, ethnicity, and religion. Caribbean people have a difficult terrain to negotiate, especially when skin-colour racism limits opportunities in every sector. The effects of these realities, in addition to their ongoing relationship with immigration because of the familial and individual settlement process, can cause Caribbean Canadians to face many crises. Not all life-altering circumstances are attributable to immigration and adaptation issues. However, having a context to understand social location and physical space can be of benefit in the counselling process. It is also essential that attention be focused not only on the individual and direct practice perspectives, but also on policy, planning, and community services.

Some studies have indicated that the transition from the Caribbean to Canada is not occurring as smoothly for the Caribbean Canadian as it had earlier (James & Walker, 1991). There are conflicting views over the reasons behind this difference (James & Walker, 1991). Today's immigrants often feel closer ties to 'home', as a result of increased mobility, improvements like direct charter flights to the Caribbean, and new communication technologies. The other major contributor continues to be racism, which is endemic to Canadian society. A recent survey indicated that Black Canadians were at the bottom of the pool in terms of employment (*Toronto Star*, 3 February 2000, section M). Race and class are cited as the major factors inhibiting full participation in Canadian society. However, it is important to note that many Canadians may not readily understand the political and social implications of racism and may repress it or deny its presence. For example, in the classroom I observe how non-White students remain on a continuum in their knowledge of structural forms of racism. In fact, some Black students are often frustrated when other Black students report that they have never experienced personal attacks of racism. The latter group is not yet aware of the structural forms of racism that soon unfold in the class through readings and discussion. Racism can create anger borne out of desperation and life circumstances. Post-coloniality, colonization, imperialism, and transnationalism are other factors that impinge on adaptation, settlement, and citizenship. Social work interventions with Caribbean Canadians will be more meaningful if, rather than focusing entirely on the problems at hand, such as child abuse, incest, and violence, they instead integrate readings and understandings of identity, post-coloniality, and larger socio-political issues that impinge on Caribbean-Canadian clients and contribute to these problems.

Identity Legacies

Constructing identities of Caribbean Canadians involves an understanding of multiplicity and fluidity. Our lives are not static but continue to be shaped by changing political and socio-economic realities. Moreover, as we have seen, Caribbean people are not homogeneous in terms of race, class, ability, age, or sexual orientation. Generation gaps are also evident in how a particular group may have experienced settlement and adaptation patterns. New generations are situating themselves differently in Canadian society. Bobb Smith (1999) researched agency among Caribbean-Canadian women and interviewed forty-five women from various ethnic, class, cultural, and racial contexts. She found that the women referred to 'home' as 'a site of learning resistance'; empowerment was a recurring theme in their stories. Home exists in the imagination as a place where the Caribbean woman fully belongs (p. 150). The dialogue among many Caribbean Canadians often includes a statement about 'going home'. They may vehemently oppose the idea of residing in their birth country, but the sense of home-ness exudes a safe and nurturing feeling. According to Bobb Smith (1999), feelings about 'home' can be romanticized: the struggles faced prior to immigration tend to be forgotten. In this research the strength and agency of the Caribbean woman are evidenced in her ability to resist and thrive via education, networking, and community activism.

Inherent in the subjective spaces of the Caribbean Canadian are traces of colonization, imperialism, and post-colonial identities. Caribbean peoples have been subjected to labelling and stereotyping, and the media has been especially harsh, typecasting Jamaicans as criminals. Black youths have an exceptionally difficult time escaping these labels and adjusting to the stigmas projected by the dominant majority. The way in which Caribbean people construe the self after immigration is critical to their adaptability and functioning in the new environment, since their identity is so negatively constructed by society. According to Bashi and McDaniel (1997): 'The immigrant's responses to racism depend on where in the racial hierarchy of the country of origin the immigrant was placed—that is, how one perceives oneself in both societies. Thus one may try (a) to pass, (b) to distinguish oneself from the group known as African Americans, or (c) to decide to bear as best one can the racist treatment in exchange for access to economic and educational opportunities better than one would face in one's home country' (p. 676).

Immigrants are usually slotted and categorized upon arrival. The African Caribbean is subsumed under Black Canadians, and Indo-Caribbeans are often categorized with South Asians. But Caribbean people share a unique blend of history and culture that distinguishes and separates them from South Asians, Black Canadians, and other groups. Furthermore, the racialization process for Caribbean Canadians continues throughout generations. According to Robinson (2000), 'The concept of racialization indicates the social construction of "race" as a significant dimension in contemporary identities. But it cannot be an inclusive personal identity. Other variables, such as gender, age, class, sexual preference and nationality are some of the other important social identities. However, racial identity may predominate and be exclusively salient on occasions. . . . Issues of "race" and ethnicity are highly salient for all minorities in American and British society throughout their life spans' (p. 4).

As new families are created in the host country, the tides of racism continue to roll in, intersecting with class, religion, sexual orientation, age, and ability and disturbing any smooth settling-in process. Even if one manages to belong to the upper class, the Black body can still be denigrated. For example, a Black male executive may employ White males and have a higher income than his White employees. However, when he is out on the street he can be targeted by the police; he therefore feels the strains of the negative media images that his White male employees will not experience. Here, race overrides class as a marker of identity and oppression.

Forging these precarious identities creates difficulties and resistance for the Caribbean Canadian. Through the power of the dominant groups, negative labelling continues to create and maintain a status that is continuously 'othered', a concept elaborated on in Chapter 5 of this book. This otherness is another reflection of post-colonial power that relegates those who do not fit the image of the White majority to the margins. Caribbean Canadians are a racialized group affected by racialized structures that impose restricted access to resources and create greater disadvantages in comparison to Whites. Ghettoization in housing is another means of relegating Caribbean Canadians to marginal status. In Toronto, for example, segregation in housing means that Caribbean Canadians can be found living in particular locations like Scarborough and the Jane–Finch corridor, and these areas have been negatively labelled as crime-ridden.

According to Small (1998), society creates images to typify the Black population. The first image relates to success, where Black people are noted in the fields of sports, music, and, to some extent, television but are far less visible in politics and business. Black failure is viewed as being the result of laziness and welfare dependency. Another image refers to 'reverse racism', where the adoption of affirmative action and employment equity initiatives is viewed as an undervaluing of credentials (Small, 1998, pp. 76–7). Such stereotyping plagues Caribbean Canadians, who are also often lumped together with their African-Canadian counterparts despite their different history and social reality. Some of these images are difficult to escape, for the discriminatory behaviours attached to them are so endemic.

In Canada, 'immigrant' is a term used to describe a Canadian-born person of colour or one who does not speak English very well (Ng, 1986). It is disconcerting always to be asked your citizenry when in fact you were born in Canada. These post-colonial practices serve to marginalize and subordinate those who do not belong to the majority group. It is therefore vital for the social worker to understand the making of these Caribbean-Canadian identities through history and present realities.

Postcolonial Understandings for Practice

Giroux (1992) argues that post-colonial theory 'provides the possibility of both challenging and transforming a cultural politics formed in binary oppositions that both silence and invite people to deskill themselves as educators and cultural workers. The challenge that postcolonialism presents to educators and cultural workers calls for new ideas, pedagogical strategies, and social movements capable of constructing a politics of difference within critical public cultures forged in the struggle to deepen and extend the promise of radical and cultural democracy' (p. 21). Caribbean Canadians have a long history of colonization, during which the colonial rulers were focused on 'civilizing' the inhabitants by instituting their own values and fully maintaining the conditions of their rule (Pieterse & Parekh, 1995). Although colonization has officially ended, the efforts to repair the damage inflicted on the colonized are further reflected on in the postcolonial period.

There is ongoing discourse around the varying meanings of post-coloniality. Social workers should be familiar with the current discourse, especially as it relates to the Caribbean Canadian.[4] Canada, although not a colonizing country, is a settler society with its own history of racism and abuse. The Caribbean Canadian is by and large cast in a subservient role; social workers, especially those from the dominant group, need to be aware of this history and not seek to mirror the colonizer–colonized relationship in their working encounters. Re-colonization can take the form of sustaining dominance and privilege in the working relationship or of working in repressive bureaucratic structures without advocating for transformation of policy and practice. Social work is also embedded within dominant White frameworks and cultures. In order for shifts to occur to incorporate difference, cultural variety, and understandings of ongoing racial formations, social workers need to learn to reconstruct integrated visions for practice, including a firm knowledge of how colonial thinking and imperialism affect theoretical and practice perspectives. Opposing grand theories when they do not fit the lives of those who are othered (McGoldrick, 1998) requires a new language to challenge the dominant power and provoke questions for vision and practice with a view to collective struggle. The Caribbean Canadian does not ever get to assimilate fully, since skin colour is a marker of identity, and identity in this case may be viewed with negativity and labelling. The ramifications are felt more acutely when Caribbean Canadians are discriminated against in the education system (Dei, 1996) and in health and social services.

Giroux (1992) states that social workers must understand the critical issues that constitute the discourse around post-colonialism. First, history and politics need to be situated within the context of colonialism to understand how privilege continues to be sustained for the majority group, and exclusion remains for those on the margins. Therefore, the social worker must know Caribbean history. Post-colonial theory allows one to 'retheorize, locate and address the possibilities for a new politics based on the construction of new identities, zones of cultural difference, and forms of ethical address that allow cultural workers and educators alike to transform the languages, social practices, and histories that are part of the colonial inheritance' (Giroux, 1992, p. 28). Social workers can extend the narrative in social work theories to include these critical concepts and engage in meaningful dialogue towards transformative change processes.

Transnational Spaces

In this section I use the work of Faist (2000) to describe the ways in which transnational spaces can be forged for the Caribbean Canadian. Although oppression is still a major obstacle, the fact that Canadians of Caribbean background occupy positions in every sector speaks to our resilience, persistence, and dogged determination to succeed despite our histories of colonization and imperialism. *Transnationalization* denotes the major shifts in world power, where multinationals dominate the economy, and technological advancements have resulted in changes in the way global capitalism is being entrenched. These shifts in world power affect the state's responses towards the social service sector, and require the social worker to contextualize social issues in a transnational context. Faist (2000) discusses three types of transnational social space that arise from international migration and flight (p. 195). I believe that his analysis is critical to allowing Caribbean Canadians to integrate their ideals regarding home and host. First, both the host country and the immigrant's place of birth should contain 'transnational kinship groups'. According to Faist, these groups afford kinship, reciprocity, and ties that could be maintained with their home country. Many Caribbean Canadians still have family they connect with in their home country,[4] and many feel the need to maintain their roots by forging philanthropic ties with the Caribbean: they may send money and donations to specific areas of need. Second, Faist refers to 'transnational circuits', whereby people repeatedly traverse the borders of immigration. Many Caribbean Canadians continue to sponsor relatives and therefore remain involved in the immigration process. The third area includes the need for 'transnational communities', which are borne out of these interactions with the home country to increase and nurture self and family and form solidarity. In Canada there are many Caribbean communities that hold sporting and cultural events and parties, as well as creating clubs, social networks, community activist groups, and educational initiatives. These are some of the sustaining influences of the Caribbean on Caribbean Canadians. The social worker again needs to understand these contexts in order to appreciate fully how cultures are re-created on different soil.

Theorizing Practice and Pedagogy

This section begins with a construction of the Caribbean-Canadian family and discussions of woman abuse. Inherent in this analysis are critiques of how social work theories can sustain dominance and superiority. These theories will be analyzed to determine their scope and relativity for working with Caribbean Canadians. It is not in the purview of this chapter to exhaust all the potential theoretical frameworks. What I hope to achieve is a broad-based interventionist approach for working with Caribbean-Canadian individuals, families, and groups in any setting —schools, workplaces, and communities.

Theoretical and practice approaches should always be grounded in the history of the peoples of the Caribbean, which includes the legacy of colonization, immigration, and transnational identity formations. I encourage the reader to always make the links with this knowledge and their work with this particular population. It is also important that various sectors involved in working with Caribbean Canadians be addressed in this chapter so that there is not the similar degeneration into binaries like macro/micro and dominant/subordinate realities where, ultimately, one binary is privileged over the other. Exclusionary practices, where the client alone is objectified without the deeper understandings of history and current social inequalities, lead to a tendency to externalize the problems of racism and oppression in society. Social workers from the dominant group need to begin to unravel racism in their own world and be comfortable with their identity. Likewise Caribbean-Canadian social workers practising within their own cultures need to understand various issues of adaptation and settlement since we all have unique lives and responses to similar situations.

The Family

It is critical for social workers working with people from the Caribbean to understand the Caribbean-Canadian family. Gopaul-McNicol (1997) researched the psychological tendencies of over eight hundred Caribbean families residing in the Caribbean, New York, Toronto, and London, England. Her methodology included interviews and analyses of those seen in therapy. She also distributed questionnaires that allowed for a profile of the Caribbean family, with emphasis on families in Trinidad and Tobago. Her research found that in the Caribbean, mood and anxiety disorders, as opposed to personality and thought disorders, often prevail (Gopaul-McNicol, 1997, p. 39). Fernando (1991) asserts that psychosocial issues manifest themselves differently for minorities than the dominant group and can be identified according to cultural norms and values. Issues around sexuality may not be overtly expressed, and other complaints like depression may be masked through psychosomatic symptoms, which elicit more compassion and concrete medical treatment (Fernando, 1991). Mental health issues can be exacerbated by immigration, adaptation, and settlement, since the norms change and the cultural climate shifts for the Caribbean-Canadian individual and family. Caribbean Canadians face the harsh realities of racism in employment, health, and education as well as in situations in their personal lives. Although many Caribbean people immigrate to improve their economic situation, they are often faced with many barriers to improving their life situation.

Caribbean Canadians realize that it is difficult to detach from what they know culturally to embrace a Western approach to understanding family problems. In the Caribbean it is customary for families to network and share within the community, the church, and the extended family. As in many developing countries, the family is characterized as a unit that should be maintained and protected. Therapy is viewed as a stain, a stigma, and a sign of failure, and the person who needs mental health counselling is often viewed as 'going mad'. Shame may create conflict for those in precarious positions who want to make change (Fernando, 1991). Al-Krewani and Graham (2000) outline some cultural factors associated with working with Arab immigrants; these factors have relevance for all immigrants with mental health problems. The authors note that stigmatizing, cultural expectations, family involvement, communication, and clients' views of mental health services are some of the critical areas to attend to for positive interventions. In Toronto, Across Boundaries, an ethno-racial mental health centre, has been established to respond to the particular needs of people of colour with mental health concerns. In order to relate to and understand Caribbean-Canadian clients, the practitioner has to understand their response to counselling (Glasgow & Gouse-Sheese, 1995). The shame and stigma attached to seeking help, especially for psycho-social problems, cause many families to rely on their community for assistance.

Sewell-Coker, Hamilton-Collins, and Fein (1985) state that therapy is a relatively new phenomenon for Caribbean people, and when problems arise in Canada, their behaviours and expectations may not fit the norm. Caribbean people tend to benefit from structured short-term counselling, can be more conservative in expressing emotions, and tend to be more formal with professionals. Sewell-Coker et al. felt that they needed to launch different types of programs to encourage more participation of Caribbean people at their agency. Caribbean people still need to be educated about counselling, and different methods of intervention should be employed rather than one main approach. Thrasher (1994) used a psychodynamic framework with an awareness of culture in her work with a 'West Indian' client. I have modified her framework of therapeutic interventions to begin a critical reflective process to work with Caribbean Canadians. History and present socio-economic and political realities relating to identity and environment are always central in any such analysis. The social worker should describe her knowledge of Caribbean culture and the realities of Caribbean peoples in Canada.

1. Social workers need to be aware of their own racial and ethnic identity, including ways in which there are commonalities with the client. This is especially crucial for the minority social worker with a Caribbean client, although there may be struggles in the working relationship for the minority worker/minority client. One area of concern is over-dependency, where the client wants to be familiar because of similar background. Another concern is that the worker may over-identify with the client, which can lead to difficulties. Awareness of these situations allows the worker to be alert and cautious in building relationships.

2. It is incumbent on the worker to acknowledge the importance of family and extended family relationships. In addition, the worker should be aware that family dynamics can change with immigration, and these changes may need to be addressed.

3. The extended family is an integral component in childrearing, and this knowledge can help the worker build trust with the client. The extended family is viewed as a source of support but can also be a source of stress. The worker

needs to determine what relationship exists among extended family members. Sometimes families in the birth country can play a major role in the lives of Caribbean Canadians.

4. Caribbean Canadians may not readily display anger in their sessions, since anger towards elders and parents is also frowned upon. The worker has to strive to recognize the ways in which the client expresses feelings. I remember working with one client who became very angry with me after the sixth visit. She projected her anger at me, since she viewed me as an accomplished person while she was feeling inadequate and powerless. This anger served as a catalyst for her further self reflection and change.
5. Immigration issues may play a role in family functioning and its dysfunction.
6. Education and employment opportunities are the main reasons for immigration; the worker can use this knowledge to motivate families.
7. The worker should acknowledge how difficult it is for the Caribbean Canadian to seek assistance, especially when the relationship between client and worker is restrained and formal. The worker can encourage and facilitate a trusting relationship.
8. The worker can provide knowledge of the dominant culture to the Caribbean family, which should help to alleviate some of the stress of immigration.
9. One of the major components in the working process is knowledge of racism and anti-racism strategies (Thrasher, 1994).

The worker should be flexible and willing to adapt various approaches for work with Caribbean Canadians. Drawing from various theories will be useful, because no one theory fully represents issues relating to race, culture, and ethnicity.[5] Gopaul-McNicol (1997) found that coaching different members of the family was indispensable to the family therapy process, since not all members are willing to attend counselling.

Violence and Betrayal

Violence is a global issue and is not limited to any particular race, group, ethnicity, country, or region. For the Caribbean Canadian, violence as a social ill needs to be contextualized within the larger framework of structural disadvantages in order to control further labelling and stereotyping of this particular group. The etiology of violence may vary with immigration, racism, and cultural influences. These contexts assist the worker/educator to understand how violence erupts within Caribbean-Canadian families, as well as some of the strategies and knowledge needed to help facilitate a change process.

The image of the Indo-Caribbean woman is also critical to understanding in the working relationship. The notion that the Indo-Caribbean woman is docile and modest needs to change (Espinet, 1993). These impressions, which ignore transitional images over time, might be unduly applied to all women of this ethnocultural background. Gopie (1993) encourages Indo-Caribbean Canadians to claim their rightful place in society and try to resist these labels.

Rooney-Bray (1999) conducted a study of women's experience of abuse and interviewed Indo-Caribbean Canadians who were originally from Trinidad and Guyana. Her findings revealed a strong correlation between a male witnessing abuse as a child and that male becoming an abuser. Her recommendations focused on education. The participants showed a tendency to trust members within their own community before resorting to reporting the abuse or going to shelters. They often felt that reporting abuse helped to perpetuate the negative myths that pervade the lives of people of colour; therefore, the violence remained a private matter. Some stated that they first reported their physical injuries to family physicians, who tended to cast a blind eye and not be supportive (Rooney-Bray, 1999). The women often preferred to enlist the assistance of a trusted friend or relative rather than alerting the police. Shelters have not been particularly sensitive to Caribbean-Canadian women, and, although various mechanisms—such as training—have been put in place to correct this attitude ongoing efforts need to reflect the reality for all Caribbean Canadians, especially regarding culture, religion, diet, and race. Caribbean Canadians have strong ties with the family, and notions of individualism that are synonymous with Western thinking may be problematic in counselling. Clients may not be ready for immediate change or may need to stay within the family for immigration and other reasons. It is also extremely difficult for a woman to break up her family: she feels the burden of keeping the family together, despite having her safety jeopardized. It is important to discuss these issues with the woman; the worker should not be harshly judgmental under these circumstances (Rooney-Bray, 1999).

It is also important to recognize behaviours and culture when working with Caribbean-Canadian men who have assaulted their partners. One co-counsellor shared some of his experiences co-leading a group of Caribbean-Canadian men who had been mandated by the law to attend counselling for partner assault. These groups are co-led with a woman counsellor.[6] The group allows the men to discuss history and to understand the nature of violence in a global context. It is particularly crucial for Caribbean-Canadian men to understand how their culture informs their behaviours. The men initially blame the environment. They have difficulty with their reduced male privilege within the family, stating, for example, that Canada is a 'woman's country'. The counsellor acknowledged the huge differences in the way Caribbean men, as opposed to White men, were treated by the authorities, and this factor was also noted by the women in the study by Rooney-Bray (1999). As a visible-minority social worker, the counsellor found that he was able to build a rapport with the men. He stated: 'I think we speak from a level of oppression that seems to bring us all together and then at the same time we try to dismantle that and say well, we do have a common theme but look at it individually.' This worker felt that the counsellors were role models for the men. Camaraderie within the group was formed fairly early in comparison to other groups. He described how Caribbean men used humour to mask social problems.

Issues around violence deserve a lengthier discussion than is given here. However, Caribbean families, especially Indo-Caribbean families, tend to be protective and private, and social workers must understand ways to intervene and work through some of these cultural norms. Issues around violence take many shapes within the Caribbean-Canadian community. One area that has been grist for the mill is childrearing attitudes and habits. The educational and child welfare system are important considerations.

Working with Children

Caribbean-Canadian youth face many barriers in Canada. They are the victims of racism, which they have to face from birth. Older immigrants may have had the foundation of belonging to a 'home' culture where they were in the majority and therefore possessed a positive identity and nationhood prior to immigration. These experiences may have assisted them to remain more secure and self-assured in an often hostile society. Caribbean-Canadian youth face overt hostilities at a far younger age, but they also have remarkable resiliency and strength to withstand the daily assaults on their identity.

James (1990) has noted that Black youths feel that they are treated differently and therefore have different opportunities from Whites and must consider race when deciding on career aspirations and other life plans. They feel that they have to be on guard because of the negative construction of Blackness in Canadian society. In James's study, youth were unable to describe the structural and systemic forms of racism and were therefore determined to overcome and sidestep the racism they viewed as being individual and institutional (1990, p. 110). Caribbean-Canadian youth and their families often have to toil harder than their White counterparts to succeed in Canadian society. Parents place a high value on education and view the school as possessing the authority to discipline their children. Their earlier British schooling in the Caribbean emphasized the authority of the teacher, and parents gave total responsibility to the school. Children who arrive in Canada from such a culture may have tremendous difficulty adjusting to an education system that values interactive learning. They may be teased because of their dialect and skin colour, and they are often downgraded within the system. It may sometimes take years for them to rebuild self-esteem and fully understand their position in the education system. In general, education forms the basis for future success, and many Black children are relegated to athletic and technical programs (James, 1990), which can again deny them access to further education since they can be easily seduced into believing they will become financially successful as, for example, a sports star.

Positive self-esteem and self-concept lead to enhanced positive identity. Robinson's (2000) research into the self-concept and self-esteem of Black adolescents led her to surmise that these two concepts are interrelated. Some young Black people may have negative feelings about their racial identity but still have a positive self-concept (p. 9).

An informal survey completed by a school board in Toronto (see Gill, 1995) revealed that among recent immigrant youths from the Caribbean, two hundred students out of every out of every thousand had behaviour problems, and in 1993 a significant number of Caribbean youth were referred for counselling. Some of the referral problems related to withdrawal, hopelessness/helplessness, depression, delinquency, truancy, aggression, anger, and theft (Gill, 1995). The social worker's understanding of how these presenting issues emerge within a White school system is indispensable to the helping process. Caribbean-Canadian youth do not see themselves reflected in the curriculum: there is an erasure of their history and character in their schooling. These issues are crucial for professionals in the social service sector to examine when working with Caribbean youth. Dei (1996) argues that 'many educators are still grappling with a comprehensive understanding of how race and the relational aspects of difference (ethnicity, class, gender, sexuality) affect the schooling and educational outcomes of youth.. .... The struggle demands that an educator is willing to be a "voice of difference", . . . willing to challenge the status quo by rupturing the racialized, hetero-patriarchal nature of educational settings and the prevailing culture of dominance' (p. 78).

School social workers need to advocate for inclusive approaches to education on a systemic and institutional level while at the same time finding ways to instill positive self-concept and images for Caribbean-Canadian youth. Meeting the family and educating them about this social system is a major task. The parents need to understand the importance of parent–teacher interviews and be coached to respond to the needs of their children. The social worker also has to be secure in her or his own racial identity to engage in discussion concerning race and subjectivity. It is especially important for workers to understand how Caribbean families discuss issues of race with their children. Sometimes race is overemphasized, for parents believe that children need to be protected and be prepared to face these ills in society. Others may believe in the liberal mentality that it is necessary to 'pull themselves up by their own bootstraps' in order to succeed. Many times parents suppress the racism they themselves encounter in order to try to avoid having their children feel the hurt and pain. Parents were not trained to educate their children about racism and survival, and there are no prescribed scripts to guide them. The school social worker has to encapsulate the presenting problem of the child within these various contexts.

Gill's (1995) analysis of a postmodern and post-structural understanding together with critical theory is indispensable for working with Caribbean clients. She asserts that social workers must be familiar with the history, culture, migration patterns, language, religious practices, and expectations regarding school performance, behaviour, and the work ethic of the Caribbean family (p. 11). According to Gill's thesis, it is particularly important for the school social worker to avoid mirroring the colonizer–colonized relationship. She explains that 'Since most immigrant African-Caribbean students expect authority figures to be directive and give advice, school social workers need to prevent mirroring the colonizer–colonized relationship. The colonizer–colonized relationship can exist along any number of polarities, including aggressive-passive, leader-follower, and dominant-submissive' (p. 14).

Critical Reflections and Transformative Principles

Social workers and educators come from diverse backgrounds. They are challenged to work with people from a variety of cultures and ethno-racial groups. Caribbean-Canadian identity is influenced by race, gender, class, age, ability, sexual orientation, negative stereotyping, and political struggles in society. Knowledge about a variety of cultures is helpful, but workers must first be comfortable with and aware of their own ethnicity and how they are implicated and complicit in forms of privilege and power. Whiteness is a signature that provides everyday forms of known and unknown privilege in society (Frankenberg, 1993). It is incumbent on all social workers to recognize their privilege as a worker within any system, private or public, and then to recognize their status within society. Adopting a colour-blind position when working with others is not acceptable: it erases unique differences that speak to subordination and marginality.

Williams (1997) speaks passionately about the denial of racial experiences that forever plague the lives of Black people, causing a 'split without and a split within': 'For white people, moreover, racial denial tends to engender a profoundly invested disingenuousness, an innocence that amounts to the transgressive refusal to know. Again, this is not to assign anything like blame, simply to observe the way in which we know race, or don't' (p. 27). Williams addresses the many situations where 'white people just didn't *know*, had just never *thought* about it' (p. 27). White social workers need to have a critical knowledge of Whiteness, where conscious and informed efforts are made for structural changes to occur. It is simply not enough to be caring and empathic with clients with Caribbean ancestry, especially when many have to suppress forms of daily violence to their character.

It is also important for the worker to reflect critically on how the newer generations of Caribbean Canadians differ from their parents in terms of how they negotiate their space in today's society. Many of these youths are not apologetic about their differences and claim their rightful status as citizens of this country. Robinson's study (2000) suggests that adolescents have positive racial attitudes that may have been nurtured by their families to equip them with skills to live in a White-dominated society.

There are many articles and texts that delineate models and describe ways for social workers to be culturally sensitive and to use cross-cultural approaches for practice (Devore & Schlesinger, 1999; Ho, 1987; Lum, 1986). While these models are useful, critical race theory for social work is also integral to work with Caribbean Canadians. I have used this theory elsewhere (Razack & Jeffery, 2002) to describe ways in which pedagogy and practice can be effected with non-White populations. First, storytelling or dialogue is an indispensable concept in this process. Storytelling can be subsumed under the notion of narrative and dialogical approaches but needs to be deconstructed when working with the Caribbean-Canadian client. It is important to listen to the client, who is the owner of the story and life history that includes the reason for being in counselling. This story needs to be heard from non-dominant, non-colonizing, and non-racist positions. These areas are challenging, especially for the White social worker whose privileged location within dominant structures needs to be unravelled and understood to avoid replicating hegemonic behaviours when hearing the narrative of the client, whether within legal, educational, employment, health, or social services. According to Healy and Leonard (2000), dialogue is not 'comfortable, harmonious and consensual' (p. 38). Dialogue structures the relationship between client and worker because of institutional notions of knowledge and power. Creating a climate of trust for the Caribbean-Canadian client can pose significant difficulties when a White worker embodies the oppression and privilege of the dominant group. The task of the worker is to try to dismantle these spaces in an honest and reciprocal way so that the client can *feel* that the historical and present struggles are understood by the worker. These understandings can then pave the way for the client to share the primary issues they are confronting in counselling.

The notion of power in the client–worker relationship is also pivotal for facilitating change processes. Healy and Leonard (2000) discuss how power operates as both a repressive and constructive process: 'the question emerges as to who is exercising power in whose interests, and who defines the interests. As power is always faced with resistance, we can expect every exercise of power to be contested. However, we cannot avoid the use of power simply because its exercise meets resistance. We would argue that critical forms of practice require not the refusal of power but rather the ongoing assessment of the operations of power within specific contexts of practice' (p. 36). It is difficult to challenge and erase colonial behaviours that include deference to authority figures, be they social workers, doctors, teachers, or others. This authority needs to be deconstructed in the working relationship. A position of overt professional superiority is harmful for the Caribbean-Canadian client.

It is also essential for the worker to advocate within the system that is oppressive and restrictive for Caribbean-Canadian clients. The worker needs to understand how Caribbean Canadians are treated within the system and adjust interventions appropriately. This adjustment may include education, advocacy, and community building. The worker needs to be knowledgeable about family systems, extended family involvement, and support systems. It is appropriate to make links with agencies that work primarily with Caribbean-Canadian clients to understand how culture, politics, and socio-economic issues affect the lives of Caribbean Canadians. There are also many Caribbean community groups where the focus is on education, advocacy, cultural production, and religious participation. Religion and spirituality are deeply embedded in the lives of Caribbean Canadians and can be significant factors in the working relationship with the practitioner.

Caribbean-Canadian social workers can be challenged in numerous ways when working with 'their own' people. First, there can be issues of over-identification when the worker knows and feels what the client is experiencing (e.g., racism and discrimination) and overcompensates by disclosing inappropriately. As a new therapist, I was especially drawn to working with Caribbean clients because I felt I understood their history and present reality. What was most difficult was maintaining the professional boundaries, especially when the client just wanted to discuss shared histories and commonalities, which could compromise the therapeutic relationship. Using critical judgment with these issues means that the social worker has to be comfortable within herself or himself or else she or he will be easily drawn into a casual working relationship. As stated earlier, the Caribbean-Canadian client can also undermine the Caribbean worker's authority and can project anger towards the worker, whom the client views as successful and powerful. These issues can affect worker–client relationships. However, the overall benefits in this dynamic far exceed potential disadvantages. Clients may feel more comfortable when there is immediate acknowledgement of shared history, understandings of immigration, culture, and race. The worker should feel comfortable with appropriate self-disclosure procedures, which can help to build trust and positive client–worker relationship.

Conclusion

Social work with Caribbean Canadians demands that the practitioner understand history and notions of race and be able to critique and challenge racism and current socio-economic realities. Moreover, critical knowledge of colonization, imperialism, and transnationalism allows the worker to contextualize social problems experienced by Caribbean Canadians. It is difficult for a White worker to understand the malaise of a Black law student who witnesses the privilege of her affluent classmates and knows that White skin opens doors. Even for the White student from a lower socio-economic position, the opportunities may be greater than for a Black middle-class student. The Black law student also has to face the backlash when the media inaccurately report the lowering of standards for Black applicants to law school. These stories may be told, but how they are heard depends on the political knowledge of the worker. The Caribbean Canadian is resilient and is ambitious to succeed in Canadian society. Many Caribbean Canadians manage to benefit and thrive within Canada; they belong to every economic sector in society. Education is one of the keys to success, and families stress the importance of achieving a higher status in society.

Many social issues that confront the Caribbean Canadian are similar to those facing to the rest of the population. Violence, depression, mental health issues, poverty, AIDS, homophobia, sexism, and classism are all prevalent issues in both Caribbean-Canadian communities and the wider society. Apart from the more common theoretical and practice interventions, there are intricate factors that social workers need to be knowledgeable about when intervening in the lives of Caribbean Canadians. This knowledge must include concepts of power and privilege and how dominance is inscribed and sustained in society. It is not enough to understand history and present-day reality; one must be actively engaged in promoting change professionally, personally, and within the larger societal structures and institutions within which oppression is so deeply embedded. Consciousness and political motivation are vital if one is to advocate for meaningful change.

Sidiqqui (2000) states that visible minorities will soon outnumber Whites in Toronto, yet their maltreatment continues. Recent studies show how racism is 'pigeonholing immigrants in poverty'. For Caribbean Canadians, non-White skin colour means that they will be visibly different, and this difference means that race and racism are always primary factors to consider in their lives. As Siddiqui so aptly states: 'The more visible you are, the more difficulties you have. This is a damning indictment' (p. 34).

Notes

1. See Razack (1999) and Ellsworth (1989) for an in-depth exploration of peda-gogical challenges in their efforts to construct an inclusive classroom.
2. For a more in-depth reading of the peoples of the Caribbean, see Magocsi (1999), who discusses the history of colonization with separate analyses of a few of the islands.
3. There are many accounts of how racism and immigration worked to sustain hegemony and power. See Henry et al. (1995), Jakubowski (1997), Fleras and Elliott (1999), Satzewich (1998).
4. See Olwig (1993) for an examination of how immigrants relate to the Caribbean nation-state of St Kitts–Nevis to create a transnational context.
5. See Devore and Schlesinger (1999) for analyses of various theoretical approaches and critiques as they pertain to and include understandings of race, culture, and ethnicity.
6. This information is based on a personal interview with a male co-counsellor who co-leads men's groups. The group is predominately for males who have been mandated by the court to attend because of domestic assault. One group is strictly for Caribbean men, and there are also mixed groups that Caribbean men are welcomed to join. The interview was transcribed and analyzed for the purposes of this paper.

References

Al-Krewani, A. & Graham, J.R. (2000). Culturally sensitive social work practice with Arab clients in mental health settings. *Health and Social Work, 25*(11), 9–25.

Ashcroft, B., Griffith, G., & Tiffin, H. (1989). *The Empire Writes Back: Theory and Practice in Post-Colonial Literature.* New York: Routledge.

Bakan, A., & Stasiulis, D. (1996). *Structural Adjustment, Citizenship, and Foreign Domestic Labour: The Canadian Case.* Toronto: University of Toronto Press.

Baksh-Soodeen, R. (1998). Issues of difference in contemporary Caribbean. *Feminist Review, 59,* 74–85.

Barrow, C. (1996). *Family in the Caribbean: Themes and Perspectives.* Kingston, Jamaica: Ian Randle Publishers.

Bashi, V., & McDaniel, A. (1997). A theory of immigration and racial stratification. *Journal of Black Studies, 27*(5), 668–82.

Bobb Smith, Y. (1999). There is no place like home: Caribbean women's feminism in Canada. In A. Hetlinger (Ed.), *Emigre Feminism: Transnational Perspectives* (pp. 149–72). Toronto: University of Toronto Press.

Brown, L. (1996). Anti-racism as an ethical norm in feminist therapy practice. In J. Adleman & G. Enguidanos (Eds), *Racism in the Lives of Women* (pp. 137–48). New York: Harrington Park Press.

Calliste, A. (1996). Anti-racism organizing and resistance in nursing: African Canadian women. *Canadian Review of Sociology and Anthropology, 33*(3), 361–90.

Calliste, A., & Dei, G.J. (Eds) (2000). *Anti-Racist Feminism: Critical Race and Gender Studies.* Halifax: Fernwood.

Dei, G.S. (1996). *Theory and Anti-Racism Education.* Halifax: Fernwood

Devore, W., & Schlesinger, G. (1999). *Ethnic-Sensitive Social Work Practice.* 5th ed. Toronto: Allyn and Bacon.

Edmondson, L. (1974). Caribbean nation-building and the internationalization of race: Issues and perspectives. In Wendell Bell (Ed.), *Ethnicity and Nation-Building: Comparative, International and Historical Perspectives.* Beverley Hills, CA: Sage.

Ellsworth, E. (1989). Why doesn't it feel empowering? Working through the repressive myths of critical pedagogy. *Harvard Educational Review, 59*(3), 297–324.

Espinet, R. (1993). Representation and the Indo-Caribbean woman in Trinidad and Tobago. In F. Birbalsingh (Ed.), *Indo-Caribbean Resistance* (pp. 42–61). Toronto: TSAR Publications.

Faist, T. (2000). Transnationalization in international migration: Implications for the study of citizenship and culture. *Ethnic and Racial Studies, 23*(2), 191–222.

Fernando, S. (1991). *Mental Health, Race and Culture.* Basingstoke, UK: Macmillan.

Fleras, A., & Elliott, J.L. (1999). *Unequal Relations: An Introduction to Race, Ethnic, and Aboriginal Dynamics in Canada.* 3rd ed. Toronto: Prentice Hall Allyn Bacon.

Frankenberg, R. (1993). *White Women, Race Matters: The Social Construction of Whiteness.* Minneapolis: University of Minnesota Press.

Gill, O. (1995). *The Role of School Social Workers in Facilitating the Success of Immigrant African-Caribbean Students in Canadian Schools.* Unpublished MA thesis, York University, Toronto.

Giroux, H. (1992). *Border Crossings: Cultural Workers and the Politics of Education.* New York: Routledge

Glasgow, G.F., & Gouse-Sheese, J. (1995). Themes of rejection and abandonment in group work with Caribbean adolescents. *Social Work with Groups, 17*(4), 3–27.

Glick, L. (1985). Epilogue: The meanings of ethnicity in the Caribbean. *Ethnic Group, 6,* 233–48.

Gopaul-McNicol, S.A. (1997). Family therapy in Trinidad and Tobago. *International Journal of Sociology of the Family, 27*(1), 35–44.

Gopie, K.J. (1993). The next Indo-Caribbean generation in Canada. In F. Birbalsingh (Ed.), *Indo-Caribbean Resistance* (pp. 62–6). Toronto: TSAR Publications.

Healy, K., & Leonard, P. (2000). Responding to uncertainty: Critical social work education in the postmodern habitat. *Journal of Progressive Human Services, 11*(1), 23–48.

Hernandez-Ramdwar, C. (1994). Ms Edge Innate. In C. Camper (Ed.), *Miscegenation Blues: Voices of Mixed Race Women* (pp. 2–7). Toronto: Sister Vision Press.

Henry, F. (1999). Caribbean peoples. In P.R. Magocsi (Ed.). *Encyclopedia of Canadian Peoples.* Toronto: University of Toronto Press.

Henry, F., Tator, C., Mattis, W., & Rees, T. (1995). *The Colour of Democracy.* Toronto: Harcourt Brace.

Ho, M.K. (1987). *Family Therapy with Ethnic Minorities.* Newbury Park, CA: Sage.

Jakubowski, L.M. (1997). *Immigration and the Legalization of Racism.* Halifax: Fernwood.

James, C.E. (1990). *Making It: Black Youth, Racism and Career Aspirations in a Big City.* Oakville, ON: Mosaic Press.

James, W., & Walker, T.G. (1991). *The West Indians in Canada.* Waterloo, ON: Wilfrid Laurier University Press.

Lum, D. (1986). *Social Work Practice and People of Color: A Process Stage Approach.* Pacific Grove, CA: Brooks/Cole.

Margolin, L. (1997) *Under the Cover of Kindness: The Invention of Social Work.* Charlottesville: University Press of Virginia.

McGoldrick, M. (Ed.) (1998). *Re-visioning Family Therapy: Race, Culture, and Gender in Clinical Practice.* New York: Guildford Press.

Mohammed, P. (1998). Towards indigenous feminist theorizing in the Caribbean. *Feminist Review, 59,* 6–33.

Ng, R. (1986). Immigrant women in Canada: A social constructed category. *Resources for Feminist Research, 15*(1), 13–14.

Olwig, K.F. (1993). Defining the national in the transnational: Cultural identity in the Afro-Caribbean diaspora. *Ethnos, 58*(3–4), 361–76.

Pieterse, J.N. & Parekh, B. (Eds). (1995). Shifting imaginaries: decolonization, internal decolonization, postcoloniality. *The Decolonization of Imagination: Culture, Knowledge and Power.* London: Zed. 1–19.

Razack, N. (1999). Anti-discriminatory practice: Pedagogical struggles and challenges. *British Journal of Social Work, 29,* 231–50.

———. (2000). Shifting positions: Making meaning in social work. In L. Napier & J. Fook (Eds), *Breakthroughs in Practice: Theorising Critical Moments in Social Work* (pp. 116–30). London: Whiting and Birch.

———. (2001). Diversity and difference in the field education encounter: Issues and challenges of racial minority students. *Social Work Education, 19*(2), 219–32.

Razack, N., & Jeffery, D. (2002). Critical race discourse and tenets for social work. Re-submitted to *Canadian Social Work Review.*

Razack, S. (1995). The perils of talking about culture: Schooling research on South and East Asian students. *Race, Gender and Class, 2*(3), 66–82.

———. (1998) *Looking White People in the Eye: Gender, Race and Culture in Classrooms and in Courtrooms.* Toronto: University of Toronto Press.

————. (2000). Your place or mine? Transnational feminist collaboration. In A. Calliste & G.J. Dei (Eds). *Anti-Racist Feminism: Critical Race and Gender Studies* (pp. 39–53). Halifax: Fernwood.

Richmond, A.H. (1993). Immigrants in Metropolitan Toronto. *New Community, 19*(2), 263–80.

Robinson, L. (2000). Racial identity attitudes and self-esteem of Black adolescents in residential care: An exploratory study. *British Journal of Social Work, 30,* 25–36.

Rooney-Bray, D. (1999). *Indo Caribbean-Canadian women's experiences of woman abuse.* Unpublished MA thesis, York University, Toronto.

Satzewich, V. (Ed.) (1998). *Racism and Social Inequality in Canada: Concepts, Controversies and Strategies of Resistance.* Toronto: Thompson Educational Publishing.

Selvon, S. (1979) Three into one can't go: East Indian, Trinidadian, West Indian. Opening address to the East Indians in the Caribbean Conference, University of the West Indies, Trinidad.

Sewell-Coker, B., Hamilton-Collins, J., & Fein, E. (1985). Social work with West Indian Immigrants. *Social Casework, 66*(9), 563–8.

Sidiqqui, H. (2000). Immigrants should boycott Canada. *Toronto Star,* 14 September, A34.

Simmons, A. (1998). Racism and immigration policy. In V. Satzewich (Ed.), *Racism and Social Inequality in Canada: Concepts, Controversies and Strategies of Resistance* (pp. 87–114). Toronto: Thompson Educational Publishing.

Small, S. (1998). The contours of racialization: Structures, representation and resistance in the United States. In V. Satzewich (Ed.), *Racism and Social Inequality in Canada: Concepts, Controversies and Strategies of Resistance* (pp. 69–86). Toronto: Thompson Educational Publishing.

Thakur, S. (1994). Domino: Filming the stories of interracial people. In C. Camper (Ed.), *Miscegenation Blues: The Voices of Mixed Race Women* (pp. 345–9). Toronto: Sister Vision Press.

Thrasher, S.P. (1994). Psychodynamic therapy and culture in the treatment of incest of a West Indian immigrant. *Journal of Child Sexual Abuse, 3*(1), 37–52.

Williams, P. (1997). *Seeing a Color-Blind Future: The Paradox of Race.* New York: Noonday Press.

Williams, P. & Chrisman, L. (Eds) (1994). *Colonial Discourses and Post-Colonial Theory: A Reader.* New York: Columbia University Press.

Chapter 15

The Context of Culture: Social Work Practice with Canadians of South Asian Background

Sarah Maiter

While attending a recent conference on multicultural social work, a hospital social worker asked me for advice concerning appropriate provision of culturally sensitive services for a South Asian–Canadian woman who was being treated for breast cancer. Barbara wanted to provide her client, Mrs Singh, with individual counselling and to arrange for her to participate in an ongoing hospital support group in order that she could receive the necessary help in dealing with her feelings about the nature and extent of her disease as well as the emotional and physical consequences of chemotherapy. Unfortunately, Barbara's objective was thwarted by Mr Singh's insistence on accompanying his wife during her bi-weekly hospital sessions and his tendency to speak and to make decisions on her behalf. Indeed, he refused to allow his wife to address any aspect of her circumstances on her own. Given the Singh's traditional dress and appearance, Barbara was inclined to interpret their behaviour and relationship in culturally specific terms. Her assumptions about South Asian culture led her to question whether Mrs Singh was being emotionally abused and physically controlled by her husband.

Aware of my professional interest in South Asian culture and my South Asian heritage and appearance, Barbara specifically inquired about how to deal with Mr Singh's dominance over his wife and how to empower Mrs Singh to assert control over her destiny. Although I was not sufficiently informed to assess the Singh family dynamics comprehensively, I asked Barbara whether or not she had considered the possibility that Mr Singh's apparently overbearing behaviour reflected his genuine concern for the health and well-being of his wife. Barbara admitted that she had overlooked this consideration and expressed her appreciation to me for making her aware of an alternative perspective and the numerous possibilities that it opens up for multicultural social work.

I do not yet know whether my advice helped Barbara to address the needs of her client more effectively, but this encounter illustrates the limitations of focusing on culture rather than on context in social work practice. Barbara was well-meaning in attempting to understand the cultural influences on family dynamics. She had progressed beyond earlier social work practice, which tended to ignore or under-estimate the need for culturally sensitive services. Over the past two decades, research in the field (for example, Hines, Garcia-Preto, McGoldrick, Almeida, & Weltman, 1992; McGoldrick, 1982; McGoldrick, Pearce, & Giordano, 1996) has urged social workers to become more knowledgeable about the culture of groups in order to provide appropriate services. Although a broad understanding of the specific values and customs of the client's culture is useful, the danger of trying to gain culturally specific understanding of groups can result in a number of critical errors in service assessment and provision. For example, social workers may not be able to understand the intricacies of another culture; culturally specific knowledge can easily be misapplied in service; and, most importantly, the focus on culture can prevent workers from assessing essential contextual issues that affect the lives of clients. Factors such as racism, structural inequities, and power differentials in both society and the social services become all too easily hidden and ignored.

Accordingly, social work must move beyond the perception of culture to con-sider the context of culture in order to provide appropriate services for diverse populations. My research and practice experience with South Asian Canadians, in addition to my personal background as a South Asian Canadian, enables me to demonstrate the problematic tendency of social work to rely on cultural percep-tion more than contextual reality.

Diversity among South Asians in Canada

The 1996 national census estimates that nearly 600,000 people of South Asian descent reside in Canada, representing a little over 2 per cent of the population. Most of this diverse cultural group is concentrated in the provinces of Ontario, with nearly 400,000 people of South Asian descent, and British Columbia, with almost 160,000 (Statistics Canada, 1996). As a result of the steady flow of immigration, these numbers will rise considerably in the national census in 2001. The term *South Asian* has been socially constructed to refer to people who have immigrated or are descendants of immigrants from Bangladesh, Bhutan, India, Maldives, Pakistan, and Sri Lanka. South Asian can also refer to individuals from Africa, Mauritius, Fiji, the Caribbean, Guyana, Great Britain, and European countries who trace their ori-gins to the aforementioned South Asian countries. Some South Asians may prefer, however, to be known by their country of origin; for example, people from Sri Lanka may prefer to be known as Sri Lankan, while those from Bangladesh may pre-fer Bangladeshi, rather than be designated by the generic term South Asian. Others from the Indian diaspora may feel little connection with the Indian subcontinent and may prefer to identify with their more recent country of origin. South Asians in Canada have also been referred to as Indo-Canadian and East Indian.

Because of the regional vastness and national distinctions captured by the term South Asian, considerable cultural differences exist within it, and these are further complicated by language and religion. The South Asian region is home to almost a billion people, who speak a wide variety of languages and dialects. In India alone, people speak fifteen major languages (including Hindi, the national language) and approximately four hundred dialects (Israel, 1999a). Along with Hinduism, the dominant religion practised, other major religions include Islam, Buddhism, Jainism, Zoroastrianism, Sikhism, Judaism, and Christianity. The population of Pakistan and Bangladesh is primarily Muslim, while Sri Lanka has a large contingency of Buddhists. Added to these regional, linguistic, religious, and cultural differences are intersecting contextual diversities such as socio-economic status, gender, ability, and age.

Thus, it would be a sweeping generalization to assume that a monolithic South Asian culture exists. On the whole, culture should be viewed less as a static entity within a group of people and more as lived experiences within a multiplicity of contexts. In effect, there is no authentic culture to understand, nor is there one way in which a culture is lived. Indeed, the dynamic interaction of culture, ethnicity, and race needs to be understood within the current context that minority groups experience.

A Contextually Based Framework for Understanding Cultural Diversity

In her article, 'Training to Think Culturally: A Multidimensional Comparative Framework' (1995), Celia Jaes Falicov offers an analytical perspective designed to assist family therapists in assessing the needs of and providing appropriate services to culturally diverse populations. She advocates a multidimensional approach that recognizes the potential complexity of the cultural background or circumstances of both the family and the service provider and that encourages a more inquisitive and open-minded strategy, rather than relying on preconceived or stereotypical ethnic-focused information. Her multidimensional position 'goes beyond the one-dimensional definition of culture as ethnicity and aims at a more comprehensive definition of culture that encompasses other contextual variables' (1995, p. 375). Falicov includes in her multidimensional definition of culture 'those sets of shared world views, meanings and adaptive behaviors derived from simultaneous membership and participation in a multiplicity of contexts, such as rural, urban or suburban setting; language, age, gender cohort, family configuration, race, ethnicity, religion, nationality, socioeconomic status, employment, education, occupation, sexual orientation, political ideology; migration and stage of acculturation' (p. 375). In applying this perspective to Mexican families, Falicov (1996) outlines four parameters that 'become roadmaps to facilitate travel in the clients' culturally patterned interactions': migration/acculturation, ecological context, family organization, and family life cycle (Falicov, 1995, p. 378). My research suggests that these parameters are applicable, with some modifications, to South Asian immigrants as well as to Canadian-born South Asians.

Falicov suggests that two perspectives inform her multidimensional framework for assessment and service provision: cultural diversity, which accepts that diversity exists and views Eurocentric practice as problematic; and social construction, which moves beyond mere interpretative analysis to a critical perspective about existing theories and practices. To Falicov's perspectives, I would add reflexivity and self-awareness. In looking at diverse cultures, it becomes all too easy to forget that the observer, in this case the social service practitioner, also has a culture that processes information. On the one hand, all social workers share a culture. The institutions in which we work, the theories that we learn, the laws that govern our work, all come from what we call in the West the 'dominant culture'. On the other hand, the information processed is also judged from the perspective of one's own cultural lens. As Herberg (1993) notes, 'One of the most important facets of the concept, culture, refers to the patterned nature of behaviour, beliefs, values, customs and institutions. Pattern, it should be pointed out, cannot be seen directly; there is an abstracting process that must be done before the pattern appears . . . [and] the product of abstracting may be an observation, consciously or unconsciously done, that certain behaviours are different from one's own. Further, these differences will be negatively or positively evaluated' (p. 3).

Even if we fear that we may indeed not be able to keep all our assumptions under control, it is better to be aware that they may be interfering in our assessments than not to be aware of this perspective at all. Social workers from diverse ethnic and racial background also need to be wary of the process of abstracting and the difficulty that they may experience in acknowledging that certain unacceptable behaviours are occurring in a family from the same background as themselves (Devore & Schlesinger, 1996).

Migration/Acculturation

According to Falicov, contextual factors arising from migration and acculturation of individuals and families form an important part of social work assessment when working with people from diverse backgrounds. The migration/acculturation parameter acknowledges diversity of where the family members came from, when, how and why they came, how they live, and what their future aspirations are. Migration results in the disruption of both internal and external meaning systems. Internal meaning systems include separations and reunions, trauma and crisis, grief and mourning, disorienting anxieties, and cultural identity. External meaning systems include language, social networks, institutions, and values. Figure 15.1 shows the above elements.

In moving to a new country, immigrants leave behind familiar social support networks, which Williams (1998) calls 'plausibility structures'. These structures 'provide a foundation for knowledge, customs, morals, leadership styles and commitments, supporting civic order and personal health' (Williams, 1998, p. 186). In the process, individuals and families suffer from a loss of meaning systems that are embedded in one's culture and that influence relationships with others (Falicov,

Figure 15.1   Migration/Acculturation

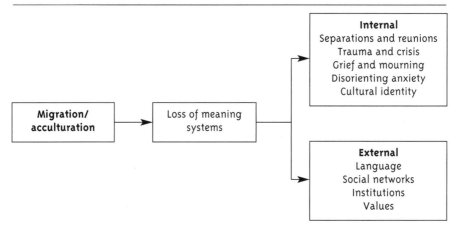

1996). Being uprooted from meaning systems can result in psychological distress, including culture shock; a sense of marginalization, isolation, and alienation; psychosomatic symptoms such as palpitations, dizziness, and insomnia; anxiety and depression; and post-traumatic stress (Doyle & Visano, 1987; Garza-Guerro, 1974; Grinberg & Grinberg, 1989; Herberg, 1993; Naidoo & Edwards, 1991; Steiner & Bansil, 1989). Other practical dilemmas that can leave immigrants, both new and old, feeling disempowered include raising children in a cultural context that is different from the one in which they were raised, and being dependent on their children serving as interpreters of both language and dominant cultural expectations. Staggered migration, whereby family members arrive at different times, also presents challenges, such as different levels of acculturation, language acquisition, reformulation of the family, and emotional issues regarding reasons for family members being left behind.

Few immigrants are prepared for the uprooting and turmoil that migration causes. Indeed, the initial response to the prospect of migration tends to focus on the hope and excitement of a better life ahead, while little attention is paid to a vague sense of loss that is also felt at leaving behind family members and familiar structures. Immigrants work at establishing new meaning systems and plausibility structures as they adjust to their new country. They become involved in religious and other social organizations that provide them with opportunities to develop new contacts and meaning systems. According to Williams (1998), immigrants gravitate to familiar social structures, not so much to separate themselves from settled society but to give themselves breathing space in familiar settings and to develop new plausibility structures for themselves and their children. As newcomers settle and adjust to the new country, find employment, become familiar with their surroundings, gain fluency in the English language, and establish new relationships, many of the original psychological distresses may decrease.

In a study that I conducted in the late 1990s on child abuse and neglect in the South Asian community (CERIS, 1998), South Asian parents identified cultural differences in childrearing approaches, differences in expectations for their children, raising children in a society that does not support these expectations, the overwhelming presence of mainstream values in basic social institutions such as schools and community organizations, and lack of an extended family and kinship ties as some of the stressful consequence of migration (Maiter, 1999). When social workers encounter South Asian parents who are experiencing problems related to their children, they should explore how issues of migration are influencing parent–child interactions. Parents resort to a range of responses in their attempts to compensate for the common consequences of migration. While some find a middle ground, adjusting values and approaches to parenting, others experience problems in making such changes. Supportive and culturally relevant social networks increase the ability to make the needed changes.

For some families, lack of financial resources and community networks increases the sense of alienation and isolation and can result in family dysfunction and violence. These families should be linked to supports in the community. In some instances, however, a sense of failure and shame at not succeeding in the settlement process may cause families to resist being linked with their community network. Care needs to be taken that such families do not remain isolated. Mr and Mrs C., recent immigrants from a rural village in India, with little knowledge of English, were reported to the local Children's Aid Society for neglect of their two young boys. The social worker assessed that the family was isolated and that linking them with culturally based community resources would help to relieve some of their stress. The social worker hoped that the children and parents would find friends and would become involved in community recreational activities. Contrary to the social worker's suggestions, the C. family refused to be linked with groups of the same ethnic background as themselves. The social worker did not want to press the issue, noting that many individuals and families did not necessarily want to remain connected with their cultural communities. Although correct in her assessment, it is important that special efforts continue to be made to link the family with some networks. Leaving this family without supports can result in increased isolation and alienation, with detrimental effects on the family. It is critical that the worker recognize that, although the family did not want to be linked with community supports from their cultural background, they may not have the resources to establish links with mainstream institutions; conversely, many mainstream institutions are often not equipped to provide culturally relevant services.

Different levels of acculturation can influence a family's ability to access help. Those South Asians from large urban settings, who had access to Western education and have greater fluency in English, will find the transition to the new country easier (Assanand, Dias, Richardson, & Waxler-Morrison, 1990). Others from rural settings, where the opportunity to learn English and Western ways is limited, will likely have greater difficulty with acculturation to a new environment, particularly a large city. The social worker, therefore, will encounter South Asian clients with different degrees of acculturation that depend on their personal, social, and economic situation in their original country, the region from which they migrated, and the duration and location of residence in the new country. Still, so much variation exists in the degree of acculturation for a South Asian individual or family that social workers need to develop understanding of the client through each individual encounter.

Families may choose to retain many cultural ways and norms over several generations. For example, the K. family, who immigrated to British Columbia in the 1960s and chose to reside in a neighbourhood with a substantial South Asian population, conduct their daily transactions among South Asians and exert strong pressure on their children to marry among the group. Mr K.'s brother and sister-in-law desire to retain many aspects of the culture but are open to their children marrying outside the group as long as their partner is of the same faith. Yet another brother, who has been transferred to Calgary for work, has decided that assimilation works best for him and has no restrictions on the choice of marriage partners for his children. However, his wife prefers greater involvement with the South Asian community and with members of their particular religion.

Adding to the complexity of social work assessments is the lack of a clear linear progression from less acculturation to greater acculturation. Mr and Mrs T. have been in Canada since the 1960s and have five children and several grandchildren born and raised in Canada. Mr and Mrs T. recently decided that they missed the sense of comfort that they got from living in their original cultural milieu. They therefore bought a house in Pakistan, where they plan to reside for several months in a year. The varied nature of acculturation among South Asians and likely among other diverse cultural groups leads to a questioning of past social work efforts that focused on encouraging newcomers to shed old ways and to assimilate to the ways of the adopted country. Indeed, acculturation theory suggests that retaining old customs results in increased mental health risks for immigrants (Falicov, 1996). However, the bicultural approach, wherein individuals retain their culture while learning to cope with living in a new context, is now considered to have better mental health outcomes (Lessinger, 1995).

If a family appears to be struggling with migration/acculturation issues, social work services should be directed at two levels. First, clients should be assisted with practical issues of settlement, which invariably involves services such as advocacy for housing, day care, English-as-a-second-language classes, and mediation between school and the family. Second, families who have lost the support networks of the extended family can be assisted to find new support structures.

Initially, families are too busy with practical issues of finding employment and housing to focus on forming new relationships. Still, having these support systems can ease the issues around settlement. Families are often accustomed to built-in support networks in their home country and may not realize that these have now to be consciously established. Social workers can explore with their clients support networks that would be meaningful to them. Many South Asian respondents in my study note that even if they have extended family in their adopted country, distances prevent a close relationship with these members. Many of them develop closer relationships with friends of similar cultural backgrounds who are in close proximity to them, and they call on these friends for help rather than on family members from whom they have grown apart. Yet others relied entirely on family for support and help. Thus, the emerging support networks are not necessarily replicas of systems that existed in the country of origin. Finding supports in geographic locations that do not have large numbers of South Asians can pose added problems.

Other studies are also beginning to focus on successful settlement patterns of immigrants, and findings from the studies are useful in helping individuals and families who are struggling with such issues. For example, Chicoine, Charbonneau, Rose, & Ray (1997), focusing on research with women in Montreal who had immigrated from three regions, Poland, South Asia, and Latin America, note that immigrant women's networks are generated in close proximity to their residence. All thirty-seven women interviewed in the study reported that most of their support networks consisted of women from their home country. These women formed networks with the aid of intermediaries whom they contacted through their husband or their associates at work or school, in addition to other sources that change over time. The study suggests that cultural issues, residential space, and support networks are closely related. The researchers' observation that immigrant men create networks largely through work has implications for those who are unemployed. Unemployment may prevent immigrant men from establishing supportive relationships through work; at the same time, they may also have fewer resources and opportunities than do the women in the study to establish support networks in their neighbourhoods.

Thus, my research and experience with the migration/acculturation patterns of South Asians in Canada, both Canadian born and immigrants, whether long-settled or newly arrived, suggest that services to the group must be considered in multicontextual rather than strictly cultural terms. Because they are not monolithic constructs having uniform consequences for individuals and families, migration/acculturation factors present challenges to social work assessment. Social workers need to assess the individual effects of migration and the level of acculturation of clients to determine the nature of service provision.

Ecology/Environment

Falicov further recommends that social workers providing therapeutic services to diverse families consider their *ecological context*—that is, where and how the family lives and how it fits into its environment. The various factors that form the family's ecological context include interaction with the community in terms of ethnicity, religion, race, and social networks; the living environment, including housing and neighbourhood and their safety; work, which includes income, schedule, stability, satisfaction, and discrimination; school, which includes achievement, discipline, parent involvement, race, and ethnicity; and other institutions such as legal, medical, and mental health. These ecological elements, illustrated in Figure

15.2, encompass the 'total field' of a problem, providing a framework for understanding the individual or family interactions with outside institutions.

Because they are relatively recent immigrants to Canada, South Asians are still dealing with issues of settlement and inclusion. The first South Asians who arrived in Canada around the begining of the twentieth century confronted accusations that they were 'contaminating' the purity and virtue of an essentially White Anglo-Saxon Protestant society (Johnston, 1999). Discriminatory legislation in British Columbia resulted in the loss of basic civil rights for South Asians in 1907 and eventually halted their further immigration by 1919. Although South Asians struggled on their own to gain the rights that were natural for immigrants from Europe and Britain, they remained disenfranchised until 1947, when the restrictions on their immigration were partially lifted. A significant change for South Asians came in 1967, when, like other residents of Canada, they were permitted to sponsor more distant relatives. As a result, the mass of South Asian immigration to Canada has occurred since the 1960s. Increasingly, South Asians have established religious and social service agencies that not only ease their settlement but also lobby on behalf of newcomers for access to relevant services.

South Asians generally find that migration has transported them to a vastly different community environment. Cultural, religious, racial, and language differences contribute to making the community environment different for South Asians. Many, even those of the second generation, choose to live in areas that have greater numbers of South Asians in order to enjoy proximity to familiar surroundings as well as social and cultural amenities, such as music, movies, restaurants, shops carrying South Asian goods, places of worship, recreational facilities, and home

Figure 15.2   Ecology/Environment

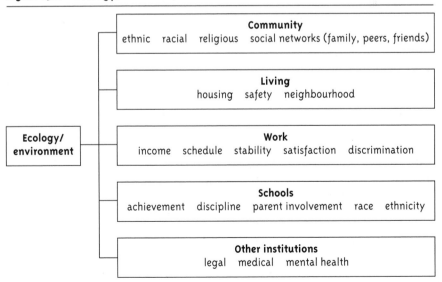

language and religious classes for children. Residing in an ethnic neighbourhood forms a buffer against culture shock while meeting the needs of the group and making access to companionship and support networks more readily available. Still, South Asians also live away from ethnic neighbourhoods—some out of choice; others because of employment. Some younger South Asians are making a choice to leave ethnic neighbourhoods as they are finding that residing in such neighbourhoods can restrict their choice of lifestyle. Others who had left the neighbourhood missed the supports that they used to enjoy and have returned. For example, Mr and Mrs A., with their four children ranging from six to twelve years of age, moved from the apartment in which they had resided for the first eight years after their arrival in Canada. Both were employed and felt that moving to a better neighbourhood would provide more opportunities for their children to become familiar with Canadian ways. The family, however, decided to move back to their old apartment building not only because the children were unhappy at being away from friends and family who also lived in the apartment building but also because the parents were experiencing considerable stress in arranging after-school care for their children. Care for their children was easily available in the apartment but posed a problem in their new area of residence.

Living in close proximity to extended family members offers many supports. Grandparents, uncles, and aunts are available to help transmit and support group values, thereby relieving stress on parents who are endeavouring to provide the atmosphere in which they grew up but without the supports that were available to their parents. Under such circumstances, husband–wife and parent–child relationships can be burdensome. Without relief from parental responsibilities, parents can become overly restrictive with their children, especially when their children are adolescents and are striving for more independence. Under similar circumstances in the home country, grandparents often act as the voice of reason to diffuse the tension between parents and children. Pettys and Balgopal (1998) found in their study of multigenerational conflicts among South Asians in the United States that grandparents in India who maintained strong links with their children and grandchildren in the United States continued to play this mediating role. Indeed, grandparents cautioned parents about becoming overly restrictive with their children and encouraged them to understand that their children were now American and had to learn to live in the North American context.

Relocation not only results in the immediate disruption of support networks, but also presents the challenge to establish new support networks that are often unlike the ones in the home country. Models of support systems that worked in the original country do not always have relevance in the adopted country as neither the context nor the resources are the same as in the original country. Mr and Mrs S., who moved to Canada with their three children ranging from seven to seventeen years of age, are feeling overwhelmed caring for their adolescent son, who is severely mentally challenged. In the home country, many family members would often provide informal relief for the parents. In Canada, this support network is not available to the parents. Through government programs, the son is entitled to relief care once a month, but the parents feel guilty when they use this resource because it appears to isolate him from family. In the home country, the support that they received was in the context of their son spending time with cousins and other family members rather than the parents being provided with relief from caring for him.

Differences relating to race, ethnicity, religion, and language combined with the reality of South Asians being a more recent immigrant group has implications for the fit between the environment and the person or family with respect to living situation and interactions at work, at school, and with other institutions. Since the change in immigration policy that allows more diverse groups of South Asians to come to Canada, South Asians with limited resources have settled in increasing numbers. The result is that impoverished South Asians are faced with living in neighbourhoods that are considered unsafe and less conducive to raising children. Parents have to be extra vigilant in such situations, with the result that levels of stress increase. South Asians, like other visible minority groups, can also encounter discriminatory practices in their attempts to obtain adequate housing. Landlords may be disinclined to rent to South Asian tenants because they believe negative stereotyping that suggests that they make undesirable tenants. Bias in renting also exists because of fear that existing tenants may move out because of the presence of certain ethnic or racial groups (Quann, 1979).

In assessing the ecological context, social workers must consider the work context of clients. Exploring with clients issues such as job satisfaction, job stability, adequacy of income for family needs, flexibility of the work schedule, and the nature and extent of discriminatory experiences at work contributes to a greater understanding of the individual's or the family's situation. Some newcomers to the country face an environment in which their professional and skilled-trades qualifications are not recognized, educational credits are not always granted equivalent status, and the requirement of Canadian experience puts barriers to finding employment (Israel, 1999b). They then take up other employment but are often dissatisfied at having to endure lower standards than those which they had set for themselves. Many also miss working in their profession, yet other advantages gained by making the move prevent a return to the country of origin. Some South Asians also find that bias in the workplace has denied them access to certain jobs and opportunities for advancement. Although the research on South Asians specifically is scant, a study of visible minorities generally shows that the average wage offer for minority males, both immigrant and non-immigrant combined, was 28.5 per cent less than that for White males. For minority females, it was 45.8 per cent lower than for White males and 9.4 per cent lower than for White females. Only about 30 per cent of the gap could be accounted for by productivity differences (Christofides & Swidinsky 1994). A number of studies (Abella, 1984; Bambrough, Bowden, & Wien, 1992; Billingsley & Musynski, 1985; Canada, 1984; deSilva, 1992; Henry & Ginzberg, 1984; Jain, 1985; Rees, 1991; Reitz, Calzavara, & Dasko, 1981) confirm discrimination in the employment practices of companies as well as by employment agencies with respect to visible minorities.

Assessments of South Asian families should also include an understanding of the children's school environment, the consequences of race and ethnicity within that environment, the level of parent involvement in the school environment, the children's school achievement, and disciplinary concerns at school. Because of their racial and ethnic minority status, South Asian families encounter within the school system issues relating to a Eurocentric curriculum, racial harassment, lack of representation, racially biased practices of teachers and administrators, and devaluation of the role and participation of the parents and the community (Henry, Tator, Mattis, & Rees, 1995). Newer South Asian immigrants attempt to make sense of contextual differences between the school environment of the home country and the adopted country. Such contextual differences include a higher degree of parental involvement, greater expectations for children to express their opinions, more discussion of social matters such as sex education, and a generally more liberal atmosphere in the school system than in the home country (Assanand et al., 1990).

South Asian parents who wish to retain their cultural expression within the home encounter more difficulty once children attend public school (Lessinger, 1995). Parents often respond by taking the positives from both cultures and finding a middle ground (Pettys & Balgopal, 1998). Those who have difficulty accommodating both cultures may struggle more with their children, who may resent the imposition of cultural norms that differ from those of their school friends. These conflicts can become unresolvable, resulting in the need for social work intervention, including child protection if violence is involved. Families who want to retain values and norms of their religion, and can afford to do so, may send their children to parochial school. Many of these schools are full and have long waiting lists. These schools allow easier transmission of values, protect children from feeling different, and provide positive role models within their culture.

When South Asians interact with mainstream social institutions, they confront barriers relating to language, race, ethnicity, and familiarity, which inhibit full access to equitable services. Child protection social workers in my study note that the lack of culturally appropriate resources for South Asians necessitated a more intrusive and directive approach with these families. Social workers fear that the lack of resources for these families leaves them without appropriate supports and places them at increased risk of abusing their children. Because mainstream agencies dealing with mental and public health problems are not necessarily equipped to meet the needs of their South Asian clients, ethno-specific agencies have been inaugurated to provide more culturally relevant services. But these alternative services are not always adequately funded and therefore continue to function on the margins, in comparison to mainstream agencies.

Consideration of a client's ecological context is a fundamental aspect of any comprehensive social work assessment. If this assessment detects the family's inability to cope with its particular environment, the social worker can act as an intermediary with outside institutions (Falicov, 1995) or, alternatively, can offer counselling that can enhance the client's responsiveness. Clients from diverse cultural backgrounds inevitably have differential coping abilities and strategies to interact with people, who, in turn, have a broad range of responses to them. Thus, as is the case for migration/acculturation, the ecological context requires individualized assessment and intervention.

Family Organization

Therapeutic services to culturally diverse individuals and families, according to Falicov, must also be provided within the context of family organization. Family organization can differ according to socio-economic level, urban or rural setting, and ethnicity. Falicov uses the 'dominant dyad', or the dominant valued relationship, to facilitate the understanding of family organization. Western family organization is based primarily on the husband–wife dyad, and the nuclear family is considered to be the ideal. In some diverse cultures, however, dyads such as the parent–child, the father–son, the mother–son within the context of an extended family system, are given high status. Falicov notes that these dyads influence the boundaries that dictate who is included or excluded from the family, what the power balance is across gender and generations within families, what the values are relating to personal individuation and family connectedness, whether communication styles are direct or indirect, and whether emotional expressivity between family members and outsiders is high or low.

In the traditional Western nuclear family, according to Falicov, the central husband–wife dyad has clear and exclusive boundaries around it, egalitarian relations are the ideal, direct communication style is the norm, individuation is favoured, and intergenerational coalitions are considered a threat. In Eastern cultures, the dominant dyad is more often the parent–child dyad within an extended family. According to Falicov, boundaries around the parent–child dyad are clear but inclusive, relationships are hierarchical, communication styles are indirect, connectedness is greatly emphasized, and same-generation alliances can be a threat. She further notes that the concepts of both dyads are not dichotomous but need to be understood as extending along a continuum.

Table 15.1 compares the traditional Western family organization with the typical South Asian family organization. The South Asian family organization can be further understood through the constructs of collectivism and individualism. Although South Asians come from vastly different traditions, values, and world views that are further influenced by such factors as socio-econmic status and regional location, Triandis (1994) insists that they tend to come from a collectivist culture. Collectivist cultures are those that organize their subjective experiences around one or more collectives such as the family, religious group, or kinship network (Triandis, 1994). A collectivist culture defines identity by group membership (Pettys & Balgopal, 1998) and emphasizes the internalization of group values, norms, and roles (Shor, 1998). South Asians in Canada find themselves to be immersed in an individualistic culture, in which personal identity is based primarily on individual characteristics. Since the self is largely independent and separate

Table 15. 1   Family Organization

Western	Eastern
husband–wife dyad (nuclear family)	parent–child dyad (extended family)
clear and exclusive (boundaries)	clear but inclusive (boundaries)
egalitarian relationships (hierarchies)	hierarchical relationships (hierarchies)
direct (communication style)	indirect (communication style)
individuation (values)	connectedness (values)
intergenerational coalitions (threat)	same-generation alliances (threat)

from groups, autonomy and individuation are the developmental tasks of individuals (Triandis, Brislin, & Hui, 1988). While an individual can be a member of many groups in individualistic cultures, no single group fully defines one's identity nor determines one's behaviour. In collectivist cultures, by contrast, people are attached to fewer groups, but these attachments have significant influence in defining one's identity (Hui, 1988).

Collectivism and individualism prescribe different ways of rearing children, caring for the elderly, and cultivating relationships within groups. In collectivist cultures, values such as family integrity, security, obedience, and conformity are more highly valued, while achievement, pleasure, and competition are favoured by individualist cultures. Collectivists emphasize attributes such as harmony and saving face, preferring homogeneous in-groups while requiring that disagreements are not shared with out-groups (Triandis et al., 1988). Childrearing emphasis is on obedience, duty, respect for elders, and sacrifice for the group (Shor, 1998). Parenting tasks include responsibility for behaviours of children even into adulthood and ensuring the happiness and security of adult children through finding appropriate marriage partners (Assanand et al., 1990).

Although the constructs of individualism and collectivism are valuable for understanding broad differences among cultures, researchers are now finding considerable intragroup differences that must be factored into discussions of the constructs. Freeman's (1997) research shows that higher socio-economic status and occupational status, urban residence, and higher levels of education correlates with higher levels of individualism in Sri Lanka. Freeman's study suggests that, even though the constructs of individualism and collectivism are useful in understanding cultural differences, they should not be seen as applying universally to particular groups. Indeed, his research shows that aspects of both constructs are often found in families. He thus cautions against seeing the constructs as opposite ends of a single bipolar dimension. The extent to which South Asian–Canadian families and individuals are individualistic or collectivist varies considerably. Families may choose to be individualistic in many aspects in order to compete in a society where individualistic characteristics are valued, but they may still retain many aspects of collectivist values.

Determining the extent to which a family adheres to individualistic or collectivist values and norms can be further complicated by the fact that many South Asians, particularly the more recently arrived immigrants, are still in a state of transition, whereby values of the extended family are being replaced by values of the nuclear family. Some of these families struggle with divided loyalties about whether to uphold values that support individualism or those that support collectivism, while these loyalties become even more complicated by expectations from different family members about which values should be given prominence. Social workers can learn much from their clients not only about the fit between a family's current structure and the needs of its various members but also about the conflicts members may be experiencing in renegotiating values and norms (Falicov, 1995).

Social workers will, therefore, need to remain open to the variety of South Asian family structures and household types. In Canada, as in the home country, households typically range from nuclear families comprising husband, wife, and children to extended families including parents, children, married sons and their families. If married daughters and their husbands do not establish a separate household, it is customary for them to move in with their in-laws. Boundaries around family households are permeable, allowing for the inclusion of family members in need. For example, it is common for a widowed daughter and her children to move back into the home of her parents. In most circumstances, unmarried children, even if they are considerably older, will continue to reside with the family of origin. Nuclear families often choose to live in close proximity to extended family members and maintain close links with them, even on a daily basis. Extended family households provide built-in support networks for family members with respect to the nurturing of children, financial responsibilities, and advice on significant issues. Aside from extended household units, South Asian families tend to maintain large extended kinship networks within which much of their social, cultural, recreational, and economic transactions are conducted (Israel, 1999a, 1999b).

Migration can result in a disruption of familiar family patterns and ties, with resultant changes in roles and responsibilities of individual members. Yet no single model captures changes that take place in family organization resulting from families living in a different cultural context. In some families, the traditional support role and high value of elderly family members become disrupted, especially if they have joined their children in Canada at a later date. They find that their children and grandchildren are busy with hectic schedules and, although respect for the elderly remains, they are consulted less frequently on significant social and family matters. Some elders may become upset at these changes, whereas others see an opportunity to enjoy a different lifestyle. The lack of extended kin in close proximity and a less active social life than that enjoyed in the home country can result in loneliness for many elderly people.

For newer immigrants, roles are also challenged when children act as interpreters and assist parents with unfamiliar transactions. The role can be demanding for children and disrupting to the authority of parents. Children may also question the traditional authority given to extended kin. Thus, if parents ask for intervention from extended kin on a matter such as a teenager's misbehaviour, the teenager might respond by questioning the person's authority (Assanand et al., 1990). Change of family structure for young couples is also occurring, although not as a linear process. Many couples enjoy an initial period of relief at not having as many responsibilities to extended family but, subsequently, some experience a sense of loss at not having family members with whom they can interact and from whom they and their children can receive support. When they do not have anyone with whom to share parenting responsibilities, young parents can feel very taxed. Because of the many changes in family structure, the reliance on outside help for family issues, in the form of social service providers, is increasing.

In providing services for South Asian families, the social worker needs to remain mindful of two realities. First, the social worker who is unduly influenced by a Eurocentric perspective may be prone to stereotyping or sweeping generalization based on the assumption that South Asian family organization is predominantly collectivist in nature and features a large extended kinship network. Indeed, South Asian families, like their counterparts in other cultures, are undergoing a certain measure of organizational transformation that probably defies simple categorization or definition. Second, South Asian families are just as likely to be operating on the assumption that they conform or should conform to a 'traditional' structure, often unaware of the changing context of family life within their own culture. The result is bound to be a degree of tension between the social worker, who genuinely seeks to help, and the family, which is perhaps embarrassed or ashamed to find itself in the position of needing help from outsiders. Such is the complexity of cultural context.

Family Life Cycle

Finally, according to Falicov, social workers providing services to culturally diverse families need to realize that developmental stages and transitions in the family life cycle are culturally patterned. Therapists use the concept of family life cycle to understand individual and family age-appropriate behaviour; transitional points in families such as birth, marriage, raising children, and death; and changes in rules occurring at such times. Figure 15.3 captures issues related to developmental stages and transitions in families.

The definitions, stages, and rituals of the family life cycle of South Asian families are influenced by collectivist values, respect for authority, large family networks, expectation of lifelong parent–child interconnectedness, and religion. The realities and necessities of life in a new context, however, mediate the family cycle for South Asians in Canada. Since family life-cycle stages and rituals are passed on from one generation to the next (McGoldrick, 1982), South Asian–Canadian parents are confronted with this internalized understanding of what it means to raise children, to impart values, and to help children move through life-cycle stages. Yet in the new context, parents recognize that other dimensions have to be included in the rearing of their children in order to help them to meet the requirements of the society within which they are living as well as to handle effectively the overwhelm-

Figure 15.3   Family Life Cycle

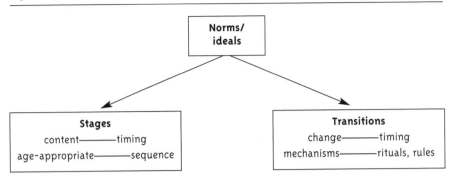

ing influences of a culture that is different from their own. Although, to some extent, all parents make changes from one generation to the next, South Asian parents and their children confront unique challenges: parents are raising children in a culture so different from the one in which they were raised, and children are confronted with making sense of two very different sets of values and norms. Family life-cycle stages and transitions also have implications for parents themselves and for grandparents, who are also confronted with a context that is different from the one in the home country. Life-cycle stages, like other cultural issues, are further mediated by poverty, education, and need.

At various stages of the family life cycle, social workers will need to be responsive to diverse cultural values. For example, South Asians tend to value interdependence between parents and children, although the nature, extent, and quality of this interdependence will vary in each family. Some families expect a higher degree of obedience from their children than do others. The personality of the child and parents as well as family experiences can influence the degree of interdependence in the family. What may appear to a social worker trained in Western theories of family life cycle to be an over-involved and enmeshed relationship between the parent and the child is likely to be the norm within South Asian culture. Problems can arise when parents try to maintain the same norms but do not have the built-in structure to support the practice of the norm. For instance, parents may feel guilty that they are unable to do all that their parents did for them because of the constraints of not having extended family members to share the responsibility. The need for both parents to work also prevents exercising the accepted norm of the family. Leaving children in daycare with strangers can be a source of guilt for many South Asian parents who may be concerned about cultural differences in child management or dietary differences that could be upsetting for the child. Many South Asian parents have resolved these difficulties by residing in neighbourhoods with a large concentration of South Asians from which they can access support. As well, daycare facilities in such areas tend to have South Asian staff, thereby increasing the comfort level of parents.

With the emphasis on interdependence, South Asian parents are less inclined to embrace concepts of adolescent separation and individuation. Parents encourage their adolescent children to learn the responsibilities of adulthood within the context of retaining a high degree of connectedness with the family. Adolescents are expected to learn the cultural values of maintaining family unity, privacy, and integrity. Pressures on teenage children can be particularly strong as parents become concerned about the erosion of the values that they see as providing long-term security for their children. Meanwhile, the children are learning to incorporate aspects of both cultures, while also responding to the many adolescent needs for friendship, fun, and experimentation.

Conflict in which the teenage children want the degree of freedom that their non–South Asian peers appear to have can be particularly complicated. South Asian youth can be vulnerable as they try to negotiate their identity in two very different cultures. Parents, for their part, may become extremely cautious about giving their teenaged children freedoms because they fear that they will lose their vital family connection, that the South Asian culture will be overwhelmed by the influence of Western culture, and, ultimately, that the children will be left isolated with no sense of belonging to any family or culture. From a Western perspective, it may appear to the social worker that the teenager's requests for more freedom and independence are reasonable, but this stance can invalidate the parents' knowledge of child-rearing. Parental authority can be acknowledged as parental responsibility, so that parents may feel empowered to provide the structure that their children require. Research by Pettys and Balgopal (1998), who explored multigenerational conflicts among South Asian parents and their teenaged children, indicates that parents are willing to adjust their parenting approaches to incorporate North American family values. Thus, the challenge for social workers is to keep in mind that culture and personality—of the parent and the child—inevitably factor into the intensity of the conflict and the prospects for resolving it.

At the other end of the life cycle, care and support for South Asian elders in the home country is an integral function of the extended family household and kinship network. The elderly command authority and respect within the extended South Asian family. They have an important role in such family matters as counselling parents and children, resolving family disputes, introducing marital partners, and helping to raise grandchildren (Assanand et al., 1990). The eldest son usually continues to reside with his parents after marriage, and he, together with his family, are responsible for parental care. Other siblings and their families often vie for visits from parents and thereby contribute to their care. The active role of elders in the affairs of their kin provides a social and recreational function, further easing the burden on immediate family members.

The variety of South Asian household types in Canada results in different ways of caring for the elderly. Some families establish households that are similar to the ones in the home country wherein, subsequent to his marriage, the eldest son, together with his wife, continues to reside with his parents, whereas other children establish separate households. Those who establish separate households experience issues common to many Canadian families endeavouring to provide care for their aging parents, especially as health problems become an increasing concern. South Asian families are not inclined to rely on institutional care as a primary option in caring for their elderly for two reasons. First, within the culture, institutional care is not regarded as a viable way of expressing respect and of fulfilling duties to an aging parent. Second, few of these institutions can be said to be truly responsive to cultural diversity. For South Asian elders, the most fundamental culturally based needs would include diet, interaction with peers of a similar language and religion, and visitation privileges for a large extended family and kinship network.

Migration and changing family patterns also have implications for the role of the South Asian elderly within their families. For example, a South Asian elder whose migration to Canada is sponsored by his or her son or daughter is presumed by government and society to be dependent. Unfamiliarity with the language and culture of the new homeland only serves to reinforce this sense of dependence (Assanand et al., 1990). Some elderly people may be able to accept their dependent status in the family and to make an easier transition to their new circumstances if they live in neighbourhoods with a large concentration of South Asians (Lessinger, 1995). Within more familiar surroundings, the elders tend to have a greater sense of comfort and to find companionship that combats loneliness and replaces the social network traditionally provided by kin. But for South Asian elders who do not have access to such family, kinship, and community ties, the reversal of their traditional role from authority to dependence can erode self-esteem and result in loneliness and depression.

The challenge for social workers is to find ways to help South Asian families balance both cultural and contextual considerations in different stages of the life cycle. Although family life-cycle stages are culturally patterned, such patterns do not apply universally. Families have internalized ways to negotiate different family life-cycle stages from experiences within their own families, which is further influenced by the personalities of the family members. Even when these life-cycle stages are in flux because of contextual considerations, families may welcome or resist, to varying degrees, the consequent changes to their culturally patterned existence. Indeed, understanding the nature and extent of change that clients will want or will tolerate is the ultimate challenge of multicultural social work practice.

Conclusion

Research about and practice within the South Asian–Canadian community raise doubt about the value of the cultural literacy approach to social work that prevailed from the early 1970s to the late 1990s. Cultural literacy was instrumental in alerting social workers to the colour- and culture-blind nature of social work theories and practice, highlighting their Eurocentric and ethnocentric bias, while questioning the applicability and relevance of traditional social work approaches for culturally/racially diverse clients. More recently, however, the cultural literacy approach has been criticized for the 'logistical' problem 'with respect to exploding national diversity', 'the potential for overgeneralization', and the emphasis on 'the abstract over the experiential and phenomenological' (Dyche & Zayas, 1995, pp. 390–1). Another critic has further noted:

> One limitation is the tendency to oversystematize and stereotype the notion of shared meanings by assuming that ethno-cultural groups are more homogeneous and stable than they actually are. Ethnic values and identity are strongly modified by a host of within-group variables: education, social class, religion, stage of acculturation, and so forth. Furthermore, many ethnic traits are in flux, stimulated by cultural evolution and by exposure to or imposition of the dominant culture. Another limitation is the assumption that the observer, the person making the social description, is completely objective and has no effect on the conclusions about the group being observed. (Falicov, 1995, p. 375)

The limitations of the cultural literacy approach have stimulated the emergence of the experiential-phenomenological approach as an alternative. This process-oriented approach recommends that social workers learn from their clients about aspects of their culture that are important to them as unique individuals who may differ from other members of their cultural group. In effect, the experiential-phenomenological approach encourages social workers to understand contextual diversity within cultural diversity. The social worker learns to understand the relationship between cultural and contextual diversity by adopting an attitude of 'cultural [and contextual] naivete and respectful curiosity [that] are given equal importance to knowledge and skill' (Dyche & Zayas, 1995, p. 389).

In other words, social workers should be engaged in a constant struggle to keep an open and inquisitive mind in their interactions with their clients, whether they are culturally diverse or not. Keeping an open mind requires that social workers recognize the inevitable presence of bias in their observations and in their understanding of situations and problems. Bias comes from our lived understanding of reality and the values that we hold to be acceptable. Still, diverse contexts provide others with their own reality. Accepting that other realties are just as valid is essential to controlling our bias and remaining objective in our understanding of clients. Careful listening to clients can result in learning from them about their contextual reality and their perspectives, thereby contributing to an interactive assessment of their situation. Within a framework of collaboration, the social worker can be committed to learning from clients about their situation, to be conscious of preconceived ideas, and to assess situations through engagement with the client. Indeed, keeping an open mind, controlling biases and assumptions, learning from clients, accepting their perspective, engaging with clients to arrive at interactive assessments of their situations, and co-planning intervention strategies are essential elements of effective cross-cultural practice.

References

Abella, R. (1984). *Report of the Commission on Equality in Employment.* Ottawa: Supply and Services Canada.

Assanand, S., Dias, M., Richardson, E., & Waxler-Morrison, N. (1990). The South Asians. In N. Waxler-Morrison, J. Anderson, & E. Richardson (Eds), *Cross-Cultural Caring: A Handbook for Health Professionals in Western Canada* (pp. 141–80). Vancouver: UBC Press.

Bambrough, J., Bowden, W., & Wien, F. (1992). *Preliminary Results from the Survey of Graduates from the Maritime School of Social Work.* Halifax: Maritime School of Social Work, Dalhousie University.

Billingsley, B., & Musynski, L. (1985). *No Discrimination Here.* Toronto: Social Planning Council of Metro Toronto and the Urban Alliance on Race Relations.

Canada (1984). *Equality Now: Report of the Parliamentary Taskforce on the Participation of Visible Minorities in Canada.* Ottawa: Queen's Printer.

CERIS (1998). *Building Bridges: The Collaborative Development of Culturally Appropriate Definitions of Child Abuse and Neglect for the South Asian Community.* Funded by the Joint Centre of Excellence for Research on Immigration and Settlement. Toronto.

Chicoine, N., Charbonneau, J., Rose, D., & Ray, B. (1997). The reconstruction process of immigrant women's social networks in Montreal. *Recherches-Feministes, 10*(2), 27–48.

Christofides, L.N., & Swidinsky, R. (1994). Wage determination by gender and visible minority status: Evidence from the 1989 LMAS. *Canadian Public Policy, 20*(1), 34–51.

deSilva, A. (1992). *Earnings of Immigrants: A Comparative Analysis.* Ottawa: Economic Council of Canada.

Devore, W., & Schlesinger, E.G. (1996). *Social Work with Minorities.* 3rd ed. Toronto: Merrill.

Doyle, R., & Visano, L. (1987). *A Time for Action! Access to Health and Social Services for Members of Diverse Racial and Cultural Groups.* Toronto: Social Planning Council of Metropolitan Toronto.

Dyche, L., & Zayas, L.H. (1995). The value of curiosity and naivete for cross cultural psychotherapists. *Family Process, 34,* 389–99.

Falicov, C.J. (1995). Training to think culturally: A multidimensional comparative framework. *Family Process, 34,* 373–88.

———. (1996). Mexican families. In M. McGoldrick, J. Pearce, & J. Giordano (Eds), *Ethnicity and Family Therapy.* 2nd ed. (pp. 169–82). New York: Guildford Press.

Freeman, M. (1997). Demographic correlates of individualism and collectivism: A study of social values in Sri Lanka. *Journal of Cross-Cultural Psychology, 28*(3), 321–41.

Garza-Guerro, A.C. (1974). Culture shock: Its mourning, and the vicissitudes of identity. *Journal of the American Psychoanalytic Association, 22,* 408–29.

Grinberg, L., & Grinberg, R. (1989). *Psychoanalytic Perspectives on Migration and Exile.* New Haven, CT: Yale University Press.

Henry, F., & Ginzberg, E. (1984). *Who Gets the Work? A Test of Racial Discrimination in Employment.* Toronto: Urban Alliance on Race Relations and the Social Planning Council of Toronto.

Henry, F., Tator, C., Mattis, W., & Rees, T. (1995). *The Colour of Racism: Racism in Canadian Society.* Toronto: Harcourt Brace.

Herberg, D.C. (1993). *Frameworks for Racial and Cultural Diversity: Teaching and Learning for Practitioners.* Toronto: Canadian Scholars' Press.

Hines, P.M., Garcia-Preto, N., McGoldrick, M., Almeida, R., & Weltman, S. (1992). Intergenerational relationships across cultures. *Families in Society: The Journal of Contemporary Human Services, 73*(3), 323–37.

Hui, C.H. (1988). Measurement of individualism-collectivism. *Journal of Research in Personality, 22,* 17–36.

Israel, M. (1999a). South Asians. In P.R. Magocsi (Ed.), *Encyclopedia of Canada's People* (pp. 1204–8). Toronto: University of Toronto Press.

———. (1999b). Pakistanis. In P R. Magocsi (Ed.), *Encyclopedia of Canada's People.* (pp.1027–37). Toronto: University of Toronto Press.

Jain, H. (1985). *Anti-Discrimination Staffing Policies: Implications of Human Rights Legislation for Employers and Trade Unions.* Ottawa: Secretary of State.

Johnston, H. (1999). Sikhs. In P.R. Magocsi (Ed.), *Encyclopedia of Canada's People* (pp. 1148–64). Toronto: University of Toronto Press.

Lessinger, J. (1995). *From the Ganges to the Hudson.* Boston: Allyn and Bacon.

Maiter, S. (1999). *Immigration Research Update: Understanding South Asian Approaches to Parenting.* Paper presented at the Ontario Association of Agencies Serving Immigrants, Orillia.

McGoldrick, M. (1982). Ethnicity and Family Therapy. In M. McGoldrick, J. Pearce & J. Giordano (Eds), *Ethnicity and Family Therapy* (pp. 3–28). New York: Guilford Press.

McGoldrick, M., Pearce, J., & Giordano, J. (Eds). (1996). *Ethnicity and Family Therapy.* 2nd ed. New York: Guildford Press.

Naidoo, J.C., & Edwards, R.G. (1991). Combatting racism involving visible minorities: A review of relevant research and policy development. *Canadian Social Work Review, 8*(2), 211–35.

Pettys, G.L., & Balgopal, P.R. (1998). Multigenerational conflicts and new immigrants: An Indo-American experience. *Families in Society: The Journal of Contemporary Human Services, 76*(4), 410–23.

Quann, D. (1979). *Racial Discrimination in Housing.* Ottawa: Canadian Council on Social Development.

Rees, T. (1991). Racial discrimination and employment agencies. *Currents: Readings in Race Relations, 7*(2), 16–19.

Reitz, J., Calzavara, L., & Dasko, D. (1981). *Ethnic Inequality and Segregation in Jobs.* Toronto: Centre for Urban and Community Studies, University of Toronto.

Shor, R. (1998). The significance of religion in advancing a culturally sensitive approach towards child maltreatment. *Families in Society: The Journal of Contemporary Human Services, 79*(4), 400–9.

Statistics Canada (1996). *Visible Minority Population in Canada.* Retrieved from www.statcan .ca/english/Pgdb/People/Population/demo40a.html

Steiner, G., & Bansil, R. (1989). Cultural patterns and the family systems in Asian Indians: Implications for psychotherapy. *Journal of Comparative Family Studies, 20*(3), 371–5.

Triandis, H.C. (1994). *Culture and Social Behavior.* New York: McGraw-Hill.

Triandis, H.C., Brislin, R., & Hui, C.H. (1988). Cross-cultural training across the individualism-collectivism divide. *International Journal of Intercultural Relations, 12,* 269–89.

Williams, R.B. (1998). Asian American and Pakistani religions in the United States. *Annals: The American Academy of Political and Social Sciences, 558,* 178–95.

Index